Distributed by:

Frontier Press

15 Quintana Drive
Galveston, TX 77554-9350
(409) 740-0138

VIRGINIA
NORTHERN NECK
LAND GRANTS

Volume IV

1800-1862

VIRGINIA
NORTHERN NECK
LAND GRANTS

Volume IV

1800-1862

Compiled by

Gertrude E. Gray

Baltimore
GENEALOGICAL PUBLISHING CO., INC.
1993

TABLE OF CONTENTS

INTRODUCTION

Northern Neck grants issued by the Commonwealth of Virginia were continued in separate books and kept in a separate collection from Virginia land grants until 1862, when the area that is now West Virginia withdrew from the Commonwealth and entered the Union. This cut off the largest source of vacant land in Virginia. The last grant book in the Northern Neck series is designated 1847 - 1862 but there are eighteen additional grants recorded as late as 1874. Beginning with Grant Book E-2, 1838 - 1846, Virginia began the use of printed forms for the grants. All books contain an index of grantees at the beginning except A-2 and B-2, which have no grantee index at all.

Abstracts in this fourth and final volume of Northern Neck land grants give grant book designation, page number, name of grantee, place of residence until Virginia began issuing grants, number of acres, location of grant, adjoining landowners, and sometimes warrant number with issue date and survey date. Names have been copied as they appear in the grant, or as near as could be deciphered from the writing, and have been abbreviated only when and as they were in the original document except for Junior and Senior. Since these grants were measured by "metes and bounds," a number of mistakes occurred in the measurements, thus making it necessary to issue another grant correcting the mistake. The majority of these grants were in the area of Frederick, Shenandoah, Culpeper, Loudoun, and Madison counties, Virginia, and Hampshire, Hardy, and Berkeley counties (now West Virginia). These abstracts have been kept brief, but every name was extracted. If an ancestor is located in any of the grants, it is advised that you secure a copy of the original and read the complete document.

The original grant books are to be found as "Northern Neck Grants 1690 - 1874," Land Office (Record Group 4), Archives Branch, Virginia State Library, Richmond, Virginia. Microfilms of the original grant books, made by the Photographic Laboratory of the Virginia State Library, were used in making these present abstracts. Copies of the microfilms are available also through L.D.S. Family History Centers throughout the country.

Abstracts of Virginia's Northern Neck Warrants and Surveys by Peggy Shomo Joyner (4 vols., 1985, 1986, 1987) may contain information on some of the grants issued before the death of Lord Fairfax. Warrant and survey records used by Mrs. Joyner are in the Virginia State Library and at present are not available on microfilm.

Copies of the original grants may be secured from the Virginia State Library. Specify name of collection, name of grantee, volume and page number. Send a self addressed, stamped envelope for a price quote, limiting requests to two items per letter. Do not include money with orders. Write to: Virginia State Library, Capitol Square, Richmond, Virginia 23219-3491.

The compiler wishes to thank the Virginia State Archives for permission to use the Northern Neck Grant Books for this project, the L. D. S. Family History Center of Burien, Washington, for the use of the microfilm, microfilm readers, the assistance given by the staff, especially Alice Montgomery, and for the encouragement of friends and fellow genealogists.

ABBREVIATIONS:

A., Acres
Actg., Acting
Adj., adj., Adjoining, Adjacent
Adm., Administration
admr., administrator
Agt., Agent
asne., assignee
Atty., Attorney
bet., between
Bk., Book
Br., Branch,
Bro., Brother
Bros. Brothers
Brs., Branches
Capt., Captain
Ch., Children
Clk., Clerk
Co., County
Cos., Counties
Col., Colonel
Cr., Creek
Ct., Court
dau., daughter
daus., daughters
dec'd, deceased
def., defendant
desc., descendant
descs., descendants
Dir., Director
Dl'd., Delivered to
Dpty., Deputy
dup., duplicate
dvse., devisee
dvses., devisees
E., East
Esq., Esquire
est., estate
Exc., Executive
Exg., Exchange
exr., executor
exrs., executors
exx., executrix
f., folio
ff'd, forfeited
Ft., Fort
Gen., General

Gent., Gentleman
gfather., grandfather
Gov., Governor
h's., heirs
inc., including
J.P., Justice of the Peace
M., Mile
m., married
Md., Maryland
M.G., Minister of the Gospel
M.H., Meeting House
Maj., Major
N., North
N.N., Northern Neck
O.B., Order Book
P/A., Power of Attorney
Par., Parish
Penn., Pennsylvania
Per., Perches
plt., plaintiff
Po., Pole, Poles
Pres., President
Prop'r., proprietor
R., River
Rd., Road
Reexg., Reexchange
rep., representatives
Rg., Ridge
Ro., Rod, Rood, Roods
RR., Railroad
Rs., Rivers
Rt., Right
S., South
s., son
s'd, said
Srvr., Surveyor
Surv., Survey
Surv'd, Surveyed
Sw., Swamp
T.W., Treasury Warrant
T.Ws., Treasury Warrants
W., West
w., wife
wid., widow
wit., witness
Wt., Warrant

A.(date), Date of survey.
/ Indicates more than one spelling in the same record.
? Indicates uncertainty as to spelling.
= issued (T.W. issued)
(see Bk. N) Northern Neck Book N first page, unnumbered.
[Grant delivered to]

VIRGINIA
NORTHERN NECK
LAND GRANTS

Volume IV

1800-1862

Z-1: T.W.2706=3 June 1799 Paul McKeever 500 A.(19 June 1799) in Hampshire Co. on Great Cacapheon where he now lives, near Adam Kline. 11 Nov 1800

Z-1: T.W.2229=14 July 1797 John Higgins & Michael Labenger 400 A.(20 June 1798) in Hampshire Co. in Green Spring Valley, Fishers Run, adj. James Donaldson, Anthoney Buck, Jeremiah Sullivant, Robert Buck dec'd. 11 Nov 1800

Z-2: 244 1/4 A. by T.W.2229=14 July 1797 & 114 3/4 A. by T.W.14,647=12 Oct 1782 John Higgins & James Higgins 359 A.(20 Oct 1799) in Hampshire Co. on Little Capecapheon adj. Moses Henderson, Stewarts Run, wid. Oliver, David Henderson. 12 Nov 1800

Z-3: T.W.2226=12 July 1797 George Martin Jr. 182 A.(8 Mar 1798) in Hampshire Co. on Gibbons's Run of N. R. adj. Samuel Todd, Joseph Sivel, John Chisholm, Rece Prichard, Graper, Adam Hair. 8 Oct 1800

Z-4: T.W.14,647=12 Oct 1782 John Higgins asne. of Daniel Jones 90 A.(21 Oct 1799) in Hampshire Co. on S. Br. Mt. adj. Simeon/Simon Taylor, George Rogers, Elsey. 13 Nov 1800

Z-5: T.W.21017=1 Dec 1783 Thomas Ruckman 158 A.(19 Nov 1797) in Hampshire Co. on Little Capecapheon Mt. adj. his plantation, William Williamson. 9 Oct 1800

Z-6: T.W.2311=7 Nov 1797 Jacob Pence (s. of Henry) 183 A.(6 Apr 1799) in Shenandoah Co. at foot of the Blue Rg. on Hawksbill Cr. adj. Henry Pence, George Hatick, Henry Deeley, Augustine Piper formerly Baylis. 17 Nov 1800

Z-7: T.W.2369=6 Jan 1798 John Carson 83 A.(12 Feb 1798) in Hardy Co. Co. adj. Joseph Nevill on Mannings run, William Rennick, Edward Shawnessey, Robert Means. 7 Nov 1800

Z-8: T.W.17361=26 June 1783 John Huddle 5 A.(2 Oct 1798) in Shenandoah Co. on N. R. of Shenandoah at mouth of Stoney Cr. adj. Darbey Downey, Downey's purchase of Farling Ball. 2 Sep 1800

Z-9: T.W.1243=26 Mar 1795 Daniel Huddle(river) 13 A.(1 Sep 1797) in Shenandoah Co. on N. R. of Shenandoah adj. George Cop purchase of John Huddles Heirs, Michael Hamman, Jacob Cofman, Benjamin Shoe. 1 Oct 1800

Z-10: T.W.15,867=8 May 1783 Thomas Flora 91 A.(1 June 1797) in Hampshire Co. on Potowmack R. adj. Robert Rogers formerly Lewis Throckmorton, John Ester, his own land, Pawpaw Rg. 1 Nov 1800

Z-11: T.W.428=7 May 1794 Samuel Levesque asne. of Ebenezer Leeth 320 A.(29 Nov 1799) in Shenandoah Co. on S. R. of Shenandoah adj. Hite & Co. Grant, Meriday Kennedy, land formerly George Leeth dec'd. 17 Mov 1800

Z-11: T.W.1736=21 Dec 1795 Ulrick Waggoner 475 A.(4 Sep 1798) in Shenandoah Co. near Mill Cr. adj. William Good, John Brock, Abraham Sherfig, Daniel Walter. 1 Oct 1800

Z-12: T.W.515=22 May 1793 George Shoemaker 130 A.(30 July 1798) in Shenandoah Co. on Ryals Run adj. John Ryman, John Beck, Henry Rinker, said Shoemaker, Henry Spoore now Daniel Webb, Ulrick Nease. 6 Oct 1800

Z-13: 70 A. by T.W.1596 & 15 A. by T.W.1597 both=22 Sep 1795 George Millslagel 85 A.(12 July 1797) in Hampshire Co. on Tear Coat adj. John Cannon, John Stoolsman, Rd. from Romney to Winchester, McBride formerly David Corbin. 1 Nov 1800 [Dl'd Jacob Jenkins 22 Sep 1801]

Z-14: T.W.2468=4 May 1798 Joseph Hedges & John Hedges 300 A.(21 Nov 1798) in Berkeley Co. on Meadow Br. & Dirt hill Mt. adj. John R. Hedges, Sleepy Cr. Mt. 4 Nov 1800 [Dl'd James Stephenson Jan 19, 1801]

Z-15:   T.W.797=18 Oct 1794 Elon Miller 320 A.(31 Aug 1796) in Berkeley Co. near mouth of Back Cr. adj. Alexander Anderson, Phillip Miller, Adam Hay, Rench, Andrew Bowman, Moses Harlin, Tunis Newkirk, N. Mt. 17 Nov 1800 [Dl'd James Stephenson Jan 19, 1801]

Z-17:   T.W.1709=28 Nov 1795 Gasper Snyder 234 A. 2 Ro. 22 Po.(22 Oct 1796) in Berkeley Co. on Back Cr. & Third Hill, adj. J. G. Honekey, William Cherry, Scott's heirs. 16 Nov 1800 [Dl'd James Stephenson Jan 19, 1801]

Z-18:   T.W.21,017=1 Dec 1783 David Corbin 125 A.(23 Feb 1798) in Hampshire Co. on little Capecapheon adj. James Murphey, said Corbin, Richard Nelson, Robert French, John Thompson. 29 Oct 1800 [Dl'd Jacob Jenkins 22 Sep 1801]

Z-19:   24 A. by T.W.2277=21 Sep 1797 & 176 A. by T.W.2457=6 Mar 1798 John Rosbough 200 A.(29 July 1798) in Hampshire Co. on Great Cacapheon adj. Smith, Dry run, Phillip Bush, Hotzenpillar, Jacob Hoober. 14 Nov 1800 [Dl'd A. Magill 17 Jan 1801]

Z-20: T.W.21,477=28 Dec 1783 John McMeckin 400 A.(28 Aug 1797) in Hampshire Co. on Little Capecapheon adj. John Thompson, David Corbin, Robert Alexander. 3 Nov 1800 [Dl'd Osburn Sprigg 23 Jan 1801]

Z-21: T.W.19,599=26 Sep 1783 John Pearsall 100 A.(18 Apr 1798) in Hampshire Co. on Sugar Camp Run of Pattersons Cr. adj. his own land. 9 Oct 1800 [Dl'd Abel Seamour 29 Oct 1801]

Z-22:   T.W.428=26 Apr 1791 John Blue 225 A.(3 May 1797) in Hampshire Co. on S. Br. adj. John Pancake, his own land, Robert Ryght, Jacobus Hinis, Paris Drew, William Beakman. 13 Oct 1800

Z-23:   T.W.19,312=12 Sep 1783 William Armstrong 400 A.(8 June 1790) in Hampshire Co. on N. R. adj. Stophle Spring Tract, Relf, Benjamin Stone, Wharton. 18 Oct 1800 [Dl'd Hugh Holms 12 Mar 1802]

Z-24:   T.W.2338=11 Dec 1797 Laurence McKearnan Jr. 35 1/2 A.(30 Mar 1799) in Berkeley Co. on Sleepy Cr. adj. Andrew Brouse, wid. Fleece, Andrew Michael, John Henderson. 4 Nov 1800 [Dl'd Jno Sherrard 6 Dec 1820]

Z-25:   T.W.8740=9 Nov 1781 William C. Williams 500 A.(27 Oct 1798) in Shenandoah Co. in Powells little Ft. adj. Ft. Mt., William Elzey, Jacob Gochenour. 1 Oct 1800 [Dl'd Prop'r 6 June 1801]

Z-26:   T.W.2338=11 Dec 1797 Laurance McKearnan Jr. 38 A.(12 Mar 1799) in Berkeley Co. on middle S. fork of Sleepy Cr. adj. Edward Crabb, Stephen Miller. 5 Nov 1800 [Dl'd Jno Sherrard 6 Dec 1821]

Z-27:   Duplicate T.W.23,086=14 May 1794 William Bryan 37 1/2 A.(27 Dec 1797) in Culpepper Co. on Oven top Mt. adj. said Bryan, Thomas Morris. 7 Nov 1800 [Dl'd Maj. Roberts 4 Feb 1802]

Z-28:   T.W.626=16 Aug 1794 Thomas Willson 16 A. 2 Ro.(19 June 1799) in Berkeley Co. being two small Islands in the Shenandoah R. adj. Samples. 14 Nov 1800

Z-29:   T.W.806=22 Oct 1794 Elenor Mason(late Elenor Chenowith) 107 A.(22 Nov 1799) in Berkeley Co. on Middle Cr. adj. Robert Lyle, Henry Bishop, said Elenor Mason, Jesse Fulkner, Pitzer. 7 Nov 1800

Z-30:   T.W.2159=25 Mar 1797 John Hunter 183 A.(8 Mar 1799) in Berkeley & Hampshire Cos. on Warm Spring Rg. adj. late Lord Fairfax, Thomas Embly now Palmer, Michael Davis, Langan, Thomas Hamlin now Robert Sherrard, Barrett now Col. Hilton, William Johnson, Richard Marquis, Alexander Henry now Plunket Phillips. 5 Nov 1800 [Dl'd Hugh Holmes 13 Mar 1801]

Z-31:   T.W.2683=17 Apr 1799 Phillip Pendleton 129 A.(26 Nov 1799) in Berkeley Co. on Warm Spring Run adj. said Pendleton, Dixon, John Gustin, John Miller, Lord Fairfax. 16 Nov 1800 [Dl'd Peter Lawson per order 5 Nov 1801]

Z-32: T.W.9078=22 Nov 1781 Alexander Smith 321 A.(25 Nov 1792) in Hardy Co. adj. Pryor S. Robey on Abrahams Cr. 30 Jan 1801 [Dl'd John Hoye 26 Mar 1804]

Z-33: T.W.19,681=2 Oct 1783 Reubin Thornhill asne. of Benjamin Lillard asne. of said Reubin Thornhill 267 A.(7 Nov 1797) in Culpepper Co. on Hughes R. adj. Alexander Rider, said Thornhill. 5 Mar 1801 [Dl'd Prop'r 5 Mar 1801]

Z-34: T.W.1284=13 Apr 1795 Hugh Holmes asne. of Phillip Pendleton 2600 A.(7 May 1794) in Hampshire Co. on S. Br. Mt. & Little Capen adj. Drew, Reager, Robert Parker, John Taylor, the Waggon Rd. 14 Mar 1801 [Dl'd Prop'r 18 Mar 1801]

Z-35: T.W.1284=13 Apr 1795 Hugh Holmes asne. of Phillip Pendleton 3550 A.(12 May 1795) in Hampshire Co. on S. Br. Mt. adj. William Buffington, Nathaniel Kirkendall, Job Parker, Isaac Means, Mill Cr. Surv. includes 400 A. of prior claims exclusive of above. 14 Mar 1801 [Dl'd Prop'r 18 Mar 1801]

Z-37: T.W.1284=13 Apr 1795 Hugh Holmes asne. of Phillip Pendleton 840 A.(11 May 1795) in Hampshire Co. adj. John Mercer, Aaron Steed, Taylor, Winchester to Frankfort Rd., John Swinfield, John Russaw. 14 Mar 1801 [Prop'r 18 Mar 1801]

Z-38: T.W.1284=13 Apr 1795 Phillip Pendleton 1586 A.(8 May 1795) in Hampshire Co. on S. Br. Mt., Little Capecapeon near town of Romey adj. his own land, Newman, Pendleton, Formans Rd. 16 Mar 1801 [Dl'd Hugh Holmes 18 Mar 1801]

Z-39: T.W.1284=13 Apr 1795 Phillip Pendleton 1300 A.(13 May 1795) in Hampshire Co. on Frankfort to Winchester Rd. adj. Robert Walker, John Donalson, Dobson, S. Br. of Powtomack, Samuel Boyd, Andrew Walker. 15 Mar 1801 [Holmes 18 Mar 1801]

Z-40: T.W.1284=13 Apr 1795 Phillip Pendleton 1200 A.(11 May 1795) in Hampshire Co. on S. Br. Mt. adj. Isaac Means, Isaac Person, William Smith, Mill Cr., Colvans Gap. 17 Mar 1801 [Dl'd Hugh Holmes 18 Mar 1801]

Z-41: T.W.1284=13 Apr 1795 Phillip Pendleton 266 A.(9 May 1795) in Hampshire Co. adj. Aron Steed, Thomas Baker on Hopkins's lick Run & Little Capecaheon, John Meshe. 17 Mar 1801 [Dl'd Hugh Holmes 18 Mar 1801]

Z-42: T.W.962=11 Dec 1794 Thomas Newell asne. of Jacob Rinker & Robert Mackey exrs. & Sarah Zane exx. under last will of Isaac Zane dec'd 140 A.(21 June 1798) in Shenandoah Co. along foot of Little N. Mt. adj. Thomas Newell, Christian Niswanger, said Zane. 3 Apr 1801 [Dl'd Philip Snapp 6 Apr 1801]

Z-43: Exg.T.W.804=13 July 1797 Edward Luttrell 14 3/4 A.(5 Apr 1800) in Fauquier Co. adj. Richard Bryley, Nath'l Greeves, Thom's Brahan/Braham, Lewis Prichard. 20 Apr 1801 [Dl'd Enoch Reno of Dumfies 29 Apr 1801]

Z-44: T.W.22,729=24 Dec 1783 Enoch Reno 5 A. 3 Ro. 30 Po.(29 Aug 1799) in Pr. William Co. adj. Jameson, McMillian, Graham. 17 Apr 1801 [Dl'd Enoch Reno of Dumfies 29 Apr 1801]

Z-44: T.W.22,729=24 Dec 1783 James Foley 42 A. 1 Ro.(15 Aug 1799) in Pr. William Co. adj. Phillip Daws, Cocke, the Spring Br. 17 Apr 1801 [Dl'd the Prop'r 8 June 1801]

Z-45: T.W.1746=24 Dec 1795 Michael Haas 100 A.(11 Oct 1799) in Shenandoah Co. at Shavers gap adj. John Kingan, Cedar Cr. 22 Apr 1801 [Dl'd Danl. Maderea 31 Dec 1807]

Z-46: Inclusive surv. by order of Hampshire Co. Ct. 5 Jan 1800 William Dunkin 424 A. (400 A. granted him 9 Mar 1779 & 24 A. by T.W.2842=13 Dec 1799) in Hampshire Co. adj. David Corbin, Samuel Williamson. 21 Apr 1801 [Dl'd William C. Williams 6 June 1801]

Z-47: T.W.8740=9 Nov 1781 William C. Williams 730 A.(28 Oct 1799) in Shenandoah Co. on Jeremys Run at the Blue Rg. adj. James Barbour, Henry Hershbarger now John Hockman, William Nail, Frederick Herberger, John McCarty, Jacob Follis, Thomas Jones. 21 Apr 1801 [Dl'd the Prop'r 6 June 1801]

3

Z-48:   T.W.426=7 May 1794 John Allensworth 41 1/2 A.(24 Sep 1799) in Shenandoah & Frederick Cos. on Happy Cr. adj. Denny Fairfax, Gooney run mannor, Russell, Joseph Hoepwell, Christopher Criser. 21 Apr 1801 [Dl'd Isaac Samuel 18 Sep 1801]

Z-49:   T.W.11,446=16 May 1782 Robert Leewright & David Willson 74 A.(27 Sep 1799) in Shenandoah Co. near Jeremys Run adj. Daniel Mark purchase of Jos: Barnes, Hites & Co., Meridy Kennady, Samuel Levesque purchase of Spencer Breeding, Jacob Follis. 22 Apr 1801 [Dl'd Hugh Holmes Esq. 22 Jan 1802]

Z-50:   T.W.515=22 May 1793 John Carter asne. of William Davis 100 A.(29 Oct 1799) in Shenandoah Co. on Stoney Run in the Blue Rg. adj. Rockingham Co. line, George Hetich. 22 Apr 1801

Z-51:   T.W.1192=21 Feb 1795 Lewis Conner 42 A.(8 Apr 1800) in Culpepper Co. adj. James Hudson, said Conner, John Slaughter, Benjamin Thomas. 21 Apr 1801 [Dl'd Mr. Aylett Hawes 9 Dec 1802]

Z-51:   T.W.375=6 Mar 1794 Nicholas Walter 100 A.(20 Nov 1799) in Frederick Co. on S. fork of Paddys Run adj. Nicholas Walter, Robertson. 24 Apr 1801 [Dl'd Philip Snap 23 May 1801]

Z-52:   T.W.1702=28 Nov 1795 William Elzey 3167 A.(25 Nov 1799) in Shenandoah Co. on Ft. Mt. adj. Joseph Miller in Powells little Ft., William C. Williams, Rd. from John Huddle's on N. R. of Shenandoah to Powells Ft., said Elzey, John Stover, George Feather, Martin Betz, Abraham Bird, John Moore Jr., Lewis Moore, David Willson, Aaron Moore. 23 Apr 1801 [Dl'd John Hopkins 27 Jan 1802]

Z-54:   T.W.2363=30 Dec 1797 Lewis Moore & David Wilson 500 A.(24 Oct 1799) in Shenandoah Co. on Short Arse Mt. adj. John Moore Jr., Joseph Hawkins, John Henning, Isaac Bond, Aaron Allen. 24 Apr 1801 [Dl'd Lewis Moore 11 Dec 1801]

Z-55:   T.W.14,163=10 Sep 1782 Collan Mitcham 28 A.(19 June 1799) in Shenandoah Co. on S. R. of Shenandoah adj. Abraham Heastand formerly Strickler. 24 Apr 1801

Z-56:   T.W.1979=5 Sep 1796 Samuel Carpenter 200 A.(1 Jan 1800) in Madison Co. adj. Robert Thomas, the German Gleebe, said Carpenter. 23 Apr 1801 [Dl'd Capt. Early 11 Dec 1802]

Z-57:   T.W.2175=17 Apr 1797 Thomas McGraw 81 A.(19 Sep 1799) in Hampshire Co. adj. Morris McGraw, Phillip Groves, Melon Pugh, George Hurtish, William Adams. 23 Apr 1801 [Dl'd Phillip Snap 23 May 1801]

Z-57:   T.W.2911=19 Mar 1800 John Clark 50 A.(26 Apr 1800) in Frederick Co. adj. said Clark. 24 Apr 1801 [Dl'd Phil. Snap 23 May 1801]

Z-58:   17 A. by T.W.20,227=31 Oct 1783 & 33 A. by T.W.375=6 Mar 1794 Phillip Snapp asne. of John Cook 50 A.(31 Oct 1798) in Frederick Co. on Paddies Run of Ceder Cr. adj. land Maj. Lewis Stephens sold Samuel Weeks, Paddies Mt. 27 Apr 1801 [Dl'd the Prop'r 23 May 1801]

Z-59:   T.W.375=6 Mar 1794 Henry Clark 100 A.(26 Oct 1798) in Frederick Co. adj. said Clark's purchase of John Weeks, Big N. Mt., Paddys Run. 24 Apr 1801 [Dl'd P. Snap 23 May 1801]

Z-60:   T.W.1363=12 May 1795 Joseph Baker asne. of Henry Dick Jr. asne. of John Mason 200 A.(24 June 1795) in Frederick Co. on Sugarts Run of Sleepy Cr. adj. Gen. Isaac Zane, Capt. Elisha Boyd, Joseph Baker. 23 Apr 1801

Z-61:   T.W.375=6 Mar 1794 Shepherd Collins 100 A.(28 Apr 1800) in Frederick Co. adj. said Collins on Paddys Run, N. Mt., Henry Clark. 24 Apr 1801 [Dl'd Philip Snap 23 May 1801]

Z-62:   T.W.16,339=12 May 1783 Hezekiah Daggs asne. of Joseph Allfree 50 A.(8 Nov 1794) in Hardy Co. adj. David Welton, said Alfree. 23 Apr 1801

Z-62:   T.W.2882=24 Jan 1800 Nicholas Walter 100 A.(25 Apr 1800) in Frederick Co.

on Paddys Run inc. two Licks in the little Cove, adj. Phillip Snap. 27 Apr 1801 [Dl'd Phillip Snap 23 May 1801]

Z-63: T.W.8740=9 Nov 1781 William Reading 9 A.(20 June 1799) in Shenandoah Co. on S. R. of Shenandoah adj. Casper Miller, James Barbour. 23 Apr 1801 [Dl'd W. Dulaney 8 Dec 1801]

Z-64: T.W.19,803=7 Oct 1783 Francis Deakins 1800 A.(29 June 1798) in Hardy Co. on Stoney R. above the Furnace Rd. adj. his own land, Andrew Bruce, Robys Mill Run, William Bowness, Jacob Stingley, Anthony Baker, Prior Robey, Rich'd Seymore. 7 May 1801 [Dl'd John Hopkins 27 Jan 1802]

Z-66: 200 A. by T.W.2302=23 Oct 1797 & 106 1/2 A. by T.W.2415=12 Feb 1798 William Williamson Jr. 306 1/2 A.(13 June 1798) in Hampshire Co. on Tare Coat & Little Capecapeon adj. Steel, Stoney lick Br., Job Shepard, Pigman, Daniel Corbin, Richard Taylor, Beals. 6 May 1801

Z-67: T.W.1080=15 Jan 1795 John Hastings 150 A.(1 Sep 1800) in Frederick Co. on Cedar Cr. near foot of Big N. Mt. adj. land Richard Longacre sold John & Jacob Tevalt near wid. Richards, Gen. Isaac Zane dec'd heirs, Brushy Rg. 8 May 1801

Z-68: T.W.2882=24 Jan 1800 Phillip Snap 90 A.(29 Apr 1800) in Frederick Co. adj. Henry Clark, said Snap. 5 May 1801 [Dl'd the Prop'r 23 May 1801]

Z-69: T.W.375=6 Mar 1794 Phillip Snap 67 A.(3 Jan 1800) in Frederick Co. adj. John Weeks, Big N. Mt., Little Cove, said Snap. 4 May 1801 [Prop'r 23 May 1801]

Z-70: Exg.T.W.867=25 Mar 1799 Benjamin Partlow 149 A.(20 May 1799) in Culpepper Co. adj. William Reece, John Strother, Odells Mt., Thomas Jones, William Reece. 5 May 1801 [Dl'd the Prop'r 22 Jan 1802]

Z-71: T.W.8740=9 Nov 1781 Derick Pennybaker 395 A.(26 Oct 1799) in Shenandoah Co. bet. Peter Ruffner & Edwin Young's heirs, Richard Patton, Martin Coffman. 8 May 1801 [Dl'd Isaac Samuel 18 Sep 1801]

Z-72: Exg.T.W.867=25 Mar 1799 Benjamin Partlow 167 A.(20 May 1799) in Culpepper Co. on Rg. little pass Rg., adj. Thomas Jones, Odells Mt. 5 May 1801 [Dl'd the Prop'r 22 Jan 1802]

Z-73: T.W.19,803=7 Oct 1783 Francis Deakins 740 A.(25 June 1798) in Hardy Co. on Abrahams Cr. adj. his surv., Thomazen Ellzey, Alexander Smith, Francis & William Deakins, Hutchingson. 7 May 1801 [Dl'd John Hopkins 27 Jan 1802]

Z-74: T.W.21,477=23 Dec 1783 Daniel Dollahon 100 A.(25 Mar 1797) in Hampshire Co. on Mill Cr. adj. his own land, Benjamin Normin, Davisson, John Normin, Phillip Pendleton. 6 May 1801 [Dl'd Robt. Means 16 June 1801]

Z-75: T.W.19,803=7 Oct 1783 Francis Deakins 600 A.(17 Aug 1798) in Hampshire Co. on Maple Swamp Run of N. Br. of Potowmack adj. Ravencroft, Ellzey, William Fox, Deakins. 7 May 1801 [Dl'd J. Hopkins 27 Jan 1802]

Z-76: T.W.14,647=12 Oct 1782 Robert Williams 140 A.(23 Aug 1799) in Hampshire Co. adj. Jacob Purget, John Spinner. 18 May 1801 [Dl'd the Prop'r 5 Jan 1802]

Z-77: T.W.19,543=27 Sep 1783 Richard Ward 27 A.(21 June 1799) in Shenandoah Co. on S. R. of Shenandoah adj. land formerly Michael Blancumbaker, John Strickler. 7 May 1801

Z-78: T.W.21,028=1 Dec 1783 William Williamson & Richard Taylor 143 A.(8 Mar 1798) in Hampshire Co. on little Capecapheon adj. said Taylor, Williamson, Thomas Ruckman. 5 May 1801

Z-79: Exg.T.W.533=5 Aug 1793 John Moore Jr. 184 A.(23 Oct 1799) in Sheanandoah Co. on three topt Mt. adj. Joseph Hawkins, William Newland, Abraham Bird. 7 May 1801 [Dl'd Prop'r 9 July 1801]

Z-80:   T.W.2311=7 Nov 1797 Aaron Moore 217 A.(21 Oct 1799) in Shenandoah Co. at the Short Arse Mt. & N. R. of Shenandoah adj. John Moore, William Moore, James Murphy, Adam Kiger,Joseph Allen, Isaac Bond. 8 May 1801 [Mr. Moses Warton 1828]

Z-82:   T.W.2102=20 Jan 1797 Peter Bunn 21 1/2 A.(6 Feb 1798) in Berkeley Co. on Mile Cr. adj. McCrea, said Bunn, Jacob Pulse, Nathaniel Morrisson. 6 May 1801

Z-83:   T.W.2310=7 Nov 1797 George Smith asne. of Peter Smith 11 A.(21 June 1799) in Shenandoah Co. on S. R. of Shenandoah adj. Michael Blancumbaker now Peter Smith, wid. Heback formerly Deobald Crissler, George Bongamon. 8 May 1801

Z-84:   T.W.18,365=6 Aug 1783 Charles Hill 170 A.(29 Dec 1797) in Hardy & Hampshire Cos. on John Johnstons run adj. Vanmeter. 8 May 1801

Z-85:   T.W.1731=15 Dec 1795 Samuel Ferguson 66 A.(7 May 1797) in Culpepper Co. on Goard vine R., said Freguson, Henry Pendleton, Cotton, Benjamin Furgeson. 6 May 1801 [Dl'd Philip Snap 4 Mar 1804]

Z-86:   T.W.169=11 Dec 1793 George Gilpin 94 A.(21 Feb 1798) in Hardy Co. Co. adj. his own land on Pattersons Cr., Stephen Ross, Smith, Richard Woods, Paul Hagerty. 8 May 1801 [Dl'd with Rec't taken 21 Aug 1803]

Z-87:   Exg.T.W.537=29 Aug 1793 Ephraim Lowman 100 A.(9 Oct 1797) in Berkeley Co. on Sleepy Cr. adj. Smith, Matth. Swim, William Neal or Lowman, John Hixon. 5 May 1801 [Dl'd Hugh Hoomes Esq. 22 Jan 1802]

Z-88: $1216.00 (one third paid to Augustin Green, Escheator, & remainder sold on Credit.) Grant to John Minor 280 A.(28 Sep 1801) in Culpeper Co. adj. Owen Campbell, W. Brook, Tombolin, Martin Pickett, Richmond Rd., property of Samuel Abbott sold by Green, Escheator for said Co., to John Minor by acts of General assembly 13 Nov 1792 & 3 Jan 1798. 31 Oct 1801

Z-89:   Exg.T.W.606=28 July 1794 George Newkirk, Reubin Newkirk, John Newkirk, James Newkirk, Joseph Newkirk, & Isaac Newkirk, ch. & heirs of Margaret Newkirk late Margaret Miles, sister & legal rep. of George Miles dec'd, 251 A.(22 Nov 1798) in Berkeley Co. on Goffs run of Back Cr. adj. Teter Barns, Jacob Foster, Grays heirs, Rd. from Johnsons Mill to Londers ferry, Burchum, David Volgamot, Dunn. 21 Oct 1801 [Dl'd Mr. Coleman 6 Nov 1801]

Z-91:   Exg.T.W.606=28 July 1794 George Newkirk, Reubin Newkirk, John Newkirk, James Newkirk, Joseph Newkirk, & Isaac Newkirk, ch. & heirs of Margaret Newkirk late Margaret Miles, sister & legal rep. of George Miles dec'd, 40 A.(15 Feb 1799) in Berkeley Co. on N. Mt. adj. Tunis Newkirk. Elon Millar, Robert Stephen, George Millar. 22 Oct 1801 [Dl'd Mr. Coleman 6 Nov 1801]

Z-92:   T.W.from late Prop'rs office of the N. N. & $3.33 1/3, William Bailey & Wendal Froushour 143 A.(8 Sep 1770) in Frederick Co. adj. them on S. fork of Sleepy Cr., Froushour, Riggs, Martin Hoover. 3 Nov 1801 [W. Rector 20 June 1802]

Z-93:   T.W.2967=6 Aug 1800 Alexander Smyth 200 A.(13 Nov 1800) in Berkeley Co. on Cherrys Br. & Tilhances Br. adj. Comptons Rg., said Smyth, Edward Conner, Daniel Blohrer, Robert Jones, Frederick Free.   20 Oct 1801 [Dl'd Hugh Hoomes Esq. 22 Jan 1802]

Z-95:   T.W.2323=24 Nov 1797 Samuel Hampton 70 1/2 A.(19 Apr 1800) in Fairfax Co. on Sandy Run adj. s'd Hampton, Carter. 24 Nov 1801 [Nich's Fitzhugh 15 Dec 1801]

Z-96:   T.W.2323=24 Nov 1797 William Mills & William Payne, said Payne asne. of said Mills 69 1/4 A.(14 June 1800) in Fairfax Co. on Occuquan R. adj. Robert Singleton. 24 Nov 1801 [Dl'd Nich's Fitzhugh 15 Dec 1801]

Z-97:   T.W.2039=17 Nov 1796 George Bell 406 1/2 A.(4 Aug 1800) in Frederick Co. adj. Manor of Leeds, John Pauner?, Groves, Griffith Thomas, William Clayton. 2 Dec 1801 [Dl'd Mr. Castleman 14 Dec 1801]

Z-98:   T.W.9982=18 Dec 1781 Phillip Dawe asne. of George Mills 4 A. 3 Ro. 20

6

Po.(15 May 1800) in Pr. William Co. on Neabsco Run adj. said Dawe, Mr. Tayloe, Cocke. 5 Dec 1801 [Dl'd the Prop'r 20 Dec 1801]

Z-99: T.W.1629=14 Oct 1795 Andrew Glassell 38 A.(24 June 1800) in Madison Co. adj. Robinson R., Tanner, William Chapman, s'd Glassell, Zimmermon. 14 Dec 1801

Z-100: T.W.1629=14 Oct 1795 Lewis Crigler 6 A.(26 June 1799) in Madison Co. adj. Ephraim Utz, George Rouse, said Crigler, Robert Thomas, George Cook. 2 Dec 1801

Z-101: T.W.1629=14 Oct 1795 William Smith 20 A.(31 Dec 1799) in Madison Co. on German Rg., Philips, said Smith. 1 Dec 1801

Z-102: T.W.1629=14 Oct 1795 James Shotwell 25 A.(14 June 1798) in Madison Co. adj. William Shotwell, Henry Lewis, Col. Hill, Thomas Sampson. 2 Dec 1801

Z-102: T.W.1629=14 Oct 1795 William Crow 14 A.(2 Apr 1800) in Madison Co. on Robinson R., adj. Dennis Crow. 1 Dec 1801

Z-103: T.W.18.085=26 July 1783 Elias Roby 70 A.(25 Apr 1794) in Hardy Co. bet. Abrahams Cr. & Stoney R. adj. Prior Roby, Joseph Nevill. 12 Dec 1801

Z-104: T.W.1629=14 Oct 1795 William Crow 141 A.(1 Apr 1800) in Madison Co. adj. Robinsons R., Sheltons Spring Br., Weatherall. 2 Dec 1801

Z-105: T.W.2109=31 Jan 1797 Jacob Fry 35 3/4 A.(9 Sep 1800) in Frederick Co. adj. said Fry, Jacob Seabourt, Isaac Zane dec'd, Mordecai Bean. 28 Nov 1801

Z-106: T.W.2109=31 Jan 1797 Jacob Fry 14 1/4 A.(9 Sep 1800) in Frederick Co. adj. Jacob Seabourt, John Cackley, Isaac Zane dec'd., Jacob White. 28 Nov 1801

Z-107: T.W.2175=12 Feb 1798 Joseph Wood asne. of Gabriel Throckmorton 140 A.(12 May 1798) in Hampshire Co. in Cove at foot of N. Mt., on Warm Spring Run adj. Elisha C. Dick, Watson, Warm Spring Rg. 28 Nov 1801

Z-107: T.W.21,477=23 Dec 1783 Solomon Newman asne. of Michael Smith 200 A.(2 Aug 1797) in Hampshire Co. on S. Br. & Little Cacapehon adj. William Carder, Andrew Wodrow, Piney Mt., Henderson, wid. Beers. 4 Dec 1801

Z-108: T.W.2797=31 Oct 1799 James Laramore 76 A.(27 June 1800) in Hampshire Co. on Little Cacapehon Mt. adj. his own land, Benjamin Mishe. 4 Dec 1801

Z-109: T.W.2175=17 Apr 1797 Timothy Smith asne. of Owen Williams 200 A.(5 June 1800) in Hampshire Co. near end of Short arse Mt. adj. Timothy Smith, Elisha C. Dick, Col. Magill. 30 Nov 1801

Z-110: T.W.20,537=10 Nov 1783 Joseph Davis 50 A.(19 Apr 1798) in Hampshire Co. on N. R. & N. R. Mt. adj. said Davis, Van-simmons, John Taylor. 30 Nov 1801

Z-111: T.W.1753=29 Dec 1795 John Thompson 100 A.(23 Aug 1797) in Hampshire Co. on Little Cacapehon adj. his own land, wid. Powles, Robert Alexander, David Corban, William Ellery. 3 Dec 1801

Z-112: 143 A. by T.W.2391=25 Jan 1798 & 145 A. by T.W.2870=14 Jan 1800 Luther & Samuel Colvan 288 A.(18 June 1800) in Hampshire Co. on S. Br. of Potomack adj. Joshua Colvan, William Inskip, Bufffaloe run. 3 Dec 1801

Z-113: T.W.20,701=10 Nov 1783 William J. Hager 8 A.(7 June 1800) in Hardy Co. on N. R. adj. Benjamin Marshall, Joseph Thompson, Caleb Evans. 7 Dec 1801

Z-114: T.W.20,701=10 Nov 1783 William J. Hager 196 A.(7 June 1800) in Hardy Co. on N. R. adj. Thomas Magill, Francis Combs, Hunting Rg., Thompson & Evans, Benjamin Marshall, Robert Means. 7 Dec 1801

Z-115: T.W.17,308=25 June 1783 Conrod Idleman 323 A.(4 Nov 1800) in Hardy Co. on Brushy Run adj. his land, David Miles, Peter Reeves, Jacob Randall. 2 Dec 1801

Z-116:   T.W.2459=10 Apr 1798 Rawleigh Colston 950 A.(22 Aug 1800) in Hampshire
Co. on Pattersons Cr. Mt. adj. John Plumb, Richard Hollsdy, Cold spring run
below Salt Petre Cave, Hampshire & Hardy Cos. line. 30 Nov 1801 [Dl'd Wilson
Allen 10 Jan 1802]

Z-117:   T.W.17,308=25 June 1783 William Davis 23 A.(8 Sep 1800) in Hardy Co.
adj. Charles Wilson on S. fork, James Machir. 2 Dec 1801

Z-118:   T.W.2262=1 Sep 1797 Paul Taylor 18 1/4 A.(7 May 1799) in Berkeley Co. on
Back Cr. adj. Peter Fletcher, Thomas Romines. 4 Dec 1801

Z-119:   Exg.T.W.956=7 Dec 1799 Jacob Price asne. of John James 67 A.(6 Oct 1800)
in Berkeley Co. adj. N. Mt. Elisha Boyd, Jacob Price now Fletcher. 28 Nov 1801

Z-119:   T.W.626=16 Aug 1794 Joseph Evans asne. of Elon Miller 5 A. 1 Ro. 30
Po.(11 Nov 1800) in Berkeley Co. on Opeaquon Cr. adj. William Burns, Michael
McKewan, James Strode dec'd heirs, Joseph Evans. 30 Nov 1801

Z-120: T.W.2262=1 Sep 1797 Paul Taylor 200 A.(29 May 1800) in Berkeley Co. on N.
Mt. & Back Cr. adj. Daniel Hainer, Robert Powell, William Nowland. 5 Dec 1801

Z-121:   T.W.956=7 Dec 1799 Joseph Bell Sr. asne. of John James 19 A.(5 May 1800)
in Berkeley Co. on Bear Garden Rg. adj. William Johnson now said Bell, Michael
Pulse, formerly Hiett now said Joseph Bell, Crane now Bell. 28 Nov 1801

Z-122:   T.W.14,647=12 Oct 1782 John McMeekin 120 A.(17 Dec 1799) in Hampshire
Co. on Pattersons Cr. & near N. Br. of Potowmack adj. John Keder, James Martin,
six mi. So. of Cumberland, near Old Town, near Frankford. 30 Nov 1801

Z-122:   T.W.377=19 Dec 1796 Robert Gustin 244 A.(23 Dec 1800) in Berkeley &
Hampshire Co. on Sleepy Cr. adj. said Gustin, Underwood Run, H. Crone, Johnson,
James Wilson. 25 Nov 1801

Z-123:   T.W.2109=31 Jan 1797 James Davison 25 A.(11 Sep 1800) in Frederick Co.
on Bear Run of Hoye Cr. adj. Jacob Trout now John Kingan, heirs of Gen. Isaac
Zane dec'd, Bennit Hall, George Carpenter formerly John Allen. 27 Nov 1801
[Dl'd Hugh Hoomes Esq. 22 Jan 1802]

Z-125: 31 1/2 A. by T.W.2477=26 May 1798 & 38 A. by Exg.T.W.585=7 Feb 1794 John
Orndorff 69 1/2 A.(10 June 1800) in Frederick Co. on Cedar Cr. adj. Jacob R.
Whiteman. 27 Nov 1801 [Dl'd Archibald Magill 22 Oct 1802]

Z-125:   T.W.1948=25 June 1796 George Booker 250 A.(25 Aug 1800) in Frederick Co.
adj. Little N. Mt., Richard Fossett, Joseph Snap, Mordecai White, Michael
Tumley, Jacob Snap. 27 Nov 1801 [Dl'd Archibald Magill 22 Oct 1802]

Z-126:   T.W.2312=7 Nov 1797 Martin Walter asne. of Michael Clems 50 A.(26 Apr
1800) in Shenandoah Co. in Powells Big Ft. on Passage Cr. adj. Michael Stover,
said Clems. 30 Nov 1801

Z-127:   T.W.2312=7 Nov 1797 Adam Poke 128 A.(3 Apr 1800) in Shenandoah Co. on
Stony Cr. adj. Jacob Pideler, Adam Barb purchase of Daniel Coffelt, Peter Drum,
said Poke, Jacob Barb. 1 Dec 1801

Z-128:   T.W.1401=30 May 1795 George Moyer 84 A.(28 Mar 1800) in Shenandoah Co.
in Powells Big Ft. on Passage Cr. adj. said Moyer. 1 Dec 1801

Z-129:   T.W.1401=30 June 1795 William Hurt 5 A.(20 Oct 1800) in Shenandoah Co.
adj. Reuben Moore, John Will, Richard Patton now James Allen. 30 Nov 1801

Z-129:   T.W.586=25 July 1794 Daniel Webb 25 A.(3 May 1800) in Shenandoah Co. on
Stoney Cr. Rg. adj. said Webb, Adam Poke. 1 Dec 1801

Z-130:   T.W.2312=7 Nov 1797 Catherine Rider, Peter Rider & Jacob Rider 180 A.(3
June 1800) in Shenandoah Co. on Stoney Cr. & Ryals Run adj. Henry Weatherholt,
George Shoemaker, Adam Poke, John Conn, Christian Funkhouser. 30 Nov 1801

8

Z-131:   T.W.2109=31 Jan 1797 Moses Russell & Philip P. Booker 286 3/4 A.(4 Sep 1800) in Frederick Co. on Duck Run of Cedar Cr. adj. Col. William Deakins, John Haystings/Hastings, Elias Kackley, John Richards son & devisee of Henry Richards dec'd, John Lee, John Tevault. 27 Nov 1801

Z-132: T.W.2175=17 Apr 1797 John Perrel 360 A.(12 May 1798) in Hampshire Co. on Great Cacapehon & Lonoms Br. adj. Jacob Pugh, top of Timber Rg., Jesse Anderson. 3 Dec 1801

Z-133:   T.W.5770=24 June 1780 William M. Sterret 400 A.(30 Aug 1800) in Hampshire Co. on Lanoms Br. & Dry Run adj. Elisha C. Dick, said Sterrett, on Timber Rg., Jesse Anderson, John Perrel Jr., Hotzerpiller, Jacob Hoober. 26 Nov 1801 [Dl'd Francis White 8 Oct 1802]

Z-134: T.W.3034=8 Dec 1800 William Shields asne. of David Kennedy 16 A. 2 Ro.(2 Apr 1801) in Berkeley Co. on Back Cr. adj. said Daniel Kennedy, Jacob Cilar, William Faris, Robert Snodgrass. 14 Jan 1802

Z-135: T.W.185=12 Dec 1793 John McMeekin 203 A.(22 Oct 1799) in Hampshire Co. on N.R. adj. David Corbin, Clay lick Run, Richard Neelson, Job Shepard. 30 Nov 1801

Z-136:   T.W.548=8 July 1794 William Kabler 18 1/2 A.(29 Jan 1800) in Culpeper Co. adj. Potatoe Run, Levy Lucaus, said Kabler, Cleaver. 24 Nov 1801 [Dl'd Ro. Pollard 3 Apr 1802]

Z-136:   T.W.3022=1 Dec 1800 Thomas Shirley, Zacheus Shirley, & Joel Yowel 106 A.(8 Jan 1801) in Madison Co. on Forked Mt. near head of white Oak Run, adj. Heywood, path to Tuff hollow, Robinson R. 25 Nov 1801

Z-137:   T.W.3022=1 Dec 1800 Thomas Shirley & Zacheus Shirley 164 A.(5 Jan 1801) in Madison Co. adj. Jebod Heywood, Fork Mt., Joel Yowel. 25 Nov 1801

Z-138: T.W.2381=17 Jan 1798 William Williamson in his own right one moiety & as asne. of Richard Taylor the other moiety of 9 A.(12 July 1798) in Hampshire Co. on Little Cacapeon adj. said Williamson, William Eley/Ely, Thomas Williamson. 4 Dec 1801 [Dl'd to Judge 10 June 1803]

Z-138: T.W.2797=31 Oct 1799 William Jones 150 A.(17 Apr 1800) in Hampshire Co. on Nobly Mt., on New Cr. adj. Samuel Davis, Kennady, Henry Miller. 4 Dec 1801 [Dl'd Dan'l Collins 21 Sep 1802]

Z-139:   T.W.3022=1 Dec 1800 Thomas Shirley, Zacheus Shirley, & Joel Yowel 95 A.(10 Jan 1801) in Madison Co. on S. prong of Robinsons R. 25 Nov 1801

Z-140:   T.W.2797=31 Oct 1799 Richard Wilson 100 A.(25 June 1800) in Hampshire Co. on Alleganey Mt., N. Br. of Potomack adj. John Abernathey. 30 Nov 1801

Z-141:   50 A. by T.W.2298=21 Oct 1797 & 20 A. by T.W.2223=10 July 1797 Stephen Pilcher 70 A.(7 Apr 1800) in Hampshire Co. on Mill Run of Pattersons Cr. adj. his own land, Stephen Creek. 7 Dec 1801 [Dl'd Micajah Barkley 27 Sep 1802]

Z-141: T.W.3022=1 Dec 1800 Thomas Shirley, Zacheus Shirley & Joel Yowel 32 A.(7 Jan 1801) in Madison Co. on Tuff hollow under the Hawkbill Mt. 25 Nov 1801

Z-142:   13 3/4 A. by T.W.2229=14 July 1797 & 62 1/4 A. by Exg. T.W.721=8 Dec 1796 John Vanpelt asne. of Michael Lanbinger 76 A.(10 Feb 1798) in Hampshire Co. on Dillings Run of Great Cacapepon adj. John Perrel Sr., Horn, John Perrel, Henry Bowers. 4 Dec 1801 [Dl'd Jos. Higgins 26 Sep 1806]

Z-143:   T.W.2223=10 July 1797 Stephen Pilcher 50 A.(14 Nov 1799) in Hampshire Co. on Mill & Dry Runs adj. his own land bought of Isaac Good, the Manor line, Peter Good. 7 Dec 1801 [Dl'd Micajah Barkley 27 Sep 1802]

Z-144:   T.W.3022=1 Dec 1800 Thomas Shirley & Joel Yowel 84 A.(3 Jan 1801) in Madison Co. adj. James Hurt on N. prong of Robinson R., Robinson Mt., Cedar Run Mt. 25 Nov 1801

Z-145: T.W.2298=21 Oct 1797 Stephen Pilcher 300 A.(13 Nov 1799) in Hampshire
Co. on Cabbin Run of Pattersons Cr. adj. Dent, George Miller.   25 Nov 1801
[Dl'd Micajah Barkley 27 Sep 1802]

Z-146: T.W.14,647=12 Oct 1782 Matthew Pigman 400 A.(15 Aug 1799) in Hampshire
Co. inc. the Clay Lick on Tear Coat. 26 Nov 1801

Z-147: T.W.1691=25 Nov 1795 Moses Russell 8 3/4 A.(26 Aug 1800) in Frederick
Co. on Duck Run adj. said Russell, Henry Richert/Richards. 28 Nov 1801

Z-147: T.W.143=11 June 1791 John Macrae 13 A. 3 Ro. 8 Po.(5 Aug 1800) in
Stafford Co. adj. John Stark, on Chappawamsick Run, Thomas Chapman. 4 Dec 1801
[Dl'd James Dawe 17 May 1804]

Z-148: T.W.1691=25 Nov 1795 Philip P. Boogher 23 A.(2 June 1800) in Frederick
Co. adj. Cedar Cr. Barnabas Tisbanate, Henry Richard, Elias Kackley. 28 Nov 1801

Z-149: 75 A. by T.W.2506=18 June & 5 A. by T.W.2516=30 July both 1798 John R.
Hedges 80 A.(20 Nov 1798) in Berkeley Co. on Dirt Hill Mt. adj. Thomas Payne.
22 Jan 1802 [Dl'd Hugh Holmes 23 Jan 1802]

Z-150: T.W.2769=18 Sep 1799 William Hill 73 A.(11 Oct 1800) in Hampshire Co. on
Pattersons Cr. inc. land now in possession of William Smith. 25 Jan 1802

Z-150:   213 A. by T.W.3032=9 Dec, 291 1/4 A. by T.W.2966=6 Aug & 93 A. by
Exg.T.W.1000=30 Dec all in 1800 John Turner 597 1/4 A.(27 Feb 1801) in Berkeley
Co. on Whites Br. adj. John R. Hedges, Brian Bruin, Frederick Free, Alexander
Smith. 26 Jan 1802

Z-152: T.W.2591=13 Dec 1798 James Robertson 234 A.(13 June 1800) in Berkeley
Co. on Tilchances Br. adj. Bryan Bruin, Charles Young, Teter Barnes, Arthur
Faris, Robert Pinkerton, Cornelius Kelly. 27 Jan 1802

Z-153: T.W.2591=13 Dec 1798 James Robertson & William Pennybaker 94 A.(10 June
1800) in Berkeley Co. on Tilchances Br. adj. Fredderick Free, George Kygar,
Harper, Shields, Stephenson, William Johnson. 27 Jan 1802

Z-154: T.W.2769=18 Sep 1799 Leroy Hill 9 1/2 A.(2 July 1800) in Hampshire Co.
on Mill Run adj. Peter Putman, Samuel Jones, said Leroy Hill. 25 Jan 1802

Z-155: T.W.2945=29 May 1800 Ephraim Lowman 268 A.(21 Nov 1800) in Berkeley Co.
on Sleepy Cr. adj. said Lowman, George Hoofman, Henry Hoofman. T. Elzey, John
Alenburger, Picket. 27 Jan 1802

Z-156: T.W.2769=18 Sep 1799 Joseph Jacobs 27 A.(25 June 1800) in Hampshire Co.
at foot of Knobly Mt. adj. Henry Miller, Robert Follar, Samuel Jones, George
Gilpin, Thomazon Elzey. 25 Jan 1802

Z-157: T.W.823=8 Dec 1798 Charles Yates 83 A.(6 May 1798) in Culpeper Co. on
middle fork of Thorntons R. adj. said Yates, Thomas Jones, Thomas Morris,
William Bryan. 15 Jan 1802 [Dl'd Maj. Roberts 4 Feb 1802]

Z-158: T.W.602=13 July 1794 Wharton Rector asne. of John Rosbough 200 A.(23 May
1800) in Hampshire Co. on Cold spring Run adj. Showler, Joseph Watson. 11 Feb
1802 [Dl'd the Prop'r 16 Feb 1802]

Z-159: T.W.16,620=28 May 1783 James Claypool 100 A.(20 May 1795) in Hardy Co.
on W. f'k of Lost R. adj. his land. 22 Mar 1802 [Dl'd Jacob Baker 22 June 1802]

Z-159: T.W.21,396=19 Dec 1783 Andrew Webster 33 A.(23 Nov 1791) in Orange Co.
on Rd. to Brocks Bridge, adj. Holliday, James Carter. 7 May 1802 (This land
not in N.N., Grant improperly Recorded in this Book. In Book No. 49 page 617)

Z-160: T.W.20,318=5 Nov 1783 Cornelius Kelly asne. of John R. Hedges 1000 A.(1
July 1801) in Berkeley Co. on Potomac adj. heirs of late Lord Fairfax, George
Huffman, Henry Huffman, Nicholas Leonard heirs, Thomson Elsey. 7 May 1802

Z-161: 300 A. by T.W.2426=1 Mar 1798 & 70 A by Exg.T.W.721=8 Dec 1796 James Reed 370 A.(2 Sep 1800) in Hampshire Co. on Lonams Br. adj. Jacob Clutter, William McVicar. 1 May 1802

Z-162: 300 A. by T.W.494 & 65 1/2 A. by T.W.493 both=31 May 1794 Michael McKewan 365 1/2 A.(23 Oct 1800) in Berkeley Co. on Dry Run of Potomack adj. McCollough, Rd. from Warm Springs to Martinsburg, John Cotter, R.B. Lee now Hunter. 1 May 1802 [Dl'd Hugh Holmes Esq. 1 Aug 1804]

Z-163:   Exg.T.W.459=14 Dec 1791 Leonard Lonas 200 A.(24 May 1800) in Shenandoah Co. adj. Stoney Cr., Ryals Run his land, George Lonas, Mathias Sivy. 5 May 1802

Z-164:   323 A. by T.W.1710=28 Nov 1795 & 31 A. by Exg.T.W.1067=13 Apr 1801 Elisha Boyd 354 A.(10 May 1801) in Berkeley Co. on Short hill Mt. & E. fork of Meadow Br. adj. Beeson now George Lanan, George Everhart, Gasper Snyder now Rynerfield. 10 May 1802 [Dl'd Ab'm Devenport 20 Sep 1802]

Z-166:   T.W.2318=15 Nov 1797 John R. Hedges 237 A.(25 July 1801) in Berkeley Co. on Stoney lick Run of Tilehances Br. adj. Bryan Bruin, John Turner, Robert Pinkerton, Cornelius Kelley. 10 May 1802 [Dl'd Maj. Devenport 19 May 1803]

Z-166:   T.W.2252=14 Aug 1797 John Swisher 100 A.(8 July 1800) in Hampshire Co. on Dillings Mt. adj. Thomas Williams. 5 May 1802 [Dl'd Thos. Dunn 9 May 1803]

Z-167:   T.W.426=7 May 1794 Moses Syver 30 A.(22 May 1800) in Shenandoah Co. in Powells Big Fork adj. Frederick Macinturf, said Syver. 4 May 1802

Z-168:   T.W.2758=31 Aug 1799 Benjamin Rufner 80 A.(20 May 1800) in Shenandoah Co. near Hawksbill Cr. adj. Christian Hoffman, said Rufners purchase of Samuel Comer & Elizabeth his w., Christian Grove. 5 May 1802

Z-168:   T.W.2463=13 Apr 1798 William Lane Jr. 65 1/2 A.(3 May 1800) in Fairfax Co. on Great Rocky Cedar Run adj. Coleman Brown, Woster said to be tenant to Carter, said William Lane. 4 May 1802

Z-169:   T.W.2758=31 Aug 1799 Elizabeth Snider & James McCalister 110 A.(23 Oct 1800) in Shenandoah Co. on Hawksbill adj. Jacob Shaver, John Griffeth, Piney Mt., Philip Summers, George Gamser. 5 May 1802

Z-170:   T.W.2552=18 Oct 1798 Jonathan Dainty 40 A.(28 May 1800) in Fairfax Co. on Pohick Rooling Rd. adj. Ravensworth, John Ward, Dyal now Grimsley, Edward Washington. 3 May 1802

Z-171:   T.W.21,017=1 Dec 1783 Elijah Greenwell 75 A.(26 Dec 1797) in Hampshire Co. on Reasoners Run of Pattersons Cr. adj. heirs of Jacob Reasoner dec'd, William Turner, said Greenwell, Abraham Thompson. 5 May 1802

Z-172:   T.W.2552=18 Oct 1798 Zebede Cumpton 1 1/8 A.(28 May 1800) in Fairfax Co. adj. Conner, Melton, William Barker dec'd, Pohick Run. 3 May 1802

Z-172:   T.W.2552=18 Oct 1798 James Carlin 18 1/8 A.(4 Dec 1800) in Fairfax Co. adj. John Dulin, Sommers, Ravensworth, Alexandria to old Ct. Hs. Rd. 4 May 1802

Z-173:   T.W.105=27 Sep 1788 Wm. Shepherd 49 1/4 A.(24 Mar 1801) in Fairfax Co. on Difficult Run adj. Fairfax, Corville, heirs of Gen. George Washington dec'd. 3 May 1802

Z-174:   Exg.T.W.537=29 Aug 1793 Michael Widmeyer 240 A.(29 Oct 1799) in Berkeley Co. on Sleepy Cr. & Warm Spring Rg. adj. James Wilson, Keyes, John Miller, Jesse Foster. 7 May 1802 [Dl'd Francis White 8 Oct 1802]

Z-175:   T.W.14,163=10 Sep 1782 Daniel Webb 50 A.(27 May 1800) in Shenandoah Co. on Ryals Run adj. Henry Weatherholt, Francis Rinehart, Col. Isaac Zane, Christian Funkhouse heirs. 5 May 1802

Z-175:   Exg.T.W.850=13 Dec 1798 Michael Wydmire 100 A.(20 June 1801) in Berkeley

Co. on Warm Spring Rg. adj. Sleepy Cr. James Willson, Kees, Widmire, Anderson. 7 May 1803

Z-176: T.W.2159=25 Mar 1797 William Rankins asne. of Matthias Swim Jr. 66A.(7 Mar 1801) in Berkeley Co. on Sleepy Cr. adj. William Rankins, Thomazan Elzey, Matthias Swim Sr., Joseph Duckwall formerly B. Bruan. 7 May 1802

Z-177: T.W.33=17 Dec 1787 John Gray 8 A.(19 Nov 1800) in Berkeley Co. on Mill Cr. of Opeckon Cr. adj. said John Gray. 1 May 1802

Z-178: T.W.2672=14 Mar 1799 Thomas Shore 50 A.(25 June 1800) in Hampshire Co. on the Allegany Mt. adj. Thomas Cooper, John Abernathy. 1 May 1802

Z-178: T.W.19,888=14 Oct 1783 William Neale 92 A. 2 Ro.(9 Mar 1801) in Berkeley Co. on Sleepy Cr. adj. Thomas Morgan, Mathias Swaim, Ephram Lowman, Michael McKewan, William Jackson. 11 May 1802 [Dl'd Robert Page 24 Oct 1803]

Z-180: Reexg.T.W.2=4 May 1798 Harmon Utterback asne. of John Mauzy asne. of Henry Mauzy 8 1/2 A.(10 Nov 1799) in Fauquier Co. on Cedar Run adj. Hudnall, Bell, Wright. 7 May 1802 [Dl'd Randolph Spiecer 3 Sep 1803]

Z-180: Reexg.T.W.2=4 May 1798 John Mauzy Jr. asne. of Henry Mauzy Jr. 25 1/2 A.(10 Nov 1799) in Fauquier Co. on Cedar Run adj. Hudnall, Bell, Wright. 6 May 1802 [Dl'd Randolph Spiecer 3 Sep 1803]

Z-181: T.W.2591=13 Dec 1798 Peter Michael 40 A.(7 Dec 1800) in Berkeley Co. on Sleepy Cr. adj. James Cowden formerly Caldwell, William Youst, John Baker, Peter Michael. 14 May 1802 [Dl'd Wm. Smith 30 Oct 1811]

Z-181: T.W.3056=20 Dec 1800 Isaac Means 300 A.(4 June 1801) in Hampshire Co. on Mill Cr. adj. Job Parker, Hugh Balantine. 7 May 1802 [Daniel Collins 2 Sep 1802]

Z-182: Reexg. T.W.2=4 May 1798 John Ball 276 1/2 A.(17 Apr 1801) in Fauquier Co. on Licking Run adj. George Chilton, Robert Lewis, Mann Page, Rd. to Ball's mill. 6 May 1802 [Rec't taken 10 June 1802]

Z-183: Exg.T.W.867=25 Mar 1799 William Slaughter asne. of John McKenny 14 3/4 A.(23 Apr 1800) in Culpeper Co. on Red Oak Mt. adj. Benjamin Johnson, said McKenny. 1 May 1802 [Dl'd Aylett Hawes 9 Dec 1802]

Z-184: Exg.T.W.850=13 Dec 1798 Peter Storm 400 A.(6 Dec 1800) in Berkeley Co. near Sleepy Cr. Mt. adj. Stephen Fenner, John Bailey, Anderson, John Spup or Shup, John Freshour, Peter Hoof. 10 May 1802

Z-185: Reexg.T.W.2=4 May 1798 Robert Hinson Sr. 12 1/2 A.(15 Nov 1799) in Fauquier Co. adj. Benjamin Dod, Jennings, Nathaniel Dod. 7 May 1802 [Dl'd A. Jennings 27 Dec 1802]

Z-185: 1000 A. by T.W.3064=26 Dec 1801 & 119 A. by T.W.404=4 June 1794 Morris Fox 1119 A.(27 Mar 1801) in Fairfax Co. on Dufficult Run adj. Thomas L. Lee now William Lyles, Davis, Fairfax, Turberville, Carter. 13 May 1802 [Thos. Pollard at Fairfax Ct. House 7 July 1802]

Z-186: T.W.2391=25 Jan 1798 Daniel Lantz asne. of William Hargis 35 A.(15 Aug 1799) in Hampshire Co. on Green Spring Valley Run of N. Br. adj. heirs of William Dabson dec'd, Pendleton. 14 May 1802

Z-187: Exg.T.W.900=10 June 1799 William Payne 8 A. 16 Po.(27 Apr 1801) in Pr. William Co. adj. his own land, Warner, Crupper, Singleton, Grigg. 14 May 1802

Z-188: T.W.17,361=26 June 1783 Michael Romich asne. of Abraham Sherffig 18 A.(22 Oct 1799) in Shenandoah Co. on Mill Cr., Little N. Mt. adj. said Sherffig, John Brock, Matthias Zehring. 6 May 1802 [Dl'd Sam'l Garger 20 June 1803]

Z-189: T.W.2797=31 Oct 1797 Stephen J.? Tarry 50 A.(18 Apr 1800) in Hampshire Co. on Knobley Mt. adj. his surv. 6 May 1802 [Dl'd Daniel Collins Sep 21, 1802]

Z-189: T.W.2870=14 Jan 1800 John Mitchell Jr. 90 A.(26 July 1801) in Hampshire Co. on Wiggins Run adj. Job Shepherd, Isaac Dawson, John Akeman. 17 May 1802

Z-190: Exg.T.W.1067=13 Apr 1801 Thomas Turner 46 A.(17 June 1801) in Berkeley Co. adj. Thomas Turner, his purchase of John Turner, Joseph Turner, heirs of John Willson dec'd. 21 May 1802

Z-191: T.W.2806=7 Nov 1799 Joseph Butler Sr. 127 A.(5 Sep 1800) in Hampshire Co. on Potomac R. adj. Richard Marquis, David Simpson, Joseph Butler, William Bennett. 21 May 1802

Z-192: Exg.T.W.1019=23 Jan 1801 John McCleary 435 A.(6 Oct 1801) in Berkeley Co. on Stoney Lick Run & Dirt Hill Mt. adj. John R. Hedges, Robert Pinkerton, Ephraim Gather, John Turner. 20 May 1802 [Dl'd Mr. Tate 20 Dec 1802]

Z-193: T.W.2870=14 Jan 1800 Jacob Millslagel 148 1/2 A.(1 Jan 1801) in Hampshire Co. on N. R. & Timber Mt. adj. Henry Baker, Andrew Millslagel, Elisha C. Dick. 17 May 1802

Z-194: T.W.1362=12 May 1795 James McGinnis 97 A.(1 Aug 1801) in Frederick Co. adj. said McGinnis, Alexander Henderson Esq. 18 May 1802

Z-195: Exg.T.W.1019=23 Jan 1801 John McCleary 370 A.(5 Oct 1801) in Berkeley Co. on Whites Br. & Dirt Hill Mt. adj. Alexander Henderson, John Turner, John R. Hedges, Joseph Hedges. 20 May 1802 [Dl'd Mr. Tate 20 Dec 1802]

Z-196: T.W.2705=3 June 1799 William Mills asne. of Jacob Umstott 50 A.(10 Sep 1799) in Hampshire Co. adj. Job Parker on Mill Cr. 18 May 1802

Z-196: T.W.21,028=1 Dec 1783 Frederick Michael 40 A.(24 Mar 1798) in Hampshire Co. on Great Cacapehon adj. said Michael, George Lynn. 18 May 1802

Z-197: T.W.21,028=1 Dec 1783 Frederick Michael 60 A.(24 Mar 1798) in Hampshire Co. on Great Cacapehon adj. his former surv., James Alexander, Elisha C. Dick. 17 May 1802

Z-198: T.W.2967=6 Aug 1800 Joseph Turner 33 A. 1 Ro. 33 Po.(18 June 1801) in Berkeley Co. adj. Thomas Turner, said Joseph Turner, Vanmeters Marsh, Thomas Turner's purchase of heirs of John Willson dec'd, Jacob Williamson. 21 May 1802

Z-199: T.W.2953=19 June 1800 Thomas Williams 5/8 A.(12 Sep 1800) in Hampshire Co. on Great Cacapehon R. inc. a small island. 21 May 1802

Z-199: T.W.1361=11 May 1795 John Williams asne. of George Hammat 3 Ro. 27 Po.(20 Dec 1800) in Loudoun Co. on Tuskaroro Br. adj. Peter Carr(part of Middleton Shaw patent), Coleman, John Williams. 19 May 1802 [Dl'd Amos Thompson 12 May 1803]

Z-200: T.W.2928=29 Apr 1800 Edward Southood 20 A.(4 Mar 1801) in Berkeley Co. on Opeckon Cr. adj. heirs of Moses Hunter dec'd, said Southood, John Mark. 21 May 1892 [Dl'd Marquis Tate 6 Dec 809]

Z-201: Exg.T.W.867=25 Mar 1799 John Slaughter 12 1/4 A.(9 Apr 1800) in Culpeper Co. adj. James Stephenson, said Slaughter. 20 May 1802 [Aylett Hawes 9 Dec 1802]

Z-201: T.W.2870=14 Jan 1800 Frederick Secrest 64 A.(18 June 1800) in Hampshire Co. adj. Great Cacapehon his land, Valentine Swisher, Daniel Jones. 18 May 1802

Z-202: T.W.2928=29 Apr 1800 William Burns Jr. 14 A.(24 Mar 1801) in Berkeley Co. on Opeckon Cr. adj. said William Burns, Edward Southood, James Crane, heirs of Jacob Hite dec'd. 21 May 1802 [Dl'd Geo. Burnes 18 May 1807]

Z-203: T.W.1171=10 Feb 1795 Thomas Binns asne. of Charles Binns 8 A. 3 Ro. 36 Per.(13 Sep 1800) in Loudoun Co. on Tuskaroro Br. adj. William Diggs now Carlile, Chandler now Ansley, Mead. 19 May 1802 [David Evans 2 Apr 1803]

Z-204:   T.W.2065=8 Dec 1796 William D. Bell 6 A. 2 Ro. 34 Po.(10 Dec 1800) in Loudoun Co. adj. Elk Lick Run, Meek, Asbury Bland now Ellzey. 18 May 1802

Z-205:   T.W.1687=24 Nov 1795 George Feckley Jr. 30 A.(22 Jan 1801) in Shenandoah Co. on N. R. of Shenandoah adj. Peter Black, George Feckley's purchase of John Waddle, Snapp. 19 May 1802 [Dl'd Philip Snapp 12 Feb 1804]

Z-206:   T.W.1171=10 Feb 1795 Thomas Fouch asne. of Charles Binns Jr. 6 A. 2 Ro. 1 Pl.(2 Feb 1801) in Loudoun Co. above Goose Cr. adj. Thomas Moss formerly Bryant Allison, Carter, John Hough now William Cotton. 19 May 1802 [Dl'd James McElhaney 1 Mar 1803]

Z-206:   T.W.1687=24 Nov 1795 George Feckley Jr. 6 A.(23 Jan 1801) in Shenandoah Co. on N. R. of Shenandoah adj. George Feckley, Feckley's purchase of John Waddle. 19 May 1802 [Dl'd Philip Snapp 12 Feb 1804]

Z-207:   T.W.21,028=1 Dec 1783 George Ohaver 50 A.(24 Mar 1798) in Hampshire Co. on Great Cacapehon adj. Grabriel Nourse. 17 May 1802

Z-208:   T.W.3059=20 Dec 1800 John Cooper 50 A.(29 Jan 1801) in Hampshire Co. on N. R. adj. Timber Mt., Elisha C. Dick, Jacob Millslagel, Henry Baker, George Cooper, Andrew Millslagel. 18 May 1802

Z-209:   T.W.1361=11 May 1795 George Hammat 3 A. 3 Ro. 38 3/4 Po.(20 Dec 1800) in Loudoun Co. on Tuskaroro Br. adj. Middleton Shaw, Joshua Daniels, William Means. 19 May 1802 [Dl'd Wm. Woody 25 Mar 1805]

Z-210:   T.W.1171=10 Feb 1795 George Hammat asne. of Charles Binns 13 A. 1 Ro. 1 Per(27 Dec 1800) in Loudoun Co. on Catocton Mt. adj. Messrs. Cock & Mercer, William Means, John Hough. 20 May 1802 [Dl'd Wm. Woody 25 Mar 1805]

Z-210:   28 A. by T.W.21,028, 13 A. by T.W.21,013 & residue by T.W.21,017 all=1 Dec 1783 Baziel Beal 44 A.(7 Aug 1799) in Hampshire Co. on N. Br. adj. Ashby, Inskeep & others, Roberts. 9 Oct 1802 [Dl'd Rob't Williams 11 Oct 1802]

Z-211:   Ann McDonald Exx. of Angus McDonald dec'd, by last will of said Angus McDonald 370 A.(11 Dec 1765) in Hampshire Co. adj. Andrew Friend, the Long Bottom on Potomack. 24 Sep 1802 [Dl'd G. Taylor 25 May 1803]

Z-212:   Ann McDonald Exx. of Angus McDonald dec'd, last will of said Angus McDonald 445 A.(12 Dec 1765) in Hampshire Co. on Pappaw Rg. opposite John Friend. 24 Sep 1802 [Dl'd G. Taylor 25 May 1803]

Z-213:   Ann McDonald Exx. of Angus McDonald dec'd as by last Will of said Angus McDonald 110 A.(15 Apr 1770) in Hampshire Co. adj. Michael Cresap, land formerly Province Williams, N. Br. of Potomack. 24 Sep 1802 [Dl'd G. Taylor 25 May 1803]

Z-214:   Ann McDonald Exx. of Angus McDonald dec'd as by last Will of said Angus McDonald 452 A.(12 Dec 1765) in Hampshire Co. opposite Bell bottom on Potomack. 24 Sep 1802 [Dl'd G. Taylor 25 May 1803]

Z-215:   Exg.T.W.867=25 Mar 1799 William Bryan 36 1/2 A.(9 Dec 1800) in Culpeper Co. adj. Owen Smith, Jason Thomas, John Yates. 20 Oct 1802

Z-215:   Exg.T.W.867=25 Mar 1799 William Bryan 285 A.(12 Feb 1801) in Culpepper Co. on Little Pass Mt. & the Blue Rg., adj. said Bryan, William Bowen, Henry Manifee. 19 Oct 1802

Z-217:   T.W.449=17 May 1794 Samuel Sidwell 97 A.(1 Sep 1801) in Frederick Co. on Apple pie Rg. adj. said Sidwell, Richard Follis, heirs of Undrell Barton dec'd, John McClain. 11 Oct 1802 [Dl'd Arch'd Magill 18 Feb 1812]

Z-218:   T.W.3054=20 Dec 1800 James Singleton 36 A.(3 Apr 1801) in Frederick Co. adj. James G. Dowdall, Joseph Wood, heirs of Joseph Jones dec'd, Joseph Glass now Col.J. G. Dowdall. 11 Oct 1802 [Dl'd Ew'd Taylor 26 Sep 1803]

Z-219: T.W.2813=15 Nov 1799 Jacob Cline/Clyne 110 A.(25 Aug 1801) in Frederick Co. adj. Peter Funk, Thomas Steel, Jesse Taylor, Enos McCoy, Jacob Weaver, John Smith. 11 Oct 1802

Z-219: T.W.2814=15 Nov 1799 Richard Glover 132 A.(8 Sep 1801) in Frederick Co. on Hoge Cr. adj. John Lupton formerly John Pickering, Bennett Hall, Phillip Miller, Robert White, George Carpenter. 11 Oct 1802 [Joseph Sexton 6 Dec 1802]

Z-221: Exg.T.W.900=10 June 1799 Hamilton Thrift 3 1/4 A.(16 Apr 1801) in Fairfax Co. on Scotts Run adj. Thrift's purchase of John Jackson being part of Savages land, Scott & Anderson, Gunnell, Alexander now said Thrift. 11 Oct 1802

Z-221: Exg.T.W, 900=10 June 1799 John Coffer 7 1/2 A.(10 Apr 1801) in Fairfax Co. on Occoquan adj. Carter, Charles Green now Lindsay, Borem now Waggoner. 11 Oct 1802

Z-222: T.W.2382=17 Jan 1798 George Beatty 320 A.(14 May 1800) in Hampshire Co. adj. his own land on Mill Cr. Knobs, Isaac Vanmeter. 13 Oct 1802

Z-223: T.W.2797=31 Oct 1799 William Gray 14 A.(6 Sep 1800) in Hampshire Co. on Potomack R., on Warm Spring Rg., adj. Higgins gap, James Dixson, John Guston. 13 Oct 1802

Z-224: T.W.999=22 Dec 1794 Zachariah Sutton 80 A.(12 Aug 1801) in Hampshire Co. on N. R. adj. John Jones formerly Relphs. 13 Oct 1802

Z-225: T.W.2797=31 Oct 1799 Reubin Millar 50 A.(13 May 1800) in Hampshire Co. on Mill Cr. adj. Craybill, Henry Millar, Fowler, Cooper. 13 Oct 1802

Z-226: T.W.1171=10 Feb 1795 Jesse Janney asne. of Charles Binns 10 A. 2 Ro. 3 Po.(27 Dec 1800) in Loudoun Co. on Goose Cr. adj. Gidney Clark, John Mead now James Dillon, John Anderson, Thomas Janney. 8 Oct 1802

Z-227: T.W.2687=26 Apr 1799 Jesse Janney 69 A.(26 Nov 1800) in Loudoun Co. on the Blue Rg. adj. John Hough, Suden, Warner, Kilpatrick, Fairfax. 8 Oct 1802

Z-228: T.W.2687=26 Apr 1799 Jesse Janney 23 1/4 A.(21 Aug 1801) in Loudoun Co. adj. John Hough, George Lewis, Thomas Dent, Updike, Isaac Nichols. 8 Oct 1802

Z-228: T.W.2687=26 Apr 1799 John Nixon asne. of Jesse Janney 7 3/4 A.(13 Nov 1801) in Loudoun Co. adj. Seconels Br., William Diggs, Benjamin Grayson, Moreland. 8 Oct 1802

Z-229: T.W.2705=3 June 1799 John Jones 276 A.(31 Jan 1801) in Hampshire Co. on N. R. of Great Cacapehon adj. land formerly Samuel Allen. 14 Oct 1802

Z-230: T.W.17,468=27 June 1783 John Kelly 82 A.(27 Nov 1801) in Fauquier Co. on Summer duck Run & Browns Run, on Rd. to Normans ford, adj. Henry Chalffer now George Chapman, Linfield Sharp, George Blackwell, Robert Emry. 8 Oct 1802 [Dl'd Augustin Jennings 27 Dec 1802]

Z-231: T.W.11,367=11 Mar 1782 Joseph Davis 100 A.(29 May 1801) in Hampshire Co. on N. R. adj. Caleb Evans, Dunmore, Edward Cockrell, Samuel Davis, John Wolf. 15 Oct 1802

Z-232: T.W.18,393=6 Aug 1783 William Clark 50 A.(30 Aug 1800) in Hampshire Co. adj. his own land. 15 Oct 1802

Z-233: T.W.1694=27 Nov 1795 Thomas Graves Sr. 12 A.(9 Nov 1800) in Madison Co. adj. said Graves, Church Mt., Lewis. 12 Oct 1802

Z-234: T.W.2993=23 Oct 1800 William Means 21 A.(23 Apr 1801) in Loudoun Co. on Tuskorora adj. Diggs now Carliles, Charles Binns, McGeath, Middleton Shaw. 9 Oct 1802 [Dl'd Rev. Amos Thompson 24 Oct 1803]

Z-235: T.W.2529=10 Sep 1798 Zachariah Fowler 100 A.(13 May 1800) in Hampshire

Co. on Mill Cr. adj. James Cooper, John High. 12 Oct 1802 [Amos Thompson 12 May 1803]

Z-236: T.W.2797=31 Oct 1799 Robert McBride 69 A.(13 Dec 1800) in Hampshire Co. on Tear Coat Cr. adj. Robert McBride, Thomas McBride, Bryan Bruin, Jacob Sevier, George Millslagel. 16 Oct 1802

Z-236: 100 A. by T.W.2797=31 Oct & 75 A. by T.W.2703=3 June both 1799 William Buffington 175 A.(4 Feb 1801) in Hampshire Co. on S. Br.of Potomack. 16 Oct 1802

Z-237: T.W.2702=3 June 1799 Philip Putman 142 A.(15 Aug 1801) in Hampshire Co. on Knobly Mt. adj. Samuel Thompson purchase of Edward Amory, Robert Crissup, Peter Putman. 16 Oct 1802

Z-238: T.W.3059=20 Dec 1800 William Grant 50 A.(11 Apr 1801) in Hampshire Co. on Tear Coat Cr. adj. Adam Hall, Samuel Collins, Thomas Mason, William Grant. 16 Oct 1802

Z-239: T.W.14,148=9 Sep 1782 Michael Laubinger 63 A.(23 Aug 1801) in Hampshire Co. on Green spring Run adj. Robert Walker, John Donaldson. 14 Oct 1802

Z-240: Resurv 28 Aug 1801 John Douthart 311 1/2 A. [300 A. granted by late Prop'r of N.N. 10 Mar 1761 to Siles Hedges who conveyed to Douthart alias John Douthit 8 Dec 1761 & 11 1/2 A.surplus by T.W.15,213=2 Apr 1782 in Hampshire Co. on Pattersons Cr. adj. land formerly Joseph Carrol, the Waggon Rd. 18 Oct 1802

Z-241: T.W.2379=17 Jan 1798 Andrew Humes 76 A.(5 Feb 1801) in Hampshire Co. on S. Br. adj. Simon Ersom, John's Run. 12 Oct 1802

Z-242: T.W.2959=26 June 1800 Jacob Read 250 A.(18 Apr 1801) in Hampshire Co. Adj. Pattersons Cr. Manor on Wild Meadow Run. 14 Oct 1802

Z-242: T.W.2381=17 Jan 1798 Thomas Williamson 150 A.(20 June 1798) in Hampshire Co. on Little Cacapehon adj. John Wallis, Paris Drew dec'd, William Eley, wid. Williamson. 14 Oct 1802

Z-243: T.W.14,148=9 Sep 1782 Michael Laubenger 247 A.(23 Aug 1801) in Hampshire Co. adj. S. Br. of Potomack, Conway Rector, James Parson dec'd, S. Br. Mt. 14 Oct 1802

Z-244: 50 A. by T.W.2713=18 June 1799 & 35 A. by T.W.3031=9 Dec 1800 Robert Snodgrass Jr. 85 A.(16 Oct 1801) in Berkeley Co. on Back Cr. adj. Samuel Winning, Robert Snodgrass, James Hammond, John Cunningham, William Johnson. 19 Oct 1802 [Dl'd Capt. Tate 24 Dec 1802]

Z-246: T.W.242=29 Jan 1794 Gilbert Combs asne. of Robert D. Combs 22 1/2 A.(4 Nov 1801) in Culpeper Co. adj. Peter Hoffman, Peter Deal, Adam Outz. 20 Oct 1802 [Dl'd the Prop'r 26 Nov 1802]

Z-247: Exg.T.W.867=25 Mar 1799 Gilbert Combs asne. of William Bryan 120 A.(11 Feb 1801) in Culpeper Co. on Oven top Mt. adj. John Skinner, William Reece, Francis Brandom, John Brandom. 20 Oct 1802 [Dl'd the Prop'r 26 Nov 1802]

Z-248: Exg.T.W.867=25 Mar 1799 William Bryan 27 A.(4 Mar 1801) in Culpeper Co. on Oventop Mt. adj. said Bryan, Thomas Morris, Charles Yates. 20 Oct 1802

Z-248: T.W.2380=17 Jan 1798 James Welch asne. of John Dixon 303 3/4 A.(21 Jan 1801) in Berkeley Co. on Sleepy Cr. adj. Jacob Hoover, Philip Pendleton formerly Hogan, Miller. 18 Oct 1802 [Dl'd Mr. Worden? 28 Sep 1803]

Z-249: Exg.T.W.1038=3 Mar 1801 John Shewmaker 233 A.(4 Nov 1801) in Hardy Co. Co. on Great Cacapehon adj. his land, John Tevolt, Thomas Littler. 21 Oct 1802

Z-251: T.W.2312=7 Nov 1797 Catharine Rider, Peter Rider & Jacob Rider 140 A.(5 Aug 1800) in Shenandoah Co. on Suppenlick Mt. adj. John Holver. 19 Oct 1802

16

Z-252:   T.W.2311=7 Nov 1797 John Holver 72 A.(3 Apr 1800) in Shenandoah Co. on
Mill Cr. adj. said Holver, George Richards, Little N. Mt. 18 Oct 1802

Z-253:   T.W.2758=31 Aug 1799 John Holver 28 A.(4 Apr 1801) in Shenandoah Co. on
Mill Cr. adj. said Holver, Martin Rup. 18 Oct 1802

Z-253:   T.W.2758=31 Aug 1799 Daniel Webb 67 A.(2 May 1801) in Shenandoah Co. on
Little N. Mt. adj. Thomas Ryan, Col. Isaac Zane's purchase of Joseph Pugh. 18
Oct 1802

Z-254:   T.W.695=24 Sep 1796 Daniel Zimmerman 69 A.(5 Mar 1801) in Shenandoah Co.
on Little Line Run adj. John Norman, Frederick Stoneberger, George Hetick, John
Heastant. 19 Oct 1802

Z-256:   T.W.2759=31 Aug 1799 Jacob Good 5 1/2 A.(25 Feb 1801) in Shenandoah Co.
near Holemans Cr., adj. Joseph Moore, Jacob Good, Michael Hannigan. 19 Oct 1802

Z-256:   T.W.2758=31 Aug 1799 Jonathan Mauk 15 A.(12 Mar 1801) in Shenandoah Co.
on N. R. of Shenandoah adj. said Mauk, Christian Graybill, George Feckley Jr.,
Henry Hiser. 19 Oct 1802

Z-257: T.W.242=29 Jan 1794 Edward Willey 34 /12 A.(27 Apr 1801) in Culpeper Co.
on little battle Run adj. said Willey, William Duncan, Slone, William Roberts.
20 Oct 1802

Z-258:   Exg.T.W.1038=3 Mar 1801 John Talbot & James Cunningham 168 A.(2 Nov
1801) in Hardy Co. on Patterson Cr. adj. Job Welton, James Machir, Relph, John
Bishop. 21 Oct 1802

Z-259: T.W.242=29 Jan 1794 Joseph Browning 51 A.(28 Dec 1801) in Culpeper Co.
adj. Charles Tull. 21 Oct 1802

Z-260: T.W.242=29 Jan 1794 Daniel Brown 12 A.(6 June 1801) in Culpeper Co. adj.
said Brown, John Creel, George Parsons, James Kelby. 21 Oct 1802

Z-261:   T.W.242=29 Jan 1794 Jason Thomas Jr. 25 A.(28 Apr 1801) in Culpeper Co.
on Pignut Rg. adj. Jason Thomas Sr., Joshua Morris, William Poutter. 20 Oct 1802

Z-261:   Exg.T.W.1038=3 Mar 1801 Van Simmons 42 A.(4 Nov 1801) in Hardy Co. in
Chrismans gap adj. his land, N. R. Mt. 21 Oct 1802

Z-262:   Exg.T.W.1038=3 Mar 1801 William McDaniel 9 A.(10 Nov 1801) in Hardy Co.
Co. on Great Cacapehon adj. his own land, George Shoemaker. 21 Oct 1802

Z-263:   100 A. by T.W.2492=6 June 1798, 47 A. by T.W.1985=24 Sep 1796 & 100 A.
by Exg.T.W.515=22 May 1793 Isaac Strickler 247 A.(24 July 1799) in Shenandoah
Co. in Messennotten adj. Benjamin Stricklers heirs sold Henry Forrer, Philip
Boyer now Philip Long, John Chamberlain, Samuel Sugden. 7 Jan 1803 [Dl'd Mr.
James Allen 8 Jan 1803]

Z-264:   T.W.748=3 Oct 1794 James Watts 180 A.(6 Jan 1795) in Hampshire Co. adj.
Frederick Finks, his own land, Thomzen Elzey, on state Rd., by Bever Run. 15
Jan 1803

Z-265:   T.W.20,542=10 Nov 1783 William Vause 103 A.(10 Nov 1798) in Hampshire
Co. on Pattersons Cr. adj. said Vause, John Dowthart. 27 Jan 1803

Z-266:   700 A. by T.W.536=19 June 1794, 400 A. by T.Ws.2528 & 2530 both=10 Sep
1798, 230 A. by T.W.3098=25 Feb 1801, 400 A. by T.W.2940=22 May 1800 & residue
T.W.22,480=24 Dec 1783 Valentine Peyton & John West 1753 A.(30 June 1801) in Pr.
William Co. on Neabsco Run & Bever dam Br. of Occoquan R. adj. Mr. Tayloe, Daw,
Foley, Graham & Silkmare, Capt. Elliott, Dorsey, Ashton, Jackson, James Peake,
Thomas Chapman. 1 Mar 1803   [Dl'd Wm. Moncure 1 Mar 1803]

Z-268:   200 A. by T.W.3011=3 Nov 1800 & 83 A. by T.W.3051=20 Dec in same year
Richard Nelson asne. of John Griffin Nelson 283 A.(12 Aug 1801) in Hampshire &

Hardy Cos. on Horn camp Run, adj. Plumb lick Mt., Frederick Starkey, George Gilpin, James Martin, William J. Hayger. 15 Mar 1803 [Enclosed to Rich'd Nelson Romney by post 20 Apr 1803]

Z-270: T.W.1710=28 Nov 1795 James Faulkner asne. of George Everheart 500 A.(2 Mar 1801) in Berkeley Co. on Short hill Mt. adj. John G. Konnekee, Scott, Sniveley. 14 Mar 1803 [Inclosed the Prop'r at Martinsburg 18 Apr 1804]

Z-271: 1000 A. by T.W.14,647=12 Oct 1782 & 122 A. by T.W.413=28 Apr 1794 James Tucker asne. of William Johnston asne. of Peter Williams 1122 A.(8 Nov 1799) in Hampshire Co. on S. Br. of Potomack adj. Peter Williams, Andrew Humes, Earrsom, Murphey, Medannil, Andrew Wodrow, George Gilpan. 1 June 1803 [Dl'd Wm. Wiseham 22 June 1803]

Z-273: T.W.14,647=12 Oct 1782 James Tucker asne. of William Johson asne. of Peter Williams 600 A.(19 Apr 1800) in Hampshire Co. on S. Br. of Potomack adj. Fielding Calmes, William Fox, Wait, Williams. 1 June 1803 [Dl'd Wm. Wiseham 22 June 1803]

Z-274: T.W.7453=20 Oct 1781 Joseph Tomlinson 200 A.(26 Nov 1802) Ohio [Recorded here through mistake]

Z-275: 200 A. by T.W.166=10 Dec 1793 & 239 A. by T.W.253=6 Feb 1794 David Hunter 439 A.(22 Jan 1802) in Berkeley Co. on Meadow Br. & Sleepy Cr. Mt. adj. Jacob Morgan, Philip Pendleton, John R. Hedges. 9 June 1803 [10 June 1803]

Z-276: T.W.2759=31 Aug 1799 Lawrence Pitman 5 A.(30 Oct 1801) in Shanandoah Co. on N. R. of Shanandoah adj. Peter Black, said Pitman. 11 June 1803 [Dl'd Mr. Snap 15 June 1803]

Z-277: T.W.3069=5 Jan 1801 James Stinson asne. of James Mathes Sr. 100 A.(22 Aug 1801) in Shanandoah Co. near S. R. of Shanandoah adj. Benjamin Mathes, James Mathes. 11 June 1803 [Dl'd Mr. Snap 15 June 1803]

Z-278: T.W.2759=31 Aug 1799 George Feather asne. of Peter Weaver 116 A.(24 June 1801) in Shanandoah Co. on N. R. of Shanandoah, adj. Martin Betz, William Smith dec'd, Abraham Bird, Daniel Newland, Peter Snider. 11 June 1803 [Dl'd Mr. Snap 15 June 1803]

Z-280: Exg.T.W.914=7 Oct 1799 Alexander Quarrier for 1/2 & David Robertson as Exr. of Duncan McRae dec'd asne. of said Quarrier for other half of 381 3/4 A.(5 Sep 1801) in Hampshire Co. adj. William Abernathy, Earson. 24 May 1803 [Dl'd Alex'r Quarrier 23 June 1803]

Z-280: Exg.T.W.914=7 Oct 1799 Alexander Quarrier for 1/2 & David Robertson as Exr. of Duncan McRae dec'd asne. of said Quarrier other half of 66 1/4 A.(3 Sep 1801) in Hampshire Co. on N. Br. of Potomack on side of Knobly Mt., adj. John Dawson. 24 May 1803 [Dl'd Alex'r Quarrier 23 June 1803]

Z-281: 50 A. by T.W.3058=20 Dec 1800, 150 A. by T.W.3264=29 Oct 1801 & 61 A. by T.W.3327=23 Jan 1802 William Naylor 261 A.(20 Jan 1802) in Hampshire Co. on S. Br. of Potowmack adj. Andrew Woodrow, Adam Hall, John Jack. 24 June 1803

Z-283: T.W.2901=26 Feb 1800 Henry Wilson 600 A.(6 Nov 1801) in Hardy Co. Co. on Waitses's run of Great Cacapehon, on Andersons Rg., adj. Johnston, Robert Means. 16 June 1803

Z-284: T.W.2901=26 Feb 1800 George Hulver 64 A.(4 Apr 1801) in Hardy Co. on Lost R. adj. Andrew Bauhman, Samuel Slater. 16 June 1803

Z-285: T.W.19,223=10 Sep 1783 William Bryan 673 A.(15 Feb 1801) in Culpeper Co. on Thorntons R. adj. Henry Poinder, Henry Manifee, Charles Yates, said Bryan, Benjamin Partlow, Love, Thomas Jones, Henry Swindler. 16 June 1803 [Dl'd Philip Snap 17 Mar 1804]

Z-287: T.W.2901=26 Feb 1800 George Hulver 283 A.(4 Apr 1801) in Hardy Co. adj.

Andrew Bouhman, William Robinson. 16 June 1803

Z-288: T.W.2794=25 Oct 1799 Henry Settle 10 A.(2 Nov 1801) in Loudoun Co. adj. John Kimbler, Benjamin James, John Ashford, ___ Oden. 16 June 1803 [Dl'd Wm. B. Harrison 9 Dec 1803]

Z-289: T.W.2901=26 Feb 1800 David Smith 24 A.(6 Nov 1801) in Hardy Co. on Pattersons Cr. Mt. 27(17) June 1803

Z-290: T.W.2792=31 Oct 1799 Amos Poland 50 A.(27 May 1801) in Hampshire Co. on Kuyhandalls mill Run adj. wid. Beer, John Jack, Kuykendall. 17 June 1803

Z-291: T.W.2901=26 Feb 1800 William J. Hager 100 A.(6 Nov 1801) in Hardy & Hampshire Cos. on Secret lick Run of N. R. adj. Thompson, Evans. 17 June 1803

Z-292: T.W.2901=26 Feb 1800 James Thompson 300 A.(3 Sep 1801) in Hardy Co. on Scaggs Run adj. Francis Combs, Benedict Jarbo, James Been, Joseph Obannon. 17 June 1803

Z-293: 50 A. by T.W.3058 & 30 A. by T.W.3051 both=20 Dec 1800 Amos Poland 80 A.(24 Aug 1801) in Hampshire Co. on Piney Mt., on Kuykendalls mill run adj. John Poland, John Goff. 17 June 1803

Z-294: T.W.19,223=10 Sep 1783 William Bowen 145 A.(13 Feb 1801) in Culpeper Co. adj. William Bryan, Henry Manifee. 18 June 1803 [Dl'd Philip Snap 17 Mar 1804]

Z-295: T.W.19,223=10 Sep 1783 Charles Asher 28 A.(16 Apr 1801) in Culpeper Co. adj. William Lovell, Asher. 18 June 1803

Z-296: T.W.19,223=10 Sep 1783 Thomas Jones 57 A.(6 Apr 1801) in Culpeper Co. on Piggnut Rg., adj. John Strother, Jason Thomas, grant of late Capt. John Strother, N. Thornton R. 18 June 1803

Z-298: T.W.19,223=10 Sep 1783 William Bowen 54 A.(14 Feb 1801) in Culpeper Co. on N. Fork of Thorntons R. opposite Henry Manifee, adj. William Bryan. 18 June 1803 [Dl'd Philip Snap 17 Mar 1804]

Z-299: 20 A. by T.W.2415=12 Feb 1798 & 100 A. by T.W.2703=3 June 1799 John Lay 120 A.(31 Jan 1801) in Hampshire Co. on Knob Rg. & Sandy Lick Hollow adj. Daniel Lay, John Stephenfought, John Combes. 20 June 1803

Z-300: Exg.T.W.1067=13 Apr 1801 Lewis Duckwall 29 A.(31 July 1801) in Berkeley Co. on Sleepy Cr. adj. White, Daniel Royer, Frederick Duckwall, Lewis Duckwall. 20 June 1803

Z-301: T.W.2682=17 Apr 1799 George Tedrick 351 A.(5 June 1800) in Berkeley Co. on Potomack R. adj. Ann Moody now Dr. Jaques, Christopher Tedrick, Michael McKewan, C. Lowman, Hoffman, John Huffman formerly Gragg. 20 June 1803

Z-302: 300 A. by T.W.2467=4 May 1798 & 75 A. by T.W.2339=11 Dec 1797 Joseph & John Copp 375 A.(16 Sep 1801) in Berkeley Co. on Sleepy Cr. adj. Michael McKearnan heirs, Yellow spring run, Bryan Bruin now Joseph Duckwall, George Wisenburg, F. Duckwall, Christian Miller, George Dyche, Edmuson, Swim, Fitzchew. 20 June 1803 [Dl'd Abm. Devenport 20 Sep 1803]

Z-304: T.W.419=1 May 1794 William Brown asne. of Thomas Allen 2 A.(7 Feb 1801) in Culpeper Co. adj. William Thornton, William Brown. 20 June 1803 [Dl'd Dr. Hawsthe 8 Dec 1803]

Z-305: T.W.3036=9 Dec 1800 Christopher Tedrick 100 A.(5 June 1801) in Berkeley Co. on Potowmack R. adj. Ann Moody now Dr. Jaques, George Tedrick, Michael McKewan. 20 June 1803

Z-306: 47 A. by T.W.141=1 June 1791 & 38 1/2 A. by T.W.2158=25 Mar 1797 William Rankins 85 1/2 A.(24 Mar 1802) in Berkeley Co. on Sleepy Cr. Mt. adj. Matthias Swim Jr., said Rankins, Matthias Swim(third). 21 June 1803 [Dl'd John Sherwood

5 Dec 1820]

Z-307:   T.W.1333=16 Mar 1795 Conrod Lodman asne. of Matthias Swim asne. of Phillip Pendleton 200 A.(18 Sep 1801) in Berkeley Co. on Sleepy Cr., Sleepy Cr. Mt. near White's gap adj. John Miller, Conrod Lutsman.   21 June 1803

Z-308:   T.W.2318=15 Nov 1797 John Oferrall asne. of John R. Hedges 143 A.(3 Sep 1801) in Berkeley Co. on Back Cr. adj. John Turner, Michael Bitzer, William Snodgrass.   21 June 1803 [Dl'd Abm. Devenport 20 Sep 1803]

Z-310:   T.W.875=29 Nov 1794 John Hunter asne. of Philip Pendleton 184 A.(18 Sep 1801) in Berkeley Co. on Sleepy Cr. Mt. adj. Alexander, Swim(third), Frederick Froushour, George Wisenberg, Philip Pendleton.   21 June 1803

Z-311:   T.W.2759=31 Aug 1799 Michael Spiegle 41 A.(29 Oct 1801) in Shenandoah Co. on N. R. of Shenandoah adj. said Spiegle, Ulrich Stover.   22 June 1803

Z-312:   T.W.1333=16 Mar 1795 John Conwell 132 A.(2 Dec 1801) in Berkeley Co. on N. Mt. adj. John Watson.   22 June 1803 [Dl'd Abram Devenport 21 Sep 1803]

Z-313:   T.W.378=11 Mar 1794 Gabriel Hays 600 A.(10 May 1802) in Hampshire Co. on Great Cacapehon Mt. adj. George Thompson, William Jackson.   22 June 1803

Z-314:   T.W.2785=3 Oct 1799 Richard Keen asne. of John Spencer 5 A. 2 Ro. 11 Po.(29 Mar 1802) in Loudoun Co. on Goose Cr. adj. Lewis Ellzey, John Keen, Mary Bolon.   22 June 1803 [Dl'd Joseph Blincoe 17 Sep 1803]

Z-315:   T.W.2759=31 Aug 1799 Moses Siever 35 A.(18 Nov 1801) in Shenandoah Co. in Powells big Ft. adj. said Siever, Michael Clem, Martin Walter, Michael Stover.   22 June 1803

Z-316:   T.W.2759=31 Aug 1799 David Clem 100 A.(18 Nov 1801) in Shenandoah Co. in Powells big Ft. adj. Moses Siever, Clem's purchase of Christian Perkipile.   23 June 1803

Z-318:   T.W.16326=12 May 1783 Jacob Copperstone 48 A.(5 Nov 1801) in Shenandoah Co. in Powells big Ft. adj. George Hawn, said Copperstone, wid. Munch, Jacob Lechliter, the Grant line.   23 June 1803

Z-319:   T.W.2490=6 June 1798 George Fravell 20 A.(25 May 1802) in Shenandoah Co. near Mulberry run adj. Hieronymas Baker, Thomas Newell, Daniel Beam formerly Samuel Blackburn.   23 June 1803 [Dl'd Philip Grymes 20 Sep 1803]

Z-320:   T.W.16,326=12 May 1783 Henry Burner 177 A.(3 Nov 1801) in Shenandoah Co. in Powells big Ft. adj. Henry Burner, William Mordock, William Ellzey, David Golladay, Jacob Binner or Binnes.   23 June 1803

Z-322:   T.W.16,326=12 May 1783 Jacob Coppersone 12 A.(5 Nov 1801) in Shenandoah Co. in Powells big Ft. on Carriers Run adj. said Copperstone, George Hawn.   23 June 1803

Z-323:   T.W.16,326=12 May 1783 John Smith(Carpinter) 328 A.(16 Feb 1802) in Shenandoah Co. in Powells big Ft. on Passsage Cr. adj. John Denton.   23 June 1803

Z-324:   T.W.2252=14 Aug 1797 John Mitchell Jr. 146 A.(2 Feb 1801) in Hampshire Co. on Wiggins run of Potowmack R. adj. Cornelius Ferrees, Job Shepard, John Aikman, Nooney.   24 June 1803

Z-325:   T.W.748=3 Oct 1794 John Mitchell Jr. 411 A.(20 June 1797) in Hampshire Co. on Great Cacapehon adj. Evan Jenkins, Peter Ougan, Thomas Fry, Ellzey formerly Heath, McBride.   24 June 1803

Z-327:   T.W.2910=19 Mar 1800 Philip Snapp 150 A.(29 June 1801) in Frederick Co. adj. Maj. Lewis Stephens, Nicholas Walters.   24 June 1803 [Prop'r 24 Sep 1803]

Z-328:   T.W.2882=24 Jan 1800 Philip Snapp 71 A.(27 Apr 1801) in Frederick Co.

adj. purchase of Maj. Lewis Stephens in the little cove, Nicholas Walters. 24 June 1803 [Dl'd the Prop'r 21 Sep 1803]

Z-329: T.W.2759=31 Aug 1799 Moses Siever 100 A.(20 Nov 1801) in Shenandoah Co. in Powells big Ft. adj. said Moses Siever, David Clem, Frederick Macinturff. 22 June 1803

Z-331: T.W.2882=24 Jan 1800 Nicholas Walters 50 A.(27 Apr 1801) in Frederick Co. adj. Samuel Weeks, Copen Mt., Robertson. 24 June 1803 [Dl'd Philip Snapp 24 Sep 1803]

Z-332: T.W.546=7 July 1794 Edward Rumsey & Joseph Gill 600 A.(3 Sep 1801) in Berkeley Co. on Sleepy Cr. Mt. adj. Swearengen, William Hixson, John Hixson, Jerome Williams. 25 June 1803 [Dl'd Griffin Taylor 10 May 1804]

Z-334: T.W.626=15 Aug 1794 John McPherson asne. of Elon Miller 3 A.(12 Feb 1802) in Jefferson Co. adj. heirs of Gerard Alexander dec'd, Christopher Beelor now John McPherson, Battaill Muse. 5 June 1803 [Dl'd George Tate 12 Dec 1803]

Z-335: T.W.6026=15 Aug 1794 Daniel McPherson asne. of Elon Millar 11 A. 1 Ro. 34 Po.,the lowermost Island in Shenandoah R.(13 Feb 1802) in Jefferson Co. 25 June 1803 [Dl'd George Tate 12 Dec 1803]

Z-336: T.W.14,647=12 Oct 1782 John Spencer 44 1/2 A.(18 Sep 1800) in Hampshire Co. on Knobly Mt., Cabbin Run, adj. said Spencer, Francis & William Deakins. 25 June 1803

Z-338: T.W.546=7 July 1794 Edward Rumsey & Joseph Gill 200 A.(4 Sep 1801) in Berkeley Co. on Sleepy Cr. Mt. adj. Swim, Dawson. 25 June 1803 [Dl'd Griffin Taylor 10 May 1804]

Z-339: T.W.2370=6 Jan 1798 Alexander Smith 1/2 & John Hay asne. of said Smith the other half 1000 A.(22 Mar 1802) in Hardy Co. on Urams Cr. adj. his own land, Alexander Lard, Bruce, Abrams Cr., John Champ, Isaac Vanmeter, Benjamin Chambers, Deakins, Edward McGuire. 25 June 1803

Z-341: T.W.2115=14 Feb 1797 Gabriel Ross & Absalom Chinoweth asne. of Joseph Baker 650 A.(22 Mar 1802) in Berkeley Co. on Back Cr. adj. Samuel Dunan?, Nathan Litler, Joseph Henderson, Peter Fletcher, William Douglas heirs. 28 June 1803

Z-342: T.W.3011=3 Nov 1800 Richard Nelson 47 A.(11 Dec 1801) in Hampshire Co. on Stonylick fork of little Cacapehon, adj. Harbert Cool, Brian Bruin. 28 June 1803 [Dl'd Sam'l Howard 29 Sep 1803]

Z-343: Exg.T.W.1229=22 Jan 1802 Adam Boarer 80 A.(8 Apb 1802) in Berkeley Co. on Buffaloe Lick run of Sleepy Cr. adj. Andrew Hoyle heirs, William Stephenson, George Corrick, William Williams. 28 June 1803 [James Campbell 10 Dec 1803]

Z-345: Exg.T.W.1229=22 Jan 1802 Adam Boarer 30 A.(1 Apr 1802) in Berkeley Co. on Sleepy Cr. adj. William Williams, heirs of Andrew Hoyle, Matthias Trotter heirs. 28 June 1803 [Dl'd Ja's Campbell Esq. 10 Dec 1803]

Z-346: Exg.T.W.1229=22 Jan 1802 Adam Boarer 20 A.(1 Apr 1802) in Berkeley Co. on Sleepy Cr. adj. Thomas Talbert, Lewis Wolf heirs, George Corrick. 28 June 1803 [Dl'd James Campbell 10 Dec 1803]

Z-347: T.W.3011=3 Nov 1800 John G. Nelson asne. of Richard Nelson 128 A.(11 Dec 1801) in Hampshire Co. bet. Hardikens fork & Stony Lick fork of little Cacapehon adj. Brian Bruin, Steel. 28 June 1803 [Dl'd Sam'l Howard 29 Sep 1803]

Z-348: 1000 A. by T.W.2957 & 150 A. by T.W.2959 both=26 June 1800 Alexander Monroe 1150 A.(12 Aug 1801) in Hampshire Co. on little Cacapehon & Tearcoat Crs. adj. Richard Nelson, Elisha Beal, Matthew Pigman, Job Sheperd dec'd, Daniel Corbin, James Murphy, Steel, Stony Mt. 29 June 1803 [Dl'd John Slane 1 Dec 1803]

Z-351: T.W.2797=31 Oct 1799 Daniel Carmichael asne. of Francis White 12 A. 12

Po.(25 Apr 1800) in Hampshire Co. on N. R. adj. White, Dr. Crage. 29 June 1803

Z-352: 500 A. by T.W.2958 & 200 A. by T.W.2959 both=26 June 1800 Alexander Monroe 700 A.(12 Aug 1801) in Hampshire Co. on Hangan rock run of N. R. adj. heirs of Francis Kees dec'd, Rd. from Romney to Winchester, Henry Baker, John Parks, Jacob Vanpelt, Elias George. 29 June 1803 [Dl'd John Slane 1 Dec 1803]

Z-354: 50 A. by T.W.2391=25 Jan 1798 & 50 A. by T.W.2797=31 Oct 1799 John Hiett 100 A.(20 Oct 1800) in Hampshire Co. on Gibbons run of N. R. adj. Dr. Craick, George Shorf. 29 June 1803 [Dl'd Sam'l Howard 29 Sep 1803]

Z-356: Exg.T.W.377=19 Dec 1796 Robert Gustin 19 A.(15 Dec 1801) in Berkeley Co. on Sleepy Cr. adj. Pike, Edward Crabb, Peter Light. 1 July 1803

Z-357: Exg.T.W.377=19 Dec 1796 Robert Gustin 166 A.(13 Mar 1802) in Berkeley Co. on Sleepy Cr. & Sleepy Cr. Mt. adj. Peter Hoof/Hoop, Philip Pendleton heirs, Jacob Hoover, Freshour heirs. 1 July 1803

Z-358: T.W.3012=6 Nov 1800 Rawleigh Colston 45 A.(31 Jan 1801) in Loudoun Co. on Goose Cr. adj. Rawleigh Colston, Samples or Aylett, Henry Peyton. 1 July 1803 [Inclosed to R.Colston 31 July 1804]

Z-359: T.W.3012=6 Nov 1800 Rawleigh Colston 39 A.(31 Jan 1801) in Loudoun Co. on Goose Cr.adj. Samples or Aylett, Henry Peyton, Cocke, Dr. Green. 1 July 1803 [Inclosed to R.Colston 31 July 1804]

Z-360: T.W.242=29 Jan 1794 Daniel Mock 93 A.(1 May 1802) in Culpeper Co. adj. said Mock, Hogg Camp Br. 1 July 1803 [Dl'd Philip Snap 17 Mar 1804]

Z-362: T.W.2540=4 Oct 1798 Daniel Field Sr. 36 1/2 A.(31 May 1802) in Culpeper Co. adj. James Sims, William Powel, William Newton, Benjamin Leavel. 2 July 1803 [Dl'd Dan'l Field, the Bearer of Prop'r's rec't 30 Oct 1812]

Z-363: T.W.2540=4 Oct 1798 Joseph Stewart & William Powel 88 A.(30 Oct 1801) in Culpeper Co. adj. said Powel & Stewart, William Newton, Daniel James, Beverlys line. 2 July 1803

Z-364: T.W.3012=6 Nov 1800 Joseph Land asne. of Rawleigh Colston 13 A. 1 Ro. 30 Per.(24 Nov 1801) in Loudoun Co. on Goose Cr. adj. Richard Beason now Stephen C. Roszell, John Hough, John Lasswell, Glebe land of Par. of Shelburn, Richard Brown, John Hough now Philip Vansickle. 2 July 1803

Z-365: Exg.T.W.427=26 Apr 1791 Alexander Smith 25 A.(16 Mar 1793) in Hardy Co. on N. Br. of Potomack adj. Norman Bruce. 1 Oct 1803 [Dl'd Mr. Deane of Monongalia 4 Oct 1803]

Z-366: 816 A. by T.W.875=29 Nov, 2000 A. by 823=1 Oct & 1164 A. by T.W.817=29 Oct all 1794 Eliz'th Hunter, Nancey C. Kennedy, Philip C. Pendleton. James Pendleton, Sarah Pendleton, Edmund Pendleton, Marie Pendleton & Wm. Henry Pendleton ch. & heirs of Philip Pendleton dec'd 3980 A.(10 Nov 1801) in Berkeley Co. inc. part of Sleepy Cr. Mt. adj. Rumsey, Gill, Cartwright, Williams, Mathias Swim, William Rankin, William Alexander, said Pendleton, John Miller, Stanley, Jacob Hoover, John Freshour, Dr. Sniveley, George Corman, Jacob Morgan. 24 Oct 1803 [Dl'd David Hunter 26 Oct 1803]

Z-369: T.W.3264=29 Oct 1801 Jost Stimbel 35 A.(9 Oct 1802) in Hampshire Co. on Mill Cr. adj. his own land, Jacob Piser, Stimbel, Rodtruck. 8 Dec 1803

Z-371: T.W.3051=20 Dec 1800 Christopher Sheffer 116 A.(28 Nov 1801) in Hampshire Co. on Nill Cr. adj. Henry Purget, Frederick High. 8 Dec 1803

Z-372: T.W.3083=21 Jan 1801 William Tate 38 A.(8 May 1802) in Madison Co. adj. Churchill Blakey, Jonathan Coward, William Booten, Jacob Souther, John Blalkey. 29 Dec 1803

Z-373: T.W.3312=2 Jan 1802 Michael Yager 50 A.(30 Sep 1802) in Madison Co. on spur of Double top Mt. adj. Elizabeth Yager, Thomas Bohannon. 26 Dec 1803

Z-375:   T.W.2797=31 Oct 1799 Henry Baugh 200 A.(20 May 1800) in Hampshire Co. on Great Cacapehon Mt., Warm spring Rg., adj. Michael Whidmier, said Baugh, William Anderson. 26 Dec 1803

Z-376:   T.W.21,475=23 Dec 1783 Andrew Leese asne. of Jehu Lewis asne. of George Wolf 350 A.(25 Mar 1790) in Hampshire Co. on Lick run adj. Bryan Bruin, Thompson, John Huff. 7 Dec 1803

Z-377:   100 A. by T.W.748=3 Oct 1794, 100 A. by T.W.18,348=6 Aug & 44 A. by T.W. 21,017=1 Dec both 1783 William Taylor 244 A.(13 May 1798) in Hampshire Co. on Great Cacapehon & Swtizers run, adj. Rudolph Bomgarner, Throckmorton, Winterton, Switzer. 9 Dec 1803

Z-379:   T.W.2797=31 Oct 1799 Robert Allen 39 A.(29 Dec 1800) in Hampshire Co. on town hill adj. Nathan Huddleston, John Wallis, Robert Allen. 9 Dec 1803

Z-380:   T.W.3057=20 Dec 1800 William Taylor 26 A.(7 June 1802) in Hampshire Co. on Lonams Br. adj. Jacob Clutter, Duncan McVicker, John Chenowith. 9 Dec 1803

Z-381:   T.W.20,670=10 Nov 1783 George Hetner asne. of George Shoemaker 86 A.(12 Oct 1792) in Hardy Co. on Hemseys run of Lost R. of Capecapon, adj. Hetner, John Cline, Claylick run of Kemseys run. 7 Jan 1804 [Jacob Claypool 16 Jan 1804]

Z-383:   148 A. by T.W.3011=3 Nov 1802 & 200 A. by T.W.3210=21 Aug 1801 John Largent 348 A.(14 Nov 1801) in Hampshire Co. on N. R. adj. Crooked Run, William Lockhart, James Slain, the Chimney tract, Boyd, Triplett. 9 Dec 1803

Z-384:   62 A. by T.W.23,086=14 May 1794 & 116 A. by T.W.19,223=10 Sep 1783 Benjamin Partlow asne. of William Bryan 178 A.(26 Nov 1801) in Culpeper Co. on Broad Br. adj. said Benjamin Partlow, said Bryan, Overtop Mt., Thomas Jones, John Loinbarger. 28 Dec 1803

Z-386:   T.W.3058=20 Dec 1800 Michael Gillispie 100 A.(3 June 1801) in Hampshire Co. on Beaver run adj. said Gillispie, Samuel Thomas, Henry Fink, Andrew Rodtruck, Arnel. 22 Dec 1803

Z-387:   T.W.3057=20 Dec 1800 John Rosbrough 143 A.(10 June 1801) in Hampshire Co. at foot of N. Mt. on Warm Spring run adj. Hodzenpiller, Philip Bush, Watson, Elisha C. Dick. 9 Dec 1803

Z-389:   T.W.2490=6 June 1798 John Sine 14 A.(19 May 1802) in Shenandoah Co. near Stony Br. adj. Abraham Barb, Nathaniel Siron now John Lechliter, Adam Smith, John Bushong Jr. dec'd, Isaac Zane dec'd. 2 Jan 1804

Z-390:   T.W.16,326=12 May 1783 Joshua Horner 53 A.(24 June 1802) in Shenandoah Co. on Jeremies Run adj. Moses Moody, Nehemiah Woods. 2 Jan 1804 [Dl'd James Allen 19 Jan 1804]

Z-391:   T.W.2490=6 Aug 1798 Jonathan Mauk 10 1/2 A.(4 Mar 1802) in Shenandoah Co. near N. R. of Shenandoah adj. Andrew Summer, said Mauk. 2 Jan 1804

Z-392:   T.W.2759=31 Aug 1799 Adam Lechliter 15 A.(16 Feb 1802) in Shenandoah Co. in Powells Big Ft. adj. said Lechliter, William Williamson, Burners mill run, the Grant line, Eagles line, John Lechliter. 28 Dec 1803

Z-393:   T.W.3083=21 Jan 1801 Churchill Blakey 31 A.(14 Apr 1802) in Madison Co. adj. land James Kirtley sold Jonathan Coward 20 Apr 1764, Piney Mt. John Blakey. 13 Jan 1804   [Dl'd John F. Price 14 Jan 1804]

Z-395:   34 A. by T.W.2490=6 June 1798 & 50 A. by T.W.2758=31 Aug 1799 Andrew Kyser 84 A.(28 Jan 1802) in Shenandoah Co. on S. R. of Shenandoah adj. his land, John D. Moyers, Michael Rinehart dec'd, said Kyser. 28 Dec 1803

Z-396:   T.W.2758=31 Aug 1799 John Allen 38 A.(23 Apr 1802) in Shenandoah Co. on dry run of S. R. of Shenandoah adj. Benjamin Woods, mine run. 28 Dec 1803

Z-397: T.W.2759=31 Aug 1799 Christian Crebill 3 A.(5 Mar 1802) in Shenandoah Co. on N. R. of Shenandoah adj. John Hockman, David Crebill, Christian Crebill. 28 Dec 1803

Z-399: T.W.3286=11 Dec 1801 William Osburn asne. of John Kain 140 sq. Po.(6 Mar 1802) in Jefferson Co. adj. Osburn, Vardier, heirs of Moses Hunter. 24 Dec 1803

Z-399: Exg.T.W.1173=5 Nov 1801 William Harper asne. of James Robinson 16 A. 2 Ro.(17 Feb 1802) in Berkeley Co. on Tilehances Br. adj. William Harper, William Johnson, James Harper, Robert Jones. 29 Dec 1803

Z-401: T.W.3220=14 Sep 1801 Joshua Carney 11 1/2 A.(10 June 1802) in Stafford Co. on N. run of Chappawamsick adj. Green, Swan Jones, said Carney, Sudden, Horton. 26 Dec 1803 [Dl'd Mr. French 11 Dec 1807]

Z-402: T.W.2903=13 Mar 1800 Paul Taylor 750 A.(23 Mar 1802) in Berkeley Co. on third hill Mt. adj. James McGowan, said Taylor, Abraham Shocky, Thomas Dobbins, Daniel Grande, Exrs. of William Duglas. 29 Dec 1803

Z-404: Exg.T.W.1003=5 Jan 1801 Paul Taylor 153 3/4 A.(11 June 1802) in Frederick Co. on Brush Cr. adj. pack horse Rd., John Millor, Samuel Ruble, Sleepy Cr. Mt., Samuel Goodnight, heirs of Thomas Talbott dec'd. 29 Dec 1803

Z-405 Resurv. 13 Nov 1801 Phebe Seaman 720 A.(granted 10 July 1762 by Prop'r of N.N. to Jonathan Seaman who devised to his sister by certificate of H. Bedingers, Clk. of Berkeley Co. Ct.) in Berkeley Co. on Opeckon Cr. 28 Dec 1803

Z-407: T.W.3031=9 Dec 1800 Joseph Foreman asne. of James Foreman 17 A.(6 July 1802) in Berkeley Co. below mouth of Back Cr. on Potowmack R. adj. John Daugherty, Moses Harlan. 24 Dec 1803

Z-408: T.W.3031=9 Dec 1800 Joseph Foreman asne. of James Foreman 5 A. 2 Ro 14 Po.(16 Dec 1801) in Berkeley Co. inc. an Island in Potowmack R. near Virginia Shore at mouth of Back Cr. 24 Dec 1803

Z-409: T.W.3286=11 Dec 1801 John Kain 5 3/4 A. 26 Po.(18 Feb 1802) in Jefferson Co. adj. late William Darke, Edward Lucas. 24 Dec 1803

Z-410: T.W.1022=23 Jan 1801 John McCleary 500 A.(17 May 1802) in Berkeley Co. on Cherrys Br. & Dirt Hill Mt. adj. Thomas Payne, John R. Hedges, Alexander Henderson, Edward Conner, heirs of George Brent dec'd, Michael McKewan & John Bailey, Palmer, Thomas Swearingen. 26 Dec 1803 [Dl'd the Prop'r 1 Jan 1804]

Z-412: T.W.164=10 Dec 1793 Moses Collins & John Roberts 300 A.(7 Apr 1802) in Berkeley Co. on Meadow Br. adj. Sniveley, third hill Mt., Elisha Boyd. 26 Dec 1803 [Dl'd P.C.Pendleton 20 Jan 1807]

Z-413: T.W.2759=31 Aug 1799 William Conner asne. of John Flemming 50 A.(8 Mar 1802) in Shenandoah Co. on Cedar Cr. & Bennetts hill. 26 Dec 1803 [Dl'd Philip Snapp 12 Feb 1804]

Z-414: T.W.2102=20 Jan 1797 Thomas Noland 4 A.(1 Dec 1801) in Berkeley Co. on Back Cr. adj. Thomas Middleton, said Noland, James Quick, Alexander Fleming. 26 Dec 1803

Z-415: T.W.3055=20 Dec 1800 Moses Dimmett 500 A.(20 Nov 1801) in Hampshire Co. on Great Cacapehon adj. said Dimmett, Peter Bruner. 17 Jan 1804

Z-417: T.W. from late Prop'rs office of the N.N., Thomas Swearingen, Van Swearingen & Andrew Swearingen dvses. of Thomas Swearingen dec'd 330 A.(23 May 1767) in Berkeley Co.(formerly Frederick) adj. William Jackson, Lucas Hood on Mt. Run of Sleepy Cr., Turd Hill, St.Johns Rd., Sleepy Cr. Mt. 23 Jan 1804

Z-419: Inclusive surv. 14 June 1800 by order of Ct. of Hampshire Co. John

Swisher 809 A.(250 A. thereof by 68 A. by T.W.18,365=6 Aug 1783 & 190 A. by T.W.2457=6 Apr 1798 & residue 330 A.=28 Aug 1788 & 239 A.=29 June 1789) in Hampshire Co. adj. Samuel Hickle, Daniel Jones, Elisha C. Dick. 16 Jan 1804

Z-421: T.W.3347=29 Jan 1802 John J. Jacobs 8 1/10 A.(13 Oct 1802) in Hampshire Co. adj. his own land, James Praytor. 17 Jan 1804

Z-422 85 A. by T.W.2175=17 Apr 1797 & 50 A. by T.W.3051=20 Dec 1800 Gabriel Throckmorton & William Winterton 135 A.(12 Aug 1801) in Hampshire Co. on Great Cacapehon adj. John Winterton, Rudolph Bomgarner. 13 Jan 1804

Z-424: T.W.20,039=17 Nov 1796 Frederick Cooper 53 3/4 A.(11 Aug 1800) in Frederick Co. on Lick Br. of Cedar Cr. adj. William Hastings, said Cooper, John Tevault, Henry Trenner. 13 Jan 1804

Z-425: T.W.2252=14 Aug 1797 Adam Kline asne. of Gabriel Throckmorton 25 A.(9 Apr 1801) in Hampshire Co. on Great Cacapehon Mt. adj. Jacob Cline, Paul McKever, Elisha C. Dick. 13 Jan 1804

Z-427: T.W.11,367=11 Mar 1782 Archibald Watts 59 A.(25 Nov 1801) in Hampshire Co. on Middle Rg. & Mill Cr. adj. s'd Watts, st. Rd. to Morgantown. 14 Jan 1804

Z-428: Exg.T.W.1260=23 Mar 1802 Stephen Ross 24 A.(13 July 1802) in Hardy Co. adj. his own land. 17 Jan 1804

Z-429: Exg.T.W.1260=23 Mar 1802 Thomas Marshall 32 A.(16 July 1802) in Hardy Co. on Br. Mt. adj. his own land, John Burch, Robert Means. 18 Jan 1804

Z-430: Exg.T.W.1260=23 Mar 1802 Christopher Martin 116 A.(5 July 1802) in Hardy Co. on Knobly Mt. adj. Stone Lick surv., Thomas Hanks, James Ryan. 18 Jan 1804

Z-431: Exg.T.W.1260=23 Mar 1802 Alexus Hays 70 A.(5 July 1802) in Hardy Co. adj. his own land under foot of new Cr. Mt., James McDavit. 17 Jan 1804

Z-432: Exg.T.W.1260=23 Mar 1802 Conrad Carr 58 A.(13 July 1802) in Hardy Co. on S. Br. adj. heirs of Henry Lancisco, Carr bought of Bagart, Jonathan Watts. 17 Jan 1804

Z-433: Exg.T.W.1260=23 Mar 1802 George Weese 33 A.(27 July 1802) in Hardy Co. on N. fork adj. Peter Hose, Edward Breathed. 16 Jan 1804

Z-434: Exg.T.W.1260=23 Mar 1802 John Webb 70 A.(3 July 1802) in Hardy Co. on Paterson Cr. Mt. 17 Jan 1804

Z-435: T.W.2901=26 Feb 1800 Andrew Bauhman 29 A.(4 Nov 1801) in Hardy Co. adj. his own land, Joseph Cockanall, Bell. 9 Jan 1804

Z-436: Exg.T.W.1260=23 Mar 1802 Thomas Oglevie 35 A.(14 July 1802) in Hardy Co. on Vanmeters mill run adj. Isaac Vanmeter. 9 Jan 1804

Z-437: Exg.T.W.1260=23 Mar 1802 William Hersha 124 A.(19 July 1802) in Hardy Co. on Patterson Cr. Mt. adj. his own land , David Welton, James Machir. 16 Jan 1804 [Dl'd Philip Snapp 16 May 1804]

Z-439: T.W.11,367=11 Mar 1782 Henry Fink 100 A.(9 June 1802) in Hampshire Co. on Sugar Run adj. Thomazon Elzey & others, Andrew Rodtruck, Corder. 16 Jan 1804

Z-440 600 A. by T.W.21,397=19 Dec 1783, 144 A. by T.W.2175=17 Apr 1797 & 156 A. by T.W.3051=20 Dec 1800 Gabriel Throckmorton, William Winterton & Robert Rogers 900 A.(12 Aug 1801) in Hampshire Co. on Great Cacapehon adj. Jacob Hoober, Shular, John Rosbrough, Joseph Watson, Hodzenpiller. 17 Jan 1804

Z-441: Exg.T.W.1196=19 Dec 1801 James Patterson 81 1/2 A.(23 Apr 1802) in Hampshire Co. on Little Cacapehon adj. Paris Drews dec'd, said Pattersons purchase of Thomas Williamson. 17 Jan 1804

Z-443: T.W.11,367=11 Mar 1782 John Mitchel Jr. 150 A.(5 Jan 1802) in Hampshire Co. on Sidling hill adj. Daniel Rogers, by Richards path, Andrew Woodrow, Samuel Berry. 21 Jan 1804

Z-444: T.W.11,367=11 Mar 1782 John Mitchel Jr.20 A.(9 Mar 1802) in Hampshire Co. on Pattersons Cr. adj. Thomas Emmerson, William Adams. 21 Jan 1804

Z-445: T.W.20,333=6 Nov 1783 John Mitchel Jr. 450 A.(24 June 1802) in Hampshire Co. on Mill Cr. adj. Jacob Fidler, Peter Cline, George Fidler, John Bishop formerly John Plum/Plumb. 18 Jan 1804

Z-447: T.W.11,367=11 Mar 1782 Willim Pilcher 148 A.(15 Mar 1801) in Hampshire Co. on Dry run inc. the dry lick adj. Isaac Welche, Abraham Good. 24 Jan 1804

Z-448: T.W.77=28 Apr 1788 Joseph Long asne. of George W. Long 40 A.(12 Nov 1799) in Hampshire Co. at Knobley Mt. in Johns Gap adj. David Long. 31 Jan 1804

Z-449: 100 A. by T.W.2456=3 Apr 1798 & 90 A. by T.W.3057=20 Dec 1800 Jacob Hutzerpiller asne. of John Rosebrough 190 A.(10 June 1801) in Hampshire Co. on Dry Run of Great Cacapehon adj. Phillip Boush, said Rosbrough, Timber Rg., John Perrel, William M. Sterrett, Thomas Vowel, Smith. 2 Feb 1804 [Mr. Philip Snapp 2 Apr 1811]

Z-451: T.W.2590=12 Dec 1798 William Withers 15 3/4 A.(16 Jan 1802) in Culpeper Co. adj. James Williams now David Hudson, said Withers. 21 Feb 1804 [Dl'd Philip Snap 17 Mar 1804]

Z-452: T.W.2705=3 June 1799 John Howard asne. of Levi Mathew 43 A.(29 May 1800) in Hampshire Co. on Great Cacapehon opposite Abraham Dowson, John Athey, said Mathew. 20 Feb 1804

Z-453: T.W.2131=2 Mar 1797 James Holliday asne. of Jesse Carney 296 A. 1 Ro. 24 Po.(5 Dec 1802) in Pr. William Co. on Quantico adj. Ashmore, Farrow, Berryman, Harrison, Davis. 21 Feb 1804 [Dl'd Jas. Holliday Dumbries 22 Sep 1804]

Z-454: T.W.2279=21 Sep 1797 Jacob Stiegel 5 A.(20 Mar 1802) in Shenandoah Co. on N. R. of Shenandoah adj. said Stiegel purchase of Lewis Rinehart, George Houbert, Balser Hup. 15 Feb 1804

Z-455: 227 A. by T.W.2591=13 Dec 1798, 100 A. by T.W.3037=9 Dec 1800 & 65 A. by Exg.T.W.1029=2 Mar 1801 James Robertson 392 A.(25 June 1802) in Berkeley Co. on Cherry's Br. of Potowmack, adj. David Gerringer, heirs of Alexander Smyth dec'd, Thomas Cherry, Joseph Forman, Adam Leppert, Stephen Snodgrass, Matthias Angle, George Brent, Daniel Blotner, Warm Spring Rd., Low. 16 Feb 1804

Z-457: T.W.2490=6 June 1798 Henry Kern 18 A.(27 May 1802) in Shenandoah Co. on Narrow Passage Run adj. George Mavis, said Kern, David Rodenheffer, Jacob Crable. 17 Feb 1804

Z-458: T.W.3417=26 June 1802 Downin Smith 4 A.(27 Aug 1802) in Madison Co. adj. said Smith, David Snyder. 21 Feb 1804

Z-459: T.W.2490=6 June 1798 Peter Boyer 33 A.(18 Feb 1802) in Shenandoah Co. in Powells big Ft. adj. William Ellzey, Denton, Henry Walter, George Aumiller. 17 Feb 1804 [Dl'd P. Snapp 6 Oct 1804]

Z-460: T.W.16,326=12 May 1783 Peter Boyer asne. of Peter Peters 17 A.(17 Feb 1802) in Shenandoah Co. in Powells Big Ft. on Passage Cr. adj. Jacob Galladay, Denton. 16 Feb 1804 [Dl'd P. Snapp 6 Oct 1804]

Z-461: 100 A. by T.W.2490=6 June 1798 & 207 A. by T.W.3023=2 Dec 1800 Daniel Henry 307 A.(28 Jan 1803) in Shenandoah Co. adj. Benjamin Mathew, James Mathews, the Grant line, Philip Spangler. 24 Feb 1804 [Dl'd Mr. Abbott 21 Sep 1804]

Z-462: T.W.2759=31 Aug 1799 John Griffith 7 A.(24 Oct 1801) in Shenandoah Co. on Dry run adj. said Griffith, Frederick Decius, Roadcap. 16 Feb 1804

Z-463:   Exg.T.W.969=29 Apr 1800 Israel Robertson 10 A.(14 Dec 1801) in Berkeley Co. adj. Back Cr. James Robertson, Israel Robertson, John Shields. 16 Feb 1804

Z-464: T.W.3417=26 June 1802 Thomas Sampson 28 1/2 A.(20 Aug 1802) in Madison Co. on Little New R. & N. Fork of Robinson R. adj. William Chapman, Henry Hill formerly Powell. 21 Feb 1804 [Dl'd John Malone 7 May 1804]

Z-465: T.W.203=22 Jan 1794 Gabriel Green 140 A.(10 June 1802) in Culpeper Co. adj. Hedgman R., David Corbin, Alexander Gordan, William Miller. 16 Mar 1804

Z-466: T.W.2538=20 Sep 1798 Henry Manifee 150 A.(1 June 1802) in Culpeper Co. adj. said Manifee. 16 Mar 1804

Z-467: Exg.T.W.1023=23 Jan 1801 Richard McSherry asne. of James Faulkner 858 A.(30 Nov 1802) in Berkeley Co. on Third hill adj. Henry Sniveley, George Everheart, Elisha Boyd, John Renerfelt, John G. Koneky. 16 Apr 1804 [Inclosed to Jas. Faulkner at Martinsburg 18 Apr 1804]

Z-469: T.W.3328=23 Jan 1802 Martin Doctor 50 A.(30 Sep 1802) in Shenandoah Co. on S. R. of Shenandoah adj. Henry Cain, Joshua Cain, Charles Sexton. 11 May 1804 [Dl'd Philip Snapp 16 May 1804]

Z-470:   40 A. by T.W.3328=23 Jan 1802 & 77 A. by T.W.3526=24 Jan 1803 Martin Doctor 117 A.(1 Mar 1803) in Shenandoah Co. at Three Mile Gap run adj. Conrod Smith, Joshua Cain, William Ellzey, Christian Stover. 11 May 1804 [Dl'd Philip Snapp 16 May 1804]

Z-471: T.W.3023=2 Dec 1800 Jacob Beam 75 A.(25 Sep 1802) in Shenandoah Co. on Pass Run adj. said Jacob & Tobias Beam, Peter Kibler. 11 May 1804 [Dl'd Philip Snapp 16 May 1804]

Z-471: T.W.3023=2 Dec 1800 Tobias Beam 200 A.(25 Sep 1802) in Shenandoah Co. on the Blue Rg. adj. his other land. 11 May 1804 [Dl'd Philip Snapp 16 May 1804]

Z-472: T.W.3023=2 Dec 1800 David Coffman (river) 29 A.(6 May 1802) in Shenandoah Co. on Messanotten Mt., Rd. from white house to New Market. 11 May 1804 [Dl'd Philip Snapp 16 May 1804]

Z-473: T.W.16,326=12 May 1783 Adam Ross 100 A.(29 Sep 1802) in Shenandoah Co. on Ruddell's run of Passage Cr. adj. land Adam Ross purchased of John Evans, John Messer. 12 May 1804 [Dl'd Philip Snapp 16 May 1804]

Z-474: T.W.16,326=12 May 1783 Frederick Mac-inturf 84 A.(12 July 1802) in Shenandoah Co. in Powells Big Ft. adj. said Mac-inturf. 12 May 1804 [Dl'd Philip Snapp 16 May 1804]

Z-474: T.W.3136=27 Apr 1801 Enoch Renow 20 A.(25 Apr 1803) in Pr. William Co. adj. Fielder, Macmillian. 16 May 1804 [Enclosed to Prop'r 23 May 1804]

Z-475: T.W.2369=6 Jan 1798 George Renick 200 A.(25 Apr 1800) in Hardy Co. on Vanmeters mill run adj. Abel Seymore, Isaac Vanmeter. 23 May 1804 [Dl'd John Welton 23 May 1804]

Z-476:   Exg.T.W.444=4 Oct 1791 John Steward 22 3/4 A.(30 Nov 1802) in Westmoreland Co. Par. of Washington adj. John Washington, Thomas Hill, Isaac Pollock, John Rose formerly Richard Watts. 18 June 1804

Z-477: T.W.2891=5 Feb 1800 Robert B. Voss 18 1/4 A.(31 Jan 1803) in Culpeper Co. adj. Thomas Knox now Thomas Fitzhugh, John Thom, near Mt. Run, Thornton's Rd., said Voss. 3 Aug 1804

Z-477: T.W.3498=30 Dec 1802 James Holliday 40 A. 20 Po.(1 Mar 1803) in Pr. William Co. on Chappawamsic adj. Grinstead, Wells, said Holliday. 2 Aug 1804 [Dl'd James Holliday, Dumfries 22 Sep 1804]

Z-478: T.W.3500=1 Jan 1803 Ferdinand Fairfax 26 1/2 A.(1 Mar 1803) in Hampshire

Co. on N. Br. of Potowmac adj. land formerly Henry Hains, Benjamin Wiley, March. 2 Aug 1804 [Dl'd Moses Myers 22 Sep 1804]

Z-479: T.W.3031=9 Dec 1800 Wallace Reid asne. of James Forman 9 A. 1 Ro.(27 Jan 1803) in Berkeley Co. on Waggon Br. of Back Cr. adj. Wallace Reid, James Winning, Frederick Shawn. 2 Aug 1804

Z-480: T.W.2490=6 June 1798 John Kemp 62 A.(23 Aug 1802) in Shanandoah Co. on Mill Cr. & Ryals Run adj. Henry Baughman, Big John Fry, Michael Circle, John Click. 2 Aug 1804 [Dl'd James Allen 26 Jan 1805]

Z-481: T.W.2832=5 Dec 1799 John Taylor 28 1/2 A.(26 Oct 1802) in Berkeley Co. on Sleepy Cr.adj. Philip Bush, Thomas Talbert. 2 Aug 1804 [Sam'l Boyd 6 Dec 1804]

Z-482: T.W.376=6 Mar 1794 Abraham Bird 142 A.(19 Oct 1798) in Shanandoah Co. adj. his own land, Three Topt Mt. 3 Aug 1804 [Dl'd Isaac Samuels 21 Sep 1805]

Z-483: T.W.1401=30 May 1795 Abraham Bird 100 A.(19 Oct 1798) in Shanandoah Co. on N. R. of Shanandoah adj. said Bird, Martin Betz. 3 Aug 1804 [Dl'd Isaac Samuels 21 Sep 1805]

Z-484: T.W.3467=29 Nov 1802 Thaddeus Norris 15 A.(15 Dec 1802) in Fauqueir Co. adj. Charles Lee Esq., John Hitt, Cedar Run, Bell. 3 Aug 1804 [Dl'd Mr. J. Love 17 Jan 1807]

Z-485: T.W.3033=9 Dec 1800 Robert Kennedy Sr. 27 A.(5 May 1802) in Berkeley Co. on Back Cr. & N. Mt. adj. Andrew Yates, said Kennedy, Ebenezer Sutton, Elisha Boyd. 3 Aug 1804

Z-486: T.W.3033=9 Dec 1800 Robert Kennedy Jr. 29 A.(5 May 1802) in Berkeley Co. on N. Mt. & Back Cr. adj. George Robertson, Hugh Douglas, Elisha Boyd, Andrew Yates. 6 Aug 1804

Z-486: T.W.19,681=2 Oct 1783 Henry Cowgill 1 1/4 A.(11 May 1797) in Culpeper Co. adj. s'd Cowgill, Reubin Zimmerman. 6 Aug 1804 [Dl'd Micajah Crews 30 Dec 1804]

Z-487: T.W.3083=21 Jan 1801 John Blakey Sr. 20 A.(8 May 1802) in Madison Co. adj. deed from Thomas Staunton to John Blakey dec'd 29 Jan 1762, Jacob Souther, Curchill Blakey, William Tates Spring Br. 6 Aug 1804 [Jos. Clark 30 Mar 1805]

Z-488: T.W.2490=6 June 1798 Bernard Peal 300 A.(20 Oct 1802) in Shanandoah Co. bet. Smith's Cr. & Messenetton Mt. adj. Walter Newman, Abraham Savage, Jacob Hershberger, James Barber. 6 Aug 1804

Z-490: T.W.11,367=11 Mar 1782 David & Hannah Pugh 86 1/2 A.(5 June 1801) in Hampshire Co. on N. R. Mt. adj. Jesse Pugh. 6 Aug 1804 [Dl'd Lewis McCorel? 27 Sep 1805]

Z-491: 418 A. by T.W.2587=8 Dec 1798 & 281 3/4 A. by T.W.2262=1 Sep 1797 Paul Taylor 699 3/4 A.(4 Dec 1801) in Berkeley Co. on Sleepy Cr. Mt. inc. Strodes Stone Quarry & head springs of Brush Cr., adj. Thomas Dobbins, Abraham Shocky, James McGowan, path from Back Cr. to Sleepy Cr. 6 Aug 1804

Z-493: Resurv. 20 May 1803 (order of Shanandoah Co. Ct.) Henry Hottel 240 A., 225 A. granted John Fry by Prop'r of N.N. 2 Oct 1777. Fry conveyed to Henry Hottel 11 Sep 1802 & 15 A. surplus, by T.W.3289=14 Dec 1801 in Shenandoah Co. on Stoney Cr. adj. Charles Byrnes, William Barr now Jacob Rinker & George Rinker, Joseph Ryman, Christopher Lindamude, John Painter Jr. formerly George Rinehart, Jacob Imsweeler formerly Philip Daringer. 7 Aug 1804

Z-494: T.W.2454=31 Mar 1798 James Sangster 9 1/2 A.(20 Feb 1802) in Fairfax Co. adj. Richard Wheeler, David Loughborough, Geo. Williams. 9 Nov 1804 [Dl'd Thomas Pollard Jr. Fairfax Ct. House 9 Nov 1804]

Z-495: T.W.760=6 Oct 1794 James Songster 36 A.(7 Jan 1800) in Fairfax Co. adj. Elzey, Giles Tillett, Simpson. 9 Nov 1804 [Dl'd 9 Nov 1804 by post to Thos.

Pollard Jr. Fairfax Ct. House]

Z-496:   Inclusive Surv. 6 June 1800 (order of Ct. of Berkeley Co.) William
Faris 108 A. (40 A. granted Faris by Prop'r of N.N. 1 Sep 1773, 23 A. to Faris
by patent 22 Mar 1790 & 45 A. by T.W.165=10 Dec 1793) in Berkeley Co. on Back
Cr. adj. Daniel Kenniday/Kennaday, Silar, Robert Snodgrass, Samuel Kenneday,
said Faris. 5 Dec 1804 [Dl'd Mr. Elisha Boyd 5 Dec 1804]

Z-497:   T.W.3421=24 July 1802 Hugh Atwell 13 A. 70 Po.(17 Nov 1802) in Stafford
Co. adj. Mr. Stephen French, Mr. Payne formerly Ashby, survey by Mr. Philip Daw
& Benj'n & Jesse Carney, Bernard Botts. 6 Dec 1804 [Mr. Foster 7 Dec 1804]

Z-498:   Exg.T.W.1406=14 Apr 1803 Amos Nichols 25 A.(8 Sep 1803) in Berkeley Co.
on Opeckon Cr. adj. George Williams, Jeremiah Strode dec'd, said Nichols. 26
Dec 1804 [Dl'd Mr. E. Boyd 31 Dec 1804]

Z-499:   Exg.T.W.1406=14 Apr 1803 John Small 18 A.(20 Sep 1803) in Berkeley Co.
on Opeckon Cr. adj. Morgan Bryan, Amos Nichols, heir of Conrod Rosey?, William
Orrick. 24 Dec 1804 [Dl'd Mr. E. Boyd 31 Dec 1804]

Z-500:   Exg.T.W.1020=23 Jan 1801 John Fernoe asne. of James Robinson 110 A.(24
Oct 1803) in Berkeley Co. on N. Fork of Sleepy Cr. & Underwood or Rock Gap Run
adj. John Fernoe, Lord Fairfax, John Overton, Elzey, William Smith. 24 Dec 1804
[Dl'd Mr. E. Boyd 31 Dec 1804]

Z-501:   Exg.T.W.1020=23 Jan 1801 Isaac Smyth one moiety & John Smyth as asne. of
said Isaac Smith the other moiety 285 A.(20 Oct 1803) in Berkeley Co. on Stony
lick Run & Tilehansies Br. adj. Cornelius Kelley, John R. Hedges, heirs of
Alexander Smyth, Whites Br., Frederick Free, James Robertson, William
Pennybaker, Compton, Charles Young. 26 Dec 1804 [Dl'd Mr. E. Boyd 31 Dec 1804]

Z-503:   T.W.11,367=11 Mar 1782 Samuel Ruckman asne. of Samuel Williamson 40
A.(18 Sep 1802) in Hampshire Co. on Stoney Mt. adj. Alex'r Henderson, Thomas
Ruckman. 8 Dec 1804

Z-504:   T.W.2982=3 Oct 1800 Samuel Adams Jr. 6 3/4 A.(24 Nov 1803) in Fairfax
Co. adj. Little Pimits Run, Henry Watsdon, Turberville, Thomas Lee, Taylor now
Turberville. 28 Dec 1804 [Dl'd Mr. Hunter 14 Jan 1805]

Z-505:   T.W.2797=31 Oct 1799 Mary Williamson, Thomas Williamson, Andrew
Williamson, Samuel Williamson, Timothy Williamson, James Williamson, Elizabeth
Williamson, Margaret Williamson, Sarah Williamson, Susanna Williamson & Jeremiah
Williamson 139 1/4 A.(29 Dec 1800) in Hampshire Co. on Little Cacapehon adj.
William Elsy, said Thomas Williamson, John Wallis. 8 Dec 1804

Z-506:   T.W.2960=26 June 1800 John Selvey 50 A.(16 May 1801) in Hampshire Co. at
foot of N. R. Mt. adj. Dunmore. 19 Dec 1804

Z-507:   Exg.T.W.1196=19 Dec 1801 Solomon Hoge 75 A.(24 Apr 1802) in Hampshire
Co. on S. Br. Mt. adj. John McCave, said Solomon Hoge. 19 Dec 1804

Z-507:   Exg.T.W.1196=19 Dec 1801 Solomon Hoge 25 A.(23 Apr 1801) in Hampshire
Co. on S. Br. Mt. adj. James Lanamore formerly Elzey, John Taylor, said Solomon
Hoge. 19 Dec 1804

Z-508:   T.W.3051=20 Dec 1800 Jeremiah Thompson & Michael Whitinger 60 A.(12 Apr
1803) in Hampshire Co. on Constant Run of Great Cacapehon adj. Jeremiah
Thompson, Peter Bruner. 20 Dec 1804

Z-509:   T.W.3529=24 Jan 1803 Jeremiah Thompson 136 A.(9 Apr 1803) in Hampshire
Co. on Great Cacapehon adj. Jacksons path, Thompson, Moses Dimmet. 19 Dec 1804

Z-510:   T.W.11,367=11 Mar 1782 George M. Laubinger asne. of Elisha Loyd asne. of
David Fairley 100 A.(3 June 1801) in Hampshire Co. on Sugar Camp Run & Clay Lick
Run adj. Elisha Collins. 27 Dec 1804

Z-511: Exg.T.W.1196=19 Dec 1801 John McBride 20 A.(23 Apr 1802) in Hampshire Co. adj. William Anderson, Joseph Reeder, Watson. 6 Dec 1804

Z-512: 41 A. by T.W.3051=20 Dec 1800 & 71 A. by 3590=9 May 1803 John Poland 112 A.(24 Aug 1803) in Hampshire Co. on Piney Mt. adj. said Poland, Michael Smith, wid. Beers. 7 Dec 1804

Z-513: T.W.196 A. by T.W.2406=30 Jan 1798 & 40 A. by 3011=3 Nov 1800 Jesse Pugh 236 A.(29 Nov 1801) in Hampshire Co. on Great Cacapehon adj. said Pugh, Wm. Hayden, Philip Groves, Wm. Adams, Frederick & Hampshire Cos. line, Anderson, John Copper. 20 Dec 1804

Z-515: T.W.3591=9 May 1803 Elijah Roberts 30 A.(10 Nov 1803) in Hampshire Co. on Mykes run of Pattersons Cr. adj. John Douthard, Geo. Gilpin, Richard Hollady, William Roberts. 31 Dec 1804

Z-516: Exg.T.W.1278=7 May 1802 Adam Winegardner 8 A.(4 Oct 1803) in Shenandoah Co. adj. mill Cr. Moses Walton's purchase of John Corly? heirs, Jacob Funkhouser heirs, Herbert Winegardner. 27 Dec 1804 [Dl'd James Allen 26 Jan 1806]

Z-517: Exg.T.W.1278=7 May 1802 Thomas Tuckwiler 141 A.(19 May 1803) in Shenandoah Co. at the Blue Rg. adj. his former surv. 27 Dec 1804 [Dl'd James Allen 26 Jan 1805]

Z-518: T.W.20,670=10 Nov 1783 Alexander Pearson 41 A.(2 Oct 1792) in Hardy Co. on Moses Run of Cacapehon adj. Whitehead, land formerly Dr. Savage. 5 Dec 1804

Z-519: T.W.3051=20 Dec 1800 Christopher Shaffer 60 A.(21 Oct 1802) in Hampshire Co. on Mill Cr. adj. his own land, John Foley, George Fidler, Henry Hartman, Henry Miller. 11 Dec 1804

Z-520: Exg.T.W.1278=7 May 1802 Isaac Overall 385 A.(14 Nov 1803) in Shenandoah Co. at Matthes's arm of Blue Rg. adj. William A.? Booth's mine tract, Charles Sexton, said Overall's purchase of Hite Woodson & others, McKay. 26 Dec 1804 [Dl'd James Allen 26 Jan 1805]

Z-521: 35 A. by T.W.2960=26 June 1800 & 24 A. by 3265=29 Oct 1801 Archibald Linchacum 59 A.(26 Dec 1802) in Hampshire Co. on N. R. adj. his own land, Joseph Tucker, Rasmus Tucker, Thomas Tucker bought of Thompson, land Linchacum bought of A. King. 29 Dec 1804

Z-522: 50 A. by T.W.2960=26 June 1800 & 50 A. by T.W.3458=9 Nov 1802 Alexander Doran 100 A.(3 Dec 1802) in Hampshire Co. on N. R. adj. his land bought of Eli Beall, John Baker, Robert Rogers. 31 Dec 1804

Z-523: Exg.T.W.1207=5 Jan 1802 Samuel Ravenscraft Jr. 30 A.(22 Jan 1803) in Hampshire Co. on N. Br. of Potomack adj. Edward McCarty formerly Thomas Bond, Nicholas Severs. 8 Dec 1804

Z-524: T.W.3289=14 Dec 1801 John Bower 35 A.(16 Apr 1803) in Shenandoah Co. near Stoney Cr. adj. Henry Bower, Abraham Barb, Nicholas Reader, George Miller, Henry Bower Jr. 22 Dec 1804

Z-525: T.W.2544=5 Oct 1798 George Baker 100 A.(20 Aug 1802) in Shenandoah Co. on Little N. Mt. adj. Thomas Newell, George Lind. 22 Dec 1804 [Dl'd Philip Snap 21 Mar 1805]

Z-526: Exg.T.W.1278=7 May 1802 John Jordan 30 A.(23 May 1803) in Shenandoah Co. on Toms Brook adj, said Jordan, Christian Wohlgemuth, Frederick Bozzerman Jr. 27 Dec 1804 [Dl'd James Allen 26 Jan 1805]

Z-527: T.W.3264=29 Oct 1801 Thomas Hollenback 441 1/4 A.(17 Dec 1802) in Hampshire Co. at foot of Knobley Mt. below Ices gap, adj. Peter Putman, John Lyon. 21 Jan 1805 [Dl'd Dr. Snyder 2 Dec 1805]

Z-528: T.W.3318=11 Jan 1802 Jeremiah McCoy 120 A.(17 May 1803) in Shenandoah

Co. on Blue Rg. at end of Knob Mt. formerly surv'd for Isaac McCoy & Jeremiah McCoy adj. Josiah Leath. 22 Dec 1804 [Dl'd P. Snap 21 Mar 1805]

Z-529: T.W.3023=2 Dec 1800 William Bozzerman 5A.(26 Feb 1803) in Shenandoah Co. on Shenanadoah R. adj. heirs of David Stover dec'd. 11 Dec 1804 [Dl'd Philip Snap 21 Mar 1805]

Z-530: T.W.2490=6 June 1798 George Lonas 35 A.(6 Apr 1803) in Shenandoah Co. on Supper lick Mt. adj. said Lonas. 11 Dec 1804 [Dl'd Philip Snap 21 Mar 1805]

Z-531: T.W.3185=18 June 1801 John Ball 100 A.(30 Aug 1802) in Madison Co. adj. McCoal, Hawkins, Stonehouse Run, John Battern, Benjamin Myrtle, said Ball, John Rush, German Congregation. 17 Dec 1804

Z-532: T.W.3023=2 Dec 1800 Peter Fiesinger 26 A.(14 Mar 1803) in Shenandoah Co. on Buck Hill adj. his own land, Deedrick Fernsler, Jacob Hamman, Christian Click, heirs of Jacob Hunsberger dec'd. 11 Dec 1804 [Dl'd P. Snap 21 Mar 1805]

Z-533: Exg.T.W.1278=7 May 1802 David Galladay 87 A.(21 May 1803) in Shenandoah Co. in Powels Big Ft. on Passage Cr. adj. Jacob Burner, Jacob Galladay dec'd, William Ellzey. 24 Dec 1804 [Dl'd Philip Snap 21 Mar 1805]

Z-534: Exg.T.W.812=26 Sep 1797 Lambert Kimble 113 A.(4 Aug 1803) in Hardy Co. adj. Sickman Homan. 15 Dec 1804

Z-535: 200 A. by T.W.3518=22 Jan 1803 & 46 A. by Exg.T.W.1044=3 Mar 1801 George Bishop 246 A.(26 July 1803) in Hampshire Co. on Grassy Lick Run adj. Robert French, Reeves. 15 Dec 1804

Z-536: Exg.T.W.812=26 Sep 1797 Joseph Thompson 100 A.(28 Sep 1803) in Hardy Co. on Br. Mt. adj. Bennet Been. 15 Dec 1804

Z-537: 100 A. by T.W.3436=21 Sep 1802 & 200 A. by 3518=22 Jan 1803 George Bishop 300 A.(3 June 1803) in Hampshire Co. on Grassey Lick Run adj. his land bought of Combes Marshall & others, John Lock, Benjamin Marshall. 14 Dec 1804

Z-539: Exg.T.W.812=26 Sep 1797 George Bradfield 406 A.(28 June 1803) in Hardy Co. adj. William Devour, on Wardens run, the Little Rg. 15 Dec 1804

Z-540: Exg.T.W.812=26 Sep 1797 George Johnston 106 A.(29 June 1803) in Hardy Co. on Kimseys Run of Lost R. near Hunting Rg. 15 Dec 1804

Z-540: T.W.2615=29 Dec 1798 John Foley 250 A.(28 Mar 1803) in Hampshire Co. on Long Rg., Mill Cr. adj. Ft. Pleasant Rd., Henry Purget, Isaac Vanmeter, Henry Hinzman, John Foley. 11 Dec 1804

Z-542: T.W.2797=31 Oct 1799 Leonard Bomcruts asne. of George Hains 50 A.(14 Mar 1802) in Hampshire Co. on Mill Cr. adj. Zachariah Fowler, John High, Isaac Vanmeter. 21 Dec 1804

Z-543: T.W.2870=14 Jan 1800 John Ester 50 A.(11 Sep 1800) in Hampshire Co. on Grants Run of Potowmack R. adj. s'd Ester sold Casler, West, Floras. 21 Dec 1804

Z-544: T.W.3529=24 Jan 1803 Jeremiah Thompson 53 A.(7 July 1803) in Hampshire Co. on Great Cacapehon adj. Peter Bruner, Jesse Harland. 19 Dec 1804

Z-545: 200 A. by Exg.T.W.1196=19 Dec 1801 & 115 A. by T.W.3590=9 May 1803 Thomas Ruckman 315 A.(28 June 1803) in Hampshire Co. on S. fork of Little Cacapehon adj. Daniel Corbin, Alexander Monroe, Murphey, Thomas Ruckman. 7 Dec 1804

Z-547: T.W.18,365=6 Aug 1783 Henry Hartman 139 A.(14 June 1800) in Hampshire Co. on Mill Cr. adj. his own land, Coopers Gap, James Cooper. 5 Dec 1804

Z-548: T.W.1597=22 Sep 1795 Joseph Leigh asne. of Daniel Harris 33 A.(27 Apr 1797) in Hampshire Co. on Tear coat adj. Col. Wodrow, John Peters, John Vitset, Jacob Reader. 17 Dec 1804

Z-548: T.W.15,213=2 Apr 1783 Evan James asne. of Jeremiah Ashby asne. of William Abernathy 15 3/4 A.14 Apr 1801) in Hampshire Co. on N. Br. of Potowmack adj. Jeremiah Ashby, Moses Tetchanet. 8 Dec 1804

Z-549: Resurv. 6 Apr 1802 by order of Hampshire Co. Ct. Abraham Inskeep 112 A. in Hampshire Co. being land in tract of 133 A. granted said Inskeep 11 Sep 1788. On New Cr. adj. Col. McCarty (formerly Bruin). 6 Dec 1804

Z-550: T.W.15,213=2 Apr 1783 George Beard asne. of Michael Youghtam? 47 A.(23 Mar 1802) in Hampshire Co. on Mykes Run adj. Peter Beaver, Christian Hilkey. 8 Dec 1804

Z-551: Resurv. by Hampshire Ct. George Myers 272 A.(1 Sep 1803 contained in tract granted said Myers 30 June 1790) in Hampshire Co. adj. John Barret formerly Andrew Parks, Thomas Hillard formerly John Dever. 23 Jan 1805

Z-552: Resurv. 21 Aug 1799 ordered by Ct. of Hampshire Co. Duncan McVicar 258 A. granted John McMeil by late Prop'r of N.N. 26 Aug 1771 who conveyed to John Barnhouse 26 & 27 Feb 1784. Barnhouse & wife conveyed to said McVicar 15 Sep 1791. 138 A. surplus in tract is taken by T.W.2175=17 Apr 1797 in Hampshire Co. adj. said McVicar, Paul M. Renuer. 29 Jan 1805

Z-553: T.W.3591=9 May 1803 Frederick High 150 A.(20 Aug 1803) in Hampshire Co. on Poughs Camp Run of Mill Cr. adj. John Bishop, Hugh Malone, William Smith. 31 Dec 1804

Z-555: Exg.T.W.1029=2 Mar 1801 Henry Welchance 8 A. 2 Ro.(10 Oct 1803) in Berkeley Co. on Opechon Cr. adj. heirs of Copenhaver, George Tapler, Jacob Morgan. 28 Dec 1804 [Dl'd Magnus Tate 11 Dec 1809]

Z-556: T.W.2477=26 May 1798 Ann Neill wid. of John Neill dec'd 13 A. 1 Ro.(14 July 1802) in Frederick Co. on Opecquon Cr. & Great Rd. from Winchester to Battletown adj. said Ann Neill, heirs of Jas. Carter, John Neill dec'd, Abraham Neill, Frederick Conrad dec'd. 22 Dec 1804 [Dl'd Dan'l Abbot 6 May 1806]

Z-557: T.W.3756=9 Nov 1803 George Creamer 22 1/2 A.(22 Nov 1803) in Berkeley Co. on Warm Spring Run adj. Peter Wisser, Elisha Boyd, said Creamer. 28 Dec 1804 [Dl'd Magnus Tate 11 Dec 1809]

Z-558: T.W.1490=8 Nov 1803 Jacob Silar 199 A.(18 Nov 1803) in Berkeley Co. on Back Cr. adj. land late of David Kenedy, Robert Dunn, Henry Ryner, John Shields, Myers part of John Jenkins land. 21 Dec 1804

Z-559: T.W.3289=14 Dec 1801 Joseph Longacre 230 A.(23 Apr 1803) in Shenandoah Co. on Little N. Mt. adj. Elizabeth McFarlan, George Lind, John Croudson, Isaac Zane, Turkey Run, Jacob Pugh, George Baker. 28 Dec 1804 [Dl'd Ch's McCormack bearer of receipt 20 Oct 1815]

Z-561: T.W.537=19 June 1794 William Bower 52 A.(10 Oct 1803) in Fauquier Co. on Marsh Run adj. James Hord/Hoard, said Bower, wid. Morgan, Bowers purchase of George Chapman. 28 Dec 1804 [Dl'd Jos. Blackwell 9 Mar 1805]

Z-562: T.W.16,326=12 May 1783 Jacob Golladay 70 A.(16 Feb 1802) in Shenandoah Co. in Powells Big Ft. on Passage Cr. adj. John Smith formerly John Grove (Tanner), said Golladay, Denton, Peter Boyer. 31 Dec 1804 [Dl'd Adam Sheannan 13 Oct 1806]

Z-563: T.W.165=10 Dec 1793 David Hunter 158 A.(26 Oct 1803) in Berkeley Co. on N. Mt. near Jerrards town adj. Chinneith, heirs of James Strode dec'd, Bazel Lucas, Peter Fletcher. 24 Dec 1804 [Dl'd Mr. Faris 11 Jan 1809]

Z-564: T.W.242=29 Jan 1794 Robert Garrot 75 A.(27 Nov 1801) in Culpeper Co. on Pignut Rg. adj. said Garrot. 28 Dec 1804 [Dl'd Wm. Ward 5 Oct 1808]

Z-565: T.W.2713=18 June 1799 James Forman 10 A.(7 Oct 1803) in Berkeley Co. (island in Potomack R. near Va. shore), adj. Abraham Lingenfeller. 21 Dec 1804

Z-566:   T.W.3344=28 Jan 1802 Andrew Walker 100 A.(22 Apr 1802) in Hampshire Co.
in the Green Spring Valley adj. said Walker at S. Br. Mt. 31 Dec 1804

Z-567:   Exg T.W.1326=21 Sep 1802 Philip Snapp 50 A.(24 Feb 1804) in Frederick
Co. on N. Mt on the Big Cove adj. Philip Snapp, Cedar Cr., Lewis Stephens. 13
Mar 1805 [Dl'd P. Snap 21 Mar 1805]

Z-568:   T.W.3592=9 May 1803 John Brown 200 A.(3 Apr 1804) in Frederick Co. on
Opequan Cr. adj. said Brown, Thomas Butterfield dec'd, Joseph Hackney, 12 Nov
1735 patent by George II to Alexander Ross, Ignatious Perry, Francis Stribling,
Ths. Berry now Levi Smith. 13 Mar 1805 [Dl'd P. Snap 29 Mar 1805]

Z-569: Exg.T.W.1327=21 Sep 1802 David Brown 21 A.(22 Feb 1804) in Frederick Co.
on Shenandoah R. adj. land formerly R. Carter. 20 Feb 1805 [Prop'r 21 Mar 1805]

Z-570:   T.W.3564=22 Mar 1803 Enoch Renno & Enoch Jameson 323 A.(16 Jan 1804) in
Fauquier & Stafford Cos. on Beaverdam & Dorrel's Runs adj. Brenttown Rd.,
Alexander Jameson now James Cowles, Fitzhugh, Toalson, Butler, Robertson,
Philips, McCoy. 8 Apr 1805 [Dl'd Ph: Dawe 16 Apr 1805]

Z-571:   T.W.2348=19 Dec 1797 Christopher Heiskell & Henry Bell asne. of William
Helm Sr. 180 A.(28 June 1804) in Frederick Co. adj. Col. Thomas Parker, John
Parmer, George Bell, Manor of Leeds, on Shenandoah R. 4 May 1805 [Dl'd Henry
Bell 4 May 1805]

Z-572:   Exg.T.W.1173=5 Nov 1801 James Robertson 19 A. 3 Ro.(14 Apr 1803) in
Berkeley Co. on N. Mt. adj. John Park, Rd. from Back Cr. to Martinsburg, Elisha
Boyd, William Douglass, Edward Tabb. 21 Dec 1804

Z-573: T.W.3206=17 Aug 1801 William Crow 100 A.(2 Apr 1903) in Madison Co. adj.
Dennis Crow. 11 Dec 1804 [Dl'd Mr. Hill 21 Jan 1806]

Z-575:   Exg.T.W.1196=19 Dec 1801 Isaac Johnson 119 1/2 A.(4 Oct 1802) in
Hampshire Co. at foot of a Mt., adj. heirs of William Dobson dec'd, said
Johnson's purchase of Parker, Andrew Walker. 7 Dec 1804

Z-577: T.W.11,367=11 Mar 1802 John Poulison asne. of Robert French 40 A.(20 Sep
1802) in Hampshire Co. on Little Cacapehon adj. his own land, heirs of Francis
Taggard dec'd, Robert French, Steel. 17 Dec 1804

Z-578: T.W.19,599=26 Sep 1783 Joseph Thompson 100 A.(21 Apr 1798) in Hampshire
Co. on TearCoat Cr. adj. John Muzey, John Cunningham. 6 Dec 1804

Z-579:   T.W.3082=19 Jan 1801 John Mitchell Jr. 24 A. 28 Po.(9 Dec 1802) in
Hampshire Co. on Warm Spring Run of Great Cacapehon adj. Henry Boush, Joseph
Watson, town of Watson or Bath, John Rosebrough, Henry Bushe. 6 Dec 1804 [Dl'd
Alex'r King 27 Sep 1805]

Z-580:   50 A. by T.W.11,367=11 Mar 1782 & 48 1/2 A. by 3529=24 Jan 1803 Solomn
Park asne. of John Park 98 /12 A.(18 Mar 1803) in Hampshire Co. on Sandy Rg.
adj. Park, Abraham Rinckart, Andrew Millslagel, Baker. 7 Dec 1804

Z-582: T.W.11,367=11 Mar 1782 John Goff 10 1/4 A.(28 May 1801) in Hampshire Co.
on Piney Mt. & Kuykendall's mill run adj. Amos Poland, said Goff. 27 May 1805

Z-583: Resurv. 14 Oct 1803 by Ct. of Hampshire Co. Edward Emery 400 A. in tract
of 400 A. granted said Emry 13 Mar 1789 in Hampshire Co. on Allegheny Mt. adj.
Thomazen Elzey, Abrams Cr. 16 May 1805 [Dl'd Heiskell 20 Sep 1806]

Z-584: T.W.1629=14 Nov 1795 John George Tanner 4 A.(10 June 1802) in Madison
Co. adj. Adam Wayland, John Blankenbeker, Huffman. 22 May 1805 [Dl'd David
Mickie 30 Apr 1806]

Z-585:   T.W.3803=28 Dec 1803 John Burrough 50 A.(7 Feb 1804) in Madison Co. on
Church Mt. adj. Adam Banks, Thomas Graves Sr., Thomas Graves.   16 May 1805
[Dl'd Wm. Madison 24 Dec 1805]

Z-586:   Exg.T.W.1506=13 Apr 1803 John Prill 35 A.(6 Dec 1803) in Berkeley Co. on Sleepy Cr. aj. said Prill, John Dixon. 16 May 1805

Z-587:   Exg.T.W.1306=10 Dec 1802 Jacob Davis 3 A. 1 Ro. 27 Po.(7 May 1804) in Berkeley Co. on Tullisses Br. adj. James Davis (King's patent), John Davis, heirs of John Ellis dec'd. 16 May 1805

Z-588:   T.W.3088=26 Jan 1801 Robert Gustin 49 A.(16 Dec 1803) in Berkeley Co. on Sleepy Cr. adj. Andrew Brouse, Rev's Riand, Rd. from Warm-springs to Winchester, William Smith. 21 May 1805 [Dl'd 1 Mar 1819 Mr. Robinson]

Z-589:   T.W.3665=28 June 1803 Eli Nichols 15 A.(10 Mar 1804) in Stafford Co. on main S. run of Acquia, adj. Carter, Henry Harding's 20 May 1725 grant now Nicholas, John Preston. 22 May 1805 [Dl'd Mr. Peter Daniel 29 Sep 1805]

Z-590:   T.W.2764=12 Sep 1799 John West 45 3/4 A.(10 May 1804) in Stafford Co. adj. said West(formerly Hinson), heirs of John James, Col. Enoch Mason, Norman, Adams. 22 May 1805 [Dl'd Peter Daniel 12 Dec 1805]

Z-592:   Exg.T.W.1184=14 Dec 1801 Henry Knipe 30 A.(26 Oct 1803) in Frederick Co. beg. at stake shewed by Joseph Langley to be corner to heirs of William Vance dec'd, Capt. William Elzey, heirs of Strother Jones dec'd. 23 May 1805 [Dl'd Jno. Sanp 2 Sep 1805]

Z-593:   Exg.T.W.1479=24 Sep 1803 James Holliday 9 A. 8 Po.(30 Dec 1803) in Pr. William Co. on Chappawamsick run adj. Bennett, Fristoe now Holliday, Carney, Lee. 17 May 1805 [Inclosed to George Carney 25 June 1805, Dumfries]

Z-594:   Exg.T.W.1479=24 Sep 1803 Benjamin Carney 15 A. 2 Ro. 4 Po.(10 May 1804) in Pr. William Co. on Quantico run adj. Abraham Farrow, Francis Jackson, Ewell's old mill dam, William Bennet. 17 May 1805 [Geo. Carney 25 June 1805, Dumfries]

Z-595:   Exg.T.W.1479=24 Sep 1803 Benjamin Carney 8 A. 3 Ro. 36 Po.(10 May 1804) in Pr. William Co. on Quantico run adj. John Bennet, Jackson, said Carney. 17 May 1805 [Inclosed to Geo. Carney 25 June 1805, Dumfries]

Z-596:   T.W.3328=23 Jan 1802 Martin Doctor 3 1/2 A.(28 Nov 1803) in Shenandoah Co. adj. Jacob Weaver, Joseph Stover, said Martin Doctor. 6 June 1805

Z-597:   Resurv 22 Nov 1803 by order of Ct. of Frederick Co. David Devo heir at law of Conrad Devo dec'd 116 1/2 A. in bounds of 60 A. granted Conrad Devo by Prop'r of N.N. 17 May 1777, 56 1/2 A. surplus in bounds by T.W.3530=24 Jan 1803 in Frederick Co. adj. shown by Isaac Painter to be Conrod Devo's, Jacob Roads formerly Mich'l Gardner, David Wilson formerly Trautvine, John Painter, Samuel Ewing & his bro. Thomas Ewing. 21 May 1805 [Dl'd Hugh Holmes Esq. 9 Dec 1805]

Z-598:   79 A. by T.W.3088=26 Jan 1801; 40 A. T.W.3461=17 May 1802 &60 A. by T.W.3749=24 Oct 1803 Robert Gustin 179 A.(27 Dec 1803) in Berkeley Co. on Sleepy Cr. adj. John Miller, Matthias Swim, Mathias Swim Jr., William, McKewan, Rumsey, Gill formerly Hickson now Malon Combs, Edmund Goodman, John Swim. 21 May 1805 [Dl'd Mr. Robinson 1 Mar 1819]

Z-600:   T.W.2217=26 June 1797 Jacob Raish asne. of John Brennon 43 A.(10 June 1802) in Frederick Co. on Lick Br. of Back Cr. adj. said Brannon, Nathan Litler. 22 May 1805 [Grant inclosed by mail to the Prop'r 7 Apr 1806]

Z-601:   150 A. by T.W.2476=24 May 1798 & 74 A. by Exg.T.W.986=3 Nov 1800 James Higgins 224 A.(9 Mar 1802) in Hampshire Co. on road from Claytons to mouth of Little Cacapehon, adj. Edward Beats, Thomas Clayton, Rinker, Larramore, Carlin, Elias Poston. 16 May 1805 [Dl'd Christopher Hieskell 2 Jan 1806]

Z-603:   T.W.2879=24 Jan 1800 William Donaldson 97 A.(14 Oct 1802) in Hampshire Co. on Green spring run adj. Bruin, Feilding Calmes, Walker, said Donaldson. 16 May 1805 [Dl'd the Prop'r 4 Dec 1805]

Z-604:   Resurv. 4 Oct 1803 by order of Ct. of Hampshire Co. Rawleigh Colston

9314 A. being same contained in bounds of tract of 10,000 A. granted by Prop'r of N.N. to Philip Martin 21 Aug 1767 who conveyed to said Colston by deed 21 Mar 1794 (recorded at Winchester 15 Apr 1795) in Hampshire Co. on Pattersons Cr. adj. Maj. Wm. Vause, Landis Spring Run, Benjamin Parker, Benjamin Rawlings. 20 May 1805 [Dl'd Gen'l Jno. Marshall 2 July 1805]

Z-606: T.W.3561=15 Mar 1803 Josias Stone 20 A. 1 Ro. 27 Po.(20 Aug 1803) in Pr. William Co. adj. Swan Jones now said Stone, John McMillian, the Dumfries Rd., John Bennett now Sam'l Feilder, Enoch Renoe. 16 May 1805 [Mr. Linton 21 Sep 1805

Z-607: T.W.8740=9 Nov 1781 Andrew Wimer asne. of Archibald Finley 61 A.(27 Sep 1798) in Shenandoah Co. on Cedar Cr. adj. Josiah Jenkins. 6 Nov 1805 [Dl'd Lewis Wolfe Esq. 28 Jan 1806]

Z-608: Exg.T.W.812=26 Sep 1797 Vanentine Cooper 100 A.(10 Dec 1803) in Hardy Co. Co. on S. Mill Cr. adj. said Cooper bought of Isaac Scott, Michael Allkier. 7 Nov 1805 [Dl'd Christ: Simons Jan 1806]

Z-609: Exg.T.W.983=2 Oct 1800 William Kabler 42 A.(6 Dec 1803) in Culpeper Co. adj. Levi Lucans, said Kabler, Frederick Kabler, Henry & John Cox, Wallis/Wallace. 4 Nov 1805 [Dl'd Mr. Strawther 9 Jan 1809]

Z-610: T.W.3831=1 Feb 1804 Daniel Gick 100 A.(29 Aug 1804) in Hampshire Co. on Mill Cr. adj. John Mitchell Jr., Richard Airs, John Plumb. 6 Nov 1805

Z-611: T.W.1235=18 May 1782 Frederick Watts 75 A.(7 Dec 1803) in Culpeper Co. adj. William Kabler, Henry Cox, Watts,, Charles Carter formerly Thompson. 6 Nov 1805 [Dl'd Mr. Strawther 9 Jan 1809]

Z-612: 50 A. by T.W.3509=8 Jan 1803 & 22 1/2 A. by Exg.T.W.1549=24 Jan 1804 Nathaniel White 72 3/4 A.(17 May 1804) in Berkeley Co. on N. Mt. adj. Nathan Bull, Robert Bull, William Chenowith. 6 Nov 1805 [Prop'r 17 Mar 1807 by post]

Z-613: T.W.3058=20 Dec 1800 David Bookless 80 A.(2 Feb 1803) in Hampshire Co. on Castlemans Run of S. Br. of Potowmac R. adj. Ephraim Harriott, Peter Williams, David Bookless. 6 Nov 1805

Z-614: T.W.3501=4 Jan 1803 Elias Christler 70 A.(30 Sep 1803) in Madison Co. on German Rg. adj. Henry Christler, said Elias Christler, John Blankenbeker, George Utz. 7 Nov 1805 [Dl'd Mr. Hill 10 Dec 1806]

Z-615: T.W.3971=19 July 1804 John Tayloe 160 A.(29 Oct 1804) in King George Co. adj. land called Nanzattico formerly granted Ralph Wormley now part belongs to said Taylor on Sincoteague Cr. 7 Nov 1805 [By post to Prop'r 13 Aug 1806]

Z-616: T.W.2797=31 Oct 1799 John Hill Price asne. of Argalon Price 91 A.(20 May 1802) in Hampshire Co. on Pattersons Cr. adj. Stephen Pilcher, the Manor line. 7 Nov 1805

Z-617: T.W.95=27 Aug 1788 Bazel Beal 47 A.(13 Apr 1801) in Hampshire Co. on Allegany Mt. & N. Br. of Potowmac R. adj. George Kiger, said Beal, Jeremiah Ashby. 7 Nov 1805

Z-618: T.W.3501=4 Jan 1803 Michael Wilhoit 14 A.(21 Oct 1803) in Madison Co. adj. Adam Snyder, Cabbin Br. on Double Top Mt. 7 Nov 1805 [Mr. Hill 10 Dec 1806]

Z-619: 60 A. by T.W.3058=28 Dec 1800 & 48 A. by T.W.3458=9 Nov 1802 Ferdinand Gulick 108 A.(18 Nov 1802) in Hampshire Co. on Little Cacapehon adj. John Steel, Benjamin Kuykendall, Alexander Henderson, Haidekins fork of Little Cacapehon, Brian Bruin, Hugh Murphy, Gulicks old surv. 9 Nov 1805

Z-620: T.W.3344=28 Jan 1802 William Florrance Jr. 243 A.(23 Apr 1802) in Hampshire Co. on Cabbin Run adj. Abraham Good, George Miller, Thomazon Elzey. 8 Nov 1805 [Dl'd Mr. Vance 19 Jan 1833]

End of Book Z 1800-1801

A2-1: T.W.3501=4 Jan 1803 Joel Grayson 20 A.(13 Nov 1803) in Madison Co. adj. Daniel Cook, Andrew Gaar, Carpenter, wid. Campbell. 8 Nov 1805 [Dl'd Mr. John Clore 11 Nov 1806]

A2-1: 50 A. by T.W.3058 & 33 A. by T.W.3051 both=20 Dec 1800 Daniel Corbin 83 A.(24 July 1801) in Hampshire Co. on Little Cacapehon adj. Thomas Ruckman, Steel, Elisha Beal, Richard Taylor, Williamson. 8 Nov 1805

A2-2: T.W.3501=4 Jan 1803 John Blankenber 30 A.(1 Oct 1803) in Madison Co. adj. said Blankenbeker, John Yager, Andrew Goar, Henry Wayman, Samuel Blankenbeker. 8 Nov 1805 [Dl'd Mr. Hill Dec 1806]

A2-3: T.W.1694=27 Nov 1795 Thomas Graves 9 A.(27 Aug 1803) in Madison Co. adj. said Graves, Bear hunting Rg. 12 Nov 1805

A2-4: T.W.586=25 July 1794 John Daniel Moyer 103 A.(28 July 1804) in Shenandoah Co. on S. R. of Shenandoah adj. his other land, Andrew Kyser, Michael Rinehart dec'd, the Sandy lick, John Conrad Aleshite. 12 Nov 1805

A2-5: T.W.3439=30 Sep 1802 John McMillian 17 1/2 A.(4 Feb 1803) in Fauquier Co. on Tow run adj. William Hackney, Charles Brent, Michael Durmont. 15 Nov 1805 [Dl'd Mr. Linton 27 Sep 1806]

A2-6: T.W.2270=21 Sep 1797 Lewis Zirchel Jr. 5 3/4 A.(8 June 1804) in Shenandoah Co. on Third Hill adj. Lewis Rineheart, Conrad Pence. 12 Nov 1805

A2-7: T.W.586=25 July 1794 Jacob Barb Sr. 245 A.(26 July 1804) in Shenandoah Co. near Stony Cr. adi. Gabriel Sayger, Peter Sayger formerly George Harrison, Jacob Anderick. 12 Nov 1805

A2-8: T.W.2958=26 June 1800 George Miller asne. of George Hill & Stephen Pilcher asnes. of Alex'r Monroe 194 A.(25 Jan 1802) in Hampshire Co. on Mill run & Patterson's Cr. adj. Patterson's Cr. mannor, William Hill, Jacob Read. 11 Nov 1805

A2-9: T.W.3591=9 May 1803 Jonathan Parker 50 A.(9 May 1804) in Hampshire Co. on Mill Cr. adj. Job Parker, John P. Titus, William Mills. 11 Nov 1805

A2-10: 161 A. by T.W.2879=24 Jan 1800 & 39 A. by T.W.3590=9 May 1803 John Dimmett 200 A.(7 July 1803) in Hampshire Co. on Rd. Rg. adj. his own land, Elliott, Dimmett bought of Archibald Wiggins. 13 Nov 1805

A2-11: T.W.3465=26 Nov 1802 Randolph Spicer 156 A.(23 Dec 1803) in Culpeper Co. on Giants Castle Mt., adj. the late Jonathan Jones, Samuel Clagett, Browning, Kindell/Kendel,   said Spicer, Frederick Duncan, Wiston, Garner. 14 Nov 1805 [Dl'd Jas. W. Gardner 4 Feb 1808]

A2-13: Exg.T.W.1205=4 Jan 1802 Gilbert Combs asne. of William Bryan 186 A.(15 Jan 1804) in Culpeper Co. adj. Fodder stack Mt., Colbert, William Deatheridge, Robert Beverley, Henry Miller. 14 Nov 1805 [Dl'd Mr. Roberts Mar 1808]

A2-14: T.W.12,035=18 May 1782 Benjamin Tutt 56 A.(3 Dec 1803) in Culpeper Co. adj. Tolliver, Isaac Stone, Hansford Tutt. 13 Nov 1805 [Dl'd Will'm Broaddus bearer of recpt. 1 Nov 1811]

A2-15: Exg.T.W.570=1 Jan 1794 Martin Coffman(River) 222 A.(14 Aug 1802) in Shenandoah Co. on main Rd. from the white house to Thornton's gap, near Daniel Mauk's mill, adj. George Underwood, Derrick Pennybaker, Edwin Young. 13 Nov 1805

A2-16: T.W.2490=6 June 1798 Adam Mavis 12 1/4 A.(19 May 1804) in Shenandoah Co. near Pugh's run adj. Abraham Kochenour, Loenard Mowrer, Jacob Hottel, John Mavis. 12 Nov 1805 [Dl'd Philip Snapp 17 Dec 1806]

A2-17: Exg.T.W.1205=4 Jan 1802 William Deatheridge asne. of William Bryan 4 1/2

A.(15 Dec 1803) in Culpeper Co. adj. said Deatheridge, Robert Beverly, Ralls Bigby. 13 Nov 1805 [Dl'd Jno Roberts Mar 1808]

A2-17:   T.W.3465=26 Nov 1802 John Broombock 247 A.(2 Jan 1804) in Culpeper Co. adj. Henry Manifee, Daniel Mock. 14 Nov 1805 [Dl'd Jno Roberts Mar 1808]

A2-19:   T.W.19,223=10 Sep 1783 William Bryan 40 A.(14 May 1804) in Culpeper Co. adj. Baxter, said Bryan, Thomas Sims, Michael Yates. 14 Nov 1805 [Dl'd Jno Roberts Mar 1808]

A2-20:   Exg.T.W.1205=4 Jan 1802 Gilbert Combs asne. of William Bryan 228 A.(16 Jan 1804) in Culpeper Co. on Nixon's Arm adj. Henry Miller, Robert Beverly, the late Armistead White, Jacoby. 14 Nov 11805 [Dl'd Jno Roberts 31 Mar 1808]

A2-21: T.W.12,035=18 May 1782 Daniel Compton 147 A.(12 Dec 1803) in Culpeper Co. adj. Thornton, Thomas Hickman, Burgess R. 14 Nov 1805 [Jno Roberts Mar 1808]

A2-22:   T.W.19,846=13 Oct 1783 John Gibson 383 A.(26 June 1790) in Fairfax Co. adj. Bull run, John Linton, James Waugh, Sampson, Turly, Wm. Payne now Abednego Adams, Nathaniel Russell now Col. Thomas Blackborn. 8 Apr 1806 [Dl'd Benjamin Botts 20 May 1806]

A2-23:   John Tompson 297 A.(29 Aug 1785) in Hampshire Co. on Little Cacapehon adj. David Corbin, Robert Alexander. 8 Apr 1806

A2-24:   50 A. by T.W.21,330=13 Dec 1783 & 50 A. by T.W.185=12 Dec 1793 George Ellifrit asne. of Thomas McMasters asne. of William Pell 100 A.(29 Aug 1795) in Hampshire Co. on Patterson's Cr. adj. Thomas Allen and Bros., William Lindsey. 8 Apr 1806

A2-25:   100 A. by T.W.2227=12 July 1797 & 77 A. by T.W.21,017=1 Dec 1783 Joseph Stern & Nicholas Baker 177 A.(19 Nov 1797) in Hampshire Co. on Little Cacapehon adj. John Williamson, their own land, Patterson, Willis, Town hill, their land bought of John Pancake. 8 Apr 1806

A2-26:   T.W.18,821=21 Aug 1783 Bernard Gallagher 53 1/4 A.(6 Apr 1805) in Pr. William Co. near head waters of Neabsco, Crooked Br. of Occoquan adj. said Gallagher, Jackson, Rd. from Bacon-race M.H. to Dumfries, Rd. from Davis's ford to Occoquan mills. 5 Sep 1806 [Dl'd John Linton 29 Sep 1806]

A2-27:   T.W.18,821=21 Aug 1783 Bernard Gallagher 42 A.(4 Apr 1805) in Pr. William Co. on Neabsco, adj. said Gallagher, Mr. John Tayloe, Rexey's run, Champe, Hazlerig, stump shown by James Peake & Obediah Calvert as corner to said Gallagher. 5 Sep 1806 [Dl'd John Linton 29 Sep 1806]

A2-28:   T.W.2552=18 Oct 1798 Richard Ratcliffe 8 A. 80 Po.(13 June 1804) in Fairfax Co. on E. Br of Popeshead run adj. Alexandria Rd., Griffin Ellzey, Moor/Moore, Lewis Saunders. 5 Sep 1806 [Dl'd Thompson Violett 1 Oct 1806]

A2-29:   T.W.2977=20 Sep 1800 John Bowen 22 1/4 A.(9 May 1805) in Frederick Co. on Opequan adj. land sold to Hugh Tate &c, Robert Reece land sold to Russell, Bennett now Neal Christy, William Lynn. 11 Sep 1806

A2-30:   Exg.T.W.1360=8 Dec 1782 John Neff asne. of William H. Pritchett & Jacob Hidleback 36 A.(8 June 1804) in Shenandoah Co. at Turkey Hill adj. John Will, James Allen, John Hup. 1 Sep 1806

A2-31:   T.W.3508=8 Jan 1803 Jacob Rinker 15 A.(29 Aug 1803) in Frederick Co. adj. Joseph Steer, James Wood, said Rinker. 1 Sep 1806

A2-33:   Exg.T.W.819=21 Oct 1797 George Chapman Jr. 11 1/2 A.(15 Dec 1803) in Fauquier Co. on Broad run bet. John Toward now George Champan Jr. & Bryan Obannon now Peter Lamkin. 1 Sep 1806 [Original by post to prop'r 26 Apr 1808]

A2-34:   Exg.T.W.1371=17 Dec 1802 Leonard Stump Jr. 8 A.(2 Mar 1805) in Hardy Co. adj. heirs of Michael Stump dec'd. 1 Sep 1806 [Christian Simons 29 Dec 1806]

A2-35: 350 A. by T.W.3405=31 May 1801 & 40 A. by T.W.382=28 Mar 1794 Charles Sexton 390 A.(20 Apr 1804) in Shenandoah Co. on S. R. adj. said Sexton, heirs of John Philip Booker dec'd, Charles Buck, William Ellzey. 1 Sep 1806

A2-36: T.W.12,367=19 June 1782 Reuben Crafford 78 A. 2 Ro. 24 Po.(25 Apr 1804) in Pr. William Co. near Stafford Co. line adj. Blackburn now Fitzhugh, Willougby Newton. 1 Sep 1806 [Dl'd Wm. T. Banks 2 Feb 1807]

A2-37: T.W.2994=23 Oct 1800 Wilson Cary Seldon 13 A. 1 Ro. 4 Po.(25 Aug 1804) in Loudon Co. on Broken hills, Cool Spring Br. adj. John Richardson, Byrns, Francis Aubrey. 2 Sep 1806 [Dl'd Stephen C. Russell 18 Dec 1806]

A2-38: T.W.1371=17 Dec 1802 Leonard Stump Jr. 10 A.(1 Mar 1805) in Hardy Co. on S. fork. 2 Sep 1806 [Dl'd Christian Simons 29 Dec 1806]

A2-39: T.W.2994=23 Oct 1800 Mahlon Combs asne. of Wilson C. Seldon 3 A.(29 Nov 1804) in Loudoun Co. on Goose Cr. adj. Combs, Hough, Studdarth, Bernard Taylor sold Combs. 2 Sep 1806 [Dl'd Richard H. Henderson 26 June 1812]

A2-40: 25 A. by T.W.165=10 Dec 1793 & 6 A. by T.W.3731=11 Oct 1803 Isaac Peters 31 A.(16 May 1804) in Berkeley Co. on Sleepy Cr. adj. s'd Peters, Peter Whisner, Michael Gray, Jacob Fleece heirs. 2 Sep 1806 [Dl'd Moses Collins 28 Sep 1807]

A2-41: T.W.2215=26 June 1797 Conrad Hieronymus 3 1/2 A.(12 Apr 1805) in Frederick Co. on Lick Br. of Isaacs Cr. adj. said Hieronymus, Robert McKee, Rout. 3 Sep 1806 [Dl'd Joseph Sexton 18 Dec 1819]

A2-42: Exg.T.W.1073=23 Apr 1801 William Doster 400 A.(27 Apr 1800) in Frederick & Berkeley Cos. on Little N. Mt. adj. John McClain, John Holt, Back Cr., Richard Follis, Adam Snapp, William Penneybaker, Frederick Haner, Nathan Bull, Barton heirs. 3 Sep 1806 [Dl'd Mr. Heiskill 19 Sep 1807]

A2-44: T.W.2216=26 June 1797 Jacob Weaver 19 A. 20 Po.(2 May 1805) in Frederick Co. on Hodge Cr. near the old Barrack's adj. Peter Bear, said Weaver, Meridith Darlington dec'd, the Great Rd. from Winchester to Romney. 4 Sep 1806

A2-45: T.W.2216=26 June 1797 Jacob Weaver 13 A. 2 Ro.(3 May 1805) in Frederick Co. on Gap Run of Hoge Run adj. John Knott, heirs of Isaac Zane dec'd, Charles Johnston, George Glaze. 4 Sep 1806

A2-46: T.W.2216=26 June 1797 Joseph Baker 135 1/4 A.(7 June 1802) in Frederick Co. on Brush Cr. adj. Samuel Ruble, John Miller, heirs of Thomas Talbot dec'd, Pack Horse Rd., Third Hill Mt., Samuel Goodnight, Frederick & Berkeley Cos. line. 4 Sep 1806

A2-47: T.W.2216=26 June 1797 Joseph Baker 19 A.(8 May 1805) in Frederick Co. on Poplar Run of Hoge Cr. adj. said Baker, George Lamp, Henry Millhorm. 4 Sep 1806

A2-48: Exg.T.W.1444=14 June 1803 Nicholas Walter 75 A.(16 Apr 1804) in Frederick Co. adj. s'd Walter in Big cove. 5 Sep 1806 [Dl'd Philip Snapp 28 Oct 1806]

A2-49: Exg.T.W.1441=8 June 1803 Philip Snapp 250 A.(16 Apr 1804) in Frederick Co. on Paddy's run adj. Shepherd Collins in Big Cove, Big N. Mt., said Snap, Henry Clark. 5 Sep 1806 [Dl'd the Prop'r 28 Oct 1806]

A2-51: 100 A. by T.W.3812, 50 A. by T.W.3813 both=16 Jan 1804 & 14 A. by Exg.T.W.1080=25 Apr 1801 Robert Moss 164 A.(1 Apr 1805) in Fairfax Co. bet. Holmes & Dogues Runs adj. West, Pearson & Harrison patent now R.M. Scott, William Cash, Mason, Matthews now Penelope French & others. 5 Sep 1806 [To Prop'r 22 Oct 1806 by post to Alexan'dr]

A2-52: T.W.2216=26 June 1797 Joshua Gore 7 3//4 A.(28 May 1804) in Frederick Co. on Sleepy Cr. adj. said Gore, Robert Leatrell/Lutrell, heirs of John Dick dec'd, Wall, George Robertson, Benjamin Jolly. 11 Sep 1806

A2-53: 50 A. by T.W.2381=17 Jan 1798 & 13 A. by Exg.T.W.986=3 Nov 1800 John

Melick 63 A.(24 May 1802) in Hampshire Co. adj. John Watford/Wolford, George Martin, Abram Pugh, Caswell, George Martin Sr. 11 Sep 1906

A2-54: T.W.3265=29 Oct 1801 James Thompson 15 1/2 A.(6 June 1804) in Hampshire Co. on N. R. adj. Joseph Hutchan, John Thompson, William Millburn. 11 Sep 1806

A2-55: T.W.2460=11 Apr 1798 Joseph Longacre Sr. 57 1/2 A.(4 Aug 1803) in Frederick Co. adj. John Wisegarber, Gen. Isaac Zane dec'd, John Whitzel, Jacob Spilman. 11 Sep 1806

A2-56: T.W.17,532=27 June 1783 John Russell 200 A.(27 Dec 1804) in Shenandoah Co. on Stoney Cr. adj. George Miller, Zane, William Hough. 14 Oct 1806

A2-57: Exg.T.W.987=10 Nov 1800 Jane Barker 121 A. 3 Ro. 15 Po.(17 Dec 1804) in Pr. William Co. adj. John Hedges, Henry Tyler, Thornton, Bennett, Glinn, Dumfries Rd. 1 Oct 1806

A2-59: Exg.T.W.987=10 Nov 1800 James Grinstead 1 A. 15 Po.(30 Dec 1804) in Pr. William Co. on Chappawamsic, adj. Holiday, Grinstead. 1 Oct 1806

A2-60: T.W.3508=8 Jan 1803 David Lupton 10 A.(27 Sep 1803) in Frederick Co. on Babb's marsh adj. said Lupton, Philip Babb, William Lupton, Thomas Babb, William Rennols now Joseph Steers. 1 Oct 1806 [Dl'd Judge Holmes 13 June 1807]

A2-61: Exg.T.W.1325=20 Sep 1802 Andrew Hoffman 125 A.(29 Jan 1805) in Shenandoah Co. on Dry Run of Hawksbill Cr. adj. Jacob Shaver, John Comer, Thomas Tuckwiler. 11 Oct 1806

A2-62: Exg.T.W.1325=20 Sep 1802 Peirceson Judd 250 A.(30 Jan 1805) in Shenandoah Co. in the Piney Mt. adj. David Baker, John Griffith, James McCallister, Philip Summers, David Coffman, said Daniel Baker. 11 Oct 1806

A2-63: Exg.T.W.1325=20 Sep 1802 Michael Crouse 80 A.(21 Aug 1805) in Shenandoah Co. on Stoney Cr. adj. David Barb & Adam Barb Jr. purchase of Zane's exrs, Jacob Norden. 13 Oct 1806

A2-64: Exg.T.W.1325=20 Sep 1802 Wendel Melcher 90 A.(29 Jan 1805) in Shenandoah Co. on Stoney Cr. adj. said Melcher's purchase of Jacob Funkhouser, Orkney Spring land, Jacob Norden. 13 Oct 1806

A2-66: Exg.T.W.1325=20 Sep 1802 Wendel Melcher 45 A.(20 Jan 1805) in Shenandoah Co. on Stoney Cr. adj. said Melcher purchase of Jacob Funkhouser, James Machin. 13 Oct 1806 [Dl'd Mr. Strickler 14 May 1808]

A2-67: T.W.17,532=27 June 1783 John Russell 370 A.(26 Dec 1804) in Shenandoah Co. on the Three mile Mt. & Stony Cr. adj. James Rusell, Jacob Wolf heirs, Jacob Stults, Ulirck Waggoner, Adam Smith, Henry Bower Sr., Henry Bower Jr., George Coffman formerly Jacob Wolf. 14 Oct 1806

A2-68: Exg.T.W.1378=24 Dec 1802 Benjamin Forman 295 A.(30 July 1804) in Hampshire Co. on Great Cacaphon R. adj. Thomas Bennett, Cornelius Ferrie, Thomas Williams. 14 Oct 1806 [Dl'd Ric'd Clagget 5 June 1822]

A2-70: Exg.T.W.1549=24 Jan 1804 Edward Beeson 1 A.(16 Nov 1805) in Berkeley Co. on Tuscarora Br. adj. s'd Beeson, Moses Hunter dec'd, David Hunter. 16 Oct 1806

A2-71: Exg.T.W.1549=24 Jan 1804 Edward Beeson 24 A. 34 Po.(15 Nov 1805) in Berkeley Co. on Back Cr. adj. said Beson, William Douglas, Matthias Bitzer. 16 Oct 1806 [Dl'd Moses Collins 25 Oct 1809]

A2-72: Exg.T.W.1016=23 Jan 1801 Jacob Hess 6 A. 2 Ro. 25 Po.(29 Oct 1805) in Berkeley Co. on Opeckon Cr. adj. said Hess, Jacob Middlecalf, William Burns Sr. 23 Oct 1806 [Dl'd Mr. George Porterfield 5 Dec 1810]

A2-72: Exg.T.W.1017=23 Jan 1801 John Miller 62 A.(18 Nov 1805) in Berkeley Co. on Tilehances Br. adj. Isaac Compton, William Johnson, heirs of Zachary Miller dec'd, James Orr, Charles Young, James Robertson, Isaac Smith. 23 Oct 1806 [Dl'd A. Faris 31 Dec 1807]

A2-74: 137 A. by T.W.2632=12 Jan 1799 & 146 A. by T.W.2323=24 Nov 1797 Samuel Farr 283 A.(20 July 1805) in Fairfax Co. on Popeshead & Pohick runs adj. Lewis Sanders, Lewis Ellzey, Thomazen Ellzey, Grayson now Francis Adams, Richard Ratcliff formerly Lewis Sanders. 23 Oct 1806 [Dl'd 15 Sep 1809]

A2-75: Exg.1549=24 Jan 1804 Henry Everhard 50 A.(4 Apr 1805) in Berkeley Co. on Back Cr. adj. George Myers, John O'Ferrall, James Carr, George Everhard. 23 Oct 1806 [Dl'd Mr. George Porterfield 5 Dec 1810]

A2-76: T.W.3546=29 July 1803 David Cristler 198 A.(1 May 1805) in Madison Co. adj. William Roebuck, Benajah Rice, Henry Waylands, William Tate, Trippits Rg. path, George Harrison. 24 Oct 1806 [Dl'd Gen. Madison 9 Feb 1810]

A2-77: Exg.T.W.1371=17 Dec 1802 Jacob Ketterman 52 A.(5 Apr 1805) in Hardy Co. adj. his own land, near head of Elkhorn, Abraham Dehart. 23 Oct 1806

A2-77: T.W.3546=29 Feb 1803 Zachary Shurley & Thomas Shurley 38 A.(1 Oct 1805) in Madison Co. adj. Henry Hill, Frog & Wallace, Yowell's 1779 patent, Yager. 24 Oct 1806 [Dl'd Prop'r 9 Dec 1809]

A2-78: T.W.4192=30 Mar 1805 William Kirkley 500 A.(26 Apr 1805) in Madison Co. adj. Job Breading, Robert Baker, Theophilus Edins, heirs of James Collins dec'd, Reubin Clark, Isaac Smith dec'd. 24 Oct 1806 [Dl'd Edwin Nichols 27 Sep 1808]

A2-79: T.W.3830=1 Feb 1804 Patrick Fleming 9 1/4 A.(13 Nov 1804) in Hampshire Co. adj. his own land, George Miller, Ft. Pleasant Rd., Josiah Smoat, heirs of Abraham Noff dec'd. 25 Oct 1806

A2-80: Exg.T.W.1707=4 Jan 1805 Henry Fleck 18 1/2 A.(28 May 1805) in Hampshire Co. on Cabbin Run adj. land Fleck bought of Dan'l Jones, John Spencer, land Fleck bought of Whitehead. 25 Oct 1806

A2-81: Exg.T.W.1707=4 Jan 1805 George Beard Jr. 13 3/4 A.(27 Mar 1805) in Hampshire Co. adj. George Taylor, Absalom Parker, George Beard Sr. 27 Oct 1806 [Dl'd Mr. McCarty 26 Nov 1814]

A2-82: Exg.T.W.1654=27 June 1804 Isaac Lupton 73 A.(9 May 1805) in Hampshire Co. on Sandy Rg., N. R. adj. Benjamin Johnson, Baker. 27 Oct 1806 [Dl'd G. Sharf 16 Nov 1814]

A2-82: 100 A. by T.W.3884=1 Feb & 14 A. by Exg.T.W.1654=27 June both 1804 John Plum Sr. 114 A.(17 Apr 1805) in Hampshire Co. on Hog Run of Mill Cr. adj. William Sandford heirs, said Plum, Philip Cline, Henry Hawk. 28 Oct 1806

A2-83: 50 A. by T.W.3529=24 Jan 1803 & 50 A. by Exg.T.W.1654=27 June 1804 Jacob Hartman 100 A.(20 Mar 1805) in Hampshire Co. on Mill Cr. adj. John High Jr., George Hains, Jacob Purget, John Foley, Isaac Vanmeter. 28 Oct 1806

A2-85: Exg.T.W.985=3 Nov 1800 Thomas Leazenby asne. of Wm. Leazenby 128 3/4 A.(11 Dec 1804) in Hampshire Co. on Mykes Run of Pattersons Cr. adj. said Leazenby, Christian Utt. 28 Oct 1806

A2-86: T.W.3082=19 Jan 1800 John Mitchell Jr. 33 1/2 A.(22 Sep 1803) in Hampshire Co. on Cabbin Run adj. Henry Prutzman, Thomas Buffington, David Long, Wharton, Jacob Purgett. 28 Oct 1806

A2-87: Exg.T.W.985=3 Nov 1800 Gersham Roberts 58 1/2 A.(10 Dec 1804) in Hampshire Co. on S. fork of Mykes Run of Pattersons Cr. adj. Stephen J.? Terry, Samuel Jacobs, Geo. Gilpin. 29 Oct 1806 [Dl'd Christopher Hyskill 31 Oct 1812]

A2-88: Exg.T.W.1654=27 June 1804 Peter Williams 90 A.(4 Mar 1805) in Hampshire Co. on Fox's Mill Run of S. Br. of Potowmack adj. Ephraim Harriott, William Fox. 29 Oct 1806

A2-89: 48 A. by T.W.3591=9 May & 90 A. by T.W.3722=29 Sep both 1803 James Caudy 138 A.(3 Nov 1805) in Hampshire Co. on Dillings Run adj. Henry Baker, William Carlyle, George Littal, George Gilpin, George Homs?, Park's Mt. 29 Oct 1806

A2-90: T.W.3458=9 Nov 1802 James Caudy 50 A.(2 Apr 1803) in Hampshire Co. on Mills Br. of Great Cacapehon adj. David Shin, Labinger heirs, Rd. from Moorfeild to Winchester, Bogan, Nelson. 29 Oct 1806

A2-91: T.W.3529=24 Jan 1803 Samuel Parks 80 A.(7 Mar 1805) in Hampshire Co. on Tear Coat Cr. adj. Eli Ashbrook, Henry Hillburn, s'd Parks, Gaither. 29 Oct 1806

A2-92: Exg.T.W.1707=4 Jan 1805 James Cunningham 300 A.(16 Oct 1805) in Hampshire Co. on S. Br. Mt. adj. Henry Piper, Conrad Huffman. 29 Oct 1806

A2-93: Exg.T.W.1709=4 Jan 1805 Isaac Wolverton asne. of George Taylor 87 A.(27 Mar 1805) in Hampshire Co. on Pattersons Cr. adj. John Dowden. 30 Oct 1806

A2-93: 45 A. by T.W.2960=26 June 1800 & 12 A. by Exg.T.W.1555=24 Jan 1804 Joseph Thompson 57 A.(22 Apr 1804) in Hampshire Co. on N. R. Mt. adj. his own land bought of Gen. John Marshall, Joseph Tucker, Joseph Thompson, John Marshall. 1 Aug 1807

A2-95: T.W.1710=12 June 1783 Jacob Clutter 193 A.(16 Nov 1805) in Hampshire Co. on Lanoms Br. adj. George Reid, Jacob Clutter, John Perrel, Jesse Anderson. 1 Aug 1807

A2-96: Exg.T.W.1555=24 Jan 1804 Abraham Dawson Jr. 23 A.(22 Nov 1804) in Hampshire Co. on Great Cacapehon adj. Abraham Dawson Sr., Levi Mathew. 1 Aug 1807

A2-97: T.W.3906=12 Mar 1804 Abraham Pennington 84 1/2 A.(17 May 1804) in Hampshire Co. on Little Cacapehon adj. Jacob Pennington. 1 Aug 1807

A2-98: Exg.T.W.1707=4 Jan 1805 Andrew Tevalt 50 A.(29 Mar 1805) in Hampshire Co. on N. R. Mt. adj. said Tevalt, Abraham Cline, Joseph Thompson. 1 Aug 1807

A2-99: T.W.3722=29 Sep 1803 Isaac Asberry 100 A.(21 Nov 1804) in Hampshire Co. on N. R. adj. Bryan Bruin, John Wolford. 1 Aug 1807 [Wm. Donaldson 7 Dec 1808]

A2-101: Exg.T.W.1196=19 Dec 1801 Jeremiah Ashby 50 A.(20 Apr 1804) in Hampshire Co. on the Allegany Mt. adj. Benjamin Ashby, Samuel Kite. 1 Aug 1807

A2-102: T.W.11,367=11 Mar 1782 Aaron Ashbrook asne. of James Nelson 75 A.(3 Mar 1803) in Hampshire Co. on Tearcoat Cr. adj. Clay lick Run, Ashbrook bought of Nelson, John Lock. 1 Aug 1807 [Dl'd Mr. Donaldson 16 Dec 1808]

A2-103: T.W.3010=3 Nov 1800 William Pool 150 A.(17 May 1804) in Hampshire Co. on S. Br. of Potowmac R. 6 Aug 1807

A2-104: T.W.3830=1 Feb 1804 John Powelson 22 1/4 A.(18 June 1804) in Hampshire Co. on Rd. from Romney to Winchester, adj. Robert French, David Corbin, James Murphy, Taggard. 6 Aug 1807

A2-105: T.W.3529=24 Jan 1803 John Selby 50 A.(5 June 1804) in Hampshire Co. on N. R. Mt., adj. said Selby, Dunmore, Adam Huffman, Joseph Huffman, Stack's gap run. 6 Aug 1807 [Dl'd Mr. Higgins 28 Dec 1807]

A2-107: 20 A. by T.W.3590 & 60 A. by T.W.3591 both=9 May 1803 John Howard 80 A.(22 Nov 1804) in Hampshire Co. on Great Cacapehon adj. said Howard bought of Levi Matthews, Charles Robison. 6 Aug 1807 [Dl'd Geo: Miller 23 Jan 1809]

A2-108: T.W.3906=12 Mar 1804 Jonathan Pownell 157 A.(17 May 1804) in Hampshire Co. on S. Br. of Potowmac R. adj. Isaac Pownell, Jacob Pennington. 6 Aug 1807

A2-109: T.W.2917=16 Apr 1800 Henry Wayman 17 A.(7 May 1804) in Madison Co. adj. John Gaar, said Wayman, Blankenbeker. 6 Aug 1807

A2-110:   T.W.2917=16 Apr 1800 John Wright asne. of Peter Cook 23 A.(5 May 1804) in Madison Co. on Carpenter's Mt. adj. Andrew Gaar, Samuel Carpenter, said Cook. 6 Aug 1807 [Dl'd Robert Hill 5 Feb 1808]

A2-111: For $90.00 paid by Isaac Strickler to Jacob Rinker escheator of Shenandoah Co.   90 A. to Strickler in Shenandoah Co. on S. R. of Shenandoah granted Philip Swyger by late Prop'r of N.N. 6 June 1780. Adj. Joseph Strickler, Isaac Strickler. Swyger now dec'd without heirs. 7 Apr 1807   [James Allen Jan 1809]

A2-113:   T.W.3508=8 Jan 1803 James Davison 14 1/4 A.(7 Mar 1805) in Frederick Co. on Rd. from Winchester to Zane's old furnace, adj. Judge Robert White, James Laurence, on Hoge Cr. 7 Aug 1807 [Dl'd Chas. Brent 20 Jan 1809]

A2-114:   T.W.1568=25 Jan 1804 Isaac Crisman 2 1/4 A.(2 Oct 1705) in Frederick Co. adj. said Crisman, Peter Good, Thomas Steel. 7 Aug 1807   [Dl'd Chas. Brent Esq. 9 Feb 1808]

A2-115:   T.W.2215=26 June 1797 Jacob Baker 10 A.(13 Apr 1805) in Frederick Co. on Isaac's Cr. adj. heirs of John Peyton dec'd, said Baker, near Long Lick. 7 Aug 1807 [Dl'd H.W. Baker 21 May 1810]

A2-116:   Exg.T.W.1556=24 Jan 1804 Joseph Longacre Jr. 354 A.(7 Mar 1805) in Frederick Co. on Cedar Cr. adj. heirs of Isaac Zane dec'd, John Orndorf, Rudolph Whiteman, Leburt's run, Long Rg., John Wetzel, John Light, George Bowers, George Renner, Henry Conrad, Frederick Strowsnyder. 7 Aug 1807 [Mr. Brent 27 Dec 1808]

A2-118:   T.W.3975=1 Aug 1804 Benjamin DuVal 41 A.(20 Sep 1805) in Madison Co. adj. s'd DuVal, Thomas Bohannon, Double Top Mt. 8 Aug 1807 [Prop'r 25 Jan 1808]

A2-119:   T.W.2713=18 June 1799 Abraham Morgan 9 A. 20 Po.(1 June 1802) in Jefferson Co. adj. Stephen Stanley, Potowmac R., Abraham Shepherd, Jacob Bedinger, said Morgan. 19 Aug 1807 [Dl'd John B. Henry 25 Oct 1809]

A2-121:   Exg.T.W.1707=4 Jan 1805 Daniel Collins 42 A. 2 Ro. 20 Po.(20 Dec 1805) in Hampshire Co. on N. Br. of Potowmac R., Knobly Mt., adj. George Gilpin. 19 Aug 1807

A2-122:   T.W.3494=24 Dec 1802 Thomas Bohannon 81 A.(6 May 1805) in Madison Co. adj. said Bonannon, Dr. Benjamin DuVal, Milan's pass on Double Top Mt., Mrs. Lewis, Cap. Thomas Wallace, Tom's Mt. 19 Aug 1807

A2-124:   Exg.T.W.1325=20 Sep 1802 Lewis Zirchel Jr. 86 A.(25 Apr 1805) in Shenandoah Co. on Mill Cr. adj. Rudolph Brock now John Hepner, William Good, Michael Zirchel. 20 Aug 1807

A2-125:   T.W.4288=19 Dec 1805 Cornelius Wayland 100 A.(4 Feb 1806) in Madison Co. adj. George Harrison, top of German' Rg., Edmund Gaines, Mrs. Teppett, Jonathan Coward, James King. 21 Aug 1807 [Dl'd Mr. Madison 18 Feb 1809]

A2-127:   Exg.T.W.1205=4 Jan 1802 Gilbert Combs asne. of William Bryan 70 A.(11 May 1805) in Culpeper Co. adj. Ezekiel Brandom, John Skinner, Adams. 21 Aug 1807 [Dl'd Maj. Roberts 1 Aug 1808]

A2-128:   Exg.T.W.2=17 May 1798 William Barber 19 A.(1 Dec 1801) in Fauquier Co. on Deep Run adj. Samuel Earle, Alexander Beache. 20 Aug 1807 [Prop'r 4 Aug 1808 to Stafford Co.]

A2-129: Exg.T.W.2=17 May 1798 William Barber 11 A.(13 Nov 1801) in Fauquier Co. on Deep Run adj. Alexander Beach, Samuel Earle, Blackwell, Robert Jones. 20 Aug 1807 [Dl'd To Prop'r by post 4 Aug 1808]

A2-130:   Exg.T.W.2=17 May 1798 William Barber 58 A.(4 Feb 1806) in Fauquier Co. on Deep Run adj. Samuel Earle, William Prim, Washington, Kerr, Latimore. 20 Aug 1807 [Dl'd To Prop'r 4 Aug 1808 by post to Stafford Co.]

A2-132:   T.W.3702=15 Aug 1803 Samuel Gordon 33 A. 131 Po.(23 Oct 1805) in

Stafford Co. adj. Carter, Turberville now Gordon, Adams formerly Brooks, Lee now Hewitt, Morson. 21 Aug 1807 [Dl'd Mr. D. Briggs 1 Feb 1813]

A2-133:   Exg.T.W.1205=4 Jan 1802 James Woodward asne. of William Bryan 95 A.(12 Apr 1805) in Culpeper Co. adj. Adams, Woodard, Francis Brandom. 21 Aug 1807 [Dl'd Maj. Roberts 1 Aug 1808]

A2-134:   T.W.22,728=24 Dec 1783 John Fox asne. of Langhorn Dade 6 A. 1 Ro. 8 Po.(14 Mar 1805) in Pr. William Co. adj. George Gray now Renoe, Grant. 22 Aug 1807 [Dl'd Prop'r 16 Feb 1809]

A2-135:   150 A. by T.W.4165=29 Jan 1805 & 70 A. by Exg.T.W.1325=20 Sep 1802 Bernard Peal 220 A.(18 June 1805) in Shenandoah Co. on Smith's Cr., Messennetten Mt. adj. William McDowell, John Heep, Rockingham Co. line. 22 Aug 1807

A2-137: 40 A. by T.W.3945=29 May & 20 A. by Exg.T.W.1549=24 Jan both 1804 Jacob Shockey 60 A.(18 Dec 1805) in Berkeley Co. on Middle fork of Sleepy Cr. adj. said Shockey, John Ambrose, Hagerty, Isburn. 22 Aug 1807 [Dl'd Smith Slaughter Esq. 6 Dec 1808]

A2-138:   T.W.8740=9 Nov 1781 Benjamin Horner & Elizabeth his w., Joel Martin & Rebecca his w., Benjamin Wood & Sarah his w., William Fallis, John Vaughn & Phoebe his w., Susanna Fallis & Isaac Fallis,(said Elizabeth, Rebecca, Sarah, William, Phoebe, Susanna, & Isaac are ch. & heirs of Jacob Fallis dec'd) 4 A.(2 Mar 1797) in Shenandoah Co. on Jeremy's run near said Fallis's grist mill, adj. Hite & Co., said Fallis. 30 Dec 1807

A2-140:   100 A. by T.W.3528=24 Jan & 94 A. by T.W.3731=11 Oct both 1803 Michael Whitmire 194 A.(30 Apr 1805) in Berkeley Co. on Sleepy Cr. on Warmspring Rg., adj. McIntire now Francis Titus, John Hollinger, Thomas McIntire. 22 Aug 1807 [Inclosed to Prop'r by mail 18 Apr 1809]

A2-141: T.W.3722=29 Sep 1803 Robert Parker Jr. 150 A.(24 Sep 1804) in Hampshire Co. on S. Br. of Potowmac R. on S. Br. Mt. adj. Robert Parker Sr. 18 Jan 1809

A2-142: Exg.T.W.1370=17 Dec 1802 George Seymour 70 A.(13 Feb 1806) in Hardy Co. on Loonies Cr. adj. Pool, William Norman. 26 Jan 1809

A2-143:   Exg.T.W.1549=24 Jan 1804 Richard Morgan 3 Ro. 29 Po.(2 Apr 1805) in Berkeley Co. on Swam ponds adj. William Maxwell, heirs of Richard Claggett, Richard Morgan. 26 Jan 1809 [Dl'd Mr. Slaughter 31 Jan 1809]

A2-144:   T.W.4292=2 Jan 1806 Conway Rector 38 A.(27 June 1806) in Hampshire Co. on S. Br. of Potowmac R. inc. a small island, adj. John Taylor, said Rector. 21 Jan 1809

A2-145: 200 A. by Exg.T.W.1654=27 June 1804 & 64 A. by T.W.1708=4 Jan 1805 David Parsons 264 A.(20 Nov 1805) in Hampshire Co. on S. Br. Mt. adj. Hugh Valentine, George Utts, Isaac Means, Job Parker heirs. 31 Jan 1809 [Mr.Donalson 6 Feb 1809]

A2-147:   Exg.T.W.1554=24 Jan 1804 Samuel Fawcett & Joseph Fawcett 431 A. 3 Ro. 36 Po.(1 Mar 1808) in Frederick Co. adj. Thomas Fawcett, Joseph Snapp, George Booker, Isaac Zane, Jonathan Lupton, George Clevenger, on Cedar Cr. 7 Feb 1809 [Dl'd Charles Brent 7 Feb 1809]

A2-148:   Exg.T.W.1185=14 Dec 1801 William Vestal asne. of William Little 18 A.(12 Nov 1807) in Jefferson Co. adj. Thomas Wilson, late John Vestal, Shenandoah R. 7 Feb 1809 [Dl'd Mr. Slaughter 7 Feb 1809]

A2-150:   Exg.T.W.1734=5 Apr 1805 Israel Janney 5 A. 3 Ro. 26 Po.(15 Dec 1805) in Loudoun Co. adj. William Suddeth, Philip Vanscikle, Nickols. 17 Feb 1809 [Dl'd Mr. Russell 17 Feb 1809] (T.W.should be 25 Apr.)

A2-151:   T.W.4322=12 Feb 1806 Samuel McQuin 115 A.(30 Apr 1806) in Culpeper Co. on Bessibell run adj. William Duncan, Frederick Duncan, Jesse Garner, John Davis. 23 Feb 1809 [Dl'd Maj. Jno. Roberts 7 Mar 1809]

A2-152 62 A. by Exg.T.W.997=24 Dec 1800 & 50 A. by T.W.3320=15 Jan 1802 Daniel Corbin 112 A.(25 June 1803) in Hampshire Co. on Grassy lick run of N. R. adj. Robert French, Alexander Henderson. 23 Feb 1809 [Christopher Haskins 26 Oct 1809]

A2-153: Exg.T.W.822=6 Dec 1797 Mark Finks 73 A.(14 Mar 1806) in Madison Co. on Ragged Mt. adj. William Hurts formerly Richard Burdiue. 22 Feb 1809

A2-154: Exg.T.W.822=6 Dec 1797 May Burton adm. of Ambrose Medley dec'd for use of legatees of s'd dec'd 224 A.(11 Apr 1806) in Madison Co. adj. Ambrose Jones, land Johnathan Terrel sold Ambrose Medley, land Bunton sold Medley. 23 Feb 1809

A2-156: Exg.T.W.822=6 Dec 1797 Mark Finks 190 A.(1 Oct 1806) in Madison Co. adj. William Terrell's grant of 3 Oct 1734 now Joseph Eddins, Conway R., John Jarrett formerly Maxwell, Joseph Rogers. 22 Feb 1809

A2-157: Exg.T.W.1739=24 May 1805 Joseph Baker 6 3/4 A.(20 Nov 1806) in Frederick Co. on Hog Cr. adj. land leased to Enoch & Ezekiel Marples, John White, Robert White, John Peyton dec'd, said Baker. 24 Feb 1809 [Dl'd H. W. Baker 25 May 1810]

A2-158: Exg.T.W.1739=24 May 1805 Joseph Baker 133 1/4 A.(20 Nov 1806) in Frederick Co. on Hog Cr. adj. said Joseph Baker, John White, John Lupton, Philip Miller, George Green, Rd. from Winchester to Hampshire Co. Ct. House, Purtlebaugh. 24 Feb 1809 [Dl'd H. W. Baker 21 May 1810]

A2-160: Exg.T.W.1707=4 Jan 1805 Ebenezar Davis 50 A.(28 May 1805) in Hampshire Co. on N. Br. of Potowmac adj. Jeremiah Ashby. 24 Feb 1809 [Dl'd Randolph Spicer 20 Oct 1810]

A2-161: Exg.T.W.1821=28 Jan 1806 Thomas Carseaden 250 A.(22 Apr 1806) in Hampshire Co. on Stags run of Pattersons Cr. adj. the manor line. 24 Feb 1809

A2-162: Exg.T.W.1171=27 Oct 1801 William Carr 44 A. 2 Ro. 13 Po.(22 May 1806) in Loudon Co. on Tuskarora adj. George Hammat, John Williams, Shaw, McGath, Coleman. 24 Feb 1809

A2-163: Exg.T.W.1708= 4 Jan 1805 Richard Dever 22 3/4 A.(15 May 1806) in Hampshire Co. on Bakers run of Potowmac R. adj. Stephen West, James Bryan, William Pool, his own land, land Devers bought of Fryback. 24 Feb 1809

A2-164: T.W.963=11 Dec 1794 Jacob Rider 300 A.(22 Mar 1806) in Shenandoah Co. on Straight Br. of Mill Cr., on Suppenlick Mt., adj. Catharine Rider, John Holver, Michael Hannigan, John Welty. 24 Feb 1809

A2-166: 230 A. by T.W.1765=27 Sep 1805 & 170 A. by T.W.1708=4 Jan 1805 Isaac Kuykendall 400 A.(26 Nov 1805) in Hampshire Co. on S. Br. Mt. adj. James Dailey, said Kuykendall, James Cunningham. 24 Feb 1809 [Col.Edward McCarty 31 Jan 1818]

A2-167: 88 A. by Exg.T.W.1555=24 Jan 1804 & 32 A. by T.W.4292=18 Mar 1806 Joseph Thompson 120 A.(22 Mar 1806) in Hampshire Co. on N. R. Mt. adj. Andrew Tevault, Abraham Cline. 24 Feb 1809 [Dl'd Christopher Haskins 26 Oct 1809]

A2-169: T.W.963=11 Dec 1794 Henry Weatherholt 100 A.(15 Mar 1806) in Shenandoah Co. on Ryals Run of Stony Cr. adj. said Weatherholt, George Shoemaker, Funkhouser, William Craike. 24 Feb 1809

A2-170: T.W.3508=8 Jan 1803 Benjamin Fenton 5 1/2 A.(4 Apr 1805) in Frederick Co. near Long Marsh adj. Patrick Royce, Jacob Stone, said Martin, John Reagan now Jacob Stone. 24 Feb 1809

A2-171: Exg.T.W.1018=23 Jan 1801 Jonathan Lovett 492 A.(16 Nov 1806) in Frederick Co. on Back Cr. adj. Joseph Wharton, Morris Reese, Robert Lockhart, Cobb Seal. 24 Feb 1809 [Dl'd Joseph Sexton 18 Dec 1809]

A2-173: T.W.2216=30 Apr 1805 Jonathan Lovett 26 1/2 A.(3 May 1805) in Frederick

Co. on Laurel Run of Back Cr. & Bear Rg., adj. Northrop Marple, Wharton, James Kile. 24 Feb 1809 [Dl'd Joseph Sexton 18 Dec 1809]

A2-174:   T.W.2917=16 Apr 1800 Joel Wayland 60 A.(10 May 1804) in Madison Co. on Main Ragged Mt. adj. Fenly McAllister, Pophams run. 25 Feb 1809 [Dl'd Samuel Estes 28 Aug 1811]

A2-176:   T.W.2479=26 May 1798 William Farmer Sr. 21 A.(3 Aug 1806) in Frederick Co. on Isaacs Cr. adj. said Farmer, John Edwards, William Adams, Frederick Light. 24 Feb 1809

A2-177:   Exg.T.W.1739=24 May 1805 Mordecai Bean 13 A.(15 Aug 1806) in Frederick Co. on Hog Cr. adj. Jacob Secret, said Bean, Isaac Zane dec'd. 25 Feb 1809

A2-178:   T.W.2621=1 Apr 1799 Jacob Larrick 15 1/2 A.(29 May 1805) in Frederick Co. on Hog Cr. adj. Henry Clowzer, Leand?, heirs of Isaac Zane dec'd, Ezekiel Cleavers, David Jones now Larrick. 25 Feb 1809

A2-180: T.W.2759=31 Aug 1799 Michael Perkipile 16 A.(19 Nov 1801) in Shenandoah Co. in Powells big Ft. on Passage Cr. adj. David Clem, Moses Siever. 25 Feb 1809

A2-181:   Exg.T.W.1185=14 Dec 1801 Leonard Harbaugh & William Little 5 3/4 A.(29 Sep 1806) in Jefferson Co. Littles falls in Shenandoah R. adj. William Little. 25 Feb 1809 [Dl'd Mr. Bennet Taylor 14 May 1810]

A2-182:   Resurv. 3 Apr 1806 on order of Frederick Co. Ct. George Lamp 335 A. 3 Ro. 15 Po. part being surplus in 320 A. granted Lamp 22 Sep 1791 in Frederick Co. on Poplar run of Hog Cr. adj. John Whitzel formerly Simon Taylor, Joseph Baker, Little N. Mt., Nicholas Hipe. 25 Feb 1809

A2-183:   Exg.T.W.1460=29 June 1803 Dennis Crow 30 A.(19 Mar 1806) in Madison Co. on Robinson R. adj. Mrs Hurst, Mrs Weatherall.   25 Feb 1809 [Dl'd Thos. Shearley 9 Dec 1809]

A2-185:   Exg.T.W.1460=29 June 1803 Zachry & Thomas Shearley 120 A.(17 Mar 1806) in Madison Co. on S. fork of Robinson R. adj. George Row's 1796 grant now said Shearley, James Baytes, Ichabod Heywood, said Zachry & Thomas Shearley. 4 Mar 1809 [Dl'd Prop'r 9 Dec 1809]

A2-187:   Exg.T.W.1460=29 June 1803 James Baytes 11 A.(17 Mar 1806) in Madison Co. adj. George Row's 26 Mar 1770 tract now said Baytes, Zachry & Thomas Shearley, Ichabod Heywood. 4 Mar 1809 [Dl'd Thomas Shearley 9 Dec 1809]

A2-188:   Exg.T.W.1016=23 Jan 1801 John Roberts 100 A.(13 Mar 1806) in Brekeley Co. on Back Cr. & Third Hill Mt. adj. Paul Taylor, James Campbell, William K. Blue. 4 Mar 1809 [Dl'd Moses Collins 25 Oct 1809]

A2-189:   Exg.T.W.1733=5 Apr 1805 William Triplett 32 A.(20 July 1805) in Fauquier Co. on Cedar run, Cedar Run Rd. adj. Debuts now Henry Hoe. 4 Mar 1809

A2-191:   Exg.T.W.911=31 Aug 1799 James Woodard 60 A.(28 Nov 1806) in Culpeper Co. adj. James Taylor White, John Strother, Samuel Young, Thomas Bragg. 4 Mar 1809 [Dl'd Mr. Turner Feb 1820]

A2-192:   Exg.T.W.1185=14 Dec 1801 William Little 2 1/2 A.(25 July 1806) in Jefferson Co. being an island in Lyttles Falls in Shenandoah R. near Potowmac Company Canal. 4 Mar 1809 [Dl'd Mr. Bennet Taylor 14 May 1810]

A2-193:   Exg.T.W.1185=14 Dec 1801 William Little 7 1/2 A.(9 Aug 1806) in Jefferson Co. being an island in Shenandoah R. on Little's falls adj. Ferdinand Fairfax. 4 Mar 1809 [Dl'd Mr. Bennet Taylor 14 May 1810]

A2-194:   Exg.T.W.1185=14 Dec 1801 William Little 6 3/4 A.(29 Aug 1806) in Jefferson Co. being an island in Shenandoah R. on Little's falls adj. John Downey's sawmill. 4 Mar 1809 [Dl'd Mr. Bennet Taylor 14 May 1810]

A2-195:   T.W.20,728=13 Nov 1783 Peter Trone 39 1/2 A.(6 June 1807) in Pr. William Co. on S. Br. of Neabsco Run adj. said Trone, DuVall, John Langfitt. 7 Mar 1809 [Dl'd Mr. Botts 10 Sep 1820]

A2-196: T.W.20,728=13 Nov 1783 Edward Dickenson 22 A.(6 June 1807) in Pr. William Co. adj. John McMillian, Townsend Dade, Swan Jones. 6 Mar 1809 [Dl'd James C. Heathe 18 July 1810 for Surv. destroyed.]

A2-197 T.W.4349=5 June 1806 Robert Luttrell 10 A. 1 Ro.(6 June 1807) in Pr. William Co. adj. Bayles Renoe, said Luttrell. 6 Mar 1809

A2-198: T.W.3485=12 Dec 1802 Enoch Renoe 205 A.(6 June 1807) in Pr. William Co. adj. Hebron Ralls, Baylis Renoe, William Ashmore, John Fox, James Jemmison. 6 Mar 1809 [Dl'd Mr. Linton 17 May 1813]

A2-199:   T.W.21,477=23 Dec 1783 John Brown 640 A.(6 Dec 1803) in Hampshire Co. on Wiggins's Run of Potowmac R. adj. John Demmitt, Rd. from forks of Great Cacapehon to Bath(or Warm) springs, Kinalloway hill. 6 Mar 1809 [Dl'd Howe Peyton 18 Jan 1810]

A2-200: T.W.4332=18 Mar 1806 Amos Clayton 85 A. 2 Ro. 17 1/2 Po.(23 Aug 1806) in Loudon Co. on the Blue Rg. adj. Reps. of William Ludwell Lee, Washington, Manor of Leeds, Brooks Clayton. 6 Mar 1809

A2-201:   T.W.2244=9 Aug 1797 William B. Harrison asne. of William Hough 29 A. 1 Ro. 10 Po.(19 Nov 1806) in Loudon Co. adj. land Russell sold Ellzev, Green, Piles, Fairfax patent line. 6 Mar 1809 [Dl'd Mr. Rozell 29 Dec 1809]

A2-203:   T.W.2244=9 Aug 1797 James Campbell asne. of William Hough 52 A. 2 Ro. 13 Po.(23 Aug 1806) in Loudon Co. under the Blue Rg. adj. Brooks Clayton, William L. Lee, Overfield. 6 Mar 1809

A2-204: T.W.4358=29 Sep 1806 John Linton 21 A. 2 Ro. 34 Po.(30 May 1806) in Pr. William adj. Jacob Langher, John Tyler dec'd, said Linton, Thomas Larkin. 7 Mar 1809 [Dl'd Prop'r 29 May 1809]

A2-205: T.W.4358=29 Sep 1806 John Linton 13 A. 1 Ro. 26 Po.(13 May 1807) in Pr. William Co. on Piney Br. of Broad Run adj. Bernard Hooe, said Linton, Henry Washington. 7 Mar 1809 [Dl'd Prop'r 29 May 1809]

A2-206:   T.W.4358=29 Sep 1806 Jacob/John Linton 4 A. 2 Ro. 17 Po.(30 May 1807) in Pr. William Co. on Broad Run adj. John Tyler dec'd, Jacob Langher. 7 Mar 1809 [Dl'd Prop'r 29 May 1809]

A2-207: Exq.T.W.1739=24 May 1805 Jacob Marll 4 1/2 A.(10 Nov 1806) in Frederick Co. on Hog Cr. adj. George Lamp, Nicholas Hipes, James Singleton. 8 Mar 1809 [Dl'd Mr. David Castleman 26 Oct 1810]

A2-208:   Exg.T.W.1739=24 May 1805 Jacob Marll 40 1/2 A.(19 Nov 1806) in Frederick Co. on Hog Cr. adj. James Singleton Esq., George Lamp, John Wetsel. 8 Mar 1809 [Dl'd Mr. David Castleman 26 Oct 1810]

A2-209:   Exq.T.W.1018=23 Jan 1801 Jonathan Lovett 100 A.(7 Aug 1807) in Frederick Co. on Lick Br. of Back Cr. adj. Joseph Wharton, Deant, Richard Holliday, Jacob Weaver, Joseph Baker, Morris Rees, Robert Lockheart. 8 Mar 1809 [Dl'd Joseph Sexton 18 Dec 1819]

A2-209:(2)   Exg.T.W.1676=21 Sep 1804 Benjamin Williams 64 A.(28 May 1807) in Frederick Co. on the Gravel spring Run of Cedar Cr. adj. Frederick Cooper, Henry Trenner, the Crab Gully, George & Jacob Wolfe. 8 Mar 1809 [Dl'd Charles McCormack 19 Oct 1809]

A2-210:   Exg.T.W.992=15 Dec 1800 George Leps 29 1/2 A.(1 Sep 1806) in Hampshire Co. in cove bet. N. Mt. & Cool Spring Rg. adj. Stephen Prichard formerly Gabriel Throckmorton, Elisha C. Dick, Joseph Watson. 9 Mar 1809 [Dl'd Warner Throckmorton 26 Jan 1821]

A2-212: T.W.2480=26 May 1798 James Laing 78 A.(4 June 1807) in Frederick Co. on Brush Cr. adj. land formerly Thomas Sands, Peter Dick, wid. Trotter. Elisha Boyd, Pack Horse Rd., Samuel Burton. 9 Mar 1809 [Dl'd Willm. Smith 4 Feb 1812]

A2-213: Exg.T.W.1370=17 Dec 1802 John Foley Sr. 710 A.(2 May 1805) in Hardy Co. on Vanmeters Mill Run adj. his own land, Joseph Vanmeter, Hientzman, Rd. from Moorefield to Frankfort, High, Isaac Vanmeter. 9 Mar 1809

A2-215: T.W.4188=25 Mar 1805 Henry Bell 120 A.(21 Sep 1807) in Frederick Co. at foot of the Blue Rg. adj. John Palmer, Joseph Groves, George Bell, on Shenandoah R., Pigeon hollow Run. 9 Mar 1809

A2-216: Exg.T.W.1370=17 Dec 1802 Isaac Vanmeter 284 A.(14 May 1807) in Hardy Co. on Patterson Cr. Mt. adi. his land, Able Seymour, George Rennick. 9 Mar 1809

A2-218: Exg.T.W.1370=17 Dec 1802 George & Abraham Sites 117 A.(12 May 1807) in Hardy Co. adj. Deep spring surv. on Deep Spring Run of S. Mill Cr. 9 Mar 1809

A2-219: 18 1/4 A. by T.W.1691=25 Nov 1795 & 13 1/4 A. by T.W.2109=31 Jan 1797 Philip P. Bucker 31 1/2 A.(1 Apr 1802) in Frederick Co. on Cedar Cr. adi. Frederick Strownyder/Strowsnyder, Hugh Holmes, John Orndoff. 9 Mar 1809

A2-220: T.W.85=11 June 1788 Thomas Lewis 1 A.(27 Aug 1807) in Frederick Co. on Opeckon Cr. adi. his own land, land Lewis bought of Joseph Wood, Samuel Glass, James Marks, wid. Jones. 9 Mar 1809

A2-221: Exg.T.W.1370=17 Dec 1802 Christian Halterman 85 A.(9 May 1807) in Hardy Co. on Cove Run of Lost R. adj. heirs of Frederick Fout. 9 Mar 1809

A2-222: T.W.4400=2 Mar 1807 Joel Hurt 14 A.(3 Apr 1807) in Madison Co. on Great Ragged Mt., adi. Mark Fink 1806 surv. 10 Mar 1809 [Robert Hill 1 Feb 1811]

A2-223: T.W.4291=2 Jan 1806 John Swisher 154 A.(18 Apr 1807) in Hampshire Co. on N. R. Mt. on Moores Run of Great Cacapehon adj. James Alexander, Thompson's Mill Path. 10 Mar 1809 [Dl'd Christopher Haskins 26 Oct 1809]

A2-224: 150 A. by T.W.4295=2 Jan 1806 & 124 A. by T.W.17,110=12 June 1783 John Fleck 274 A.(21 Nov 1807) in Hampshire Co. on Cabin Run adj. Henry Fleck, Knobley Mt., Gen. Lee, Oneal's gap. 10 Mar 1809

A2-225: T.W.4295=2 Jan 1806 Margaret Crawfice 100 A.(26 Feb 1807) in Hampshire Co. on Plum Run and Pattersons Cr. adj. land formerly Benjamin Scritchfield, Balsor Shelhorn. 10 Mar 1809

A2-226: 100 A. by T.W.4314=4 Feb 1806 & 64 A. by Exg.T.W.1796=18 Dec 1805 Benjamin Lillard 164 A.(18 Sep 1807) in Madison Co. on Rocky Run, Fork Mt. adj. Benjamin Delany (10 Nov 1798 surv.) now Peter Fox, Great Ragged Mt. 10 Mar 1809

A2-228 T.W.4291=2 Jan 1806 James Parsons 4 A.(12 Nov 1807) in Hampshire Co. on S. Br. of Potowmac R. opposite his own land, adj. William Forman heirs, John Forman heirs. 11 Mar 1809

A2-229 T.W.4291=2 Jan 1806 Henry Fawver 100 A.(29 May 1807) in Hampshire Co. on Bennetts Run of Potowmac R. adi. Joseph Watson, John Dimmett. 11 Mar 1809 [Dl'd Christopher Haskins 26 Oct 1809]

A2-230: Exg.T.W.721=8 Dec 1796 Edward Perrell 19 1/2 A.(13 May 1806) in Hampshire Co. on Dillings Run adi. his own land, John Devers, Rd. from Winchester to Moorfield, Joseph Perrell. 11 Mar 1809

A2-231 T.W.4295=2Jan 1806 Richard Slone 100 A.(8 May 1807) in Hampshire Co. on Mill Cr. adj. wid. Ludwick, Jacob Piser, said Slone. 30 Mar 1809

A2-232: T.W.4293=2 Jan 1806 William Baker asne. of James Ravenscroft 200 A.(30 May 1807) in Hampshire Co. on Allegany, New Cr. adj. John Baker, Joseph Hall, Thomas Whitecar, Elisha C. Dick, Teavaults run, Nicholas Tevault. 30 Mar 1809

A2-233:   T.W.963=11 Dec 1794 John Conrad Ehlshite 12 1/2 A.(29 Oct 1806) in Shenandoah Co. on S. R. of Shenandoah adj. John Daniel Myer, John Roads, said Ehlshite. 30 Mar 1809

A2-234:   T.W.4293=2 Jan 1806 John Ravenscroft asne. of James Ravenscroft 172 A.(14 May 1807) in Hampshire Co. on Alleqany Mt. on Abram's Cr., Copper spring Run, adi. Jacob Vanmeter. 30 Mar 1809

A2-235:   Exg.T.W.1548=24 Jan 1804 Matthias Swim Jr. 100 A.(20 May 1807) in Brekeley Co. on Sleepy Cr. adj. Matthias Swim Sr., McDonald, Thornton, Thompson Elzey. 30 Mar 1809 [Dl'd Mr. Tate 12 Dec 1809]

A2-236:   Exg.T.W.1030=2 Mar 1801 Matthias Swim Sr. 200 A.(20 May 1807) in Berkeley Co. on Sleepy Cr. adj. Col. Smith's heirs, Collings, Moody, Gustim, McDonald. 30 Mar 1809 [Dl'd Mr. Tate 12 Dec 1809]

A2-237:   T.W.4262=17 Aug 1805 John Palmer 45 3/4 A.(21 Sep 1807) in Frederick Co. on Blue Rg. adj. Col. Thomas Parker, on Shenandoah R., Henry Bell, said Palmer. 30 Mar 1809

A2-239:   T.W.1391=27 May 1795 Hugh Holmes 1748 A.(7 Apr 1806) in Frederick Co. on Paddys run adj. Col. William Deakins, the waggon Rd. through Duck Run Gap to Nicholas Swisher, John Holmesgale, Shepherd Collins, John Clark, John Cook now Philip Snap, Lewis Stephens now Philip Snap, Nicholas Walters, Paddy's Mt., John Rudloph, Isaac Zane. 30 Mar 1809 [Dl'd the Prop'r 14 Nov 1809]

A2-241: T.W.1391=27 May 1795 Hugh Holmes 252 A.(1 Mar 1806) in Frederick Co. on Cedar Cr. adj. John Cooper, Henry Shull, John F. Strowsnyder, John Orndoff, Jacob Hoffman, Philip P. Bucker, Jacob Wolfe. 30 Mar 1809 [Prop'r 14 Nov 1809]

A2-243: T.W.2480=26 May 1798 Henry Routsul 22 A.(7 June 1807) in Frederick Co. on Back Cr. adj. said Routsel, McDonald, William McKee. great Rd. from Weavers to Rumner. 30 Mar 1809

A2-244:   Exg.T.W.1370=17 Dec 1802 Mary Ohaver 165 A.(14 May 1807) in Hardy Co. on Waits Run of Great Cacapehon adj. Thomas Wood. 30 Mar 1809

A2-245:   T.W.20,333=6 Nov 1783 Joseph Nevill 700 A.(26 May 1800) in Hardy Co. on Stoney R., adj. Clear Meadow Run, said Nevill. 30 Mar 1809

A2-246:   Exg.T.W.1370=17 Dec 1802 John T. Veatch 96 A.(11 May 1807) in Hardy Co. on Looneys Cr. adj. his own land, John Scott heirs, John Pool, Brue. 30 Mar 1809 [Dl'd Hezekiah Veatch 28 Dec 1809]

A2-247: T.W.4293=2 Jan 1806 John Wolford 50 A.(15 Sep 1807) in Hampshire Co. on N. R. adj. said Wolford, Isaac Asberry, George Martin. 30 Mar 1809

A2-248:   Exg.T.W.1707=4 Jan 1805 John Matthew 25 A.(30 May 1807) in Hampshire Co. on Great Cacapehon adj. Henry Bruner, Peter Larew. 30 Mar 1809

A2-249: T.W.3320=15 Jan 1802 John Petters asne. of Daniel Corbin 45 A.(25 Oct 1805) in Hampshire Co. on Little Cacapehon adj. Thomas Ruckman, Richard Taylor, said Daniel Corbin. 30 Mar 1809

A2-250: T.W.3541=29 Jan 1803 Eli Ashbrook 91 A.(13 May 1805) in Hampshire Co. on Tear Coat Cr. adj. Henry Hillburn. 30 Mar 1809

A2-251:   T.W.1270=7 Apr 1795 Henry Hickle asne. of George Lafollet 85 A.(31 Dec 1806) in Hampshire Co. on Great Cacapehon adi. Philip Cline, Hickel, Jesse Puqh, Melon Pugh. 30 Mar 1809

A2-252: T.W.4294=2 Jan 1806 William Hamilton 50 A.(29 Apr 1807) in Hampshire Co. on Great Cacapehon adj. his purchase of Thomas Simms, James Leath. 30 Mar 1809

A2-253: 125 A. by T.W.17,110=12 June 1783 & 72 A. Exg.T.W.1707=4 Jan 1805 George Sharp 197 A.(27 Oct 1806) in Hampshire Co. on N. R. at foot of Grape Rg. adj.

48

Daniel Loy, Francis White, Gap run, William Moorland, Henry Baker. 30 Mar 1809

A2-254:   280 A. by T.W.4293 & 20 A. by T.W.4291 both=2 Jan 1806 Robert Colvin 300 A.(8 Aug 1806) in Hampshire Co. on Litttle Cacapehon on Town hill adi. John Critton Sr., said Colvin bought of Jonas Hidge, Christopher Errett or Evrett, John Johnson. 30 Mar 1809

A2-255:   T.W.2781=27 Sep 1799 Jacob Critten 79 A.(4 Sep 1805) in Hampshire Co. on Little Cacapehon adj. John Johnson, John Darrow, John Critten Sr. 30 Mar 1809

A2-256:   Exg.T.W.1839=28 Mar 1807 Francis Martin 246 A.(1 Oct 1807) in Fauquier Co. on Marsh Run adj. Marr's Run, Chilton Randall, Robert Green, Joseph Morgan, John & Thomas Strode. 10 Apr 1809 [Dl'd Harrison Dance 31 Oct 1809]

A2-258:   T.W.3588=3 May 1803 Robert Hening 102 A.(26 Nov 1807) in Stafford Co. on Potowmack Cr. adj. Robert Hening, land called the Bell plains. 10 Apr 1809

A2-259:   Exg.T.W.1170=27 Oct 1801 John Farensworth asne. of Charles Binns 12 A. 3 Ro. 37 Po.(28 June 1807) in Loudon Co. on Blue Rg. adj. Warner, Carter now Reps. of William L. Lee, Thomas. 10 Apr 1809

A2-260:   T.W.85=11 June 1788 Jacob Rinker 1 A. 18 Po.(7 Aug 1807) in Frederick Co. adj. James Smith, near Winchester, Gabriel Jones, Isaac Parkins's mill, Cornelious Baldwin, Jonathan Parkins. 10 Apr 1809 [Lewis Wolf 27 Jan 1810]

A2-260:   Exg.T.W.1707=4 Jan 1805 Frederick Buzzard 18 1/2 A.(27 May 1806) in Hampshire Co. on Owens Rg. adj. heirs of Jacob Jenkins dec'd., Tunis Titus, Fry. 10 Apr 1809

A2-262:   Exg.T.W.1707=4 Jan 1805 Frederick Buzzard 109 A.(26 May 1806) in Hampshire Co. on Bear-garden Rg. adj. Leamaon, Christopher Fry, Joseph Gill, Robison. 10 Apr 1809

A2-263:   Exg.T.W.1707=4 Jan 1805 Frederick Buzzard 40 3/4 A.(26 May 1806) in Hampshire Co. on Bear Garden Rg. adj. Fry, Leamon, said Buzzard. 10 Apr 1809

A2-264:   Exg.T.W.1016=23 Jan 1801 James Anderson & David Hunter 2380 A.(23 Apr 1807) in Berkeley Co. on Sleepy Cr. Mt. & Meadow Br. adj. John Overton, Ruble, Wright, Stephen Fenner, Peter Storm, Peter Huff, Elkins, Philip Pendleton dec'd, Henry Snively/Sniveley, Moses Collins, John Roberts. 10 Apr 1809

A2-266:   T.W.3354=4 Mar 1780 John Seddon 12 A. 23 Po.(18 Mar 1805) in Stafford Co. adj. Accokeek mine Co. now Francis Foushee, s'd Seldon, Downing. 10 Apr 1809

A2-267:   T.W.962=11 Dec 1794 Isaac Overall 170 A.(1 June 1807) in Shenandoah Co. adj. his other lands, Overall's purchase of John Saffer. 10 Apr 1809

A2-268:   T.W.2710=12 June 1799 Thomas Allen 38 A.(27 Nov 1806) in Culpeper Co. adj. William Thornton, Thomas Waldon, Bumgarner, said Allen. 10 Apr 1809 [Dl'd to rec't for surv. 22 Nov 1810]

A2-269:   T.W.62=23 Feb 1788 Thomas Seymour 173 A.(23 Apr 1808) in Hardy Co. on Abram's Cr. on the Allegany Mt. 10 Apr 1809

A2-270:   T.W.962=11 Dec 1794 John Overall 211 A.(2 June 1807) in Shenandoah Co. adj. his other land, Piney Mt. 10 Apr 1809

A2-272:   T.W.62=23 Feb 1788 Thomas Seymour 18 A.(23 Apr 1808) in Hardy Co. on the Allegany Mt. east of Abrams Cr. adi. heirs of Peter Srout. 10 Apr 1809

A2-273:   T.W.3912=20 Mar 1804 James Stewart 90 1/2 A.(14 Apr 1807) in Stafford Co. on Acquia Cr., Jacksons Mill Br. adj. Hope Patent, Austins Run. 10 Apr 1809

A2-274:   T.W.3267=29 Oct 1801 John Brown 198 A.(20 May 1808) in Hampshire Co. on Wiggins's Run of Potowmac R. adj. Kinaloway Hill, said Brown, Beel Dimmitt. 10 Apr 1809 [Dl'd Howe Peyton 18 Jan 1810]

A2-275:   T.W.4180=1 Mar 1805 Gustavus B. Wallace 62 A.(6 Feb 1808) in King George Co. adj. Gants Swamp or Turkeyaker run, John Rowley now Michael Wallace, Heale & Hubbard now Reuben Owens, Champe, Lurtey's estate now Michael Wallace. 10 Apr 1809 [Dl'd Prop'r at King Geo. Ct. house by mail 10 Aug 1809]

A2-276:   T.W.4418=22 Aug 1807 James Abell 10 1/4 A.(27 Apr 1808) in Pr. William Co. on Powell's run adj. said Abell, John Matthews, Capt. John McCray, Moses Lynn, John Lynn. 10 Apr 1809 [Dl'd Mr. Daw 31 Jan 1811]

A2-277:   T.W.2977=20 Sep 1800 Joshua Gore for one moiety & Peter Dick as asne. of said Gore for the other moiety 77 3/4 A.(11 Dec 1805) in Frederick Co. on Brush Cr. adj. Henry Gardner, Joseph Wear, Reason Mayson, Peter Dick, Heirs of Henry Gardner dec'd, Thomas Collins. 10 Apr 1809

A2-278:   T.W.110=7 Oct 1788 Charles McKewan 71 A.(6 Nov 1807) in Jefferson Co. on Potowmac R. adj. Isaac Chapline, Rignal Green, John Williamson. 10 Apr 1809 [Dl'd Moses Collins 25 Oct 1809]

A2-280:   Exq.T.W.1021=23 Jan 1801 John Robinson 452 A.(6 July 1808) in Berkeley Co. on Sleepy Cr., Rd. from Martinsburg to Bath, adi. Theodorus Shaw, William Rankin, Carter, Thomas Fields, Jerome Williams, Matthias Swim, Robert Gustin, Southwood, his own land, Oven lick Rg.   29 Sep 1809 [Dl'd Prop'r by mail at Clarksburg 18 Oct 1809]

A2-282:   T.W.1021=23 Jan 1801 John Robinson 302 A.(17 Oct 1808) in Berkeley Co. adj. McDonald, Robert Gustin, Edward Southwood, James Throckmorton, Dry Run, land formerly Pendleton. 29 Sep 1809 [Prop'r by mail to Clarksburg 18 Oct 1809]

A2-283:   T.W.85=11 June 1788 Jacob Rinker 6 A. 2 Ro. 35 Po.(2 Nov 1808) in Frederick Co. adj. Winchester, John Will, Gabriel Jones, Wolfe's heirs, Lupton. 29 Sep 1809 [Dl'd Lewis Wolfe 27 Jan 1810]

A2-284:   Exg.T.W.1185=14 Dec 1801 Thomas Flagg & William Gibbs asne. of William Little 6 1/2 A.(18 Feb 1808) in Jefferson Co. adj. Malon Anderson, Jervis Shirley, Charles Washington. 29 Sep 1809

A2-285:   84 A. by Exg.T.W.1562=24 Jan 1804, 100 A. by T.W.4490=22 Sep 1808 & 60 A. by T.W.81=23 May 1788 John Hutchinson 244 A.(25 Nov 1808) in Frederick & Hampshire Cos. on Bear Garden Rg. adj. John Rodgers, Owen Rodgers, Thompsons heirs, Joseph Berry heirs, William Smith, Sleepy Cr. 29 Sep 1809   [Dl'd Mr. Brent 12 Dec 1810]

A2-287:   400 A. by T.W.4324=17 Feb 1806 & 81 1/2 A. by T.W.4190=26 Mar 1806 George Smith 481 1/2 A.(6 June 1807) in Frederick Co. on Isaac's Cr. at Horselick place adj. William Garman, Abraham Keckley, Jacob Oats, Joseph Fletcher, McKee, Carr, Henderson. 29 Sep 1809

A2-289:   T.W.4190=26 Mar 1805 George Smith 6 A.(7 June 1807) in Frederick Co. on Isaac's Cr. adj. said Smith, Carr, Henderson. 29 Sep 1809

A2-290:   300 A. by T.W.4486=26 Aug 1808 & 55 A. by Exq.T.W.1573=25 Jan 1804 Edward O. Williams 355 A.(22 Nov 1808) in Berkeley Co. adj. the late Lord Fairfax, George Williams, Green, Houte, Richard Margan/Morgan. 29 Sep 1809

A2-292:   Exg.T.W.1261=23 Mar 1802 Isaac Brake 90 A.(4 Nov 1808) in Hardy Co. adj. his own land, William Radcliff. 29 Sep 1809

A2-293:   Exg.T.W.813=26 Sep 1797 James Morrow & David Morrow 45 A.(4 Nov 1808) in Hardy Co. adj. their own land, Valentine Cooper. 29 Sep 1809 [Dl'd Mr. Adam Fisher 26 Mar 1811]

A2-294:   Exg.T.W.1562=24 Jan 1804 Charles McCormick 5 3/4 A.(20 Sep 1808) in Frederick Co. on Great Rd. from Snickers Ferry to Winchester adj. Ambrose Barnett, Edward Adams, George H. Norris called the Hermitage tract, Nevil's corner, Densil. 29 Sep 1809

A2-296: Exg.T.W.1261=23 Mar 1802 Andrew Harvey 9 A.(2 Nov 1808) in Hardy Co. on the Alegany Mt. adj. his own land near Alder Swamp Run. 10 Oct 1809 [Dl'd Mr. Adam Fisher 26 Mar 1811]

A2-297: T.W.3267=29 Oct 1801 Jonathan Purcall 210 A.(26 May 1808) in Hampshire Co. on S. Br. of Potowmac R. adj. Isaac Kuykendall, James Cunningham formerly Jonathan Purcall. 1 Nov 1809

A2-298: T.W.3058=20 Dec 1800 Hezekiah Linthecum asne. of Richard Taylor 50 A.(24 May 1801) in Hampshire Co. on N. R. at foot of Short arse Mt., adj. Morefield Rd., Evans. 1 Nov 1809

A2-299: T.W.4454=29 Feb 1808 Thomas Pollard 18 A.(3 Oct 1808) in King George Co. at mouth of Lamb Cr. adj. John & George Mott now said Pollard, marsh or pocoson on Rappahannock R. 1 Nov 1808 [Dl'd Prop'r 21 Nov 1809]

A2-300: T.W.3267=29 Oct 1801 John Higgins 77 A.(17 May 1808) in Hampshire Co. on Great Rd. from Frankfort to Winchester, on Little Cacapehon, adj. John Brawn, Higgins formerly Linzey, Robert Daugherty. 1 Nov 1809 [M.A. King 22 Dec 1809]

A2-301: Exg.T.W.1707=4 Jan 1805 Alexander King 50 A.(30 Mar 1808) in Hampshire Co. on Great Rd. from Frankfort to Winchester adj. Daniel Black, John Lyon, Patrick Savage, Colbert Chew, Heirs of James McAlister dec'd. 1 Nov 1809 [Dl'd the Prop'r 22 Dec 1809]

A2-302: T.W.4436=7 Dec 1807 Daniel Hollenback 100 A.(18 Mar 1808) in Hampshire Co. on Pattersons Cr. adj. William Cowen formerly Ogan, James Mitchell, Colsons run, Hollenbacks heirs. 1 Nov 1809 [Dl'd Mr. Frederick Sheets 18 May 1813]

A2-304: T.W.963=11 Dec 1794 John Koontz Jr. 10 A.(31 Mar 1808) in Shenandoah Co. on S. R. of Shenandoah, adj. said Koontz. 1 Nov 1809

A2-305: T.W.3590=9 May 1803 Samuel Poston asne. of George McManing 30 A.(31 Aug 1803) in Hampshire Co. on great Rd. from Romney to Winchester adj. David Shin, Elias Lovit/Lovett, Labinger. 1 Nov 1809

A2-306: Exg.T.W.1707=4 Jan 1805 Thomas Mulledy 50 A.(9 Dec 1807) in Hampshire Co. on Mill Cr. adj. his own land, Richard Sloan formerly John Norman, his land bought of Dollehan. 1 Nov 1809

A2-308: T.W.4438=8 Dec 1807 Richard Sloan 190 A.(23 Mar 1808) in Hampshire Co. on Mill Cr. adj. his own land, Thomas Mullidy, wid. Ludwick, Jacob Piser, Daniel Botruck. 1 Nov 1809

A2-309: T.W.2322=23 Nov 1797 Jeremiah Reed 17 1/2 A.(10 May 1805) in Hampshire Co. on Lorroms Br. adj. said Reed, Jesse Anderson. 1 Nov 1809 [Dl'd A. King 22 Dec 1809]

A2-310: Preemption T.W.2128=24 Apr 1782 John Johnson 60 A.(5 Jan 1801) in Hampshire Co. on Rock gap run in warm spring valley adj. said Johnson, Henry Crone, Robert Gustin. 1 Nov 1809 [Dl'd William Smith 4 Feb 1812]

A2-311: Exg.T.W.913=21 Sep 1790 William Lewis 81 A.(2 Apr 1808) in Madison Co. adj. Henry Lewis, Double top Mt. 1 Nov 1809

A2-313: T.W.4294=2 Jan 1806 Richard Blue 52 A.(28 Apr 1808) in Hampshire Co. on S. Br. Mt. & S. Br. adj. Newmans heirs. 1 Nov 1809

A2-314: Exg.T.W.1572=25 Jan 1804 Charles Sexton 340 A.(1 Apr 1808) in Shenandoah Co. adj. William Ellzey, said Sexton, Martin Doctor. 1 Nov 1809

A2-316: T.W.962=11 Dec 1794 Peter Baker 44 A.(12 Jan 1808) in Shenandoah Co. on Stony Cr. near Little N. Mt., adj. heirs of Peter Baker dec'd, Paul Hamman heirs, James Machir. 1 Nov 1809

A2-318: 247 A. by T.W.4291=2 Jan 1806 & Exg.T.W.1831=13 Feb 1806 William Naylor

355 A.(13 May 1808) in Hampshire Co. on S. Br. of Potowmack R. adj. Buffingtons knob, John Jack, said Naylor, Adam Hall, David Parsons, William Buffington. 1 Nov 1809 [Dl'd Chris't Hyshill 31 Oct 1812]

A2-320: T.W.963=11 Dec 1794 John Conrad Elkshite 20 A.(22 Jan 1808) in Shenandoah Co. on S. R. of Shenandoah adj. John Daniel Moyer, Sandy lick, Michael Renchart now Andrew Kyser, said Elkshite. 1 Nov 1809

A2-322: T.W.40=5 Jan 1788, T.Ws. 53 & 54=23 Jan 1788 in name of David Hunter, grant to Robert Stephen asne. of David Hunter 2144 A.(30 May 1788) in Berkeley Co. on Potomack R. adj. Robert Stephen, George Chapman, John Potts, John Davis, Thomas Adams, Sir John's Rd., Thomas Curtis. 10 Jan 1810 [Dl'd Philip C. Pendleton 22 Jan 1810]

A2-324: T.W.45=5 Jan 1788 & 54=23 Jan 1788 David Hunter 400 A.(5 June 1780) in Berkeley Co. on Potomack R. opposite mouth of Conogocheague Cr. & Williams's port in Maryland, adj. Nicholas Harman, James Jack, Ross heirs, Rd. to Watkins's ferry. 10 Jan 1810 [Dl'd Philip C. Pendleton 22 Jan 1810]

A2-326: T.W.53 & 54=23 Jan 1788 David Hunter 1500 A.(4 June 1788) in Berkeley Co. on Potomack R. adj. Jeremiah Jack, Basore, Michael Shiveley, Thomas Adams, Sir John's Rd. 10 Jan 1810 [Dl'd Philip C. Pendleton 22 Jan 1810]

A2-327: T.W.41=5 Jan 1788, Wts. 54 & 59=23 Jan 1788 David Hunter 1050 A.(10 June 1788) in Berkeley Co. on Potomack R. adj. Stephen Boyles, Warm Spring Run. 10 Jan 1810 [Dl'd Philip C. Pendleton 22 Jan 1810]

A2-329: T.W.4292=2 Jan 1806 Thomas Mulledy asne. of Abbot Carder 200 A.(27 Jan 1807) in Hampshire Co. on Town Run near Romney adj. Adam Heiskell, John Jack, Henry Heinzman, Andrew Wodrow. 10 Jan 1810

A2-330: 100 A. by T.W.1196=19 Dec 1801 & 62 1/2 A. by T.W.3722=29 Sep 1803 George Myers asne. of Thomas Hillyard 162 1/2 A.(20 Feb 1804) in Hampshire Co. on Edwards Run adj. said Hillyard's land bought of Deven, George Myars, John Turner, John Park, George Bethell. 10 Jan 1810

A2-332: 258 A. by T.W.4379=9 Dec 1806 & 350 A. by T.W.4376=4 Dec 1806 Thomas Strode of Culpeper Co. 608 A.(13 Feb 1809) in Fauquier Co. on marsh run adj. Alexander now Suddoth, Reuben Wright, Skinker, Parnals spring, Thornton now Strode. 30 May 1810 [Dl'd the Prop'r 30 May 1810]

A2-333: T.W.4339=18 Apr 1806 James Bowen 90 A.(5 Jan 1808) in Fauquier Co. on Marsh Run adj. John Smith now said Bowen, Thornton now Downman, George Wheatley. 6 June 1810 [Dl'd James Booksright? 6 June 1810]

A2-335: Charles Lee asne. of Thomas Bryan Martin as heir at law to Thomas Lord Fairfax dec'd and as agent for Denny Fairfax of Great Britain a dvse. under will of said Thomas Lord Fairfax by the name of Denny Martin, 1109 A.(29 Aug 1766) in Frederick Co. adj. the Prop'r, James Boyle, Lord Fairfax, Baker. 11 July 1810 [Dl'd Mr. William Dandridge 12 July 1810]

A2-337: Charles Lee asne. of Thomas Bryan Martin (see A2-335:) 1614 A.(20 Apr 1752) in Frederick Co. on Potowmac R. bet. Watkins's ferry & mouth of Back Cr., adj. Richard Wells, Jacobus Hogland. 27 Oct 1810 [Raw. Colston Esq. 23 Nov 1820]

A2-338: Charles Lee asne. of Thomas Bryan Martin(see A2-335) 1045 A.(21 Dec 1751) in Frederick Co. in barrens near Potowmac R. adj. Lord Fairfax, Richard Wells. 27 Oct 1810 [Dl'd Raw. Colston Esq. 23 Nov 1820]

A2-340: 100 A. by T.W.3996=10 Oct 1804 & 92 A. by T.W.4447=28 Jan 1808 Valentine Peyton & Benjamin Ashby 192 A.(15 Feb 1808) in Stafford Co. adj. Thomas Botts, Cedar Run old rolling Rd., Bridewell, Newton, Ashby. 26 Nov 1810

A2-342: T.W.3320=15 Jan 1802 John Peters 43 A.(10 Nov 1809) in Hampshire Co. on Stoney Lick Run of Tear coat Cr. adj. Daniel Corbin sold to John Peters, Matthew Pigman, Joseph Taylor. 17 Oct 1810

A2-343: Exg.T.W.1831=13 Feb 1806 for 200 A. & 60 A. by Exg. T.W.1998=3 Feb 1809 Herbert Cool 260 A.(3 Nov 1809) in Hampshire Co. on Little Cacapehon adj. heirs of Henry Baker, Samuel Parks. 17 Oct 1810

A2-345: T.W.4292=2 Jan 1806 John House 15 A.(3 June 1806) in Hampshire Co. on Bird's Run of N. Br. of Potowmac R. adj. George Leighliter, wid. Slagil?. 17 Oct 1810

A2-346: Exg.T.W.1848=6 June 1806 Thomas Lewis asne. of William Jenkins Hager 160 A.(14 Oct 1808) in Hampshire Co. on Tear Coat Cr. adj. Samuel Park/Spark, Job Shepherd. 17 Oct 1810

A2-347: 200 A. by T.W.4502=30 Nov 1808 & 116 A. by Exg.T.W.1573=25 Jan 1804 Edward O. Williams 316 A.(10 Feb 1809) in Berkeley Co. on Opeckon Cr. adj. Thompson, Strode heirs, Nichols, Stephenson, Williams, Green. 17 Oct 1810

A2-348: T.W.4391=19 Jan 1807 Nicholas Orrick 30 A.(12 June 1809) in Hampshire Co. on Potowmac R. adj. Dixon, Smith, Pendleton, Smoot. 23 Nov 1810

A2-349: Exg.T.W.1893=20 Jan 1807 John Fleming 71 A.(22 Feb 1808) in Hampshire Co. adj.Tear coat Cr. Crooked Run, John Caswell dec'd, Abraham Pugh. 17 Oct 1810

A2-351: Exg.T.W.1707=4 Jan 1805 John Largent asne. of George W. Price 14 A.(14 Oct 1808) in Hampshire Co. below forks of Great Cacapehon adj. John Copsey, Abraham Larue, James Largent. 17 Oct 1810

A2-352: T.W.3722=29 Sep 1803 John Cumpton asne. of Samuel Howard 200 A.(23 Nov 1804) in Hampshire Co. on Great Cacapehon, bet. Great Cacaphon Mt. & little Mt. adj. Jeremiah Thompson. 17 Oct 1810

A2-353: T.W.4291=2 Jan 1806 Jacob Parker 100 A.(3 Jan 1809) in Hampshire Co. on Mill Crr. adj. his own land, Tidball. 17 Oct 1810

A2-355: T.W.4476=11 July 1808 William Tippet 41 A.(17 Apr 1809) in Fauquier Co. on Dorrel's Run adj. William Coppedge dec'd, James Stark, Brenttown tract. 17 Oct 1810

A2-356: T.W.4536=29 May 1809 John Downey 51 A.(16 June 1809) in Jefferson Co. adj. Walker now Benjamin Beeler, New Bloomary land, Thomas Smith now William B. Page. 26 Oct 1810

A2-357: T.W.4536=29 May 1809 John Downey 17 A.(17 June 1809) in Jefferson Co. on Shenandoah R. adj. James Hammond dec'd, Nathaniel Craigwell. 26 Oct 1810

A2-359: Exg.T.W.1873=3 Dec 1806 Benjamin Price asne. of Aaron Sanders 6 A. 13 Po.(28 Dec 1809) in Loudoun Co. adj. Wood now Tibbs, Shepherd, land Clapham sold Beaty, Sinclair. 26 Oct 1810

A2-360: Exg.T.W.1999=4 Feb 1809 Jacob Halterman 183 A.(6 July 1809) in Hardy Co. on Big Cove of Lost R., adj. Abraham Delawder, Christopher Halterman. 17 Oct 1810

A2-361: Exg.T.W.1999=4 Feb 1809 Christopher Halterman 72 A.(2 Oct 1809) in Hardy Co. on Lost R. adj. his own land. 17 Oct 1810

A2-362: Exg.T.W.1999=4 Feb 1809 Christopher Halterman 75 A.(6 July 1809) in Hardy Co. on Big Cove of Lost R. adj. Nicholas Bearly, Jacob Halterman. 17 Oct 1810

A2-363: Exg.T.W.1999=4 Feb 1809 Christopher Halterman 24 A.(6 July 1809) in Hardy Co. on big Cove run of Lost R. adj. his own land, Delawder. 17 Oct 1810

A2-364: Exg.T.W.1999=4 Feb 1809 Lionel Branson 23 A.(4 July 1809) in Hardy Co. adj. Mathias Wilkins heirs, James Russell. 17 Oct 1810

A2-365: Exg.T.W.1999=4 Feb 1809 Lionel Branson 52 A.(4 July 1809) in Hardy Co.

on Cove run of Lost R. adj. Jacob Miller, his own land, Chrisman, Cove Mt. 17 Oct 1810

A2-367: Exg.T.W.1999=4 Feb 1809 Jacob Miller 68 A.(4 July 1809) in Hardy Co. on Cove run of Lost R. adj. his own land, Lionel Branson. 17 Oct 1810

A2-368: Exg.T.W.1998=3 Feb 1809 Henry Bails 3 A.(25 June 1809) in Hampshire Co. on Potowmac R. adj. Thomas Williams, heirs of McKerney formerly Ross. 23 Nov 1810 [Dl'd Will'm Smith 30 Oct 1811]

A2-369: T.W.4378=9 Dec 1806 John Clarke 3 A. 1 Ro. 11 Po.(1 June 1809) in Frederick Co. adj. his own land, Mauk, land mortgaged by James McDonald to Josiah Thompson, on Opeckon Cr. 17 Oct 1810

A2-370: 2000 A. by T.W.1392=27 May 1795, 1000 A. by T.W.2428=1 Mar 1798 & 1000 A. by Exg.T.W.1552=24 Jan 1804 Hugh Holmes 4000 A.(21 Oct 1808) in Shenandoah & Hardy Cos. on Great & Lesser N. Mts., Cedar Cr., adj. Joseph Longacre, Pears, Thomas Newell's purchase of Jenkins, Josiah Jenkins, Henry Conrad, Zane's Grindstone Quarry tract, John Kingan, Michael Haas, Jacob Ott, James Machir, Switzer's run, Thomas Wood. 17 Oct 1810 [Dl'd Prop'r 11 June 1811]

A2-373: Exg.T.W.1923=24 Sep 1807 William Shaw 21 A.(20 June 1809) in Pr. William Co. adj. James Anderson dec'd, Charles Tyler. 17 Oct 1810 [Dl'd the Prop'r 9 Oct 1811]

A2-374: Exg.T.W.1707=4 Jan 1805 John Hawking Sr. 90 A.(13 Sep 1808) in Hampshire Co. on N. R. Mt. below the Ice Caves adj. Daniel Lay's land bought of John Hawkins, John Slone. 17 Oct 1810 [Dl'd Wm. Dever bearer of rec't 12 June 1811]

A2-375: Exg.T.W.1923=24 Sep 1807 Walter Warder 3 A. 15 Po.(4 July 1809) in Pr. William Co. adj. Charles Tyler's mill dam, Bernard Hooe Sr., Walter Warder, Capt. William Tebbs. 17 Oct 1810 [Dl'd Wm. Shaw 9 Oct 1811]

A2-376: Exg.T.W.1923=24 Sep 1809 William Shaw 2 A.(20 June 1809) in Pr. William Co. adj. Willoughby Tebbs heirs, his own land, Henry Washington. 17 Oct 1810 [Dl'd Wm. Shaw 9 Oct 1811]

A2-377: Exg.T.W.1016=23 Jan 1801 John Hunter 22 3/4 A.(30 Oct 1809) in Berkeley Co. on Mountain Run of Sleepy Cr. adj. John Hogan, James Abernathy, John Miller, John Prill?. 17 Oct 1810 [Dl'd Maj. Jno. Sherrard 3 June 1822]

A2-379: T.W.3833=1 Feb 1804 Jacob Vandiver asne. of William Florance 189 A.(22 Sep 1807) in Hampshire Co. on Cabin Run of Pattersons Cr. adj. Bush, Elzey, Abraham Good, Knobley Mt., George Gilpin, Thomazon Elzey. 17 Oct 1810

A2-380: T.W.4293=2 Jan 1806 Samuel Davis 50 A.(5 Oct 1808) in Hampshire Co. on Abram's Rg., his own land. 17 Oct 1810 [Dl'd Christopher Haiskell 24 Oct 1811]

A2-381: T.W.2384=19 Jan 1798 Elias Martin 22 A.(16 Jan 1810) in Fauquier Co. on Licking Run bet. Garner now Yellis Johnson & Catesby Cocke now said Martin. 26 Oct 1810 [Dl'd Mr. Will'm McDaniel 13 June 1811]

A2-382: T.W.403=16 Apr 1794 Collam Mitcham 35 A.(1 Nov 1809) in Shenandoah Co. on the Messennotta Cr. adj. Reuben Long formerly Jonathan Watson, Solomon Kessner, James Barbour, Reuben Long purchase of Christian Shelley. 26 Oct 1810 [Dl'd Jas. Allen 8 Nov 1813]

A2-384: T.W.403=16 Apr 1794 John Hockman 7 A.(6 Sep 1809) in Shenandoah Co. on Pass Run adj. Hockman's purchase of Peter Fox, Jacob Stamback. 26 Oct 1810

A2-385: T.W.403=16 Apr 1794 Henry Walter 24 A.(27 Oct 1809) in Shenandoah Co. in Powell's Big Ft. adj. his land, Jacob Burner's purchase of Peter Boyer, Aumiller, Christian Smith. 26 Oct 1810

A2-387: Surv. 19 Oct 1809 ordered by Ct. of Berkeley Co. Morris Rees 310 A. (207 A. is part of 1315 A. granted John Mills 12 Nov 1735 who conveyed to his s.

Henry Mills 9 Mar 1743. On 18 & 28 Apr 1753 Henry Mills conveyed to Morris Rees Sr. who by will 16 Mar 1800 devised land to his s. Morris Rees & 103 A. by T.W.3002=29 Oct 1800 in Berkeley Co. on Mill Cr. adj. Thomas Rees, John Gray, James Willson, Magowan. 26 Oct 1810 [Dl'd Mr. Waggoner 14 Jan 1812]

A2-389: T.W.403=16 Apr 1794 Charles Specht 163 A.(26 Oct 1809) in Shenandoah Co. in Powells Big Ft. on Passage Cr. adj. land he bought of Jacob Rinker, William Ellzey, William Mordock, George Syver. 26 Oct 1810

A2-390: T.W.403=16 Apr 1794 Samuel Kern 6 A.(10 Aug 1809) in Shenandoah Co. an island in N. R. of Shenandoah opposite where he lives. 26 Oct 1810

A2-401: T.W.4508=15 Dec 1808 Theodosius Hansford 7 1/2 A.(4 Apr 1809) in King George Co. adj. Sydney Wishart, tract held by Michael Wallace being same conveyed by John Grigsby and w. to William Rowley, Hansford's own land. 28 Dec 1810 [Dl'd the Prop'r 30 Jan 1811]

A2-402: Resurv.8 Apr 1803 by order of Ct. of Hampshire Co. John Matthew 198 1/2 A. granted John Larew for 205 A. 3 Sep 1789 & 5 Nov 1792. Isaac Larew exr. of will of said John Larew conveyed to Thomas Johnson under a power derived from said will dated 3rd Jan 1792. Johnson conveyed to said John Matthew 18 Nov 1797. In Hampshire Co. on Great Cacapehon & Little Mt. adj. William Bills now Wilson & Kelso, Abram Dawson formerly John Constant, Peter Larew. 25 Jan 1811

A2-404: T.W.by late Prop'r of N. N. Surv. for John Reno 20 Mar 1761 for 166 A. in Hampshire Co. on Patterson's Cr. adj. Rattan, Johnston. John Reno 25 May 1765 assign his right to Constantine Dougherty who sold to Thomas Barclay of Philadelphia, merchant. 16 May 1791 a Commission of Bankruptcy issued under laws of Pensylvania against Thomas Barclay, who was declared a Bankrupt, and who 3 June 1791 conveyed above land with all his other property to certain commissioners in the Commission named in trust for all his creditors, Commissioners on day & year last mentioned, by powers given them by the laws, did appoint Robert Ralston of Philadelphia, merchant, assignee of all the estate and effects of Thomas Barclay, and did convey to him, in trust, for benefit of creditors of Barclay. Robert Ralston on 22 June 1796 did sell said 166 A. to James Hopkins. Hopkins for the better perfecting of his title to same having purchased of Michael Dougherty(eldest bro. & heir at law to said Constantine Dougherty,) his right to land. Michael Dougherty 2 Aug 1796 sell & confirm to James Hopkins. 30 Jan 1811 [Dl'd Col. A. King 6 Feb 1811]

A2-407: Exg.T.W.1555=24 Jan 1804 Travis D. Croston 32 A.(22 Aug 1808) in Hampshire Co. on N. R. adj. his own land, Jacob Croston, James Higgins. 27 Mar 1811 [Dl'd Will'm Dever 13 Nov 1811]

A2-408: T.W.2552=18 Oct 1798 Thomas West 32 1/4 A.(19 Aug 1807) in Fairfax Co. adj. William Devaughn, Pearson, Carr, Simpson, Alexander. 24 Apr 1811 [Grant sent Mr. Thomas C. Nash -order from Prop'r 24 Apr 1811]

A2-409: Thomas Terry now dec'd by entry & location by T.W.2649=26 Jan 1799 had surveyed 17 Oct 1803 100 A. on Rapadan Rd. in Madison Co. adj. James Davis, John Harrison, John Jackson, Joel Graves. Thomas Terry departed this life intestate before grant was made, his right descended to his heirs & legal reps. in intestate succession. Richard Gulley who intermarried with Mary Terry a dau. & coheiress of said Thomas Terry dec'd one undivided eighth part of said tract during his life as tenant by courtesy. Richard Gulley had issue, born alive, by said Mary, & Mary since departed this life. At death of Richard Gulley the undivided eighth part to Mary Gulley, dau. sole heiress & only issue of said Mary Terry, by Richard Gulley lawfully begotten, and to Nancy Kelley w. of William Kelley, late Nancy Terry, another dau. and Coheiress of Thomas Terry dec'd, one undivided eithth part of said land, and to Joseph Terry, John Terry, Salley Terry, James Terry, William Terry, & Lucy Terry, other ch. & coheirs of said Thomas Terry dec'd, each one undivided eighth part of said land & to Richard Gulley during his life, with remaider to said Mary Gulley and her heirs, reserving to Salley Terry wid. of Thomas Terry any right of dower she may lawfully claim. 14 May 1811 [Capt.John Rouzee 15 May 1811]

A2-412: T.W.4600=8 Dec 1809 William H. Parker 41 A. 1 Ro. 15 Per.(27 June 1810) in Cople Par. Westmoreland Co. adj. Henry L. Yeattman, John Simpson, John Lyle, Peter Smith, Spencer Ball. 23 May 1811 [Dl'd Rich'd E. Parker 25 May 1811]

A2-413: T.W.403=16 Apr 1794 Richard C. Walter 158 A. 3 Ro.(28 Oct 1809) in Shenandoah Co. on Cunningham's run adj. said Walter, Charles Sexton, Ezekiel Freeman. 23 May 1811 [Dl'd Peter Adams 31 Oct 1811]

A2-414: T.W.11,376=11 Mar 1782 Westley Henderson asne. of Richard Taylor 50 A.(12 May 1801) in Hampshire Co. on Litttle Cacapehon adj. said Taylor. 23 May 1811

A2-416: T.W.2323=24 Nov 1797 Daniel Jenkins 12 A. 3 Ro.(26 May 1807) in Fairfax Co. adj. Alexander, Fairfax, Alexander Scott. 23 May 1811 [Dl'd John Ratcliffe 6 June 1812]

A2-417: Exg.T.W.1873=3 Dec 1806 Aaron Sanders 3 A. 2 Ro. 4 sq. Po.(28 Dec 1809) in Loudoun Co. on Br. of Limestone, adj. Francis Awbrey, Catesby Cock, Mercer, Clapham. 23 May 1811

A2-419: T.W.403=16 Apr 1794 William S. Walters 150 A.(4 Jan 1809) in Shenandoah Co. on Mathes's arm, adj. his own land, James Stimson. 23 May 1811 [Dl'd Peter Adams 31 Oct 1811]

A2-420: Exg.T.W.1873=3 Dec 1806 William Ellzey asne. of Aaron Sanders 17 A. 3 Ro. 21 Po.(13 Apr 1809) in Loudoun Co. adj. Lasswell, Mathews, Goose Cr., Morris, Carter. 23 May 1811 [Dl'd Richard H. Henderson 21 Feb 1812]

A2-421: T.W.1999=4 Feb 1809 Peter Sperry 102 A.(7 Mar 1810) in Hardy Co. on S. fork of N. R. adj. John Sperry. 23 May 1811

A2-422: T.W.1999=4 Feb 1809 John Sperry 30 A.(8 Mar 1810) in Hardy Co. adj. his own land on S. Fork of N. R., Peter Sperry. 23 May 1811

A2-424: T.W.1999=4 Feb 1809 Isaac Chrisman 36 A.(8 Nov 1810) in Hardy Co. on Lost R. adj. his own land, Lionel Branson, Cove Mt. 29 June 1811

A2-425: T.W.1999=4 Feb 1809 John Mathias 12 A.(8 May 1810) in Hardy Co. on Plumb run of Lost R. adj. John Hime, said Mathias, his land purchased of Roberts. 29 June 1811

A2-427: Exg.T.W.1038=3 Mar 1801 John Mathias 48 A.(8 May 1810) in Hardy Co. on Cove run of Lost R. adj. said Mathias, Blizard. 29 June 1811

A2-428: T.W.1999=4 Feb 1809 William Cornel 200 A.(5 May 1810) in Hardy Co. on Patterson's Cr. adj. James Machir, John Bishop, George Rankin, Talbot, Cunningham. 23 May 1811

A2-430: T.W.1999=4 Feb 1809 James Peck(a negro man) 124 A.(6 Nov 1809) in Hardy Co. near head of Lost R. adj. William Faylor/Taylor, John Hime. 29 June 1811

A2-431: T.W.1999=4 Feb 1809 Philip Claypole 93 A.(17 Nov 1810) in Hardy Co. on Lost R. on Cove Mt. adj. John Claypole, Anthony Miller. 29 June 1811

A2-433: Exg.T.W.1999=4 Feb 1809 Conrod Idleman 373 A.(4 Jan 1810) in Hardy Co. adj. his own land on Loonies Cr., Randel, Reeves, James Seymour, Ellzey, Bishop. 29 June 1811

A2-435: Exg.T.W.1999=4 Feb 1809 John Hime 130 A.(6 Nov 1809) in Hardy Co. on head of Lost R. 29 June 1811

A2-436: Exg.T.W.2099=7 Dec 1809 Mary Barton 32 3/4 A.(23 May 1810) in Frederick Co. near foot of little N. Mt. bet. Roger Barton & William Doster, adj. Ruble. 29 June 1811

A2-438: Exg.T.W.2099=7 Dec 1809 John Wright 1 A.(24 May 1810) in Frederick Co.

adj. Alexander Miller, Levi Smith, Joseph Hackney, Aaron Hackney, James Curl, James Scarff, on Apple Pye Rg., David Castleman, Charles McCormick, Borders. 29 June 1811

A2-439: Exg.T.W.1998=3 Feb 1809 John Higgins 134 A.(28 Mar 1809) in Hampshire Co. adj. Philip Pendleton, Simon Taylor, Moore, Rd. from Winchester to Frankford, James Larimore. 29 June 1811

A2-441: Exg.T.W.1998=3 Feb 1809 John Higgins 440 A.(29 Mar 1809) in Hampshire Co. on Little Cacapehon Mt. adj. John Spore, John & Jonas Queen on Crooked Run of Little Cacapehon, James Pownell/Powell, Rd. from Winchester to Frankford, Rinker. 29 June 1811

A2-442: Exg.T.W.1960=6 May 1808 Arron Hackney, Rachel Barrett, Polly Butterfield & John Butterfield 29 A.(8 Nov 1810) in Frederick Co. adj. Joseph Hackney, Leroy Dangerfield, Jolliffes heirs, Thomas Butterfield dec'd, which is part of A. Ross's old patent., Levi Smith. 29 May 1811

A2-444: Exg.T.W.1970=7 Dec 1808 William Charlton 9 A. 1 2/3 Po.(7 Nov 1810) in Frederick Co. adj. Zane, Perkins, Samuel Carter on Round hill. 29 June 1811 [Dl'd Mr. Arch'd Magill 21 Jan 1817]

A2-446: T.W.4292=2 Jan 1806 William Fox 10 A.(6 Oct 1807) in Hampshire Co. being two small islands in S. Br. of Potowmac R. opposite his own land and adj. William Inskep. 29 June 1811

A2-447: T.W.3237=28 Sep 1801 John Linton 12 A. 2 Ro.(20 June 1810) in Pr. William Co. adj. Carr's estate, John B. Luckett dec'd. 29 June 1811 [Dl'd William Linton 31 Jan 1812]

A2-449: T.W.2727=14 Aug 1799 James Slane 195 A.(20 Oct 1808) in Hampshire Co. on N. R. adj. Benjamin McDonald, William Lockhart, Relfe, Elijah Stone, Henry Asberry. 29 June 1811

A2-451: Exg.T.W.1848=25 June 1806 John Butcher 50 A.(30 Oct 1808) in Hampshire Co. on Great Cacapehon adj. Keith, Conrad, Boyd. 29 June 1811

A2-452: T.W.3267=29 Oct 1801 Samuel Holt 200 A.(17 Oct 1808) in Hampshire Co. on Rd. from Romney to Winchester, adj. Thomas McBride, John Crider, Robert Alexander, Henry Haines, his own land. 29 June 1811

A2-454: T.W.4294=2 Jan 1806 John Thompson 200 A.(29 Apr 1808) in Hampshire Co. on S. Br. of Potowmac and said Br. Mt. adj. Richard Blue. 29 June 1811

A2-457: Exg.T.W.1998=3 Feb 1809 Samuel Hall 31 A.(15 June 1809) in Hampshire Co. on Great Cacapehon adj. his own land, Jesse Harland/Harlin, Thompson's mill dam. 29 June 1811

A2-458: Exg.T.W.1998=3 Feb 1809 Samuel Hall 12 A.(15 June 1809) in Hampshire Co. adj. his own land, Peter Bruner. 29 June 1811

A2-459: Exg.T.W.1998=3 Feb 1809 John Melicks 185 A.(19 Apr 1809) in Hampshire Co. on Tearcoat Br. of N. R. of Great Cacapehon adj. his own land, Robert Slocum, Melicks purchase of Andrew Wadrain, Adam Hair, John Brown. 29 June 1811

A2-461: Exg.T.W.1998=3 Feb 1809 Peter Bruner 7 A.(15 June 1809) in Hampshire Co. adj. his own land, Siler, on Great Cacapehon, Samuel Hall, Thompson. 29 June 1811

A2-462: Exg.T.W.1831=13 Feb 1806 John L. Sehon asne. of John Jones 37 A.(28 Oct 1810) in Hampshire Co. adj. Bell, Howser, Thomas Dunn, Bell's purchase of Hogland. 9 Jan 1812

A2-463: Exg.T.W.1175=5 Nov 1801 Thomas Williams 210 A.(29 Oct 1810) in Hampshire Co. on Potowmac R. adj. his own land, Kelley's heirs, on Cacapehon Mt., Boiles, Mickmahon. 9 Jan 1812

A2-465:   T.W.4322=12 Feb 1806 Samuel McQuin 64 A.(11 Oct 1810) in Culpeper Co. adj. Frederick Duncan, Oder, Julian. 9 Jan 1812 [Mr. Jno. Strode 21 May 1812]

A2-465:   T.W.4322=12 Feb 1806 Samuel McQuin 56 A.(10 Oct 1810) in Culpeper Co. adj. Jesse Garner, James Monroe, late William Duncan.   9 Jan 1812 [Dl'd Mr. Jno. Strode 21 May 1812]

A2-466:   T.W.2287=7 Oct 1797 Joshua Tulles 100 A.(24 Oct 1797) in Fauquier Co. adj. Samuel Morehead, Owen Ginnnen, Carter, Hudnall, said Tulles. 9 Dec 1812 [Dl'd Joseph D. Smith 20 Mar 1812]

A2-467:   Exg.T.W.1924=26 Drp 1807 Jacob Wolfe 47 A.(2 Sep 1808) in Shenandoah Co. on S. R., of Shenandoah adj. land Isaac Overall & Edwin Young purchased of William Young, Enos McKay, Joseph Burner. 9 Jan 1812

A2-469: Exg.T.W.1555=24 Jan 1804 Frederick High 100 3/4 A.(25 Aug 1810) in Hampshire Co. adj. Henry Hawk, his own land, on Pough's Camp run, Cooper. 9 Jan 1812

A2-470: Exg.T.W.1180=8 Dec 1801 Alfred Gant asne. of William Gore 100 A.(15 May 1810) in Culpeper Co. adj. Trion, Poulter, Thomas Carter, William Porter. 9 Jan 1812 [Dl'd Maj. Roberts 1 Mar 1813]

A2-471:   Exg.T.W.3 Feb 1809 Edward Taylor 154 A.(20 May 1811) in Hampshire Co. on Mill Cr. and the middle Rg. adj. Joseph Tidball, Tytus, Smoot. 20 May 1812 [Dl'd E? Hieshell 1 Nov 1812]

A2-474:   Exg.T.W.1999=4 Feb 1809 William Buffington 40 A.(4 May 1810) in Hardy Co. adj. his own land on Adams's Cr. 20 May 1812 [Dl'd Christoper Hyskill 31 Oct 1812]

A2-475:   Exg.T.W.1180=8 Dec 1801 Silas Jenkins asne. of William Gore 115 A.(14 May 1810) in Culpeper Co. adj. said Gore, Marshal Jones, Poulter, John Jenkins. 20 May 1812 [Dl'd Mr. Turner 21 Dec 1813]

A2-476:   Exg.T.W.1999=4 Feb 1809 Jesse Davis 51 A.(29 Mar 1810) in Hardy Co. on New Cr., adj. George Moore, Joseph Davis, Kittle Lick Rg. 20 May 1812 [Dl'd Chris'r Hyskill 31 Oct 1812]

A2-478:   T.W.4518=2 Feb 1809 Edward O. Williams 27 A. 36 Po.(1 Oct 1811) in Jefferson Co. on Potomac R. adj. Abram Morgan, Richard Morgan, Moses Teague, Clement Pierce. 13 Oct 1812 [Dl'd Mr. Wagoner 2 Feb 1816]

A2-479:   T.W.4442=24 Dec 1807 Nathaniel Dodd Sr. 66 3/4 A.(9 Mar 1811) in Fauquier Co. on Marsh run adj. Darnel, Smith, Bowen, Wheatley. 13 Oct 1812 [Dl'd Mr. Buckner 24 May 1813]

A2-480:   T.W.4627=24 Mar 1810 Benjamin Dodd 3 A. 1 Ro.(7 Mar 1811) in Fauquier Co. on Rappahannoc adj. Jonas Williams now said Dodd, Carter now William Sinckler, Rd. from Chester's gap to Falmouth. 13 Oct 1812   [Dl'd Mr. Buckner 24 May 1813]

A2-481:   T.W.22,751=24 Dec 1783 John Johnson 30 A. 2 Ro. 22 Po.(27 Sep 1811) in Loudoun Co. on Goose Cr. Br. out of Blue Rg. thro Keys gap, adj. Peter Romine, Lewis, representatives of William L. Lee dec'd, Martin Overfelt. 13 Oct 1812 [Dl'd Mr. Robert Beadon 8 Dec 1817]

A2-482:   78 3/4 A. by Exg.T.W.1998=3 Feb 1809 & 58 A. by T.W.4611=29 Jan 1810 Henry Asberry 136 3/4 A.(22 Sep 1810) in Hampshire Co. adj. John Starn, his own land, on Sideling Hill, Joseph Asberry. 13 Oct 1812

A2-484:   50 A. by T.W.4611=29 Jan 1810 & 17 A. by Exg.T.W.1998=3 Feb 1809 William Alderton 67 A.(26 Apr 1811) in Hampshire Co. on Easter's run adj. Philip Chrsman/Chrismal, John Kesler, John Easter, West, Tobe Curtis. 13 Oct 1812

A2-485:   T.W.4291=2 Jan 1806 Frederick Buzzard 159 A.(28 Mar 1811) in Hampshire Co. adj. James Slane, Andrew Woodrow, John Largent, Berry. 13 Oct 1812

A2-486: Exg.T.W.1998=3 Feb 1809 John Allaback 9 3/4 A.(3 Apr 1811) in Hampshire Co. adj. Joseph Abril, Stephen Powers. 13 Oct 1812 [Dl'd G. Sharfe 16 Nov 1814]

A2-487: Exg.T.W.1998=3 Feb 1809 Isaac Dilliplane 29 1/4 A.(1 July 1811) in Hampshire Co. on N. R. adj. Rees, Prichard, Armstrong, Crumpton, Hockin. 13 Oct 1812

A2-488: T.W.4602=8 Jan 1810 Ransom Day 32 1/4 A.(30 Apr 1811) in Hampshire Co. on Little Cacapehon adj. Smoot, Paterson, Joseph Starn. 13 Oct 1812 [Dl'd Chris'r Hyskill 31 Oct 1812]

A2-489: Exg.T.W.1998=3 Feb 1809 Frederick Buzzard 12 A. 3 Ro. 30 Po.(18 Nov 1810) in Hampshire Co. adj. his own land, Jacob & John Buzzard, on Mills Br. of Great Cacapehon. 13 Oct 1812

A2-490: T.W.4602=8 Jan 1810 Joseph Starn 95 5/8 A.(16 May 1811) in Hampshire Co. adj. Armstrong, John Starn, Slane?. 13 Oct 1812

A2-491: Exg.T.W.1695=4 Dec 1804 George McColley 71 3/4 A.(9 Mar 1811) in Hampshire Co. on N. R. Mt. adj. his own land, Frances? White formerly Kees. 13 Oct 1812

A2-493: 20 A. by T.W.4573=31 Oct 1809 & 3 A. by T.W.4627=24 Mar 1810 Minor Winn Sr. 23 A.(1 July 1811) in Fauquier Co. on Little R. adj. Flourence, Carr, Holtzclaw now Elijah Griffith, Barton now Griffith. 13 Oct 1812 [Dl'd Mr. Burr Powell 24 Jan 1814]

A2-494: T.W.1998=3 Feb 1809 John Stump 240 A.(12 Sep 1811) in Hampshire Co. on Little Cacapehon adj. Vestal, William Sterrett, Speake. 13 Oct 1812

A2-496: T.W.1555=24 Jan 1804 Jacob Jenkins 106 1/2 A.(2 Sep 1811) in Hampshire Co. on Keyth's run of Big Cacapehon adj. Roye, Spring gap Rg. 13 Oct 1812

A2-497: T.W.18,382=6 Aug 1783 Jacob Emet asne. of John Malick 77 A.(11 Mar 1811) in Hampshire Co. adj. Emmets, Kees, Baker, William Mires, Pepper. 13 Oct 1812

A2-498: T.W.4602=8 Jan 1810 John Starn 184 A.(23 Sep 1811) in Hampshire Co. on N. R. adj. Asberry, Davis, Williamson, White, Gardener, M'Donal. 13 Oct 1812

A2-500: T.W.2226=12 July 1797 Travis D. Croston 55 A.(25 Aug 1808) in Hampshire Co. on N. R. adj. Jacob Compston, said Croston, George Sharp. 13 Oct 1812 [To rec't Oct 1812]

A2-501: Exg.T.W.1997=3 Feb 1809 Adam Hider 402 5/8 A.(10 Sep 1810) in Hampshire Co. on Kellers run of Pattersons Cr. adj. ONeal, John Clawson, Alexandria King, Andrew Woodrow, Rd. from Winchester to Frankfort. 13 Oct 1812

A2-502: T.W.2651=26 Jan 1799 James Tidball asne. of Joel Longstrath 251 A.(7 Dec 1805) in Hampshire Co. on Potomack R. adj. Elinor McDonal. 13 Oct 1812

A2-503: Exg.T.W.1999=4 Feb 1809 Henry Nicholas asne. of Jacob Nicholas 269 A.(4 July 1811) in Hardy Co. on Town run. 13 Oct 1812 [Mr. Thomas Kearn 12 Aug 1813]

A2-505: Exg.T.W.813=26 Sep 1797 Jonathan Branson 61 A.(31 Oct 1811) in Hardy Co. on Cove run of Lost R. adj. Lionel Branson heirs, Jacob Chrisman. 13 Oct 1812

A2-506: T.W.813=26 Sep 1797 Casper Hite 165 A.(1 Oct 1811) in Hardy Co. on N. fork of Patterson's Cr. 13 Oct 1812

A2-507: T.W.813=26 Sep 1797 Hezekiah Wheeler Jr.(of George) 100 A.(2 Oct 1811) in Hardy Co. on New Cr. adj. Ignatius Wheeler, Kettle lick surv. 13 Oct 1812

A2-508: Exg.T.W.2100=8 Jan 1810 George Urise 60 1/2 A.(1 Mar 1811) in Hampshire Co. adj. Adam Flick, John Spencer, foot of Knobly Mt., Henry Flick. 13 Oct 1812

A2-510: T.W.4598=5 Dec 1809 John Culp 6 A.(13 June 1811) in Hampshire Co. at foot of Knobly Mt. adj. his surv., George Culp. 13 Oct 1812

A2-511:   T.W.4598=5 Dec 1809 John Culp 13 3/8 A.(13 June 1811) in Hampshire Co. at foot of Knobly Mt. adj. his surv. 13 Oct 1812

A2-512:   Exg.T.W.813=26 Sep 1797 Elias Shewmaker 25 A.(4 Oct 1811) in Hardy Co. adj. his own land. 13 Oct 1812

A2-513:   T.W.2100=8 Jan 1810 Godfrey Ship 18 1/4 A.(14 Mar 1811) in Hampshire Co. on Plum Run adj. his own land, Stephen's. 13 Oct 1812

A2-514:   200 A. by T.W.4611=29 Jan 1810 & 115 1/4 A. by Exg.T.W.1998=3 Feb 1809 James House 315 1/4 A.(25 Apr 1811) in Hampshire Co. on Sideling hill adj. M' Donnal, Perry Pink. 13 Oct 1812

A2-515:   50 A. by T.W.4436= 7 Dec 1807 & 43 A. by Exg.T.W.2100=8 Jan 1810 Ann Akers 93 A.(5 Nov 1810) in Hampshire Co. adj. Warton, Purget at foot of Knobly Mt. adj. Purget now Ann Akers. 13 Oct 1812

A2-517:   Exg.T.W.2100=8 Jan 1810 Godfrey Ship 19 1/4 A.(14 Mar 1811) in Hampshire Co. on Plum run adj. his own land, Israel Stallcup, Thomas Dunn. 13 Oct 1812

A2-518:   Exg.T.W.1707=3 Jan 1803 Jonathan Jones 64 1/8 A.(23 Oct 1811) in Hampshire Co. on Paterson's Cr. adj. Abel Seemore, Isaac Vanmeter's purchase of John Jones dec'd, McGuire. 13 Oct 1812

A2-519:   Exg.T.W.1998=3 Feb 1809 Jacob Doll 115 1/2 A.(22 Aug 1811) in Hampshire Co. bet. Knobly & New Cr. Mts. adj. David Hatton, John Doll. 13 Oct 1812

A2-521:   Exg.T.W.1998=3 Feb 1809 William French 148 5/8 A.(28 May 1811) in Hamp- shire Co. on S. Br. of Potomack R. adj. Taylor's heirs, Callemees. 13 Oct 1812

A2-522:   T.W.4391=19 Jan 1807 Walter Davis 18 A.(29 Apr 1811) in Hampshire Co. on S. Br. of Potomack adj. his own land, Copsey. 13 Oct 1812

A2-523:   Exg.T.W.2068=21 Aug 1809 Lewis Tutt & Hansford Tutt 206 A.(2 Oct 1811) in Culpeper Co. adj. Fields, Miller, Waddle, Strode, Cooper, Foster, Daniel Fields. 13 Oct 1812 [John Mallory 23 Dec 1814]

A2-524:   Exg.T.W.813=26 Sep 1797 George Stingly 44 A.(30 Sep 1811) in Hardy Co. adj his own land, George Shells. 13 Oct 1812

A2-525:   Exg.T.W.813=26 Sep 1797 Joseph Davis 6 A.(2 Oct 1811) in Hardy Co. on New Cr. adj. his own land, Jesse Davis, on Kettle lick Rg. 13 Oct 1812

A2-526:   105 A. by Exg.T.W.1874=3 Dec 1806 & 200 A. by T.W.4609=22 Jan 1810 the Legatees of James Lyndsey dec'd 305 A.(18 Apr 1811) in Madison Co. on Middle prong of N. fork of Rapidan R. adj. Michael Clores formerly John Weaver, Wallace, James Lyndsey dec'd. 13 Oct 1812

A2-527:   Exg.T.W.813=26 Sep 1797 James Harriss 125 A.(21 Nov 1811) in Hardy Co. adj. his land purchased of Richard Wood on Patterson's Cr. 13 Oct 1812

A2-529:   Exg.T.W.1555=24 Jan 1804 Richard Short 90 7/8 A.(26 Apr 1811) in Hampshire Co. on Spring gap Rg. adj. Thomas Stradford, McDonnald. 13 Oct 1812

A2-530: T.W.4735=30 Apr 1811 Henry Hartman 163 1/4 A.(5 June 1811) in Hampshire Co. on Mill Cr. adj. John Foley, James Reed, his own land. 13 Oct 1812

End of Book A2 1805-1812

B2-1:   Exg.T.W.813=26 Sep 1797 Martin Hawk 206 A.(1 Oct 1811) in Hardy Co. adj. his land, John Hawk, Thomson Elzey.   13 Oct 1812   [Col.Jethro Nevill 4 Dec 1822]

B2-1:   Exg.T.W.813=26 Sep 1797 Martin Garbar 71 A.(19 Nov 1811) in Hardy Co. on S. Mill Cr. adj. his purchase of Christian Eyeman, N. N. line.   13 Oct 1812 [Dl'd Col. Mullen 3 Jan 1836]

B2-2:   T.W.3011=3 Nov 1800 Jacob Jinkins asne. of Edward Swann 128 1/2 A.(3 Sep 1811) in Hampshire Co. on Sideling hill adj. Jakson's path, James Cowden?.   13 Oct 1812

B2-3:   T.W.4612=12 Feb 1811 John Gray 3 A. 2 Ro.(10 Apr 1811) in Berkeley Co. adj. William Baldwin now James Wilson, William Sherrerd, Gilbert McKowan, James Wilson now said Gray.   25 Nov 1812

B2-4:   Exg.T.W.1998=3 Feb 1809 Isaac Johnson 5 1/4 A.(24 Apr 1811) in Hampshire Co. in Greenspring Valley on N. Br. of Potomac adj. Sprigs, Short, his own land, Jacobs, Dobson, Johnson.   25 Nov 1812

B2-4:   Exg.T.W.1170=22 or 27 Oct 1801 John Hamiilton asne. of Charles Binns 23 A. 16 Po.(16 Jan 1812) in Loudoun Co. adj. William Bowell, Obed Pierpoint, Cavans, Fairfax.   25 Nov 1812

B2-5:   T.W.4533=15 May 1809 Moses Garriott 16 A.(9 Nov 1811) in Madison Co. adj. Copelands run, his own land, Thomas Bohannon, Crane, James Shotwell.   25 Nov 1812 [Dl'd Mr. Tho's Shearley 5 Apr 1813]

B2-6:   Exg.T.W.1571=25 Jan 1804 Joseph Miller 22 3/4 A.(29 July 1811) in Frederick Co. adj. Joseph Stover formerly Niswander, William Adams, Mattox, Miller's purchase of Charles Barnes.   25 Nov 1812

B2-7:   T.W.4291=2 Jan 1806 Robert Rogers 76 1/4 A.(30 Mar 1811) in Hampshire Co. near Wilson's Mill, Sherreds store, on Blumery Run, Wilson, Lewis.   25 Nov 1812

B2-7:   T.W.4541=2 June 1809 Simon Bradford 24 3/4 A.(6 Oct 1810) in Fauquier Co. on Marsh Run adj. McBee, Daniel Bradford, Eustace.   9 Mar 1813   [Dl'd Mr. Buckner 24 May 1813]

B2-8:   T.W.4816=23 Jan 1812 Thomas Hunton 13 A.(2 Mar 1812) in Fauquier Co. on Broad Run adj. said Hunton's purchase of Dr. David Stuart, Joseph Minter, Hunton purchase of Chilton, Duff.   9 Mar 1813

B2-9:   T.W.4541=2 June 1809 Peter Conway Sr. 13 1/2 A.(27 Sep 1810) in Fauquier Co. on Marsh Run adj. Wheatley, Crump.   9 Mar 1813

B2-10:   Exg.T.W.2139=9 Oct 1811 John Lee 13 A. 1 Ro. 31 sq. Po.(13 Mar 1812) in Pr. William Co. adj. Cousellor Robert Carter, Bernard Hooe formerly Hainy. 9 Mar 1813 [Dl'd William R. Chapman 13 Oct 1815]

B2-10:   T.W.3039=10 Dec 1800 Alexander McMaken 8 A. 3 Ro. 23 Per.(28 Mar 1812) in Loudoun Co. on Tuskorora, adj. Chandler, Cock, Pedrick now Mead, Hague. 9 Mar 1813   [Dl'd the Prop'r 12 July 1814]

B2-11:   T.W.4798=14 Dec 1811 George Bailey 142 A.(3 Feb 1812) in Madison Co. on Stanton R. adj. Zachariah Lewis 1756 grant, the Fork Mt., Elizbeth Wilhoite's Sta_?_rd? tract, Edward Bryan. 9 Mar 1813 [Dl'd Mr. Wm. W. Hening 21 Apr 1813]

B2-12:   T.W.4798=14 Dec 1811 Peter Garrett 112 A.(17 Apr 1812) in Madison Co. adj. William Kirtlett, Garth's Run, John Booton formerly Pickett, Garth's Spring Mt., Terrel's Bluff. 9 Mar 1813 [Dl'd Mr. Linn Banks 4 Dec 1822]

B2-13:   T.W.4798=14 Dec 1811 the Legatees of Reuben Baytes dec'd 21 A.(7 Feb 1812) in Madison Co. adj. Shearer now Campbell, Elias Campbell now John Campbell 16 Apr 1792, Frog & Wallace grant 23 May 1751. 9 Mar 1813

B2-14: T.W.4798=14 Dec 1811 William Lewis & Abraham Lewis 77 A.(4 Feb 1812) in Madison Co. adj. Richard Maulden patent of 28 Sep 1728, James Shotwell, Thomas Bohannon. 9 Mar 1813 [Dl'd Mr. Wm. W. Hening 21 Apr 1813]

B2-15: T.W.4401=2 Mar 1807 George Withers 140 Per.(21 Mar 1812) in Stafford Co. adj. Alexander now Daniel, Heirs of Thomas Sedden. 30 Mar 1813 [Dl'd Mr. P. N. Daniel 20 May 1813]

B2-16: Exg.T.W.1998=3 Feb 1809 Warner Throckmorton 106 1/2 A.(19 Feb 1812) in Hampshire Co. on S. Br. of Potomack, S. Br. Mt. adj. John Inskeep, William Inskeep. 27 May 1813 [Dl'd Mr. Abraham W. Inskeep 26 Oct 1813]

B2-17: Exg.T.W.1998=3 Feb 1809 Thomas McBride & Joel Ward 53 3/4 A.(28 Aug 1811) in Hampshire Co. on Big Cacapehon adj. Corlisl?, Thomas McBride Sr., Baregarden Rg. 27 May 1813 [Dl'd Mr. Chris't Erskine 31 Oct 1814]

B2-17: Exg.T.W.2083=5 Oct 1809 Jacob Langyher 17 A. 2 Ro.(18 Sep 1811) in Pr. William Co. on Broad Run adj. his land, Charles Ming, Dan'l Tebb. 27 May 1813

B2-18: Exg.T.W.2083=5 Oct 1809 Jacob Langyher 11 A. 1 Ro. 10 Po.(15 Sep 1811) in Pr. William Co. adj. Joseph Thurman, Daniel Tebb. 27 May 1813

B2-19: Exg.T.W.2083=5 Oct 1809 Charles Ming 4 A.(17 June 1811) in Pr. William Co. on Broad Run adj. Jacob Langyher, said Ming formerly Holtzclaw. 27 May 1813 [Dl'd Mr. Chrs't Erskin 31 Oct 1814]

B2-19: 100 A. by T.W.4444=7 Jan 1808 & 60 A. by Exg.T.W. 1569=25 Jan 1804 William Buffington 160 A.(19 Sep 1812) in Hampshire Co. on S. Br. Mt. adj. Daily's mill lott, Parson's. 27 May 1813

B2-20: T.W.4489=22 Sep 1808 Daniel Abbott & John Bowen 59 A.(19 Apr 1812) in Frederick Co. adj. James Russell, James Scott, Daneil Royer, Green Spring Mt., Bunkers hill, James Scott, Holt. 27 May 1813

B2-21: Exg.T.W.2083=5 Oct 1809 William Shaw 29 A.(30 Sep 1811) in Pr. William Co. adj. Hogan, William Tebb, Holtzsclaw, Atwell, Stone & Moss. 27 May 1813

B2-22: Exg.T.W.1998=3 Feb 1809 William Deaver 44 A.(3 Feb 1812) in Hampshire Co. near N. R. adj. Compstone, Crooston, his own land. 27 May 1813 [Dl'd 19 Dec 1814 to bearer of rec't.]

B2-23: Exg.T.W.900=10 June 1799 William Payne asne. of Tully R. Payne 4 1/4 A.(20 Aug 1807) in Fairfax Co. adj. Simon Pearson, John Trammel, Gunnel. 27 May 1813

B2-23: 400 A. by T.W.4611=29 Jan 1810 & 30 3/8 A. by T.W.1707=4 Jan 1805 Peter Mauzey 430 3/8 A.(3 Apr 1811) in Hampshire Co. adj. William Parrish, Joseph Lemman/Leman, Timber Rg., Great Cacapehon, Walter Wilson. 27 May 1813

B2-24: 122 1/8 A. by T.W.4611=29 Jan 1810 & 48 A. by T.W.4249=2 Jan 1806 Richard Blue 170 1/8 A.(19 Oct 1811) in Hampshire Co. on S. Br. of Potomack adj. John Michel, Pownal, Colven. 27 May 1813

B2-25: T.W.4916=29 June 1812 John Bradford 19 A.(18 Sep 1812) in Madison Co. adj. John A. Yager, William Earley, Robert C. Carter, Col. Beale. 1 Aug 1813 [Dl'd Mr. L. Banks 23 Nov 1814]

B2-26: T.W.4193=30 Mar 1805 Frederick Sowers 180 A.(16 Nov 1812) in Madison Co. in fork of S. fork of Robinson R., Shenandoah & Madison Co. line. 1 Aug 1813 [Dl'd Mr. Doyke 3 Jan 1814]

B2-27: T.W.4929=3 Sep 1812 William P. Craighill 2 1/2 A.(21 Oct 1812) in Jefferson Co. Island in Littles fall on Shennandoah R. near upper end of Potomac Co.'s Canal, William Little. 1 Aug 1813 [Dl'd George M. Umphreys 6 Jan 1814]

B2-28: T.W.4813=18 Jan 1812 Frederick Macinturf 7 A.(6 Apr 1812) in Shenandoah

Co. in Powells Big Ft. adj. said Macinturf, Jacob Koverstine, Michael Clem, Moses Syver. 1 Aug 1813

B2-29: T.W.4793=7 Dec 1811 Robert Kyle 200 A.(17 Mar 1812) in Hampshire Co. on Ises Run of Georges Run of Patterson's Cr. adj. Wharton, McBride, his own land. 1 Aug 1813 [Dl'd Mr. Throckmorton Feb 1816]

B2-30: T.W.4780=29 Oct 1811 Jacob Shaver Sr. 3 3/4 A.(22 May 1812) in Shenandoah Co. at place called the Forest, adj. Philip Shaver's purchase of Samuel Overholser, said Jacob Shaver Sr. purchase of George Wills. 1 Aug 1813

B2-31: Exg.T.W.1175=5 Nov 1801 Thomas Williams 11 1/2 A.(22 Apr 1812) in Hampshire Co. on Canolaway Hill adj. his own land. 1 Aug 1813

B2-32: 50 A. by T.W.4762=1 Aug 1811 & 33 A. by Exg.T.W.3320=15 Jan 1802 Herbert Cool 83 A.(24 Mar 1812) in Hampshire Co. on Little Cacapon adj. Baker. 1 Aug 1813 [Dl'd Mr. G. Sharf 16 Nov 1814]

B2-33: Exg.T.W.2156=28 Jan 1812 Israel Stallcup 64 A.(26 Feb 1812) in Hampshire Co. on Plumb Run adj. Andrew Monrow, his own land, Knobly Mt., John Litchliter. 1 Aug 1813

B2-34: T.W.4913=25 June 1812 John Culp 75 A.(24 Oct 1812) in Hampshire Co. on Knobly Mt. adj. George Culp, his own land. 1 Aug 1813

B2-35: T.W.4913=25 June 1812 Daniel Combs 43 3/4 A.(21 Sep 1812) in Hampshire Co. on George's Run of Patterson's Cr. adj. Spencer, Purget, Huper. 1 Aug 1813

B2-36: T.W.4671=20 Nov 1810 Jacob Crisman 11 1/4 A.(8 May 1812) in Hampshire Co. near Potomack adj. White, William Alderton, John S. Kesler, Philip Crisman. 1 Aug 1813 [Dl'd Mr. Sharfs 21 Feb 1816]

B2-37: Exg.T.W.1998=3 Feb 1809 John Pownall 79 3/8 A.(2 June 1811) in Hampshire Co. on Town hill adj. McBride, Blew, Corben. 1 Aug 1813 [By mail 23 Mar 1814]

B2-38: T.W.4873=26 Mar 1812 Philip Fahs Sr. 56 3/4 A.(22 Aug 1812) in Hampshire Co. on N. R. adj. Wolford, his own land, the School house tract, Lee, Morelan, Asberry. 1 Aug 1813 [Dl'd Mr. Vance 19 Jan 1833]

B2-39: T.W.4762=1 Aug 1811 Evan Caudy & John Cheshire 100 A.(2 May 1812) in Hampshire Co. on Bare garden Rg. adj. James Caudy, David Shin, Edward's, their own land. 1 Aug 1813

B2-40: Exg.T.W.1997=3 Feb 1809 Adam Hider 60 A.(9 Sep 1812) in Hampshire Co. on Mill Cr. adj. Franks, McGuire, in Parker's gap. 1 Aug 1813

B2-41: T.W.4745=24 May 1811 Adam Hair 36 A.(1 June 1811) in Hampshire Co. on two lick run adj. Powelson, Slack, Combs, his own land on Town hill, Allon, Dunkin. 1 Aug 1813 [Dl'd Mr. Vance 19 Jan 1833]

B2-42: Exg.T.W.1998=3 Feb 1809 George Myre 50 7/8 A.(27 Aug 1811) in Hampshire Co. on Sandy Rg. adj. Richard George, Bethel, Turner. 1 Aug 1813

B2-43: 190 A. by T.W.4739=10 May 1811 & 16 1/2 A. by Exg.T.W. 1707=4 Jan 1805 Jacob Myre 206 1/2 A.(26 Aug 1811) in Hampshire Co. on Dividing Rg. bet. Parks & Dillens Run adj. Ingle, George Myers, Horn. 1 Aug 1813

B2-45: T.W.4745=24 May 1811 Jacob Ruckman in his own right one moiety & as asne. of Peter Ruckman the other moiety 52 A.(23 Mar 1812) in Hampshire Co. on head drains of Little Cacapehon adj. Bell, Steel, and others. 1 Aug 1813

B2-46: T.W.4873=26 Mar 1812 Frederick Secrist? 69 A.(23 May 1812) in Hampshire Co. on Great Cacapehon adj. John Swisher and others, Jones. 1 Aug 1813

B2-47: T.W.615=17 Sep 1794 Elisha Moorland 27 A.(2 Jan 1812) in Hardy Co. on N. fork of Paterson's Cr. adj. James Marquess, his land, the Allegany. 1 Aug 1813

B2-47:   T.W.615=17 Sep 1794 George Strout 197 A.(18 Feb 1812) in Hardy Co. on Middle fork of Paterson's Cr. adj. Wharton. 1 Aug 1813

B2-48:   T.W.615=17 Sep 1794 Isaac Wilson 64 A.(9 Oct 1812) in Hardy Co. on Mill Mt., Lost R. adj. Godfry? Wilkins, John Wilson. 1 Aug 1813

B2-49:   T.W.615=17 Sep 1794 John Wilson 120 A.(9 Mar 1812) in Hardy Co. on Lost R. adj. his own land, on Mill Mt., George Wilkins. 1 Aug 1813

B2-50: T.W.615=17 Sep 1794 George Wilkin Sr. 77 A.(30 Mar 1812) in Hardy Co. on Mill Run of Lost R. adj. his own land. 1 Aug 1813

B2-51: T.W.615=17 Sep 1794 Christian Hilkey 100 A.(2 Dec 1811) in Hardy Co. on Walkins Rg. adj. Alexis Hays, Benjamin Chambers, his own land, Dividing Rg. bet. head drains of New Cr. & Paterson's Cr. 1 Aug 1813

B2-52: T.W.615=17 Sep 1794 Christopher Martin 149 A.(16 Apr 1812) in Hardy Co. adj. his own land adj. Sarah Reed, James Ryan. 1 Aug 1813

B2-53: T.W.615=17 Sep 1794 Christopher Martin 214 A.(16 Apr 1812) in Hardy Co. adj. his own land on Knobly Mt., William Harriss, Thomas Salts, Peter Putonun, Sarah Reed. 1 Aug 1813

B2-54: T.W.615=17 Sep 1794 James Lyon 35 A.(1 Jan 1812) in Hardy Co. adj. William Stingly, James McDavit, his own land. 1 Aug 1813

B2-55: Exg.T.W.1261=23 Mar 1802 William Warden 123 A.(18 Feb 1812) in Hardy Co. on S. fork of N. R. adj. Michael Switcher. 1 Aug 1813

B2-56: T.W.615=17 Sep 1794 James McDavit 241 A(2 Dec 1811) in Hardy Co. on N. fork of Pattersons Cr. adj. his own land, Benjamin Chambers, McDavit's mill run, Walker's Rg., Samuel Roby, Archibald Stewart. 1 Aug 1813

B2-58: T.W.615=17 Sep 1794 James McDavit 149 A.(2 Dec 1811) in Hardy Co. on Walkers Rg. bet. spout spring surv. & Mary Barrett. 1 Aug 1813

B2-59: Exg.T.W.2138=24 June 1811 Elias Martin 9 A.(28 Apr 1812) in Fauquier Co. on Licking Run adj. Garner, Catesby Cocke, said Elias Martin. 4 Jan 1814 [Dl'd Alex'd D. Kelly 12 Dec 1815]

B2-60:   T.W.2293=16 Oct 1797 Henry Gunnell 10 A.(29 July 1812) in Fairfax Co. near Difficult Run adj. T. Fairfax, Guy Broadwater dec'd lately John Tramell now James Coleman. 4 Jan 1814 [Dl'd Mr. Jno. Sangster 10 Dec 1814]

B2-61:   50 A. by Exg.T.W.2156=28 Jan 1812 & 52 1/2 A. by Exg.T.W.1831=13 Feb 1806 Amos Poland 102 1/2 A.(22 Mar 1812) in Hampshire Co. on S. Br. of Potomack adj. Shanks, Thomas Watkins, John Poland, his own land. 4 Jan 1814 [Dl'd Mr. Chris't Erskin 31 Oct 1814]

B2-62:   50 A. by Exg.T.W.2156=28 Jan 1812 & 63 /12 A. by T.W. 4856=24 Feb 1812 Amos Poland 113 1/2 A.(21 Mar 1812) in Hampshire Co. on S. Br. adj. John Jack, Smith, his own land, Leasues run. 4 Jan 1814 [Mr. Chris't Erskin 31 Oct 1814]

B2-64: 50 A. by T.W.4762=1 Aug 1811 & 40 1/2 A. by 4856=24 Feb 1812 Amos Poland 90 1/2 A.(18 Aug 1812) in Hampshire Co. on Piney Mt. adj. John Polan, Smith. 4 Jan 1814 [Dl'd Mr. Chris't Erskin 31 Oct 1814]

B2-65: 50 A. by Exg.T.W.1707=4 Jan 1805 & 40 A. by T.W. 4856=24 Feb 1812 Samuel House 90 A.(17 Mar 1812) in Hampshire Co. on Knobly Mt. adj. his land purchased of Robert Momrow. 4 Jan 1814 [Dl'd Mr. McCarty 21 Nov 1814]

B2-66: T.W.4848=20 Feb 1812 John Dulin Sr. 65 A.(21 Sep 1812) in Fauquier Co. on Carters Run adj. John Dagg, Thomas Stone, Monroe, Fairfaxes line. 4 Jan 1814 [Dl'd Col. Thornton Buckner 20 Dec 1814]

B2-67: T.W.4827=1 Feb 1812 Stephen Cook 15 A. 3 Ro. 21 Po.(6 Feb 1813) in

Loudoun Co. on Goose Cr. adj. Lee, Warner now Cook, late Thomas L. Lee purchase from estate of George Carter dec'd. 4 Jan 1814 [George Porterfield 23 Nov 1816]

B2-68:   Exg.T.W.1793=11 Dec 1805 Valentine Ayle 12 A.(14 Nov 1812) in Berkeley Co. on Opeckon Cr. adj. Lewis Coffenberger, Joseph Gorrell, George Burns, Alexander Cooper, James Strode. 4 Jan 1814

B2-69:   Exg.T.W.1024=23 Jan 1801 Andrew Jenkins 1 A. 2 Ro. 15 Po.(25 Aug 1812) in Berkeley Co. on Potomack R. adj. Joseph Forman. 4 Jan 1814 [Dl'd Geo. Porterfield 23 Nov 1816]

B2-70:   T.W.4642=7 June 1810 James Forman 2 A. 3 Ro. 20 Po.(15 June 1812) in Berkeley Co. on Opeckon Cr. adj. Edward Strode now said James Forman, John Strode. 4 Jan 1814 [By mail to Prop'r 28 May 1814]

B2-71: T.W.4623=28 Feb 1810 Henry Fairfax 614 A.(5 Mar 1813) in Pr. William Co. on Chappawamsick Cr. adj. Benjamin Edia dec'd, the stage Rd., place shown by Allen Duffy as Carter's line, Harrison's Rd., Thomas Harrison. 4 Jan 1814 [Dl'd Mr. Z'h Beach 16 July 1814]

B2-73:   Exg.T.W.2168=5 Dec 1812 Thomas Bohannon 37 A.(18 Mar 1813) in Madison Co. adj. his land, Adam Clore, Moses Garriett, land James Yowell, Henry Creamer & wife deeded to Nicholas Leatherer 29 Oct 1778, Rouse. 25 Oct 1814 [Dl'd Mr. Dan'l Field 7 Nov 1814]

B2-74: T.W.961=11 Dec 1794 Thomas Williams & Abraham Williams 154 A.(6 Nov 1810) in Shennandoah Co. on Ft. Mt., adj. David Allen, William Ellzey, John Overall, Woods. 25 Oct 1814 [Dl'd Joseph Spangler 30 Oct 1816]

B2-75:   T.W.4495=30 Sep 1808 Philip Stout 50 A.(22 May 1812) in Berkeley Co. on Sleepy Cr. adj. said Stout, Serwas?. 25 Oct 1814 [Dl'd 6 Dec 1814]

B2-76:   T.W.4291=2 Jan 1806 Abraham Good 80 A.(30 Dec 1812) in Hampshire Co. on Patersons Cr. adj. Welch, his own land. 25 Oct 1814 [Mr. Throckmorton Feb 1816]

B2-77:   T.W.4225=2 Oct 1807 John Hampton 77 A.(27 Mar 1813) in Fauquier Co. on Broad run, inc. part of top of Bisquet Mt., adj. Welch, said Hampton, Dent now Welch, Chapman, John Morgan, James Morgan, Pinkstone, Lawler. 25 Oct 1814 [Dl'd Mr. Foster 6 Dec 1814]

B2-78:   T.W.4518=2 Feb 1809 Edward O. Williams 2 A. 2 Ro. 31 Po.(28 Oct 1812) in Jefferson Co. adj. Joseph Chapline now heirs of Frederic Molers, late Richard Mercer. 25 Oct 1814 [Dl'd Mr. Humphrey 27 Oct 1814]

B2-79:   569 A. by Exg.T.W.1971=9 Dec 1808, 268 3/4 A. by Exg. T.W.1180=8 Dec 1801, & 12 1/4 A. by Exg.T.W.1269=14 Apr 1802 Tobias Beam asne. of Aquilla Combs 850 A.(26 Apr 1813) in Culpeper Co. adj. said Beam, Manefee, Odells Mt., Benjamin Partlow, William Bryan. 25 Oct 1814 [Dl'd Mr. Z. Turer 6 Dec 1814]

B2-81:   Exg.T.W.1270=26 Apr 1802 Michael Whitmire 27 A.(7 Mar 1812) in Berkeley Co. on Sleepy Cr. & Warm Spring Rg., his land, Foster, Henry Bough. 25 Oct 1814 [Dl'd John Sherrard 1 Feb 1821]

B2-82:   Exg.T.W.1998=3 Feb 1809 Henry Asberry 4 1/2 A.(22 Sept 1810) in Hampshire Co. adj. Thomas Slane, his own land. 20 Dec 1814

B2-83:   Exg.T.W.1998=3 Feb 1809 John Starn 57 7/8 A.(22 Sep 1810) in Hampshire Co. adj. his own land formerly Smith's, John Davis. 20 Dec 1814 [Dl'd Mr. Sharfe 21 Feb 1816]

B2-83:   By entry 17 Nov 1783 William Ravenscroft asne. of James McDonail 313 A.(22 Apr 1784) in Hampshire Co. on Knobly Mt. in N.N. of Virginia. 20 Dec 1814 [Dl'd Edw'd McCarty 28 Dec 1816]

B2-84:   T.W.4913=25 June 1812 Daniel Lyons asne. of Elisha Lyons 40 A.(28 Aug 1812) in Hampshire Co. on S. Br. of Potomack adj. Walter Davis, Simon Taylor,

Copey, Inskep, opposite Frenches Neck, Break Neck Hill. 20 Dec 1814 [Dl'd Mr. Sharfe 21 Feb 1816]

B2-85: Surv. 28 June 1811, 20 A. by T.W.4622=29 Jan 1810 & 16 3/4 A. by Exg.T.W.1707=4 Jan 1805 William Naylor 36 3/4 A. in Hampshire Co. on Bridge run of S. Br. of Potowmac adj. his own land, David Parsons, Adam Hall's heirs, near Romney. 20 Dec 1814 [Dl'd Mr. Throckmorton Feb 1816]

B2-86: Surv. 3 Oct 1811 by Exg.T.W.2068=21 Aug 1809 Lewis & Hansford Tutt 110 A. in Culpeper Co. adj. Stone, Almond Vaughn, Archibald Tutt, Daniel Field, Lewis Tutt. 20 Dec 1814 [Dl'd 30 Sep 1816 to rec't]

B2-87: For $43 paid to Treas. of Commonwealth; Betsy Johnston, Nancy Dawe, Philip Deverex Dawe & William Dawe, for use & benefit of ch. & deves. of Philip Dawe dec'd as by last will & testament of said Philip Dawe dec'd., lots 28 & 31 in Town of Dumfries in Pr. William Co. Lots bear date of 15 May 1808 & 26 Nov 1812 & escheated for defect of heirs of Thomas Atkin dec'd. Sold at public auction 30 April 1808 to Philip Dawe. 10 Apr 1815 [Peyton Norvell 25 May 1816]

B2-89: Surv. 24 July 1813 by T.W.4802=24 Dec 1811 Robert Daniel 4 A. 2 Ro. 12 Po. in Berkeley Co. adj. heirs of Richard Evans, James Stevenson, Thomas & John Gill, Levi Hanshaw, John Tate. 26 Apr 1815 [Dl'd Meverill Locke 18 Oct 1815]

B2-90: Surv. 7 May 1813 by T.W.4769=9 Oct 1811 Edward Smith 1 A. 21 Po. in town of Winchester, Frederick Co. being surplus land in his lot(#33). 26 Apr 1815

B2-91: Surv. 7 May 1813 by T.W.4769=9 Oct 1811 Edward McGuire 2 A. 3 Ro. 23 Po. in town of Winchester, Frederick Co. surplus in his lot(#43) adj. Hazlett, Rd. to Martinsburg, William Holliday. 26 Apr 1815

B2-92: Surv. 6 May 1813 by T.W.4769=9 Oct 1811 Robert Macky 1 A. 2 Ro. 36 Po. surplus in his lot(#58) in Winchester, Frederick Co., adj Mackys other lands, Edward McGuire. 26 Apr 1815

B2-93: Surv. 7 May 1813 by T.W.4769=9 Oct 1811 John Baker 3 A. 3 Ro. 4 sq/Po. in Winchester, Frederick Co. Surplus in his lot(#41). 26 Apr 1815

B2-94: Surv. 1 Oct 1813 by T.W.3321=16 Jan 1802 Daniel Payne 14 A. 1 Ro. in Fauquier Co. on Great run adj. Rd. from Fauquier Ct. House to Chesters gap, Peter Kemper, Buckner & Willis, Michael Mildrum, Kemper now Timberlake. 26 Apr 1815 [Dl'd Mr. James W. Kelley 31 Oct 1817]

B2-95: Surv. 7 May 1813 by T.W.4769=9 Oct 1811 Daniel Lynn 1 A. 2 Ro. 6 sq. Po. in Winchester, Frederick Co. Surplus in his out lot(#42) on Rd. from Loudon St. through Knaves Town, Holliday, Cameron St. 26 Apr 1815

B2-96: Surv. 10 Sep 1813 by Exg.T.W.1016=23 Jan 1801 Nathaniel Blue 7 A. in Berkeley Co. on Turkey buzzard run of Opeckon Cr. adj. Edward Southwood, heirs of Alexander Reyley, Henry Bedinger. 26 Apr 1815

B2-97: Surv. 22 Mar 1813 by T.W.4867=17 Mar 1812 Jacob Weaver 6 A. 3 Ro. 23 Po. in Berkeley Co. adj. John Myers, said Weaver. 26 Apr 1815 [Dl'd Maj. And. Waggoner during session of 1815,'16]

B2-98: Surv. 18 Dec 1812 by Exg.T.W.1024=23 Jan 1801 Jacob Weaver 5 A. 16 Po. in Berkeley Co. on Opeckon Cr. adj. Jacob Weaver, George Tabler. 26 Apr 1815 [Dl'd Maj. And. Waggoner during session of 1815,'16]

B2-99: Surv. 2 Nov 1813 by T.W.2833=5 Dec 1799 John Fernoe 21 A. in Berkeley Co. on Sleepy Cr. adj. Horseman's heirs, Charles Lee. 26 Apr 1815 [Dl'd Maj. And. Waggoner during session of 1815,'16]

B2-100: Surv. 3 Nov 1813 by T.W.2833=5 Dec 1799 John Fernoe 9 A. 2 Ro. 20 Po. in Berkeley Co. on Sleepy Cr. adj. said Fernoe. 26 Apr 1815 [Dl'd Maj. And. Waggoner during session of 1815,'16]

B2-101: Surv. 22 Jan 1813 by Exg.T.W.1017=23 Jan 1801 John Miller 10 A. in Berkeley Co. on Tilhances Br. adj. William Shields, John Shield heirs, Zachariah Miller, said John Miller. 26 Apr 1815 [Dl'd Israel Robinson 15 Dec 1818]

B2-102: Surv. 20 Aug 1813 by T.W.4913=25 June 1812 Benjamin Evens & Elizabeth Bozelley 40 A. in Hampshire Co. on New Cr. Mt. adj. Elzey, Bozelley, Vandiver, said Evens. 26 Apr 1815 [Dl'd Edw'd McCarty 27 Dec 1816]

B2-103: Surv. 23 Aug 1813 by T.W.4889=13 May 1812 George Spero 8 A. 1 Ro. 24 Po. in Berkeley Co. on Opeckon Cr. adj. said Spero, Sam Fetter, Moses Hunter heirs, Jacob Weaver. 26 Apr 1815 [Dl'd Mr. Shaer/Shaerr Jan 1816]

B2-104: Surv. 22 Sep 1813 by T.W.5065=21 Apr 1813 Jesse Harlan 95 A. in Hampshire Co. on Great Cacaphon Mt. adj. his own land. 26 Apr 1815 [Dl'd Edw'd McCarty 28 Dec 1816]

B2-105: Surv. 6 Feb 1812 by Exg.1998=3 Feb 1809 Josias More 22 1/2 A. in Hampshire Co. on S. Fork of Mikes Run of Paterson's Cr. adj. Hibs & Bakehom. 26 Apr 1815 [Dl'd Mr. Throckmorton Feb 1816]

B2-106: Surv. 1 June 1813 by Exg.T.W.1967=12 July 1808 Francis Martin 16 1/2 A. in Fauquier Co. on Marrs Run adj. Daniel Marr patent of 25 Jan 1727/8, William Blackwell & John Woodside. 26 Apr 1815 [Dl'd Mr. John P. Kelley 31 Oct 1817]

B2-107: 50 A. by T.W.4934=12 Sep 1812 & 40 A. by T.W.4913=25 June 1812 Isaac Ingle 90 A.(15 Dec 1812) in Hampshire Co. on S. Br. Mt. adj. Fox, Lee, the heirs of Herrod dec'd, Utt. 26 Apr 1815 [Dl'd Chris: Heiskell 1 Nov 1815]

B2-109: Surv. 23 June 1813 by T.W.5065=21 Apr 1813 Arthur Kerscadden 70 A. in Hampshire Co. on Pattersons Cr. adj. Thomas Kerscadden, George Stagg, his own land. 26 Apr 1815 [Dl'd Edw'd McCarty 27 Dec 1816]

B2-110: Surv. 23 June 1813 by T.W.5065=21 Apr 1813 George Stagg 13 3/4 A. in Hampshire Co. on Patterson's Cr. adj. Arthur Kerscadden, his own land, Kerscadden formerly Murphy. 26 Apr 1815 [Dl'd Frederick Sheetz 22 Nov 1815]

B2-111: Surv. 23 June 1813 by T.W.5065=21 June 1813 George Stagg 44 A. in Hampshire Co. on Patterson's Cr. adj. Kerscadden, his own land. 26 Apr 1815

B2-112: Surv. 22 June 1813 by T.W.5065=21 Apr 1813 Abraham Leatherman 62 A. in Hampshire Co. on Patterson's Cr. adj. Peter Umstott, Daniel Leatherman, Daniel Wip, wid. Millar, his own land. 26 Apr 1815 [Dl'd Frederick Sheetz 22 Nov 1815]

B2-113: Surv. 7 Oct 1813 by T.W.5057=2 Apr 1813 Philip Shaver 45 A. in Shenandoah Co. on Dry Run adj. said Shaver's purchase of Jacob Baker, Dr. Frederick Tisiues, Peter Blauser. 26 Apr 1815 [Dl'd Mr. Lovell Feb 1816]

B2-114: Surv. 11 Oct 1813 by T.W.5057=2 Apr 1813 Christian Baumgardner 450 A. in Shenandoah Co. on S. R. of Shenandoah adj. said Baumgardner, Andrew Kyser, William Ellzey, Andrew McKay. 26 Apr 1815 [Dl'd Mr. Lovell Feb 1816]

B2-116: Surv. 5 Oct 1813 by T.W.5057=2 Apr 1813 James Stinson 11 3/4 A. in Shenandoah Co. adj. deed from Lord Fairfax to Alexander Mathews in 1750 now David Lockhart, said Stinson. 26 Apr 1815 [Dl'd Col. Wm. Carson 2 Sep 1815]

B2-117: Surv. 12 Oct 1813 by T.W.5057=2 Apr 1813 Peter Blauser Jr. 100 A. in Shenandoah Co. on Dry Run at foot of Blue Rg. adj. Peter Blauser. 26 Apr 1815 [Dl'd Judge Lowell 17 June 1816]

B2-118: Surv. 9 Oct 1813 by T.W.5057=2 Apr 1813 Jacob Koverstine 25 A. in Shenandoah Co. in Powells Big Ft. on Passage Cr. adj. said Koverstine, David Ross, Martin Walter, Michael Clem, Frederick Macinturff, John Moore. 26 Apr 1815 [Dl'd Mr. Lovell Feb 1816]

B2-119: Surv. 4 Oct 1813 by T.W.5057=2 Apr 1813 James Stinson 100 A. in Shenandoah Co. on the Round Mt., Derby's Run adj. said Stinson, Joseph Stover,

John Blackwood, wid. Marks. 26 Apr 1815 [Dl'd Col. Wm. Carson 2 Apr 1815]

B2-120: Surv. 20 Oct 1813 by T.W.5057=2 Apr 1813 Daniel Hoffman 4 A. in Shenandoah Co. on S. R. of Shenandoah adj. said Hoffman, Casper Good formerly Collam Mitcham, Phebe McGown formerly Benjamin Grigsby. 26 Apr 1815 [Dl'd Mr. Lovell Feb 1816]

B2-121: Surv. 6 Apr 1813 by T.W.615=17 Sep 1794 Jonathan Tucker 300 A. in Hardy Co. on N. R. adj. Joseph Obannon, Jefferson's Knob, Aaron Tucker, Day. 26 Apr 1815 [Dl'd Mr. Simons 7 Feb 1816]

B2-122: Surv. 15 Aug 1812 by T.W.615=17 Sep 1794 Thomas Topen asne. of Gabriel Bradigum 180 A. in Hardy Co. on Capen Run of Shenandoah adj. William Maloan, Cove Run, Christian Hinegarner. 26 Apr 1815 [Dl'd Mr. Simons 4 Jan 1816]

B2-124: Surv. 25 June 1813 by T.W.5065=21 Apr 1813 Jacob & Coonrod Umstotts 3 3/4 A. in Hampshire Co. on Patterson's Cr. adj. the manor, their own land, Plumb. 26 Apr 1815 [Dl'd Christoper Heiskell 1 Nov 1815]

B2-125: Surv. 8 Apr 1813 by T.W.615=17 Sep 1794 David Ogden 47 A. in Hardy Co. on Waits Run of Great Cacaphon adj. Switcher, Savage, said Ogden. 26 Apr 1815 [Dl'd Mr. Simons 4 Jan 1816]

B2-126: Surv. 6 Apr 1813 by T.W.615=17 Sep 1794 Aaron Tucker 214 A. in Hardy Co. on Mt. Run of N. R. adj. Joseph Tucker, James Orme. 26 Apr 1815 [Dl'd Mr. Simons 4 Jan 1816]

B2-127: Surv. 7 Apr 1813 by T.W.615=17 Sep 1794 Henry Coler 312 A. in Hardy Co. on Pattersons Cr. Mt. adj. Isaac VanMeter, Able Seymour. 26 Apr 1815 [Dl'd Mr. Simons 4 Jan 1816]

B2-128: Surv. 6 Apr 1813 by T.W.615=17 Sep 1794 Aaron Tucker 67 A. in Hardy Co. on Jeffersons Knob, N. R. adj. Joseph Obannon, Bean, Day, Jonathan Burch. 26 Apr 1815 [Dl'd Mr. Simons 4 Jan 1816]

B2-129: Surv. 18 Feb 1813 by Exg.T.W.1997=3 Feb 1809 Thomas Burket 276 A. in Hampshire Co. on Little Cacapehon adj. Swinfield Cavender, Miller, John Brown, Larramore, Townhill, Combs. 26 Apr 1815 [Dl'd Mr. White Jan 1819]

B2-130: Surv. 7 Oct 1813 by T.W.5065=21 Apr 1813 Jeremiah Monroe 463 A. in Hampshire Co. on Tare coat Br. of N. R. adj. Timothy Smith, Elisha C. Dick, George Horn, John Peters, Parks, Dunmore, Chersher. 26 Apr 1815 [Dl'd Mr. Sharfe 21 Feb 1816]

B2-132: Surv. 30 Mar 1812 by Exg.T.W.1998=3 Feb 1809 Henry Bringman 50 A. in Hampshire Co. on Sideling Hill. 26 Apr 1815 [Dl'd Mr. Vance 1834]

B2-133: Surv. 28 Oct 1813; 250 A. by T.W.4982=1 Dec 1813 & 129 A. by T.W.5065=21 Apr 1813 John Loy 379 A. in Hampshire Co. on Tare-coat of N. R. adj. George Horn, Jeremiah Monrow, Samuel Parks, his own land. 26 Apr 1815 [Dl'd Mr. Sharfe 21 Feb 1816]

B2-134: Surv. 13 May 1813 by T.W.4969=2 Nov 1812 Samuel Dew 100 A. in Hampshire Co. on S. Br. of Potomack and on Kuykendolls Mill Run adj. Samuel Dew dec'd, Charles Vowel, Jonathan Purcell, Nathaniel Kuykendoll dec'd, James Dailey, Cunningham. 26 Apr 1815 [Dl'd Mr. Sharfe 21 Feb 1816]

B2-136: Surv. 29 Apr 1813 by T.W.818=29 Oct 1794 Jonathan Lovett 30 A. in Frederick Co. adj. Joseph Wharton, Joseph Baker now Larrick, Anderson, Capper on Timber Rg., John Carlile, M. Capper. 26 Apr 1815 Mr. Sharfe 21 Feb 1816] [Dl'd Joseph Sexton 18 Dec 1819]

B2-137: Surv. 12 Mar 1813 by T.W.4891=20 May 1812 Thomas Norman 42 3/4 A. in Culpeper Co. adj. said Norman, Mason, poor Town tract, Adams formerly Garner & Norman. 26 Apr 1815 Mr. Sharfe 21 Feb 1816] [Dl'd Page Finnie 12 Dec 1816]

B2-138: Surv. 13 Mar 1806 by T.W.4292=2 Jan 1806 John Hammack & Thomas Yonaly asnes. of Joseph Parrill otherwise called Parrel 83 1/2 A. in Hampshire Co. on Dillings Run adj. Edward Perrel, Holmes. 26 Apr 1815 [Mr. Sharf 21 Feb 1816]

B2-139: Surv. 22 Jan 1813 by T.W.4873=26 Mar 1812 Jacob Millslagle 43 A. in Hampshire Co. adj. John Cooper, his own land. 26 Apr 1815 [Dl'd Mr. Sharf 15 Dec 1815]

B2-140: Surv. 28 & 29 Apr 1813 12 1/2 A. by T.W.4190=26 Mar 1805, 408 A. by Exg.T.W.1018=23 Jan 1801 & 1640 1/2 A. by T.W.13,832=15 Aug 1782 Jonathan Lovett 2061 A. in Frederick Co. adj. Wharton, Anderson, Dr. Dick, N.Mt., Back Cr., Bear Rg., Mahlen Pugh, Jesse Anderson, White Pine Rg., James Anderson, Lonams Br., Frederick & Hampshire Co. line. 26 Apr 1815 [Dl'd Joseph Sexton 18 Dec 1819]

B2-142: Surv. 5 Nov 1813 by T.W.4813=18 Jan 1813 Nicholas Shumucker 13 A. in Shenandoah Co. adj. George Wisman, said Schumucker, Peter Schmucker, Matthias Schmutz. 26 Apr 1815 [Dl'd Mr. Lovell Feb 1816]

B2-143: Surv. 12 June 1813 by T.W.4813=18 Jan 1812 Adam Ridenour(s. of Adam) 27 A. in Shenandoah Co. in Powells Big Ft. adj. Jacob Lechliter, John Carrier now Frederick Macinturf, David Clem's purchase of the wid. Miller, Henry Ridenour purchase of Jacob Copperstone. 26 Apr 1815 [Dl'd George F. Utt 30 Oct 1816]

B2-144: Surv. 10 Apr 1813 by T.W.961=11 Dec 1794 Adam Baker 75 A. in Shenandoah Co. on Little Mt. adj. Henry Borrer dec'd. 26 Apr 1815 [Mr. Lovell Feb 1816]

B2-145: Surv. 29 Apr 1813; 400 A. by T.W.23,063=24 Dec 1783 & 28 1/2 A. by 818=29 Oct 1794 Jonathan Lovett 428 1/2 A. in Frederick Co. adj. William McKee, John Routt, Thomas Anderson on Timber Rg., Elzey, said Lovett, Thomas Dent, Romney Rd., William Adams. 26 Apr 1815 [Dl'd Joseph Sexton 18 Dec 1819]

B2-146: Resurv. 23 June 1813 by order of Shenandoah Co. Ct. John Nicholas Knop 227 A. in Shenandoah Co. adj. John Brenner, Jacob Humbert formerly called the prop'r's manor, Peter Foutz purchase of John Roler, David Oroark, heirs of Michael Zerckel dec'd. Grant for 320 A. by Thomas Lord Fairfax 22 Dec 1774 to Conrod Cool who by his last will 4 Dec 1794, recorded in Co. Ct. of Shenandoah Co., directed to be sold by John Cool & Michael Branner Exrs. of said will. Sold to said Knop 8 Apr 1800 & 22 Oct 1801. 26 Apr 1815 [Dl'd Mr. Lovell Feb 1816]

B2-148: Surv. 14 Jan 1814 by T.W.4736=3 Apr 1811 Ambrose Barnett 2 A. in Frederick Co. adj. his own land formerly Neavill, Lindsay now George H. Norris, land formerly Morris, Calmeas. 22 May 1815 [Dl'd Mr. Castleman Mar 1831]

B2-149: Surv. 24 May 1813 by Exg.T.W.1024=23 Jan 1801 Luke McManus 6 A. in Berkeley Co. on Back Cr. adj. John Dokes, William Johnston?, Barnes. 22 May 1815 [Dl'd Maj. And: Waggoner during Session of 1815'16]

B2-150: Surv. 14 Jan 1814 by T.W.4730=3 Apr 1811 George Barnett 8 A. in Frederick Co. adj. his own land formerly Neavill, Madden now Litler, Hugh West now Adams, Fairfax Rd. 22 May 1815 [Dl'd Mr. Castleman Mar 1831]

B2-151: Surv. 28 Aug 1813 by T.W.212=23 Jan 1794 Henry Nicholas 367 A. in Hardy Co. on Town Ft. Run of S. Br. of Potomac adj. George Harness, James Machir, James Cunningham. 22 May 1815 [Dl'd Thos. Keerean 19 Sep 1815]

B2-152: Surv. 5 Nov 1812 by T.W.4898=27 May 1812 Joseph Glass 3 A. 2 Ro. 17 1/2 Po. in Frederick Co. adj. his own land, Martin Cartmell, heirs of Solomon Cartmill, late Col. Dowdall now Thomas Kramer & Jane Dowdall, said Glass formerly Joseph Glass dec'd, John Beckett, fork of Opeckon, Samuel Glass now Joseph Glass, David Glass. 22 Apr 1815 [Dl'd Dawson McCormick 23 Oct 1816]

B2-154: Surv. 10 Jan 1814 by T.W.5065=21 Apr 1813 John Baker 30 1/4 A. in Hampshire Co. on N. R. adj. John Pepper, John Candy, his own land, Jacob Baker, Kees. 22 June 1815 [Mr. Dunn 1831]

B2-155: Surv. 13 Apr 1814 by T.W.5220=29 Mar 1814 William Morrison 200 A. in

Frederick Co. adj. James Cochran. Peter Milhorn, Peter Ham. James Singleton, Jacob Marl, Hotson. 22 June 1815 [By mail to Wm. Morrison 12 Sep 1815]

B2-156: Surv. 20 Jan 1814 by T.W.5008=5 Jan 1813 Spencer Hendrickson asne. of William Hill 100 A. in Hampshire Co. on Pattersons Cr. adj. Gilpin, Leroy Hill. 22 June 1815 [Dl'd Chris: Heiskell 1 Nov 1815]

B2-157: Surv. 1 July 1814 by T.W.3483=18 Dec 1802 Walker Reid 91 A. 39 Po. in Fairfax Co. on Great Cedar Rocky Run adj. Walker, Thomas, Carter, Ashton, Johnson now Talbott. 22 June 1815 [Dl'd Maj. Waugh 7 Dec 1815]

B2-157: Surv. 8 Jan 1813 by T.W.4982=1 Dec 1812 John House 24 A. in Hampshire Co. on N. Br. of Potomack R. adj. John House, Fairfax. 22 June 1815 [Dl'd Mr. William Naylor 9 Dec 1817]

B2-158: Surv. 11 Jan 1814 by T.W.5108=26 Aug 1813 John Swisher 124 A. in Hampshire Co. on Hughs Mill Run of Great Cacapehon adj. Abraham Cline, John Swisher Sr., his own land, Alozanaces?. 22 June 1815 [Dl'd Mr. Throckmorton Feb 1816]

B2-159: Surv. 5 July 1814 by T.W.5086=25 May 1813 Jacob Jenkins 42 7/8 A. in Hampshire Co. on Bear garden Rg. adj. his own land, Buzzard, Robert Rogers. 22 June 1815 [Dl'd Mr. Sharfe 21 Feb 1816]

B2-160: Surv. 19 Nov 1813 by T.W.4889=13 May 1812 Thomas Bryerly 4 A. in Berkeley Co. adj. Richard Bryerley, Robert Steuart, Sybert. 22 June 1815

B2-161: Surv. 25 Nov 1813 by Exg.T.W.1399=15 Mar 1803 Elias Oden 2 1/2 A. in Berkeley Co. adj. Carlile, Richard Butt heirs, said Elias Oden. 22 June 1815 [Dl'd Mr. Shearer Jan 1816]

B2-161: Surv. 29 Sep 1814 by T.W.5176=24 Jan 1814 Edward McCarty 66 A. in Hampshire Co. on Knobly Mt. adj. Means, his own land. 22 June 1815 [27 Dec 1816]

B2-162: Surv. 5 Mar 1814, 75 A. by T.W.4913=25 June 1812 & 55 A. by T.W.4856=24 Feb 1812 Thomas Davis 130 A. in Hampshire Co. on Sideling hill adj. John Starn, John Davis, Henry Bringman. 22 June 1815 [Dl'd Mr. Sharfe 21 Feb 1816]

B2-163: Surv. 4 Jan 1814 by Exg.T.W.1793=11 Dec 1805 Elizabeth Sylar 3 A. 2 Ro. 22 Po. in Berkeley Co. on Stookeys Spring Run of Back Cr. adj. Jacob Stookey, Andrew Sylar. 22 June 1815 [Dl'd Maj. And: Waggoner at 1815'16 session]

B2-164: Surv. 16 Apr 1814 by Exg.T.W.1822=29 Jan 1806 John Riner 19 A. in Madison Co. adj. heirs of William Roberts dec'd, Razor, land Ambrose Powell deeded Christian Riner & Ebehart Riner 21 Mar 1750, Solomon Carpenter, John Riner, Ambrose Jones dec'd. 22 June 1815 [Dl'd Geo. H. Allen 5 Dec 1815]

B2-165: Surv. 12 Nov 1813 by T.W.4642=7 June 1810 Joseph Forman 8 A. 3 Ro. 20 Po. in Berkeley Co. on Back Cr. adj. said Forman, Potomack R. 22 June 1815

B2-166: Surv. 26 Nov 1813 by T.W.4780=29 Oct 1811 James Stinson 286 A. in Shenandoah Co. on S. R. of Shenandoah adj. Thomas Allen, Philip Spingler, Daniel Henry, Bingham, Stover. 22 June 1815 [Dl'd Col. Wm. Carson 2 Sep 1815]

B2-167: Surv. 9 June 1814 by T.W.5190=8 Feb 1814 Esther Reese 27 A. in Shenandoah Co. on N. R. of Shenandoah adj. said Esther Reese, Samuel Kerns, heirs of Alexander Stockslager dec'd, Esther Reese purchase of Jacob Bird. 22 June 1815

B2-168: Surv. 25 Jan 1814 by T.W.5108=26 Aug 1813 Peter Calrick 173 A. in Hampshire Co. on Dry Run of Pattersons Cr. adj. Buskark, Welch. 22 June 1815 [Dl'd Mr. Throckmorton Feb 1816]

B2-169: Surv. 1 Oct 1814 by T.W.212=23 Jan 1794 George Rankins 245 A. in Hardy Co. on Pattersons Cr. adj. Felix Welton, Christian Cosner, Job Wilton. 22 June 1815 [Dl'd Mr. Jacob Miller 24 Dec 1817]

B2-170: Surv. 14 May 1814 by T.W.212=23 Jan 1794 Jacob Wolford & Jacob Hawk 68 A. in Hardy Co. on Loones Cr. adj. George Harness Sr., Martin Hawk. 22 June 1815 [Dl'd S. Niville 8 Dec 1823]

B2-171: Surv. 12 May 1814 by T.W.212=23 Jan 1794 Conrod Idolman 46 A. in Hardy Co. on Allegany Mt. & Isle? Run adj. his own land, Joseph Neville, Upton Brnes?. 22 June 1815 [Dl'd Mr. Simons 18 Dec 1815]

B2-172: Surv. 9 Nov 1813 by Exg.T.W.1021=Jan 1801 James Harmison 15 A. in Berkeley on Potomack R. adj. James Fisher, John Miller. 22 June 1815 [Dl'd Mr. Shearer Jan 1816]

B2-172: Surv. 20 Apr 1814 by T.W.5079=21 May 1813 Maj. Benjamin Folson or Tolson 13 A. in Stafford Co. on Chappawamsick Run adj. Harrison, Brent, Hedges. 22 June 1815 [Dl'd Peter Daniel 30 Oct 1815]

B2-173: Surv. 23 June 1814 25 A. by T.W.5081=21 May 1813 & 2 A. by T.W.5133=11 Mar 1814 Joshua Owens 27 A. in Fauquier Co. on Leather Coat Mt. adj. Henderson, Ewel, Nevel. 22 June 1815 [Dl'd Col. Buckner 21 Feb 1816]

B2-174: Surv. 31 May 1813 by T.W.5058=2 Apr 1813 John Overall 205 A. in Shenandoah Co. adj. grant line, Benjamin Wood, said Overall, Thomas & Abraham Williams, William Ellzey. 22 June 1815 [Dl'd Col. Wm. Carson 2 Sep 1815]

B2-175: Surv. 12 May 1814 by T.W.212=23 Jan 1794 Solomon Michael 38 A. in Hardy Co. on Loonies Cr. and Walkers Rg. adj. Martin Hawk, George Harness. 3 Aug 1815 [Dl'd Mr. Simons 4 Jan 1816]

B2-176: Surv. 11 Aug 1814 by T.W.452=17 May 1794 John Snider & Nathan Dillon 16 1/2 A. in Frederick Co. adj. James Russell, Abbott, Scott now Wryht, Banett. 3 Aug 1815

B2-177: Surv. 20 Dec 1814 by T.W.4196=8 Apr 1805 George Rennoe 10 A. 1 Ro. 37 Po. in Pr. William Co. adj. Mrs. Cure?, Lutteral, Enoch Rennoe. 3 Aug 1815 [Dl'd Mr. John Gibson 13 Jan 1816]

B2-177: Surv. 13 July 1813 by T.W.20,541=10 Nov 1783 Michael Briel 24 1/4 A. in Frederick Co. on Cedar Cr. adj. John Orndoff, Henry Briel Sr., Henry Briel Jr. 3 Aug 1815 [Mr. A. Magill 15 Jan 1816]

B2-178: Surv. 18 Feb 1814 by T.W.4890=14 May 1812 George Blakemore 2 A. 1 Ro. 18 Po. in Frederick Co. adj. Hewitt formerly Handsecker, his own land originally Nevill, Smith. 18 Oct 1815 [Dl'd Mr. Augustine Smith 21 Nov 1815]

B2-179: Surv. 30 Apr 1814 by Exg.T.W.1017=23 Jan 1801 Adam Boarer 143 A. in Berkeley Co. on S. fork of Sleepy Cr. adj. William Shank formerly Hoof, William Summers formerly John Fenner, Gasper Shafner. 18 Oct 1815 [Dl'd Maj. And: Waggoner at session of 1815'16]

B2-180: Surv. 29 Apr 1814 by Exg.T.W.1017=23 Jan 1801 Adam Boarer 122 1/2 A. in Berkeley Co. on S. fork of Sleepy Cr. adj. Lewis Shockey formerly Daniel Lynn, Davis, Fenner. 18 Oct 1815 [Dl'd Maj. And: Waggoner at session of 1815'16]

B2-181: Surv. 28 Apr 1814 by Exg.T.W.1017=23 Jan 1801 Adam Boarer 23 1/2 A. in Berkeley Co. on S. fork of Sleepy Cr. adj. heirs of John Ridenhour/Ridenour, Lewis Shockey formerly Daniel Lynn, Davis. 18 Oct 1815 [Dl'd Maj. And: Waggoner at session of 1815'16]

B2-182: Surv. 3 May 1815 by Exg.T.W.2165=10 June 1812 Jacob Weaver Jr. 11 A. 1 Ro. in Fauquier Co. on Marsh Run adj. tract conveyed to said Weaver by Col. Joseph Blackwell, Armistead Blackwell, Talliafero Shumate. 16 Nov 1815 [Dl'd Col. Buckner 26 Feb 1816]

B2-183: Surv. 30 Mar 1814 by Exg.T.W.2165=10 June 1812 William Fitzhugh Carter 13 A. 3 Ro. in Fauquier Co. on Cedar Run, Licking Run, Owl Run, adj. Hon'ble Robert Carter now said William F. Carter & William Triplett. 16 Nov 1815

[Dl'd Mr. Williams Carter 8 July 1816

B2-185:   Surv. 15 Feb 1815 by T.W.5104=11 Aug 1813 George B. Pickett 9 A. 3 Ro.
in Fauquier Co. on Watry Mt., Great Run, N. Br. of Rappahannock R. adj. Buckner
& Willis, Col. Martin Pickett, Henderson, Barry. 16 Nov 1815 [3 Apr 1816]

B2-186:   Surv. 27 Nov 1813 by Exq.T.W.2131=12 Feb 1811 John Hutchinson 54 3/4 A.
in Frederick Co. adj. Abner Clarke, Jacob Allamong, Jacob Groves, on Isaac's
Cr., Warm spring Rd., Babb, Kern formerly Elisha Boyd, Rinker, Jasper Cather.
16 Nov 1815 [Dl'd Jared Williams 12 Feb 1816]

B2-188:   Surv. 22 Sep 1814 by Exg.T.W.2165=10 June 1812 Charles Kemper Jr. 16 A.
in Fauquier Co. on Carter's Run adj. Thomas Stone, Monroe, Thomas Jackman. 16
Nov 1815 [Dl'd Col. Thornton Buckner 17 Feb 1816]

B2-189:   Surv. 11 June 1814 by Exg.T.W.2165=10 June 1812 Isham Obannon 4 A. 3
Ro. in Fauquier Co. on Little R. adj. Winn, Holtzclaw, Scott now Tyler,
Hampton's Mill Pond. 16 Nov 1815 [Dl'd Col. Buckner 21 Feb 1816]

B2-191:   Surv. 20 Mar 1814 by T.W.4890=14 May 1812 David Lupton 1 A. 17 sq. Po.
in Frederick Co. adj. his own land, Edward Mercer, Babb now said Lupton. 16 Nov
1815 [Dl'd Mr. Alfred H. Powell 24 Jan 1816]

B2-192:   Surv. 24 June 1814 by Exg.T.W.2165=11 May 1812 Maj. John Kemper 22 A.
in Fauquier Co. on Cedar Run adj. Bush now Chichester, Henry Mauzy, Barbour,
Kemper, Grubb. 16 Nov 1815 [Dl'd the Prop'r 6 Jan 1816]

B2-194:   Surv. 1 June 1812 by Exg.T.W.2156=28 Jan 1812 John Sloan 100 A. in
Hampshire Co. on Mill Cr. adj. Smawley, Richard Sloan, Means, Taylor. 22 Feb
1816 [Dl'd Jas. Daily 24 Jan 1817]

B2-195:   Surv. 27 May 1812 by T.W.4873=26 Mar 1812 Abraham Cline 18 1/2 A. in
Hampshire Co. on N. R. Mt. adj. John Swisher Jr., Paul Coffman, his own land.
22 Feb 1816 [Dl'd Mr. Magill Mar 1819]

B2-196:   Surv. 21 Aug 1811 27 A. by Exg.T.W.1695=4 Dec 1804, 83 A. by
T.W.1710=19 June 1783, & 13 3/8 A. by Exg.T.W.1997=3 Feb 1809 John McDowell 123
3/8 A. in Hampshire Co. on Mikes Run of Pattersons Cr. adj. Beaver, Christian
Hilkey, and others, Youkams. 22 Feb 1816 [Dl'd Jas. Daily 24 Jan 1817]

B2-197:   Surv. 24 Mar 1812 by T.W.4671=20 Nov 1810 John Powelson asne. of Amary
Day 186 1/2 A. in Hampshire Co. on Little Cacapehon adj. Elisha Bell, Ruckman,
Steel, Parks, Pigeon lick Run of said Cacapehon. 22 Feb 1816 [Dl'd James
Gibson 8 June 1818]

B2-198:   Surv. 15 Feb 1812 95 1/2 A. by Exg.T.W.1997=3 Feb 1809 & 168 A. by
T.W.3906=12 Mar 1804 John Swisher Sr. 263 1/2 A. in Hampshire Co. on Hughes Run
of Great Cacapehon adj. George, John Swishers Jr., Frederick Michael, formerly
James Alexander, N. R. Mt., Elisha C. Dick. 22 Feb 1816 [Dl'd Mr. William
Naylor 9 Dec 1818]

B2-199:   Surv. 5 May 1815 by T.W.5078=20 May 1813 Jacob Baker 64 A. in
Shenandoah Co. in forks of Shenandoah R. adj. Joseph Stovers, John Catlett. 22
Feb 1816 [9 July 1816]

B2-200:   Surv. 29 Nov 1804 by T.W.21,664=24 Dec 1783 Jonathan Wilson 360 A. in
Campbell Co. on Big Falling R. & Long Mt. adj. Alexander, Forbish. 22 Feb 1816
(Grant marked out. This book for grants the N.N. only, grant to Jonathan Wilson
for 360 A. in Campbell was improperly recorded in this book; this record is
therefore erased. Recorded in proper book. Wm. Pendleton Reg'r

B2-201:   Surv. 5 Oct 1814 by T.W.4916=29 June 1812 Daniel James 25 A. in Madison
Co. adj. David Yowell, Jack Yowell, Paul Leatherer, John Carpenter. 18 Mar 1816
[Dl'd Mr. L. Taylor 1 May 1816]

B2-202:   Surv. 24 8th Month 1815 by T.W.4868=17 Mar 1812 Braxton Davenport 1 A.

3 Ro. 18 Po. in Jefferson Co. being an island in Shenandoah R. in the Bulls falls. 19 Aug 1816 [Dl'd Dan'l Morgan 23 Nov 1816]

B2-203:   Surv. 24 8th Month 1815 by T.W.4868=17 Mar 1812 Braxton Davenport 3 A. 3 Ro. 17 Po. in Jefferson Co. being an island in the Shenandoah R. opposite Stryder's Mill. 19 Aug 1816 [Dl'd Dan'l Morgan 28 Nov 1816]

B2-204:   Surv. 24 8th Month 1815 by T.W.4868=17 Mar 1812 Braxton Davenport 2 A. 17 Po. in Jefferson Co. being an island in Shenandoah R. in the Bulls falls. 19 Aug 1816 [Dl'd Dan'l Morgan 23 Nov 1816]

B2-205:   Surv. 16 of 8th Month 1815 by T.W.4868=17 Mar 1812 Braxton Davenport 19 A. 3 Ro. 20 Po. in Jefferson Co. being an island in Shenandoah R. in the Bulls falls. 19 Aug 1816 [Dl'd Dan'l Morgan 23 Nov 1816]

B2-206:   Surv. 10 Sep 1806 by T.W.4261=4 Aug 1805 James Gunnel asne. of Richard Ratclife 4 A. 120 sq. Po. in Fairfax Co. adj. Lewis Ellzey, Dunbar, David Waugh, Thomas Ford. 19 Aug 1816 [Dl'd Mr. Hunter 4 Feb 1816]

B2-207:   Surv. 29 Aug 1815 byT.W.212=23 Jan 1794 Henry Nicholas 377 A. in Hardy Co. on Powder lick Run adj. George Harness, Updegraff heirs, Bullet & Higgins, Seymour, Cunningham. 19 Aug 1816 [Dl'd John Lewis 30 Oct 1820]

B2-208:   Surv. 29 Aug 1815 by T.W.212=23 Jan 1794 Henry Nicholas 12 A. in Hardy Co. on Cornwell's Run adj. Abel Seymour, Harness McCarty. 19 Aug 1816 [Dl'd John Lewis 30 Oct 1820]

B2-209:   Surv. 10 Apr 1815 by T.W.212=23 Jan 1794 James Wilson 181 1/2 A. in Hardy Co. on Middle Rg. & Trout Run of Cacapon adj. his own land, Jacob Pugh, Wheeler Gillett formerly William Wilson. 19 Aug 1816 [Jacob Rinker 20 Dec 1816]

B2-210:   Surv. 24 Oct 1815 by T.W.5279=27 Oct 1814 James Hurst 110 A. 1 Ro 12 Po. in Jefferson Co. adj. George Pemberton, James Hurst formerly George Washington, Tully McKenny, James Coyl, Creamer, Blackburn now James Hurst, Samuel Davenport. 19 Aug 1816 [Dl'd Dan'l Morgan 23 Nov 1816]

B2-211:   Surv. 20 May 1815 by T.W.5086=25 May 1813 Benjamin McDonal 34 A. in Hampshire Co. on N. R. adj. Cotrill, his own land. 19 Aug 1816 [Dl'd Mr. William Naylor 9 Dec 1817]

B2-212:   Surv. 6 Nov 1815 by T.W.5359=2 Mar 1815 Adam Cristler 51 A. in Madison Co. adj. Adam Cristler, Mrs. Smith, George Harrison, William Tate's path, Henry Cristler dec'd. 19 Aug 1816 [Dl'd Mr. Linn Banks 22 Feb 1817]

B2-214:   Surv. 27 Oct 1815 30 A. by T.W.506=21 Apr 1813 & 32 A. by T.W.5176=24 Jan 1814 Arthur Kerscadden 62 A. in Hampshire Co. on Pattersons Cr. adj. Thomas Kerscadden, George Stagg, his own land, Savour. 19 Aug 1816 [Edw'd McCarty 27 Dec 1816]

B2-215:   Surv. 10 Sep 1815 by T.W.4011=29 Jan 1810 John Poland 70 A. in Hampshire Co. on Little Capecapon and Piny Mt. adj. Henderson, White, Smith, Amos Poland. 19 Aug 1816 [Dl'd James Daily 24 Jan 1817]

B2-216:   Surv. 12 Apr 1815 by T.W.212=23 Jan 1794 William Heath asne. of Samuel Kennedy 251 A. in Hardy Co. on Turn Mill Run adj. William Heath, Patterson's Cr. Mt., John Smith, Isaac Vanmeter, Isaac Hite, Arnold. 2 Sep 1816 [Dl'd Jacob Miller 24 Dec 1817]

B2-217:   Surv. 14 Apr 1815 by T.W.212=23 Jan 1794 James McDavid 255 A. in Hardy Co. on S. fork of New Cr. & Walkers Rg. adj. Christian Hilkey, New Cr. Mt., Kettle Lick Run, Charles Lee. 2 Sep 1816 [Dl'd Mr. Inskeed 29 Oct 1823]

B2-218:   Surv. 12 Mar 1815 by T.W.212=23 Jan 1794 Martin Peterson 50 A. in Hardy Co. on N. Mill Cr. adj. his own land, Alt. 2 Sep 1816 [Jacob Miller 24 Dec 1817]

B2-219:   Surv. 11 May 1814 by T.W.212=23 Jan 1794 George Stingly 323 A. in Hardy

Co. on Loonies Cr. adj. Thomas Wharton heirs, George Shell formerly Thomas Gaven, Joseph Wharton, said Stingly. 2 Sep 1816 [Mr. Jacob Miller 24 Dec 1817]

B2-220: Martin Peterson 50 A. in Hardy Co. Twice issued & Recorded through mistake; original cancelled; see other ent'e page 318. Wm. G. Pendleton, Regs'r

B2-221: Surv. 13 Oct 1815 by T.W.212=23 Jan 1794 George Judy 17 A. in Hardy Co. adj. his own land on S. Mill Cr., his Weese Tract. 20 Sep 1816 [24 Dec 1817]

B2-222: Surv. 30 Aug 1815 by T.W.212=23 Jan 1794 Hugh Murphy 67 A. in Hardy Co. on Allegany Mt. on Abraham's Cr. adj. Alexander Smith, Bruce, John Champ heirs, Vandaver. 20 Sep 1816 [Dl'd Mr. Jacob Miller 24 Dec 1817]

B2-223: Surv. 13 Oct 1814 by T.W.212=23 Jan 1794 John Judy 12 A. in Hardy Co. adj. his own land on S. Mill Cr. adj. George Judy. 20 Sep 1816 [Dl'd Mr. Jacob Miller 24 Dec 1817]

B2-223: Surv. 18 Apr 1815 by T.W.212=23 Jan 1794 Solomon Groves 16 A. in Hardy Co. on Loonies Cr., New Cr. Mt. & Walkers Rg. adj. his own land, Martin Hawk. 20 Sep 1816 [Dl'd Mr. William Hutchinson 2 Sep 1822]

B2-224: Surv. 18 Apr 1815 by T.W.212=23 Jan 1794 Samuel Roby 14 A. in Hardy Co. on N. fork of Paterson's Cr. & Walker's Rg. adj. Henry Smith, his own land. 20 Sep 1816 [Dl'd Mr. Jacob Miller 24 Dec 1817]

B2-225: Surv. 20 Jan 1815 by T.W.212=23 Jan 1794 Jonathan Branson 19 A. in Hardy Co. on Mill Run of Lost R. adj. Matthias Wilkins heirs, George Wilkins. 20 Sep 1816 [Dl'd Mr. Jacob Miller 24 Dec 1817]

B2-227: Surv. 14 Oct 1815 by T.W.212=23 Jan 1794 George Sites 40 A. in Hardy Co. on S. Mill Cr. adj. his land. 20 Sep 1816 [Mr. Jacob Miller 24 Dec 1817]

B2-228: Surv. 1 Sep 1815 by T.W.212=23 Jan 1794 William Rodgers 163 A. in Hardy Co. on Great Cacapon adj. Abram Fry, James Stewart. 20 Sep 1816 [Dl'd Mr. Jacob Miller 24 Dec 1817]

B2-229: Surv. 14 Apr 1815 by T.W.212=23 Jan 1794 William Stingley 24 A. in Hardy Co. on N. fork of Paterson's Cr. adj. his own land, Gasper Hite, Beur?, New Cr. Mt. 20 Sep 1816

B2-230: Surv. 14 Apr 1815 by T.W.212=23 Jan 1794 Gasper Hite 70 A. in Hardy Co. on New Cr. Mt. aj. his own land, William Stingley, Byrne. 20 Sep 1816 [Dl'd Mr. Jacob Miller 24 Dec 1817]

B2-231: Surv. 20 Dec 1814 by T.W.5058=2 Apr 1813 Joseph Ellis 300 A. in Shenandoah Co. on the Blue Rg., near Thornton's gap, adj. Martin Shenk, Lewis Myers formerly Windle Shank, Tobias Beam. 20 Sep 1816 [Jac. Rinker Jr. 22 Jan 1817]

B2-232: Surv. 29 Apr 1815 by T.W.5058=2 Apr 1813 Reuben Long 44 A. in Shenandoah Co. on Messenutten Cr. adj. said Long, Strickler, Turnpike Rd., Isaac Strickler, Samuel Sugden heirs, Long's purchase of Jonathan Watson. 20 Sep 1816 [Dl'd Jac. Rinker Jr. 22 Jan 1817]

B2-233: Surv. 4 May 1815 by T.W.5058=2 Apr 1813 Casper Miller 2 1/4 A. in Shenandoah Co. on S. R. of Shenandoah adj. Casper Miller, Joseph Louderback. 20 Sep 1816 [Dl'd Jac. Rinker Jr. 22 Jan 1817]

B2-234: Surv. 9 Mar 1815 by T.W.5140=7 Dec 1813 Adam Barb Jr. 131 A. in Shenandoah Co. on Stoney Cr. adj. David Barb, said Adam Barb Jr., Michael Crouse, John Sheetz. 20 Sep 1816 [Dl'd Jac. Rinker Jr. 22 Jan 1817]

B2-235: Surv. 21 Jan 1815 by T.W.5023=5 Feb 1813 John Bowman(blacksmith) 167 A. in Shenandoah Co. on Mill Cr. adj. Jacob Hamman, Philip Roushe, Michael Romick, George Hamman, Henry Wocker, George Weaver. 20 Sep 1816 [Dl'd Jac. Rinker 22 Jan 1817]

B2-237: Surv. 4 Mar 1815 by T.W.4813=18 Jan 1812 George Philip Pence 3/4 A. in Shenandoah Co. in the Forest adj. said Pence's purchase of John Nease, Jacob Zerfas, John Boot?. 20 Sep 1816 [Dl'd Jac. Rinker 22 Jan 1817]

B2-237: Surv. 11 Aug 1814 by T.W.5141=7 Dec 1813 Andrew Kizer 150 A. in Shenandoah Co. on S. R. of Shenandoah adj. Christian Bumgarner, said Kizer, Elsey, David Mumau. 20 Sep 1816 [Dl'd Jac. Rinker 22 Jan 1817]

B2-239: Surv. 10 Nov 1814 by T.W.4813=18 Jan 1812 John Miller 94 1/2 A. in Shenandoah Co. at the Blue Rg. adj. said Miller, Peter & Abraham Prince, George Hettick. 20 Sep 1816 [Dl'd Jacob Rinker 22 Jan 1817]

B2-240: Surv. 20 May 1814 by T.W.5023=5 Feb 1813 John Varner 48 A. in Shenandoah Co. in the Piney Mt. adj. George Prince, Samuel Hersberger, his own line. 20 Sep 1816 [Dl'd Jac. Rinker Jr. 22 Jan 1817]

B2-241: Surv. 12 May 1814 by T.W.5141=7 Dec 1813 Philip Shaver 275 A. in Shenandoah Co. at the Blue Rg. on Dry Run adj. Thomas Tuckwiller, Piercen Judd, Peter Blausser/Blosser, said Shaver. 20 Sep 1816 [Dl'd Jac. Rinker Jr. 22 Jan 1817]

B2-242: Surv. 29 Apr 1815 by T.W.5058=2 Apr 1813 Reuben Long 26 A. in Shenandoah Co. on Messenotten Cr. adj. Isaac Strickler, Solomon Kessney, Jonathan Watson now said Long. 20 Sep 1816 [Dl'd Jac. Rinker 22 Jan 1817]

B2-243: Surv. 30 Apr 1815 by 5140=7 Dec 1813 Reuben Long 142 A. in Shenandoah Co. on Messennotten Cr. adj. Christian Shelley now s'd Long, Turnpike Rd., Jonathan Watson now Long, Samuel Sugden, James Barbour. 20 Sep 1816 [Dl'd Jac. Rinker Jr. 22 Jan 1817]

B2-245: Surv. 13 May 1815 by T.W.4740=13 May 1811 Samuel Light 6 A. 1 Ro. 17 Po. in Berkeley Co. on Opekon Cr. adj. John Myer/Myers, Samuel Harrison heirs, Samuel Light. 20 Sep 1816 [Dl'd Mr. Porterfield 6 Dec 1817]

B2-246: Surv. 18 Apr 1815 by T.W.212=23 Jan 1794 James Marquis 26 A. in Hardy Co. on Walker's Rg. & N. fork of Pattersons Cr. adj. his own land bought of Thomas Dent, Rannells. 20 Sep 1816 [Dl'd To Rec't 1830]

B2-247: Surv. 13 Apr 1815 by T.W.212=23 Jan 1794 John Smith 113 A. in Hardy Co. on Mudlick run adj. Isaac Vanmeter. 20 Sep 1816 [Dl'd Col. Mullen 19 Jan 1836]

B2-248: Surv. 24 May 1815 by Exg.T.W.1362=9 Dec 1802 Paul Taylor 286 A. in Berkeley Co. on N. Mt. adj. James Campbell, Samuel Chenoweth, Pitzer, William Orr, Henry Bower. 20 Sep 1816 [Dl'd Israel Robertson 21 Jan 1818]

B2-250: Surv. 13 Apr 1815 by T.W.212=23 Jan 1794 John Smith 206 A. in Hardy Co. on Turn mill Tun adj. William Heath, Isaac Hite, Joseph Vanmeter. 20 Sep 1816 [Dl'd Col. Mullen 19 Jan 1836]

B2-251: Surv. 30 Sep 1815 by Exg.T.W.1017=23 Jan 1801 James W. Wheat asne. of Adam Bohrer(Adam Boarer) 86 A. in Berkeley Co. on Warm spring Run of Potomac R. adj. Nicholas Orrick, Doctor Gustin, Morton. 20 Sep 1816 [Mr. Porterfield 16 Dec 1818]

B2-252: Surv. 30 May 1815 by T.W.5086=25 May 1813 Benjamin McDonal 65 1/4 A. in Hampshire Co. on N. R. adj. Sutton, his own land. 20 Sep 1816 [Dl'd William Naylor 9 Dec 1817]

B2-253: Surv. 30 May 1815 by T.W.4841=18 Feb 1812 John Starn 506 A. in Hampshire Co. on N. R. adj. John Davis, Samuel Williamson, Henry Bringman, top of Negro Mt. 20 Sep 1816 [Dl'd Mr. White 1 Aug 1818]

B2-254: Surv. 1 July 1814 50 A. by T.W.4913=23 June 1812, 25 A. by T.W.5119=29 Oct 1813 & 25 A. by T.W.4982=1 Dec 1812 Samuel Probasco 100 A. in Hampshire Co. on N. R. adj. Carter, Stone Williamson, John Starn and his own land, Negro-Mt. 20 Sep 1816 [Dl'd Mr. Armstrong Feb 1819]

B2-255: Surv. 12 June 1815 by T.W.5149=15 Dec 1813 John Caudy 45 A. in Hampshire Co. on N. R. adj. Carmikle, said Caudy, on N. R. Mt. 20 Sep 1816 [Dl'd Mr. William Naylor 9 Dec 1817]

B2-257: Surv. 12 June 1815 by T.W.5268=8 Aug 1814 John Wolford 57 A. in Hampshire Co. on N. R. Mt. adj. Emmert, White, his own land. 30 Dec 1816 [Dl'd Col. Edward McCarty 31 Jan 1818]

B2-258: Surv. 24 Dec 1814 by T.W.5149=15 Dec 1813 John Caudy 60 1/2 A. in Hampshire Co. on N. R. adj. John Hiett, Carmikel, Busbey, Flanninghan, his own land. 30 Dec 1816 [Dl'd Mr. William Naylor 9 Dec 1817]

B2-259: Surv. 4 July 1814 by T.W.4913=25 June 1812 Jacob Creeke 55 A. in Hampshire Co. on Great Capecapon adj. Foxcraft, John Nave, John Rodgers, Joseph Stone. 30 Dec 1816 [Dl'd Joseph Sexton 22 Jan 1817]

B2-260: Surv. 4 Apr 1814 by T.W.5119=29 Oct 1813 Joseph Thompson & Joseph Martin 200 A. in Hampshire Co. on N. R. 30 Dec 1816 [Dl'd Mr. White 1 Jan 1819]

B2-260: Surv. 10 Oct 1815 by T.W.4891=20 May 1812 Mary Lowen 20 1/2 A. in Culpeper Co. adj. John Porter, said Mary Lowen, Tureman, Winston, Thornton Foushee, legatees of John Foushee dec'd. 30 Dec 1816 [Rob. C. Smith 22 Jan 1817]

B2-261: Surv. 30 June 1813 by T.W.4598=5 Dec 1809 William Alderton asne. of David Alderton 13 1/2 A. in Hampshire Co. on Potomac R. adj. Fryback, Greenwall, Nicholas Friend. 30 Dec 1816 [Dl'd Jas. Daily 24 Jan 1817]

B2-262: Surv. 20 May 1815 by T.W.5384=17 Apr 1815 George Latham 20 A. 3 Ro. 35 Po. in Stafford Co. on Potowmac run adj. Washington, Carter, Harding. 30 Dec 1816 [Dl'd Mr. Thomas Hill 31 Oct 1817]

B2-263: Surv. 14 Apr 1815 by T.W.212=23 Jan 1794 James Machir & Jacob Tevebaugh asne. of John Coffill 41 A. in Hardy Co. on Middle Mt. & S. fork, adj. Jacob Stover, Abel Seymour. 30 Dec 1816 [Dl'd Mr. James Russell 29 Oct 1817]

B2-264: Surv. 29 Aug 1815 by T.W.212=23 Jan 1794 Jacob Tevebaugh & James Machir asnes. of John Coffill 32 A. in Hardy Co. on S. fork adj. Abel Seymour, Jacob & Peter Hutton's Hite tract, Simpson, Michael Neff. 30 Dec 1816 [Dl'd Mr. James Russell 29 Oct 1817]

B2-265: Surv. 17 Mar 1812 by T.W.4151=8 Jan 1805 Henry Tyler 9 A. 2 Ro. 12 sq. Po. in Pr. William Co. adj. Richard Davis, Richard Fristoe. 30 Dec 1816 [Dl'd Mr. Foster 25 Jan 1817]

B2-265: Surv. 18 Mar 1812 by T.W.4151=8 Jan 1805 Henry Tyler 50 A. 3 Ro. 26 Po. in Pr. William Co. adj. Lewis Dickerson, Junckeson, Br. of Cappawamsick Cr., Richard Davis. 30 Dec 1816   [Dl'd Jas. E. Heath 19 Sep 1817]

B2-266: Surv. 10 Oct 1815 by T.W.4963=22 Oct 1812 Ann, Margaret, & Catherine S. Hencock 22 A. 1 Ro. 17 Po. in Pr. William Co. adj. Tayloe formerly Benbridge, Tayloe formerly Markham & Harrison, Colchester Rd., Grayson, Downman. 30 Dec 1816 [Dl'd Mr. Heath 7 June 1817]

B2-267: Surv. 20 Aug 1813 by T.W.5065=21 Apr 1813 Andrew Ernholt 75 A. in Hampshire Co. on New Cr. adj. Deen, Bowman, James, Tib's run. 30 Dec 1816 [Dl'd James Daily 24 Dec 1816?]

B2-268: Surv. 16 Jan 1816 by T.W.4913=25 June 1812 John Thompson 5 A. in Hampshire Co. on N. R. adj. John T. Summers. 30 Dec 1816 [Dl'd Mr. Carscadon 1832]

B2-269: Surv. 3 Jan 1814 by T.W.5008=5 Jan 1813 James Graham 60 A. in Hampshire Co. on Pattersons Cr. adj. Flood, his own land. 30 Dec 1816 [Ephraim Dunn 4 Dec 1821]

B2-270: Surv. 21 June 1814 by T.W.5065=21 Apr 1813 Frederick Purget 100 A. in Hampshire Co. on Mill Cr. adj. Frederick Hoke, John Shofe, on Pattersons Cr. Mt.

30 Dec 1816 [Dl'd James Daily 24 Jan 1817]

B2-271: Surv. 8 June 1815 by T.W.4982=1 Dec 1812 William McPowell 62 A. in Hampshire Co. on Little Cacapehon adj. John Powner, his own land, Town Hill. 30 Dec 1816 [Dl'd James Daily 24 Jan 1817]

B2-272: Surv. 11 Jan 1815 by T.W.5065=21 Apr 1813 Elisha Lyons 100 A. in Hampshire Co. on Cobbon Run of Patterson's Cr. adj. John Culp, Warton, Fairfax, Knobly Mt. 30 Dec 1816 [Dl'd James Daily 24 Jan 1817]

B2-273: Surv. 25 Jan 1814 by T.W.4982=1 Dec 1812 Isaac Welch 21 A. in Hampshire Co. on Patterson's Cr. adj. Abraham Good, his own land. 30 Dec 1816

B2-274: Surv. 7 Jan 1814 by T.W.5119=29 Oct 1813 Joseph Johnson (s. of John) asne. of William Critton 100 A. in Hampshire Co. on Little Cacapehon adj. his own land & others. 30 Dec 1816 [Dl'd Warner Throckmorton 26 Jan 1821]

B2-275: Surv. 29 Dec 1814 by T.W.5149=15 Dec 1813 John Hiett 32 A. in Hampshire Co. on N. R. adj. Henderson, Lee, Sharf, Wolford, Caudy and his own land. 30 Dec 1816 [Dl'd Mr. William Naylor 9 Dec 1817]

B2-276: Surv. 31 May 1814 by T.W.21,013=1 Dec 1783 John T. Summers 34 A. in Hampshire Co. on N. R. adj. Dunmore, Tucker, his own land, John Thompson. 30 Dec 1816

B2-277: Surv. 29 Aug 1815 by T.W.212=23 Jan 1794 Wheler Gelett 14 A. in Hardy Co. on Rg. bet. Trout Run & Capcapen adj. his own land, Jacob Pugh. 30 Dec 1816

B2-278: Surv. 9 Sep 1815 by T.W.5431=1 Aug 1815 Richard Henry Henderson & Thomas Henderson Exrs. of last will of Alexander Henderson late of Dumfries, dec'd, as expressed in said last will, 45 A. 1 Ro in Pr. William Co. on Powell's Run, adj. Matthews, John Lynn dec'd. 30 Dec 1816 [James E. Heath 18 Jan 1817]

B2-279: Surv. 24 June 1815 by T.W.4831=18 Jan 1812 Samuel Rodeheffer 1 3/4 A. in Shenandoah Co. adj. his other land, Matthias Smootz, John Cohenour. 30 Dec 1816 [Dl'd Jac. Rinker Jr. 22 Jan 1817]

B2-280: Surv. 17 Dec 1814 50 A. by T.W.4913=25 June 1812, 25 A. by T.W.5008=5 Jan 1813, & 35 A. by T.W.5065=21 Apr 1813 Thomas Allon 110 A. in Hampshire Co. on Patterson's Cr. adj. Hollenback, his own land. 30 Dec 1816 [Dl'd Mr. Vance 19 Jan 1833]

B2-281: Surv. 20 Sep 1815 by T.W.212=23 Jan 1794 Elisha E. Russell & Wheeler Gillett 197 A. in Hardy Co. on Great Capcapen adj. James Stewart Sr., hiers of George Shewmaker, their own land, William Richardson heirs. 1 Nov 1816 [Dl'd Col. Carson 22 Nov 1816]

B2-282: Surv. 19 Sep 1815 by Exg.T.W.2159=21 Feb 1811 John Snyder, Joseph C. Kellar & Josiah Crampton asnes. of Charles Binns 22 A. 1 Ro. 12 Po. in Loudoun Co. on Potomac R. adj. Fairfax, Tankerville, John Colvill 6 Oct 1742 grant, Little Dutchman's Run, Awbrey. 30 Dec 1816 [Dl'd Rob't Moffett 22 May 1818]

B2-283: Surv. 2 Dec 1815 by Exg.T.W.1915=10 Sep 1807 Ferdinando Fairfax 10 A. 3 Ro. 16 Po. in Loudoun Co. near Short hill adj. Kittokton Cr., Francis Awbrey, Catsby Cock. 30 Dec 1816 [Dl'd Rob't Moffett 22 May 1818]

B2-284: Surv. 19 Oct 1815 by Exg.T.W.2220=2 Oct 1815 Robert Ratcliffe 10 A. in Fairfax Co. adj. Stone now Henry S. Halley, Lewis Elzey now B. R. Davis. 30 Dec 1816 [Mr. Hunter 4 Feb 1817]

B2-285: Surv. 14 Oct 1814 100 A. by T.W.5023=5 Feb 1813 & 34 A. by T.W.5275=19 Aug 1814 Piercen Jedd & Peter Heastand Jr. 134 A. in Shenandoah Co. on Pass Run adj. the Blue Rg., heirs of Martin Kaufman dec'd. 30 Dec 1816 [Jac. Rinker Jr. 22 Jan 1817]

B2-286: Surv. 16 Apr 1814 by T.W.961=11 Dec 1794 George Gander 28 1/2 A. in

Shenandoah Co. adj. Blackford Arthur & Co., heirs of Martin Kaufman(river) dec'd, Jonas Ruffner. 30 Dec 1816 [Dl'd Jac. Rinker Jr. 22 Jan 1817]

B2-287: Surv. 16 Aug 1815 by T.W.5236=17 May 1814 Jeremiah & Thomas Hall 18 A. in Culpeper Co. adj. Thomas Hall dec'd, Robert Patton, Marshall Petty, Russel Vaughan. 30 Dec 1816 [Dl'd Mr. Philip Slaughter 24 Nov 1817]

B2-288: Surv. 15 Mar 1816 80 A. by Exg.T.W.2214=12 May 1815 & 14 A. by T.W.4133=17 Dec 1804 Willis Cummins 94 A. in Fauquier Co. on Brenttown Run adj. John Nelson, the Rg. Rd., James Cox, Elijah Hansborough, Stephen French. 10 May 1817 [Dl'd Col. Buckner 3 Dec 1817]

B2-289: Surv. 21 June 1814 by T.W.5070=17 May 1813 Henry H. Halley 11 A. 1 Ro. 33 Po. in Fairfax Co. on S. Run adj. Halley, Godfrey, Washington, Cox, William Simpson. 10 May 1817 [Dl'd Mr. Thompson (of Farifax) 13 Dec 1817]

B2-290: Surv. 13 July 1813 by T.W.20,541=10 Nov 1783 Michael Briel 81 3/4 A. in Frederick Co. on Cedar Cr. adj. Hoffman, Longacre, Orndurff, Henry Briel, Philip Poker. 10 May 1817

B2-291: Surv. 3 Apr 1813 by Exg.T.W.1707=4 June 1805 John Allaback 18 1/2 A. in Hampshire Co. on Great Cacaphon adj. James Leath, Foxcraft, Bear-Waller Pond, his own land and others. 10 May 1817 [Dl'd Mr. White 28 Dec 1818]

B2-292: Surv. 6 June 1814 by T.W.5070=17 May 1813 Richard S. Windsor 20 A. 2 Ro. 2 Po. in Fairfax Co. on Middle Run adj. Auberry, Thomas Windsor, Hall. 10 May 1817 [Dl'd Geo. Millan 30 Oct 1817]

B2-293: Surv. 3 Feb 1816 100 A. by T.W.4845=19 Feb 1812, 200 A. by 4986=4 Dec 1812, 200 A. by T.W.5123=30 Oct 1813, 500 A. by T.W.5138=6 Dec 1813 & 200 A. by T.W.5543=22 Dec 1815 Isaac Overall 1200 A. in Shenandoah Co. on Dry Run & John Overall's Mill Run at the Blue Rg., adj. Richard Waters, Fielding Thompson, Charles Saxon, James Stinson, Isaac Overall's purchase of Thomas Allen, said Overrall bought of Shaffer, Young's heirs, James Barbour, Freeman. 10 May 1817 [Dl'd Col. Carson 24 Dec 1817]

B2-296: Surv. 5 July 1814 100 A. by T.W.3011=3 Nov 1800, 33 3/4 A. by T.W.3541=29 Jan 1803 & 100 A. by T.W.5086=25 May 1813 Jacob Jinkins 233 3/4 A. in Hampshire Co. on High tops & Ivory Run of Great Cacapehon adj. John Rogers. 10 May 1817 [Dl'd Mr. Throckmorton 24 Jan 1820]

B2-297: Surv. 20 Sep 1815 200 A. by 5112=13 Sep 1813 & 52 A. by 5120=29 Oct 1813 William Steenbergen 252 A. in Shanandoah Co. at the Short Arse Mt. & Big Mt. Run of Smith's Cr. adj. said Steenberhgen's purchase of Robert Patton, Benjamin Pennybacker, Charles Moore, Aaron Moore. 10 May 1817 [The Prop'r 8 Jan 1818]

B2-298: Surv. 24 Nov 1815 500 A. by T.W.5294=3 Nov 1814 & 465 A. by T.W.5275=19 Aug 1814 James Kendal 965 A. in Shenandoah Co. on Blue Rg. adj. Benjamin Wood, John Allen, Piney Mt., John Wood, said Kendal, Senate Atwood, Mitchell Robinson, Jones, James Barbour, Emanuel McNight, Zane now Wood. 1 Nov 1817 [Dl'd Col. Carson 24 Dec 1817]

B2-300: Surv 1 Apr 1815 by T.W.5226=27 Apr 1814 George Oakley 150 A. in Shenandoah Co. near head of Land's Run, on Ivy Hill. 1 Nov 1817

B2-300: Surv. 28 Aug. 1816 by Exg.T.W.1035=3 Mar 1801 John Lawson Eastham 69 1/2 A. in Fauquier Co. on Brown's Run adj. John Hudnall, John Morehead now John Frogg, Marsh Rd., John Hopper. 1 Nov 1817 [Dl'd Col. Buckner 3 Dec 1817]

B2-301: Surv. 27 Jan 1816 by T.W.4813=18 Jan 1812 David Mummau (So. river) 60 A. in Shenandoah Co. bet. S. R. of Shenandoah & Ft. Mt., adj. William S. Marye, Andrew Kyser, Fodder House Mt., Buck Run, John Road. 1 Nov 1817 [Dl'd Mr. Jacob Rinker Jr. 5 Dec 1817]

B2-303: Surv. 21 Mar 1816 by Exg.T.W.2171=18 Dec 1812 Thornton Stringfellow 11 3/4 A. in Fauquier Co. on Rock Run adj. Benjamin West, said Stringfellow, James

Steglar. 1 Nov 1817 [Dl'd Maj. B. Ficklin 3 Dec 1817]

B2-303: Surv. 21 Feb 1816 by T.W.212=23 Jan 1794 James Snodgrass 178 A. in Hardy Co. on Huckleberry Rg. adj. heirs of David Welton, and others, Sarah Smith, heirs of Felix Welton. 1 Nov 1817 [Dl'd Jessee Cunningham 9 Feb 1819]

B2-304: Surv. 29 Jan 1814 by T.W.1243=26 Mar 1795 Jonas Crabill asne. of John Reager 6 A. 3 Ro. 15 Per. in Shenandoah Co. bet. Ft. Mt. & N. R. of Shenandoah adj. Jacob Stover, Jonas Graybill. 1 Nov 1817 [Mr. Wm. Anderson 26 Oct 1818]

B2-305: Surv. 26 Aug 1816 by T.W.5500=6 Nov 1815 Richard Ratcliffe 39 A. 32 Po. in Fairfax Co. on Accotink Run adj. oak shewn by John Moore & W. H. Moore as beginning of grant to George Mason Jr. for 1930 A. 5 Jan 1714/5, on Hatmark Br., Gladdins now heirs of Joseph Powell dec'd, ODaniel's Br., William ODaniel, Stephen ODaniel now said Ratcliffe. 1 Nov 1817 [Mr. Henning 13 Dec 1817]

B2-306: Surv. 24 Nov 1815 100 A. by Exg.T.W.2100=8 Jan 1810 & 8 A. by T.W.4842=18 Feb 1812 George Little 108 A. in Hampshire Co. on N. R. & N. R. Mt. adj. George McColley, Wood. 1 Nov 1817 [Dl'd Col. Edward McCarty 31 Jan 1818]

B2-307: Surv. 9 Sep 1816 60 3/4 A. by T.W.5587=12 Feb 1816 & 52 A. by T.W.4611=29 Jan 1810 William Kyte 112 3/4 A. in Hampshire Co. on Alleghany Mt. adj. Samuel Kyte. 1 Nov 1817 [Dl'd Mr. Armstrong Feb 1819]

B2-308: Surv. 16 Aug 1816 by T.W.5119=29 Oct 1813 Samuel Shinn 23 A. in Hampshire Co. on Great Cacapon adj. John Thomas, Evan Caudy, John Chesher, heirs of David Shinn dec'd, Bare Garden Rg., John Caudy. 1 Nov 1817

B2-309: Surv. 18 Sep 1816 157 A. by T.W.4602=8 Jan 1810, 300 A. by T.W.4598=5 Dec 1809, 93 A. by T.W.5268=8 Aug 1814, 11 A. by Exg.T.W.1997=3 Feb 1809, & 50 A. by T.W.5119=29 Oct 1813 Henry Heinzman 611 A. in Hampshire Co. on S. Br. of Potomac adj. Miller, Pancake, Kuykendoll, Huffman, Pendolton. 1 Nov 1817 [Dl'd Col. Edward McCarty 31 Jan 1818]

B2-310: Surv. 1 Aug 1816 by T.W.5086=25 May 1813 Jacob Ziler 20 A. in Hampshire Co. on Great Cacapon adj. Peter Bruner Sr., Thompson, his own land. 1 Nov 1817 [Dl'd Mr. Armstrong Feb 1819]

B2-311: Surv. 12 Sep 1816 177 1/2 A. by Exg.T.W.1569=25 Jan 1804, 100 A. by T.W.5571=2 Feb 1816, 39 A. by T.W.5587=12 Feb 1816 & 11 A. by T.W.5119=29 Oct 1813 Frederick Purget 327 1/2 A. in Hampshire Co. on Mill Cr. adj. Hoke, Foaley. 1 Nov 1817 [Dl'd Warner Throckmorten 24 Jan 1821]

B2-312: Surv. 24 May 1816 by T.W.5065=21 Apr 1813 Abraham Leatherman 13 A. in Hampshire Co. on Patterson's Cr. adj. Hershman, his own land, the Manor land. 1 Nov 1817 [Dl'd Jas. Gibson 3 Nov 1821]

B2-313: Surv. 30 May 1815 T.W.5268=8 Aug 1814 John Higgins 37 A. in Hampshire Co. on Crooked Run of Little Cacapon adj. Larramore, Brown, Richard Morlan, John Queen, Higgins, Rinker, Powelson. 1 Nov 1817 [Col. Edward McCarty 31 Jan 1818]

B2-314: Surv. 6 Nov 1816 50 A. by T.W.4842=18 Feb 1812 & 50 A. by Exg.T.W.428=26 Apr 1791 John Higgins 100 A. in Hampshire Co. on Little Cacapon adj. Taylor, Stroud, Nicholas R. More formerly Bills, Hopkins Lick Run. 1 Nov 1817 [Dl'd Col. Edward McCarty 31 Jan 1818]

B2-315: Surv. 3 Sep 1816 by Exg.T.W.992=15 Dec 1800 John Umstots 9 A. in Hampshire Co. on Patterson's Cr. adj. Peter Umstot, James Watts Sr., Abner Bain. 1 Nov 1817 [Dl'd Col. Edward McCarty 31 Jan 1818]

B2-316: Surv. 7 Sep 1816 by T.W.4982=1 Dec 1812 Robert Slocom 27 1/2 A. in Hampshire Co. on Tear Coat adj. Roberson, Wetsall, Brown, Melick. 1 Nov 1817 [Dl'd Col. Edward McCarty 31 Jan 1818]

B2-317: Surv. 7 Nov 1816 16 A. by T.W.5086=25 May 1813, 221 A. by T.W.5775=29 Oct 1816, & 100 A. by Exg.T.W.1707=4 Jan 1805 Luther Martin Jr. 337 A. in

Hampshire Co. on S. & N. Brs. of Potomac adj. Luther Martin of Baltimore, Michel, Tapley, Tidball, Magloclin, Murphy's heirs, Taylor, Br. Mt. 1 Nov 1817 [Dl'd Gibson 7 Nov 1818]

B2-319: Surv. 25 Oct 1816 263 A. by T.W.5572=2 Feb 1816 & 100 A. by T.W.4842=18 Feb 1812 William Naylor 363 A. in Hampshire Co. on S. Br. adj. Huffman, heirs of Wharton dec'd, Trough hill. 1 Nov 1817 [Dl'd Prop'r 9 Dec 1817]

B2-320: Surv. 26 Aug 1816 50 A. by T.W.5119=29 Oct 1813 & 50 A. by T.W.5634 =8 Mar 1816 Aaron Harlan 100 A. in Hampshire Co. on Great Cacapon adj. The Mt. Surv. 1 Nov 1817 [Dl'd Mr. Armstrong Feb 1819]

B2-321: Surv. 27 Apr 1816 by T.W.5571=2 Feb 1816 Absalom Shingleton 34 A. in Hampshire Co. on Little Cacapon adj. Foxcraft, Hall, Joshua Powner. 1 Nov 1817 [Dl'd Col. Edward McCarty 31 Jan 1818]

B2-322: Surv. 22 June 1814 by T.W.5017=28 Jan 1813 Edward McCarty, James Dailey, John McDowell & William Naylor asnes. of John Plum Sr. 26 1/2 A. in Hampshire Co. on Patterson's Cr. adj. John Plum Sr. 1 Nov 1817 [Dl'd Col. Edward McCarty 31 Jan 1818]

B2-323: Surv. 29 Oct 1815 by T.W.5286=1 Nov 1814 Edward McCarty, William Naylor, James Dailey & John McDowell 645 A. in Hampshire Co. on Pattersons Cr. adj. Rawleigh Colston, their own formerly John Shofe & John Plumb Sr., Muddy run Mt., Purget. 1 Nov 1817 [Dl'd Col. Edward McCarty 31 Jan 1818]

B2-324: Surv. 22 June 1814 by T.W.5017=28 Jan 1813 Edward McCarty, James Dailey, William Naylor & John McDowell asnes. of John Plum Sr. 15 A. in Hampshire Co. on Patterson's Cr. adj. said Plum, Patterson's Cr. Mt. 1 Nov 1817 [Dl'd Col. Edward McCarty 31 Jan 1818]

B2-325: Surv. 23 June 1814 by T.W.5017=28 Jan 1813 Edward McCarty, James Dailey, John McDowell & William Naylor asnes. of John Shofe 86 A. in Hampshire Co. on Patterson's Cr. Mt. adj. John Plumb Sr., John Shofe. 1 Nov 1817 [Dl'd Col. Edward McCarty 31 Jan 1818]

B2-326: Surv. 20 Nov 1815 by T.W.5065=21 Apr 1813 John Blue 50 A. in Hampshire Co. on S. Br., near Hanging Rock Rg. adj. heirs of Uriah Blue dec'd, his own land. 1 Nov 1817 [Dl'd Mr. Vance 19 Jan 1833]

B2-327: Surv. 10 Aug 1816 by T.W.5065=21 Apr 1813 William Mills 15 A. in Hampshire Co. on S. Br. of Potomac adj. Vanmeter, Hawk, Dobbons. 1 Nov 1817 [Dl'd Mr. McCarty 26 Feb 1821]

B2-328: Surv. 10 Aug 1816 50 A. by T.W.5017=28 Jan 1813 & 28 A. by T.W.5065=21 Apr 1813, William Mills 78 A. in Hampshire Co. on S. Br. of Potomac adj. Vanmeter. 1 Nov 1817 [Dl'd Mr. McCarty 26 Feb 1821]

B2-329: Surv. 10 Sep 1816 by T.W.212=23 Jan 1794 Benjamin Beshor asne. of Jacob Cullers 60 A. in Hardy Co. in upper Cove, on Lost R. adj. George H. Lindemoot, N. Mt. 1 Nov 1817 [Dl'd Mr. Jacob Miller 24 Dec 1817]

B2-330: Surv. 23 Oct 1816 by T.W.5578=5 Feb 1816 Daniel McCoy 12 A. 2 Ro. in Berkeley Co. on Potomac R. adj. McPherson, Breim?, Robert Roach. 1 Nov 1817

B2-331: Surv. 8 Mar 1816 by T.W.4982=1 Dec 1812 Samuel Cockrill 131 A. in Hampshire Co. on Patterson's Cr. adj. Paw, Flanigan, Greenwell, his own land. 1 Nov 1817 [Dl'd Mr. Armstrong Feb 1819]

B2-332: Surv. 18 June 1816 268 A. 1 Ro. 23 Po. by Exg.T.W. 2216=15 May 1812 & 157 A. 3 Ro. 15 Po. by T.W.5665=16 May 1816 William Adams 426 A. 38 sq. Po. in Frederick Co. adj. his own land, Joseph Baker, Jacob Null called Hannah Cook Surv., Fen Fenton, on Isaac's Cr. of Back Cr., David Adams, John Evert, Patrick Reynolds dec'd, Peter Babb. 1 Nov 1817

B2-333: Surv. 18 Sep 1815 by Exg.T.W.2159=21 Feb 1812 Jacob Wartman asne. of

Charles Binns 9 A. 3 Ro. 3 Po. in Loudoun Co. on Potomac R. adj. land Colvill sold Fairfax now Jacob Wartman, Jacob Lowrey, Dutchman Run, Surv. made for Bazil Dever by Md., surv. for said Wartman by Md., Tankerville. 1 Nov 1817 [Dl'd Rob't Moffett 22 May 1818]

B2-334: Surv. 16 May 1813 60 A. by Exg.T.W.1021=23 Jan 1801 & 26 A. by T.W.4897=27 May 1812 Stephen Snodgrass 86 A. in Berkeley Co. on Back Cr. adj. said Stephen Snodgrass, Michael Pitzer, Andrew Paul, Richard Rigg, Richard Wood, Lowery. 1 Nov 1817 [Dl'd Mr. Israel Robertson at session of 1817'18]

B2-336: T.W.4745=24 May 1811 Peter Ruckman one moiety & as asne. of Jacob Ruckman the other moiety 39 1/4 A.(23 Mar 1812) in Hampshire Co. on Little Cacapehon adj. Steel, Ruckman. 30 Mar 1818 [Dl'd Mr. Gibson Sr. 7 Nov 1818]

B2-337: Surv. 28 Sep 1814 by T.W.5176=24 Jan 1814 Edward McCarty 63 A. in Hampshire Co. on Nobly Mt. adj. Means. 30 Mar 1818 [Dl'd W. Armstrong Feb 1819]

B2-338: Surv. 29 Nov 1816 by T.W.5722=10 Aug 1816 Charles Bruce 6 A. in Stafford Co. adj. Alexander, Newton. 10 June 1818 [Dl'd Jno. Taliaferro 11 Dec 1818]

B2-339: Surv. 17 Dec 1816 by T.W.5785=11 Nov 1816 Henry Carter 106 A. in Loudoun Co. adj. Janney now Dulaney, Benjamin Grayson, Thomas Dodd, Cox now Humphries. 10 June 1818

B2-340: Surv. 8 Jan 1816 by T.W.5544=22 Dec 1815 George Britton & Enos McRay 272 A. in Shenandoah & Culpeper Cos. on Blue Rg. adj. said McRay's purchase of Tobias Beam, Joseph Elliss, John Shenk, the Turnpike Rd., heirs of John Pettit dec'd. 10 June 1818 [By mail to Mr. James Modesitt 3 July 1818]

B2-341: Surv. 20 Mar 1816 by T.W.5552=30 Dec 1815 Frederick Decious & Richard Ransbottom 300 A. in Shenandoah Co. on Piney Mt. near Blue Rg. adj. John Griffy, John Freez, Adam Fox, Blackford, Arthur & Co., John Hockman. 10 June 1818 [By mail to Mr. James Modesitt 3 July 1818]

B2-343: Surv. 7 Aug 1816 by T.W.5509=25 Nov 1815 John W. Abbott 28 1/2 A. in Shenandoah Co. on Big line Run adj. George Kettick, David Dovel, John Carter. 10 June 1818 [Dl'd Mr. Wm. Anderson 26 Oct 1818]

B2-344: Surv. 15 Mar 1816 by T.W.4780=29 Oct 1811 John Oferbocher Jr. 190 A. in Shenandoah Co. at the Blue Rg. near little Hawksbill Cr. adj. John Snider, Peter Hays, John Fronk, George Ketick, Balie's Mt., Martin Kite, Henry Dealey. 10 June 1818 [Dl'd Mr. James Modesitt 3 July 1818]

B2-346: Surv. 10 Jan 1816 500 A. by T.W.4922=12 Aug 1812 & 8 1/2 A. by T.W.5544=22 Dec 1815 George Britton 508 1/2 A. in Shenandoah Co. at the Blue Rg. near Pass Run adj. James Barber, James Bryant, Tobias Beam, Jacob Beam, Enos McRay, Britton's mill dam, Britton formerly Christian Forrer, Philip Kibler, John Mundle, Wm. C. Williams. 10 June 1818 [Mr. James Modesitt 3 July 1818]

B2-349: Surv. 13 Sep 1815 by T.W.5419=1 July 1815 John Brumback 9 3/4 A. in Shenandoah Co. near Pass Run adj. Lewis Pence, said Brumback, Rd. from Lurdy to Thornton's Gap, Brumback now Blackford, Arthur & Co. 10 June 1818 [Dl'd Mr. James Modesitt 3 July 1818]

B2-350: Surv. 27 Feb 1816 by T.W.5552=30 Dec 1815 Frederick Decious 50 A. in Shenandoah Co. at the Blue Rg. adj. said Decious. 10 June 1818 [Dl'd Mr. James Modesitt 3 July 1818]

B2-351: Surv. 21 Feb 1816 by T.W.5419=1 July 1815 Frederick Decius 100 A. in Shenandoah Co. on Dry Run near the Blue Rg. adj. said Decius. 10 June 1818 [Dl'd Mr. James Modesitt 3 July 1818]

B2-353: Surv. 27 July 1815 by T.W.4813=18 Jan 1812 John Kyser 3 1/8 A. in Shenandoah Co. on S. R. of Shenandoah adj. said Kyser. 10 June 1818 [Mr. James Modesitt 3 July 1818]

B2-354: Surv. 30 Aug 1815 by T.W.212=23 Jan 1794 George Lowderman 7 A. in Hardy
Co. on N. Mill Cr. adj. Jesse Stump, Peter Lowderman, heirs of George Steffe,
Adam Steffle. 10 June 1818 [Dl'd Jesse Cunningham 9 Feb 1819]

B2-355: Surv. 11 Apr 1817 by T.W.5107=25 Aug 1813 Jacob Kackley 18 A. 27 sq.
Po. in Frederick Co. on Cedar Cr. adj. Samuel Vance, Michael Humble, his own
land. 10 June 1818 [Dl'd Mr. Barton 1 Mar 1824]

B2-357: Surv. 10 Apr 1817 by T.W.5107=25 Aug 1813 Jacob Kackley 7 A. 3 Ro. 18
sq. Po. in Frederick Co. on Cedar Cr. adj. Jacob Wolfe, Geo: Snapp, Michael
Humbert. 10 June 1818 [Dl'd Mr. Barton 1 Mar 1824]

B2-358: Surv. 9 Nov 1816 by Exg.T.W.1880=2 Jan 1807 Geo: Clevenger 46 A. 3 Ro.
3 Po. in Frederick Co. on Cedar Cr. adj. Joseph Fawcett, Sarah Zane, Thornbury,
Mordecai Whitestone. 10 June 1818 [Dl'd Mr. McComick 14 Oct 1818]

B2-359: Surv. 14 Aug 1816 by T.W.452=17 May 1794 John Haner 365 A. 1 Ro. 27 Po.
in Frederick Co. on Green Spring Run of Back Cr. adj. Smith now Bull, Dr. Bull's
purchase of Jno. Wright, Nathan Ross, Robert Powell, Wm. Penabaker, Richard
Morris. 10 June 1818 [Dl'd Mr. Magill Mar 1819]

B2-360: Surv. 16 Aug 1816 by T.W.5688=20 June 1816 John Wright 3 A. 1 Ro. 20
Po. in Frederick Co. on Back Cr. bet. Jacob Butler, Joseph Fenton, Thomas
Barett/Barrett, Chas. Street. 10 June 1818

B2-361: Surv. 2 Apr 1816 by Exg.T.W.1230=22 Jan 1802 William McCawly in his own
right for one moiety and asne. of Elias Clarke who was asne. of John S. Campbell
for the other moiety 9 1/2 A. in Frederick Co. adj. Jonathan Brown dec'd,
William Vance heirs now William Hoover, heirs of William Chepley dec'd on Lick
Run of Opeckon. 10 June 1818 [Dl'd Mr. Magill 11 Mar 1819]

B2-362: Surv. 8 May 1817 by T.W.5109=1 Sep 1813 William M. Wiley 100 A. in
Culpeper Co. on the Washington Rd. adj. Henry Rightenour, Gabriel Wiley, Lewis
Fosset, Peter Lawrence, Bird Eastham, George Haney, Wm. Lane. 10 June 1818
[26 Aug 1818 by mail to Gaines's X Roads, Culpeper, as by letter of 16 Apr 1818]

B2-363: Surv. 10 May 1817 by T.W.5778=30 Oct 1816 Samuel Baker 70 A. in
Culpeper Co. adj. Bird Eastham, Wm. M. Wiley, Farrow, John Morrison, George
Haney. 10 June 1818 [Dl'd Mr. Robert G. Ward 1 Nov 1820]

B2-364: Surv. 14 May 1817 by T.W.5188=7 Feb 1814 Charles Shackelford 319 A. in
Culpeper Co. on Peaked Mt. adj. Moses Gibson, John Warner, John Morrison,
Barbour. 10 June 1818 [Dl'd Maj. Roberts 15 Apr 1819]

B2-366: Surv. 13 May 1817 by T.W.5188=7 Feb 1814 Charles Shackelford 70 1/4 A.
in Culpeper Co. on Dade's R. adj. George Compton, Richard Jackson, Richard Duke,
John Morrison, Dade's Gap Rd. 10 June 1818 [Dl'd Maj. Roberts 15 Apr 1819]

B2-367: Surv. 26 Nov 1816 by T.W.4897=27 May 1812 Stephen Snodgrass 48 A. in
Berkeley Co. on Potomack R. adj. Joseph Forman, John Miller, said Snodgrass,
Adam Leppert. 10 June 1818 [Dl'd Israel Robinson 15 Dec 1818

B2-367: Surv. 14 Aug 1816 by Exg 1893=20 Jan 1807 John Monroe 50 A. in Hampshire
Co. on N. R. Mt. adj. Smith, Claton, his own land. 10 June 1818 [Mr. G. Cross
1 Nov 1819]

B2-368: Surv. 15 Oct 1816 by T.W.16,972=12 June 1783 William Catlett 41 A. in
Berkeley Co. on Middle fork of Sleepy Cr. adj. Stephenson, Bush, Ungar. 10 June
1818 [Dl'd Mr. Porterfield 15 Dec 1818]

B2-369: Surv. 25 Apr 1817 by T.W.5817=24 Dec 1816 Thomas Hall 122 A. in
Culpeper Co. adj. Samuel Slaughter, said Thomas Hall, Dr. Carter, Pittenger. 10
June 1818 [Dl'd to Prop'r by mail 24 July 1818]

B2-370: Surv. 4 Apr 1816 by T.W.5119=29 Oct 1813 John Young 66 A. in Hampshire
Co. on Great Capecapon adj. Harlan, his own land, Cornelious Free. 10 June 1818

[Dl'd John Sherrard 1 Feb 1821]

B2-371: Surv. 3 May 1817 by T.W.5586=12 Feb 1816 John Malic 29 1/2 A. in Hampshire Co. on Tear Coat Cr. of N. R. adj. his own land, Gen. John Brown conveyed to him by John Prunty, Ferren formerly Foxcraft & Thompson. 10 June 1818 [Mr. White Jan 1818]

B2-372: Surv. 7 Mar 1817 by T.W.5359=2 Mar 1815 Mark Finks 94 A. in Madison Co. adj. Maj. Jones, Dulaney, Landrum's run, Henry Jenkins. 10 June 1818 [Dl'd Mr. Barton 20 Oct 1818]

B2-373: Surv. 12 June 1816 by T.W.5562=18 Jan 1816 Samuel Dew 390 A.. in Hampshire Co. on S. Br. of Potomac adj. James Dailey, James & David Parsons, said Dew, on Sulivants & School House or Hanted Lick Runs, James Cunningham, Jonathan Purcell now James & David Parsons, James Daily originally Giles Sulivant now Isaac Kuykendoll, Nathan Kuykendoll. 10 June 1818 [Dl'd Mr. Gibson 7 Nov 1818]

B2-374: Surv. 24 Nov 1817 by T.W.212=23 Jan 1794 John Snyder 60 A. in Hardy Co. adj. Fouts heirs on Mud lick run of Cove Run of Lost R., Jacob Snyder. 1 Oct 1818 [Dl'd Mr. Machir 25 Jan 1819]

B2-375: Surv. 21 Aug 1817 by T.W.212=23 Jan 1794 Benjamin Besher 27 A. in Hardy Co. on Cove Run of Lost R. adj. Christopher Hatterman, Abraham Delawter, N. Mt. 1 Oct 1818 [Dl'd Mr. Jos. S. Spangler 6 Dec 1819]

B2-375: Surv. 26 Nov 1816 by T.W.2470=1 Feb 1798 Michael Roney 73 A. in Berkeley Co. on Cherry's Br. adj. said Roney's purchase of heirs of Alexander Smith, Compton's Bridge, Daniel Plotner, Barret. 1 Oct 1818 [Dl'd Mr. Porterfield 16 Dec 1818]

B2-376: Surv. 17 June 1817 by Exg.T.W.2235=25 Nov 1816 Capt. John Kelly 62 1/2 A. in Fauquier on Marsh Run adj. Thomas Hooper now Carter, Phillip Ludwell, said Kelly. 1 Oct 1818 [Dl'd Thos. Brown 21 Dec 1818]

B2-377: Surv. 14 June 1817 by T.W.5666=16 May 1816 William Adams 41 A. 2 Ro. 7 Po. in Frederick Co. adj. Samuel Strobridge, Martin Riley, Graham on Brush Cr. 1 Oct 1818 [Dl'd Mr. Sexton 3 Feb 1820]

B2-379: Surv. 8 Nov 1816 by T.W.4889=13 May 1812 John McKown 3 A. 1 Ro. 31 Po. in Berkeley Co. adj. Jacob Rees, David Rees, James Russell, Morgan, said John McKown. 1 Oct 1818 [Dl'd Israel Robinson 5 Dec 1818]

B2-379: Surv. 11 Aug 1816 200 A. by T.W.5077=20 May 1813 & 100 A. by T.W.5704=22 July 1816 Jesse Wood 300 A. in Shenandoah Co. on Gooney Run adj. Gooney Mannor at the Blue Rg., Isaac Overall. 1 Oct 1818 [Dl'd Mr. Hupp 20 Oct 189(1819)]

B2-381: Surv. 13 Aug 1816 by T.W.5704=22 July 1816 Jesse Wood 60 A. in Shenandoah Co. at the Blue Rg. adj. Benjamin Wood, Isaac Overall, heirs of John Young dec'd. 1 Oct 1818 [Dl'd Mr. Hupp 20 Oct 1819]

B2-382: Surv. 3 Jan 1817 by T.W.5806 =11 Dec 1816 Charles Humphrey 72 A. 1 Ro. 28 Po. in Stafford Co. adj. Robert Carter, Laurence Washington & Augustine Washington now Lewis Ficklen. 1 Oct 1818

B2-383: Surv. 13 June 1816 by T.W.4813=18 Jan 1812 Jacob Koverstine 10 A. in Shenandoah Co. in Powells Big Ft. on Passage Cr. adj. said Koverstine, Martin Walter, heirs of Mosses Siver dec'd. 1 Oct 1818 [Mr. Steinbarger 26 Dec 1818]

B2-384: Surv. 21 Mar 1817 by T.W.5409=2 June 1815 Absalom Rinker & Joshua Foltz Jr. 300 A. in Shenandoah Co. on Stoney Cr. & Narrow Passage Cr. adj. George Houdeshelt now John Gochenour, John Zimmerman formerly William Hough, John Arthur & Co. purchase of Exrs. of Isaac Zane dec'd, John Russell. 1 Oct 1818 [Dl'd Mr. Jos. S. Spangler 6 Dec 1819]

B2-385: Surv. 22 Feb 1816 by T.W.5140=7 Dec 1813 Daniel Munch 25 A. in Shenandoah Co. in Powell's Big Ft. on Passage Cr. adj. Adam Lechliter, said Munch,

Solomon Vanmetre, George Kniseley. 1 Oct 1818 [Dl'd Sam'l Bare 5 Dec 1821]

B2-386: Surv. 1 Nov 1817 by T.W.212=23 Jan 1794 Conrad Sager 34 A. in Hardy Co. on Cove Run of Lost R. adj. his own land, John Mathias/Matthias. 1 Oct 1818

B2-387: Surv. 18 Dec 1816 by T.W.5187=7 Feb 1814 Henry Menifee Jr. 30 A. in Culpeper Co. adj. Thomas Jones, Henry Menifee Sr. 1 Oct 1818

B2-387: Surv. 2 Oct 1815 by Exg.T.W.2168=5 Dec 1812 Joel Grayson 10 1/4 A. in Madison Co. adj. Andrew Gaar 1734 grant, heirs of said Gaar dec'd, Cook, George Tetor 10 Jan 1735 grant. 1 Oct 1818 [Dl'd Mr. Jos. S. Spangler 6 Dec 1819]

B2-388: Surv. 25 Aug 1817 by Exg.T.W.2237=5 Dec 1816 John L. Eastham 12 1/2 A. in Fauquier Co. adj. John Hudnall, Brown's Run. 1 Oct 1818 [Dl'd Mr. Allen 15 June 1819]

B2-389: Surv. 31 Dec 1816 by Exg.T.W.2229=16 Mar 1816 James & Andrew Bickers 6 A. in Madison Co. adj. Jonathan Pratt, Crooked Run. 1 Oct 1818 [Dl'd Rob't Hill 23 Feb 1819]

B2-390: Surv. 14 Dec 1816 by T.W.5528=11 Dec 1815 Thomas Buck 1 A. 70 Po. in Shenandoah Co. being an Island in S. fork of Shenandoah R. 1 Oct 1818 [Dl'd Mr. Magill 11 Mar 1819]

B2-391: Surv. 28 Mar 1817 by T.W.5826=3 Jan 1817 Daniel Lewis 8 A. 23 Po. in Hampshire Co. on Little Cacapehon, S. Br. Mt. adj. his own land, John Carder, Charles Powelson, Duncan now John Carder, Dobson now said Lewis. 1 Oct 1818 [Dl'd Mr. Armstrong Feb 1819]

B2-392: Surv. 6 Nov 1816 by 137 A. by T.W.5571=2 Feb 1816 & 227 A. by T.W.5775=29 Oct 1816 William Clark 364 A. in Hampshire Co. on Mill Run of Patterson's Cr. adj. Henderson, Gilpon, Chamberlane. 1 Oct 1818 [Dl'd Mr. Armstrong Feb 1819]

B2-393: Surv. 21 Feb 1817 by T.W.615=17 Sep 1794 Leonard Stump Jr. 63 A. in Hardy Co. on S. fork of S. Br., on Fork Mt., adj. said Stump, George Nave, John Stump. 1 Oct 1818 [Dl'd Mr. Leonard Neff 3 June 1823]

B2-394: Surv. 11 Sep 1817 by T.W.5902=to Edward McCarty & Co. 20 Feb 1817. Edward McCarty & James Dailey in Hampshire & Hardy Cos. 521 A. on Muddy Run Mt. & Pattersons Cr. Mt., Muddy Run or Furnace Run of Patterson's Cr. adj. Rawleigh Coulston, said McCarty, William Naylor, James Dailey, John McDowell, Alibar? Spring. 1 Oct 1818 [Dl'd Mr. Armstrong Feb 1819]

B2-395: Surv. 22 May 1816 by T.W.5571=2 Feb 1816 William Clark 43 A. in Hampshire Co. on Patterson's Cr. adj. William Clark Sr., William Leach. 1 Oct 1818 [Dl'd Mr. Armstrong Feb 1819]

B2-396: Surv. 14 Mar 1816 by T.W.5571=2 Feb 1816 William Pool 9 A. in Hampshire Co. on S. Br. of Potomac adj. Pennington Tuley, his own land. 1 Oct 1818 [Dl'd Mr. Armstrong Feb 1819]

B2-397: Surv. 4 Nov 1815 by T.W.15,198=6 Mar 1783 John Stoker 70 A. in Hampshire Co. on Little Capecapon adj. Dickens, his own land. 1 Oct 1818 [Dl'd Col. White 14 Feb 1820]

B2-398: Surv. 4 Nov 1815 50 A. by T.W.21,437=23 Dec 1783 & 34 A. by T.W.5065=21 Apr 1813 John Stoker 84 A. in Hampshire Co. on Little Capecapon adj. Higgins, Bolsor, Stoker, his own land. 1 Oct 1818 [Dl'd Col. White 14 Feb 1820]

B2-399: Surv. 10 Oct 1816 50 A. by T.W.5119=29 Oct 1813 & 50 A. by T.W.5572=2 Feb 1816 Alexander Poston 100 A. in Hampshire Co. on Tear Coat adj. Dunmore, Smith, Monroe. 1 Oct 1818 [Dl'd Col. White Jan 1820]

B2-400: Surv. 15 Oct 1816 by T.W.4672=20 Nov 1810 Garret W. Blue Jr. 146 A. in Hampshire Co. on S. Br. of Potomac adj. heirs of John Blue dec'd, Powellson, heirs of Uriah Blue dec'd. 1 Oct 1818 [Dl'd Col. Wm. Throckmorton 19 Feb 1823]

B2-401: Surv. 14 Mar 1816 by T.W.5571=2 Feb 1816 Abraham Pennington 23 A. in Hampshire Co. on Little Capacapon adj. Stroud, Pool, his own land. 1 Oct 1818 [Dl'd Mr. White Jan 1818]

B2-402: Surv. 18 Dec 1816 by T.W.5106=14 Aug 1813 William Gore 30 A. in Culpeper Co. on Wolf Mt. adj. Reubin Sims, James Miller, James Jones estate, Thomas Segg. 1 Oct 1818 [Dl'd George Ficklin 24 Feb 1820]

B2-403: Surv. 30 July 1817 by T.W.5775=29 Oct 1816 George Little 50 A. in Hampshire Co. on Riggs's Hollow a drain of N. R., N. R. Mt., Timber Mt. adj. Richard Wood, George Sharff. 1 Oct 1818 [Dl'd Mr. Armstrong Feb 1819]

B2-404: Surv. 21 Dec 1816 by T.W.5023=5 Feb 1813 Jacob Funkhouser(Stoney Cr.) 100 A. in Shenandoah Co. bet. Stoney Cr. & Stoney Cr. Rg., adj. said Funkhouser, Wendel Melcher, George Lonas. 1 Oct 1818 [Dl'd Wm. Page 17 Dec 1818]

B2-405: Surv. 5 Nov 1813 by T.W.1839=5 Mar 1796 Marshall Petty asne. of George Haywood Jr. 39 1/2 A. in Culpeper Co. adj. Robert Patton, Thomas Hall dec'd, said Haywood now Marshall Petty, Russel Vaughan, Mount Poney, Reubin Pierce formerly Inskeep. 1 Oct 1818 [Dl'd A. P.Hill 1 Dec 1818]

B2-406: Surv. 13 June 1817 by T.W.5209=15 Feb 1814 Joseph Evans 113 A. in Shenandoah Co. bet. Hawksbill Cr. & Mill Run, adj. George Rothgeb, heirs of Benjamin Ruffner dec'd. 28 Nov 1818 [Dl'd to Prop'r 5 Dec 1818]

B2-407: Surv. 9 Dec 1817 by Exg.T.W.2226=19 Feb 1816 Richard Coleman asne. of Charles Binns 35 A. 10 Po. in Loudoun & Fairfax Cos. adj. Carter, Fitzhugh. 1 Dec 1818 [Dl'd Mr. John Washton 30 Jan 1819]

B2-408: Surv. 3 Mar 1818 by Exg.T.W.2226=19 Feb 1816 Elizabeth Stocks, w. of William Stocks, & Stephen Sands asnes. of Charles Binns 10 A. in Loudoun Co. adj. reps. of late Jacob Sands, Cock now Hixon. 1 Dec 1818 [Mr. Rust 19 Feb 1829

B2-409: Surv. 20 Feb 1818 100 A. by T.W.6107=8 Dec 1817 & 50 A. by T.W.6147=22 Jan 1818 George Smith 150 A. in Frederick Co. adj. John Giffin, Jenkins, White, Robert Muse, said Smith, Romney Rd., Henderson. 1 Dec 1818 [Dl'd George Smith 16 Jan 1819]

B2-410: Surv. 14 May 1818 by Exg.T.W.2226=19 Feb 1816 Robert Mofett asne. of Charles Binns 47 1/2 A. in Loudoun Co. on Goose Cr. adj. Binks, Secolin Br., Carter now Oayter, Carter. 1 Dec 1818 [Dl'd Townsend McVay 2 Nov 1819]

B2-411: Surv. 21 Apr 1817 by T.W.5830=9 Jan 1817 Daniel Fink in his own right one moiety & as asne. of John Rankin the other moiety, 129 1/2 A. in Hampshire Co. on Patterson's Cr. adj. the manor belonging to Coulson, Thomas Carskaden who sold to said Rankin, Jesse Baine, Lewis Vandiver, Arthur Carskadon. 1 Dec 1818 [Dl'd Wm. Armstrong 14 Feb 1820]

B2-412: Surv. 13 Apr 1816 by T.W.5360=2 Mar 1815 Nimrod Jenkins 65 A. in Madison Co. adj. Stephen Jenkins on Rugged Mt., said Nimrod Jenkins. 10 Feb 1819 [Dl'd Linn Banks 9 Mar 1819]

B2-413: Surv. 10 Jan 1814 by T.W.4735=30 Apr 1811 Jonathan Hiett 10 A. in Hampshire Co. on N. R. adj. Jonathan Pugh, Even Hiett, John Martin. 10 Feb 1819 [Dl'd Mr. White Jan 1819]

B2-413: Surv. 7 Feb 1818 by T.W.4460=21 Mar 1808 Thomas Sedden 36 A. in Stafford Co. on Accokeek, near Mountjoy's old Mill path, adj. Sedden now Mitchel, Leachman now Mason, Mary James, Norman. 12 Apr 1819 [Mr. Ustice 14 May 1819]

B2-414: Surv. 10 Oct 1817 by T.W.5419=1 July 1815 Philip Kibler 10 1/2 A. in Shenandoah Co. on S. R. of Shenandoah, adj. Kibler, John Kizer. 12 Apr 1819 [Dl'd Mr. Hupp 20 Oct 1819]

B2-415: Surv. 20 Mar 1818 by Exg.T.W. 2232=1 Nov 1816 Joel S. Graves 85 A. in Madison Co. adj. Banks, Breading, on Harvey's Mt., heirs of William Harvey dec'd, said Graves. 12 Apr 1819 [Dl'd Linn Banks 11 Feb 1820]

B2-416: Surv. 9 Oct 1817 by T.W.5704=22 July 1816 George Prince Sr. 50 A. in Shenandoah Co. on Piney Mt. adj. John Kiblinger, Henry Prince, said George Prince, Jacob Koontz. 12 Apr 1819 [Dl'd Mr. Hupp 20 Oct 1819]

B2-417: Surv. 5 May 1817 by T.W.5552=30 Dec 1815 Benjamin Wood 327 A. in Shenandoah Co. bet. Ft. Mt. & S. R. of Shenandoah adj. said Benjamin Wood, John Wood, Hite & Co. now John Wood. 12 Apr 1819 [Dl'd Mr. Hupp 20 Oct 1819]

B2-418: Surv. 28 May 1816 by T.W.5274=19 Aug 1814 John Gatewood Sr. 500 A. in Shenandoah Co. bet. S. R. of Shenandoah & Ft. Mt. adj. Daniel Stover, land Isaac Strickler sold heirs of John Strickler dec'd, Daniel Kaufman. 12 Apr 1819 [Dl'd Dan'l Anderson 20 May 1823]

B2-419: Surv. 10 Dec 1815 37 A, by Exg.T.W.1831=13 Feb 1806 & 20 A. by T.W.4856=24 Feb 1812 John Flood 57 A. in Hampshire Co. on Patterson's Cr. adj. Alkier, Dunn, Dickins, Emberson. 12 Apr 1819 [Dl'd Mr. Heiskill 2 Nov 1820]

B2-420: Surv. 18 July 1817 T.W.5978=11 July 1817 in favor of John P. Duvall for benefit of Mrs. Elizabeth Tebbs ch. Grant to Thomas F. Tebbs, Foushee? Tebbs, Mary F. Spence, Margaret C. Triplett, Ann F. Duvall, Willougby Wm. Tebbs, & Samuel John Tebbs, only ch. of Mrs. Elizabeth Tebbs, 88 A. in Stafford Co. adj. Toleson, Nun's Br., George Smith, Brent Town Rd., heirs of Knox. 12 Apr 1819

B2-421: Surv. 10 Sep 1817 by T.W.5433=5 Aug 1815 Henry St.George Tucker 110 A. in Berkeley Co. adj. Abraham Vanmetre, Abraham Vanmetre Jr., Elizabeth Gibbons formerly James Watson, John Baker formerly John Markes, Strode, said Henry St.George Tucker. 12 Apr 1819 [Dl'd Proprietor 8 Feb 1820]

B2-422: Surv. 6 July 1818 by T.W.6013=14 Aug 1817 John Macrae 24 A. in Pr. William Co. adj. heirs of John Macrae dec'd., Wood, Golf now Trone, Hornsby. 1 June 1819 [Dl'd Gen. John Hunter 8 Feb 1820]

B2-423: Surv. 25 Aug 1818 92 1/4 A. by T.W.6166=5 Feb 1818 & 23 A. by T.W.6129=31 Dec 1817 Jacob Myers 115 1/4 A. in Hampshire Co. on Patterson's Cr. adj. his own land bought of John Hill Price, the Manor line, land Jacob Vandiver bought of Jacob Putman, Arjalon Price land sold by John Hill Price to said Myers. 1 June 1819 [Dl'd Wm. Armstrong Jr. 14 Feb 1820]

B2-424: Surv. 4 May 1816 40 A. by T.W.4873=26 Mar 1812 & 40 A. by T.W.4913=25 June 1812 John S. Kesler 80 A. in Hampshire Co. on Potowmac adj. Florah, Tidball, his own land, Easter. 1 June 1819

B2-425: Surv. 14 Apr 1818 by T.W.6039=14 Oct 1817 Idaiah Corbin Sen. 114 A. in Culpeper Co. adj. said Corbin, William Major, Green now Rice. 1 June 1819 [Dl'd George Ficklin 24 Feb 1820]

B2-426: Surv. 2 July 1816 100 A. by T.W.5571=2 Feb 1816 & 100 A. by Exg.T.W.992 =15 Dec 1800 John Rosebrough 200 A. in Hampshire Co. on Great Capecapon adj. Fry originally Woodfin, Rudolph, Huver. 1 June 1819 [Dl'd Philip Kline 1 Sep 1820]

B2-427: Surv. 10 Apr 1816 by T.W.5544=22 Dec 1815 George Britton Sr. 138 A. in Shenandoah Co. at the Blue Rg., adj. Pass Run, heirs of Hawksbill Martin Kauffman dec'd, Piercen Judd. 1 June 1819 [Dl'd Mr. Hupp 20 Oct 1819]

B2-428: Surv. 2 Apr 1816 by T.W.5544=22 Dec 1815 George Britton Sr. 43 1/2 A.in Shenandoah Co. on Blue Rg. adj. Joseph Elliss, Jacob Beam, Tobias Beam. 1 June 1819 [Dl'd Mr. Hupp 20 Oct 1819]

B2-429: Surv. 19 Aug 1817 by T.W.5704=22 July 1816 Abraham Spidler Jr. 7 3/4 A. in Shenandoah Co. on Little line Run adj. John Carter, Jacob Plume, John Nowman, John George. 1 June 1819 [Dl'd Mr. Hupp 20 Oct 1819]

B2-430:   Surv. 4 Dec 1816 by T.W.5552=30 Dec 1815 Abraham Spidler Jr. 150 A. in
Shenandoah Co. at the Round Head Mt. adj. Henry Aleshite, John Nowman, George
Hetich, John Kibler, John Snider. 1 June 1819 [Dl'd Mr. Hupp 20 Oct 1819]

B2-432:   Surv. 7 Nov 1816 by T.W.4295=2 Jan 1806 Samuel Thompson & Alexander
Doran 300 A. in Hampshire Co. on N. R. adj. Smith, Dunmore, Emmert, Doran,
Elkhorn Run. 1 June 1819 [Dl'd Mr. G. Cross 1 Nov 1819]

B2-433:   Surv. 6 June 1817 by T.W.5544=22 Dec 1815 Joel Finks 24 1/4 A. in
Shenandoah Co. on Little Hawksbill Cr. adj. said Finks, Martin Kite, Stoney Run,
George Hetick, Mill Mt. 1 June 1819 [Dl'd Mr. Hupp 20 Oct 1819]

B2-435:   Surv. 28 May 1817 by T.W.5704=22 July 1816 Peter Prince & Abraham
Prince 5 1/2 A. in Shenandoah Co. at Piney Mt. near Big Hawksbill Cr. adj. Henry
Prince, Balsor Sour, George Prince. 1 June 1819 [Dl'd Mr. Hupp 20 Oct 1819]

B2-436:   Surv. 26 Dec 1816 by T.W.5704=22 July 1816 Jacob Koontz 230 A. in
Shenandoah Co. on the Piney Mt. bet. the Blue Rg. & the little Hawksbill Cr.
adj. Peter Metz Sr., George Prince. 1 June 1819 [Dl'd Mr. Hupp 20 Oct 1819]

B2-437:   Surv. 3 Aug 1817 by T.W.5419=1 July 1815 John Miller 48 1/2 A. in
Shenandoah Co. at the Blue Rg. on Dry Run adj. Thomas Tuckwiller, Peter
Blausser, Philip Shaver, Frederick Decier, John Griffy. 1 June 1819 [see B2-436]

B2-439:   Surv. 25 Mar 1816 by T.W.4813=18 Jan 1812 John Shenks, son of Martin,
54 A. in Shenandoah Co. on Pass Run near the Blue Rg. adj. Martin Stumback, John
Hockman, John Alther bought of wid. Wilson & John Mundell. 1 June 1819 [Dl'd
Mr. Hupp 20 Oct 1819]

B2-441:   Surv. 30 Dec 1816 by T.W.5409=2 June 1815 Christian Bumgarner 187 A.
in Shenandoah Co. bet. the Massanetin Mt. & S. R. of Shenandoah adj. Enos McRay,
said Bumgarner, Elsie. 1 June 1819 [Dl'd Mr. Hupp 20 Oct 1819]

B2-443:   Surv. 15 May 1817 by T.W.5122=30 Oct 1813 Joshua Ruffner 500 A. in
Shenandoah Co. bet. S. R. of Shenandoah & Ft. Mt. adj. Reuben Long, the Turnpike
Rd., Isaac Strickler, James Barber. 1 June 1819 [Dl'd Mr. Hupp 20 Oct 1819]

B2-445: Surv. 1 Dec 1817 by T.W.5655=20 Apr 1816 Daniel Brown 95 A. in Culpeper
Co. adj. Barbour, Hot Mt. near Madison & Culpeper line, Benjamin Lillard,
Weakley, said Dan'l Brown. 1 June 1819 [Dl'd Daniel Brown 27 July 1819]

B2-447:   Surv. 14 Apr 1817 by T.W.4813=18 Jan 1812 George Sibert 31 3/4 A. in
Shenandoah Co. in Powell's big Ft. adj. said Sibert, Wm. Moredock, heirs of
Jacob Golliday. 1 June 1819 [Dl'd Mr. Hupp 20 Oct 1819]

B2-448: Surv. 28 Feb 1817 by T.W.5704=22 July 1816 Abraham Algiers 3 A. in
Shenandoah Co. bet. the Massanettin Mt. & S. R. of Shenandoah adj. Adam
Rineheart, said Algiers, James Barber. 1 June 1819 [Dl'd Mr. Hupp 20 Oct 1819]

B2-449: Surv. 17 May 1817 16 1/4 A. by T.W.5065=21 Apr 1813 & 25 A. by
T.W.5571=2 Feb 1816 John Cundiff 41 1/4 A. in Hampshire Co. on Mill Run of
Patterson s Cr. adj. Robert Jones, Fuller, Michael Kelly, his own land, John
Ward lately Robert Fuller dec'd, Knobly Mt., Samuel Jones grant of 10 Oct 1795.
1 June 1819 [Dl'd Wm. Armstrong Jr. 14 Feb 1820]

B2-451:   Surv. 23 Jan 1818 by T.W.6073=4 Nov 1817 John Singleton 150 A. in
Hampshire Co. on Middle Rg. & Patterson's Cr. adj. Andrew Lee heirs, George
Rineheart, James Randall, Fox's path, Hall. 1 June 1819

B2-453: Surv. 3 June 1814 by T.W.5070=17 May 1813 Leonard Barker 6 A. 1 Ro. 20
Po. in Fairfax Co. on Middle Run adj. Auberry, Hall now Lee, Thomas Simpson now
Windsor, Auberry now Windsor. 1 July 1819 [Dl'd Mr. Thompson 18 Feb 1820]

B2-454:   Surv. 26 Nov 1818 by T.W.6418=20 Nov 1818 Jared Williams Jr. & Otho S.
Williams 382 A. 2 Ro 5 Po. in Frederick Co. bet. Crooked Run & N. fork of
Shenandoah R. adj. Daniel Shambaugh, McKay, Ephraim Garrison, Jack's Br.,

87

William Hand, Samuel O. Hendren. 1 July 1819 [Dl'd Mr. Sexton 6 Dec 1820]

B2-457:   Surv. 29 Oct 1818 by T.W.4889=13 May 1812 Jacob Courtney 10 3/4 A. in Berkeley Co. on Sleepy Cr. adj. Rumsey, Gill, Tedrick, the Meadow Br., John Hickson. 1 July 1819 [Dl'd John Porterfield 8 Dec 1819]

B2-458:   Surv. 1 Sep 1817 by T.W.5438=18 Aug 1815 John Keyseeker 43 A. in Berkeley Co.. on Sleepy Cr. adj. John Fronk, Jacob Ash, Lancelot Jaques, R. Breetherd. 1 July 1819 [Dl'd Mr. John Sherrard 6 Dec 1823]

B2-460:   Surv. 16 Mar 1818 by Exg.T.W.2229=16 Mar 1816 John Ford 9 A. in Madison Co. 1 July 1819   [Dl'd Ro. Hill 12 Jan 1820]

B2-461:   Surv. 17 Oct 1816 by Exg.T.W.1017=23 Jan 1801 Adam Boarer 41 A. in Berkeley Co. on Middle fork of Sleepy Cr. adj. his other land, John Deck. 1 July 1819 [Dl'd John McCleary 2 Oct 1819]

B2-462:   Surv. 9 Apr 1817 by T.W.5688=20 June 1816 James Bean 7 A. 1 Ro. 20 Po. in Frederick Co. on Hog Cr. adj. his own land, Geo: Seicriest, Jacob Lavrick. 1 July 1819 [Dl'd Mr. Burton 1834]

B2-463:   Surv. 3 Sep 1817 by T.W.4801=23 Dec 1811 James Smith 9 A. in Berkeley Co. on Lick Run of Sleepy Cr. adj. Philip Stout heirs, Henry Schriver, Claycomb. 1 July 1819 [Dl'd John McCleary Jr. 29 Oct 1819]

B2-465:   Surv. 19 Oct 1818 by T.W.5832=9 Jan 1817 Elisha Boyd 27 1/2 A. in Berkeley Co. on N. Mt. adj. Henry Bishop surv. of 25 Oct 1788, said Boyd's 8 Oct 1797 surv., John Boyd 1776 grant. 1 July 1819 [Dl'd Jno Porterfield 8 Dec 1819]

B2-466:   Surv. 22 Apr 1818 by T.W.6184=18 Feb 1818 Robert V. Snodgrass 210 A. in Berkeley Co. on Rock Gap Run of Sleepy Cr., on Warm Spring Rg. adj. R. Gustin, William Smith heirs, Johnston, McKeainin. 1 July 1819 [Porterfield 8 Dec 1819]

B2-468:   Surv. 29 Sep 1817 by T.W.4517=2 Feb 1809 Edward O. Williams 19 A. 36 sq. Po. in Berkeley Co. adj. West's heirs, said Edward O. Williams, head of the Swam Pond. 1 July 1819 [Dl'd John McCleary Jr. 29 Oct 1819]

B2-469:   Surv. 20 Aug 1818 by Exg.T.W.1948=3 Feb 1808 Michael Pentony 52 A. 1 Ro. 26 Po. in Berkeley Co. on Sleepy Cr. adj. said Pentony, heirs of Pictall, Swim Jr., Luke Pentony. 1 July 1819 [Dl'd John Sherrard 4 Dec 1820]

B2-471:   Surv. 18 Sep 1818 by T.W.5359=2 Mar 1815 Allen Yowell 30 A. in Madison Co. adj. Allen Yowell, Elijah Yowell. 1 July 1819 [Dl'd Linn Banks 11 Feb 1820]

B2-472:   Surv. 19 Jan 1818 by T.W.5641=19 Mar 1816 Leonard Lonas Jr. 100 A. in Shenandoah Co. on Stony Cr. Rg. adj. Leonard Lonas, Abraham Sonnafrank. 1 July 1819 [Dl'd Mr. John Caldwell 6 Dec 1819]

B2-475:   Surv. 19 Oct 1818 by T.W.4801=23 Dec 1811 Elisha Boyd 7 A. in Berkeley Co. on N. Mt. adj. John Miller heirs, John McClean's 1794 surv., John Boyd's 1778 surv., said Elisha Boyd. 1 July 1819 [Jno Porterfield 8 Dec 1819]

B2-476:   Surv. 24 Nov 1818 by T.W.5977=11 July 1817 Abraham Hupp 4 A. in Shenandoah Co. on N. R. of Shenandoah adj. Henry Bushong. 1 July 1819 [Dl'd Mr. John Caldwell 6 Dec 1819]

B2-478:   Surv. 22 Sep 1818 by T.W.5209=15 Feb 1814 Joseph Evans 68 1/4 A. in Shenandoah Co. on Rd. from Luray to White House adj. John Basey. 1 July 1819

B2-479:   Surv. 30 June 1817 by T.W.5552=30 Dec 1815 Joseph Little asne. of Collen Mitchum 141 A. in Shenandoah Co. bet. S. R. of Shenandoah & Ft. Mt. adj. Joshua Ruffner. heirs of Isaac Strickler dec'd. 1 July 1819 [Dl'd Mr. Steenbergen 16 Dec 1819]

B2-481:   Surv. 14 Sep 1818 by T.W.5592=15 Feb 1816 Charles Check 22 A. in Pr. William Co. adj. Charles Cornwell, Ash, Dumfries Rd. 26 Oct 1819

B2-482: Surv. 14 Sep 1818 by T.W.5592=15 Feb 1816 Daniel Kincheloe 20 A. in Pr. William Co. adj. John Davis, said Daniel Kincheloe, Rutland Johnston, John Hammitt dec'd. 26 Oct 1819 [Dl'd Bernard Hooe 11 Feb 1820]

B2-483: Surv. 22 July 1816 25 A. by T.W.4602=8 Jan 1810 & 33 A. by T.W.4913=25 June 1812 Leonard Boncrotz alias Pumcrots 58 A. in Hampshire Co. on Mill Cr. adj. Vanmeter, his own land, Thrasher's Knob. 26 Oct 1819 [Wm. Armstrong Jr. 14 Feb 1820]

B2-484: Surv. 21 Apr 1818 by T.W.6227=9 Mar 1818 William Naylor 40 1/2 A. in Hampshire Co. on Knobs of Mill Cr. Mt. adj. Thomas Taylor's purchase of Kuykendall, said Naylor. 26 Oct 1819 [Wm. Armstrong Jr. 14 Feb 1820]

B2-486: Surv. 21 Apr 1818 55 A. by T.W.5286=1 Nov 1814 & 63 A. by 5572=2 Feb 1816 William Naylor 118 A. in Hampshire Co. on S. Br. Mt., S. Br. of Potomac adj. his purchase of heirs of George Beatty dec'd, his land originally Edward Snicker, Kuykendall Mill Run. 26 Oct 1819 [Dl'd Wm. Armstrong Jr. 14 Feb 1820]

B2-488: Surv. 6 Sep 1817 by T.W.4522=15 Jan 1809 Jacob Rinker 75 A. in Hampshire Co. on Crooked run of Little Cacapehon adj. Samuel Williamson's purchase of Matthew Brown originally John Higgins's, George Fletcher formerly Gasper Rinker, Richard Moreland originally Gasper Rinker, John Larramore, Jacob Rinker, Fletcher. 26 Oct 1819 [Dl'd Wm. Armstrong Jr. 14 Feb 1820]

B2-489: Surv. 7 Sep 1816 100 A. by T.W.4762=1 Aug 1811 & 14 1/4 A. by T.W.4842=18 Feb 1812 John Arbanathy 114 1/4 A. in Hampshire Co. on Alleghany Mt. adj. wid. Riley, his own land. 26 Oct 1819 [Dl'd Wm. Armstrong Jr. 14 Feb 1820]

B2-491: Surv. 13 Dec 1817 157 3/4 A. by T.W.5065=21 Apr 1813 & 100 A. by T.W.2478=26 May 1798 Abraham Criswell 257 3/4 A. in Hampshire Co. on Dillons Mt. inc. Poplar Spring adj. George Cales, Lupton Mill Rd., Short Mt. 26 Oct 1819 [Dl'd Mr. G. Cross 2 Nov 1819]

B2-492: Surv. 23 Mar 1818 by T.W.5902=20 Feb 1817 George Urice Jr., John Urice & Peter Urice 43 1/4 A. in Hampshire Co. on Cabbin Run of Patterson's Cr. adj. said George Urice's &c 255 A. bought of John Fleak, Samuel Dobbins, Robert Allen. 26 Oct 1819 [Dl'd Wm. Armstrong Jr. 14 Feb 1820]

B2-494: Surv. 31 Mar 1818 by T.W.5571=2 Feb 1816 Stephen Fuller 50 A. in Hampshire Co. on Mill Cr. adj. George Haines bought of Jacob High, Thomas Ingmyer bought of George Hains and sold to William Fuller, Bishop's land, George Liller?. 26 Oct 1819 [Dl'd Wm. Armstrong Jr. 14 Feb 1820]

B2-495: Surv. 28 Jan 1818 370 A. by T.W.5649=1 Apr 1816 & 140 A. by T.W.5903=20 Feb 1817 William Armstrong Jr. 510 A. in Hampshire Co. on Horse Shew Rg., Broad Run of Cabbin Run of Patterson's Cr. adj. Daniel Combs, John Culp, Wharton's land. 26 Oct 1819 [Dl'd Wm. Armstrong Jr. 14 Feb 1820]

B2-497: Surv. 24 Jan 1818 by T.W.5830=9 Jan 1817 Jacob Lees 68 A. in Hampshire Co. on Barton run of Patterson's Cr. adj. Thomas Hollenback heirs, Patrick Kirk now Dr. Edward Dyer heirs. 26 Oct 1819 [Dl'd Wm. Armstrong Jr. 14 Feb 1820]

B2-499: Surv. 13 Dec 1817 100 A. by T.W.4913=25 June 1812 & 50 A. by T.W.4873=26 Mar 1812 George Cale 150 A. in Hampshire Co. on Big Cacapehon on Cacapehon Mt. & Dillon's Mt. on Rd. from Winchester to Moorfield, adj. Abraham Criswell bought of Poston's heirs, Chriswell formerly Chenoweth, Cale's own land. 26 Oct 1819 [Dl'd Col. White 14 Feb 1820]

B2-500: Surv. 29 Jan 1818 100 A. by T.W.5065=21 Apr 1813 & 107 A. by T.W.5826=3 Jan 1817 Elisha Lyons 207 A. in Hampshire Co. on Horse shew Rg. adj. Michel Baker bought of Henry Purget, James Spencer formerly Hugh Murphy 1777. 26 Oct 1819 [Dl'd Wm. Armstrong Jr. 14 Feb 1820]

B2-501: Surv. 7 Jan 1818 by T.W.5571=2 Feb 1816 Richard Hall 7 A. in Hampshire Co. on middle Rg. of S. Br. Mt. & Little Cacapehon Mt. adj. his purchase of Joshua Calvill, 1788 patent of Hugh Murphy, original patent of Benjamin Ely

89

1778, Foxcroft. 26 Oct 1819 [Dl'd Mr. Throckmorton 11 Dec 1819]

B2-503: Surv. 19 Mar 1818 by T.W.5875=11 Feb 1817 Samuel Cockrel 62 1/2 A. in Hampshire Co. on Patterson's Cr. adj. Sarah Ann Wright, Robert Lockhart heirs, surv. not finished for Thomas Carskaddon in name of Arthur Carskaddon, Daniel Fink, John Rankin, his own land bought of Lewis Vandiver. 26 Oct 1819 [Col. White 25 Feb 1823]

B2-505: Surv. 20 Mar 1818 23 A. by T.W.5775=29 Oct 1816 & 6 A. by T.W.5571=2 Feb 1816 George Staggs 29 A. in Hampshire Co. on Patterson's Cr. adj. the Manor line, his own land, Rawlins. 26 Oct 1819 [Dl'd Wm. Armstrong Jr. 14 Feb 1820]

B2-506: Surv. 30 Mar 1818 by Exg.T.W.2100=8 Jan 1810 William Fuller asne. of George Hanes 50 A. in Hampshire Co. on Mill Cr. on S. Br. Mt. or knobs of Mill Cr. Mt. adj. George Liller, said Haines, Thomas Ingmyer, William Fuller. 26 Oct 1819 [Dl'd Wm. Armstrong Jr. 14 Feb 1820]

B2-507: Surv. 29 Aug 1817 by T.W.5775=29 Oct 1816 George Robins Tasker 19 A. in Hampshire Co. on Little Alleghany Mt., Pine Swamp Run adj. his 100 A. bought of Richard Wilson & 262 A. bought of Newman Beckwith, Robert Sinclair, resurv. by Daniel Lyons. 26 Oct 1819 [Dl'd Wm. Armstrong Jr. 14 Feb 1820]

B2-509: Surv. 24 Mar 1818 by T.W.5573=2 Feb 1816 George Hill 281 1/2 A. in Hampshire Co. on Putman's & Dry Runs of Patterson's Cr. adj. Buskirk, John Hill Price, Jacob Vandiver bought of Jacob Putman, Manor line, Arjalon Price now John Hill Price, Peter Cabrick, Deakins. 26 Oct 1819 [Wm. Armstrong Jr. 14 Feb 1820]

B2-511: Surv. 5 Aug 1818 by T.W.5826=3 Jan 1817 William Critton 50 A. in Hampshire Co. on Little Cacapehon Cr. adj. Jacob Sibert's heirs originally Drumgold now Stephen Calvin, Benjamin Stump. 26 Oct 1819 [Wm. Armstrong Jr. 14 Feb 1820]

B2-513: Surv. 10 Apr 1818 by T.W.212=23 Jan 1794 John Wilson 48 A. in Hardy Co. on Mill Run of Lost R. adj. his own land, George Wilkins. 26 Oct 1819 [Dl'd Jethro Nevill 19 Jan 1820]

B2-514: Surv. 10 June 1818 by T.W.212=23 Jan 1794 Asa Ships 36 A. in Hardy Co. on Br. Mt., main Rd. from Winchester to Moorefield, adj. Thomas Birch. 26 Oct 1819 [Dl'd Jesse Cunningham 19 Jan 1820]

B2-515: Surv. 14 Apr 1818 by T.W.5922=3 Apr 1817 Charles Lobb 51 A. in Hardy Co. on Fork Mt. & Grassy Knob adj. William Cunningham, Abel Seymour. 26 Oct 1819

B2-516: Surv. 23 Nov 1818 by T.W.5922=3 Apr 1817 Charles Lobb 111 A. in Hardy Co. on Town Ft. Run of S. Br. of Potomack adj. his own land, John G. Harness, heirs of Robert Giboney. 26 Oct 1819

B2-518 Surv. 2 Nov 1818 by T.W.5065=21 Apr 1813 John Cundiff 8 A. 33 Po. in Hampshire Co. on Mill Run of Patterson's Cr. adj. John Ward late Robert Fuller, heirs of Samuel Jones dec'd. 26 Oct 1819 [Dl'd Wm. Armstrong Jr. 14 Feb 1820]

B2-519: Surv. 17 Jan 1817 by T.W.4820=30 Jan 1812 Alexander Harper & John Smith 15 A. in Berkeley Co. on Tilehance's Br. adj. James Shield, Thomas Ellis, heirs of William Johnston. 26 Oct 1819 [Dl'd Maj. John Sherrard 3 June 1822]

B2-520: Surv. 19 Jan 1817 by T.W.4820=30 Jan 1812 Alexander Harper & John Smith 15 A. in Berkeley Co. on Tilehandes Br. adj. William Johnstons heirs, Isaac Compton, John Syler or Lyler. 26 Oct 1819 [Maj. John Sherrard 3 June 1822]

B2-521: Surv. 20 Mar 1818 by T.W.4889=13 May 1812 Alexander Harper 69 A. 3 Ro. in Berkeley Co. on Tilehance's Br. adj. James Shields, said Harper & John Smith, William Johnston heirs, Jacob Miller. 26 Oct 1819 [Dl'd Maj. John Sherrard 3 June 1822]

B2-523: Surv. 13 Feb 1816 by T.W.5560=12 Jan 1816 Achilles Rogers 26 A. 1 Ro. 17 Po. in Orange Co. at the Great Mt. adj. William Blakey, Piney Mt. (Grant improperly recorded in this book; recorded in the proper book. Tho. Mercer Clk.)

B2-524: Surv. 26 Feb 1817 by T.W.4617=7 Feb 1810 John Giffin 37 1/4 A. in Frederick Co. on Isaac's Cr. adj. White formerly Nutt, George Smith, William Garner, Jenkins, Romney Rd., John Stipe, Hampshire Co. line. 26 Oct 1819 [Dl'd Mr. Sexton 1 Feb 1821]

B2-525: Surv. 19 Sep 1811 by Exg.T.W.1794=12 Dec 1805 George Smith asne. of Enock Renno & Enock Jameson 29 1/4 A. in Fauquier & Stafford Cos. on Beaver Dam Run adj. Fitzhugh, Toalson, Butler, Renno & Jameson. 18 Dec 1819 [Dl'd Mr. Fox 31 Dec 1819]

B2-526: Surv. 19 Sep 1811 by Exg 1794=12 Dec 1805 George Smith asne. of Enoch Renno & Enoch Jameson 58 3/4 A. in Fauquier Co. on Beaver dam Run adj. William Phillips, said Renno & Jameson, Butler, Robertson. 18 Dec 1819 [Dl'd Mr. Fox 31 Dec 1819]

B2-528: Surv. 1 Mar 1816 by T.W.5509=25 Nov 1815 John W. Abbott 68 1/4 A. in Shenandoah Co. bet. S. R. of Shenandoah & Hawksbill Cr. adj. heirs of Benjamin Ruffner dec'd, Blackford & Co. purchased of Jonas Ruffner, heirs of (river) Martin Kaufman dec'd, John Basey, John Underwood. 20 Jan 1820 [Dl'd Joseph S. Pointer 2 Feb 1820]

B2-529: Surv. 6 Apr 1813 by T.W.615=17 Sep 1794 Joseph Yucker 234 A. in Hardy Co. on Mountain Run of N. R. adj. Jonathan Burch, Joseph Obannon, James Orme, Aaron Tucker. 20 Jan 1820 [Dl'd Jethro Nevill 7 Feb 1820]

B2-530: Surv. 29 Oct 1812 300 A. by T.W.4745=24 May 1811 & 26 A. by Exg.T.W.1997=3 Feb 1809 Jacob Barker 326 A. in Hampshire Co. on Mill Cr. & Middle Rg. on Rd. from Parker's to Mill Cr. adj. Tidball, Mills, his own land. 20 Jan 1820 [Dl'd Ephraim Dunn 19 Dec 1822]

B2-533: Surv. 29 Apr 1818 by T.W.5070=17 May 1813 George Simpson 18 A. in Fairfax Co. on Sandy Run adj. Faulkner, Turley, Jacobs. 1 Feb 1820 [Dl'd Mr. Thompson 18 Feb 1820]

B2-534: Surv. 28 Apr 1818 by Exg.T.W.1516=16 Dec 1803 Moses Simpson 27 A. 1 Ro. 28 Po. in Fairfax Co. on S. Run of Pohick adj. Richard Simpson, Joseph Simpson, Coffer, Ellzey, Huson. 1 Feb 1820 [Dl'd Mr. Thompson 18 Feb 1820]

B2-536: Surv. 18 Sep 1818 by T.W.6085=14 Nov 1817 Thomas Johnson 51 3/4 A. in Hampshire Co. on Great Cacapehon adj. Foxcraft. 1 Feb 1820 [By mail to Robert Sherrard, Hampshire, 16 June 1820]

B2-538: Surv. 25 Nov 1817 by T.W.5778=30 Oct 1816 William Brooke 7 A. in Culpeper Co. adj. said William Brooke, Joseph Ritenour formerly Conrad Darr, George Haynie, Bumer. 1 Feb 1820

B2-539: Surv. 26 Dec 1817 by T.W.6074=4 Nov 1817 James Cunnard 12 1/2 A. in Hampshire Co. on Big Cacapehon and Sidling Hill adj. his own land originally granted William Demoss, Henry Bruner originally Elisha Cogle, John Matthews now Bruner. 1 Feb 1820 [Col. White 14 Feb 1820]

B2-540: Surv. 17 Sep 1818 by T.W.4808=13 Jan 1812 Robert Sherrard 166 1/2 A. in Hampshire Co. on Three Spring Mt., Chestnut Spring Run of Big Cacapehon adj. Foxcraft, Thompson, said Sherrard, 2 tracts of Bloomery land now William Naylor, one was patented to John Brown & other to Robert Rutherford, James Leith, Ralph, William Wilson, John Brown. 1 Feb 1820

B2-543: Surv. 8 June 1818 by T.W.6157=29 Jan 1818 Samuel Foreman 15 1/4 A. in Hampshire Co. on Edwards's Mt. adj. Thomas Edwards's heirs, Francis White Esq. bought of James Hiett, Benjamin Slane originally Henry Batten, s'd Foreman, George Foreman, Rd. from Winchester to Romney, Ellis. 1 Feb 1820 [Dl'd Col. White 14 Feb 1820]

End Book B2 1812-1820

C2-1: Surv. 26 Jan 1818 by T.W.5065=21 Apr 1813 Samuel Totten 47 A. in Hampshire Co. on Patterson's Cr. near Johnsons Mill adj. his own land, Watts, Hassel, Cabbin Run Rg., Boardman. 1 Feb 1820 [Dl'd Col. White 14 Feb 1820]

C2-1: Surv. 24 Nov 1817 by T.W.5586=12 Feb 1816 Henry Topper 125 A. in Hampshire Co. on Bear Garden or Owens Rg. & Big Cacapehon adj. James McBride, Joseph Abril, Frederick Buzzard, Thomas Allen bought of Thomas McBride & Joel Ward, his own surv., his purchase of James McBride. 1 Feb 1820 [Col. White 14 Feb 1820]

C2-3: Surv. 24 Nov 1817 by T.W.5775=29 Oct 1816 Henry Topper 12 A. in Hampshire Co. on Big Cacapehon adj. his land bought of James McBride, Thomas Allen bought of Thomas McBride & Joel Ward, Trout Hole. 1 Feb 1820 [Col. White 14 Feb 1820]

C2-4: Surv. 1 May 1818 by 6166=5 Feb 1818 Cunrad Menser 1 A. 18 Po. in Hampshire Co. on Maple run of N. R. adj. his own land, Sylvanus Bennet heirs, Wharton heirs. 1 Feb 1820 [Dl'd F. White 14 Feb 1820]

C2-4: Surv. 30 Apr 1818 by T.W.5826=3 Jan 1817 John Pepper Jr. & Henry Pepper asne. of Addison McCauley otherwise called McCalley or Key's land 21 A. 2 Ro. 22 Po. in Hampshire Co. on Bear Wallow Run of Tare Coat Cr. adj. James McFarlin bought from Cunningham, George Myers bought of Jacob Myers, Baker's land and his own land now Jacob Pepper, Cooper. 1 Feb 1820 [Dl'd Col. White 14 Feb 1820]

C2-5: Surv. 1 May 1818 by T.W.6166=5 Feb 1818 Michael Short asne. of Rees Pritchard 11 A. 3 Ro. 6 Po. in Hampshire Co. on Crooked run of Little Cacapehon & Gibbon's Run of N. R. adj. Cunrad Menser, William Philips, Isaac Heizkell, Thomas Slane, George Sharff. 1 Feb 1820 [F. White 14 Feb 1820]

C2-6: Surv. 1 May 1818, 16 3/4 A. by T.W.4735=30 Apr 1811 & 16 3/4 A. by T.W.6166=5 Feb 1818 Jonathan Pugh 33 1/2 A. in Hampshire Co. at confulence of N. R. & Tear Coat Cr. adj. his own land, John Pepper Jr., John Baker, John Pepper Sr. 1 Feb 1820 [Dl'd Col. White 14 Feb 1820]

C2-8: Surv. 2 Oct 1817 by T.W.5571=2 Feb 1816 Mary Combs asne. of Samuel Foreman in his own right one moiety & of John Foreman, David Foreman, Henry Foreman, said Samuel Foreman, Mary Foreman, Catherine Foreman, Margaretts Foreman & Abylona called Abelone Foreman heirs of Jacob Foreman dec'd the other moiety 12 3/4 A. in Hampshire Co. on Round Knob & Cold Stream of Big Cacapehon adj. heirs of John Combs dec'd bought of William McPherson, Benjamin Slane, said Samuel Foreman, Jacob Foreman heirs. 1 Feb 1820 [Dl'd Col. White 14 Feb 1820]

C2-9: Surv. 21 May 1816, 50 A. by T.W.5571=2 Feb 1816 & 16 A. by 4762=1 Aug 1811 John H. Price 66 A. in Hampshire Co. on Patterson's Cr. adj. his own land. 1 Feb 1820 [Dl'd Mr. Throckmorton 14 Feb 1820]

C2-9: Surv. 9 Sep 1818, 40 A. by 6324=6 July 1818 & 71 1/2 A. by 6295=8 June 1818 Jonathan Burch 111 1/2 A. in Hampshire Co. on Town Gap Run by Romney, S. Br. Mt., adj. Aaron Ashbrook now Moses Pettit, said Jonathan Burch, John Foreman Sr., Buffaloe Run, Rd. from Romney to Winchester. 1 Feb 1820 [Dl'd Mr. Throckmorton 14 Feb 1820]

C2-11: Surv. 27 Nov 1817 by T.W.5817=24 Dec 1816 William Wallis 36 A. in Culpeper Co. on Potato Run adj. said Wallis, James Hansbrough, Edward Voss sold Charles Bruce now said Hansbrough, Gen. James Williams, John Wharton, John Cox. 18 Feb 1820 [Dl'd A. P. Hill 21 Feb 1820]

C2-12: Surv. 12 Feb 1819 by T.W.4982=1 Dec 1812 David Corbin 2 A. in Hampshire Co. on Little Cacapehon adj. Robert French, William Wilson, s'd Corbin, Rd. from Romney to Winchester, Corbin, Kearan. 18 Feb 1820 [Mr. Armstrong 30 Nov 1824]

C2-12: Surv. 6 Apr 1819 by T.W.4889=13 May 1812 David Hunter 54 sq. Po. in Berkeley Co. on Opeckon Cr. adj. William Rush, said David Hunter, Hoover. 18 Feb 1820 [Dl'd Jno. Porterfield 6 Dec 1820]

C2-13: Surv. 26 Mar 1819 by T.W.6375=5 Oct 1818 William Sherrard 58 A. in Hampshire Co. on Bloomery Run of Big Capcapehon adj. Foxcraft, Thompson, Joseph Johnson. 18 Feb 1820 [Dl'd the prop'r 11 May 1820]

C2-13: Surv. 4 Mar 1819 by T.W.6144=20 Jan 1818 John Gochenour 200 A. in Shenandoah Co. on Narrow Passage run, gap of Little N. Mt. adj. George Houdeshelt now s'd Gochenour. 18 Feb 1820 [Mailed prop'r, Woodstock in Shenandoah 30 Apr 1820]

C2-14: Surv. 6 May 1819 by T.W.5641=19 Mar 1816 Isaac Keys & Joseph Fawcett 10 A. in Shenandoah Co. on S. R. of Shenandoah, adj. Abraham Strickler, heirs of Isaac Strickler dec'd, Philip Swyger now heirs of Isaac Strickler dec'd, Joseph Strickler. 18 Feb 1820

C2-15: Surv. 12 Nov 1816 by Exg.T.W. 1024=23 Jan 1801 Samuel Rankin asne. of William Rankin 60 A. in Berkeley Co. on Sleepy Cr. adj. Fitzhugh, said Rankin, Elisha Boyd. 18 Feb 1820 [Dl'd Wm B. King 30 May 1820]

C2-16: Surv. 12 Nov 1816 by Exg.T.W.1024=23 Jan 1801 Samuel Rankin asne. of William Rankin 48 A. in Berkeley Co. on Sleepy Cr. adj. E. Boyd Esq., William Rankin, Joseph Duckwall. 18 Feb 1820 [Dl'd Wm B. King 30 May 1820]

C2-17: Surv. 18 Apr 1818 by T.W.4801=23 Dec 1811 John Powell 3 A. 2 Ro. in Berkeley Co. adj. Obed Noland, Nathan Ross, John Yeats. 18 Feb 1820 [Dl'd Jos. Grantham 4 Dec 1820]

C2-17: Surv. 18 Apr 1818 by T.W.4801=23 Dec 1811 John Powell 8 1/2 A. in Berkeley Co. adj. John Powell, Obed Noland, Nathan Ross. 18 Feb 1820 [Dl'd Jos Grantham 4 Dec 1820]

C2-18: Surv. 17 & 18 Apr 1818 by T.W.4801=23 Dec 1811 John Powell 73 A. in Berkeley Co. on N. Mt. adj. Pennybaker, Obed Noland, Andrew Waggoner's heirs, James Barton. 18 Feb 1820 [Dl'd Joseph Grantham 4 Dec 1820]

C2-19: Surv. 22 Mar 1819 by T.W.6145=20 Jan 1818 Joseph Johnson 166 A. in Hampshire Co. on Bloomery run of Big Capcapen near foot of High Top Mt. adj. the Bloomery land. 1 Apr 1820 [Dl'd Mr. Vance 19 Jan 1833]

C2-19: Surv. 10 June 1819 by T.W.6227=9 Mar 1818 William Naylor 248 1/4 A. in Hampshire Co. on Bloomery Run called Enoch's mill Run of Big Cacapehon adj. Bloomery land formerly William Heath dec'd now William Naylor(viz: 400 A. formerly Robert Rutherford 1772 grant, 391 A. also Rutherford & 240 A. patented to Isaac Zane), Robert Sherrard's mill, Foxcraft, Thompson, Joseph Tidball sold Heath. 1 Apr 1820 [Dl'd Mr. Christopher Heiskell 1 Jan 1824]

C2-20: Surv. 27 Mar 1819 by T.W.6241=2 Apr 1818 David Ellis 35 A. in Hampshire Co. on Edwards's Mt. adj. Isaac Hollingworth, Foreman, Thomas Edwards. 1 Apr 1820 [Mailed Ro. Sherrard, Hampshire Co. 16 June 1820]

C2-21: Surv. 18 June 1819 by T.W.6406=5 Nov 1818 David Ellis 175 A. in Hampshire Co. on Big Capcapehon adj. Peter Shinholt, Francis White, Joseph Yeats, Copass. 1 Apr 1820 [Dl'd Mailed Robert Sherrard Hampshire Co. 16 June 1820]

C2-22: Surv. 19 June 1819 by T.W.6085=14 Nov 1817 Thomas Johnson 18 1/4 A. in Hampshire Co. on Big Capcapehon adj. his late surv., Foxcroft. 1 Apr 1820 [Forwarded to Robert Sherrard, Hampshire Co. 16 June 1820]

C2-22: Surv. 20 Jan 1819 by T.W.6132=8 Jan 1818 Francis Dunnington 1 A. in Pr. William adj. Town of Dumfries, Macrae. 12 May 1820

C2-23: Surv. 11 June 1818 by T.W.5641=19 Mar 1816 George Baily 23 1/4 A. in Shenandoah Co. at the Blue Rg. adj. John Kibler Jr., John Snider, Little Hawksbill Cr., Peter Hay. 12 May 1820 [Dl'd Mr. Sam'l Anderson 31 Oct 1820]

C2-23: Surv. 23 Jan 1818 by T.W.5704=22 July 1816 Elizabeth Koontz, Noah Koontz, Rebecca Koontz & Nancy Koontz 128 3/4 A. in Shenandoah Co. on Piney Mt. near the Blue Rg. adj. Frederick Huffman, Jacob Koontz, George Prince, Samuel

Hershberger, heirs of David Leonberger dec'd. 12 May 1820 [Mr. Jno Colvlle]

C2-24: Surv. 16 Oct 1817 by T.W.5704=22 July 1816 Benjamin Cave & George Tiller 192 1/2 A. in Shenandoah Co. at the Blue Rg. adj. heirs of Joseph Roads Sr. dec'd, Joseph Browning, John Kiblinger, George Hetick. 12 May 1820 [Dl'd Mr. Sam'l Anderson 31 Oct 1820]

C2-25: Surv. 29 May 1818 by T.W.5544=22 Dec 1815 George Kizer 400 A. in Shenandoah Co. bet. Ft. Mt. & S. R. of Shenandoah adj. William Elzie, Christian Bumgarner, Andrew McKay or McRay, Samuel Odell. 12 May 1820 [Dl'd Mr. Sam'l Anderson 31 Oct 1820]

C2-26: Surv. 27 July 1819 by T.W.5526=11 Dec 1815 John W. Green 1/2 A. in Culpeper Co. adj. John W. Green on Summerduck run, Freeman. 12 May 1820 [Dl'd the Prop'r 21 Jan 1821]

C2-26: Surv. 5 Oct 1819 by T.W.6664=8 June 1819 Garrett Wynekoop 4 A. 3 Ro. 10 sq.Po. in Berkeley Co. adj. heirs of Adrian Wynekoop, Henry Orndorff, Jephtha Martin, Huffman, Levi Martin. 12 May 1820 [Dl'd Mr. Daniel Morgan 11 Jan 1828]

C2-27: Surv. 30 May 1816 by T.W.961=11 Dec 1794 Abraham Spidler Jr. 5 3/4 A. in Shenandoah Co. bet. Mill run & Hawksbill Cr. adj. Abraham Rothgeb, Abraham Spidler Sr., Jacob Strickler. 12 May 1820 [Dl'd Mr. Sam'l Anderson 31 Oct 1820]

C2-27: For $44.00 Francis Smith Lot No. 81 in town of Dumfries in Pr. William Co. that escheated to Commonwealth 14 Apr 1808 for defect of heirs of Francis Rice dec'd. 13 June 1820

C2-28: James Hayes for $258.00 140 A. (commonly called Grays) in Pr. William Co. that escheated 14 Apr 1808 for defect of heirs of Francis Rice dec'd. 13 June 1820 [Dl'd Jas. E. Heath 23 Apr 1821]

C2-28: For $34.00 Thomas Chapman Lots No. 9 & 10) in town of Carrborough in Pr. William Co. escheated 15 May 1808 by defect of heirs of Christopher Russell dec'd. 13 June 1820

C2-29: Surv. 18 Jan 1819 by T.W.627=22 May 1818 Thomas Fouch asne. of Isaac Wright 7 3/4 A. in Loudoun Co. adj. Hollifield, Hugh Caldwell, Rev. Amos Thomson dec'd. 13 June 1820 [Dl'd Fayette Ball 14 Dec 1820]

C2-29: Surv. 25 Nov 1818 by T.W.5641=19 Mar 1816 Reuben Long 50 A. in Shenandoah Co. on S. R. of Shenandoah adj. said Long, George Koontz, Collan Mitcham. 17 Aug 1820 [Dl'd Moses Walton 7 Dec 1820]

C2-30: Surv. 20 Aug 1819 by T.W.6664=8 June 1819 Robert Snodgrass Jr. 50 A. in Berkeley Co. on Back Cr. adj. said Robert Snodgrass, Jacob French or Jordan's heirs, Jacob Snider, William Runner. 17 Aug 1820

C2-31: Surv. 1 May 1819 by T.W.6114=10 Dec 1817 William Harmanson 5 1/4 A. in Berkeley Co. on Sleepy Cr. adj. Henry Claycomb, Dr. Lancelot Jaques, Schriver, Claycomb formerly Miller. 17 Aug 1820 [Dl'd Jas. Porterfield Dec 1820]

C2-32: Surv. 12 May 1819 by Exg.T.W.2256=20 Aug 1817 Paul Taylor 237 A. in Berkeley Co. on Back Cr. adj. James McGowan, Duning, Grist, Little Mt., Smith, Gray, Stephenson, Townson, Riley. 17 Aug 1820 [Dl'd Mr. Joel Ward 30 Dec 1820]

C2-33: Surv. 8 June 1818 by T.W.212=23 Jan 1794 Francis Godlop 78 A. in Hardy Co. on N. R., Bucks hill adj. his own land, Nicholas Moore, Spring run. 17 Aug 1820 [Dl'd Francis White 1 Mar 1821]

C2-34: Surv. 17 June 1819, 50 A. by T.W.5826=3 Jan 1817 & 50 A. by 4611=29 Jan 1810 William Alderton 100 A. in Hampshire Co. on Potomac adj. his own land, James Allender, Abraham Branson. 17 Aug 1820 [Dl'd Francis White 1 Mar 1821]

C2-35: Surv. 17 Nov 1819, 30 A. by T.W.6241=2 Apr 1818 & 5 A. 1 Ro. 19 Po. by 6661=7 June 1819 Dade Powell asne. of Robert Sherrard 35 A. 1 Ro. 19 Po. in

Hampshire Co. on Big Rg. of Big Cacapehon Mt. partly surv'd by Samuel Dew, adj. John Harnes bought of John Darby, Thomas Allen bought of John Bond, land left Thomas McBride by his father, said Powell bought of James Leith, his land bought of William Higgins. 17 Aug 1820 [Dl'd Francis White 1 Mar 1821]

C2-36: Surv. 16 Nov 1819 by T.W.6662=7 June 1819 Robert Harrison asne. of Dade Powell 35 1/2 A. in Hampshire Co. on Big Capcaphon adj. Frederick Buzzard, Abril formerly Foxcraft, Harrison, Barney Belford. 17 Aug 1820 [Mr. Vance 19 Jan 33]

C2-36: Surv. 14 Sep 1816 by T.W.4672=20 Nov 1810 Peter Bruner 49 1/2 A. in Hampshire Co. on Great Capecapon adj. Harlan, Hall, Ziler, his own land, Thompson. 17 Aug 1820 [Dl'd Jno Sherrard 1 Feb 1821]

C2-37: Surv. 14 Jan 1819 by T.W.5826=3 Jan 1817 Elisha Gulick 6 A. 2 Ro. 18 Po. in Hampshire Co. on Bear Wallow run of Tear Coat Cr. adj. his land bought of Thomas Nicholson formerly Jacob Keizner, Richard Trouton formerly Philip Price, James Gallaway, Barney Kearan, Martin Shafer. 17 Aug 1820 [F. White 1 Mar 1821]

C2-38: Surv. 8 Apr 1819 by T.W.5065=21 Apr 1813 Daniel Bruner 41 1/4 A. in Hampshire Co. on Big Capcapen Cr. adj. said Bruner, Noah Larew, Abraham Larew, Joseph Right. 17 Aug 1820 [Dl'd John Sherrard 1 Feb 1821]

C2-39: Surv. 6 Aug 1816 by T.W.4982=1 Dec 1812 Benjamin Stump 69 A. in Hampshire Co. on Little Capecapon adj. Sherewood, heirs of Peter Stump dec'd. 17 Aug 1820 [Dl'd F. White 1 Mar 1821]

C2-40: Surv. 12 June 1819 by Exg.T.W.2280=7 Nov 1818 Robert M. Powell 7 A. 36 Po. in Hampshire Co. on Rocky Rg. near Bear Garden, adj. Frederick Co., Nathan Litler bought of Owing Rodgers, Stacy Biven & wife, his own bought of Page as agent for Robert Ferran. 17 Aug 1820 [Dl'd Francis White 1 Mar 1821]

C2-41: Surv. 14 June 1819 15 A. by T.W.5572=2 Feb 1816 & 35 A. by T.W.6512=1 Feb 1819 Henry Fauver 50 A. in Hampshire Co. on Sidling Hill, adj. Pendleton, Nicholas Fauver. 17 Aug 1820 [Dl'd Francis White 1 Mar 1821]

C2-41: Surv. 2 Oct 1819 by T.W.6074=4 Nov 1817 James Summervill 14 A. 31 Po. in Hampshire Co. on Bloomery Run of Big Cacapehon, adj. Winchester to Frankfort Rd., Abraham Weaver, said Summervill, Nathan Litler, Robert Rodgers, Peter Ogan, Ephraim Miller or John Weaver, Joseph Stone. 17 Aug 1820 [F. White 1 Mar 1821]

C2-42: Surv. 9 Apr 1819 by T.W.6241=2 Apr 1818 Daniel Slain 50 A. in Hampshire Co. on Heath's gap run of Big Capcapehon adj. Roice heirs, land formerly Kitchelo. 17 Aug 1820 [Dl'd F. White 1 Mar 1821]

C2-43: Surv. 13 May 1819 by T.W.6151=26 Jan 1818 William Grant 38 A. in Hampshire Co. on Little Capcapehon & Brushy Rg. adj. Bruin, Murphy, Arnold, Wilson. 17 Aug 1820 [Dl'd F. White 1 Mar 1821]

C2-44: Surv. 31 Dec 1817 by T.W.5572=2 Feb 1816 Nicholas Fauver 100 A. in Hampshire Co. bet. Sidling hill & Rd. Rg. adj. Henry Fauver formerly Archibald Wiggins, Philip Pendleton, Michael McUan, McDonald, James Watson. 17 Aug 1820 [Dl'd F. White 1 Mar 1821]

C2-45: Surv. 29 Dec 1817 by T.W.5572=2 Feb 1816 William Neely 146 A. in Hampshire Co. on Kanolaway Hill & Long Hollow of Potomack adj. heirs of Thomas Williams dec'd, lands of Brown called the Quaker's Surv., Cornelius Ferree. 17 Aug 1820 [Dl'd Mr. Ignatius O'Ferrel 14 Feb 1823]

C2-46: Surv. 12 Apr 1819 by T.W.5572=2 Feb 1816 William Neely 24 A. in Hampshire Co. on Big Capcapehon adj. heirs of Zedekiah Williams, Dawson. 17 Aug 1820 [Dl'd Mr. Ignatius O'Ferrel 14 Feb 1823]

C2-47: Surv. 12 July 1816 by T.W.4982=1 Dec 1812 Peter Mauzey Jr. 46 A. in Hampshire Co. on Great Capecapon adj. Frederick Buzzard, Jacob Kerns, Walter Wilson, Peter Mauzey Sr. 17 Aug 1820 [Dl'd F. White 1 Mar 1821]

C2-47: Surv. 26 Nov 1819 by T.W.6512=1 Feb 1819 Samuel Dobbins 100 A. in Hampshire Co. on Sheets run of Patterson's Cr. below Okey Johnson formerly Michael Sheets. 17 Aug 1820 [Dl'd Wm. Armstrong Dec 1820]

C2-48: Surv. 16 Apr 1819 by T.W.6443=15 Dec 1818 Benjamin Hull 41 1/4 A. in Hampshire Co. bet. N. & S. fork of Mike's run of Patterson's Cr. adj. his land, James Harrison formerly John Cundiff. 17 Aug 1820 [Mr. Armstrong 6 Dec 1820]

C2-49: Surv. 5 Oct 1819, 200 A. by T.W.6521=1 Feb 1819 & 80 1/4 A. by T.W.6662=7 June 1819 Thomas Welch 280 1/4 A. in Hampshire Co. on Cabbin Run Rg. adj. John Nesbet. 17 Aug 1820 [Dl'd Ephraim Dunn Dec 1821]

C2-50: Surv. 9 Nov 1818, 30 A. by T.W.5065=21 Apr 1813, 32 A. by T.W.5176=24 Jan 1814 & 60 1/4 A. by T.W.6166=5 Feb 1818 Arthur Carskadon & Thomas Carskadon 122 1/4 A. in Hampshire Co. on Patterson's Cr. adj. heirs of Thomas Carskadon dec'd now John Rankin, George Stagg, said Arthur Carskadon. 17 Aug 1820 [Dl'd Mr. Armstrong 6 Dec 1820]

C2-51: Surv. 18 June 1819 by T.W.6512=1 Feb 1819 Samuel Cockrell 7 A. in Hampshire Co. on Patterson's Cr. adj. Nicholas Paugh originally Christian Long, Samuel Cockrell formerly George Beard, Joseph Long. 17 Aug 1820 [Dl'd Mr. Armstrong 6 Dec 1820]

C2-52: Surv. 27 Mar 1819 by T.W.5875=11 Feb 1817 Daniel Leatherman 37 A. 3 Ro. in Hampshire Co. on Middle run of Paterson's Cr. adj. hiers of Benjamin Rawlings dec'd, Paterson's Cr. Manor, George Stagg, Peter Rawlngs. 17 Aug 1820 [Dl'd Mr. McCarty 24 Feb 1821]

C2-53: Surv. 20 Apr 1819 by T.W.6241=2 Apr 1818 Thomas Johnson 70 A. in Hampshire Co. on Big Capcapehon adj. Lewis Largent, Foxcroft, Abraham Dawson. 17 Aug 1820 [Mailed Robert Sherrard 13 Feb 1821]

C2-53: Surv. 16 Mar 1819 by T.W.6295=8 June 1818 John Huff 60 A. in Hampshire Co. on Big Capcapehon adj. said Huff, John Hardy, Henry Bruner. 17 Aug 1820 [Dl'd Rob't Sherrard 13 July 1821]

C2-54: Surv. 19 Apr 1819 by T.W.6406=5 Nov 1818 John Allen 50 A. in Hampshire Co. on Big Capcapehon adj. Copsey, his own land. 17 Aug 1820 [Dl'd Rob't Sherrard 13 July 1821]

C2-55: Surv. 24 Nov 1819, 203 3/4 A. by Exg.T.W.2280=7 Nov 1818 & 51 1/2 A. by T.W.6662=7 June 1819 Hanson Catlett 255 1/4 A. in Hampshire Co. on Horse Shoe Rg., Bone lick Hollow of Patterson's Cr. adj. William Armstrong. 17 Aug 1820 [Dl'd Ephraim Dunn 19 Dec 1822]

C2-56: Surv. 16 Jan 1819 by T.W.5065=21 Apr 1813 Michael Baker 21 A. in Hampshire Co. on George's Run of Paterson's Cr. adj. Richard Baker, heirs of Kile, his own land bought of John McBride. 17 Aug 1820 [Dl'd Mr. Vance 19 Jan 1833]

C2-57: Surv. 14 Jan 1819 by T.W.6074=4 Nov 1817 Elijah Lyons 66 A. in Hampshire Co. on George's Run of Paterson's Cr., Knobley Mt. adj. Elisha Lyons, his own surv. 17 Aug 1820

C2-57: Surv. 9 Aug 1819 by T.W.6284=1 June 1818 John Hoye 80 1/2 A. in Hampshire Co. on N. Br. of Potomack adj. George Calmes, George Gilpin, Christian Musselman. 17 Aug 1820 [Dl'd Throckmorton Jan 1821]

C2-58: Surv. 27 Jan 1819 by T.W.6166=5 Feb 1818 Warner Throckmorton 12 1/2 A. in Hampshire Co. on N. Br. of Potomack adj. heirs of Evan James dec'd. 17 Aug 1820 [Dl'd Warner Throckmorton 24 Jan 1821]

C2-59: Surv. 23 June 1819 by T.W.6073=4 Nov 1817 Okey Johnson 200 A. in Hampshire Co. on Middle Rg. & Patterson's Cr. adj. Catharine Johnson, Adam Hall, John Singleton, Fox's path. 17 Aug 1820 [Dl'd Mr. McCarty Feb 1821]

C2-60: Surv. 5 May 1819 by T.W.6295=8 June 1818 Joseph Meekins & James Meekins

250 A. in Hampshire Co. bet. Town Hill & Little Capcapehon adj. Steed now Sterrit, Meekins, Hopkins's Lick Run, James Meekins. 17 Aug 1820 [Dl'd Warner Throckmorton 24 Jan 1821]

C2-61:   Surv. 1 Sep 1819 by T.W.6072=4 Nov 1817 Vause Fox asne. of Willim Fox 100 A. in Hampshire Co. on S. Br. Mt. bet. Hanging rocks gap & Mill Cr. gap adj. said William Fox, Edward Taylor, Isaac Engle.   17 Aug 1820 [Dl'd Warner Throckmorton 24 Jan 1821]

C2-62:   Surv. 3 Oct 1819 by T.W.5418=29 June 1815 Henry Strider 14 A. in Jefferson Co. said to be ungranted (but now occupied by the United States with large Buildings), near Potomac R. 17 Aug 1820 [Dl'd Mr. Lackland 25 Aug 1820]

C2-62:   Surv. 1 Oct 1819 by T.W.5418=29 June 1815 Henry Strider 21 A. 1 Ro in Jefferson Co. adj. Robert Harper, Potowmac R., George Compton, United States Canal. 17 Aug 1820 [Dl'd Mr. Lackland 25 Aug 1820]

C2-63:   Surv. 2 Oct 1819 by T.W.5418=29 June 1815 Henry Strider 13 A. 21 Po. ungranted (but now occupoied by United States and large workshops) in Jefferson Co. near Potowmac R., adj. Robert Harper, mouth of Shenandoah, United States Canal. 17 Aug 1820 [Dl'd Mr. Lackland 25 Aug 1820]

C2-64: Surv. 18 Nov 1819 by T.W.6724=25 Oct 1819 Jesse Cunningham 78 A. in Hardy Co. near Sugar Loaf adj. James Cunningham. 17 Aug 1820 [Mr. Nevill 11 Jan 1822]

C2-64: Surv. 3 Sep 1819, 50 A.by Exg.T.W.2131=12 Feb 1811 & 50 A. by T.W.5721=10 Aug 1816 William C. Sexton asne. of John Hutchinson 100 A. in Frederick Co. on Isaac's Cr. adj. John Routt. 17 Aug 1820 [Dl'd Mr. Sexton ? Dec 1820]

C2-65: Surv. 15 Nov 1819 by T.W.6724=25 Oct 1819 John Welton 23 A. in Hardy Co. on N. Fork adj. heirs of Peter Buffenberger, Valentine Powers.   17 Aug 1820 [Dl'd Mr. Machir 6 Dec 1820]

C2-66: Surv. 16 Nov 1819 by T.W.6724=25 Oct 1819 Jacob Sites 92 A. in Hardy Co. on S. Mill Cr. adj. his land, Michael Alkier Jr., Solomon Alkier, John Roraboh, Frederick Sites, Peter Pettleyon. 17 Aug 1820 [Dl'd Christian Simon 5 Dec 1820]

C2-67:   Surv. 25 Aug 1819 by T.W.6324=6 July 1818 John Stoker 100 A. in Hampshire Co. on Little Cacapehon, adj. said Stoker bought of Isaac Cox, John Critton, Kesler. 17 Aug 1820 [Dl'd F. White 14 Mar 1821]

C2-68:   Surv. 16 Nov 1819 by T.W.6724=25 Oct 1819 George Lindemoot 33 A. in Hardy Co. on Upper Cove Run of Lost R. adj. his own land, Nicholas Bearly. 17 Aug 1820 [Dl'd Mr. Machir 6 Dec 1820]

C2-69:   Surv. 16 Nov 1819 by T.W.6724=25 Oct 1819 Joseph Walker 161 A. in Hardy Co. on N. Fork of Patterson's Cr. adj. Jacob Bishop, his land bought of James Thares, George Gilpin, Thomas B. Overton. 17 Aug 1820 [John Lewis 10 Oct 1820]

C2-70:   Surv. 16 Nov 1819 by T.W.6724=25 Oct 1819 Andrew Russell 155 A. in Hardy Co. adj. his own land, Joseph Vanmeter. 17 Aug 1820 [Dl'd Mr. Machir 6 Dec 1820]

C2-70:   Surv. 30 Aug 1815 by T.W.212=23 Jan 1794 Michael Ault 4 A. in Hardy Co. adj. N. Mill Cr. Leonard Hagler, s'd Ault. 17 Aug 1820 [Mr. Nevill 5 Dec 1823]

C2-71:   Surv. 9 June 1818 by T.W.212=23 Jan 1794 Joseph Buckley 83 A. in Hardy Co. on N. R. & Spring Lick Rg. adj. his own land, Thomas Marshall, Tommie's lick hollow. 17 Aug 1820 [Dl'd Mr. Nevill 5 Dec 1823]

C2-72:   Surv. 16 Nov 1819 by T.W.6724=25 Oct 1819 Philip Switzer 64 A. in Hardy Co. on Lost R. adj. his own land, Jeremiah Inskeep, Joseph Gohonour heirs, Thomas Wilson, George Hulver. 17 Aug 1820 [Dl'd Mr. Machi 6 Dec 1823]

C2-73:   Surv. 17 Nov 1819 by T.W.6724=25 Oct 1819 Thomas Moore 105 A. in Hardy Co. adj. his own land on Great Capcapen, Benjamin Moore. 17 Aug 1820 [Dl'd Mr. Machi 6 Dec 1823]

C2-73: Surv. 17 Nov 1819 by T.W.6724=25 Oct 1819 Thomas Moore 60 A. in Hardy Co. adj. his own land, Great Capcapen, Benjamin Moore. 17 Aug 1820 [Dl'd Mr. Machi 6 Dec 1823]

C2-74: Surv. 21 Nov 1819 by T.W.6724=25 Oct 1819 Robert Masters, Elizabeth Bean, Cloe Bean, Trefeny Masters, Diana Masters, Mary Masters, William Masters, & Cassa Masters, heirs at Law to Ezekiel Masters dec'd. 63 A. in Hardy Co. on Skagg's Run of N. R. adj. Thomas Marshall, Thomas Davis, Isaac Vanmeter, James Bean. 17 Aug 1820 [Dl'd Mr. Machi 6 Dec 1823]

C2-75: Surv. 24 Nov 1819 by T.W.6724=25 Oct 1819 Thomas Wilson (of Maryland) 188 A. in Hardy Co. on Big Run of Patterson's Cr. adj. Peter Babb, heirs of Felix Welton dec'd. 17 Aug 1820 [Dl'd John Lewis 30 Oct 1820]

C2-76: Surv. 23 Nov 1819 by T.W.6724=25 Oct 1819 John Smith 142 A. in Hardy Co. on Joseph Vanmeter's Mill Run adj. Mitchell & High. 17 Aug 1820 [Dl'd Mr. Machi 6 Dec 1823]

C2-76: Surv. 3 May 1817 by T.W.5057=2 Apr 1813 Frederick Sower 50 A. in Shenandoah Co. near Blue Rg., on Dry Run of Hawksbill Cr. adj. John Comer, Andrew Hoffman. 17 Aug 1820 [Dl'd Moses Walton 7 Dec 1820]

C2-77: Surv. 16 Apr 1819, 50 A. by T.W.6324=6 July 1818 & 42 A. by T.W.6443=15 Dec 1818 Henry Pool 92 A. in Hampshire Co. on Corn's run otherwise called Mill Run & N. fork of Mike's Run of Patterson's Cr. adj. his own land bought of John Cundiff Jr., John Matthews. 7 Dec 1820 [Dl'd Mr. Armstrong 7 Dec 1820]

C2-78: Surv. 30 Apr 1818, 10 A. by T.W.5070=17 May 1813 & 35 A. 3 Ro. by Exg.T.- W.1516=16 Dec 1803 Moses Simpson 45 A. 3 Ro. in Fairfax Co. on Occoquan adj. George Simpson, Falkner, Carter, Jacobs. 7 Dec 1820 [James Sangster 15 Dec 1820]

C2-79: Surv. 21 Dec 1816, 500 A. by T.W.5442=29 Aug 1815 & 200 A. by T.W.5380=10 Apr 1815 Joseph Lewis asne. of Francis Whitely & Elijah Arnold 700 A. in Cul- peper Co. adj. Russell's Mt. Spencer Withers, Joseph Lewis, John Finnell, Little R., Daniel Compton, Clem Hasty. 20 Dec 1820 [Dl'd Philip Slaughter Dec 1820]

C2-80: Surv. 27 Nov 1819 by T.W.6295=8 June 1818 John Martin 17 1/2 A. in Hampshire Co. on N. Br. of Potomack adj. George Mason heirs, John Hoye, Charles Ravenscraft, Martin, 20 Dec 1820 [Dl'd Col. King 11 Dec 1823]

C2-82: Surv. 20 May 1819, 70 A. by T.W.5187=7 Feb 1814 & 40 A. by T.W.5106=14 Aug 1813 George N. Ralls & Jonah Hollingsworth asne. of William Gore 110 A. in Culpeper Co. on Piney R. adj. Thomas Jones, Garret, William Yates. 8 Jan 1821 [Enclosed to prop'r 9 Jan 1821]

C2-83: Surv. 19 Mar 1818, 102 A. by T.W.4982=1 Dec 1812, 121 A. by T.W.4913=25 June 1812, 59 3/4 A. by T.W.4291=2 Jan 1806 & 214 1/4 A. by T.W.5876=11 Feb 1817 Sarah Ann Wright, Robert Lockhart Wright & Rebecca Margery Wright 497 A. in Hampshire Co. on Pattterson's Cr. adj. William Rees, John Murphy, Samuel Cockrell's purchased of Lewis Vandiver. 6 Feb 1821 [Dl'd Mr. McCarty Feb 1821]

C2-84: Surv. 15 June 1819 by T.W.4831=4 Feb 1812 Aaron Harlin asne. of Michael Widmyer 18 A. in Hampshire Co. on Big Capcapehon adj. Harlin's land, Thomson, said Widmyer, Hoy. 6 Feb 1821 [Dl'd Maj. Jno Sherrard 3 June 1822]

C2-84: Surv. 10 Mar 1820 by T.W.5359=2 Mar 1815 Richard P. Kinsey 15 A. in Madison Co. adj. Zachariah Lewis 13 Sep 1756 patent, on S. fork of Staunton R., Fork Mt., Joshua Bush, McDaniel. 6 Feb 1821 [Dl'd to receipt 1834]

C2-85: Surv. 19 May 1820 by T.W.6865=25 Feb 1820 Benjamin Graves 525 A. in Madison Co. adj. Mark Stowers 1753 grant, Staunton R., Isaac Smith 1752 grant, Elias Powell 1749 grant. 6 Feb 1821

C2-86: Surv. 17 May 1820 by T.W.6865=25 Feb 1820 Benjamin Graves 49 A. in Madison Co. adj. said Graves, heirs of Churchnill Eddins dec'd, Terrell's bluff. 6 Feb 1821 [Dl'd Alx'r Graves 23 May 1821]

C2-86: Surv. 27 May 1820 by T.W.6865=25 Feb 1820 Asa W. Graves 23 A. in Madison Co. adj. Joel Eddins, said Graves. 6 Feb 1821 [Dl'd G. Hindman 2 May 1827]

C2-87: Surv. 6 Nov 1819 by T.W.6724=25 Oct 1819 John Hagerty of Georgetown, D.C. 104 A. in Hardy Co. on Thorn Run adj. his own land, William Hersha, heirs of George Gilpin, James Harrass/Harris. 1 Mar 1821 [Dl'd Mr. Geo. Cock 25 Mar 1825]

C2-88: Surv. 29 July 1819 by T.W.5703=22 July 1816 John Garewood 1100 A. in Shenandoah Co. on Ft. Mt., adj. land formerly Collin's, said Gatewood, Marye, Elzie, Andrew Kizer. 1 Mar 1821 [Dl'd Mr. Moses Walton 13 Dec 1823]

C2-90: Surv. 24 May 1820, 100 A. by T.W.5123=30 Oct 1813 & 300 A. by T.W.5413=21 June 1815 William B. Overall 400 A. in Shenandoah Co. on Flint run near the Blue Rg. adj. Manor land, Moses Henry, Mrs. Job, James Barbour, Gimblet Mt., Mathes's Arm Mt., Elijah Roy, Edward Laurence, Conner, James Blackwood. 1 Mar 1821 [Dl'd Mr. Rob't Allen 3 Dec 1822]

C2-91: Surv. 3 Sep 1819 by T.W.5552=30 Dec 1815 Martin Alther 72 A. in Shenandoah Co. at the Blue Rg. adj. Frederick Alther, Piercen Judd, Philip Shaver, Frederick Decier, Martin Stumback. 1 Mar 1821 [Mr. Moses Walton 13 Dec 1823]

C2-92: Surv. 20 July 1819, 75 A. by T.W.5544=22 Dec 1815 & 80 A. by 5944=24 May 1817 Martin Stumback 155 A. in Shenandoah Co. on Blue Rg. adj. said Stumback, Frederick Alther, John Hockman. 1 Mar 1821 [Dl'd Mr. Moses Walton 13 Dec 1823]

C2-93: Surv. 6 Sep 1819 by T.W.5704=22 July 1816 Daniel Spidler 4 1/4 A. in Shenandoah Co. bet. Mill Run & Hawksbill Cr. adj. Abraham Spidler Sr., Groves. 1 Mar 1821 [Dl'd Mr. Moses Walton 13 Dec 1823]

C2-94: Surv. 1 Apr 1820 by T.W.6695=31 Aug 1819 Cuthbert Harris two tracts in Fauquier Co. on Rappahannock R. 13 A. 3 Ro. (Lot 1) adj. George Turbeville, & 7 A. 1 Ro.(Lot 2) adj. said Turbeville. 14 Apr 1821 [Forwarded to D. Briggs of Fredkb'g by Robt Stananrd Esq.]

C2-95: Surv. 5 Oct 1819 by T.W.6512=1 Feb 1819 William Calmes 47 1/4 A. in Hampshire Co. on S. Br. of Potomack adj. land of said William & George Calmes, Peter Williams, Quarry Run. 14 Apr 1821 [Mr. Throckmorton 1822]

C2-95: Surv. 11 May 1819 by T.W.4994=11 Dec 1812 Henry Everheart 188 A. in Berkeley Co. on Third Hill Mt. adj. Baker of Winchester, heirs of Scott, Rinerfelt now Wolford, Elisha Boyd. 15 May 1821 [Dl'd Levi Henshaw Dec 1822]

C2-96: Surv. 20 June 1819 by T.W.4994=11 Dec 1812 Henry Everheart 27 A. in Berkeley Co. on Rock Spring Run adj. James Robinson, Henry Riner, Peter Jones, Elk Rg., Thomas Robinson. 15 May 1821 [Dl'd Levi Henshaw Dec 1822]

C2-97: Surv. 13 Aug 1819, 342 A. 2 Ro. 14 Po. by Exg.T.W.1948=3 Feb 1808 & 77 A. 1 Ro. 26 Po. by T.W.4889=13 May 1812 Michael Pentony 420 in Berkeley Co. on Sleepy Cr. adj. land formerly Feilds, John Householder, Luke Pentony, E. Lowman, Michael Pentony, John Heckson. 15 May 1821 [Dl'd Maj. John Sherrard 20 Nov 1821]

C2-98: Surv. 8 June 1820 by T.W.6775=29 Dec 1819 William Heath 2000 A. in Hardy Co. on Patterson's Cr. Mt. adj. James Miles, heirs of Morris Thomas, on Coler's knob, Wm. Cornwall, Jacob Willis, Abel Seymour, Michael Daicie, Morgantown Rd., heirs of Peter Reaves, Adam Harness, heirs of Felix Welton, James Miles Buzzard & Orr tracts, heirs of John Bishop. 15 May 1821 [Dl'd J. Niville 8 Dec 1823]

C2-100: Surv. 30 Oct 1819 by T.W.5817=24 Dec 1816 Thomas Hall 3 7/8 A. in Culpeper Co. adj. said Hall, Russel Vaughan, Bishop. 15 May 1821 [Dl'd Mr. William Smith 3 June 1821]

C2-101: Surv. 23 Nov 1819, 50 3/4 A. by Exg.T.W.2280=7 Nov 1818 & 102 3/4 A. by T.W.6662=7 June 1819 Simon Taylor 153 1/2 A. in Hampshire Co. on Hog Lick Run of S. Br. of Potomack adj. his own land. 15 May 1821 [Dl'd Haskiel 6 Mar 1823]

C2-102: Surv. 25 Nov 1819, 37 A. by T.W.5527=2 Feb 1816 & 62 A. by T.W.6662=7

June 1819 John Flood 99 A. in Hampshire Co. on Plumb & Turner Runs of Patterson Cr. adj. his own land, Turner. 15 May 1821 [Dl'd Ephraim Dunn 4 Dec 1821]

C2-102: Surv. 3 May 1819 by T.W.5433=5 Aug 1815 John Powell 598 A. in Berkeley Co. on Brush Cr. of Back Cr. adj. Sleepy Cr. Mt., James McGowan, Paul Taylor, Little Mt., Riley, Pack Horse Rd. 30 July 1821 [By mail to prop'r White Hall Frederick Co.]

C2-103: Surv. 3 May 1819 by T.W.5433=5 Aug 1815 John Powell 90 A. in Berkeley Co. on Back Cr. adj. Taylor, McGowan, Pack Horse Rd., Douglas, Morrow, Dunning. 30 July 1821 [By mail to prop'r White Hall Frederick Co.]

C2-104: Surv. 4 Oct 1820 by T.W.6724=25 Oct 1819 Valentine Cooper 10 A. in Hardy Co. adj. his own land, heirs of Jacob Landers, on S. Mill Cr. 30 July 1821 [Dl'd Jacob Miller 5 July 1822]

C2-105: Surv. 4 Oct 1820 by T.W.6724=25 Oct 1819 Valentine Cooper 57 A. in Hardy Co. on S. Fork Mt. adj. David & James Morrow. 30 July 1821 [Dl'd Jacob Miller 5 July 1822]

C2-105: Surv. 8 Mar 1820 by T.W.6631=5 Apr 1819 Alfred D. Ashby 41 A. in Frederick Co. bet. Manor of Leeds, Lewis Ashby's heirs & land Benjamin Ashby sold Thomas Shepherd now Shepherd's heirs. 30 July 1821

C2-106: Surv. 3 June 1820 by T.W.5826=3 Jan 1817 James Kelsoe asne. of Absalon Davis 300 A. in Hampshire Co. on Leanam's Br. of Big Cacapehon adj. James Kelsoe, Henry Stephens, Philip Cline, Kelsoe's Mill Rd. 30 July 1821 [Dl'd Mr. Throckmorton 7 Feb 1822]

C2-107: Surv. 28 Mar 1820 by T.W.6512=1 Feb 1819 John Rankin 100 A. in Hampshire Co. on Sheetz Run of Patterson's Cr. adj. Jacob Reasoner, Major Cooper, path from Rankin's to Cabbin Run, Benjamin Ayres, land conveyed from Dayton to John Snyder and from his Exrs. to Okey Johnson, Samuel Dobbins. 30 July 1821

C2-107: Surv. 8 June 1820 by T.W.5775=29 Oct 1816 Abraham Plumb 50 A. in Hampshire Co. on Falling Run of Big Cacapehon adj. Henry Stephens formerly George Reid, Joseph Clutter, his own land bought from David Tullis formerly Jacob Clutter. 30 July 1821 [Dl'd Mr. Throckmorton 7 Feb 1822]

C2-108: Surv. 10 Aug 1820, 240 A. by T.W.6163=2 Feb 1818 & 300 A. by Exg.T.W. 2337=27 Jan 1820 George Hebner 540 A. in Shenandoah Co. on Sraight Br. of Mill Cr., Suppenlick Mt. adj. Samuel Watt purchase of Henry Moats?, said Hebner, George Lonas, John Sheetz formerly heirs of Catharine Reder dec'd, Henry Hottel formerly Rinehart Cofman. 30 July 1821 [Dl'd Moses Walton 7 Dec 1821]

C2-109: Surv. 15 Nov 1819, 50 A. by T.W.6074=4 Nov 1817, 50 A. by T.W.6295=8 June 1818 & 28 3/4 A. by T.W.6662=7 June 1819 William B. Leach 128 3/4 A. in Hampshire Co. on Cabbin Run of Patterson's Cr., Cabbin Run Rg. adj. Abraham Good, Benjamin Bailey, Peter Leatherman, Brushy Rg. 30 July 1821 [Dl'd Mr. Wm. Armstrong 21 Dec 1822]

C2-110: Surv. 14 June 1819 by T.W.5058=2 Apr 1813 Moses Walton 18 A. in Shenandoah Co. near Smith's Cr. adj. Rudolph Kagy, Joseph Strickler, said Moses Walton, Jacob Houser. 30 July 1821 [Dl'd Moses Walton 7 Dec 1821]

C2-111: Surv. 10 Jan 1820 by T.W.5641=19 Mar 1816 John Kagy(s. of Jacob) 18 3/4 A. in Shenandoah Co. on Smith Cr. adj. Jacob Kagy, Daniel Brennaman, Benjamin Pennybacker. 30 July 1821 [Dl'd Moses Walton 7 Dec 1821]

C2-112: Surv. 13 Dec 1819 by T.W.5142=7 Dec 1813 George Biller 267 A. in Shenandoah Co. on Mill Cr. adj. John Holver, said Biller, Little N. Mt., Daneil Walters. 30 July 1821 [Dl'd Moses Walton 7 Dec 1821]

C2-113: Surv. 14 Dec 1819 by T.W.5142=7 Dec 1813 George Biller 133 A. in Shenandoah Co. on Mill Cr. adj. said Biller, John Holver, Elk Lick Hollow, Patrick Okenlan, Jacob Runion, Timber Rg., Bear Run, Biller's purchase of Rupp.

30 July 1821 [Dl'd Moses Walton 7 Dec 1821]

C2-114:   Surv. 30 Sep 1820 by T.W.5057=2 Apr 1813 Jacob Koverstone Sr. 26 A. in
Shenandoah Co. in Powells Big Ft. on S. R. of Shenandoah adj. his other land,
Ellzey, David Clem. 30 July 1821 [Dl'd Moses Walton 7 Dec 1821]

C2-115:   Surv. 30 Aug 1820 by T.W.5057=2 Apr 1813 Jacob Koverstone Sr. 65 A. in
Shenandoah Co. in Powell's Big Ft. on S. R. of Shenandoah adj. Michael Clem,
William Ellzey, John Shenk. 30 July 1821 [Dl'd Moses Walton 11 Dec 1821]

C2-116:   Surv. 9 Oct 1820 by T.W.6724=25 Oct 1819 Joseph Hill 56 A. in Hardy Co.
on Spring Lick Rg. near N. R. adj. Thomas Marshall, his own land, Joseph
Bulkley, James Orm. 30 July 1821 [Dl'd John Lewis 18 Nov 1822]

C2-116:   Surv. 8 May 1820 by T.W.6755=9 Dec 1819 Andrew Bogle 133 A. 1 Ro. in
Hampshire Co. on Alleghany Mt. and New Cr. adj. Upton Bruce, Rd. from Michael
Fout up s'd Mt., Jonathan Edwards. 30 July 1821 [Dl'd James Gibson 1 Nov 1821]

C2-117:   17 Aug 1820 by T.W.6662=7 June 1819 David Parsons 7 A. 3 Ro. 29 Po. in
Hampshire Co. being a small island in S. Br. of Potomack near his own land. 30
July 1821 [Dl'd Ephraim Dunn Dec 1821]

C2-118:   Surv. 12 Apr 1820 by T.W.6755=9 Dec 1819 Reuben Davis asne. of Thomas
Davis 81 A. 2 Ro. 28 Po. in Hampshire Co. on New Cr. adj. heirs of Thomas Deane
dec'd, William & Aaron Thomas, Copejoy's Run, Bushy Rg., Reuben David. 30 July
1821 [Dl'd James Gibson 1 Nov 1821]

C2-119:   Surv. 10 Apr 1820 T.W.6662=7 June 1819 Joseph Crosley 424 A. 28 Po. in
Hampshire Co. on Cabbin Run of Patterson's Cr. adj. Rhodham Rodgers & John
Rodgers, David Long. 30 July 1821 [Dl'd James Gibson 1 Nov 1821]

C2-120:   Surv. 19 Nov 1819 by T.W.6166=5 Feb 1818 John Templeman 7 1/2 A. in
Hampshire Co. on N. Br. of Potomack adj. Terence Doyle sold William H. Burnes
who sold to wid.of John Neptune. 30 July 1821 [Dl'd Mr. Vance 1 Nov 1823]

C2-121:   Surv. 17 June 1820 by T.W.5209=15 Feb 1814 Joseph Evans 16 A. in
Shenandoah Co. bet. Hawksbill Cr. & Mill Run adj. heirs of Benjamin Ruffner
dec'd. 30 July 1821

C2-122:   Surv. 9 Sep 1820 by T.W.6831=21 Feb 1820 John Huffman 78 A. 3 Ro. in
Jefferson Co. adj. Richard Mercer, Frederick Moler, on Potomack R., said
Huffman. 1 Sep 1821 [Dl'd Mr. Lucas 4 Dec 1821]

C2-122:   Surv. 21 Mar 1815 by T.W.5070=17 May 1813 Francis Coffer Jr. 10 A. 3
Ro. 10 Po. in Fairfax Co. on Back Br. of N. Run of Pohick adj. James Simpson,
Francis Coffer Jr., Francis Coffer Sr. 1 Sep 1821 [James Sangster 6 Dec 1822]

C2-123:   Surv. 29 Jan 1812, 50 A. by T.W.4831=4 Feb 1812 & 50 A. by T.W.6375=5
Oct 1818 Michael Widmyer 100 A. in Hampshire Co. on Big Cacaphon adj. Peter
Bruner Esq., Vanorsdeln, Peter Bruner Jr. 1 Sep 1821 [John Sherrard 3 Jan 1824]

C2-124:   Surv. 24 Mar 1819 by T.W.4831=4 Feb 1812 Michael Widmyer 20 A. in
Hampshire Co. on Sleepy Cr. & Stoney Valley Gap of Warm Spring Rg., adj. Edward
G. Williams, William Smith. 1 Sep 1821 [Dl'd John Sherrard 3 Jan 1824]

C2-124:   Surv. 30 June 1820, 98 A. by T.W.5775=29 Oct 1816 & 47 1/4 A. by
T.W.5826=3 Jan 1817 Herbert Cool 145 1/4 A. in Hampshire Co. on Bear Wallow Run
of Tear Coat adj. William Grant, Robert Fulton, Thomas Mason, Jacob Shwiers,
said Cool, James Peters, Addison & George McCalley bought of James Galloway,
Christopher Whitsel, Dunmore, Tunie Peters, Stephen Leigh. 1 Sep 1821 [Dl'd
Mr. Throckmorton 7 Feb 1822]

C2-125:   Surv. 22 June 1819 by T.W.6295=8 June 1818 John Tharp 129 A. in
Hampshire Co. on Horn Camp Run of N. R. adj. his own land, on Hairy Mt. 1 Sep
1821 [Dl'd Mr. Parsons 7 Jan 1826?]

C2-126: Surv. 7 June 1816 by T.W.5663=9 May 1816 John Mason 220 A. in Stafford Co. on Austin's Run adj. John Knight, John Latham, Henry White, Robertson, Hancock Euctace/Eustace, Fritter. 1 Sep 1821 [Dl'd Mr. Alex'r Botts 8 Nov 1821]

C2-127: Surv. 22 Mar 1815 by T.W.4287=18 Dec 1805 Fanny B. Wilson(w. of Richard Wilson), Mary Coffer & Thomas Coffer heirs at law of John Coffer the Elder dec'd of Harriot Parsons dec'd (infant dau. & sole heiriss of Harriot E. Parsons dec'd and also one of the heirs of John Coffer the younger dec'd. and also John Coffer the younger dec'd. Said Fanny B., Mary, Thomas, Harriot E. & John Coffer the younger were ch. & only heirs at law of John Coffer the elder dec'd. Reserving to Solomon Parsons husband of said Harriot E. Parsons dec'd any right as tenant which he may be entitled to: 12 A. 118 Po. in Fairfax Co. on S. run of Pohick adj. Jos. Simpson's land left him by his father, land bought of George Simpson, Bond Veal, Howard. 1 Sep 1821 [Dl'd Wm. Smyth 29 Sep 1821]

C2-128: Surv. 16 Nov 1820 by T.W.6755=9 Dec 1819 John Junkins 71 1/4 A. in Hampshire Co. on N. Br. of Potomack, Slab Camp Run adj. heirs of William Vance dec'd. 10 Oct 1821 [Carsdaken 1829]

C2-129: Surv. 31 May 1820 by T.W.6662=7 June 1819 Benjamin Junkins 67 A. in Hampshire Co. on N. Br. of Potomack inc. mouths of Deep Run & Howell's Run adj. Wm. Fox. 10 Oct 1821 [Dl'd Ephraim Dunn 8 Dec 1821]

C2-130: Surv. 30 May 1820 by T.W.6755=9 Dec 1819 Reazin Harvey 31 3/4 A. in Hampshire Co. on N. Br. of Potomack adj. his land bought of Edward Emery. 10 Oct 1821 [Dl'd Ephraim Dunn 19 Dec 1822]

C2-131: Surv. 24 May 1806 by T.W.15,516=18 Apr 1783 Robert Gustin 187 A. in Morgan Co. (formerly Hampshire) in Warm Spring Valley at foot of Great Cacapehon Mt. adj. Thomizin Elzey, John Casler, Johnson, Burk, William Alexander. 10 Oct 1821 [Dl'd Ignatious O Ferrall 12 Feb 1822]

C2-132: Surv. 22 Dec 1820 by T.W.6724=25 Oct 1819 William Cunningham Jr. 47 A. in Hardy Co. on Patterson's Cr. Mt. adj. his own land, James Machir. 10 Oct 1821 [Dl'd Jacob Miller 5 Jan 1822]

C2-133: Surv. 29 Sep 1820 by T.W.6241=2 Apr 1818 David Ellis 30 1/2 A. in Hampshire Co. on Oewn's Rg. & Big Cacapehon adj. Nathan Littler, Robert Rodgers, John Kearan, Peter Ogan, Frederick Buzzard, Jacob Jinkins. 1 Nov 1821 [Dl'd Col. White Mar 1823]

C2-133: Surv. 28 Aug 1820 by T.W.6406=5 Nov 1818 David Ellis asne. of William Sherrard 140 A. in Hampshire Co. on Bloomery Run of Big Cacapehon adj. William Naylor, Joseph Johnson, High Top Mt., Robert Rutherford 1778 grant now Naylor, Royce now Naylor, Isaac Zane. 1 Nov 1821 [Dl'd Col. White Mar 1823]

C2-134: Surv. 25 Aug 1820 by T.W.6241=2 Apr 1818 Robert Sherrard 17 A. 3 Ro. in Hampshire Co. on Bloomery Run adj. Robert Rodgers, Sherrard's Mill tract surv. for Richard Collier, Foxcraft, William Naylor, Henry Lewis, Ross. 1 Nov 1821 [Dl'd Col. White 2 Mar 1822]

C2-135: Surv. 6 June 1820 by T.W.5902=20 Feb 1817 Thomas Racey 75 A. in Hampshire Co. on Timber Rg. & Loanam's Br. of Big Cacapehon adj. said Racey's land bought of Robert Hellier, Jeremiah Reed, George Reed's Lick, William Lafollet. 5 Dec 1821 [Dl'd Mr. Odell 14 Dec 1840]

C2-136: Surv. 6 June 1820 by Exg.T.W. 2280=7 Nov 1818 Jesse Anderson 100 A. in Hampshire Co. on Loanam's Br. of Big Cacapehon adj. Joseph Clutter, Stephens, James Kelsoe, William Layfollet, Thomas Racey. 5 Dec 1821 [Mr. Odell 29 Jan '38]

C2-137: Surv. 12 June 1820 by T.W.6295=8 June 1818 Joel Ellis 4 A. in Hampshire Co. on Big Cacapehon Mt. adj. Elijah Pennington, his own land bought of William Perril, Dr. Elisha C. Dick, John Perril. 5 Dec 1821

C2-137: Surv. 25 Aug 1819, 100 A. by 6151=26 Jan 1818 & 73 A. by 6295=8 June 1818 Luther Calvin & John Johnson 173 A. in Hampshire Co. on Spring Gap Mt. &

Little Cacapehon adj. Braddock's Old Rd., John Critton, Daniel Lyon, Breakneck Rd., Short now Ginnevan, William Burges. 5 Dec 1821 [Dl'd F. White 1822]

C2-138: Surv. 1 June 1820 by 6755=9 Dec 1819 James Anderson Sr. 85 A. 2 Ro 29 Po. in Hampshire Co. on Cramberry Rg. of Little Alleghany Mt., Cramberry Run of Deep Run of N. Br. of Potomack. 5 Dec 1821

C2-139: Surv. 31 Dec 1820 by T.W.6724=25 Oct 1819 John Snyder 46 A. in Hardy Co. adj. Jacob Chrisman, Cove of Lost R., heirs of Frederick Fout, Cove Run. 12 Feb 1822 [Dl'd Mr. Leonard Neff 12 June 1822]

C2-139: Surv. 31 Dec 1820 by T.W.6724=25 Oct 1819 John Snyder 10 A. in Hardy Co. on Cove Run of Lost R. adj. heirs of Frederick Fout, Jacob Chrisman. 12 Feb 1822 [Dl'd Mr. Leonard Neff 12 June 1822]

C2-140: Surv. 19 Sep 1821 by T.W.7106=21 July 1821 David Sphor & John Mullen 161 A. in Hardy Co. on Turn Mill Run adj. Isaac Vanmeter, John Smith, William Heath, Thomas Oglevie. 15 May 1822 [Dl'd Mr. John Lewis 15 Aug 1822]

C2-141: Surv. 31 Aug 1820 by T.W.6512=1 Feb 1819 Susanna Dew 77 3/4 A. in Hampshire Co. on Dillons Mt. & Big Cacapehon drain bet. Short Mt. & Big Cacapehon Mt. adj. Abraham Criswell, John Swisher. 16 May 1822 [Col. White 25 Feb 1823]

C2-142: Surv. 20 Apr 1819 by T.W.6166=5 Feb 1818 Hendriks Clark 48 A. in Hampshire Co. on Cabbin Run of Patterson's Cr. adj. Benjamin Baley formerly Thomas Toys. 16 May 1822 [Dl'd James Gibson 1 Nov 1822]

C2-142: Surv. 28 Oct 1821 by T.W.6786=5 Feb 1820 Conrod Lutman 7 1/2 A. in Morgan Co. on Sleepy Cr. adj. heirs of George Wisenburgh dec'd, George Lutman, Isaac Caw. 10 June 1822 [Dl'd John Sherrard 6 Dec 1823]

C2-143: Surv. 24 Sep 1821 by T.W.7119=27 Aug 1821 David Moler, Henry Moler, Mary Moler & Adam Moler 8 A. 2 Ro. 24 Po. in Jefferson Co. on Potomac R. adj. John Hufman, John Brian, Moler heirs. 10 June 1822 [Daniel Morgan 31 Dec 1822]

C2-143: Surv. 6 Aug 1821 by T.W.6443=15 Dec 1818 John Brady 98 1/2 A. in Hampshire Co. on Swishers Run of Smith's Mill Run of S. Br. of Potomack, adj. Fielding Calmes heirs, Reynolds heirs. 10 June 1822 [Ephraim Dunn 19 Dec 1822]

C2-144: Surv. 23 Sep 1820 by T.W.6513=2 Feb 1819 William Clark 480 A. in Hampshire Co. on Mill Run & Mike's Run of Patterson's Cr. adj. Clark, wid. Harris. Coulson formerly Reed now Vincent Vandiver, Meadow Run. 10 June 1822 [Dl'd Ephraim Dunn 19 Dec 1822]

C2-146: Surv. 19 June 1819 by T.W.6512=1 Feb 1819 Thomas Carskaddon 200 A. in Hampshire Co. on Middle Rg. & Patterson's Cr. adj Frederick Sheetz, James Watts, his own land. 10 June 1822 [Dl'd Ephraim Dunn 19 Dec 1822]

C2-146: Surv. 3 May 1821 by T.W.6747=6 Dec 1819 Jacob Beidler 634 A. in Shenandoah Co. in Powell's little Ft. & Three Top Mt. adj. William Ellsey, Henry Linn, Jacob Gochenour, William C. Williams. 10 June 1822 [Mr. Samuel Bare 5 Feb 1823]

C2-148: Surv. 26 Oct 1821 by T.W.5023=5 Feb 1813 George Hottel (tanner) 4 A. in Shenandoah Co. near N. Mt., on Funk's Mill Run adj. Abraham Smutz, said George Hottel, Jacob Syver, John Hottel. 10 June 1822 [Dl'd Mr. Samuel Bare 5 Feb 1823]

C2-148: Surv. 24 Mar 1821 by T.W.6114=10 Dec 1817 Robert Murphy 1 A. 2 Ro. 15 Po. in Berkeley Co. on Back Cr. adj. said Robert Murphey, Abraham Robinson. 10 June 1822 [Dl'd Mr. Levi Henshaw 20 Dec 1822]

C2-149: For $440 Osmond Johnson 300 A. by estimation in Richmond Co. being same which Thomas Morse dec'd, an alien died seized. Inquest 1 Sep 1819 found land to Escheat. Sold 30 Mar 1822 to Johnson. 16 July 1822 [Dl'd Prop'r 13 Aug 1822]

C2-149: Surv. 1 May 1821 by T.W.5712=29 July 1816 Henry Linn 700 A. in Shenandoah Co. in Powell's Little Ft. adj. Charles Lee, William Ellzey, John Geyer,

Jacob Gochenour, Isaac Overall. 1 Oct 1822 [Dl'd Mr. Rob't Allen 3 Dec 1822]

C2-151: Surv. 17 Aug 1821 by Exg.T.W. 2357=5 Dec 1820 Samuel Walton 100 A. in Shenandoah Co. on Suppen Lick Mt. adj. Oakney Spring Rd., George Lonas, George Hebner, John Sheetz's purchase of Catharine Rider dec'd heirs, Jacob Funkhouser. 1 Oct 1822 [Dl'd Mr. Moses Walton 13 Dec 1822]

C2-152: Surv. 23 Feb 1820 by T.W.5826=3 Jan 1817 Jacob Swires asne. of Herbert Cool 33 A. in Hampshire Co. on Bear Wallow Run of Tear Coat adj. Jacob Shwier bought of Thomas Mason, John Bailey, Jacob Buzzard, James Galloway, James Powell, Shwiers formerly James Peters. 1 Oct 1822 [Dl'd Col. White 25 Feb 1823]

C2-153: Surv. 3 Apr 1820 by T.W.5775=29 Oct 1816 George Cannon 109 A. in Hampshire Co. on Tear Coat adj. Frederick Starkey, Thomas Lewis(surv'd for Hager). 1 Oct 1822 [Dl'd Col. White 25 Feb 1823]

C2-153: Surv. 8 Aug 1820 by T.W.6647=22 May 1819 John Higgins 22 1/2 A. in Hampshire Co. bet. S. Br. Mt. & Little Cacapehon adj. said Higgins land surv'd for Bryan Bruin, John Spore now Gonts, Thomas Burkit, Brown, Robert Dougherty. 1 Oct 1822 [Dl'd Col. White 25 Feb 1823]

C2-154: Surv. 4 May 1820 by T.W.5441=24 Aug 1815 John Loy Jr. 228 1/4 A. in Hampshire Co. on Tear Coat Cr. adj. Frederick Starkey, Thomas Lewis surv'd for Hager, George Cannon, William Loy, Hood & Ray formerly Pigman. 1 Oct 1822 [Dl'd Col. White 25 Feb 1823]

C2-156: Surv. 23 Aug 1821 by T.W.6664=8 June 1819 Jonas Hedges 120 A. in Berkeley Co. on Meadow Br. bet. Third hill & Sleepy Cr. Mt. adj. Benjamin Farman. 1 Oct 1822 [Dl'd Mr. Levi Hinshaw 20 Dec 1822]

C2-156: Surv. 10 June 1819, 44 A. by T.W.4841=18 Feb 1812 & 53 A. by T.W.5571=2 Feb 1816 Abraham Pennington & William Pool 97 A. in Hampshire Co. on Little Capcaphon adj. Jacob Pennington, Pool, on Townhill. 1 Oct 1822 [Dl'd Col. White 25 Feb 1823]

C2-157: Surv. 11 Apr 1820 by Exg.T.W. 2280=7 Nov 1818 Susanna Ruckman 90 A. 2 Ro. 36 Po. in Hampshire Co. on Little Cacapehon adj. Samuel Ruckman's heirs, Cramer, Ann Watkins formerly Henderson. 1 Nov 1822

C2-158: Surv. 10 Apr 1820, 40 A. by T.W.6157=29 Jan 1818 & 28 A. 1 Ro 30 Po. by T.W.6662=7 June 1819 John Thrush 68 A. 1 Ro 30 Po. in Hampshire Co. on Rawlings Run of Patterson's Cr. adj. his own land, heirs of Peter Putman dec'd, John Vanbuskirk & Nesbet. 1 Nov 1822 [Dl'd Col. Wm. Trockmorton 19 Feb 1823]

C2-159: Surv. 23 Aug 1820 by T.W.6512=1 Feb 1819 Thomas Edwards 77 1/4 A. in Hampshire Co. on Beargarden Mt. adj. Thomas Allen bought of Thomas McBride & Joel Ward, Henry Topper, Frederick Buzzard, Charles Carlisle & Jonathan Carlisle. 1 Nov 1822 [Dl'd Wm. Vance 13 Dec 1832]

C2-160: Surv. 1 Mar 1821 by T.W.6904=22 May 1820 Michael Caudy 69 A. in Hampshire Co. on Dillon's Mt., Dillon's Run adj. William Moreland bought from Owen Williams, Richard Lyon bought of Eli Beall both tracts originally William Engles, Betsy Ann Dew. 1 Nov 1822

C2-161: Surv. 1 Mar 1821 by T.W.6074=4 Nov 1817 William Moreland 46 6/10 A. in Hampshire Co. on Dillon's Mt. or Capehon Mt. & Dillon's Run adj. his own upper & lower tracts, one bought of Owen Williams, Michael Caudy, Carlisle. 1 Nov 1822

C2-162: Surv. 29 May 1821 by T.W.5351=14 Feb 1815 Michael Miller 124 1/2 A. in Hampshire Co. on Stoney Run of S. Br. of Potomack, adj. Cunrad Huffman's heirs, John Huffman. 1 Nov 1822 [Dl'd Col. King 11 Dec 1823]

C2-163: Surv. 13 June 1821 by T.W.6755=9 Dec 1819 Zachariah Arnold 3 A. in Hampshire Co. on Mill Cr & Patterson's Cr. adj. land he bought of John Wright, land he bought Peter Ingle & Patrick Fleming, High. 1 Nov 1822 [Dl'd Wm. Throckmorton 19 Feb 1823]

C2-164:   Surv. 21 Aug 1821, 50 A. by T.W.6662=7 June 1819 & 89 1/2 A. by
T.W.6888=17 Apr 1820 John Arnold (s. of Samuel) 139 1/2 A. in Hampshire Co. on
Mill Run of Patterson's Cr. adj. James McGuire, Jonas Chamberlin, Hogan, William
Clark. 1 Nov 1822   [Dl'd Wm. Armstrong 21 Jan 1823]

C2-165:   Surv. 17 Mar 1821 by T.W.6726=28 Oct 1819 David Null 106 A. in Morgan
Co. on Sleepy Cr. & Warm Spring Rg. adj. Charles McIntire, Cacapeon Mt., Riley
heirs(of Winchester), Richard Chenowith. 1 Nov 1822 [Dl'd Sexton 25 Jan 1825?]

C2-165:   Surv. 1 Mar 1921 by T.W.5818=30 Dec 1816 William Slaughter (s. of
William) 12 1/4 A. in Culpeper Co. on Thornton's R. adj. Col. John Thornton,
George Cheek, Lergeant, Right's Mt. 1 Nov 1822 [Dl'd Col. Ward 10 Jan 1823]

C2-166:   Surv. 15 Jan 1822 by T.W.6865=25 Feb 1820 Benjamin Graves 203 A. in
Madison Co. on Terrel's bluff, adj. William Terrel's 3 Oct 1734 grant, Elijah
Eddins, Claibourn Eddins, Mark Finks, Joseph Rogers, said Benjamin Graves, land
formerly Duval's. 1 Nov 1822 [Dl'd Mr. Garnd? 7 Apr 1824]

C2-167:   Surv. 16 June 1821 by T.W.7059=23 Mar 1821 Robert Lyle 80 A. in
Berkeley Co. on N. Mt. adj. Henry Bower's, John Lyles, Paul Taylor now Spencer.
20 Nov 1822 [Dl'd Mr. Robertson 1 Mar 1824]

C2-168: Surv. 15 June 1821 by T.W.7059=23 Mar 1821 Robert Lyle 65 A. in Berkeley
Co. on N. Mt. adj. Nicholas Hess. 20 Nov 1822 [Dl'd Mr. Robertson 1 Mar 1824]

C2-169:   Surv. 24 Sep 1795, 15,000 A. by T.W.735=29 Sep 1794 & 10,517 A. by
T.W.736=29 Sep 1794 George Hetick 25,517 A. in Shenandoah Co. on the Blue Rg. at
intersection of Shenandoah, Rockingham & Madison Cos., adj. Little Naked Cr.
Big & Little line Runs, William Davis, John Grigby now Christopher Comer,
Frederick Stoneberger, Stoney Run, Augustine Piper, David Ruffner, Little Hawksbill Cr., Joseph Strickler, Henry Nisley, Goodlove Prince, Jacob Shaver. Surv.
includes 1233 A. exclusive of above. 20 Nov 1822 [Dl'd Henry StGeorge 1822]

C2-172: Surv. 5 Apr 1822, 600 A. by T.W.7006=2 Feb 1821 & 556 A. by T.W.7114=15
Aug 1821 Robert Hord & Thomas Hord 1156 A. in Pr. William Co. on Neabsco Run &
Occoquan R. adj. Peake, Jackson, Lartin, Carr heirs, Taylor, Page, Dawe, Savage,
Dorsey, O. Byrd, Coalter, Seliaksman, Fairfax. 6 Jan 1823 [Dl'd Mr. Timberlake
16 Jan 1823]

C2-173:   Surv. 22 Aug 1821 by T.W.6907=30 May 1820 Samuel Hedges the 4th 4 A. 3
Ro 28 Po. in Berkeley Co. on Back Cr. adj. Samuel Hedges the 3rd, Samuel Hedges
the 4th. 6 Jan 1823 [Dl'd Mr. Levi Hinshaw 9 Jan 1823]

C2-174:   Surv. 3 Apr 1822, 40 A. by Exg.T.W.2338=28 Jan 1820 & 80 A. by
Exg.T.W.2348=2 June 1820 John Lyle 120 A. in Berkeley Co. on N. Mt. adj. Henry
Bowers, Nicholas Hess, Paul Taylor now Spencer Jr. 6 Jan 1823 [Dl'd Mr. Rich'd
Claggett 7 Feb 1823]

C2-175:   Surv. 26 Nov 1821 by Exg.T.W.2338=28 Jan 1820 Edward Beeson, Joseph
McFeely & John Myers 300 A. in Berkeley Co. on Meadow Br. bet. Sleepy Cr. Mt. &
Third Hill Mt. adj. Benjamin Farman, John Myers. 6 Jan 1823 [Dl'd Mr. John
Sherrard 8 Jan 1823]

C2-175:   Surv. 17 May 1821, 47 A. by T.W.5438=18 Aug 1815 & 3 A. by T.W.6930=1
Aug. 1820 John Keysucker 50 A. in Morgan formerly Berkeley Co. adj. Sleepy Cr.
Mt., William Rankir, Mathias Swim 3rd, Jerome Williams heirs, Philip Pendleton
heirs. 15 Feb 1823 [Dl'd Mr. John Sherrard 21 Feb 1823]

C2-176:   Surv. 5 Nov 1818 by T.W.5176=24 Jan 1814 Samuel Vandiver 260 A. in
Hampshire Co. on Vandiver's Run of N. Br. & Alleghany Mt. adj. Vanmeter, Harvie
formerly Edward McCarty, Col. Martin, Thomas Mulledy, Jeremiah Cockrell heirs,
his tract, John Parker. 10 Mar 1823 [Dl'd Col. White of the Senate 1 Jan 1821]

C2-177:   Surv. 20 Aug 1821 by T.W.5572=2 Feb 1816 Mary Harrison, wid. of Joseph
Harrison dec'd 44 A. in Hampshire Co. on Mikes Run of Patterson's Cr. adj. her
own land, heirs of Peter Beaver dec'd. 10 Mar 1823

105

C2-178:   Surv. 21 May 1821 by T.W.6448=17 Dec 1818 James Smith Arthur asne. of John Purkeypile 200 A. in Shenandoah Co. near the Narrow Passage Run at gap of Little N. Mt. adj. John Gochenour, Absalom Rinker, Joshua Foltz Jr. 10 Mar 1823

C2-179:   Surv. 23 May 1822 by T.W.7150=22 Nov 1821 Hancock Eustace 27 A. 15 Po. in Stafford Co. adj. Allerton, Robinson, Rocky Br., William Fritter, Whitson. 30 Apr 1823

C2-180:   Surv. 2 May 1822 by T.W.5813=21 Dec 1816 Conrad Loy 15 A. in Frederick Co. adj. Jonathan Parkins, James McCoole, John Mosee dec'd, Robert Davison, on Hunting Rg. 30 Apr 1823 [Dl'd Mr. Castleman 1829]

C2-181:   Surv. 9 Apr 1822 by T.W.6604=11 Mar 1819 Robert Montgomery, Christian Holm & William Stevenson asnes. of John Crockwell 2 Ro. 7 Per. in Frederick Co. adj. Crum, Cooper, Bruce, said Montgomery. 30 Apr 1823 [Dl'd Col. Joseph Sexton 27 June 1825]

C2-181:   Surv. 20 Mar 1822 by Exg.T.W.2401=7 Jan 1822 David Null 117 A. in Frederick Co. adj. Meshack Sexton now David Reese, Wharton now Pendleton, Joseph Baker, on Brush Cr., William Adams, Green spring Rd., Zack's Lick. 30 Apr 1823 [Dl'd Col. Sexton 25 June 1825]

C2-182:   Surv. 20 Mar 1822 by Exg.T.W.2401=7 Jan 1822 David Null 14 A. 3 Ro. 23 Per. in Frederick Co. adj. Sexton, Johnston, Harrision, on Brush Cr., Wharton now Pendleton, Fisher now Johnston, Matthew Harrison. 30 Apr 1823 [Dl'd Col. Sexton 25 June 1825]

C2-183:   Surv. 19 Mar 1822 by Exg.T.W. 2400=7 Jan 1822 John Everet 55 3/4 A. in Frederick Co. adj. Joseph Baker, John Puffengerger, Brush Cr. 30 Apr 1823 [Dl'd Col. Sexton 15 1825]

C2-184:   Surv. 19 Mar 1822 by Exg.T.W. 2400=7 Jan 1822 John Everet 20 3/4 A. in Frederick Co. adj. his own land, Grovier, Wharton now Pendleton, Brush Cr., Matthew Harrison. 30 Apr 1823 [Dl'd Col. Sexton 15 1825]

C2-185:   Surv. 20 Apr 1820 by T.W.6604=11 Mar 1819 Barbara Rinker asne. of John Crockwell 24 A. 15 sq. Po. in Frederick Co. on Babbs Cr. adj. Joseph Fry, Hannah Fenton, Benjamin Fenton. 30 Apr 1823 [Dl'd Col. Sexton 13 Jan 1824]

C2-186:   Surv. 14 June 1821 by T.W.5826=3 Jan 1817 Jacob Ludwick 15 A. 7 Po. in Hampshire Co. on Mill Cr. & Middle Rg. adj. Jacob Biser, Joseph Myers, said Ludwick, Samuel Arnold, Sloan. 30 May 1823 [Dl'd Mr. John Sloane 18 Feb 1826]

C2-187:   Surv. 1 May 1822 by T.W.7106=21 July 1821 George Shireman 130 A. in Hardy Co. in upper Cove, on Lost R. adj. Conrod Sager, Jacob Shireman. 8 July 1823 [Dl'd Neville 8 Dec 1823]

C2-187:   Surv. 8 July 1816 by Exg.T.W. 2229=16 Mar 1816 Andrew Glassell asne. of Joseph Towles 11 A. in Madison Co. adj. Fleshman, Jacob Lepp, Muscoe Newman, Abraham Utz, said Towles. 8 July 1823 [Dl'd Linn Banks 3 Jan 1824]

C2-188:   Surv. 7 Aug 1822 by T.W.6865=25 Feb 1820 Elijah Skinner asne. of John Pilcher 5 A. in Madison Co. adj. old Parson & Barnett Rds., said Pilcher, Joel Yager, Benjamin Yager, said Skinner. 8 July 1823 [Dl'd Linn Banks 3 Jan 1824]

C2-188:   Surv. 6 Sep 1822 by T.W.7260=27 May 1822 Richard Carr 5 A. 2 Ro. 15 Po. in Frederick Co. on Linestone Rg. adj. said Carr's purchase of Hugh Holmes, the Grove Tract now heirs of Adam Aldrige dec'd, Paddy pond tract, Ellis now Lewright, Lickins. 8 July 1823

C2-189:   Surv. 6 Sep 1822 by T.W.7260=27 May 1822 Richard Carr 4 3/4 A. in Frederick Co. adj. Henry Bayliss, Snapp, Carr's purchase of Hugh Holmes, on Limestone Rg., Isaac Hollingsworth. 8 July 1823

C2-190:   Surv. 16 Aug 1820 by T.W.6396=15 July 1820 Thomas M. Marshall asne. of Benjamin Marshall 240 A. in Hardy Co. on Mud lick Run of N. R. adj. his own land, Thomas Smith, tract formerly William Jeinkins Hager, Frederick Starky. 8 July 1823 [Dl'd Neville 8 Dec 1823]

C2-190:   Surv. 12 Oct 1821 by T.W.6396=15 July 1820 James Miles 1000 A. in Hardy Co. adj. Pattersons Cr. s'd Miles, James Machir, his Coomes Tract, Peter Babb, Williams's Mill tract, Charles A. Turly.   8 July 1823 [Dl'd Neville 8 Dec 1823]

C2-191:   Surv. 10 July 1821 by T.W.6396=15 July 1820 William Veatch & Jeremiah Veatch 52 A. in Hardy Co. on Loonies Cr. adj. James Seymour, heirs of Richard Seymour dec'd, the Manor line.   8 July 1823 [Dl'd Neville 8 Dec 1823]

C2-192:   Surv. 10 July 1822 by T.W.5516=1 Dec 1815 James Gray 206 A. in Hardy Co. on N. Fork of S. Br. of Potomac adj. Valentine Power, John Wilton, Peter Hive, Breathard.   8 July 1823 [Dl'd Mr. Vanmeter 2 Jan 1824]

C2-193:   Surv. 12 June 1821 by T.W.6662=7 June 1819 Richard Holliday 50 A. in Hampshire Co. on Patterson's Cr. adj. his own land, Job Wealton heirs, Vincent Williams heirs, Patterson Cr.   30 Aug 1823 [Dl'd C. Heiskel 6 Dec 1823]

C2-194:   Surv. 10 Apr 1821 by T.W.6904=22 May 1820 Moses Pettit 2 A. 3 Ro. 13 Po. in Hampshire Co. near Town Gap Run by Romney, adj. his own land bought of Philip Cool, Moses Everett bought of Darius Everitt originally Foreman, James Gibson, Warner Throckmorton, Rd. from Romney to Winchester, Foreman, Samuel Ruckman. 30 Aug 1823 [Dl'd Mr. Armstrong 27 Nov 1824]

C2-195:   Surv. 31 Aug 1820 by T.W.6074=4 Nov 1817 George Cale 50 A. in Hampshire Co. on Big Cacapehon bet. Short Mt. & Capehon Mt., Moorefield Rd., adj. Abraham Criswell. 30 Aug 1923 [Dl'd Mr. White 3 Dec 1823]

C2-195:   Surv. 18 Sep 1819, 80 A. by T.W.6166=5 Feb 1818 & 10 A. by T.W.6662=7 June 1819 James Allender 90 A. in Hampshire Co. on Little Cacapehon adj. Richard Deaver, John Cox, on Townhill.   30 Aug 1923 [Dl'd Mr. White 3 Dec 1823]

C2-196:   Surv. 5 Oct 1820 by T.W.6904=22 May 1820 Robert Nelson 52 1/4 A. in Hampshire & Frederick Cos. on Mills's Cr. of Big Cacapehon adj. Henry Michael, Jacob Jinkins, said Nelson formerly James Nelson now dec'd, William Garman, Christopher Whitsel. 30 Aug 1923 [Dl'd Mr. White 3 Dec 1823]

C2-197:   Surv. 8 June 1822 by T.W.7109=27 July 1821 Vincent Vandiver 75 A. in Hampshire Co. adj. Samuel Cockrell, Elijah Greenwell bought of John Wright that was surv'd for Robert Lockhart heirs, Thomas Carskaden, Pattersons Cr., Cabbin Run. 30 Aug 1823 [Dl'd Thomas Carskan 4 Feb 1828]

C2-198:   Surv. 1 June 1822 by T.W.7109=27 July 1821 Vincent Vandiver 150 A. in Hampshire Co. on Knobley Mt. adj. John Hammock formerly David Long. 30 Aug 1923 [Dl'd Mr. White 3 Dec 1823]

C2-199:   Surv. 5 Nov 1822 by T.W.5143=8 Dec 1813 Isaac Kuykendall 80 1/4 A. in Hampshire Co. on S. Br. of Potomac, Br. Mt. adj. Cunrad Huffman being part of grant to Jonathan Cockburn, his own land, William Naylor now Isaac Pancake formerly Piper, Mill Cr. 30 Aug 1823 [Dl'd Col. Sloan 9 Jan 1826]

C2-200: Surv. 29 Sep 1820, 150 A. by Exg.T.W.2156=28 Jan 1812, 52 1/2 A. by dup. T.W.4762=1 Aug 1811 & 292 1/2 A. by T.W.6820=16 Feb 1820 Lambert Larew 495 A. in Hampshire Co. on Big Cacapehon, Little Mt., adj. Peter Larew heirs, Carlisle, Isaac Larew, Abraham Dawson. 30 Aug 1823 [Dl'd Mr. White 3 Nov 1823]

C2-202:   Surv. 21 Aug 1822 by T.W.5409=2 June 1815 Daniel Bowman 9 A. in Shenandoah Co. on N. R. of Shenandoah adj. said Bowman, George Fravel. 30 Aug 1823 [Dl'd Samuel Beire 3 Dec 1823]

C2-203: Surv. 30 Apr 1822 by T.W.6448=17 Dec 1818 Peter Williams asne. of Jacob Barb(s. of Adam) 23 A. in Shenandoah Co. on Little N. Mt. adj. Peter Sayger, Jacob Barb, Abraham Sonnafrank. 30 Aug 1823 [Dl'd Jacob Rinker Jr. 9 Jan 1824]

C2-204:   Surv. 5 Aug 1822 by T.W.4813=18 Jan 1812 Benjamin Lear 35 A. in Shenandoah Co. on Stoney Cr. adj. heirs of Conrad Lear dec'd, John Arthur & Co., Jacob Wolfe the Elder dec'd now John McFee. 30 Aug 1823 [Dl'd Samuel Beire 3 Dec 1823]

C2-205: Surv. 12 July 1822 by T.W.4813=18 Jan 1812 Eberhart Frederick Schuttler 1 A. in Shenandoah Co. near Mill Cr. adj. John Coile, John Filsmoyer, Michael Koontz. 30 Aug 1823 [Dl'd Jacob Rinker Jr. 9 Jan 1824]

C2-205: Surv. 28 Aug 1820 by T.W.5023=5 Feb 1813 Abraham Spidler Jr. 12 A. in Shenandoah Co. on Piney Mt. adj. Philip Long, Joseph Koontz, Burnet Stoudemoier. 4 Sep 1823 [Dl'd Samuel Anderson 1 Nov 1823]

C2-206: Surv. 2 Oct 1819 by T.W.5419=1 July 1815 Benjamin Cave 67 1/4 A. in Shenandoah Co. at the Blue Rg. adj. Joseph Browning, John Kiblinger, George Hetick, Joseph Roads Sr. heirs, Henry Prince bought of McCollister. 4 Sep 1823 [Dl'd Samuel Anderson 1 Nov 1823]

C2-207: Surv. 30 Sep 1819 by T.W.5419=1 July 1815 Ephraim Jinkins 86 A. in Shenandoah Co. at the Blue Rg. adj. Joel Fink, Jacob Kite, George Hetick. 4 Sep 1823 [Dl'd Samuel Anderson 1 Nov 1823]

C2-208: Surv. 19 Nov 1819 by T.W.5641=19 Mar 1816 Christian Aleshite 5 A. in Shenandoah Co. bet. S. R. of Shenandoah & Mill Run adj. Joseph Rosenberger, Jonathan Tobins, William Maize, Caleb Cambell. 4 Sep 1823 [Dl'd Samuel Anderson 1 Nov 1823]

C2-208: Surv. 2 Nov 1820 by T.W.5641=19 Mar 1816 Daniel Walters 6 1/2 A. in Shenandoah Co. on Mill Cr. & N. Mt. adj. said Walters, John Cumphers, Jacob Kirlin. 4 Sep 1823 [Dl'd Samuel Beire 3 Dec 1823]

C2-209: Surv. 4 Oct 1819 by dup. T.W.5944=26 Oct 1818 John Oferbocher Jr. 140 A. in Shenandoah Co. at the Blue Rg. adj. John Kibler, Roberts, John Frank, Christian Farver, George Hetick, Strickler. 4 Sep 1823 [Sam'l Anderson 1 Nov'23]

C2-210: Surv. 19 Nov 1819 by dup. T.W.5944=26 Oct 1818 Henry Aleshite Sr. 46 A. in Shenandoah Co. on Big Line Run adj. John Nowman, John Kizer, George Hetick. 4 Sep 1823 [Dl'd Samuel Anderson 1 Nov 1823]

C2-211: Surv. 7 June 1820 by dup. T.W.5944=26 Oct 1818 John Mauck 1 3/4 A. in Shenandoah Co. bet. S. R. of Shenandoah & the Hawksbill Cr. adj. Philip Long, said Mauck, Jonathan Tobin. 4 Sep 1823 [Dl'd Samuel Anderson 1 Nov 1823]

C2-212: Surv. 9 Apr 1820 by T.W.5704=22 July 1816 Benjamin Graves 4 3/4 A. in Shenandoah Co. on the Blue Rg. adj. Rockingham Co. line, said Graves. 4 Sep 1823 [Dl'd Mr. Grarnet 7 Apr 1824]

C2-213: Surv. 8 May 1821 by T.W.6959=13 Nov 1820 James L. McKenna 20 A. 35 Po. inc. eight islands in Loudoun Co. in Broad Run, adj. s'd McKenney, s'd McKenna, Linton, Carter. 16 Oct 1823

C2-215: Surv. 9 Mar 1822 by T.W.5875=11 Feb 1817 Jonas Chamberlin 14 A. 35 Po. in Hampshire Co. on hills west of Pattersons Cr. near said Chambelin, adj. Elijah Greenwell, Samuel Cockrell. 16 Oct 1823 [Dl'd Mr. Parsons 10 Jan 1825]

C2-215: Surv. 2 of 5th mo. May 1822 by T.W.7220=4 Mar 1822 Anthony Kerney 2 A. 3 Po. in Jefferson Co. adj. the late Orendorf, William Butler, Jones. 16 Oct 1823 [Dl'd 1 Jan 1824]

C2-216: Surv. 23 Mar 1822 by T.W.6833=21 Feb 1820 Isaac Overall 4790 A. in Shenandoah Co. at the Blue Rg. adj. Benjamin Cave, Little Hawksbill Cr., Tanners Rg., Caspard Hess, Stoney Run, Shenandoah & Rockingham Cos. line, David Dovel, John Kizer, Frederick Stoneberger, John Kibler Jr. formerly Piper, Joseph Striekler, Christian Forver?, John Frank, Jacob Kite, Joel Fink, Joseph Roads Sr. heirs. George Teller?. 16 Oct 1823 [Dl'd Samuel Beire 3 Dec 1823]

C2-220: Surv. 3 June 1822 by T.W.6848=24 Feb 1820 Jacob Fry 14 A. in Frederick Co. adj. Isaac Zane dec'd. Mordicai Bean dec'd, said Fry, Seabert now James

108

Bean. 31 Oct 1823 [Dl'd Col. Sexton 13 Jan 1824]

C2-221: Surv. 10 Jan 1823 by T.W.6865=25 Feb 1820 Benjamin Yager 10 A. in Madison Co. on Parsons Rd., adj. John Pilcher, Swindal, Carpenter, Benjamin Yager. 31 Oct 1823 [Dl'd Linn Banks 3 Jan 1824]

C2-222: Surv. 19 June 1822 by T.W.6930=1 Aug 1820 Henry Fauver 18 1/2 A. in Morgan Co. on Demmetts Run adj. Philip Wiggins, Potomac R., his land formerly James Watson, his purchase of Thomas Oar. 31 Oct 1823 [Robert Gustin 6 Jan 1824]

C2-223: Surv. 15 June 1822 by T.W.4906=9 June 1812 Samuel Rankin 21 A. in Morgan Co. on Lick or Mt. Run adj. Conrod Lutman, James Abernathy, Richard Wood, John Hunter, Lighthizer. 31 Oct 1823 [Dl'd Robert Gustin 6 Jan 1824]

C2-223: Surv. 8 May 1822 by T.W.6443=6 Dec 1820 Tavis D. Croston 100 A. in Hampshire Co. near N. R. adj. Henry Compton, William Armstrong, William Deavers. 31 Oct 1823 [Dl'd Mr. Sloan 1833]

C2-224: Surv. 30 Oct 1822, 38 1/2 A. by T.W.6295=8 June 1818 & 29 1/4 A. by T.W.6145=20 Jan 1818 Jonathan Burch 67 3/4 A. in Hampshire Co. on Town Gap Run by Romney to S. Br. of Potomac adj. John Jack, John McDowell, Samuel Ruckman, Warner Throckmorton & James Gibson, tract surv'd for John McMeekin, said Burch, Thomas Blair, Isaac Woolverton Sr. 31 Oct 1823 [Dl'd Mr. Parsons 8 Jan 1825]

C2-226: Surv. 8 Oct 1822, 36 A. by T.W.6241=2 Apr 1818, 7 A. by T.W.6406=5 Nov 1818 & 25 1/2 A. by T.W.6375=5 Oct 1818 David Ellis 68 1/2 A. in Hampshire Co. on Edwards Run of Big Cacapehon adj. Isaac Hollngsworth Mill Tract, William Carlisle now Charles Carlisle, John Combs heirs, Samuel Foreman, David Ellis. 14 Nov 1823 [Dl'd by mail 18 Nov 1823]

C2-227: Surv. 26 June 1822, 150 A. T.W.6166=5 Feb 1818 & 388 1/2 A. by T.W.7011=12 Feb 1821 John S. Kesler 538 1/2 A. in Hampshire Co. on Little Cacapehon, Grindstone or Spring-gap Mt., Devils nose Mt. adj. Rawleigh Caulston, Jeremiah Ginnevan. [Dl'd by mail 18 Nov 1823]

C2-229: Surv. 18 June 1822, 66 A. by T.W.6151=26 Jan 1818, 14 A. by T.W.5902=20 Feb 1817 & 20 A. by T.W.4906=9 June 1812 Isaac Biggerstaff 100 A. in Morgan Co. on Potomac R. adj. his own land, Samuel Biggerstaff, John Hartley Sr. 15 Nov 1823 [Dl'd Mr. Sharrard 4 Dec 1824]

C2-230: Surv. 23 Feb 1823 by T.W.5818=30 Dec 1816 Capt. Daniel Brown 140 A. in Culpeper Co. adj. Barbour, Wildemy, Joseph Weekley, Richard Jinkins heirs. 3 Feb 1824 [Dl'd Ambrose P. Hill 4 Feb 1824]

C2-230: Surv. 25 Sep 1820 by Exg.T.W.2351=1 Sep 1820 Robert M. Powell 11 A. 2 Ro. 29 Po. in Loudoun Co. adj. Charles Green, Powell's purchase of Brown, Leven Powell now Robert M. Powell, Daniel Eaches. 7 Feb 1824 [Mr. Kerchevall 1830]

C2-231: Surv. 3 of 5th Mo.(May) 1822 T.W.7159=10 Dec 1821 Joseph McMurrin 7 A. in Jefferson Co. adj. Adam Link, Robert Buckles, Edward Lucas. 7 Feb 1824 [Dl'd Braseton Davenport 19 Feb 1824]

C2-232: Surv. 20 Nov 1822 by Exg.T.W.2307=22 Apr 1819 Enock Rennoe 92 A. 3 Ro. 19 Po. in Pr. William Co. on Chesnut Br. of Cedar Run adj. Joseph Carr formerly Grant, French formerly Rolls, Tidwell, Lucky Run. 10 Feb 1824 [Dl'd Capt. Foster 12 Feb 1824]

C2-233: Surv. 19 Apr 1823 by Exg.T.W.2307=22 Apr 1819 Enock Rennoe 14 A. 3 Ro. in Pr. William Co. adj. John Fox. 10 Feb 1824 [Dl'd Capt. Foster 12 Feb 1824]

C2-233: Surv. 9 May 1822 by T.W.6512=4 Feb 1819 John Slane 17 1/4 A. in Hampshire Co. on N. R. adj. his old land, James Brown heirs, Adam Cooper, Adam Loy, said Slane. 3 Mar 1824 [Dl'd Col. Sloan 9 Jan 182?]

C2-234: Surv. 17 Aug 1822 by T.W.4968=2 Nov 1812 James Moseley 86 A. 1 Ro. in Hampshire Co. on New Cr. adj. his land formerly heirs of Thomas Turner dec'd,

Parker or Davis gap, Rd. from said Davis to New Cr., Parrot, said Moseley. 3 Mar 1824 [Dl'd Mr. Heiskel 9 Mar 1824]

C2-235: Surv. 8 Oct 1822, 35 A. by T.W.6241=2 Apr 1818 & 55 A. by T.W.6375=5 Oct 1818 David Ellis 90 A. in Hampshire Co. on Chesnut Mt., near Great Cacapehon, adj. Robert Sherard, David Ellis, Joseph Kenney formerly Ralph, James Gray formerly Brian Bruin, James Leith. 7 Apr 1824 [Dl'd Mr. Parsons 7 Jan 1826]

C2-236: Surv. 13 Aug 1823 by T.W.6878=22 Mar 1820 Benjamin Cave 4 A. in Shenandoah Co. on Little Hawksbill Cr. near the Blue Rg., adj. Joel Finks, heirs of Joseph Roads, Lawson Berry. 31 May 1824

C2-236: Surv. 3 June 1823 by T.W.6878=22 Mar 1820 John Burner & Joseph Strickler 226 A. in Shenandoah Co. bet. Massanetten Mt. & S. R. of Shenandoah adj. John Beaver, Reuben Long, John Brewbaker, John Gatewood, said Burner. 31 May 1824 [Dl'd Mr. Bryan H. Henry 20 Oct 1824]

C2-237: Surv. 21 Apr 1821, 15 A. by T.W.5775=29 Oct 1816 & 2 A. 50 Po. by T.W.6074=4 Nov 1817 Azariah Pugh 17 A. 1 Ro. 10 Po. in Hampshire Co. on Timber Rg. adj. John Anderson, David Lupton, Jesse Pugh, Michael Capper, said Azariah Pugh formerly Jesse Pugh asne. of James Seaton. 31 May 1824 [Dl'd Mr. Parsons 10 Jan 1825]

C2-238: Surv. 21 May 1823 by T.W.5704=22 July 1816 Michel Clemm 61 A. in Shenandoah Co. in Powels little Ft. adj. Williams, said Clemm, Benjamin Pennybaker dec'd, Little Ft. Mt. 14 June 1824

C2-239: Surv. 27 May 1823 by T.W.5419=1 July 1815 Abraham Heastand 100 A. in Shenandoah Co. at the Blue Rg. on Dry Run adj. Piercen Judd, Peter Heastand, Samuel & Jacob Kaufman. 14 June 1824 [Dl'd Mr. Bryan H. Henry 20 Oct 1824]

C2-241: Surv. 9 Apr 1823 by dup. T.W.5944=26 Oct 1818 Philip Phogle 100 A. in Shenandoah Co. in Powels Big Ft. on Passage Cr. adj. David Clemm, Elsie. 14 June 1824 [Dl'd Mr. Bryan H. Henry 20 Oct 1824]

C2-241: Surv. 9 Apr 1823 by dup. T.W.5944=26 Oct 1818 James Stinson Jr. 5 A. in Shenandoah Co. on S. R. of Shenandoah adj. George Leath, James Stinson Sr. 14 June 1824 [Dl'd Mr. Bryan H. Henry 20 Oct 1824]

C2-242: Surv. 8 Apr 1823 by dup. T.W.5944=26 Oct 1818 James Stinson alias James Stinson Jr. 169 A. in Shenandoah Co. on Flint Run, adj. Elijah Roy, Thomas Allen, Long Mt., heirs of John Blackwood dec'd, Manor line. 14 June 1824 [Dl'd Mr. Bryan H. Henry 20 Oct 1824]

C2-243: Surv. 7 May 1822 by T.W.6662=7 June 1819 John Baker 41 3/4 A. in Hampshire Co. on N. R. Mt. adj. his land, John Caudey. 14 June 1824 [Mr. Dunn 1831]

C2-244: Surv. 24 Apr 1822 by T.W.6295=8 June 1818 John Tharp 21 A. in Hampshire Co. adj. Tharp on Horn Camp Run of N. R. 14 June 1824 [Mr. Parson 17 Jan 1826]

C2-244: Surv. 20 Nov 1822, 50 A. by T.W.5336=13 Jan 1815 & 25 A. by T.W.7286=3 Aug 1822 John Loy Sr. 75 A. in Hampshire Co. on Cold Stream of Big Cacapehon adj. Abraham Rinehart, his own land, Round Knob Mt. 14 June 1824 [Dl'd Mr.Pugh 8 Jan 1825]

C2-245: Surv. 20 Nov 1822, 56 A. by T.W.4934=12 Sep 1812 & 8 A. by T.W.5351=14 Feb 1815 Thomas Lewis alias Thomas Lewis Sr. 64 A. in Hampshire Co. on N. R. adj. John Hawkins, Adam Cooper, Grape Rg. 14 June 1824 [Mr. Pugh 8 Jan 1825]

C2-246: Surv. 8 May 1810 by Exg.T.W.1180=8 Dec 1801 William Gray asne. of John Yates 21 A. in Culpeper Co. adj. said Yates, Richard Yates. 31 Aug 1824 [Dl'd Mr. Turner 6 Feb 1825]

C2-246: Surv. 27 Feb 1823 by T.W.6211=26 Feb 1818 David Johnson 130 A. in Culpeper Co. on Blue Rg. adj. said Johnson, Samuel Miller, Howard Compton, Stains Run. 31 Aug 1824

C2-247:   Surv. 25 Feb 1823 by T.W.7146=31 Oct 1821 Andrew Gaunt 90 A. in
Culpeper Co. on the Blue Rg. adj. hiers of Richard Yates, Piney R., Strother,
William Gray. 31 Aug 1824 [Dl'd Mr. Turner 7 Feb 1825]

C2-248:   Surv. 29 Feb 1823 by T.W.6944=7 Sep 1820 William Bowen 200 A. in
Culpeper Co. adj. said Bowen,, Shruby Mt. Blue Rg., said Odles estate, Barbour,
John Menefee, Henry Menefee, Thornton R. 31 Aug 1824 [Mr. Turner 7 Feb 1825]

C2-250:   Surv. 13 Mar 1823, 70 1/4 A. by T.W.6295=8 June 1818 & 96 3/4 A. by
T.W.7327=18 Nov 1822 William Doran 167 A. in Hampshire Co. on N. R. adj. Brushey
Rg., Alexander Doran formerly Rogers, Elkhorn Run, Richard Poston, William
Poston, Jacob Emart, Asa Carter. 31 Aug 1824 [Dl'd James Gilson 3 Nov? 1824]

C2-251:   Surv. 24 Feb 1823 by T.W.7183=1 Feb 1822 Adam Panabaker 3 A. in
Culpeper Co. on Thorntons R. adj. Francis Brandum, said Panabaker, Rd. at
Bryants Meeting House, Henry Menefee, James Jones. 31 Aug 1824

C2-252:   Surv. 10 Dec 1822 by Exg.T.W.2280=7 Nov 1818 Michael Millar 50 A. in
Hampshire Co. on S. Br. of Potomac, S. Br. Mt. adj. his own land patented to him
by his father Isaac Millar 31 Jan 1792, Cunrad Huffman heirs, William Mills. 31
Aug 1824 [Dl'd Mr. Armstrong 30 Nov 1824]

C2-253:   Surv. 14 Dec 1822 150 A. by T.W.6484=19 Jan 1819 & 8 A. 2 Ro. 30 Po. by
T.W.5351=14 Feb 1815 Michael Millar 158 A. 2 Ro. 30 Po. in Hampshire Co. on
Stone Run & Saw Mill Run of S. Br. of Potomac adj. his land, Isaac Kuykendall
formerly Joshua Smally. 31 Aug 1824 [Dl'd Mr. Armstrong 30 Nov 1824]

C2-254:   Surv. 7 Nov 1822 225 A. by T.W.5775=29 Oct 1816, 201 A. by T.W.6166=5
Feb 1818 & 99 A. by T.W.6227=9 Mar 1815 William Mills 525 A. in Hampshire Co. on
S. Br. of Potomac, drain through Vanmeters Gap, Mills Mill Run opposite the
Glebe, Br. Mt., Middle Mt., S. Br. Mt. adj. William Naylor bought
of George Beatty heirs, Cunrad Huffman heirs formerly James Dobbins, Thomas
Taylor, Vanmeter. 31 Aug 1824 [Dl'd Mr Parsons 8 Jan 1825]

C2-256:   Surv. 7 Apr 1820 by T.W.6295=8 June 1818 John Martin 98 A. 1 Ro. 22 Po.
in Hampshire Co. on N. Br. Mt. called Martins hill, ash Cabbin Run of N. Br. of
Potomac, adj. said Martin patented by Nehemiah Martin 16 Oct 1766, John Martin
Jr. 31 Aug 1824

C2-257:   Surv. 12 Apr 1820, 33 A. 3 Ro. 24 Po. by T.W.6074=4 Nov 1817 & 35 A. 7
Po. by T.W.6295=8 June 1818 John Woolford 68 A. 3 Ro 31 Po. in Hampshire Co. on
Gibbons Run of N. R. adj. Philip Feeks, William Flemingham, John Brown, his
purchase of William Day, Reason Howard. 31 Aug 1824 [Dl'd Mr. Pugh 8 Jan 1825]

C2-259:   Surv. 25 Apr 1822 by T.W.6512=1 Feb 1819 Joseph Martin 8 A. 25 Po. in
Hampshire Co. on N. R. adj. his own land, Dunmore heirs, John T. Summers now
Joseph Martin. 31 Aug 1824 [Dl'd James Gibson 3 Nov 1824]

C2-259:   Surv. 14 Sep 1822 by T.W.6295=16 Apr 1822 William Doran 29 3/4 A. in
Hampshire Co. near N. R. on Brushy Rg. adj. Robert Fulton, Asa Carter, John
Carter, Alexander Doran. 31 Aug 1824

C2-260:   Surv. 15 Aug 1823 by T.W.7327=18 Nov 1822 William Doran 88 1/2 A. in
Hampshire Co. on N. R. Mt. adj. Levi James formerly Jacob Baker. 31 Aug 1824
[Dl'd James Gibson 3 Nov 1824]

C2-261:   Surv. 12 Oct 1822 by T.W.7104=6 July 1821 Hugh Murphey 68 A. 28 Po. in
Hampshire Co. on Abrahams Cr. of N. Br. of Potomac & Alleghany Mt. adj. James &
David Parsons, John Higgins heirs, heirs of Charles Lee dec'd, heirs of John
Johnson dec'd, heirs of Hugh Murphey dec'd. 31 Aug 1824 [Mr. Parsons 10 Jan 1825

C2-262:   Surv. 25 June 1823 by T.W.6072=4 Nov 1817 Jamima Fox, wid. of William
Fox dec'd, Ivea Decker w. of Luke Decker, late Ivea Fox, Absalom Fox, Vause Fox,
Eliza Williams w. of Joseph Williams late Eliza Fox, George Fox, Gabriel Fox,
Ann Inskeep w. of Isaac Inskeep late Ann Fox, Rebeckah Temple w. of Dr. John
Temple late Rebeckah Fox, Amos Fox, Julianna Fox, Rachel Fox, William F. Fox &

Sarah Fox ch. & heirs of s'd William Fox dec'd 980 A. in Hampshire Co. on Middle Rg., Castlemans Run of S. Br., Mill Cr. adj. Ephraim Herriott formerly William Harriott, s'd William Fox heirs, Strother McNeal, Isaac Means heirs, Peter Williams, Booklass. 31 Aug 1824 [Dl'd Col. Sloan 9 Jan 1826]

C2-263: Surv. 11 May 1822 by T.W.5571=2 Feb 1816 Alexander Poston 64 A. in Hampshire Co. on Kinsmans Mt. & N. R. adj. Edward Perrel. 31 Aug 1824 [Dl'd Mr. Caskardon 1828]

C2-264: Surv. 14 Sep 1822 by T.W.7280=17 July 1822 Lewis Emett 59 A. 3 Ro. 28 Per. in Frederick Co. adj. Stephen Myers, Thomas Steel, Dry Run of Crooked Run. 31 Aug 1824 [Dl'd Nash Legrand 10 Dec 1824]

C2-265: Surv. 6 Nov 1822 by T.W.5351=14 Feb 1815 Isaac Kuykendall 217 A. 2 Ro. 33 Po. in Hampshire Co. on Buffaloe Run of S. Br. of Potomac adj. Isaac Pancake formerly Henry Kuykendall. 31 Aug 1824 [Dl'd Col. Sloan 9 Jan 1826]

C2-266: Surv. 4 Jan 1822 29 A. by T.W.7104=6 July 1821 & 11 A. 1 Ro. 29 Po. by T.W.4873=26 Mar 1812 James Gray 40 A. 1 Ro 29 Po. in Hampshire Co. on Big Cacapehon adj. his own land, Joseph Yates, Parker. 25 Oct 1824

C2-267: Surv. 12 Nov 1823 100 A. by T.W.6808=10 Feb 1820 & 56 A. by T.W.6604=11 Mar 1819 Benjamin Fenton 156 A. in Frederick Co. adj. Jacob Wolfe, John Cooper, John Frye, Henry Shull, Joseph Holsenpiller bought of Benjamin Williams one of heirs of Jacob Woolfe dec'd, Peter Stephens 1768 grant, Cedar Cr., John Richards. 25 Oct 1824

C2-268: Surv. 24 Apr 1823 by T.W.4597=5 Dec 1809 Ruth Lowry asne. of Thomas Oglevie 157 A. in Hardy Co. on Patterson Cr. Mt. adj. John Webb, heirs of Isaac Hite, Daniel Arnold. 25 Oct 1824

C2-269: Surv. 13 Nov 1823 by Exg.T.W.2434=30 Oct 1822 Michael McKewan 101 A. in Berkeley Co. on N. Mt. adj. Baldwin, Lemon, Robert Daniels. 25 Oct 1824 [Dl'd Mr. Coulston 26 Jan 1825]

C2-270: Surv. 2 May 1822 by T.W.6245=8 Apr 1818 John Brannon 98 A. in Frederick Co. adj. Abraham Miller, James Barr, David Greenlee, heirs of John Brannon Sr. dec'd. 25 Oct 1824 [Dl'd Col. Sexton 15 ___ 1825]

C2-270: Surv. 27 Nov 1823, 194 A. by T.W.5681=17 June 1816 & 6 A. by T.W.7213=1 Mar 1822 John Rudloph asne. of Jacob Garrett 200 A. in Frederick & Shanandoah Cos. adj. Peter Harbough, George Hup, Samuel Shell, Samuel Orndurff, Cedar Cr., Jacob Garret, Paddys Run, Jacob Rudolph. 25 Oct 1824 [Capt. Shipp 8 Dec 1824]

C2-272: Surv. 17 Oct 1822 by T.W.5725=19 Aug 1816 George Karns asne. of Jacob Hierronimus 2 3/4 A. in Frederick Co. adj. George Kearnes, Caster Allamong, Isaacs Cr., Conrod Hierronimus now said Allamong, McKee, Rout. 25 Oct 1824 [Dl'd Col. Sexton 28 Dec 1824]

C2-272: Surv. 26 Nov 1823 by T.W.7213=1 Mar 1822 Jacob Garret 92 A. in Frederick Co. adj. Samuel Orndurff, Rudolph heirs, said Garret, on Cedar Cr., Squiles, Jacob Kackley formerly James?, Paddy, John Rudloph, Peter Hurbough, Paddys Run. 25 Oct 1824 [Dl'd Capt. Shipp 8 Dec 1824]

C2-274: Surv. 23 May 1823 by T.W.7104=6 July 1821 Christian Utta asne. of Abraham Reed 16 A. 34 Po. in Hampshire Co. on Miles Run of Patterson's Cr. adj. Christian Utta, Halliday. 17 Nov 1824

C2-274: Surv. 18 Aug 1823 by Exg.T.W.2444=22 Feb 1823 Simeon Turner 72 A. 1 Ro. in Berkeley Co. adj. Powell, James S. Lane. 11 Nov 1824

C2-275: Surv. 12 Apr 1822 by Exg.T.W.2349=20 June 1820 Morton Bourne alias Bourn asne. of Joseph Castleman 55 A. 1 Ro. 2 Po. in Berkeley Co. on Back Cr. adj. Morton Bourne, Robert Powell, Nathan Ross. 11 Nov 1824 [Dl'd Mr. LeGrand]

C2-275: Surv. 13 June 1823 by Exg.T.W. 2280=Nov 1818 Jonathan Burch 37 A. 39

sq. Po. in Hampshire Co. on Bald Hill, adj. Samuel Ruckman, Little Cacapehon, Abbit Carder formerly Thomas Mulledy, Wilson Ruckman, William Naylor, Perez Drew heirs. 11 Nov 1824

C2-276: Surv. 23 Feb 1824 by T.W.7266=6 June 1822 Thomas Selectman 125 A. in Pr. William Co. on Occaquan R., adj. Swan Point tract, Gravelly Br., said Selectman, Mill Tract. 11 Nov 1824 [Dl'd Wm. Clarke 20 Dec 1824]

C2-277: Surv. 28 Apr 1796 by T.W.1836=6 Mar 1796 Mary Forbes, Catharine Forbes, Nancy Forbes, Elizabeth Forbes, John Forbes, Martin Forbes & James Forbes only ch. & heirs of John Forbes late of Berkeley Co. dec'd, 11 A. 23 sq. Po. in Berkeley Co. adj. Daniel Kenneday, Henry Riners, John G. Konnekey, George Mires. 17 Jan 1825

C2-278: Surv. 14 June 1814 by T.W.5641=19 Mar 1816 Jacob Sheetz & John Mourer, in trust, and their successors 1/2 A. in Shanandoah Co. on Narrow Passage Cr. (for school house & Seminary for inhabitants in neighborhood of Narrow Passage Cr.) adj. Philip Williams, John Mourer, George Grandorff. 15 Feb 1825

C2-279: Surv. 1 May 1824 by Exg.T.W.2472=23 Feb 1824 Dugal Campbell 151 A. in Berkeley Co. on N. Mt. adj. Dutton, James Barton, Holt, Russell, Land's heirs, Swingle, Cagle heirs, Hartstock heirs. 14 Feb 1825

C2-280: Surv. 27 Aug 1823 by T.W.7453=24 Mar 1823 Peter Kabrick 59 1/2 A. in Hampshire Co. on Dry Run of Pattersons Cr. adj. Andrew Nisbet, Abraham Good, Sylvester Welsh, heirs of Peter Kabrick Sr. dec'd, Rd. from Burlington to Paddy Town, Nisbit formerly Buskirk. 23 Mar 1825 [Dl'd Col. Slone 9 Jan 1826]

C2-281: Surv. 10 Jan 1824 by Exg.T.W.1795=12 Dec 1805 Richard H. Barnes, Helen Mary Barnes, Thomas Beale Barnes, Catherine Ann Barnes, Alexander Beale Barnes, Elizabeth Thomas w. of Addison N. Thomas & William Barnes only heirs of William Barnes dec'd, 88 A. 1 Ro, 29 Po. in Pr. William Co. on Neabsco Run adj. Tayloe, Tibbs, William Barnes. 20 Apr 1825 [Dl'd James E. Heath 13 June 1825]

C2-281: Surv. 1 Nov 1823 by T.W.5944=24 May 1817 Ethanus Campher 89 1/2 A. in Shenandoah Co. on N. Mt. adj. Peter Frenster, John Campher, John Bowers, Abraham Jones, John Holver, George Billers, Daniel Walters. 4 May 1825 [Dl'd Ethanmous Campher 26 Jan 1826]

C2-282: Surv. 3 Aug 1824 by T.W.7735=13 July 1824 Godfrey Wilkin 5 A. in Hardy Co. on Kimseys Run of Lost R. adj. his own land, Joseph Wilkin. 4 May 1825 [Dl'd Joseph Inskeep 28 Oct 1825]

C2-283: Surv. 2 Aug 1824 by T.W.7735=13 July 1824 John Wetzel 88 A. in Hardy Co. on Kimseys Run of Lost R. adj. John Duffield heirs. 4 May 1825 [Dl'd Joseph Inskeep 28 Oct 1825]

C2-283: Surv. 12 Apr 1824 by T.W.6724=25 Oct 1819 Joseph Davis 152 A. in Hardy Co. on New Cr. adj. Jesse Davis, New Cr. Mt. 7 May 1825 [Col. Sloan 9 Jan 1826]

C2-284: Surv. 15 Jan 1824 by T.W.6735=4 Nov 1819 Leornard Boncrot Jr. 13 A. 20 sq. Po. in Hampshire Co. bet. Mill Cr. & S. Br. of Potomack near Threshers knob adj. Leornard Boncrot Sr., John & Nicholas Leatherman formerly John High, Zachariah Fowler. 7 May 1825 [Dl'd Col. Sloan 9 Jan 1826]

C2-285: Surv. 27 Apr 1824 by T.W.5129=9 Nov 1813 George M. Pennybacker & Joel Pennybacker Exrs. of last will of Benjamin Pennybacker dec'd 30 A. in Shenandoah Co. on Smiths Cr. adj. Benjamin Pennybaker formerly Benjamin Fawcett, James Allen, Solomon Kingree. 4 June 1825 [Dl'd Robert Allen 5 Dec 1825]

C2-285: Surv. 1 May 1824, 500 A. by Exg.T.W.2352=28 Sep 1820 & 296 A. by T.W.5129=9 Nov 1813 George M. Pennybacker & Joel Pennybacker Exrs. of last will of Benjamin Pennybacker dec'd 796 A. in Shenandoah Co. on Big Mt. Run of Smiths Cr. & Passage Cr. in Powells Ft. adj. Charles L. Moore formerly Jacob Moore, Messennutten Mt., Short Arse Mt., Benjamin Pennybaker purchase of Clem, the Dividing Rg. 4 June 1825 [Dl'd Robert Allen 5 Dec 1825]

C2-286:   Surv. 15 Dec 1823 by T.W.6832=21 Feb 1820 George Hottle 400 A. in Hampshire Co. on Frys Run of Big Cacapehon, near Fry's Rd., Bear Rg.   4 June 1825 [Dl'd M. Bear 26 Jan 1826]

C2-287: Surv. 6 Nov 1824, 500 A. by T.W.7514=3 Nov 1823 & 64 A. by 7465=1 May 1823 James Vance 564 A. in Hampshire Co. on N. Mt., Loanans Br. adj. William Lafollet, John Lafollet, Bear Rg., David Stepehs, Jesse Anderson. 4 June 1825

C2-288:   Surv. 3 Sep 1823 by T.W.7118=23 Aug 1821 Charles Tackett 117 A. in Fauquier Co. bet. Benjamin Ficklin now Charles Tackett, William Carr heirs now Tibbs, Francis Latham, Stephen French, Humfrey heirs, Woods Br. 23 Aug 1825 [Dl'd Capt. T. _?_ 31 Oct 1825]

C2-288: Surv. 18 Jan 1824 by Exg.T.W.1795=12 Dec 1805 Richard H. Barnes, Helen Mary Barnes, Thomas Beale Barnes, Catherine Ann Barnes, Alexander Beale Barnes, Elizabeth Thomas w. of Addison N. Thomas & William Barnes heirs of William Barnes dec'd, 17 A. 30 Po. in Pr. William Co. by Dumfres Rd., adj. heirs of Col. Ewell dec'd, Tayloe, Tomas, & 71 A. 22 Po in said Co. adj. Woods, Ruses now Ewels. 23 Aug 1825

C2-289:   Surv. 8 Oct 1824 by T.W.7735=13 July 1824 John Homan 162 A. in Hardy Co. on Limestone Rg., & Lost R. adj. his own land, George Hulver, Boughmans Rd. 15 Sep 1825 [Dl'd Mr. Mullen 23 Feb 1830]

C2-290: Surv. 14 Apr 1824 by T.W.5519=1 Dec 1815 George Lowderman 53 A.   in Hardy Co. on N. Mill Cr. adj. Jesse Stump, s'd Louderman, Michael Alt, Stombough. 15 Sep 1825 [Dl'd Mr. Neff 1828]

C2-290: Surv. 26 Feb 1824 by Exg.T.W.2348=2 June 1820 Michael McKewan & John Lyle 316 A. in Berkeley Co. on N. Mt. adj. Boyd, Mengham, Bailey, McKewan, Pulse, Spencer, Lyle. 15 Sep 1825

C2-291: Surv. 17 July 1824 by T.W.7649=16 Feb 1824 Thomas J. Bullett 1 A. in Pr. William Co. on Quantico Cr. adj. Potomac R., town of Newport. 15 Sep 1825 [Dl'd Mr. Harrison 5 July 1827]

C2-292: Surv. 14 Apr 1824 by T.W.6724=25 Oct 1819 Jacob Barkdoll in his own right one moiety and as asne. of Jacob Kellerman the other moiety 56 A. in Hardy Co. on N. Mill Cr. adj. heirs of Martin Peterson. 15 Sep 1825

C2-292: Surv. 14 Apr 1824 by T.W.5516=1 Dec 1815 Adam Boots & Jesse Stump 130 A. in Hardy Co. adj. N. Mill Cr. Martin Peterson heirs, Philip Yokum. 15 Sep 1825

C2-293: Surv. 2 Aug 1824 by T.W.5519=1 Dec 1815 Michael Brake 40 A. in Hardy Co. on S. Fork of S. Br. of Potomack adj. N.N. line, heirs of George Mongold dec'd, said Brake. 15 Sep 1825

C2-293: Surv. 20 Mar 1824 by T.W.5641=19 Mar 1816 Jacob Funkhouser (Mill Cr.) 3 1/2 A. in Shenandoah Co. on Mill Cr. adj. Ephraim Rinker, said Funkhouser, heir of David Funkhouser dec'd. 15 Sep 1825 [Dl'd Bearer 26 Jan 1826]

C2-294:   Surv. 10 Mar 1824 by T.W.7384=18 Jan 1823 Daniel Funkhouser 200 A. in Shenandoah Co. adj. said Funkhouser, Pugh, E. Feely. 15 Sep 1825 [Dl'd Mr. Bear 26 Jan 1826]

C2-294:   Surv. 1 Sep 1824 by T.W.5641=19 Mar 1816 John Zirkle 8 A. 2 Ro. 27 Po. in Shenandoah Co. on N. fork of Shenandoah R. adj. said Zirkle, David Olinger, Benjamin Zirkle. 15 Sep 1825 [Dl'd Mr. Bear 26 Jan 1826]

C2-295:   Surv. 24 June 1824 by T.W.6966=9 Dec 1820 John Rankin 49 A. 3 Ro. 35 Po. in Hampshire Co. on Reasoners & Sheets Runs of Pattersons Cr. adj. his land, Samuel Dobbins, Cooper. 19 Sep 1825 [Dl'd Mr. Parsons Jan 7 1826]

C2-295: Surv.7 Apr 1824 by T.W.5351=14 Feb 1815 William Clark 20 A. 1 Ro. 22 Po. in Hampshire Co. on Mill Run of Pattersons Cr. adj. Thomas Rees, said William Clark, heirs of George Miller dec'd. 19 Sep 1825 [Dl'd Mr. Parsons Jan 7 1826]

C2-296:   Surv. 1 June 1824 by T.W.4968=2 Nov 1812 Thomas Sollars 50 A. in
Hampshire Co. on New Cr. on Tibs Run, the Mt. Rd., Andrew Aronhalt, Rd. to wid.
Deanes. 19 Sep 1825 [Dl'd Mr. Parsons Jan 7 1826]

C2-296:   Surv. 8 Apr 1824 by T.W.6073=4 Nov 1817 Thomas Rees 50 A. in Hampshire
Co. on Pattersons Cr. & Middle Rg. adj. Arganal Price 1795 grant, Daniel
Hollingback, Rd. from Pattersons Cr. to S. Br. of Potomack. 19 Sep 1825 [Dl'd
Mr. Parsons Jan 7 1826]

C2-297:   Surv. 30 Oct 1823 by T.W.5572=2 Feb 1816 Eli Moore 23 A. in Hampshire
Co. on Mikes Run of Patterson's Cr. adj. his surv., Hardy Co. line. 19 Sep 1825
[Dl'd Mr. Parsons Jan 26 1826]

C2-298: Surv. 27 Oct 1824, 47 A. by T.W.6755=9 Dec 1819 & 2 A. by T.W.6166=5 Feb
1818 Hendrix Clark 49 A. in Hampshire Co. on Clark's Mill Run adj. Thomas Rees,
Daniel Clark. 19 Sep 1825 [Dl'd Henderson Clark by Mr. Parsons Jan 7 1826]

C2-298:   Surv. 16 Apr 1824 by T.W.7104=6 July 1821 John Darby 4 A. 3 Ro. in
Hampshire Co. on big Cacapehon adj. Francis White, said Darby bought of William
Hamilton, Dade Powell, Thomas Allen heirs. 19 Sep 1825 [Mr. Parsons 7 Jan 1826]

C2-299: Surv. 1 July 1824 by T.W.6662=7 June 1819 Ann Harrison wid. & relict of
James Harrison dec'd, Joseph Harrison & Sarah Ann Harrison ch. & heirs of said
James Harrison dec'd 34 A. 6 Po. in Hampshire Co. on Mikes Run of Pattersons Cr.
adj. Primm now heirs of said James Harrison, William Fuller formerly Benjaman
Hults, Knobley Mt., Primm. 19 Sep 1825 [Dl'd Mr. Parsons 7 Jan 1826]

C2-300:   Surv. 27 May 1824, 150 A. by T.W.7109=27 July 1821 & 29 A. by 7483=25
July 1823 Vincent Vandiver 179 A. in Hampshire Co. on Knobley Mt. adj. John
Hammock formerly David Long, Ravenscraft, Edward McCarty, Johns Gap, said
Vandiver. 19 Sep 1825 [Dl'd Mr. Parsons 7 Jan 1826]

C2-300:   Surv. 27 Apr 1824 by T.W.5641=19 Mar 1816 John Spitler 30 A. in Shenandoah Co. on Stoney Cr. adj. Daniel Stout now said Spitler, Joshua Voltz, Adam
Sine, John Sine, Peter Craig formerly Daniel Stouts, John Hottell. 19 Sep 1825

C2-301:   Surv. 10 Jan 1825, 50 A. by T.W.7496=12 Sep 1823 & 5 A. by T.W.7019=16
Feb 1821 Thomas L. Moore 55 A. in Fauquier Co. on Carters Run adj. Scott,
Rappahannock Mt., Anderson, Fairfax line, George Chapman. 5 Oct 1825 [By mail
to Prop'r 6 Oct 1825]

C2-302:   Surv. 11 Sep 1824 by T.W.7501=30 Sep 1823 Samuel Dobbins 146 A. in
Hampshire Co. on Cabbin Run, Cabbin Run Rg. adj. his own land, Cooper, Allen,
Reasoners Run. 19 Sep 1825 [Dl'd Mr. Parsons 7 Jan 1826]

C2-302:   Surv. 31 Mar 1824 by T.W.5535=15 Dec 1815 Jacob Burner Jr. 10 A. in
Shenandoah Co. in Powells Big Ft. on Passage Cr. adj. heirs of John Spangler
dec'd, Dr. Jacob Keller, George Bowman. 19 Sep 1825

C2-303:   Surv. 1 Apr 1824 by T.W.5535=15 Dec 1815 Jacob Burner Jr. 10 A. in
Shenandoah Co. in Powells Big Ft. on Passage Cr. adj. William Moordock, Fergus
Cron now Michael Burner, Burner formerly Denton, heirs of John Spangler dec'd.
19 Sep 1825

C2-303:   Surv. 31 Mar 1824 by T.W.5535=15 Dec 1815 Jacob Burner Jr. 7 A. in
Shenandoah Co. in Powells Big Ft. on Passage Cr. adj. said Burner formerly
Denton, John Spangler dec'd heirs, Henry Walter, Dr. Jacob Kellar. 19 Sep 1825

C2-304:   Surv. 26 May 1824 by T.W.7303=1 Oct 1822 Moses Walton 8 3/4 A. in
Shenandoah Co. bet. Smiths Cr. & Messsenotten Mt. adj. Henry Kagy, Rudolph Kagy,
Samuel Strickler. 19 Sep 1825 [Dl'd Col. Allen 4 Jan 1826]

C2-304:   Surv. 8 June 1824 by T.W.7453?=24 Mar 1823 Michael Caudy 39 1/4 A. in
Hampshire Co. adj. Parker Mt. George Oats. 19 Sep 1825 [Mr. Parsons 7 Jan 1826]

C2-305:   Surv. 14 Apr 1824 by T.W.5571=2 Feb 1816 Samuel Williamson 19 3/4 A. in

Hampshire Co. on Crooked Run of Little Cacapehon adj. Richard Moreland, John Millison. 19 Sep 1825 [Dl'd Mr. Parsons 7 Jan 1826]

C2-306:   Surv. 12 Feb 1824, 100 A. by T.W.4763=7 Aug 1811 & 8 A. by T.W.6661=7 June 1819 Cornelius Williamson 108 A. in Hampshire Co. on Crooked Run of Little Cacapehon adj. Samuel Hott, Edward Knott, Dividing Rg., path to Thompsons Mill. 19 Sep 1825 [Dl'd Mr. Parsons 7 Jan 1826]

C2-306:   Surv. 30 Dec 1823, 200 A. by T.W.5571=2 Feb 1819 & 71 1/2 A. 1 Feb 1819 Richard Blue 271 1/2 A. in Hampshire Co. on Sugar Run of S. Br. of Potomack adj. Henry Powellson, John Thompson, Blue's Rd. to Newman Town. S. Br. Mt. 19 Sep 1825 [Dl'd Mr. Parsons 7 Jan 1826]

C2-307:   Surv. 12 Jan 1824 by T.W.6776=31 Dec 1819 John Brant 35 A. 3 Ro. in Hampshire Co. on N. Br. of Potomack, Pine Swamp Run opposite Brants factory inc. 1793 surv. of Moses Tichinal never patented, adj. Newman Beckwith. 19 Sep 1825

C2-308:   Surv. 13 Jan 1824 by T.W.6776=31 Dec 1819 John Brant 14 1/4 A. in Hampshire Co. on N. Br. of Potomack adj. Ohio Bottom surv. of Burns's heirs. 19 Sep 1825 [Dl'd Mr. Carskaddon 1828]

C2-309:   Surv. 26 Oct 1824 by T.W.7202=27 Feb 1822 William Clark 98 A. 3 Ro. in Hampshire Co. on Mill Run of Pattersons Cr. adj. Hickman, said Clark, heirs of George Miller dec'd, Abraham Reed. 19 Sep 1825 [Dl'd Mr. Parsons 7 Jan 1826]

C2-309:   Surv. 2 July 1824 by T.W.5441=24 Aug 1815 Joshua Bethel 39 A. in Hampshire Co. on Kenman Mt. bet. N. R. & Dillons Run adj. heirs of Benjamin Johnson dec'd bought of George Edgington, Jesse Lupton, Parril, Starkey. 19 Sep 1825 [Dl'd Mr. Jas. Gibson 28 Dec 1826]

C2-310:   Surv. 24 May 1824 by T.W.4781=20 Apr 1824 Jacob Fout & William Fout 37 A. in Hampshire Co. on New Cr. adj. Andrew Aronhalt. 19 Sep 1825 [Dl'd Mr. Parsons 7 Jan 1826]

C2-311:   Surv. 20 Dec 1823 by T.W.6904=22 May 1820 Henry Brill 28 3/4 A. in Hampshire Co. on Dry Run of Cacapehon Spring Br. adj. Jacob Pugh's 1778 surv., John Bell, John Lucan. 19 Sep 1824 [Dl'd Mr. Vance 1833]

C2-311:   Surv. 7 Sep 1824, 22 3/4 A. by T.W.6904=22 May 1820 & 13 3/4 A. by T.W.7453=24 Mar 1823 Michael Caudy 36 1/2 A. in Hampshire Co. on Dillons Run and Winding Rg. adj. Jesse Lupton, Isaac Lupton, William Carlyle formerly Bowers. 19 Sep 1825 [Dl'd Mr. Parsons 7 Jan 1826]

C2-312:   Surv. 2 Sep 1824 by T.W.7501=30 Sep 1823 John Jeremiah Jacobs 61 1/2 A. in Hampshire Co. adj. his land, Praters Run of N. Br. of Potomack, Middle Rg., path from s'd Jacobs to Frankfort. 19 Sep 1825 [Dl'd Mr. Parsons 7 Jan 1826]

C2-313:   Surv. 26 Aug 1824 by T.W.5775=29 Oct 1816 James Pennington 10 A. 34 Po. in Hampshire Co. adj. Big Cacapehon Joel Ellis, Elijah Pennington. 19 Sep 1825

C2-314:   Surv. 11 Sep 1824 by T.W.7501=30 Sep 1823 Solomon Elifritz 100 A. in Hampshire Co. on Pattersons Cr. adj. Samuel Dobbins. 19 Sep 1825 [Mr. Parsons 7 Jan 1826]

C2-314:   Surv. 4 June 1824, 60 A. by T.W.7109=27 July 1821 & 34 1/4 A. by T.W.6904=22 May 1820 Vincent Vandiver & John McVicker 94 1/4 A. in Hampshire Co. on Loanams Br. of Big Cacapehon adj. James Kelsoe, Henry Stevens, Philip Kline, Joseph Clutter. 19 Sep 1825 [Dl'd Mr Thomas Carskardon 4 Feb 1828]

C2-315:   Surv. 6 Dec 1823 by T.W.6904=22 May 1820 Margaret Racy relict of Thomas Racy, Elizabeth Racy, Madison Racy, Mana Racy, Nacy Racy, Sarah Racy, John Racy & Lewis Racy heirs & ch. of said Thomas Racy dec'd, 25 3/4 A. in Hampshire Co. on Loanams Br. of Big Cacapehon adj. William Lafollet, Timber Rg., Jesse Anderson, said Thomas Racy. 19 Sep 1825 [Dl'd Mr. Odell 7 Dec 1840]

C2-315:   Surv. 19 Nov 1823 by T.W.6787=5 Feb 1820 Daniel Hollingback 17 A. in

Hampshire Co. on Pattersons Cr. & Middle Rg., adj. John Pearsall now Eleenezer
Mcnary, Henry Hazel now Stephen Chandler heirs. 4 Oct 1825 [Dl'd Mr. Parsons 7
Jan 1826]

C2-316: Surv. 5 Nov 1823 by T.W.6787=5 Feb 1820 Daniel Hollingback 250 1/4 A.
in Hampshire Co. on Middle Rg., Pattersons Cr. adj. Ebenezer Mcnary formerly
John Pearsall, Stephen Chandler, Wm. Armstrong, Arjilon Price. 4 Oct 1825
[Dl'd Mr. Parsons 7 Jan 1826]

C2-317: Surv. 3 Oct 1820 by T.W.6406=5 Nov 1818 Thomas Hook asne. of Michael
Pugh asne. of David Ellis 18 A. in Hampshire Co. on Timber Rg. adj. Charles
Simmons, David Caudy, Thomas Hook, Haden, Loanams now said Simmons, John Brown
now Thomas Hook. 4 Oct 1825 [Dl'd Mr. Vance 19 Jan 1833]

C2-318: Surv. 8 Jan 1925 by T.W.7467=12 May 1823 Jacob Reichard 12 A. in Morgan
Co. on Sleepy Cr. adj. said Reichard, Fitzchew, John Burn. 4 Oct 1825 [Dl'd
Mr. Sherrard Nov 1827]

C2-318: Surv. 5 Nov 1824 by T.W.7692=9 Mar 1824 Elizabeth Burk 59 1/2 A. in
Morgan Co. adj. Warm Springs Run, Jacob Pinkins, Elisha Boyd, William Sherrard,
George Orrich, William Neely. 4 Oct 1825 [Dl'd Mr. Sherrard 8 Dec 1825]

C2-319: Surv. 17 Feb 1824 by T.W.5509=25 Nov 1815 John Mauck 129 A. in
Shenandoah Co. bet. Mill Run & S. R. of Shenandoah adj. Calib Cambill, Jonathan
Tobin, said Mauck. 4 Oct 1825 [Dl'd Mr. Morton 16 Jan 1826]

C2-319: Surv. 4 Apr 1824 by dup. T.W.5944=26 Oct 1818 John Mauck 17 A. in
Shenandoah Co. on Stony Run adj. heirs of Lewis Stonebeger dec'd. 4 Oct 1825
[Dl'd Mr. Morton 16 Jan 1826]

C2-320: Surv. 28 June 1823, 150 A. by T.W.7166=15 Dec 1821 & 466 A. by
T.W.7372=26 Dec 1822 John Brant asne. of George R. Tasker 616 A. in Hampshire
Co. on N. Br. of Potomac adj. Alexander Riley, Newman Beckwith, John Warwick,
William McChesney. 5 Oct 1825 [Dl'd Mr. Carskaddon 1828]

C2-321: Surv. 14 Apr 1824 by T.W.6724=25 Oct 1819 George Sites 36 A. in Hardy
Co. on Fork Mt. & Mill Cr. 5 Oct 1825 [Dl'd Mr. James Murury 26 Nov 1827]

C2-321: Surv. 13 Feb 1824 by T.W.6512=1 Feb 1819 John Arnold 100 A. in
Hampshire Co. on Little Cacapehon adj. Humphrey Corbin, Joseph Mason now John
Arnold, David Corbin, Cornelious Williamson. 5 Oct 1825

C2-322: Surv. 26 Oct 1823? by T.W.7312=21 Oct 1822 William Lynn 8 A. 3 Ro. 20
Po. in Pr. William Co. on Powels Run adj. William Lynn dec'd, King, Bland's Rd.
5 Oct 1825

C2-322: Surv. 14 Nov 1824 by T.W.6930=1 Aug 1820 Dennis OBrian 17 1/2 A. in
Morgan Co. on Warm Spring Rg., Capt. Johns Run adj. John Castler, Michael
McKewan, William Neely, William Johnson. 5 Oct 1825 [Dl'd Mr. Sherrard 1828]

C2-323: Surv. 10 Oct 1824 by T.W.7735=13 July 1824 George Fisher & Adam Fisher
70 A. in Hardy Co. on Elkhorn adj. heirs of Elias Shoemaker, Barkdoll, heirs of
Adam Fisher dec'd, near main Rd. 5 Oct 1825 [Dl'd Mr. Neff 19 __ 1927]

C2-323: Surv. 23 Apr 1824 by T.W.5534=15 Dec 1815 Daniel Munch 3 1/2 A. in
Shenandoah Co. in Powells Big Ft. on Passage Cr. adj. Dr. Jacob Keller, Adam
Lechliter, said Daniel Munch, Christian Shipe. 5 Oct 1825 [Dl'd Mr. Sam'l Bare
14 Dec 1827]

C2-324: Surv. 1 Dec 1823 by T.W.6748=6 Dec 1819 John Beeler 166 A. in
Shenandoah Co. on Little N. Mt. adj. said Beeler, Kingan, Rudloph Rosenberger,
Henry Rosenberger, heirs of Philip Brobeck dec'd. 5 Oct 1825

C2-325: Surv. 11 Sep 1824, 70 A. by T.W.6513=2 Feb 1819 & 80 A. by T.W.6129=31
Dec 1817 Teter Rawlings 150 A. in Hampshire Co. on Stovers Run & Middle Run of
Pattersons Cr. adj. Elijah Rawlings, heirs of Benjamin Rawlings dec'd, Johnson's

or Stover's Run. 30 Nov 1825 [Dl'd Col. Sloan 9 Jan 1826]

C2-325: Surv. 7 Sep 1812 by T.W.615=17 Sep 1794 Levi Claypole asne. of Jacob Miller exr. of John Claypole dec'd 75 A. in Hardy Co. on Saw Mill Run and Coalkill Run of Lost R. adj. his own land, George Lee Sr. heirs. 24 Feb 1826

C2-326: Surv. 26 June 1824, 200 A. by T.W.7651=17 Feb 1824 & 370 1/2 A. by T.W.6445=16 Dec 1818 Frederick Sheetz & Samuel Cockrell 570 1/2 A. in Hampshire Co. on Middle Rg. & Patterson's Cr. adj. Samuel Flenaghan, Joseph Long, Fox's path, Thomas Carskaddon, James Parker, Frederick Sheetz, George Utts, John Tatterer? & wife, Fillink. 2 June 1826 [Dl'd Mr. James Gibson 28 Dec 1826]

C2-328: Surv. 8 Apr 1825 by T.W.7878=16 Feb 1825 Branson Poston 97 A. in Hampshire Co. on Poston's & Hammock's Mill Runs of N. R. adj. Joseph Thompson. 2 June 1826 [Dl'd Mr. Carskaddon 1828]

C2-328: Surv. 3 Dec 1823 by T.W.7409=17 Feb 1823 Jacob Rudolph 117 A. in Shenandoah Co. on Little N. Mt. & Dry Run of Cedar Cr. adj. Philip Peer, Benjamin Williams. 2 June 1826

C2-329: Surv. 31 May 1819 by T.W.5775=29 Oct 1816 Samuel Williamson 75 A. in Hampshire Co. on N. R. Mt. adj. Anthony Orr. 2 June 1826 [To Rect. 1829]

C2-329: Surv. 10 Dec 1824 by T.W.4813=18 Jan 1812 Herman Webb 36 A. in Shenandoah Co. on Stony Cr. Rg. adj. Christina & Mary Rider, Daniel Webb, Peter Rider, said Herman Webb. 2 June 1826

C2-330: Surv. 25 Oct 1824 by Exg.T.W.2175=25 Mar 1813 Joseph R. Lynn 78 A. 1 Po. in Pr. William Co. on Quantico Cr. adj. Holliday heirs, Dr. Spence, Berryman. 2 June 1826 [Dl'd Mr. Sinclair? Feb 1827]

C2-330: Surv. 26 Nov 1824 by T.W.7056=8 Mar 1821 John Bark & Samuel Johnson 56 A. in Morgan Co. on Warm Spring Run adj. McKewan, Neely, Robert Gustin, Alburdi Gustin, Henry Boyle dec'd heirs purchased of Hoskins, William Boyle. 2 June 1826 [Dl'd Benjamin Orrick 22 Jan 1827]

C2-331: Surv. 25 Nov 1824 58 A. by T.W.6662=7 June 1819 & 66 1/4 A. by T.W.4968=2 Nov 1812 Benjamin Junkins 124 A. 1 Ro. in Hampshire Co. adj. his land on N. Br. of Potomack. 2 June 1826 [Dl'd Mr. Gibson Jan 1827]

C2-331a: Surv. 2 Aug 1825 by T.W.7960=30 June 1825 John Hart 200 A. in Frederick Co. on Hoge Cr. adj. Adam Hart, Casper Rinker's dvse. Ruth Jackson, Nathan Littler, John Holliday, Williamson. 2 June 1826 [Dl'd Mr. Mason 1 Mar 1827]

C2-331a: Surv. 7 Apr 1825 by T.W.5641=19 Mar 1816 Adam Barb(s. of Abraham) 100 A. in Shenandoah Co. on Little Stoney Cr. adj. Joshua Barb, heirs of Abraham Barb dec'd sold to John Arthur & Co., N. Mt., John Bower. 1 Sep 1826

C2-332: Surv. 16 Dec 1824 by T.W.5641=19 Mar 1816 Peter Grim 3 A. 2 Ro. 20 Per. in Shenandoah Co. on N. R. of Shenandoah, on Mt. Br., adj. heirs of Jonathan Hull dec'd, George Rynard. 1 Sep 1826

C2-333: Surv. 30 Dec 1824 by T.W.7820=20 Dec 1824 Joel Williams 115 A. in Shenandoah Co. on Cedar Cr., N. Mt. called Bonnets hill adj. Israel Orndorff dec'd, Shells & Wymer's Runs, Longacre, Strosnider, William Conner. 1 Sep 1826

C2-333: Surv. 5 Apr 1825 by T.W.7878=16 Feb 1825 David Foreman & John Combs 77 1/2 A. in Hampshire Co. on Sandy Rg. on Edwards Mt. adj. Carlysle, Amos Park, Abraham Rinehart, George Park formerly John Park. 1 Sep 1826 [Dl'd Mr. Jas. Gibson 28 Dec 1826]

C2-334: Surv. 20 May 1825, 80 A. by Exg.T.W.2406=15 Jan 1822 & 54 A. by T.W.6662=7 June 1819 Benjamin Slane 134 A. in Hampshire Co. on N. R. of Great Cacapehon adj. Travis D. Crosston, William Deaver, William Lockheart, Christopher Heiskel. 1 Sep 1826 [Dl'd Mr. Jas. Gibson 28 Dec 1826]

C2-335:   Surv. 11 Dec 1824 by T.W.7567=19 Jan 1824 Ebenezer McNary 1 A. 1 Ro. 4 Po. in Hampshire Co. on Patterson's Cr. adj. his own land bought of John Pearsaul heirs, heirs of William Armstrong Sr. dec'd, McBride, McNary. 1 Sep 1826 [M. Slone? 24 Jan 1822]

C2-336: Surv. 22 Mar 1825, 47 3/4 A. by T.W.6443=15 Dec 1818 & 11 3/4 A.=17 June 1819 William Loy 59 1/2 A. in Hampshire Co. on Dividing Rg. near Tear Coat Cr. adj. John Horn, said Loy, Elisha Bell, John Ruckman. 1 Sep 1826 [Dl'd Mr. Jas. Gibson 28 Dec 1826]

C2-336:   Surv. 8 Nov 1824 by T.W.7501=30 Sep 1823 Elias Jones 20 A. in Hampshire Co. in Senates Gap of Knobley Mt. adj. his own land bought of Samuel Kenedy. 1 Sep 1826   [Dl'd Mr. Jas. Gibson 28 Dec 1826]

C2-337:   Surv. 4 Apr 1825 by T.W.7829=28 Dec 1824 George Park 74 1/2 A. in Hampshire Co. on Sandy Rg. adj. his own land, Jacob Millshlagle bought of Baker. 1 Sep 1826   [Dl'd Mr. Jas. Gibson 28 Dec 1826]

C2-337:   Surv. 21 Oct 1825, 150 A. by T.W.7121=4 Sep 1821 & 2 1/4 A. by T.W.7419 =19 Feb 1823 Abraham Vanmeter 152 1/4 A. in Hampshire Co. on Stony Run of S. Br. of Potomack adj. Isaac Kuykendall, Michael Miller, Vanmeter, the Glebe formerly John Dicker, Aaron Huffman. 1 Sep 1826   [Dl'd Mr. Jas. Gibson 28 Dec 1826]

C2-339:   Surv. 17 Nov 1824 by T.W.6443=15 Dec 1818 William Loy 52 1/4 A. in Hampshire Co. on Little Cacapehon & Tear Coat adj. Dividing Rg., John Horn, Eaton, Holland, John Ruckman formerly John Powelson. 1 Sep 1826   [Dl'd Mr. Jas. Gibson 28 Dec 1826]

C2-339:   Surv. 25 June 1825 by T.W.7501=29 Oct 1824 Joseph Ridgeway 14 1/4 A. in Hampshire Co. on Great Cacapehon adj. land he bought of Abraham Vanosdeln, Daniel Bruner. 1 Sep 1826   [Dl'd Mr. Jas. Gibson 28 Dec 1826]

C2-340:   Surv. 19 May 1825 by T.W.7136=25 Oct 1821 Joseph Hiett 37 3/4 A. in Hampshire Co. on Sandy Rg. adj. John Loy, Joseph Hiett. 1 Sep 1826

C2-340:   Surv. 8 Aug 1825 by T.W.7136=25 Oct 1821 John Kidwell 10 A. 1 Ro. 25 Po. in Hampshire Co. on Coldstream of Big Cacapehon adj. Kidwell, John Hyatt's 1762 grant, Timothy Hiett, Thomas Kennedy now said Kidwell, Joseph Hiett. 1 Sep 1826   [Dl'd Mr. Jas. Gibson 28 Dec 1826]

C2-341:   Surv. 11 Dec 1824 by T.W.7567=19 Jan 1824 Ebenezer McNary 4 A. 3 Ro. 29 sq. Po. in Hampshire Co. on Patterson's Cr. adj. land he bought of John Pearsaul heirs, heirs of William Armstrong Sr. dec'd formerly Nathaniel Parker, McNary, Hollanback. 1 Sep 1826 [Dl'd Sloan 24 Jan 1827]

C2-342:   Surv. 5 Oct 1825, 50 A. by T.W.7692=9 Mar 1824 & 11 A. by T.W.7903=22 Feb 1825 Abraham Dawson 61 A. in Morgan Co. on Great Cacapeon Cr. adj. his late surv. Michael Whitmire, Abraham Vonosdal. 1 Sep 1826 [Dl'd to rec't 1828]

C2-342:   Surv. 4 Oct 1825, 100 A. by T.W.7903=22 Feb 1825 & 47 A. by T.W.4906=9 June 1812 Abraham Dawson 147 A. in Morgan Co. on Great Cacapeon Cr. adj. his own land, Israel Dawson, John Huff. 1 Sep 1826 [Dl'd to rec't 1828]

C2-344:   Surv. 29 Sep 1825 by T.W.7726=27 May 1824 Jacob Showalter 2 1/2 A. in Rockingham Co. adj. said Showalter, Jesse Harrison. (Marked out. Improperly recorded here)

C2-344:   Surv. 30 Sep 1825 by T.W.7735=13 July 1824 Jacob Berkdall 800 A. in Hardy Co. on S. fork Mt. adj. his land bought of Henry Roraboh, Jacob Sanders, Jacob Tetrick, John Roraboh, his Page place. 21 Oct 1826 [Dl'd Mr. Miller 1827]

C2-345:   Surv. 14 Nov 1825 by T.W.7735=13 July 1824 John Fout 241 A. in Hardy Co. on Cove Run of Lost R. adj. George Shireman, Jacob Snyder, Jonathan Branson, Cove Mt., John Drum. 21 Oct 1826 [Dl'd Mr. Miller 1827]

C2-346:   Surv. 15 Nov 1825 by T.W.7735=13 July 1824 Joseph M. Parker 135 A. in

Hardy Co. on Cove Run of Lost R. adj. Jonathan Branson, Jacob Chrisman, Cove Mt. 21 Oct 1826 [Dl'd Mr. Miller 1827]

C2-347: Surv. 12 Nov 1824 by T.W.7379=4 Jan 1823 Isaiah Conner 190 A. in Culpeper Co. on Withers Cheek, Barber, Ryley. 21 Oct 1826 [Dl'd 18 Oct 1827]

C2-347: Surv. 20 May 1825 by T.W.7181=30 Jan 1822 Walter Newman 1405 A. in Shenandoah Co. on Stoney Cr. & Big N. Mt. adj. Adam Barb, Jacob Funkhouser, Henry Rinker. 7 Nov 1826 [Dl'd Sam'l Lewis 23 Jan? 1827]

C2-348: Surv. 14 May 1825, 3000 A. by T.W.7061=26 Mar 1821 & 474 A. by T.W.7181=30 Jan 1822 Walter Newman 3474 A. in Shenandoah Co. on Big N. Mt. adj. John Arthur & Co., said Newman, John Link, Godfrey Miller, heirs of Isaac Funkhouser dec'd, Benjamin Dellinger, Jacob Miller, George Airon, Adam Baker, Rd. to Moorefield. 7 Nov 1826 [Dl'd Sam'l Lewis 23 Jan? 1827]

C2-350: Surv. 13 June 1825 by T.W.7692=9 Mar 1824 Hubbert Humes Jr. 3 3/4 A. in Morgan Co. on Sleepy Cr. on Little Timber Rg. adj. Frederick Householder, Hubbert Humes Sr., George Lyler. 7 Nov 1826 [Dl'd Mr. Orrick 29 Jan 1817]

C2-351: Surv. 7 Mar 1825 by T.W.5318=7 Dec 1814 Jonas Menefee 70 A. in Culpeper Co. adj. Henry Menefee Sr., William Bowen. 7 Nov 1826 [Mr. Turner 5 Feb 1827]

C2-352: Surv. 20 May 1825, 100 A. by T.W.6295=8 June 1818 & 20 A. by 4808=13 Jan 1812 John Williamson 120 A. in Hampshire Co. on N. R. adj. Samuel Probasco, Henry Asberry heirs, John Starn, John Davis, Hawkins, Kidwell. 7 Nov 1826 [Dl'd Mr. James Gibson 28 Dec 1826]

C2-352: Surv. 11 May 1825 by T.W.7181=30 Jan 1822 Walter Newman 125 1/2 A. in Shenandoah Co. on Little N. Mt. adj. Newman's purchase of Thomas Ryan, on Laurel Run, Godfrey Miller, John Link, Ephraim & Casper Rinker, John Arthur & Co. 7 Nov 1726 [Dl'd Mr. S. Lewis 23 Jan 1827]

C2-353: Surv. 18 Dec 1824 by T.W.6878=22 Mar 1820 John Hockman 407 A. in Shenandoah Co. at the Blue Rg. adj. said John Hockman, Griffie, Jacob Smith, Dry Run, Martin Stumback, heirs of John Hockman dec'd. 7 Nov 1826

C2-354: Surv. 10 Nov 1821 by T.W.7735=13 July 1824 Abram Sites 91 A. in Hardy Co. on Fork Mt. adj. Deep Spring Surv. 7 Nov 1826 [Dl'd by mail 6 May 1831]

C2-355: Surv. 3 Dec 1825 by T.W.7517=1 Dec 1823 Rowland Jenkins 100 A. in Culpeper Co. adj. Daniel Grubb, Wallis, Hazle R., Dotson. 7 Nov 1826 [Dl'd Mr. Friack? 5 Feb 1827]

C2-355: Surv. 2 Dec 1825 by T.W.7517=1 Dec 1823 William Jenkins 26 A. in Culpeper Co. adj. Ezekiel Brandum, Wallis, Adams, said William Jenkins. 7 Nov 1826 [Dl'd Mr. Turner 5 Feb 1827]

C2-356: Surv. 8 Dec 1823, 200 A. by T.W.7408=7 Feb 1823 & 65 A. by T.W.7409=17 Feb 1823 Jacob Rudolph 265 A. in Shenandoah & Frederick Cos. adj. said Jacob Rudolph, on Cedar Cr., Samuel Orndorff, Stover's heirs. 7 Nov 1826

C2-356: Surv. 26 Feb 1826 by T.W.7312=21 Oct 1822 John Tansil 296 A. in Pr. William Co. adj. Tuckam's Br., John Mills, the Barren Rg., Cockrill's Mt., Peaks Mill Dam. 13 Nov 1826 [Dl'd Mr. Sinclair 17 Feb 1827]

C2-357: Surv. 12 Jan 1826 by T.W.7312=21 Oct 1822 John Tansil 126 A. in Pr. William Co. on Neabsco Cr. near Atkinson, Tayloe, Messrs Langly & King, Goslin. 13 Nov 1826 [Dl'd Mr. Sinclair 17 Feb 1827]

C2-358: Surv. 25 Oct 1825 by T.W.6878=22 Mar 1820 Henry Farror 50 A. in Shenandoah Co. on Eastern Ft. Mt. adj. Christian Farror, John Gatewood Sr. 13 Nov 1826 [Dl'd B. Almond 23 Feb 1827]

C2-358: Surv. 25 Oct 1825 by T.W.6878=22 Mar 1820 William A. Harris 50 A. in Shenandoah Co. on Eastern Ft. Mt. adj. John Gatewood Sr. 13 Nov 1826 [Dl'd B.

Almond 23 Feb 1827]

C2-359: Surv. 25 Oct 1825 by T.W.6878=22 Mar 1820 Christian Farror 50 A. in Shenandoah Co. on Eastern Ft. Mt. adj. William A. Harris, John Gatewood Sr. 13 Nov 1826 [Dl'd Mr. Almond 23 Feb 1827]

C2-359: Surv. 25 Feb 1826 by T.W.7312=21 Oct 1822 John Hooe Jr. 18 A. 7 Po. in Pr. William Co. adj. William Branner, Yorkshire farm, William Were/Ware, Chilton. 13 Nov 1826 [Dl'd 17 Feb 1827]

C2-360: Surv. 14 Sep 1825 by T.W.7318=31 Oct 1822 Charles Bruce 49 A. 24-53 Po. in Stafford Co. adj. Tullys Oldfield, Thornton, Curtis, Fitzhugh, Brown's Spring Br., Newton. 1 Dec 1826 [Dl'd J. J. Fry 15 Mar 1827]

C2-360: Surv. 23 Apr 1825 by T.W.7851=29 Jan 1825 Daniel Mackinturff 93 A. in Shenandoah Co. in Powels Big Ft. adj. said Mackinturff, John Clem(of Michael). 14 Feb 1827

C2-361: Surv. 23 Mar 1824, 5 A. by T.W.7104=6 July 1821, 15 A. by Exg.T.W.2406=15 Jan 1822, 50 A. by T.W.6662=7 June 1819 & 3 A. by T.W.7489=25 July 1823 Samuel Flenaghan 73 A. in Hampshire Co. on Pattersons Cr. & Middle Rg. adj. said Flenaghan, Joseph Long originally John Dowden, Frederick Sheetz, Samuel Cockrell, Fox's path, Okey Johnston, Catharine Johnston. 27 Feb 1827 [Dl'd Mr. Sloan 9 Mar 1827]

C2-362: Surv. 15 Apr 1824, 7 A. by T.W.4808=13 Jan 1812, 1 1/2 A. by T.W.6375=5 Oct 1818 & 1 1/2 A. by 7489=25 July 1823 David Ellis 10 A. in Hampshire Co. on Ivy Runs adj. Jacob Jenkins, Wm. Naylor. 27 Feb 1827 [Mr. Sloan 9 Mar 1827]

C2-362: Surv. 19 Nov 1823 by T.W.7489=25 July 1823 Ebenezer McNary 59 A. in Hampshire Co. on Middle Rg. & Pattersons Cr. adj. McNary bought of Pearsall heirs, Wm. Armstrong, Daniel Hollenback. 27 Feb 1827 [Dl'd Mr. Sloan 9 Mar 1827]

C2-363: Surv. 14 Apr 1825, 160 A. by T.W.7056=8 Mar 1821 & 124 1/2 A. by T.W.7903=22 Feb 1825 John Huchison 284 1/2 A. in Morgan Co. on Great Cacapeon Cr. adj. Mosses Run, Abraham Dawson, Lambert Larue, Little Mt., Isaac Larue, Thompson. 10 Mar 1827

C2-364: Surv. 5 June 1825 by T.W.7318=31 Oct 1822 Abner Schuyller asne. of Enoch Mason 8 A. 1 Ro. 32.44 Po. in Stafford Co. adj. Seddon & Moncure, Gordon. 7 Mar 1827 [Gen. Cook 7 Mar 1827]

C2-365: Surv. 15 Dec 1825 by T.W.6878=22 Mar 1820 Reubin Ross, John Clem (of Mike), John Clem (of Teter) & John Conner 446 A. in Shenandoah Co. in Powel's Big Ft. on Passage Cr., Western Ft. Mt. adj. Adam Ross, John Valentine, John Clem of Mike, Coanston, David Ross, Teter Clem, John Conner. 25 Apr 1827 [By mail Mr. Wm. A. Almond 30 Apr 1827]

C2-366: Surv. 2 Mar 1826 by T.W.7732=19 June 1824 John W. Williams 80 A. 1 Ro. 16 Po. in Pr. William Co. on Chapawamsic Cr. adj. Wm. Able, Macrae, Carter. 24 Apr 1827 [By mail to John W. Williams 23 May 1827]

C2-366: Surv. 26 July 1826 by T.W.7513=1 Nov 1823 Leonard Love 45 A. 28 Po. in Pr. William Co. on Little Cr. adj. Groves, Enis, Payne, Ennis/Inniss. 18 May 1827 [By mail to John W. Williams 23 May 1827]

C2-367: Surv. 17 Oct 1825 by T.W.7127=4 Oct 1821 George White Jr. 38 1/2 A. in Westmoreland Co. in Irish Neck adj. estate of Park, John Payne, Task. 25 Apr 1827 [Sent to Mr. White by mail]

C2-367: Surv. 17 Oct 1825 by T.W.7127=4 Oct 1821 George White Jr. 36 A. 26 Po. in Westmoreland in the Irish Neck adj. John Payne, Henry Bowcock formerly Martin, Park's estate. 25 Apr 1827 [Dl'd Mr. White by mail]

C2-368: Surv. 4 Sep 1822, 138 A. by T.W.7260=27 May 1822, 150 A. by T.W.7273=21 June 1922 & 40 A. by T.W.7280=17 July 1822 Joshua Gore in his own right one moiety & John Finch asne. of said Gore for other moiety 328 A. in Frederick & Hampshire Cos. adj. Foxcroft & Thompson, John Neff formally Stonebridge, John Rodgers now Joshua Gore, Joseph Baker now John Finch, Cacapon Mt., Sir Johns old Rd. 10 Apr 1827 [Dl'd Mr. Ebin Milton 15 Oct 1827]

C2-369: Surv. 2 Mar 1826 by Exg.T.W.2510=31 Oct 1825 William Able 14 A. 2 Ro. 5 Po. in Pr. William Co. on Chappawamsic Cr. adj. Dumfries Rd., said Able, Harrison. 24 Apr 1827 [Dl'd Mr. James H. Reed 24 Oct 1827]

C2-370: Surv. 2 Mar 1826 by Exg.T.W.2510=31 Oct 1825 William Able 9 A. 3 Ro. 20 Po. in Pr. William Co. on Quantico Cr. adj. said Able. 24 Apr 1827 [Dl'd Mr. James H. Reed 24 Oct 1827]

C2-370: Surv. 10 Dec 1825 by T.W.6878=22 Mar 1820 Francis W. G. Thomas 100 A. in Shenandoah Co. on Eastern Ft. Mt. adj. Henry Forrer, John Gatewood Sr. 25 Apr 1827 [Dl'd Mr. Turner 1829]

C2-371: Surv. 15 Dec 1825 by T.W.6878=22 Mar 1820 Benjamin Cave 13 1/4 A. in Shenandoah Co. on Blue Rg. adj. John Brumback, John Kiblinger, George Hetick, said Cave. 25 Apr 1827

C2-372: Surv. 9 Dec 1825 by T.W.6878=22 Mar 1820 John Larey 282 1/2 A. in Shenandoah Co. in Powells Big Ft. adj. Western Ft. Mt., Middle Mt., Passage Cr. 25 Apr 1827

C2-373: Surv. 14 Dec 1825 by T.W.6878=22 Mar 1820 John Clem (of Teter) 242 A. in Shenandoah Co. in Powells Big Ft. on Western Ft. Mt., Little Mt. adj. Daniel Macingturff, George Mackingturff. 25 Apr 1827 [Dl'd to Rec't 1827]

C2-374: Surv. 20 Dec 1825, 100 A. by T.W.6387=26 Oct 1818 & 47 A. by T.W.6878= 22 Mar 1820 John Plodt 147 A. in Shenandoah Co. on S. fork of Shenandoah R., Massanutta Mt. adj. Joseph Laudenback, said Plodt, Hoffman, Rockingham Co. line, Daniel Hoffman. 25 Apr 1827

C2-375: Surv. 13 Dec 1825 by T.W.6878=22 Mar 1820 Joseph Laudenback 77 A. in Shenandoah Co. on Massanutta Mt. & S. Fork of Shenandoah R. adj. his land, John Plodt. 25 Apr 1827 [Dl'd Oct 1829]

C2-376: Surv. 13 Dec 1825 by T.W.6878=22 Mar 1820 Michael Probst 106 A. 3 Ro. in Shenandoah Co. on S. fork of Shenandoah R. & Massanutta Mt. adj. the Co. line, Daniel Hoffman, John Plodt. 25 Apr 1827 [Dl'd to rec't 1827]

C2-377: Surv. 12 Apr 1826 by T.W.6865=25 Feb 1820 Gabriel Smith 6 A. in Madison Co. adj. reps. of David Snyder dec'd, John Graves, Stanton R. 25 Apr 1827 [Dl'd Linn Banks Esq. 30 May 1828]

C2-377: Surv. 10 Dec 1825 by T.W.6878=22 Mar 1820 George Levesque 40 A. in Shenandoah Co. on S. Fork of Shenandoah R. & Eastern Ft. Mt., Sandy Lick Run adj. John C. Aleshire, William S. Marye, Andrew Keyser. 25 Apr 1827 [Dl'd Rec't 1827]

C2-378: Surv. 8 July 1826, 8 A. by T.W.6907=30 May 1820 & 100 A. by Dup.T.W.5438 =18 Aug 1815 Frank Johnson the younger 108 A. in Berkeley Co. adj. Jacob French heirs, Peter Light heirs, James Porterfield, Powson, Allen. 18 May 1827

C2-379: Surv. 10 Dec 1824 by T.W.7462=24 Apr 1824 Vincent Vandiver in his own right one moiety & as asne. of Peter Rawlings other moiety 17 A. 2 Ro. 18 Po. in Hampshire Co. on Middle Run of Pattersons Cr. adj. heirs of Benjamin Rawlings dec'd, Elijah Rawlings, Daniel Leatherman, Pattersons Cr. Manor. 18 May 1827

C2-380: Surv. 11 Mar 1826 by T.W.7951=7 June 1825 Benjamin Bradigum 15 A. 30 Po. in Hardy Co. on Big Cove Run of Lost R. adj. Jacob Shireman, John Wetsel, Isaac Chresman heirs. 18 May 1827 [Dl'd Mr. Shooke 4 Oct 1827]

C2-381: Surv. 23 Dec 1825 by T.W.6555=15 Feb 1819 Benjamin Blackford, John Arthur, Joseph Arthur, Robert Miller & James Sterrett 518 A. in Shenandoah Co.

on N.Mt. adj. Arthur & Co. purchase of Adam Smith Exrs., Walter Newman, Arthur & Co. purchase of Abraham Barb, Adam Barb, John Bowers, George Miller. 18 May 1827

C2-383: Surv. 31 Mar 1826 by T.W.7303=1 Oct 1822 John Newman 5 A. in Shenandoah Co. on Smith's Cr. adj. said Newman, Christian Kagey, Jacob Harshberger, David Homan. 29 Sep 1827 [Dl'd Col. Coalton]

C2-383: Surv. 8 May 1826, 100 A. by T.W.7558=9 Jan 1824 & 67 A. by T.W.7858=9 Feb 1825 Henry Tusing 167 A. in Shenandoah Co. on Stone Cr., on Sup & Lick Mt. adj. said Tusing, Adam Barb. 29 Sep 1827 [Dl'd Mr. Walton]

C2-384: Surv. 15 Nov 1825 by T.W.7857=9 Feb 1825 Samuel Hall 100 A. in Shenandoah Co. on Mill Cr. adj. Jacob Prophet, Daniel Walters, George Biller. 29 Sep 1827 [Dl'd Mr. Walton]

C2-385: Surv. 16 May 1826 by T.W.7558=9 Jan 1824 John Sheetz 94 A. in Shenandoah C. on Stony Cr. adj. said Sheetz, John Baisey?, Adam Barb. 29 Sep 1827 [Dl'd Mr. Walton]

C2-386: Surv. 6 Apr 1825 by T.W.7856=7 Feb 1825 Philip Peter Backer 257 A. in Shenandoah Co. on Little N. Mt. adj. John Bealer, Rudolph Rosenberger, Henry Rorer, John Bly now David Pitman, John Kingan, Henry Rosenberger. 29 Sep 1827 [Dl'd Mr. Walton]

C2-387: Surv. 17 May 1826 by T.W.6238=28 Mar 1818 John Sheetz 100 A. in Shenandoah Co. on Supenlick Mt. adj. said Sheetz. 29 Sep 1827 [Dl'd Mr. Walton]

C2-388: Surv. 15 May 1826, 100 A. by T.W.5819=30 Dec 1816 & 35 A. by T.W.6238=28 Mar 1818 John Funkhouser & Abraham Funkhouser 135 A. in Shenandoah Co. on Stony Cr. & Supenlick Mt. adj. John Sheetz, John Basey/Basy, Jacob Funkhouser, Samuel Walton. 29 Sep 1827 [Dl'd Mr. Walton]

C2-389: Surv. 29 Dec 1825, 16 1/2 A. by T.W.4292=2 Jan 1806 & 8 A. 2 Ro. 20 Po. by T.W.7410=19 Feb 1823 Caleb Evans 25 A. 20 Po. in Hampshire Co. on Stack Gap Run of N. R. adj. Huffman, Mayhall. 29 Sep 1827 [Dl'd Mr. Lupton 8 Dec '53]

C2-389: Surv. 22 Dec 1825, 23 A. 3 Ro. 6 Po. by T.W.6295=8 June 1818 & 19 A. 1 Ro. 8 Po. by T.W.5875=11 Feb 1817 John Arnold(of Zachariah) asne. of Frederick High & Henry High 43 A. 14 Po. in Hampshire Co. on Mill Cr. adj. Abraham Vanmeter heirs, John Arnold(of Samuel), Richard Sloan bought of Andrew Redeinck?, John Arnolds formerly of Andrew Cannon, Nicholas Boyce. 29 Sep 1827

C2-390: Surv. 7 Mar 1825 by T.W.7146=31 Oct 1821 Andrew Gaunt 10 A. in Culpeper Co. adj. said Gaunt, Henry Menefee Sr. 29 Sep 1827 [Dl'd Mr. Turner 1828]

C2-391: Surv. 1 Dec 1825 by T.W.7147=1 Nov 1821 Gassaway Cross 250 3/4 A. in Morgan Co. on Conoloway Hill, the Long Hollow adj. hiers of Thomas Williams dec'd. 29 Sep 1827 [Dl'd Mr. Benj. Orrick 1828]

C2-392: Surv. 9 May 1826, 250 A. by T.W.6238=28 Mar 1818 & 63 A. by T.W.7858=9 Feb 1825 Adam Barb Jr. 313 A. in Shenandoah Co. on Supen Lick Mt., Stony Cr. adj. Adam Tusing, John Sheetz, said Barb, Henry Tusing. 29 Sep 1827 [Mr. Walton]

C2-393: Surv. 13 Dec 1825, 800 A. by T.W.7518=1 Dec 1823 & 400 A. by T.W.7828=24 Dec 1827 Henry Menefee Sr. 1200 A. in Culpeper Co. adj. William Gore, the devils stair run, on the Blue Rg., Little Hogback Mt., Joshua Lampton, Broombock now Blackwell, Henry Menefee Sr., Gaunt. 29 Sep 1827 [Dl'd Mr. Turner 1828]

C2-395: Surv. 23 Apr 1826 by T.W.8055=8 Apr 1826 John Arthur 1000 A. in Shenandoah Co. on Little N. Mt. at a gap in said Mt. adj. George Coffett, George Riffey, Joseph Keckley, Henry Kearne, George Shrum, Jacob Stuttz. 29 Sep 1827 [Dl'd Mr. Walton]

C2-396: Surv. 6 Oct 1825 by T.W.7642=9 Mar 1824 William Doling 30 A. in Morgan Co. on Great Cacapheon Cr. adj. his land. 29 Sep 1827 [Mr. Benj. Orrick 1828]

C2-397: Surv. 8 Mar 1826 by T.W.6748=6 Dec 1819 Daniel Funkhouser Sr. 6 1/2 A. in Shenandoah Co. adj. said Funkhouser, Anthony Spengler, Frederick Stoner Sr. 29 Sep 1827

C2-398: Surv. 8 Mar 1826 by T.W.6748=6 Dec 1819 Frederick Stoner Sr. 1 1/4 A. in Shenandoah Co. adj. Stoner, Anthony Spangler, Daniel Funkhouser Sr. 29 Sep 1827

C2-398: Surv. 12 Apr 1826 by T.W.5023=5 Feb 1813 John Clem (s. of David Clem) 15 3/4 A. in Shenandoah Co. in Powells Big Ft. adj. Michael Fogle, John Siver, David Clem formerly Purkepile. 29 Sep 1827 [Dl'd Oct 1827]

C2-399: Surv. 2 May 1826 by T.W.5078=20 May 1813 George Miller 414 A. in Shenandoah Co. on Little Stony Cr. adj. Isaac Zane, John Bowers, Thomas Hall. 29 Sep 1827 [Dl'd Col. Rose 1828]

C2-400: Surv. 8 May 1826 by T.W.6878=22 Mar 1820 Jonas Gray 252 A. in Shenandoah Co. in Powells Big Ft. bet. Passage Cr. & Eastern Ft. Mt. adj. David Clem Sr., Jacob Koverstone, George Fravel now George Sibert. 29 Sep 1827 [Dl'd Col. Bare 1828]

C2-401: Surv. 16 May 1826 by T.W.5412=21 June 1815 James Kendal 232 A. in Shenandoah Co. bet. the Blue Rg. & S. fork of Shenandoah R. adj. Joshua Woods, McNeale, Jeremiah Odell. 29 Sep 1827 [Dl'd Col. Bare 5 Dec]

C2-402: Surv. 29 Dec 1825 by T.W.7829=28 Dec 1824 Nathan Lore 19 A. 1 Ro. 23 Po. in Hampshire & Hardy Cos. on N. R. adj. Michael Swisher, Joseph Triplett formerly John Hawk 1789 grant, said Lore, Nicholas Moore, Mayhall. 6 Oct 1827 [Dl'd Mr. C.A. Turley 1828]

C2-403: Surv. 26 Oct 1825 by T.W.7735=13 July 1824 Henry M. David 301 A. in Hardy Co. on Mt. Run of N. R. 6 Oct 1827 [Dl'd W.G. Williams 1827]

C2-404: Surv. 18 Nov 1826 by T.W.9090=2 Nov 1826 Samuel B. Davis 49 1/4 A. in Hampshire Co. in Franks Gap on New Cr. Mt. adj. James Moseley dec'd, William Duling Jr. 6 Oct 1827 [Dl'd Mr. Thomas Carksaddon 6 Feb 1828]

C2-405: Surv. 2 Nov 1826 by T.W.7903=22 Feb 1825 Pheby Catlett 6 1/2 A. in Morgan Co. on Capt. Johns Run of Potomac R. adj. John Mires, Henry Knoles, heirs of Ignathius Offerrall. 6 Oct 1827 [Dl'd Mr. Orrick 1828]

C2-406: Surv. 16 May 1826 by T.W.7692 =9 Mar 1824 Abraham Gross 38 1/2 A. in Morgan Co. on Potomac R. adj. heirs of Col. McDonald, Ephraim Langham. 6 Oct 1827 [Dl'd Mr. Benj. Orrick 1828]

C2-406: Surv. 28 May 1826, 45 A. by T.W.7692=9 Mar 1824 & 3 7/8 A. by T.W.7903 =22 Feb 1825 Archibald Flora 48 7/8 A. in Morgan Co. on Sidling Hill Mt. adj. his land, E. Langham, Robert Rodgers heirs. 6 Oct 1827 [Mr. Benj. Orrick 1828]

C2-407: Surv. 28 Mar 1826 by T.W.6878=22 Mar 1820 William Tucker 18 1/4 A. in Shenandoah Co. near Stoney Run adj. Lewis Stonebarger, Paul & Nicholas Long, John Mauck. 6 Oct 1827 [Dl'd Mr. James R. Robertson 19 June 1829]

C2-408: Surv. 27 Apr 1827 by T.W.7513=1 Nov 1823 Leonard Love 2 A. 3 Ro. 15 Po. in Pr. William Co. on Littrl Cr. adj. Love, Ennis, Payne formerly Luckitt, Enniss. 29 Nov 1827 [By mail 30 Sep 1829]

C2-408: Surv. 29 Jan 1827 by Exg.T.W.2176=25 Mar 1813 Henry Fairfax 47 A. 2 Ro. in Pr. William Co. on Hoes & Little Crs. adj. Tayloe, Hoe, Spence. 17 Nov 1827 [Dl'd Mr. Tyler 1828]

C2-409: Surv. 1 Sep 1826 by T.W.7312=21 Oct 1822 John Tansil 100 A. 2 Ro 34 Po. in Pr. William Co. on Powels Run adj. Enoe, Davis, Petty. 17 Nov 1827 [Dl'd Col. Hunton 1833]

C2-410: Surv. 1 Dec 1824 by T.W.7056=8 Mar 1821 John Burk 11 1/2 A. in Morgan Co. on Sir or Capt. Johns Run adj. Michael Burk heirs, William Johnson, Samuel

Johnson, heirs of William Alexander. 17 Nov 1827 [Dl'd Mr. Benj. Orrick 1828]

C2-410:   Surv. 14 Jan 1822 by T.W.7180=14 Dec 1826 Anthony Kerney 38 A. in Berkeley Co. adj. Wm. Short, Isaac Vandasdall, heirs of Van Bennet, Elizabeth Lucus, Jones Heirs, Kerney. 17 Nov 1827 [Dl'd Mr. Daniel Morgan 26 Dec 1827]

C2-411:   Surv. 20 Dec 1825 by T.W.4832=4 Feb 1812 Wm. Smith 22 A. in Morgan Co. on N. fork of Sleepy Cr. & Indian Run adj. his own land, P.C. Pendleton, heirs of Henry Dawson. 17 Nov 1827 [Dl'd Mr. Cross 1829]

C2-411:   Surv. 23 Aug 1825 by Exg.T.W.2315=10 Nov 1819 John Ingram 68 A. 26 Po. in Loudoun Co. on Blue Rg. adj. Henry Oram, Jesse Howell, McIlhaney. 25 Jan 1828 [Dl'd Mr. Joshua Osborne 9 Feb 1828]

C2-412:   Surv. 26 July 1825 by Exg.T.W.2315=10 Nov 1819 Alfred Holland 1 A. 4 Po. in Loudoun Co. bet. Short hill & Blue Rg., Catocton Cr. adj. Kilgore, Thomas Lasley heirs, Mrs. McIlhaney, Potts, Killgore. 25 Jan 1828 [Dl'd Mr. Joshua Osborne 9 Feb 1828]

C2-412:   Surv. 21 Apr 1813 by order of Grayson Co. Ct. Joshua Stoneman 202 A. in Grayson Co. on Chesnut Cr. of New R. adj. said Stoneman, Jeremiah Wilson, Samuel Cary, Jonathan Cary, Thomas Davis Sr. by his last will 26 Aug 1789, devised to his son, Harmon Davis, (Daniel Davis, Thomas Davis, Harmon Davis & John Davis heir & rep. of Thomas Davis dec'd,.) Harmon Davis & w. Hannah conveyed to Stoneman 1803.   10 Jan 1828 [Dl'd Mr. Blair 1828] Improperly recorded in this book. Recorded in its proper place #77 p. 412

C2-414:   Surv. 17 May 1827 by T.W.8018=27 Dec 1825 John Marshall 100 A. in Hampshire Co. on N. Br. of Potomac adj. his own land, land he bought of Benjamin Wiley, said Wiley. 24 Apr 1828 [Dl'd prop'r 8 Oct 1828]

C2-414:   Surv. 9 May 1827 by T.W.6865=25 Feb 1820 Mark Finks 22 A. in Madison Co. adj. Mark Finks, arm of Ragged Mt. 24 Apr 1828

C2-415:   Surv. 12 May 1827 by T.W.7558=9 Jan 1824 Christopher Hickle 60 A. in Shenandoah Co. on Ryan's Run near Stony Rg. adj. George Lonas, said Christopher Hickle formerly Samuel Watts, John Libby. 24 Apr 1828 [Dl'd Mr. Walton 1828]

C2-416: Surv. 26 Feb 1827, 100 A. by Exg.T.W.2173 & 38 A. 2 Ro. by Exg.T.W.2176 both=25 Mar 1813 Henry Fairfax 138 A. 2 Ro. in Pr. William Co. on Hooe's Cr. & Occaquan Rd. adj. Hooe, Tayloe. 24 Apr 1728 [Dl'd Mr. McRae 3 Dec 1828]

C2-417:   Surv. 22 Dec 1825 bu Exg.T.W.1809=13 Jan 1806 Joseph Bond 46 A. in Shenandoah Co. on Anderson's Run of Cedar Cr. adj. said Anderson, Samuel Bschm?, Zane, Henry Richard. 9 May 1828 [Dl'd Mr. Lovell 23 Feb 1829]

C2-418:   Surv. 23 Dec 1825 by Exg.T.W.1809=13 Jan 1806 Joseph Bond 44 A. in Shenandoah Co. on Cedar Cr. adj. said Bond, Longacre, Orndorff, foot of Cupola HillSwayne. 9 May 1828 [Dl'd Mr. Lovell 23 Feb 1829]

C2-419:   Surv. 14 Jan 1827 by T.W.7735=13 July 1824 Joseph McNemar 30 A. in Hardy Co. on Big Run of Patterson's Cr. adj. his own land, Jacob Cornel. 9 May 1828 [Dl'd to Rec't 1828]

C2-419:   28 July 1827 by T.W.6396=13 July 1820 Benjamin Bradigum 77 A. in Hardy Co. on Lost R. adj. Adam Lee, Woolard heirs, Jacob Shireman. 5 June 1828 [Dl'd Mr. Mullen 1829]

C2-420:   Surv. 8 May 1827 by T.W.6865=15 Feb 1820 Jeremiah McAlister 27 A. in Madison Co. adj. Fentry McAlister(1 Feb 1749 grant), John Sampson to James Yarnell 30 Aug 1777, Yager, John Smith. 23 May 1828 [Col. Banks 19 May 1829]

C2-421:   Surv. 15 Apr 1824 by T.W.5639=8 Mar 1816 John Largent 76 A. in Hampshire Co. on Big Cacapehon adj. John Copsey, Allen, William Bill. 22 Sep 1828 [Dl'd To Rec't 1830]

C2-422:   Surv. 20 Apr 1827 by T.W.8053=7 Feb 1826 Philip Umstot 50 A. in
Hampshire Co. on Knobly Mt. adj. James Randall, Thornton B. James bought of
Wharton. 22 Sep 1828 [Dl'd Mr. Cascadon]

C2-423: Surv. 28 Sep 1827, 50 A. by T.W.6662=7 June 1819 & 66 A. by T.W.7202=27
Feb 1822 Amos Poland 116 A. in Hampshire Co. on Kuykendall's saw mill run of S.
Br. of Potomac & Piney Mt. adj. John Poland heirs, his own land, William Vance
formerly Henderson, Sutton. 22 Sep 1828

C2-424:   Surv. 7 Oct 1827, 30 A. by T.W.7878=16 Feb 1825 & 10 1/4 A. by
T.W.7101=26 June 1821 Peter Shinholt 40 A. 1 Ro. in Hampshire Co. on Sandy Rg.
adj. his own land, Brown, John Hiett Sr. now said Shinholt, Adam Loy. 22 Sep
1828 [Dl'd Mr. Caskaddon 1828]

C2-425:   Surv. 6 Oct 1827, 42 1/2 A. by T.W.7878=16 Feb 1825 & 42 A. by
T.W.8074=24 Feb 1826 Peter Shinholt 84 1/2 A. in Hampshire Co. on Sandy Rg. adj.
his own land, Conrod Holt formerly Francis White, Smauel Shinholt. 22 Sep 1828
[Dl'd Mr. Caskaddon 1828]

C2-426:   Surv. 2 Oct 1827 by T.W.7419=19 Feb 1823 James Thompson 50 A. in
Hampshire Co. on N. R. & N. R. Mt. adj. John Caudy heirs, Joseph Thompson. 22
Sep 1828 [Dl'd Mr. Caskaddon]

C2-427:   Surv. 19 July 1827 by T.W.9089=2 Nov 1826 Cloe Ann Powelson 79 A. 3 Ro
in Hampshire Co. on Little Cacapehon, adj. John Powelson heirs, Patterson or
Ridwell, James French 1767 grant. 22 Sep 1828 [Dl'd Mr. Kerchivall 23 Feb 1829]

C2-428:   Surv. 26 June 1827, 107 1/2 A. by T.W.9089=2 Nov 1826 & 17 A. by
T.W.9215=6 Apr 1827 Philip More 124 1/2 A. in Hampshire Co. on Mill Cr. adj. his
own land, Henry Hartman heirs. 22 Sep 1828 [Dl'd to Rec't 1829]

C2-429:   Surv. 29 Oct 1827, 100 A. by T.W.6512=1 Feb 1819 & 18 1/2 A. by
T.W.9090=2 Nov 1826 Michael Millar 118 1/2 A. in Hampshire Co. on Sawmill Run of
S. Br. of Potomac adj. his land bought of Aaron Huffman, Abraham Vanmeter. 22
Sep 1828 [Dl'd Mr. Caskaddon 1830]

C2-430:   Surv. 5 June 1827 by T.W.7963=7 July 1825 David Gick 93 1/2 A. in
Hampshire Co. on Mill Cr. adj. Richard Sloan, his own land, Fink, Reed heirs,
Airs. 22 Sep 1828 [Dl'd Mr. Caskaddon 1829]

C2-431:   Surv. 5 Sep 1827, 72 A. by 7419=19 Feb 1823 & 28 1/2 A. by T.W.7465=1
May 1823 Jacob Shinholt 103 1/2 A. in Hampshire Co. on Gibbons Run & N. R. adj.
John Patterson, John Malick, Slocum heirs, his own land. 22 Sep 1828 [Dl'd Mr.
Caskaddon 1829]

C2-432:   Surv. 11 May 1827, 100 A. by T.W.6512=1 Feb 1819 & 28 A. by T.W.6662=7
June 1819 Okey Johnson 128 A. in Hampshire Co. on Sheetz Run of Patterson's Cr.
adj. his own land bought of Dr. John Snyder heirs or Adm'rs formerly Michael
Sheetz, Vincent Vandiver. 22 Sep 1828 [Dl'd Mr. Caskaddon 1829]

C2-433:   Surv. 9 June 1827, 48 A. by T.W.5351=14 Feb 1815 & 12 A. by T.W.9089=2
Nov 1826 Michael Millar 60 A. in Hampshire Co. on Island Hill adj. Isaac
Pancake, his own land, Blanch Mt. called Island Hill. 22 Sep 1828 [Dl'd Mr.
Caskaddon 1830]

C2-434: Surv. 6 Sep 1827, 400 A. by T.W.7998=1 Nov 1825 & 60 A. by 7101=26 June
1821 William Daugherty 460 A. in Hampshire Co. on Little Cacaphon, on main Rd.
from Winchester to Springfield, adj. Charles Taylor formerly John Higgins,
Philip Cline. 22 Sep 1828 [Dl'd to Rec't 1829]

C2-434:   Surv. 9 June 1827, 165 A. by T.W.5351=14 Feb 1815, 135 A. by
T.W.6484=19 Jan 1819, 96 A. by T.W.5587=12 Feb 1816 & 133 A. by T.W.9098=2 Nov
1826 Michael Millar 444 A. in Hampshire Co. on Saw Mill Run of S. Br. of
Potomack adj. Wharton, Brown. 22 Sep 1828 [Dl'd Mr. Caskaddon 1830]

C2-435:   Surv. 2 July 1827 by T.W.6833=21 Feb 1820 Martin Lorgen 160 A. in

Shenandoah Co. in Short hills adj. Isaac & Samuel Myers, Richard Hudson, John Sheets, John Fry, George Miller. 22 Sep 1828 [Dl'd Mr. Walton 1828]

C2-436: Surv. 29 Aug 1827 by T.W.7760=23 Feb 1824 Thomas Mulledy & Abbit Carder 77 A. in Hampshire Co. on Woodrows Run of S. Br. of Potomack adj. William Poland, Richard Poland, Amos Poland, David Parsons, John Jack, Piney Mt., John Poland heirs, Amos Beers. 22 Sep 1828 [Dl'd Mr. Caskaddon 1829]

C2-437: Surv. 15 Sep 1827 by T.W.7310=15 Oct 1822 John Tinsinger 174 A. 21 sq.Po. in Shenandoah Co. on Buck Hill adj. heirs of Christoper Lindmood dec'd, John Hansbarger, Joshua Vlotz, Magdalena Tinsinger, Jacob Fry, Andrew Lindamood. 22 Sep 1828 [Dl'd Mr. Walton 1828]

C2-438: Surv. 13 Nov 1827 by T.W.6878=22 Mar 1820 Martin Zorger 3 A. 31 Po. in Shenandoah Co. on Mill Cr. adj. John Moore, John Pence, George Will(s. of John), heirs of Jacob Shaver dec'd. 22 Sep 1828 [Dl'd Mr. Walton 1828]

C2-439: Surv. 12 Nov 1827 by T.W.7858=9 Feb 1825 Edward Walton 86 1/2 A. in Shenandoah Co. on Mill Cr. adj. Daniel Walters, Joseph Ryman, Timber Rg., George Biller heirs, Jacob Profate. 22 Sep 1828 [Dl'd Mr. Walton 1828]

C2-440: Surv. 14 June 1827 by T.W.9028=13 May 1826 William Smith & John L. Smith 142 1/2 A. in Shenandoah Co. on Little N. Mt. & Cedar Cr. adj. William McCloud heirs, George Rudloph, Richard M. Scott. 22 Sep 1828 [Mr. Walton 1828]

C2-440: Surv. 17 June 1827, 200 A. by T.W.7858?=9 Feb 1825 & 200 A. by 6144=20 Jan 1818 William Kirlin, John Pence(of Conrad), Samuel Myers, David Kerlin, Jacob Pence(of Philip), Michael Neas, Isaac Myers, Samuel Goetz, Solomon Shoter, Philip Pence(of Conrad), John Hass, Jonathan Harpine, Jacob Bower, Ephraim Rinker, Daniel Walters & John Zirkle 400 A. in Shenandoah Co. in the Short Hills, adj. Isaac & Samuel Myers, Conrad Custard, Buck Lick Run, George Hebner, John Sheetz. 22 Sep 1828 [Dl'd Mr. Walton]

C2-442: Surv. 8 Nov 1825 by T.W.6662=7 June 1819 Christoper Staggs 44 A. 2 Ro. 30 Po. in Hampshire Co. on Staggs Run of Pattersons Cr. adj. George Staggs, Thomas Wealch. 22 Sep 1828 [Dl'd Mr. Caskadden 1829]

C2-442: Surv. 5 May 1827 by T.W.9089=2 Nov 1826 Sylvester Mott 63 A. in Hampshire Co. on Mill Run of Pattersons Cr. adj. heirs of Henry Pool, John Arnold(of Samuel), Harrison formerly Jones, his own land formerly Mathews. 22 Sep 1828 [Dl'd Mr. Caskadden 1829]

C2-443: Surv. 12 May 1827, 250 A. by T.W.5441=24 Aug 1815 & 150 A. by T.W.7104=6 July 1821 Samuel Hammock asne. of John Hammock 400 A. in Hampshire Co. on Cabbin Run of Pattersons Cr. & main Rd. from Romney to Morgan town, adj. his land bought of David Long. 22 Sep 1828 [Dl'd Mr. Caskadden 1830]

C2-444: Surv. 8 Nov 1827 by T.W.8054=7 Feb 1827 George Bane & Abner Bane Jr. 100 A. in Hampshire Co. on Middle Rg. & Pattersons Cr. adj. Thomas Carskaddon. 22 Sep 1828 [Dl'd Mr. Caskadden 1829]

C2-445: Surv. 2 Nov 1827 by T.W.5351=14 Feb 1815 Isaac Kuykendall 100 A. in Hampshire Co. on Stony & Buffaloe Runs of S. Br. of Potomac adj. his own land, Michael Millar, his land bought of Sutton, his land formerly Henry Heinzman. 22 Sep 1828 [Dl'd Mr. Caskadden 1830]

C2-446: Surv. 7 Sep 1827 by T.W.7501=30 Sep 1823 Henry Barricks 44 A. in Hampshire Co. on Alleghany Mt. adj. Jessee Sharpless, John Brant. 22 Sep 1828 [Dl'd Mr. Carskaddon 1829]

C2-446: Surv. 9 May 1827 by T.W.6662=2 Aug 1826 Okey Johnson 72 A. in Hampshire Co. on Rows Run of Pattersons Cr. adj. Catharine Johnson formerly Bryan Bruin, Samuel Flannegan, his own land, 22 Sep 1828 [Dl'd Mr. Caskaddon 1829]

C2-447: Surv. 21 Apr 1827 by T.W.8006=7 Dec 1825 Philip Urice 93 1/2 A. in Hampshire Co. on Knobly Mt. adj. hiers of Elisha Lyon, Philip Umstot. 22 Sep

1828 [Dl'd Mr. Caskaddon 1829]

C2-448: Surv. 24 Aug 1827, 180 A. by T.W.7238=1 Apr 1822 & 72 A. by T.W.9215=6 Apr 1827 Thomazen Grayson 252 A. in Hampshire Co. on New Cr. Mt. & Corns Run of Pattersons Cr. adj. his own land. 22 Sep 1828 [Dl'd Mr. Carskaddon 1829]

C2-449: Surv. 30 May 1827 by T.W.7878=16 Feb 1825 Jonathan Pugh Jr. 75 A. in Hampshire Co. on Tear Coat Cr. of N. R. adj. Johathan Pugh Sr., Hall's heirs, Joseph Thompson. 22 Sep 1828 [Dl'd Mr. Karskaddon 1829]

C2-450: Surv. 21 Aug 1827 by T.W.5641=19 Mar 1816 Abraham Barb 27 A. in Shenandoah Co. on Stoney Cr. adj. said Abraham Barb purchase of John Spitlar, Joshua Foltz, John Hottle, Peter Craig, John Line. 10 Nov 1828 [Dl'd Mr. Lovell 1829]

C2-450: Surv. 20 June 1827 by T.W.7157=7 Dec 1820 Daniel Webb 110 1/2 A. in Shenandoah Co. on Stony Cr. near N. Mt. adj. Abraham Sannafrank, heirs of Powel Hammon, Jacob Funkhouser. 4 Nov 1828 [Dl'd Mr. Lovell 1829]

C2-451: Surv. 28 June 1827 by T.W.7858=9 Feb 1825 Christian Overholser 1 A. 2 Ro. 26 Per. in Shenandoah Co. adj. Philip Sayger, John Overholser, heirs of John Neas. 4 Nov 1828 [Dl'd Mr. Walton 1828]

C2-452: Surv. 7 Feb 1827 by T.W.6244=7 Apr 1818 Joshua Lampton 180 A. in Culpepper & Shenandoah Cos. adj. Broombrock now Blackwell, Minifee, Covingtons Mt., Jeremy's Run, Patick. 4 Nov 1828 [Dl'd Mr. Turner 1829]

C2-453: Surv. 12 Sep 1827 by T.W.6878=22 Mar 1820 Godfrey Miller 100 A. in Shenandoah Co. adj. said Miller, Benjamin Dillinger, David Funkhouser heirs, John Newman, Gap Mt. 4 Nov 1828 [Dl'd Mr. Lovell 1829]

C2-453: Surv. 29 Sep 1827, 50 A. by T.W.7858=9 Feb 1825 & 56 1/2 A. by 7851=29 Jan 1825 Daniel Webb 106 1/2 A. in Shenandoah Co. on Stony Cr. adj. Joseph Bedinger, John Poke, Abraham Sannafrank, Christian Murmaw. 4 Nov 1828 [Dl'd Mr. Lovell 1829]

C2-454: Surv. 10 July 1827 by T.W.7851=29 Jan 1825 John Smith(s. of Christian) 9 1/4 A. in Shenandoah Co. in Powel's Ft. adj. Christian Smith, Dennis & Thomas C. Farrell, David Smith. 4 Nov 1828 [Dl'd Mr. Lovell 1829]

C2-455: Surv. 29 Sep 1827 by T.W.7157=7 Dec 1821 Daniel Webb 5 A. in Shenandoah Co. on Stony Cr. Rg. adj. said Webb, heirs of Mumaw, Abraham Sannafrank, land Webb bought of George Mumaw. 4 Nov 1828 [Dl'd Mr. Lovell 1829]

C2-456: Surv. 10 July 1827 by T.W.6784=2 Feb 1820 George Linn 11 1/2 A. in Shenandoah Co. on N. R. of Shenandoah adj. estate of Mathias Zering dec'd, Langdon's Rg., Henry Linn. 4 Nov 1828 [Dl'd Mr. John Koontz 28 Oct 1829]

C2-456: Surv. 11 May 1827 by T.W.7558=9 Jan 1824 Catharine Mafees 3 1/4 A. in Shenandoah Co. on Sand Rg. adj. Adolph Coffman, Henry Luttz, Joseph Dobson/ Dodson, Zane's old Rd., Benjamin Hudson. 4 Nov 1828 [Dl'd to Rec't 1829]

C2-457: Surv. 5 Dec 1827 by T.W.6878=22 Mar 1820 Abraham Algier 85 1/4 A. in Shenandoah Co. bet. S. Shenandoah & Massanuttem Mt. adj. said Algier, Adam Rhinehart, Joseph Lauderback, Isaac Koontz. 10 Nov 1828 [Dl'd Mr. Lovell 1829]

C2-458: Surv. 5 Jan 1828 by T.W.6878=22 Mar 1820 Philip D.C. Jones 143 1/2 A. in Shenandoah Co. bet. Big & Little N. Mt. on Cedar Cr. adj. James Copelan, James Conner. 4 Nov 1828 [Dl'd Rec't 1829]

C2-459: Surv. 3 July 1827, 27 A. by T.W.6448=17 Dec 1818, 43 A. by T.W.7858=9 Feb 1825 & 7 1/2 A. by T.W.7851=29 Jan 1825 Jacob Barb(s. of Adam) 77 1/2 A. in Shenandoah Co. adj. Peter Williams, Abraham Sannafrank, Little N. Mt., Macker, Dry Run, Peter Williams. 4 Nov 1828 [Dl'd James R. Robertson 19 June 1829]

C2-460: Surv. 29 June 1827, 200 A. by T.W.6878=22 Mar 1820 & 300 A. by T.W.7858=9 Feb 1825 Christian Overholser 500 A. in Shenandoah Co. in the Short

Hills, adj. Isaac Six, Bear Run, Mathias Miller heirs, George Roler. 4 Nov 1828 [Dl'd Mr. Walton 1828]

C2-460: Surv. 3 July 1827, 97 A. by T.W.7858=9 Feb 1825 & 69 1/4 A. by T.W.6878=22 Mar 1820 Adam Sagger 166 1/4 A. in Shenandoah Co. adj. George Arien, Little N. Mt., Bear's Run, Rd. to Glossip's Gap, George Foltz, Elk Run, Peter Sagger. 4 Nov 1828 [Dl'd Mr. Lovell 1829]

C2-461: Surv. 2 & 3 April 1827 by T.W.7044=28 Feb 1821 Peter Speelman asne. of William Barney & William Kindrick for 2/3 & said William Barney & William Kindrick in their own right for 1/3 of 293 1/2 A. in Morgan Co. on Cacapeon Mt. adj. heirs of Richard Chenowith, David Null. 4 Nov 1828 [Dl'd Rec't 1828]

C2-462: Surv. 23 Oct 1827, 196 1/2 A. by T.W.5534=15 Dec 1815 & 364 A. by T.W.6878=22 Mar 1820 Daniel Munch 560 1/2 A. in Shenandoah Co. in Powel's Big Ft. at Crease Ft. adj. Solomon Vanmeter, Jacob Danner. 4 Nov 1828 [Dl'd Mr. Anderson 1829]

C2-463: Surv. 14 Nov 1827 by T.W.6878=22 Mar 1820 John Rudy 26 1/4 A. in Shenandoah Co. on N. R. adj. land John Adam Dortinger conveyed to Adam Dortinger in 1783, now wid. & heirs of Adam Dortinger, Jacob Miller now heirs of John Koontz, McNee's run, Henry Artz, Daniel Huddle. 10 Nov 1828 [Dl'd Mr. Robertson 1829]

C2-464: Surv. 28 July 1827 by T.W.9925=18 May 1827 George Simon 94 A. in Hardy Co. on S. fork, Fork Mt. adj. his own land. 21 Nov 1828 [Dl'd Mr. Mullen 1829]

C2-465: Surv. 28 July 1827 by T.W.5519=1 Dec 1825 James Gray 12 1/2 A. in Hardy Co. on N. Mill Cr. adj. John Stombough, Jacob Barkdoll bought of Michael Alt. 21 Nov 1828 [Dl'd Mr. Mullen 1829]

C2-465: Surv. 25 Apr 1826 by Exg.T.W.2511=21 Jan 1826 John Giffin 68 3/4 A. in Frederick Co. on Isaac's Cr. adj. Alexander Henderson, George Smith, Reese. 21 Nov 1828 [To rec't 1828]

C2-466: Surv. 5 July 1827 by T.W.7851=29 Jan 1825 Montgomery R. Elbon 50 A. in Shenandoah Co. on Three Mille Mt. adj. Christian Dellinger, Joshua Foltz, Martin Delenger, Christipher Helsley, John Arthur & Co. 21 Nov 1828 [Mr. Lovell 1829]

C2-467: Surv. 6 Feb 1827 by T.W.8094=6 Mar 1826 Vincent Colbert 41 A. 3 Ro. 29 Po. in Pr. William Co. on Occoquon adj. Reuben Colbert heirs, Hooe, Peter Trone. 22 Nov 1828 [Dl'd to Rec't 1828]

C2-468: Surv. 24 Feb 1828 by T.W.2531=10 Jan 1827 Craven Peake 23 A. 2 Ro. 10 Po. in Pr. William Co. on Neabsco Run adj. John Peake, William Peake, Bacon Race Rd., Sartin, Colbert's heirs. 21 Nov 1828 [Dl'd Col. Hoe 1834]

C2-468: Surv. 8 Mar 1828 by T.W.2510=31 Oct 1825 Moses Cockrell 7 A. in Pr. William Co. on Piny Br. of Occoquan R. adj. said Cockrell, Florence, Hicson, Johnson. 21 Nov 1828

C2-469: Surv. 2 Jan 1828 by T.W.6878=22 Mar 1820 John Craig 72 1/2 A. in Shenandoah Co. on Ryals Run adj. Henry Wetherholt, Adam Baker, William Craig, Frederick Craig, Christian Dellinger, George Dellinger, Jacob Rinker. 21 Nov 1828 [Dl'd Mr. Lovell]

C2-470: Surv. 1 June 1827 by T.W.8059=31 Jan 1826 James Summerville 145 1/2 A. in Hampshire Co. on Blomery Run of Big Cacapehon adj. Abraham Weaver, Thomas Neasmith, Joseph Stone, his own land. 21 Nov 1828 [Dl'd Mr. Carscaddon 1830]

C2-470: Surv. 25 Sep 1827, 50 A. by T.W.6448=17 Decc 1818 & 25 A. by T.W.6878=22 Mar 1820 Abramham Sannafrank 75 A. in Shenandoah Co. on hills west of Stony Cr. adj. Sannafrank's purchase of Jacob Showalter, Adam Sagger, Peter Williams now Sannafrank, Adam Poke heirs. 22 Nov 1828 [Dl'd Mr. Cauldwell 1829]

C2-471: Surv. 13 Sep 1827 by T.W.6878=22 Mar 1820 Abraham Sannafrank 90 A. in Shenandoah Co. adj. Lewis Naesselradt, Peter Baker, on Stony Cr., Thomas Hammon now Sannafrank, said Sannafrank purchase of Jacob Showalter, Adam Sagger, Peter Baker. 24 Nov 1828 [Dl'd Mr. Cauldwell 1829]

C2-472:   Surv. 21 Apr 1827 by T.W.7026=19 Feb 1825 Edward Digges 3 A. 1 Ro. 23 Po. in Fauquier Co. on Carter's Run adj. Fairfax now John Scott, heirs of William Sittle dec'd. 24 Nov 1828 [Dl'd Mr. D. Smith 19 Dec 1828]

C2-473:   Surv. 30 June 1827, 34 A. by T.W.9053=21 July 1826 & 100 A. by T.W.7181=30 Jan 1822 Daniel Dellinger 134 A. in Shenandoah Co. on Short Hills on Pewee Run adj. John Fisher now Isaac Six, Timber Rg., George Biller heirs, Christian Overholser. 24 Nov 1828 [Dl'd Mr. Cauldwell 1829]

C2-474:   Surv. 1 July 1827 by T.W.6878=22 Mar 1820 Lewis Naesselrodt 22 A. in Shenandoah Co. on Suppenlick Mt. adj. Jesse Lonas, said Naesselrodt, Jacob Funkhouser. 4 Nov 1828 [Dl'd 1831]

C2-474:   Surv. 7 Sep 1824, 40 A. by T.W.7104=6 July 1821 & 50 A. by T.W.7501=30 Sep 1823 David Foreman & Joel Ward 89 3/4 A. in Hampshire Co. on Mt. bet. Parks Hollow & Dillon's Run adj. Sam'l Guard, Eli Ball, George Oats. 10 Feb 1829 [Dl'd Mr. Carskaddon 1829]

C2-475:   Surv. 8 Aug 1825 by T.W.7419=4 Aug 1825 William Hawkins asne. of David Hawkins 40 3/4 A. in Hampshire Co. on N. R. Mt. adj. John Hawkins, Robert Williams formerly John Hawkins. 15 Jan 1829 [Dl'd Mr. Carskaddon 1829]

C2-476:   Surv. 2 Apr 1828 by T.W.9159=21 Feb 1827 Jacob Rinker 13 1/4 A. in Shenandoah Co. near Woodstock, adj. Jacob W. Miller formerly Allison, Kisely now John Effinger, Dan'l Hissey. 3 Feb 1829 [Dl'd Mr. Walton 1829]

C2-477:   Surv. 14 May 1828 by T.W.6878=22 Mar 1820 Henry Cullers & Daniel Cullers 100 A. in Shenandoah Co. in Powells Big Ft. adj. Daniel Cullers, Henry Cullers, John Bushong, Solomon Vanmeter, Daniel Munch. 25 Mar 1829 [Dl'd Mr. James R. Robertson 19 June 1829]

C2-477:   Surv. 19 Mar 1828 by T.W.6144=20 Jan 1818 Henry Cullers 69 A. in Shenandoah Co. in Powells Big Ft. adj. Daniel Cullers, John Bushong, Jacob Danner, S. Ft. Mt., Daniel Munch, Solomon Veach, Jacob Ridenour. 25 Mar 1829 [Dl'd Mr. Jas. R. Robertson 19 June 1829]

C2-478:   Surv. 17 Mar 1828, 79 A. by T.W.9932=26 June 1827 & 6 A. by T.W.9997=22 Jan 1828 Jacob Funk Sr. 85 A. in Shenandoah Co. on Passage Cr. in Powells Big Ft. adj. Jacob Lechliter, Henry Ridenour now said Funk, John Clem. 25 Mar 1829 [Dl'd Mr. James R. Robertson 19 June 1829]

C2-479:   Surv. 30 Apr 1828 by T.W.5820=30 Dec 1816 Joseph Parker 100 A. in Shenandoah Co. on Little N. Mt. adj. Henry Layman, Joseph Fawver. 25 Mar 1829 [Dl'd Dr. Magruder 23 Jan 1830]

C2-480:   Surv. 21 Feb 1828 by T.W.9932=26 June 1827 Jacob Ott otherwise Jacob Ott Sr. 321 A. in Shenandoah Co. on Little N. Mt. adj. David Huddle, said Jacob Ott, Henry Kearns, George Shrum, heirs of John Arthur dec'd. 25 Mar 1829 [Dl'd Mr. John Koontz 15 June 1829]

C2-481:   Surv. 19 Feb 1828 by T.W.6878=22 Mar 1820 John Wilkin 176 3/4 A. in Shenandoah Co. on Little N. Mt. adj. Henry Layman, Joseph Layman Sr., Joseph Fawver. 25 Mar 1829

C2-481:   Surv. 6 Feb 1828, 50 A. by T.W.6295=8 June 1818 & 236 1/4 A. by T.W.9953=31 Oct 1827 Edward Taylor 286 1/4 A. in Hampshire Co. on Mill Cr. adj. Middle Rg., William Fox heirs, Isaac Means heirs, Jacob Parker. 25 Mar 1829 [Dl'd Mr. Carskaddon 1830]

C2-482:   Surv. 25 Jan 1828 by T.W.9091=22 Nov 1826 Nathaniel Kuykendall 25 A. in Hampshire Co. on Cabbin Run of Pattersons Cr. adj. his land bought of James Leach. 25 Mar 1829 [Dl'd to Rec't 2 Oct '29]

C2-483:   Surv. 8 Dec 1827, 60 A. by T.W.7202=27 Feb 1822 & 13 A. by 9952=31 Oct 1827 William Lockheart 73 A. in Hampshire Co. on R. R. adj. his land, Deavers, Anthony Orr. 25 Mar 1829 [Dl'd Rec't Oct 1829]

C2-483:   Surv. 31 Jan 1827 by T.W.7771?=3 Nov 1824 Reubin Davis asne. of Thomas Davis 40 A. in Hampshire Co. on New Cr. Mt. adj. Moses Thomas, Henry Coleshine heirs, James Bosely. 25 Mar 1829 [Dl'd Rec't 1829]

C2-484:   Surv. 6 Mar 1828 by T.W.10,032=23 Feb 1828 Ebenezar McNary 4 A. 1 Ro. 29 Po. in Hampshire Co. on Pearsalls Run of Patterson Cr. adj. his own land, Samuel Kerchival, Hollenback heirs, McNary's purchase of Isaac Hollenback. 25 Mar 1829 [Dl'd to Rec't 1829]

C2-485:   Surv. 4 Apr 1828 by T.W.10,032=23 Feb 1828 David Parsons Jr. 152 A. in Hampshire Co. on S. Br. of Potomack adj. Isaac Pancake, James Parsons Sr. 25 Mar 1829 [Dl'd Carskaddon 1830]

C2-485:   Surv. 18 May 1827 by T.W.5826=3 Jan 1817 Abel Wiley asne. of Robert Beavers 97 3/4 A. in Hampshire Co. on N. Br. of Potomac adj. Benjamin Wiley, John Marshall. 25 Mar 1829

C2-486:   Surv. 12 Jan 1828 by T.W.9953=31 Oct 1827 George Sloan 80 1/2 A. in Hampshire Co. on Mill Cr. adj. Edward Taylor, John Parker, Thomas Mulledy, John Whiteman, Parker's Titus place. 25 Mar 1829 [Dl'd Mr. Carskaddon 1830]

C2-487: Surv. 2 Nov 1827 by T.W.6184=18 Feb 1818 William Shields 11 A. 2 Ro. 19 Po. in Berkeley Co. on Back Cr. adj. said Shields, Miller, Grantam, Jones. 5 May 1829 [Dl'd to Rec't 1829]

C2-488:   Surv. 28 May 1828 by T.W.10,096=2 May 1828 Jacob Weaver 44 A. in Fauquier Co. adj. Debut, Hogin now hiers of William Triplett, Richard Colvin, William Foote, William Hogin 1741 grant, Brenton, Weaver. 5 May 1829 [Dl'd Mr. David Briggs 31 July 1829]

C2-488:   Surv. 29 Feb 1828 by T.W.9968=21 Dec 1827 William Foote & Jacob Weaver 92 A. in Fauquier Co. on Cedar Run adj. Brenton. 5 May 1829 [Dl'd Mr. David Briggs 31 July 1829]

C2-489: Surv. 5 June 1824, 6 A. by T.W.6904=22 May 1820, 25 A. by T.W.7011=12 Feb 1821 & 23 3/4 A. by 7489=25 July 1823 William Nixon 54 3/4 A. in Hampshire Co. on Big Cacapehon Mt. adj. Rob't Pugh, said Hugh, William Nixon, Abraham Criswell, George Nixon formerly James Key. 7 May 1829 [Mr. Carskaddon 1830]

C2-490: Surv. 6 Sep 1828 by T.W.7312=21 Oct 1822 Peter Trone 76 A. 1 Ro. in Pr. William Co. on Neabsco Run adj. Clinkscale heirs, Woods, Lawson, said Trone. 7 May 1829   [Dl'd by mail 21 Oct 1829 to Mr. T. Nelson Jr.]

C2-490: Surv. 11 Dec 1827, 83 A. by T.W.5634=8 Mar 1816 & 7 A. by T.W.9952=31 Oct 1827 Benjamin McDonald 90 A. in Hampshire Co. on N. R. adj. his own land, Henry Asberry heirs. 7 May 1829 [Dl'd Mr. Carskaddon 1830]

C2-491: Surv. 12 Dec 1827, 40 A. by T.W.5634=8 Mar 1816, 60 A. by T.W.9117=17 Dec 1826 & 27 A. by T.W.9952=31 Oct 1827 Benjamin McDonald 127 A. in Hampshire Co. on N. R. adj. his own land, Henry Asberry heirs, Hiett formerly Starns, Sutton. 7 May 1829 [Dl'd Mr. Carskaddon 1830]

C2-492: Surv. 19 Apr 1828, 51 A. by T.W.5141=7 Dec 1813 & 3 A. by T.W.5023=5 Feb 1813 Jacob McClanahan 54 A. in Shenandoah Co. on Hornsbys Run in Powels Big Ft. adj. Isaac Nichols, Eazle, Jacob Keller. 7 May 1829

C2-493: Surv. 13 June 1828 by T.W.4780=29 Oct 1811 John Keyser 13 3/4 A. in Shenandoah Co. on S. R. of Shenandoah adj. George Dovill, George Bongamon, main R. Road, David Dovell, Juda Housen, said Keyser. 7 May 1829 [Dl'd 1835]

C2-493: Surv. 15 Mar 1828 by T.W.9970=22 Dec 1827 Joseph Pitman & John Pitman 100 A. in Shenandoah Co. on Short Arse Mt. adj. Lawrence Pitman, Isaac Samuels dec'd heirs. 7 May 1829 [Dl'd bearer of Rec't Feb 1831]

C2-494: Surv. 9 Jan 1828 by T.W.6878=22 Mar 1820 Daniel Huffman 302 1/2 A. in Shenandoah Co. on Massanuttn Mt. adj. Thomas Goaden, Jesse Grigsby, Adam Rineheart, Abraham Algier. 7 May 1829 [Dl'd Mr. John Koontz 28 Oct 1829]

C2-495: Surv. 30 Jan 1828 by T.W.6878=22 Mar 1820 Joseph Clarke 39 1/2 A. in Shenandoah Co. on Dry Run adj. Piercen Judd, Philip Shavers, Tean's Mt. of the Blue Rg., Peter Blauser, Benjamin Blackford, George Brittan. 7 May 1829

C2-496: Surv. 6 Mar 1828, 493 A. 3 Ro. 7 Po. by T.W.7567=19 Jan 1824 & 795 A. by T.W.10,032=23 Feb 1828 Ebenezer McNary 1288 A. 3 Ro. 7 Po. in Hampshire Co. on Pattersons Cr. adj. Daniel Hollenback, Alexander King formerly Peter Jones, Territt, Allen McCray, McNary bought of Pearsall Exr., William Armstrong heirs, Thomas Hollenback heirs, Samuel Kirchavel. 25 Mar 1829 [Dl'd Rec't 1829]

C2-497: Surv. 21 Dec 1826, 8 A. 1 Ro. 12 Po. by T.W.6755=9 Dec 1819 & 7 A. 2 Ro. 38 Po. by T.W.7771=3 Nov 1824 Reubin Davis asne. of Thomas Davis 16 A. 10 Po. in Hampshire Co. on New Cr. adj. Deans heirs, Issac James, Thomas Athey heirs, Fouts, Reubin Davis land bought of John Aronhalt, James Bosely Sr. 25 Mar 1829 [Dl'd Mr. Carskaddon 1830]

C2-498: Surv. 11 Jan 1828 by T.W.9952=31 Oct 1827 Richard Sloan 17 A. 28 Po. in Hampshire Co. on Mill Cr. adj. his own land, Thomas Mullidy, Josias Smoots. 25 Mar 1829

C2-499: Surv. 26 Aug 1828 by T.W.8006=7 Dec 1825 Elijah Hall 39 A. in Hampshire Co. on Town Hill and Little Cacaphon adj. Richard Hall bought of Joseph Powel, John Thompson heirs, William M. Powell heirs. 4 Sep 1829 [Mr. Carskaddon 1830]

C2-499: Surv. 30 June 1828, 50 A. by T.W.8006=7 Dec 1825 & 50 A. by T.W.7202=27 Feb 1822 William Harvey 100 A. in Hampshire Co. on Abrahams Cr. on Allegheny Mt. adj. Benoney Cassady formerly Elzey, Clariton. 4 Sep 1829 [Mr. Carskaddon 1830]

C2-500: Surv. 24 Jan 1828, 150 A. by T.W.7326=18 Nov 1822 & 36 3/4 A. by T.W.6157=29 Jan 1818 John Greenwalt 186 3/4 A. in Hampshire Co. adj. James Welsh formerly Putman, on Staggs & Middle Runs of Pattersons Cr. 4 Sep 1829 [Dl'd Mr. Carskaddon 1830]

C2-501: Surv. 6 Oct 1827, 25 A. by T.W.7501=30 Sep 1823 & 7 A. by T.W.8074=24 Feb 1826 Conrod Holt in his own right one moiety & as asne. of Benjamin Slane the other moiety 32 A. in Hampshire Co. on Sandy Rg. adj. said Holt, William Vance, land Holt bought of Francis White. 4 Sep 1829 [Mr. Carskaddon 1830]

C2-501: Surv. 12 May 1828, 150 A. by T.W.8019=30 Dec 1825, 57 A. by T.W.9106=7 Dec 1826 & 75 A. by T.W.6129=31 Dec 1817 Isaac Blue 282 A. in Hampshire Co. on S. Br. of Potomac adj. Abraham W. Inskeep, Samuel Kerchival Jr., Daniel Brelsford. 4 Sep 1829 [Dl'd Mr. Carskaddon 1830]

End Book C2 1820 -'29

D2-1: Surv. 6 May 1828 by T.W.7101=26 June 1821 John D. Ravenscraft 66 A. 2 Ro. in Hampshire Co. on Knobly Mt. adj. John Urice, George Urice, Peter Urice, McCarty heirs, Vincent Vandiver, David Long, John Ravenscraft heirs. 4 Sep 1829 [Mr. Carskaddon 1830]

D2-1: Surv. 12 Jan 1828 by T.W.6295=2 Nov 1826 John Parker 50 A. in Hampshire Co. on Mill Cr. adj. his own land, Thomas Mulledy, Parker's Titus place. 4 Sep 1829 [Mr. Carskaddon 1830]

D2-2: Surv. 14 Oct 1828 by T.W.9089=2 Nov 1826 Demcy Welsh Sr. 20 1/2 A. in Hampshire Co. on New Cr. adj. said Welch bought of Christopher Parrott heirs, Welsh bought of Nathan Head Sr. 4 Sep 1829 [Mr. Carskaddon 1830]

D2-3: Surv. 29 Oct 1828, 28 A. by T.W.6157=29 Jan 1818 & 69 A. by T.W.6776=31 Dec 1819 Michael Thrush 97 A. in Hampshire Co. on Staggs Run of Pattersons Cr. adj. John Thrush, Christopher Stagg. 4 Sep 1829 [Mr. Carskaddon 1830]

D2-3: Surv. 1 July 1828 by T.W.10,032=23 Feb 1828 George G. Tasker 11 1/2 A. in Hampshire Co. on N. Br. of Potomack & Allegany Mt. adj. John Brant. 4 Sep 1829 [Mr. Carskaddon 1830]

D2-4: Surv. 28 Mar 1828 by T.W. 7136=25 Oct 1821 Isaac Green & Thomas Rees 25 A. in Hampshire Co. on Dry Fork of Mill Run of Pattersons Cr. adj. the Manor, Richard Buffington bought of Thomas Rees, McDonold, Ridgly. 4 Sep 1829 [Mr. Carskaddon 1830]

D2-5: Surv. 3 Jan 1828 by T.W.9089=2 Nov 1826 John Parker 50 A. in Hampshire Co. on Mill Cr. adj. his own land, his Titus place, Jacob Parker formerly Jonathan Parker, John Parker formerly Job Parker, Richard Sloan, Thomas Muledy. 4 Sep 1829 [Mr. Carskaddon 1830]

D2-5: Surv. 29 Oct 1828, 100 A. by T.W.9988=11 Jan 1828 & 130 1/4 A. by T.W.6776=31 Dec 1819 William Stagg 230 1/4 A. in Hampshire Co. on Saggs Run of Pattersons Cr. adj. John Greenewalt, George Stagg, Paddy Town Hollow, Frederick Sheetz, Samuel Hammock, Thomas Welsh, Christopher Stagg. 4 Sep 1829 [Mr. Carskaddon 1830]

D2-6: Surv. 29 Oct 1828 by T.W.6157=29 Jan 1818 John Thrush 33 A. in Hampshire Co. on Saggs Run of Pattersons Cr. adj. his own land, Abraham Good, William Buskirk. 4 Sep 1829 [Mr. Kascadon 1831]

D2-7: Surv. 10 Aug 1828 by T.W.10,032=23 Feb 1828 Richard Sloan 98 A. in Hampshire Co. on Mill Cr. adj. Leonard Ludwick heirs, his own land, Thomas Muledy, land Muledy bought of Dollohan. 4 Sep 1829 [Mr. Carskaddon 1830]

D2-8: Surv. 27 Aug 1828, 100 A. by T.W.6074=4 Nov 1817, 100 A. by T.W.8006=7 Dec 1825 & 175 3/4 A. by T.W.9952=31 Oct 1827 William Pool 375 3/4 A. in Hampshire Co. bet. Town Hill & Little Cacaphon adj. his own land, Christopher Vandegriff formerly said Pool, Abraham Pennington, Sterritt, Luther C. Martin. 4 Sep 1829 [Mr. Carskadon]

D2-9: Surv. 12 Jan 1826 by T.W.6888=17 Apr 1810 John Whiteman 50 A. in Hampshire Co. adj. Middle Rg., Mill Cr., John Parker, Edward Taylor, Rd. from Romney to Burlington, John Parker's Titus place. 4 Sep 1829 [Mr. Carskadon 1830]

D2-10: Surv. 8 Jan 1828 by T.W.7903=22 Feb 1825 Aaron Harlan 9 A. in Morgan Co. on Cacapeon Cr. adj. his own line, Gassaway Crosser, Hustan. 4 Sep 1829 [Mr. Cross 1829]

D2-10: Surv. 9 Jan 1828 by T.W.7044=28 Feb 1821 Aaron Harlan 136 A. in Morgan Co. on Cacapehon Mt. & Cacapehon Cr. adj. Jeremiah Thompson, Jno. Bruner. 4 Sep 1829 [Mr. Cross 1829]

D2-11: Surv. 26 Mar 1828 by T.W.7903=22 Feb 1825 James Higgins Jr. 33 A. in

Morgan Co. adj. Potomac R., Cacapeon Mt., Jacob Leopard, Thomas Higgins, John Johnson. 4 Sep 1829 [Mr. Cross 1829]

D2-11: Surv. 27 Oct 1828 by T.W.10,135=14 Oct 1828 Frederick Sheetz 228 A. in Hampshire Co. on Pattersons Cr. adj. George Stagg, Rd. from Romney to Paddy Town, Vincent Vandiver, Arthur & Thomas Carscadon, Samuel Hammock. 4 Sep 1829 [Mr. Carskadon 1830]

D2-12: Surv. 24 Aug 1827 by T.W.9089=2 Nov 1826 Sylvester Welch 75 A, in Hampshire Co. on Cabbin Run & Dry Run of Pattersons Cr. adj. Wm. Welch bought of Benj. Welch, Abram Good, Isaac Welch. 4 Sep 1829 [Mr. Carscaddon 1830]

D2-13: Surv. 19 Nov 1828 by T.W.5926=11 Apr 1817 Sarah Longerbone 23 1/4 A. in Frederick Co. on Frederick & Jefferson Cos. line, adj. James Ware, Dade. 9 Sep 1829 [Mr. Castleman 1829]

D2-13: Surv. 21 May by Exg.T.W. 2508=12 Sep 1825 Alexander Lowry 116 A. in Frederick Co. on Paddys Run of Cedar Cr. adj. John Rudolph, Samuel Ornduff. 9 Sep 1829 [Mr. Castleman 1829]

D2-14: Surv. 2 Aug 1827 by T.W.9050=20 July 1826 Jacob Shook & Leonard Neff 200 A. in Hardy Co. on Cacapeon Mt. & Howards Lick Run. 9 Sep 1829 [Dl'd to Rec't 22 Dec 1829]

D2-15: Surv. 16 Oct 1828 by T.W.6136=10 Jan 1818 Charles Shackelford 120 A. in Culpeper Co. adj. John Morrison, Warner, Peaked Mt. 22 Sep 1829 [Dl'd Mr. Hill 15 Dec 1829]

D2-15: Surv. 16 Oct 1828 by T.W.5380=10 Apr 1815 Elisha Rickets 23 A. in Culpeper Co. adj. Moses Gibson, Thorntons old patent line, Bear Wallow, John Morison/Morrison. 9 Sep 1829 [Dl'd Dr. Thornton 1 Feb 1831]

D2-16: Surv. 5 June 1828 by T.W.9980=5 Jan 1828 Nathan John 16 1/2 A. in Frederick Co. adj. Andrew Huddle, Wm. Denny, W. S. Jones, Joseph Miller, Abraham Rhodes, Mattox, Mauk, Pitman, McClur formerly Dolphin Drew. 9 Sep 1829 [Mr. Castleman 1829]

D2-16: Surv. 12 Dec 1825 by T.W.6174=9 Feb 1818 William Gore 70 A. in Culpeper Co. adj. said Gore, on Little Stair Run, Hinchman, Devils Stair Clift. 22 Sep 1829 [Dl'd Jno: S. Pendleton 12 Apr 1839]

D2-17: Surv. 16 June 1828 by T.W.7691=9 Mar 1824 George Swhier & Peter Zeiler 345 A. in Frederick Co. adj. Capon Mt., Gore, Finch, Wm. & Charles McEntyre/Intire, Reley heirs, Foxcraft & Thompson, Joshua Gore, John Finch formerly Joseph Baker. 9 Sep 1829 [Mr. Castleman 1829]

D2-18: Surv. 20 Aug 1828 by T.W.6448=17 Dec 1818 John Kniesley 55 1/2 A. in Shenandoah Co. in Powels Big Ft. on Little S. Mt. adj. George Kniesly dec'd, David Crawford. 22 Sep 1829 [Col. Bare 1834]

D2-19: Surv. 8 Feb 1827 by T.W.7678=4 Mar 1824 James Norman asne. of Wm. Gore 184 A. in Culpeper Co. adj. the Devils little Stair near Benjamin Hinchman, Little Meadow Br.,the Blue Rg., Menifee. 22 Sep 1829 [Dl'd Rec't 20 Dec 1841]

D2-19: Surv. 19 Aug 1828 by T.W.6878=20 Mar 1820 Abraham Kniesley 30 A. in Shenandoah Co. in Powels Ft., on S. Ft. Mts., Rd. from Woodstock to Milford. 22 Sep 1829

D2-20: Surv. 1 Jan 1828 19 1/2 A. by T.W.7157=7 Dec 1821 & 2 7/8 A. by T.W.6878=22 Mar 1820 Daniel Webb 22 3/8 A. in Shenandoah Co. on Stoney Cr. Rg. adj. said Webb's purchase of George Mumaw, Abraham Sanafrank. 22 Sep 1829 [Dl'd to Rec't 1829]

D2-20: Surv. 4 Jan 1828 by T.W.7851=29 Jan 1825 Henry Haun 1 1/4 A. in Shenandoah Co. bet. Woodstock & the N. Mt. adj. Jacob Schmucker, Wm. W. Payne, said Haun. 22 Sep 1829 [Dl'd Mr. Robertson 1829]

D2-21:   Surv. 3 May 1828 by T.W.9053=21 July 1826 Walter Newman & Christain Dellinger 126 A. in Shenandoah Co. adj. said Newman, Isaac Funkhouser, said Dellinger, Little N. Mt., George Foltz, Beans Run of Stony Cr., Adam Sayger in Glassips Gap, George Arion. 22 Sep 1829 [Mr. Robertson 1829]

D2-22:   Surv. 7 May 1828, 21 A. by T.W.6144=20 Jan 1818 & 1/2 A. by T.W.7310=15 Oct 1822 Ephraim Rinker 22 1/2 A. in Shenandoah Co. on Stoney Cr. adj. John Fry, John Noell, Joseph Bedinger. 22 Sep 1829 [Mr. Robertson 1829]

D2-22:   Surv. 7 Apr 1828 by T.W.7310=15 Oct 1822 Daniel Lickliter 22 1/4 A. in Shenandoah Co. in Powells Big Ft. adj. heirs of Timothy Eagle, Adam Lickliter, Henry Lickliter, Jacob Keller, Hornbys Run. 22 Sep 1829

D2-23: Surv. 26 Sep 1828 by T.W.6943=2 Sep 1820 Jacob Cornell 13 A. in Hardy Co. near Pattersons Cr. adj. John Cornell, Abraham Hutton.   26 Nov 1829   [Mr. Seymore 1829]

D2-24:   Surv. 27 May 1828? by T.W.6943=2 Sep 1820 George Bishop 300 A. in Hardy Co. on N. R. & Hunting Rg. adj. Fox lick Surv., Francis J. Combs, John Martin. 26 Nov 1829 [Mr. Mullen 1830]

D2-24:   Surv. 20 Mar 1828 by T.W.10,030=23 Feb 1828 Daniel Funkhouser Jr. asne. of Stephen Hickle 214 A. in Hampshire Co. on Cacapehon Mt. adj. his own land, Sutton, George Rudolph, John Rosebrough, BumGarner. 22 Sep 1829 [Rec't 1829]

D2-25:   Surv. 16 Aug 1828 by T.W.7851=29 Jan 1825 Jacob W. Miller 16 1/2 A. in Shenandoah Co. near Woodstock, adj. land Miller bought of William Allason heirs, Joseph Freed, Jacob Rinker, Daniel Hisey. 22 Sep 1829 [Dl'd Bearer 21 June 1830]

D2-26:   Surv. 19 Mar 1828 by T.W.6784=2 Feb 1820 Solomon Veatch 100 A. in Shenandoah Co. in Powels Big Ft. adj. Michael Kniesley, Jacob Ridenour, S. Ft. Mt. 26 Nov 1829 [Mr. Anderson 1829]

D2-26: Surv. 23 Sep 1828 by T.W.7382=6 Jan 1823 Joshua Orrowhood 80 A. in Hardy Co. on Normans Run of Loonies Cr. adj. his own land & others. 26 Nov 1829 [Mr. Mullen 1830]

D2-27:   Surv. 22 Sep 1828 by T.W.10,023=16 Feb 1828 George Simon 290 A. in Hardy Co. on Middle Mt. adj. his own land, Christian Simons & others. 26 Nov 1829 [Mr. Seymore 1829]

D2-27:   Surv. 1 Oct 1828 by T.W.6943=2 Sep 1820 George Shireman 89 A. in Hardy Co. on Corr Run of Lost R. adj. Jacob Shireman. 26 Nov 1829 [Mr. Mullen 1830]

D2-28:   Surv. 4 Dec 1827 by T.W.9952=31 Oct 1827 Thomas Slane 13 A. in Hampshire Co. on Crooker Run & Taylors Run of Little Cacaphon adj. George Fletcher, Richard Moreland, his own land formerly John Higgens.   26 Nov 1829   [Mr. Kerchival 1830]

D2-29:   Surv. 13 Dec 1827 by T.W.9153=12 Feb 1827 Alexander Monroe 25 A. in Hampshire Co. on Maple Run of Little Cacaphon adj. Adams, Henderson, Burch, John Millison, McCray. 26 Nov 1829 [Mr. Kerchival 1830]

D2-29:   Surv. 30 Aug 1828 by T.W.7755=11 Sep 1824 Zorabable Galloway 17 A. 3 Ro. in Hampshire Co. on Little Cacaphon adj. Edward Kelly bought of Ferdinand Gulick, his own land. 26 Nov 1829 [Mr. Kerchival 1830]

D2-30:   Surv. 21 Sep 1827 by T.W.5775=29 Oct 1826 Silas Prather 100 A. in Hampshire Co. on Spring gap Mt. adj. Cox, Jacob Jenkins heirs.   26 Nov 1829 [Mr. Kerchival 1830]

D2-30:   Surv. 5 Jan 1828 50 A. by T.W.6755=9 Dec 1819 & 70 A. by T.W.9952=31 Oct 1827 Jacob Biser 120 A. in Hampshire Co. on Middle Rg., Beaver Run of Patersons Cr. adj. Edward Taylor, Josias Smoot, Henry Fink, John Parker, Elzey. 26 Nov 1829 [Mr. Kerchival 1830]

D2-31:   Surv. 10 Sep 1827, 50 A. by T.W.6755=9 Dec 1819 & 86 A. 3 Ro. 13 Po. by T.W.4968=2 Nov 1812 Reubin Davis asne. of Thomas Davis one moiety & Reason Harvey in his own right the other moiety 136 A. 3 Ro. 13 Per. in Hampshire Co. on Alleghany Mt. adj. Blackburn, Cooper, Mackers land, Asbys new Rd. 13 Nov 1829 [Mr. Vance 19 Jan 1833]

D2-32:   Surv. 7 Oct 1828 by T.W.7903=22 Feb 1825 John Young 3 3/4 A. in Morgan Co. on Cacaphon Cr., Conoloway Mt., adj. Bennett now said Young. 13 Nov 1829 [Mr. OFarrel 1830]

D2-32:   Surv. 6 Oct 1828 by T.W.7903=22 Feb 1825 William Hutchion 53 A. in Morgan Co. on Little Mt., Cacaphon Cr. adj. Jeremiah Thompson heirs, Thompson now Jacob Tyler. 13 Nov 1829 [Mr. OFarrel 1830]

D2-33:   Surv. 1 Nov 1828 50 A. by T.W.7692=9 Mar 1824 & 50 A. by T.W.7903=22 Feb 1825 Lewis Johnson 100 A. in Morgan Co. on Warm spring Rg. adj. John Johnson, John Hunter, Pugh, Wm. Neily, heirs of Michael McKewan, Thomas Johnson, Wm. Johnson. 13 Nov 1829 [Mr. OFarrel 1830]

D2-34:   Surv. 21 July 1828 by T.W.6786=6 Feb 1820 George Crowl 5 5/8 A. in Morgan Co. on S. & Middle forks of Sleepy Cr. adj. Ashcraft now Mathias Ambrouse, hiers of Peter Light, John Youst. 13 Nov 1829 [Mr. OFarrel 1830]

D2-34:   Surv. 18 Nov 1828 by T.W.6943=2 Sep 1820 Aaron Welton 137 A. in Hardy Co. on Lunies Cr. adj. Diamond Lick surv., Adam Harness. 13 Nov 1829

D2-35:   Surv. 18 Nov 1828 by T.W.6943=2 Sep 1820 Aaron Welton 97 A. in Hardy Co. on Flat Bush run of Lunies Cr. adj. his own land, Adam Harness, John Clark, Henry Fester. 13 Nov 1829 [Mr. Leymon 1829]

D2-36:   Surv. 22 Sep 1828 by T.W.10,023=16 Feb 1828 Christian Simon Sr. 207 A. in Hardy Co. on Middle Mt. adj. Hinkle, himself, Fredericks Gap. 13 Nov 1829 [Mr. Mullen 1830]

D2-36:   Surv. 30 Dec 1828 by T.W.10,029=22 Feb 1828 Thomas Goff 100 A. in Frederick Co. adj. James Lesinger, Eli Bean, William Bean, Armstead Wilson, Gap Run. 13 Nov 1829 [Mr. Castleman 1829]

D2-37:   "This grant recorded on page 44 this book." (Marked out)

D2-38:   Surv. 14 Nov 1827 byT.W.4863=10 Mar 1812 John Largent(of Lewis) in his own right one moiety & James Slane asne. of said Largent the other moiety 39 1/2 A. in Hampshire Co. on N. R. Mt. adj. Marjoram Belford. 26 Nov 1829 [Dl'd Mr. Carscadden 1830]

D2-38:   Surv. 13 Dec 1827, 96 1/2 A. by T.W.9153=12 Feb 1827 & 78 A. by T.W.9952 =31 Oct 1827 Peter Shaffer asne. of Alexander Monroe 174 1/2 A. in Hampshire Co. on Crooked Run of N. R. adj. Burch/Birch, Cox. 26 Nov 1829 [Mr. Kercheval 1830]

D2-39:   Surv. 14 Dec 1827, 15 A. by T.W.9153=12 Feb 1827 & 1 1/2 A. by T.W.9952=31 Oct 1827 Peter Shaffer asne. of Alexander Monroe 16 1/2 A. in Hampshire Co. on Gibbon's Run of N. R. adj. Brown heirs, Grape's heirs, Wm. Torrance, Miers, David Grape heirs. 26 Nov 1829 [Mr. Kercheval 1830]

D2-40:   Surv. 20 Feb 1823 by Exg.T.W.1795=12 Dec 1805 Jane Williams 2 A. 2 Ro. 32 Po. island in Pr. William Co. in Quantico Cr. below town of Dumfries. 26 Nov 1829 [Mr. Foster 1829]

D2-40:   Surv. 20 Feb 1823 by Exg.T.W.1795=12 Dec 1805 Jane Williams 3 A. 1 Ro. 36 Po. island in Pr. William Co. in Quantico Cr. below town of Dumfries. 26 Nov 1829 [Mr. Foster 1829]

D2-41:   Surv. 20 Feb 1823 by Exg.T.W.1795=12 Dec 1805 Jane Williams 11 A. 2 Ro. 32 Po. island in Pr. William Co. in Quantico Cr. below town of Dumfries. 26 Nov 1829 [Mr. Foster 1829]

D2-41: Surv. 28 June 1827 211 A. by T.W.4982=1 Dec 1812, 42 A. by T.W.6074=14 Nov 1817 & 140 A. by T.W.6662=7 June 1819 David Corbin 393 A. in Hampshire Co. on S. fork of Capecapeon adj. Henry Baker, John Powelson heirs. 26 Nov 1829

D2-42: Surv. 6 Dec 1827 by T.W.9952=31 Oct 1827 George Fletcher 43 1/2 A. in Hampshire Co. on Crooked Run of Little Cacaphon adj. his own land, his purchase of Jacob Rinker, Thomas Slane bought of John Higgins, Isaac Hains formerly Powell, Joseph Snapp. 26 Nov 1829

D2-42: Surv. 15 Nov 1828 by T.W.6943=2 Sep 1820 George Koone 84 A. in Hardy Co. on Big Rg. & Lost R. adj. Leonard Bradfield heirs. 26 Nov 1829 [Mr. Mullen 1830]

D2-43: Surv. 22 Sep 1828 by T.W.9925=18 May 1827 Benjamin Hull 76 A. in Hardy Co. on Pattersons Cr. adj. Zachariah Linton. 26 Nov 1829 [Mr. Mullen 1830]

D2-43: Surv. 22 Feb 1828 by T.W.7404=13 Feb 1823 George Craigen 146 A. in Hardy Co. on Fork Mt. adj. his own land, Charles Lobb, John Stump, James Russell. 26 Nov 1829 [Mr. Mullen 1830]

D2-44: By certificate from Auditor of Public Accounts, purchase money has been paid. Grant by Commonwealth to Joseph Sewell 185 A. in Fairfax Co. above Great Falls of Potomac R. on Scotts Run adj. Capt. George Turberville, Scotts Middle Run. Samuel Johnston died seized of s'd land. Inquest 23 July 1823 land found to Escheat. 23 Nov 1829 [Dl'd Mr. Eli Offiett 14 Jan 1830]

D2-45: Surv. 29 June 1828 by T.W.9980=5 Jan 1828 William Gaulph 291 A. 1 Ro. in Frederick Co. adj. James Singleton dec'd, Wm. Bean, John Miller, Thomas Ogden, Wm. Hoover, Jonathan Smith, Wm. Campbell, James Cockran, William Morrison. 12 Dec 1829 [Mr. Castleman 1829]

D2-45: Surv. 2 Aug 1827 by T.W.7382=6 Jan 1823 John Stingley & William Stingley 150 A. in Hardy Co. on Walkers Rg. adj. Henry Hawk, himself, Michael. 26 Nov 1829 [Mr. Brown 1830]

D2-46: Surv. 15 Nov 1828 by T.W.6989=9 Jan 1827 John Cornal 262 A. in Hardy Co. on Black Oak Rg., Pattersons Cr. adj. heirs of John Bishop dec'd, Babb heirs, James Machir, Charles A. Turley. 26 Nov 1829 [Mr. Seymore 1829]

D2-47: Surv. 25 Sep 1828 by T.W.6943=2 Sep 1820 Michael Coffman 300 A. in Hardy Co. on Fork Mt., Limestone Rg. adj. his own land, deep spring surv. 26 Nov 1829 [Mr. Mullen 1830]

D2-47: Surv. 29 Oct 1827 by T.W.9925=8 May 1827 Isaac Kuykendall 600 A. in Hardy & Hampshire Cos. on S. Br. of Potomac & Trough Mt. adj. Daniel McNiel. 26 Nov 1829 [Mr. Kerchaval 1830]

D2-48: Surv. 12 Feb 1829 by T.W.9932=26 June 1827 John Hutchinson 85 A. in Shenandoah Co. on Little Ft. Mt. adj. heirs of George Hutchinson dec'd, Joseph Arthur & Co., John Storey, Eli Downy. 2 Dec 1829 [Dl'd Mr. Williams Mar 1831]

D2-49: Surv. 9 Sep 1827, 84 A. by T.W.7372=26 Dec 1822 & T.W.7672=3 Mar 1824 Elizabeth Good wid. of Philip Good dec'd, John Good, Philip Good, Mary Good & Elizabeth Good, ch. & heirs of Philip Good dec'd, 591 1/4 A. in Hampshire Co. on Alleghany Mt. & N. Br. of Potomac adj. said heirs, Nally, Gumerys Run. 12 Dec 1829 [Mr. Donaldson 1829]

D2-50: Surv. 24 Dec 1825 by T.W.6820=16 Feb 1820 Henry High in his own right one moity & as asne. of Frederick High for the other moity 21 1/2 A. in Hampshire Co. on Mill Cr. adj. Abraham Vanmeter heirs, Henry High formerly Hite, Nicholas Boyce. 15 Jan 1830 [Mr. Caskadom 1830]

D2-50: Surv. 3 Apr 1828, 340 A. by T.W.7374=26 Dec 1822, 104 3/4 A. by T.W.5143=8 Dec 1813 & 35 A. by T.W.6776=31 Dec 1819 Isaac Pancake 744 3/4 A. in Hampshire Co. on Buffaloe Run & S. Br. of Potomack adj. his own land, James Parsons Sr., Little Mt., Pancake's Friend Gray tract. 25 Jan 1830

D2-51:   Surv. 18 Oct 1828, 110 A. by T.W.5188=7 Feb 1814, 100 A. by T.W.5118=28 Oct 1813, 80 A. by T.W.6136=10 Jan 1818 & 400 A. by 9212=19 Mar 1827 Charles Shackleford & James Green Jr. 590 A. in Culpeper Co. adj. Dades Spring Br., Daniel Compton, Stephen Compton. 3 Feb 1830 [Mr. Hill 1830]

D2-52:   Surv. 28 Aug 1828 by T.W.6072=4 Nov 1817 Frances Farmer 100 A. in Hampshire Co. on Spring Gap Mt. adj. her own land, John S. Rester/Kester, Robert Rogers. 30 Mar 1830 [Dl'd G.W. Mumford 31 Mar 1830]

D2-53:   Surv. 11 Nov 1828 70 A. by T.W.6241=2 Apr 1818 & 27 1/4 A. by T.W.9988=11 Jan 1828 Robert Sherrard 97 1/4 A. in Hampshire Co. near Southern Ivy Run of Great Cacaphon adj. his own land, Joseph Johnson, Zane, Jenkins heirs. 30 Mar 1830 [Dl'd G.W. Mumford 31 Mar 1830]

D2-54:   Surv. 19 Feb 1829 by T.W.6244=7 Apr 1818 Zepheniah Turner Jr. 28 A. in Culpeper Co. adj. Botts Mill Pond, Kirtley, Tutt, Crapp. 1 May 1830 [Rec't 1830]

D2-55:   Surv. 2 May 1828 by T.W.7181=30 Jan 1822 Walter Newman 53 3/4 A. in Shenandoah Co. on little Stoney Cr. adj. George Miller, heirs of Isaac Zane dec'd, John Bowers, Adam Barb, Joshua Barb. 22 Mar 1830 [Col. Bare 1832]

D2-56:   Surv. 15 Oct 1828 by T.W.7732=19 June 1824 John W. Williams 180 A. in Pr. William Co. on Chappawamsic Cr. adj. heirs of Mason, Back Br. 29 Apr 1830 [Col. Hoe]

D2-56: Surv. 28 Aug 1829 by T.W.7302=27 Feb 1822 Alexander Deaver 14 A. in Hampshire Co. on N.R. adj. his own land, Croston. 1 May 1830 [Mr. Carscadom 1831]

D2-57:   Surv. 29 Apr 1829 by T.W.9159=8 Mar 1822 John Rudolph Jr. 185 A. in Shenandoah Co. on Cedar Cr. & Little N. Mt. adj. said Rudolph, Henry Richards, Elijah Richards, James Copeland. 1 May 1830 [Dl'd Thomas Buck 26 Oct 1830]

D2-58:   Surv. 5 June 1829 by T.W.9125=10 Jan 1827 Joseph R. Gilbert 60 A. 3 Ro. 21 Po. in Pr. William Co. on Quantico Cr. below town of Dumfries agreeable to entry by said James R. Gilbert 22 July 1827. 29 Apr 1830 [Dl'd Col. Hoe 1834]

D2-59:   Surv. 6 Nov 1828, 100 A. by T.W.10,027=22 Feb 1828, 9 3/4 A. by T.W.6776=31 Dec 1819 & T.W.5775=29 Oct 1816 William H. Moreland 209 3/4 A. in Hampshire Co. on Little Cacaphon adj. Spring Gap Mt., his own land, Francis Farmer bought of Robert Rodgers, Moreland bought of Elias Poston, land Moreland bought of Higgins, Frances Farmer. 24 Apr 1830 [Dl'd Mr. Carscadom 1831]

D2-60:   Surv. 15 Oct 1828 by T.W.7513=1 Nov 1823 Leonard Love 7 A. 3 Ro. in Pr. William Co. on Quantico Cr. adj. land formerly Lucketts. 20 Apr 1830 [Dl'd to Rec't 20 May 1835]

D2-60:   Surv. 4 Nov 1828 by T.W.10,031=23 Feb 1828 John Stump 220 A. in Hampshire Co. on Little Cacaphon adj. his own land, William Vastal, George Sharp, Moreland, Queen formerly Larimon & Carlin, Haunted Lick Run. 27 Apr 1830 [Dl'd Mr. Carscardon 1831]

D2-61:   Surv. 10 Mar 1829, 100 A. by T.W.10,169=18 Dec 1828 & 21 1/4 A. by T.W.10,227=24 Feb 1829 James M. Morrison & John W. Morrison 121 1/4 A. in Frederick Co. adj. William Morrison, Joseph Baker, John Whitzle, Charles King. 25 June 1830 [Dl'd Mr. Castleman 1831]

D2-62:   Surv. 10 May 1829, 400 A. by T.W.9155 & 9156=27 Feb 1827, 102 A. 14 Po. by T.W.7312=21 Oct 1822, 100 A. by Exg.T.W. 2175=5 Mar 1813, 90 A. by T.W.2510=31 Oct 1825 & 30 A. by T.W.2174=25 Mar 1813 Henry Fairfax 722 A. 14 Po. in Pr. William Co. on Occoquan Rd., adj. said Fairfax, Mason, Crouches Rd., Taylor, Hooes Cr. 16 Apr 1830 [Col. Hooe 1834]

D2-63:   Surv. 6 Nov 1828, 100 A. by T.W.10,027=22 Feb 1828 & 3 3/4 A. by T.W.6776=31 Dec 1819 Richard Moreland 103 3/4 A. in Hampshire Co. on Little Cacaphon on Spring Gap Mt. adj. Wm. H. Moreland, Burch, Higgins tract. 17 Apr 1830 [Dl'd Mr. Carscadon 1831]

D2-64: Surv. 6 Nov 1828, 50 A. by 10,027=22 Feb 1828 & 132 A. by T.W.6776=31 Dec 1819 William H. Moreland 182 A. in Hampshire Co. on Little Cacaphon adj. his own land, Smith fork of Haunted Lick Run, Queen, John Stump, Moreland's purchase of Carlin, his land bought of Poston, his land formerly Higgins.   24 Apr 1830 [Dl'd Mr. Carscadon 1831]

D2-65: Surv. 14 Mar 1829 by T.W.6881=30 Mar 1820 Joseph Haines 19 A. 36 sq. Po. in Berkeley Co. adj. Edward O. Williams heirs, the swan pond.   20 Apr 1830

D2-65: Surv. 3 May 1828 by T.W.9053=21 July 1826 Walter Newman 17 1/2 A. in Shenandoah Co. on Stoney Cr. adj. Joshua Foltz, John Ryan, Godfrey Miller, Isaac Funkhouser.   25 June 1830 [Dl'd Mr. Harriss]

D2-66: Surv. 19 Nov 1828 by T.W.6943=2 Sep 1820 George Koone 198 A. in Hardy Co. on Vinceys Run adj. Branfield heirs.   6 Sep 1830 [Mr. J. Mullin 7 Sep 1830]

D2-67: Surv. 21 Sep 1829 by T.W.9925=18 May 1827 Jacob Stover & William Greenwood 157 A. in Hardy Co. on Fork Mt. adj. Leonard Neff, John Craigen.   6 Sep 1830 [By mail to Mr. J. Mullin 7 Sep 1830]

D2-67: Surv. 7 Sep 1829 by T.W.10,292=24 Aug 1829 George Selectman 1610 A. in Fairfax Co. adj. said Selectman, Alexander, Washington, Thomas Gassam, John Hampton, on Occoquon.   23 Apr 1830

D2-68: Surv. 5 June 1828 by Exg.T.W. 2508=12 Sep 1825 John L. Smith 7 A. 34 sq. Po. in Frederick & Shenandoah Cos. adj. Jacob Hahn, Peter Bowyers/Boyer, Isaac Hite on Cedar Cr.   26 Oct 1930 [Col. Bare 1832]

D2-69: Surv. 8 May 1829 by T.W.6943=2 Sep 1820 Jacob Brekdoll 206 A. in Hardy Co. on S. Mill Cr. adj. heirs of Thomas Parsons dec'd.   26 Oct 1830 [Mr. Seymore]

D2-69: Surv. 19 Aug 1829 by T.W.6604=11 Mar 1819 Charles McCormick 4 1/2 A. in Frederick Co. (an island in Shenandoah R. opposite land Castleman & McCormick purchased of Nobles heirs.   26 Oct 1830 [Mr. Castleman]

D2-70: Surv. 22 Feb 1828 by T.W.5518=1 Dec 1815 Leonard Dasher 110 A. in Hardy Co. adj. his own land bought of Abraham House, George Simons.   26 Oct 1830 [Dl'd Mr. Seymore]

D2-70: Surv. 22 Dec 1828 by T.W.6943=2 Sep 1820 Daniel Webb 136 A. in Hardy Co. in upper cove of Lost R. adj. Lawrence Deloder, George H. Lerdsmoot?, John Webyel, N. Mt.   25 Oct 1830 [Dl'd Mr. Williams]

D2-71: Surv. 14 July 1829 by Exg.T.W.2561=14 Feb 1828 John Piper 65 A. in Frederick Co. adj. John Ront dec'd, William Adams, Richard Holliday dec'd, on Back Cr., McKee, Dalby, Peyton.   26 Oct 1830 [Mr. Castleman]

D2-72: Surv. 2 Jan 1830 by T.W.7692=9 Mar 1824 Valentine Smith 43 A. in Morgan Co. on Potomac R., adj. Conoly hill, Gassaway Cross, William Neely.   26 Oct 1830 [Mr. OFarrell 1831]

D2-72: Surv. 30 Aug 1827 by Exg.T.W.2349=2 June 1820 Abraham Snyder 107 A. in Berkeley Co. on N. Mt. adj. said Snyder, Hammis.   26 Oct 1830 [Dl'd Mr. Wm. L. Boak 2 Dec 1845]

D2-73: Surv. 21 Sep 1829 by T.W.9925=18 May 1827 Abraham Sites 7 1/2 A. in Hardy Co. adj. Jacob Fisher, his own land, Elk horn Run, Imans Mill Run.   26 Oct 1830 [Mr. Mullen 1831]

D2-73: Surv. 6 June 1829, 25 A. by T.W.10,258=7 Apr 1829 & 4 A. by T.W.10,267=29 Apr 1829 Abraham Leatherman 29 A. in Hampshire Co. on Cabbin Run of Pattersons Cr. adj. his own land, Okey Johnson, Lick Run, Samuel Dobbins.   26 Oct 1830 [Dl'd Mr. Carscadon Mar 1831]

D2-74: Surv. 4 Mar 1829 by T.W.10,162=10 Dec 1828 Nicholas Leatherman 34 1/2 A. in Hampshire Co. on Flag Meadow Run of Mill Cr. adj. his own land, Henry

Purgett, John Ludwick, Jacob Hartman, John Foly heirs. 26 Oct 1830 [Dl'd Mr. Carscadon Mar 1831]

D2-75: Surv. 22 May 1829 50 A. by T.W.6776=31 Dec 1819 & 6 A. by T.W.10,267=29 Apr 1829 Jeremiah Lease 56 A. in Hampshire Co. on Middle Rg. adj. William Fox heirs, Ephraim Herriott. 26 Oct 1830 [Dl'd Mr. Carscadon Mar 1831]

D2-75: Surv. 19 May 1829 by T.W.9953=31 Oct 1827 Jacob Parker 50 A. in Hampshire Co. on Mill Cr. adj. his own land, Buffaloe Lick Run, Edward Taylor, Isaac Means heirs Bush Place. 26 Oct 1830 [Dl'd Mr. Carscadon Mar 1831]

D2-76: Surv. 12 June 1829 by T.W.7771=3 Nov 1824 Robert Parker 50 A. in Hampshire Co. on Mikes Run of Pattersons Cr. adj. Christian Utt. 26 Oct 1830 [Dl'd Mr. Carscadon Mar 1831]

D2-76: Surv. 20 June 1828, 150 A. by T.W.9089=2 Nov 1826, 172 A. by T.W.10,032=23 Feb 1828, 25 A. by T.W.7878=16 Feb 1825 & 61 A. by T.W.7755=11 Sep 1824 Harrison Watkins 408 A. in Hampshire Co. bet. S. fork of Little Cacaphon & Indian Camp Run adj. John Patterson, Robert McBridges, Edward Kelly bought of Ferdinand Gulick, Steel, John Creamer. 26 Oct 1830 [Mr. Carscadon Mar 1831]

D2-77: Surv. 29 Dec 1828 by T.W.10,162=10 Dec 1828 Samuel Flanagin 149 3/4 A. on Middle Rg., Pattersons Cr. adj. his own land, Sheetz, Cocherel, Fox, Okey Johnson, said Flanagin. 26 Oct 1830 [Dl'd Mr. Carscadon Mar 1831]

D2-78: Surv. 27 Aug 1829 by T.W.10,267=29 Apr 1829 Joell Ward 27 A. in Hampshire Co. in Parks Hollow adj. his own land, George Parks, Rd. from Winchester to Romney. 26 Oct 1830 [Dl'd Mr. Carscadon Mar 1831]

D2-79: Surv. 16 June 1829, 116 A. by T.W.10,217=13 Feb 1829 & 18 A. by T.W.10,267=29 Apr 1829 John Ludwick 134 A. in Hampshire Co. on Mill Cr. adj. Henry Purget, Frederick High, Wharton. 26 Oct 1830 [Mr. Carscadon Mar 1831]

D2-80: Surv. 11 Aug 1829, 300 A. by T.W.9955=31 Oct 1827 & 100 A. by 10,027=22 Feb 1828 Jacob Parker 400 A. in Hampshire Co. on Mill Cr. Mt. adj. his own land, Isaac Means heirs, Caldwell, Richard Sloan. 26 Oct 1830 [Mr. Carscadon Mar 1831]

D2-80: Surv. 25 June 1829, 50 A. by T.W.6776=31 Dec 1819 & 40 A. by T.W.7985=17 Oct 1825 Frederick Kearnes/Kearns 90 A. in Hampshire Co. on Neals Run of Little Cacaphon adj. his own land, Mathias Ginneran heirs. 26 Oct 1830 [Dl'd Mr. Carscadon 1831]

D2-81: Surv. 2 July 1829 by T.W.6295=8 June 1818 John Martin 4 A. 2 Ro. 9 Po. in Hampshire Co. on Alleghany Mt. near N. Br. of Potomac. 26 Oct 1830 [Dl'd Mr. Carscadon 1831]

D2-82: Surv. 13 May 1829, 19 A. by T.W.9953=31 Oct 1827 & 3 A. 1 Ro. 28 Po. by T.W.10,135=14 Oct 1828 Henry Hawke 22 A. 1 Ro. 28 Po. in Hampshire Co. on Mill Cr. Knob & Mill Cr. adj. Thomas Taylor. 26 Oct 1830 [Dl'd Mr. Carscadon 1831]

D2-82: Surv. 7 Mar 1829 by T.W.8006=7 Dec 1825 Jasper Foley, William Foley, Isaac Foley, Milly Moore w. of Solomon Moore late Milly Foley, Sidney Purget w. of William Purger late Sidney Foley & Catharine Foley, ch. & heirs of Wm. S. Foley dec'd 50 A. in Hampshire Co. on Mill Cr. adj. Philip Morris/More, Henry Hartman heirs. 26 Oct 1830 [Mr. Carscadon 1831]

D2-83: Surv. 1 July 1829, 15 A. by T.W.7501=30 Sep 1823 & 17 3/4 A. by T.W.6776=31 Dec 1819 Henry Barricks 32 3/4 A. in Hampshire Co. on Alleghany Mt. on Montgomerys Run of N. Br. of Potomac adj. Pea vine bottom surv. 24 Oct 1830 [Mr. Carscadon 1831]

D2-83: Surv. 28 July 1829 by T.W.10,267=29 Apr 1829 Henry Purget Sr. 50 A. in Hampshire Co. on Mill Cr. adj. his own land, John Ludwick, Frederick High, John Foley heirs. 26 Oct 1830 [Dl'd Mr. Carscadon 1831]

D2-84: Surv. 13 Apr 1829 by T.W.10,032=11 Apr 1829 Jacob Fleet 127 A. 3 Ro. in

Hampshire Co. on Bartons Run of Pattersons Cr. adj. Jacob Lee, Boyd. 26 Oct 1830 [Mr. Carscadon 1831]

D2-85: Surv. 26 Aug 1826 by T.W.8053=7 Feb 1826 Thomas Taylor 50 A. in Hampshire Co. on Mill Cr. Knobs, Mill Cr. adj. said Taylor bought of Jacob High, Fotherhouse Knob. 26 Oct 1830 [Mr. Carscadon]

D2-85: Surv. 16 May 1828 by T.W.7465=1 May 1823 Robert Beavers 37 A. in Hampshire Co. on N. Br. of Potomac adj. Benjamin Wiley. 26 Oct 1830 [Mr. Carscadon 1831]

D2-86: Surv. 26 Dec 1828 by T.W.9988=11 Jan 1828 George House 14 A. in Hampshire Co. on Knobley Mt. adj. his own land, Samuel House. 26 Oct 1830 [Dl'd Mr. Carscadon 1831

D2-86: Surv. 27 Aug 1829 by T.W.9128=16 Jan 1827 George Oats & John Shivers 25 1/4 A. in Hampshire Co. on Edward Run of Cacaphon adj. their own land, Bethell now Wilson, Jonathan Barrett, John Shivers. 26 Oct 1830 [Mr. Carscadon 1831

D2-87: Surv. 2 Apr 1829, 100 A. by T.W.9215=6 Apr 1827 & 6 A. by 10,135=14 Oct 1828 Elias Jones 106 A. in Hampshire Co. on New Cr. Mt. and Row lick Run of New Cr. adj. Henry Harrison formerly Adam Haden, Abrahams Rg. 26 Oct 1830 [Mr. Carscadon 1831

D2-88: Surv. 14 Apr 1829, 250 A. by T.W.9952=31 Oct 1827 & 96 A. by T.W.10,135=14 Oct 1828 Samuel Dobbins 346 A. in Hampshire Co. on Pattersons Cr. & Cabbin Run Hill adj. his own land, Samuel Totten, Peter Harsell Sr., Oakey Johnson, Abraham Leatherman. 26 Oct 1830 [Mr. Carscadon 1831

D2-88: Surv. 5 June 1829, 29 A. by T.W.4968=2 Nov 1812, 16 3/4 A. by T.W.6755=9 Dec 1819, 49 1/4 A. by T.W.8006=7 Dec 1825, 26 1/2 A. by T.W.10,135=4 Oct 1828 & 31 1/4 A. by 10,258=7 Apr 1829 Solomon Ellifrits 153 A. in Hampshire Co. on Pattersons Cr., Cabbin Run hill adj. Samuel Dobbins, Okey Johnson, John Rankin heirs. 26 Oct 1830 [Dl'd Mr. Carscadon 1831

D2-89: Surv. 22 Dec 1828, 50 A. by T.W.9952=31 Oct 1827 & 4 A. by T.W.6295=8 June 1818 John Parker 54 A. in Hampshire Co. on Middle Rg. adj. his own land, Edward Taylor, Jacob Biser?, Elzy heirs, Umtots heirs. 26 Oct 1830 [Mr. Carscadon 1831

D2-90: Surv. 13 Oct 1828 by T.W.7755=11 Sep 1824 Mathias Stollaberger 107 1/2 A. in Hampshire Co. on Cabbin Run of Pattersons Cr. adj. Nathaniel KuyKendall, Benjamin Bailey. 26 Oct 1830 [Dl'd Mr. Carscadon]

D2-91: Surv. 23 Dec 1828 by T.W.6295=8 June 1818 John Parker 56 A. in Hampshire Co. on Middle Rg. and Mill Cr. adj. his own land, Jacob Parker, Rd. from Romney to Morgantown. 26 Oct 1830 [Mr. Carscadon 1831

D2-92: Surv. 22 Dec 1828 by T.W.6295=8 June 1818 John Parker 27 1/2 A. in Hampshire Co. on Middle Rg. adj. Mill Cr. his own land. 26 Oct 1830 [Carscadon 1831

D2-93: Surv. 5 May 1828 by T.W.10,032=23 Feb 1828 Jacob Fleek 72 A. in Hampshire Co. on Knobly Mt. adj. his own land, John Spencer, James Randell, his land bought of Arthur Graham. 26 Oct 1830 [Mr. Carscadon 1831

D2-93: Surv. 28 Oct 1829 by T.W.9131=20 Jan 1827 George Ziler & Henry Brunner 73 5/8 A. in Morgan Co. on Cacapeon Cr. & Sideling Hill adj. Aaron Harlon, Peter Bruner formerly Jeremiah Thompson. 10 Nov 1830 [Mr. OFerrell 1831]

D2-94: Surv. 2 June 1829 by T.W.7467=12 May 1823 Samuel Rankin 24 1/2 A. in Morgan Co. on Sleepy Cr. adj. heirs of Ignatius Offerrell, Fitzhew, heirs of Thomas Elsey, said Rankin. 10 Nov 1830

D2-95: Surv. 12 May 1829 by T.W.7903=22 Feb 1825 Aaron Harlon 36 A. in Morgan Co. on the Big Rg., Cacapeon Cr. adj. said Harlon, George Bruner, George Renolds. 10 Nov 1830 [Mr. OFerrell 1831]

D2-95: Surv. 29 Oct 1829 by T.W.7903=22 Feb 1825 John Young 25 A. in Morgan Co. on Cacapeon Cr. at foot of Cacapeon Mt. adj. (Lawyer) Anderson of Maryland formerly Cornelius Fure. 10 Nov 1830 [Mr. OFerrell 1831]

D2-96: Surv. 13 May 1829 by T.W.6448=17 Dec 1818 George Riffey 2 1/4 A. in Shenandoah Co. on Little N. Mt. adj. Leonard Hart, Jacob Neiswander. 10 Nov 1830 [Col. Bare 1832]

D2-97: Surv. 22 Nov 1826 by Surv. 7828=27 Dec 1824 Andrew R. Barbee 73 A. in Culpeper Co. on the Blue Rg. near Thorntons Gap adj. Barbour, Gabriel Jordan and others. 10 Nov 1830

D2-97: Surv. 24 Dec 1829 by T.W.6388=26 Oct 1818 Jesse Veach 89 A. in Shenandoah Co. in Powells Ft. adj. Peter Coverstone, Jacob Lickliter, Michael Kniesley. 10 Nov 1830 [Dl'd Mr. Williams]

D2-98: Surv. 12 Apr 1829 by T.W.Surv. 9190=8 Mar 1827 Joseph Parker 92 3/4 A. in Shenandoah Co. adj. Walter Newman, John Russell. Henry Miller, George Miller, Isaac Zane, Little Stoney Cr. 10 Nov 1830

D2-99: Surv. 29 June 1829 by T.W.5516=1 Dec 1815 James Gray 50 A. in Hardy Co. on N. fork adj. heirs of James Machie, Peter Hire, his own land. 10 Nov 1830

D2-99: Surv. 13 Oct 1829 by T.W.9925=18 May 1827 George Miller 143 A. in Hardy Co. on Kimseys Run of Lost R. adj. his own land, Buck Rg. 10 Nov 1830 [Dl'd Mr. Mullen 1832]

D2-100: Surv. 23 Dec 1829 by T.W.5209=15 Feb 1814 Michael Kniesley 150 A. in Shenandoah Co. in Powells Ft. on Passage Cr. adj. Peter Coverstone, S. Fork Mt., Jacob Ridnour, Solomon Veach, Jacob Lichliter. 10 Nov 1830 [Dl'd Mr. Harriss]

D2-100: Surv. 8 May 1829 by T.W.7851=29 Jan 1825 Joseph P. Mahony 50 A. in Shenandoah Co. on Little N. Mt. adj. George Randolph, William & John L Smith. 10 Nov 1830 [Dl'd Mr. Wm.s]

D2-101: Surv. 7 Mar 1828 by T.W.7390=29 Jan 1823 John L. Smith 70 A. in Shenandoah Co. on Little N. Mt. adj. heirs of William McCleod, William Smith, said John L. Smith, Richard M. Scott. 10 Nov 1830

D2-102 Surv. 26 Dec 1829 by T.W.5294=3 Nov 1814 Jonathan Miller 43 A. in Shenandoah Co. on Stoney Cr. Rg. adj. Isaac Funkhouser, Phillip Miller, Christian Mumaw, Jacob Rinker, Godfrey Miller. 30 Nov 1830 [Mr. Bare 1832]

D2-102: Surv. 29 Mar 1830, 371 1/2 A. by T.W.10,362=13 Jan 1830 & 53 1/2 A. by Exg.T.W.2405=15 Jan 1822 Peter Larew 425 A. in Hampshire Co. on Tear Coat Cr. adj. Jacob Pepper, Alexander Dorins, Timothy Smith, Henderson, Cheshir, Samuel Parks. 22 Nov 1830 [Mr. Carscadon 1831]

D2-103: Surv. 26 Mar 1828 by T.W.9189=8 Mar 1827 Benjamin Hawkins 137 A. in Shenandoah Co. on Short Arse Mt. adj. Bear Wallow, Aaron Moon, William Elzey. 9 Feb 1831 [Mr. Pennebacker 1832]

D2-103: Surv. 26 Mar 1828 by T.W.9189=8 Mar 1827 Benjamin Hawkins 14 1/2 A. in Shenandoah Co. on N. Fork of Shenandoah R. adj. heirs of John Allen dec'd, Israel Allen. 9 Feb 1831 [Mr. Pennebacker 1832]

D2-104: Surv. 15 Jan 1830 by T.W.10,191=29 Jan 1829 Abraham Baker 56 A. 2 Ro. 5 Per. in Shenandoah Co. on Little N. Mt. adj. Thomas Newell, Abraham Pittman, Thomas Newell, Philip Peter Baker. 10 Apr 1831

D2-105: Surv. 12 Dec 1827 by T.W.8011=13 Dec 1825 Joseph Fawver 100 A. in Shenandoah Co. adj. Henry Layman, George & Philip Lentz, heirs of Mathias Zehring, Joseph Parker. 9 May 1831 [Col. Bare 1832]

D2-106: Surv. 16 May 1830 by T.W.9038=15 June 1826 Larkin Weaver, Theodosha Weaver, Joell Weaver, Francis Weaver, Elijah Weaver, James Weaver, Sarah Weaver,

Simeon Weaver, Juliann Weaver, Elizabeth Weaver & Alfred Weaver only heirs of Mathias Weaver dec'd 90 A. in Madison Co. adj. George Harrison, Adam Cristler, William Tate, Jonathan Coward grant of 8 June 1768. 3 Aug 1831 (This Grant was improperly recorded here. See No. 80 pa 397) Marked out.

D2-106: Surv. 29 May 1827 by T.W.8006=7 Dec 1825 William Doman 30 A. in Hampshire Co. on Little Cacapheon on Town hill adj. Norman Urton bought of Asa Everitt(formerly Thomas Pettitt). 3 Aug 1831 [Mr. Carscadon]

D2-107: Surv. 25 Sep 1830 by T.W.10,307=2 Oct 1829 Alfred Bowman 110 A. in Hampshire Co. on N. Br. of Potomac adj. James Prather. 3 Aug 1831 [Mr. Carscadon]

D2-108: Surv. 25 Aug 1830 40 A. by Exg.T.W.2429=5 Sep 1822 & 10 A. by T.W.7485 =25 July 1823 Nathan B. Brelsford 50 A. in Hampshire Co. on Knob Rg. & N. R. adj. Majoram Brelsford, John Largint(of Lewis), James Slane. 3 Aug 1831 [Dl'd Mr. Carscadon]

D2-108: Surv. 21 May 1829, 67 1/2 A. by T.W.6647=22 May 1819 & 297 A. by T.W.10,267=29 Apr 1829 James Abernathy 364 1/2 A. in Hampshire Co. on Abernathys Mill Run of S. Br. of Potomac on Valley Mt. adj. John Brady, Middle Mt., Donaldson, Campbell Mt. 3 Aug 1831 [Mr. Carscadon]

D2-109: Surv. 26 Apr 1830 by T.W.10,321=3 Nov 1829 Robert Sherrard 50 A. in Hampshire Co. on Falling Spring Run of Great Cacaphon adj. James Mathews, Daniel Royce heirs. 3 Aug 1831 [Capt. Munford 1831]

D2-110: Surv. 19 Dec 1829 by T.W.10,321=3 Nov 1829 Daniel Williams 135 A. in Hampshire Co.on Little Cacaphon adj. Chas. Taylor, William Daugherty. 3 Aug 1831

D2-111: Surv. 25 Aug 1830, 60 A. by Exg.T.W.2429=5 Sep 1822 & 54 A. by T.W.7326 =18 Nov 1822 Marjoram Brelsford 114 A. in Hampshire Co. on Knots Rg. & N. R. adj. his own land. 3 Aug 1831 [Mr. Carscadon]

D2-112: Surv. 4 June 1830 by T.W.6724=25 Oct 1819 George See 39 1/2 A. in Hardy Co. on Cove Run of Lost R. adj. John Mathias. 3 Aug 1831 [Dl'd rec't 1832]

D2-112: Surv. 20 Sep 1830 by T.W.10,191=29 Jan 1829 Abraham Pittman 34 A. 3 Ro. in Shenandoah Co. adj. Thomas Newell, Philip Peter & Abraham Baker. 3 Aug 1831 [Mr. Bare 1832]

D2-113: Surv. 11 Dec 1829 by T.W.5209=15 Feb 1814 Adam Shearman & Michael Kniesley 284 A. in Shenandoah Co. on Ft. Mt. in Powells Ft. adj. Jacob Funk now Peter Coverstone, John Coleman, George F. Hupp. 3 Aug 1831 [Col. Bare 1832]

D2-113: Surv. 10 May 1830 by T.W.10,424=23 Feb 1830 Joseph Snapp 5 1/4 A. in Frederick Co. adj. George Clevenger, Peter Gilham, Luckins formerly Richard Fawcett, Abraham Miller formerly George Clevenger, Care now Gilham. 24 Aug 1831

D2-114: Surv. 15 July 1830 by T.W.10,424=23 Feb 1830 Robert Muse 6 A. 2 Ro. 17 Po. in Frederick Co. adj. his own land, Screviner, Thomas Races now Pugh. 3 Aug 1831 [Dl'd Feb 1832]

D2-115: Surv. 6 June 1830 by T.W.10,422=23 Feb 1830 Absolum See 62 A. in Hardy Co. on Cove Mt. adj. his own land, Jacob & John Mathias. 3 Aug 1831 [Rect 1832]

D2-115: Surv. 10 Dec 1829, 50 A. by T.W.10,267=29 Apr 1829 & 153 1/2 A. by T.W.10,321=3 Nov 1829 Benjamin Williamson 203 A. 2 Ro. in Hampshire Co. on Sideling Hill adj. John Davis, Joweph & Jeremiah Hiett. 25 Aug 1831

D2-116: Surv. 23 Mar 1830 by T.W.10,362=13 Jan 1830 Samuel J. Stump 250 A. in Hampshire Co. on Little Cacaphon adj. John Stump, Sharfe, Vastal, James Meekins, Hopkins Lick Run, Sterrett, James Meekins Sr. 23 Aug 1831

D2-117: Surv. 15 May 1830, 100 A. by T.W.10,217=15 July 1829 & 200 A. by T.W.10,246=3 Mar 1829 David Ellis 300 A. in Hampshire Co. on Great Cacaphon adj. Joseph Kenney, William Naylor, James Richmond, William Richmond, George Holt,

Peter Shinholt, Samuel Shinholt, said Ellis, Parker heirs. 24 Aug 1831 [Capt. Munford 1831]

D2-118:   Surv. 4 Dec 1829, 94 A. by Exg.T.W.2248=Apr 1817 & 30 A. by T.W.10,321=3 Nov 1829 Henry Carter 124 A. in Hampshire Co. on N. R. Mt. adj. Dunmore heirs, Joseph Martin, John Thompson, John Candy heirs, James Thompson, Caleb Evans, Joseph Huffman. 24 Aug 1831 [Mr. Carscadon 1832]

D2-119:   Surv. 29 May 1828, 150 A. by T.W.7326=8 Nov 1822 & 137 A. by T.W.7109=27 July 1821 Vincent Vandiver in his own right for one moiety & as asne. of William Mitchell for the other moiety 287 A. in Hampshire Co. on New Cr. adj. Nathaniel Kuykendall, William Duling Sr. 30 Sep 1831 [Mr. Carscadon]

D2-120:   Surv. 28 May 1828 by T.W.7485=25 July 1823 Vincent Vandiver 273 3/4 A. in Hampshire Co. on Alleghany Mt. & N. Br. of Potomac adj. Reason Harvey, Elias Browning, Harveys Spring Run, Harvey formerly Davis. 13 Sep 1831 [Mr. Carscadon

D2-121:   Surv. 6 May 1828 by T.W.6512=Feb 1819 Vincent Vandiver 80 A. in Hampshire Co. on Mill Cr. adj. Stephen Fuller, George Liller, James Sparling heirs, Magill/McGill heirs. 13 Sep 1831 [Mr. Carscadon 1832]

D2-122:   Surv. 26 June 1828 by T.W.7326=18 Nov 1822 Vincent Vandiver 299 1/2 A. in Hampshire Co. on Alleghany Mt. & N. Br. of Potowmac adj. Reason Harvey, John Junkins, Stephen Cooper, Macker heirs, Wyckoff Run, Elk Garden Surv. 13 Sep 1831 [Mr. Carscadon 1832]

D2-123:   Surv. 10 July 1828, 355 A. by T.W.7009=27 July 1821 & 31 A. by T.W.7485=25 July 1823 Vincent Vandiver 366 A. in Hampshire Co. on S. Br. of Potowmac adj. the Glebe land of Williams Mills, Salt Peter Gap, Abraham Vanmeter, S. Br. Mt., Conrod Huffman Sr. heirs, William Naylor, Decker or Mills Gap. 13 Sep 1831 [Mr. Carscadon 1832]

D2-124:   Surv. 12 Sep 1827 by T.W.8006=7 Dec 1825 Francis Murphy 25 A. in Hampshire Co. on Alegany Mt. adj. And'w Bogle or Boyle?, Murpheys Glade. 13 Sep 1831 [Mr. Carscadon 1832]

D2-125:   Surv. 23 June by T.W.10,162=10 Dec 1828 John Thrush 50 A. in Hampshire Co. on Stagg Run of Pattersons Cr. adj. his own land, Elijah Buskirk. 13 Sep 1831 [Mr. Carscadon 1832]

D2-126:   Surv. 5 Apr 1830 by T.W.10,403=18 Feb 1830 George Shoemaker 51 1/2 A. in Hampshire Co. on Mud Run of Mill Cr. adj. Frederick High, Jackson, Frederick Purget, Patrick Kelly Heirs, John Ludwich. 13 Sep 1831 [Mr. Carscadon 1832]

D2-126:   Surv. 24 Aug 1830, 100 A. by T.W.10,362=15 Jan 1830 & 25 A. by T.W.7485=25 July 1823 Samuel Ruckman 125 A. in Hampshire Co. on Little Cacaphon adj. Baker, Jacob Ruckman heirs, Stabb Lick. 13 Sep 1831 [Mr. Carscadon 1832]

D2-127:   Surv. 8 Nov 1830 by T.W.10,403=18 Feb 1831 Henry Purget Jr. 52 1/2 A. in Hampshire & Hardy Cos. on Long Rg. & Mill Cr., S. Br. of Potowmac adj. his purchase of Frederick Purget, Isaac Vanmeter. 13 Sep 1831 [Mr. Carscadon]

D2-128:   Surv. 19 Jan 1830, 100 A. by T.W.10,217=13 Feb 1829 & 100 A. by T.W.10,321=3 Nov 1829 Abraham Parker 200 A. in Hampshire Co. on Mill Cr. & Middle Rg. adj. Jacob Parker, John Parker. 13 Sep 1831 [Mr. Carscadon]

D2-129:   Surv. 11 Jan 1828 by T.W.5819=30 Dec 1816 Adam Huffman 100 A. in Shenandoah Co. on Massenuten Mt. adj. Daniel Huffman, Abraham Algier, Joseph Loudeback, John Plodt. 20 Sep 1831 [Col. Bare 1832]

D2-130:   Surv. 4 June 1830 by T.W.10,422=23 Feb 1830 George See & Edmund See 142 A. in Hardy Co. on Rush Lick Run of Lost R. adj. their own land. 13 Sep 1831 [Dl'd rect 1832]

D2-131:   Surv. 19 Nov 1830 by T.W.7326=18 Nov 1822 Isaac Baker & Jacob Taylor 60 A. in Hampshire Co. on N. Br. of Potowmac adj. said Taylor, John J. Jacob, John

Craigen heirs. 13 Aug 1831 [Mr. Carscadon 1832]

D2-131:   Surv. 21 Nov 1828 67 A. by T.W.7501=30 Sep 1823 & 26 A. by T.W.6776=31
Dec 1819 Lickfrit Kabrick asne. of Stepthat? Jones 95 A. in Hampshire Co. on
Mill Run of Pattersons Cr. adj. Abraham Reed, George Millar heirs, the Manor
line, Colston bought of Jacob Reed. 29 Sep 1831 [Mr. Carscadon 1832]

D2-132:   Surv. 13 June 1829 by T.W.7749=30 Aug 1824 Lickfrit Kabrick 36 1/2 A.
in Hampshire Co. on Dry Run of Mill Run of Pattersons Cr. adj. Isaac Welch,
Peter Kabrick heirs, William Clarke, 29 Sep 1831 [Mr. Carscadon 1832]

D2-133:   Surv. 30 Mar 1830, 55 1/2 A. by T.W.10,403=18 Feb 1830 & 25 1/2 A. by
T.W.2405=15 Jan 1822 John Cheshir 79 A. in Hampshire Co. on Tear Coat Cr. adj.
Harburt Cool. 29 Sep 1831 [Mr. Carscadon]

D2-133:   Surv. 18 June 1830 by Exg.T.W.2429=5 Sep 1822 Reason Harvey 5 1/2 A. in
Hampshire Co. adj. Edward L. Blackburn heirs, his own land, Vincent Vandiver.
29 Sep 1831 [Mr. Carscadon 1832]

D2-134:   Surv. 23 June 1830 by T.W.10,403=18 Feb 1830 Daniel Leatherman 44 1/2
A. in Hampshire Co. on Cabbin Run of Pattersons Cr. adj. Knobly Mt., Peter
Leatherman bought of George Miller, Solomon Leatherman, Peter Leatherman bought
of Benjamin Bailey. 29 Sep 1831 [Mr. Carscadon]

D2-134:   Surv. 19 Sep 1829 by T.W.7501=30 Sep 1823 Peter & George Hartman 50 A.
in Hampshire Co. on Mill Cr. adj. Philip Mores, William S. Foley heirs, Henry
Hartman heirs. 29 Sep 1831 [Mr. Carscadon 1832]

D2-135:   Surv. 21 June 1830, 14 A. by T.W.5572=2 Feb 1816, 50 A. by 4781=30 Oct
1811 & 12 A. by T.W.7501=30 Sep 1823 William Boseley 76 A. in Hampshire Co. on
Alleghany Mt. adj. Sugar Camp Run, his own tract. 29 Sep 1831 [Mr. Carscadon]

D2-136: Surv. 19 Mar 1830, 11 A. by T.W.9988=11 Jan 1828, 39 A. by T.W.10,162=10
Dec 1828 & 17 A. by 10,362=13 Jan 1830 George House 67 A. in Hampshire Co. on
Knobly Mt. adj. his own surv., Marshall, Staffords line. 29 Sep 1831 [Mr.
Carscadon]

D2-137:   Surv. 21 Dec 1830 by T.W.10,481=2 Nov 1830 Gabriel Fox 90 A. in Hampshire Co. on Castleman Run of S. Br. of Potomac adj. William Fox heirs, William
Calmers, Fox heirs Castleman tract, John Wright. 19 Oct 1831 [to rec't 1831]

D2-137:   Surv. 22 Dec 1830 by T.W.10,481=2 Nov 1830 Gabriel Fox & George Fox 91
A. in Hampshire Co. on Castlemans Run & S. Br. of Potomac adj. William Fox heirs
Castleman tract, William Calmes. 19 Oct 1831 [to Rec't 1831]

D2-138:   Surv. 4 June 1830 by T.W.10,429=25 Feb 1830 Jacob Fisher 400 A.in Hardy
Co. on Cattail & Maxwells Run bet. his Maxwell's place & the Manor line, Wm.
Cunningham. 9 Nov 1831 [Mr. Mullen 1832]

D2-139:   Surv. 8 Nov 1830 by T.W.10,481=29 Oct 1830 George Harness 270 A. in
Hardy Co. on Fork Mt. adj. his own land, George Cunningham, William Cunningham
heirs, Charles Lobb. 11 Nov 1831 [Mr. Mullen 1832]

D2-139:   Surv. 4 June 1830 by T.W.10,422=23 Feb 1830 Henry Baughman 15 A. in
Hardy Co. on Lost R. adj. his own land, Jeremiah Inskeep, William Reed. 11 Nov
1831 [Mr. Mullen 1832]

D2-140:   Surv. 2 June 1830 by T.W.10,422=23 Feb 1830 Jacob Cline 85 A. in Hardy
Co. near Capon waters adj. his own land, Pierson heirs, Baker heirs, Bakers Mt.
11 Nov 1831 [Mr. Mullen 1832]

D2-141:   Surv. 4 June 1830 by T.W.10,422=23 Feb 1830 Abraham Link 37 1/2 A. in
Hardy Co. on Lost R. adj. his own land, George Hulver/Hulvert, Limestone Rg.,
John Homans, Sanders. 11 Nov 1831 [Dl'd Col. Mullen 19 Jan 1836]

D2-142:   Surv. 4 June 1930 by T.W.9139=30 Jan 1827 Henry M. Davis 155 A. in

Hardy Co. on Stone Lick Run adj. John Smith and others, Day, Perry. 11 Nov 1831 [Mr. Mullen 1832]

D2-142: Surv. 6 Mar 1830 by T.W.10,362=13 Jan 1830 Thomas Taylor 25 A. 2 Ro. in Hampshire Co. on Mill Cr. & Sink Hole Knob, adj. his own land, Leai. 11 Nov 1831 [Mr. Carscadon 1832]

D2-143: Surv. 26 Aug 1829 by T.W.10,032=23 Feb 1828 John Pugh 50 A. in Hampshire Co. on Tear Coat Cr. adj. Johnathan Pugh Sr., Johnathan Pugh Jr., Hall heirs, John Flemming. 11 Nov 1831 [Mr. Posten 1832]

D2-144: Surv. 21 Apr 1830, 100 A. by T.W.10,032=23 Feb 1828 & 4 A. by T.W.10,403=18 Feb 1830 Johnathan Hiett 104 A. in Hampshire Co. on N. R. Mt. adj. his own land, John B. White, Joseph Spotts, McCauley/McCauly. 11 Nov 1831 [Mr. Carscadon 1832]

D2-145: Surv. 30 Nov 1830 by T.W.7485=25 July 1823 Charles S. Taylor 160 A. in Hampshire Co. on Crooked Run of Little Cacapon adj. John Higgins heirs, George Sharpe, John Queen, Leith, John Smith, said Taylor. 11 Nov 1831 [Mr. Carscadon 1832]

D2-146: Surv. 30 Apr 1830 by Exg.T.W.3406=4 June 1802 Peter Fedrick Jr. & John Fedrick Jr. 43 A. in Morgan Co. on Sleepy Cr. adj. Philip C. Pendleton, Jacob Courtney, Josiah Hulse. 11 Nov 1831 [Dl'd John O'Farrell 16 Jan 1839]

D2-146: Surv. 28 Oct 1830 by T.W.9053=21 July 1826 Daniel Dellinger 46 1/2 A. in Shenandoah Co. on Short Hills adj. John Coffman, heirs of Michael Zirkle dec'd, Abraham Good. 11 Nov 1831 [Dl'd to Order 15 Sep 1835]

D2-147: Surv. 21 May 1830 by T.W.7390=29 Jan 1823 William Smith 12 1/2 A. in Shenandoah & Frederick Cos. on Cedar Cr. below Turkey Run adj. his own land, George Miller, Frederick Mowus. 11 Nov 1831 [Dl'd Mr. Bare 1832]

D2-148: Surv. 10 July 1830 by T.W.9189=8 Mar 1827 Henry Prince 58 1/2 A. in Shenandoah Co. on Rd. from Thornton's Gap to Honeyville, Piney Mt., Andrew Hoke, Peter & Abraham Prince, said Henry Prince/Price, heirs of John Kiblinger, Joseph Road heirs, heirs of John Miller dec'd. 11 Nov 1831 [Col. Bare 1832]

D2-149: Surv. 28 Sep 1830 400 A. by T.W.7345=9 Dec 1822 & 97 1/2 A. by T.W.9189=8 Mar 1827 Charles L. Moore 497 1/2 A. in Shenandoah Co. on Short Arse Mt. adj. Big Mt. run of Smith's Cr., Solomon Kingree, said Moore, opposite Evan's cabin. 11 Nov 1831 [Col. Bare 1832]

D2-150: Surv. 20 Sep 1830 by T.W.6747=6 Dec 1819 David McIntierf & George McIntierf 50 A. in Shenandoah Co. in Powels Ft. adj. their land, Martin Kibler. 11 Nov 1831 [Col. Bare 1832]

D2-151: Surv. 21 Oct 1830 by T.W.7858=9 Feb 1825 David Barb 15 A. 3 Ro. 33 Po. in Shenandoah Co. on Stoney Cr. adj. Henry Tusing, said Barb, Adam Barb. 11 Nov 1831 [Col. Bare 1832]

D2-151: Surv. 26 Feb 1830 by T.W.7851=29 Jan 1825 Andrew Keyser 26 A. in Shenandoah Co. bet. S. R. & Ft. Mt. adj. George Levesque granted him by Abraham Shue, Keyser's purchase of heirs of Michael Rhinetreat dec'd, Christian Bumtgarner, Keyser's McKnight tract, David Mumew. 11 Nov 1831 [Mr. Bare 1832]

D2-152: Surv. 28 July 1830, 150 A. by T.W.9967=19 Dec 1827 & 98 A. by T.W.9189 =8 Mar 1827 Peter Sprinkle asne. of John Huloa 248 A. in Shenandoah Co. on Short Hills & Mill Cr. adj. John Huloa Sr., John Bealer, Patrick OHenley. 11 Nov 1831 [Col. Bare 1832]

D2-153: Surv. 23 Nov 1829, 190 A. each on T.W.10,111 & 10,112 both=July 17 1828, 92 1/4 A. by T.W.7985=17 Oct 1825, 109 1/2 A. by T.W.9953=3 Nov 1829 & 834 1/4 A. by T.W.10,321=3 Nov 1829 Clement Smith 1416 A. in Hampshire Co. on Alleghany Mt. adj. Philip Good heirs, N. Br. of Potomac, Dawson. 23 Nov 1831 [Mr. Carscadon 1832]

D2-155: Surv. 9 Mar 1830 by T.W.10,362=13 Jan 1830 Thomas Taylor 24 1/2 A. in Hampshire Co. on S. Br. Mt. adj. his own land, Isaac Pancake, Lear. 15 Nov 1831 [Mr. Carscadon 1832]

D2-155: Surv. 18 June 1830 by T.W.7485=25 July 1823 Vincent Vandiver 232 A. in Hampshire Co. on Alleghany Mt. & Abrahams Cr. adj. Reason Harvey & Thomas Davis, Blackburn heirs. 15 Nov 1831 [Mr. Carscadon 1832]

D2-156: Surv. 17,18,19 & 20 May 1830 by T.W.6878=22 Mar 1820 John Koontz 2410 A. in Shenandoah & Frederick Cos. on Big N. Mt. adj. Jacob Rudloph, Michael Strasnider, Joel Williams, George Wyrmeer, Samuel Shell, Polly Orndoff, John Wymar, David Peer, Millers Run, estate of Isaac Zane dec'd, heirs of Thomas Swany dec'd, Jenkins now Peers & Beechm, Hugh Holmes, Paddy's Run, Lawrence Keller, Samuel Orndorff, Alexander Lowery. 23 Nov 1831 [Dl'd Mr. Bare 1832]

D2-159: Surv. 13 Dec 1829, 7 1/2 A. by T.W.9028=12 May 1826 & 4 1/2 A. by T.W.7390=29 Jan 1823 William Smith 12 A. in Shenandoah Co. on Turkey Run adj. Jonathan Swift now said Smith, Smith's part of Bryan Bruin tract, Isaac White now Watson heirs. 15 Nov 1831 [Dl'd Mr. Bare 1832]

D2-159: Surv. 10 Nov 1830, 15 1/4 A. by T.W.10,481=2 Nov 1830, 7 1/4 A. by T.W.10,321=3 Nov 1829 & 32 1/4 A. by T.W.7326=18 Nov 1822 Edward Taylor & Peter Hartman 54 3/4 A. in Hampshire Co. on Mill Cr. Knob adj. Joseph Shockey, Henry Hartman heirs, John Leatherman, Leonard Baumcrotz heirs, William Naylor. 15 Nov 1831 [Mr. Carscadon 1832]

D2-160: Surv. 22 June 1829 by 7501=30 Sep 1823 James Meekins 35 A. 1 Ro. in Hampshire Co. on Hopkins Lick Run of Little Cacaphon adj. M. Steritt, Vandegriff, Ren, Thomas Burkett. 15 Nov 1831 [Mr. Carscadon 1832]

D2-160: Surv. 22 Dec 1829 25 A. by T.W.10246=3 Mar 1829 & 7 1/4 A. by T.W.10,321=3 Nov 1829 Edward Taylor & Peter Hartman 32 A. 1 Ro. in Hampshire Co. on Mill Cr. adj. Phillip More, Henry Hartman heirs, George & Peter Hartman. 15 Nov 1831 [Mr. Carscadon 1832]

D2-162: Surv. 19 Sep 1829 by T.W.7985=17 Oct 1825 Peter Hartman 75 A. in Hampshire Co. on Mill Cr. adj. Henry Hartman heirs, Henry Hawk heirs, Magill heirs. 15 Nov 1831 [Mr. Carscadon 1832]

D2-162: Surv. 6 Jan 1830, 14 1/4 A. by T.W.10,321=3 Nov 1829 & 51 3/4 A. by T.W.7672=3 Mar 1824 Nicholas Biser 66 A. in Hampshire Co. on Middle Rg. adj. Jacob Biser, John Parker, Edward Taylor, Nicholas Biser. 15 Nov 1831 [Mr. Carscadon 1832]

D2-162: Surv. 4 Dec 1829, 1 A. by T.W.10,032=23 Feb 1828 & 2 Ro. 32 Po. by T.W.10,321=3 Nov 1829 Isaac N. Wilson 1 A. 2 Ro. 32 Po. in Hampshire Co. on N. R. adj. his own land, Synthicant, Sutton, said Wilson. 15 Nov 1831 [Mr. Carscadon 1832]

D2-163: Surv. 30 Sep 1829, 50 A. by 10,403=18 Feb 1830 & 70 A. by T.W.7104=6 July 1821 James Ravenscraft 120 A. in Hampshire Co. on Knobley Mt. adj. John D. Ravenscraft, Banks, said James Ravenscraft, Michael Thrash bought of Isaac Means, Vincent Vandiver. 15 Nov 1831 [Mr. Carscadon 1832]

D2-163: Surv. 22 June 1830, 7 1/4 A. by T.W.6776=31 Dec 1819, 70 A. by 10,403=18 Feb 1830 & 62 3/4 A. by T.W.2429=5 Sep 1822 Henry Barrick 140 A. in Hampshire Co. on Montgomeries Run on Alleghany Mt. adj. his own land, Jesse Sharpless, Pleaudn surv., N. Br. of Potomack, Phillip Good heirs. 15 Nov 1831 [Mr. Carscadon 1832]

D2-164: Surv. 15 Apr 1830 by T.W.7672=3 Mar 1824 Joseph Shockey 122 A. in Hampshire Co. on Mt. bet. S. Br. of Potomac & Mill Cr. adj. Wm. Naylor, Michel Millar, Wm. Mills, Thomas Taylor. 15 Nov 1831 [Mr. Carscadon 1832]

D2-165: Surv. 30 Apr 1831 by T.W.6878=22 Mar 1820 Edward Levell 75 1/2 A. in Shenandoah Co. in Blue Rg. on Pass Run adj. Abraham Heastand/Heasland, Samuel

Coffman, George Hetick, George Britton dec'd. 29 Nov 1831 [Dr. Robertson 1832]

D2-165: Surv. 29 Apr 1831 by T.W.5057=2 Apr 1813 Elijah Pettit, Elizabeth Edwards late Elizabeth Pettit & Rachel Flemings late Rachel Pettit only heirs of Johnthan Pettit dec'd 106 3/4 A. in Shenandoah Co. at the Blue Rg., on Elder Mt. near Thorntons Gap adj. Sam'l & Jacob Haufman, John Shenk, Piersin Judd, Peter Heastead. 27 Nov 1831 [Dr. Robertson 1832]

D2-167: Surv. 28 June 1830, 55 A. by T.W.2406=15 Jan 1822, 30 A. by T.W.7489=25 July 1823, 115 A. by T.W.7501=30 Sep 1723 & 19 A. by T.W.10,027=22 Feb 1828 Stephen Bird 219 A. in Hampshire Co. on S. Br. Mt. adj. Thomas Burkett and others, Edward Trickle, Treely or Freely, Francis Murphy heirs. 27 Nov 1831 [Mr. Carscadon 1832]

D2-168: Surv. 20 Nov 1830 by T.W.7513=1 Nov 1823 Leonard Love 12 A. 2 Ro. 2 Po. in Pr. William Co. on Neabcos Run adj. said Love, Bell Air tract. 27 Nov 1831 [Dl'd to Rec't 20 May 1835]

D2-169: Surv. 9 Dec 1829 by T.W.10,246=3 Mar 1829 Jacob Cooper 19 1/2 A. in Hampshire Co. on N. R. & Sandy Rg. adj. John Cooper, Adam Cooper. 13 Sep 1831 [Dl'd Mr. Carscadon]

D2-169: Surv. 24 Aug 1827, 203 A. by T.W.7489=25 July 1823 & 65 A. by T.W.7465=1 May 1823 Vause Fox 268 A. in Hampshire Co. on Middle Rg. & Castle Run adj. William Fox heirs, John Wright, Herriott. 27 Feb 1832 [Mr. Carscadon]

D2-170: Surv. 10 Feb 1827 by T.W.6244=7 Apr 1818 Andrew Gannt 17 A. in Culpeper Co. adj. said Gannts purchase of Yates, Gray. 21 Mar 1832 [Mr. Broaddus 1832]

D2-170: Surv. 17 July 1830 by T.W.8094=6 Mar 1826 William Garner 32 A. 1 Ro. 21 Po. in Pr. Wm. Co. near Occoquan, adj. Occoquan Rd., Fairfax, Davis. 2 Mar 1832

D2-171: Surv. 10 Nov 1829 by T.W.7678=4 Mar 1824 William Gore 16 A. in Culpeper Co. adj. John Miller, said Gore, Green, Peyton, Flinchman. 10 Mar 1832 [Mr. Broadus 1832]

D2-171: Surv. 5 Dec 1827, 60 A. by T.W.7104=July 1821 & 65 A. by T.W.7166=15 Dec 1821? Joseph Snapp 125 A. in Hampshire Co. on Crooked Run of Little Cacaphon adj. his own land, land he bought of Job Cooper, George Fletcher, Isaac Hains formerly Powell. 12 Mar 1832 [Dl'd Mr. Carscadon]

D2-173: Surv. 16 Apr 1830, 30 A. by T.W.7672=3 Mar 1824 & 36 A. by T.W.10,403=18 Feb 1830 Joseph Shockey 66 A. in Hampshire Co. on Mill Cr.Knob adj. Wm. Naylor, Coopers Gap, Henry Hartman heirs, in Hartman Gap. 11 Nov 1831 [Mr. Carscadon]

D2-174: Surv. 30 Dec 1828 by T.W.10,133=2 Oct 1828 Armistead Wilson 58 A. 2 Ro. 24 Po. in Frederick Co. adj. William Beard, Joseph Marpole, Henry Crowger, Thomas Goff, William Bean, James Lesenger, Henry Clowzer. 13 Mar 1832 [Maj. Opie 1832]

D2-174: Surv. 13 July 1831, 861 3/4 A. by T.W.7181=30 Jan 1822, 169 1/2 A. by T.W.9053=21 July 1826 & 43 3/4 A. by T.W.6448=17 Dec 1818 Walten Newman 1075 A. in Shenandoah Co. on Little Stony Cr. & Sugar Hill, adj. George Miller, James Russell. 17 Mar 1832 [Col. Bare 1832]

D2-174a: Surv. 3 Mar 1828 110 A. by T.W.5636=13 Mar 1816 & 18 A. by T.W.7145=31 Oct 1831 Joseph Embry 128 A. in Culpeper Co. adj. said Embry, Hubert Elkin, Wharton, William Corbin, John Southard, John Fletcher. 6 Dec 1831 [Dl'd Mr. Broaddus 1832]

D2-175: By Certificate from Auditor of Public Account, purchase by Gilbert Deavers 108 A. in Fairfax Co. on Accotink adj. Ravensworth, Boggess, John Ward, Zebedee Compton. 8 Mar 1831 [Dl'd Mr. Chichestr Mar 1831]

D2-175a: Surv. 4 Aug 1831 by T.W.10,463=7 Aug 1830 James Sterrett asne. of

Valentine Simmons 371 A. in Hardy Co. on Waite's Run of big Cacapon adj. Wilson, heirs of Robert Mins dec'd. 19 Sep 1832 [Dl'd A.M. Sterrett 20 Sep 1832]

D2-176: Surv. 3 June 1831 by T.W.10,523=12 Feb 1831 Churchill Berry 6 1/4 A. in Culpeper Co. adj. Samuel Dennis, heirs of William Johnson dec'd, Joseph Johnson dec'd legatee of William Johnson dec'd now C. Berry, Benjamin Johnson, Bessybell Mt. 19 Oct 1832 [Dl'd Col. Hill 18 Feb 1833]

D2-176: Surv. 4 June 1830 by T.W.10,422=23 Feb 1830 Philip Wisman 272 A. in Hardy Co. on Big Capeon adj. his own land, Abraham Littler, Micle, Hittler. 17 Oct 1832 [Dl'd Col. Bare 8 Feb 1833]

D2-176a: Surv. 15 July 1831 by T.W.5552=30 Dec 1815 Joseph Fawver 105 A. in Shenandoah Co. on Little N. Mt. adj. Mathias Zering, Elizabeth Rudolph, said Fawver. 18 Oct 1832 [Dl'd Col. Bare 8 Feb 1833]

D2-177: Surv. 16 July 1831 by T.W.5552=30 Dec 1815 Joel Williams 100 A. in Shenandoah Co. on Cedar Cr. bet. Big & Little N. Mts. adj. Samuel Shell, Polly Orndoff, said Williams, Michael Strosnider heirs. 18 Oct 1832 [Dl'd 1833]

D2-177a: Surv. 23 Aug 1828 by T.W.6878=22 Mar 1820 Wharton Jones 22 3/4 A. in Shenandoah Co. adj. his own land, Ulrick Biedner formerly Breeding, Benjamin Wood formerly James Botts. 18 Oct 1832 [Dr. Robertson 1833]

D2-177a: Surv. 26 May 1831 by T.W.10,539=26 Mar 1831 Peter Shinholt 85 1/2 A. in Hampshire Co. on Sandy Rg. adj. Conrod Holt, Peter Shinholt, John Hiett, Jonathan Hiett. 18 Oct 1832 [Dl'd Mr. Vance 19 Feb 1833]

D2-178: Surv. 23 Apr 1830, 5 A. by T.W.10,246=3 Mar 1829 & 3 1/4 A. by T.W.10,321=3 Nov 1829 Owen Delaplain 8 1/4 A. in Hampshire Co. on N. R. adj. Aalexander Monroe, George & Alexander Deavr/Deaver, Bennitt, said heirs, William Torrance. 18 Oct 1832 [Dl'd Mr. Sloan 1833]

D2-178a: Surv. 17 Oct 1831 by T.W.10,508=10 Jan 1831 Cromwell Orrick 14 A. in Morgan Co. on Potomac R. adj. Grasshopper hollow run, said Orrick, heirs of Gustin. 18 Oct 1832 [Dl'd Maj. Sherrard Mar 1835]

D2-178a: Surv. 29 Apr 1831 by T.W.5944=24 May 1817 Enos McKay 73 A. in Shenandoah Co. at foot of Glue Rg. adj. Abraham Beahm Jr., heirs of Jacob Beahm dec'd. 18 Oct 1832 [D. Robertson 1833]

D2-179: Surv. 8 Apr 1831 by T.W.9039=16 June 1826 John Walden 3 A. 1 Ro. 31 Po. in Fauquier Co. on Cedar Run adj. Colson now John Blackwell, said Walden, Hudnall, Taylor. 18 Oct 1832

D2-179a: Surv. 7 Nov 1831, 51 1/4 A. by T.W.7903=22 Feb 1825 & 19 1/4 A. by T.W.10,508=10 Jan 1831 John Young 70 1/2 A. in Morgan Co. on Potomac adj. Martin Bilmire, George Renolds. 18 Oct 1832 [Dl'd Mjr. Sherrard 11 Dec 1832]

D2-179a: Surv. 7 Nov 1831 by Surv. 4906=9 June 1812 Lewis B. Johnson 78 A. in Morgan Co. on Potomac R. adj. Sidling Hill, Nichaolas Fawon, Henry Fawver, Philip C. Pendleton. 18 Oct 1832 [Dl'd Mr. Vance 1833]

D2-180: Surv. 16 Dec 1831 by T.W.10,424=23 Feb 1830 William Bywaters 5 A. 3 Ro. 12 1/2 Po. in Frederick Co. adj. his other land, Joseph Dolly, land formerly Lewis McCoole. 18 Oct 1832 [Dl'd Col. Smith Mar 1834]

D2-180a: Surv. 9 July 1831 by T.W.10,289=10 Aug 1829 Zachariah Allen, Mary Ann Long & Richard Allen 100 A. in Pr. William Co. on Potomac R. 26 Oct 1832 [Col. Hoe 1834]

D2-180a: Surv. 6 Aug 1831 by T.W.10,289=10 Aug 1829 William Allen 383 A. 3 Ro. in Pr. William Co. on Powels Run & Potomac R. 26 Oct 1832 [Dl'd 1834]

D2-181: Surv. 18 May 1831 by T.W.10,489=9 Dec 1830 Daniel Williams 8 A. in Hampshire Co. on Little Cacaphon adj. S. fork of Haunted Run, John Stump, said

149

Williams purchase of William H. Moreland, George Sharp. 18 Oct 1832 [Mr. Vance]

D2-181:   Surv. 22 Nov 1831 by T.W.10,258=7 Apr 1829 Henry Harrison 11 A. in Hampshire Co. on New Cr. adj. John Head formerly George Six, Joseph Davis heirs. 29 Oct 1832 [Dl'd Mr. Vance 1833]

D2-181a: Surv. 15 May 1831 by T.W.10,539=26 Mar 1831 John Urice & Peter Urice 50 A. in Hampshire Co. on Knobley Mt. adj. Henry Fleek, George John, Peter Urice, Neils Gap. 29 Oct 1832 [Mr. Sloan 1833]

D2-182:   Surv. 30 Mar 1831 by T.W.9952=31 Oct 1827 Thomas Slane 31 A. in Hampshire Co. on Maple Run of N. R., Rd. from forks of Great Cacaphon to Romney, said Slane, Jerimiah Hiett, wid. Asbury & Joseph Asbury heirs, Peter Stump. 29 Oct 1832 [Mr. Vance 1833]

D2-182:   Surv. 28 Mar 1831, 22 1/2 A. by T.W.7485=25 July 1823 & 78 1/2 A. by T.W.10,489=9 Dec 1830 Peter Mauzy Sr. 101 A. in Hampshire Co. on Timber Rg., Mills Br. adj. Mason heirs, Wilson/Witson, Elijah Fletcher, said Peter Mauzy. 29 Oct 1832 [Mr. Vance 1833]

D2-182a: Surv. 9 Nov 1827 by T.W.9089=2 Nov 1826 Adam Sultzer 100 A. in Hampshire Co. on Mill Cr. adj. Abraham Vanmeter, Leonard Bauncrotz, Piss Ant Hill. 29 Oct 1832 [Mr. Sloan 1833]

D2-183: Surv. 10 Mar 1831 44 A. by T.W.10481=2 Nov 1830 & 100 A. by 7104=6 July 1821 Jacob Miller Jr. 144 A. in Hampshire Co. on Knobly Mt. 1 Nov 1832 [Mr. Sloan 1833]

D2-184:   Surv. 22 Jan 1831 by T.W.6747=6 Sep 1819 Henry Forror 33 3/8 A. in Shenandoah Co. on Hawksbill Cr. adj. Michael Baracker bought of Gabriel Tutt, Michael Shaler bought of Christian Forror, Samuel Forror & Christian Forror bought of Joseph Ruffner, John Conway. 2 Nov 1832 [D. Robertson 1833]

D2-185: Surv. 23 Dec 1831 by T.W.10,508=10 Jan 1831 James Bayles 17 A. 3 Ro. 15 Po. 6 parts of a Po. in Morgan Co. on Potomac R. adj. his own land, land formerly Thomas Kelly now heirs of William McCandliss. 4 Nov 1832 [Dl'd Mjr. Sherrard 11 Dec 1832]

D2-186: Surv. 20 Aug 1830 by Exg.T.W.1793=12 Dec 1805 Col. John Gibson 128 A. 3 Ro. 20 Po. in Pr. William Co. on Beam Dam Br. of Occoquan R. adj. Coalter, said Gibson, Joseph R. Gilbert heirs, Hays, Selectman. 10 Nov 1832 [Dl'd Mr. Gibson 8 Dec 1832]

D2-187:   Surv. 4 Dec 1830 by T.W.10,481=2 Nov 1830 Isaac Critton 69 A. in Hampshire Co. on Clay Lick Rg. & Little Cacaphon adj. John Kalor, Benjamin Stamp, George Moreland, William Critton, Isaac Critton bought of George Moreland, Alla Kalor. 2 Nov 1832 [Mr. Vance 1832]

D2-188:   Surv. 26 June 1829 by T.W.10,162=10 Dec 1828 Silas Prather 100 A. in Hampshire Co. on Little Cacaphon adj. Joseph Stump, Little Cacaphon Mt., Peter Stump, Pearce Noland, John Stump, Elizabeth More heirs. 2 Nov 1832 [Mr. Sloan 1933]

D2-189:   Surv. 24 June 1829 by T.W.10,162=10 Dec 1828 Silas Prather 75 A. in Hampshire Co. on Little Cacaphon adj. John Jinkens heirs, Benj. Stump, Taylor, formerly Largent, John Critton bot of James Miles. 2 Nov 1832

D2-190:   Surv. 20 Apr 1831 by T.W.9997=22 Jan 1828 Adam Socksman 5 A. 3 Ro. 27 Per. in Shenandoah Co. bet. two Great Roads from Woodstock to Winchester adj. George Haun, Socksman bought of John & George Alterfer, Jacob Good, John Hopaflent. 2 Nov 1832 [Dl'd Col. Bare 1833]

D2-191:   Surv. 14 Apr 1831 by T.W.9997=22 Jan 1828 Adam Socksman 3 A. 1 Ro. 12 Per. in Shenandoah Co. adj. said Socksman bought of John & George Altaifer, Joseph Swartze. 2 Nov 1832 [Dl'd Col. Bare 8 Feb 1833]

D2-192:   Surv. 2 Aug 1831 by T.W.1795=12 Dec 1805 Benjamin Pridman 5 A. 8 Po. in Pr. William Co. adj. Fergason, said Pridman. 2 Nov 1832 [P. William]

D2-193:   Surv. 6 Jan 1831 by T.W.10,481=29 Oct 1830 Jesse Stump 50 A. in Hardy Co. adj. his own land bought of heirs of John Linkins/Lekins, on Mill Cr., Ward, Green, Wise. 2 Nov 1832 [Mr. Mullen 1833]

D2-194:   Surv. 25 June 1829 by T.W.7985=17 Oct 1825 John Kaler 20 A. in Hampshire Co. on Little Cacaphon adj. George Moreland, Alla Kaler, Benjamin Stump. 2 Nov 1832 [Dl'd Mr. Vance 19 Feb 1833]

D2-195:   Surv. 12 July 1831 by T.W.6878=22 Mar 1820 John Koonts 516 A. in Shenandoah Co. on Narrow Passage Cr. adj. said Koonts' Samuel Nizely tract, Adolph Coffman, Philip Sheets formerly Lewis Stephens, Henry Sheets, Jacob Huddle, David Hisey, William Philips, Abraham Lambert, James Diceit, Blackford Arthur & Co. 2 Nov 1832 [Dl'd Col.Bare 8 Feb 1833]

D2-196:   Surv. 13 Apr 1831 by T.W.10,362=13 Jan 1830 Richard Sloan 13 1/2 A. in Hampshire Co. on Mill Cr. adj. Henry Hawks heirs, Abraham Vanmeter heirs, Biser heirs, Richard Sloan bought of Rickey, Sloan bought of McNeal & Henry Hawks heirs. 3 Nov 1832 [Mr. Sloan 1833]

D2-197:   Surv. 11 Mar 1831 by T.W.10,481=2 Nov 1830 James Allen 107 A. in Hampshire Co. on Pattersons Cr. near Middle Rg. adj. Ashford Rees, Thomas Allen, Daniel Hollenback. 3 Nov 1832 [Mr. Sloan 1833]

D2-197:   Surv. 18 Mar 1831 by T.W.10,481=2 Nov 1830 Solomon Leatherman 53 A. in Hampshire Co. on Cabin Run adj. Peter Leatherman Sr., William Welsh, Sylvester Welsh, Abraham Good. 3 Nov 1832 [Mr. Sloan 1833]

D2-198:   Surv. 18 Nov 1831 by T.W.10,539=26 Mar 1831 Samuel Caldwell 150 A. in Hampshire Co. bet. Mill Cr. & S. Br. of Potomac. 3 Nov 1832 [Mr. Vance 1833]

D2-199:   Surv. 9 Mar 1831 by T.W.10,481=2 Nov 1830 Peter Leatherman Jr. 120 A. in Hampshire Co. on Knobley Mt. adj. Peter Leatherman Sr bought of Benjamin Bailey, Daniel Leatherman, Peter Leatherman Sr. bought of George Millar, William Welsh. 3 Nov 1832

D2-200:   Surv. 3 Dec 1831 by T.W.10,591=15 June 1831 Jacob Myers 10 A. in Berkeley Co. on Opockon Cr. adj. John Muger, John Leght, Henry Myers. 4 Nov 1832

D2-201:   Surv. 28 Apr 1831 by T.W.5944=24 May 1817 Enos McKay 163 A. in Shenandoah Co. on Blue Rg. adj. said McKay, David McKay bought of Heritage Blackwell, near Elk hollow, Jeremies Run. 4 Nov 1832 [Dl'd Dr. Robertson 1833]

D2-202:   Surv. 25 Mar 1831 by T.W.9117=17 Dec 1826 William Largent 144 A. in Hampshire Co. on N. R. Mt. adj. Benjamin McDonald, Absolam Millar. 4 Nov 1832 [Dl'd Mr. Vance 22 Jan 1833]

D2-203:   Surv. 7 Mar 1831 by T.W.7382=6 Jan 1823 Thomas Lyon & John Hilkey 100 A. in Hardy Co. on New Cr. & Walkers Rg. adj. their own land bought of Williamson. 4 Nov 1832 [Mr. Mullen 1833]

D2-203:   Surv. 4 June 1830 by T.W.10,422=23 Feb 1830 Godfrey Wilkins 36 1/2 A. in Hardy Co. on Kinnsey's Run of Lost R. adj. Martin Miller, Chambers. 4 Nov 1832 [Mr. Mullen 1833]

D2-204:   Surv. 19 Nov 1831 by T.W.9952=31 Oct 1827 John Neff 200 A. in Hampshire Co. on Abram's Rg. adj. Thomazen Grayson. 4 Nov 1832 [Mr. Sloan 1833]

D2-205:   Surv. 17 Nov 1831 by T.W.9997=22 Jan 1828 Philip Ludwick 11 A. in Shenandoah Co. on Beesons Br. adj. said Ludwick, Peter Sine, William Rinker, Absolam Rinker. 4 Nov 1832 [Dl'd Col. Bare 8 Feb 1833]

D2-205:   Surv. 10 Feb 1831 by T.W.10,481=29 Oct 1830 Henry Switzer 247 A. in Hardy Co. on S. fork of N. R. adj. his own land, John Sperry. 4 Nov 1832 [Dl'd

Mr. Mullen 1833]

D2-206:   Surv. 15 Nov 1831 by T.W.9189=8 Mar 1827 Reuben Walton 7 A.   3 Ro. 29
Po. in Shenandoah Co. adj. Kagays, Moses Walton, Strickler.   4 Nov 1832
[Pennybaker 1833]

D2-207:   Surv. 20 Apr 1829 by T.W.6437=14 Dec 1818 Samuel Frye asne. of John
Babb, Peter Babb, William Babb, Samuel Babb, Lydia Babb(now Lydia Frye w. of
Samuel Frye) & Levi Babb heirs & devisees of Peter Babb dec'd, 500 A. in Hardy
Co. on Anderson's Rg. and Big Capon adj. John Fulkerson, Joseph Wells, Christian
Haw, Christian Hull, John Funkhouser. 19 Dec 1832 [Dl'd Col. Mullin 20 Dec 1832]

D2-208:   Surv. 18 July 1831 by T.W.5944=24 May 1817 Joshua Summers 8 A. on Punk
Run at the Blue Rg. in part of Shenandoah Co. that is now part of Page Co. Adj.
John Varner, Henry Sour, Hetick, George Prince, Eve Pointer. 4 Nov 1832 [Dl'd
Dr. Robertson 1833]

D2-208:   Surv. 13 May 1831 by T.W.10,481=2 Nov 1830 John Spencer 50 A. in
Hampshire Co. on Knobley Mt. adj. Jacob Miller. 4 Nov 1832 [Mr. Sloan 1833]

D2-209:   Surv. 8 June 1830 by T.W.10,422=23 Feb 1830 Godfrey Wilkins 57 A. in
Hardy Co. on Lost R. adj. his own land, Thomas Elswick, spur of Little Rg. 4
Nov 1832 [Mr. Mullen 1833]

D2-210:   Surv. 7 Dec 1829 by Surv. 8061=15 Feb 1826 John Sevier 40 A. 1 Ro. in
Hampshire Co. on Big Cacaphon adj. Samuel Beckwick, Abraham Plum, Jacob Cump,
Frederick Secrites. 4 Nov 1832 [Mr. Sloan 1833]

D2-210:   Surv. 10 Feb 1831 by T.W.10,481=29 Oct 1830 Henry Wise 98 A. in Hardy
Co. on N. R. adj. heirs of Frederick Wise dec'd, Henry Gochenonet, Jonathan
Taylor. 4 Nov 1832 [Mr. Mullen 1833]

D2-211:   Surv. 7 Mar 1831 by T.W.10,422=23 Feb 1830 Daniel Sites 99 A. in Hardy
Co. on High Knob of Middle Mt. bet. N. & S. Mill Cr. 4 Nov 1832 [Mr.Mullen 1833]

D2-212:   Surv. 5 Mar 1831 by T.W.10,481=2 Nov 1830 Alexander Page 93 1/2 A. in
Hampshire Co. on Grape Knob adj. William Bonmoratz, Isaac Vanmeter. 4 Nov 1832
[Dl'd Mr. Vance 19 Jan 1833 & afterwards to Mr. Mullen]

D2-212:   Surv. 2 Dec 1831 by T.W.9189=8 Mar 1827 Elijah Evans 100 A. in
Shenandoah Co. on Massanotten Mt. adj. heirs of Benjamin Pennybacker dec'd. 4
Nov 1832 [Dl'd to Bare Mar 1836]

D2-213:   Surv. 24 Jan 1832 by T.W.6662=7 June 1819 Frederick High 25 A. in
Hampshire Co. on Mill Cr. adj. said High, Henry Hawk heirs, Hiram High bought of
Magills Exr., Richard Sloan heirs, Joseph Ludwick bought of Henry Hawk. 4 Nov
1832 [Mr. Soan 1833]

D2-214: Surv. 11 Mar 1831 100 A. by T.W.7319=1 Nov 1822 & 180 A. by T.W.10,489=9
Dec 1830 Ashford Rees 280 A. in Hampshire Co. on Middle Rg. & Patterson's Cr.
adj. Hazle Run, Jacob Miller, Thomas Allen. 4 Nov 1832 [Mr. Vance 1833]

D2-215:   Surv. 4 June 1830 by T.W.10422=23 Feb 1830 Martin Miller 173 1/2 A. in
Hardy Co. on Kinseys Run of Lost R. adj. George Miller. 4 Nov 1832 [Mr. Mullen
1833]

D2-216:   Surv. 9 Feb 1832 by T.W.6295=8 June 1818 Henry High 39 1/2 A. in
Hampshire Co. on Mill Cr. adj. Adam Niff heirs, Horse lick Run, Patrick
Flemming, Zachariah Arnold heirs, Angus W. McDonald bought of Abraham Vanmeter
heirs, John Arnold. 4 Nov 1832 [Mr. Sloan 1833]

D2-217:   Surv. 17 May 1831, 25 A. by T.W.6443=15 Dec 1818, 175 A. by T.W.9953=31
Oct 1827 & 5 A. by T.W.10,539=26 Mar 1831 Richard Blue 205 A. in Hampshire Co.
on S. Br. Mt., S. Br. of Potomac adj. Isaac Blue, William Inskeep, said Richard
Blue, John Pownall. 4 Nov 1832 [Mr. Vance 1833]

D2-218:   Surv. 1 Dec 1830 by T.W.10,481=29 Oct 1831 William Campbell 1043 A. in
Hardy Co. on Big Cacapon adj. John Bushby/Busby, Michael Shoemaker, Gillets &
Russil, Jeremiah Stewart, Richardson. 4 Nov 1832 [Col. Mullen 10 Jan 1833]

D2-219:   Surv. 20 Mar 1831 337 A. by T.W.5826=3 Jan 1817, 86 A. by T.W.7010=12
Feb 1821, 50 A. by T.W.6166=5 Feb 1818 & 100 A. by T.W.7465=1 May 1823 John S.
Kesler 573 A. in Hampshire Co. on Little Cacaphon Cr. adj. James Taylor,
Allender, Town hill, Ginnevan Mill, John Cuttin heirs. 4 Nov 1832 [Vance 1933]

D2-220:   Surv. 1 July 1829, 134 A. by T.W.10,217=13 Feb 1829, 203 1/2 A. by
10,258=7 Apr 1829, 159 A. by T.W.10,162=10 Dec 1828 & 28 1/2 A. by T.W.10,032=23
Feb 1828 George G. Tasker & Benjamin Tasker 525 A. in Hampshire Co. on Alleghany
Mt. & Stony Run of N. Br. of Potomac adj. their own land, their Wilson tract,
James McCorneack, Thomas Shores, the Mossy Springs, James Junkin, Martin,
Nalley, George R. Tasker. 4 Nov 1832 [Mr. Vance 1833]

D2-221:   Surv. 4 June 1830 by T.W.9925=18 May 1827 William Campbell 614 A. in
Hardy Co. on Andersons Rg., Big Cacapon adj. James Sterret, Daniel Babb, George
Lynn, Abraham Jittles, Mins. 4 Nov 1832 [Dl'd Col. Mullin 10 Jan 1833]

D2-222:   Surv. 18 July 1831 by T.W.5944=24 May 1817 William Bradley asne. of
Barnett Stondemoyer 53 1/2 A. on Piney Mt. in Shenandoah now Page Co. adj. Jacob
Koonts, William Bradley's purchase of John Buswell, George Prince, Henry Prince,
John Bromback, John Kibbiner heirs. 4 Nov 1832 [Dl'd Mr. Robertson 1833]

D2-223:   Surv. 9 May 1832, 104 1/2 A. by T.W.10,359=8 Jan 1830, 96 1/2 A. by
T.W.10,424=23 Feb 1830 & 8 A. by T.W.10,563=19 Apr 1831 Reuben Zeiler & Joshua
Gore 209 A. in Frederick Co. adj. Sleepy Cr. Bryan Bruin, John Sugedut, Timber
Rg., Shiriff now Slade, Johnston, Jolley, Catlett, James Luttrel. 1 Feb 1833

D2-224:   Surv. 8 Nov 1830, 790 A. by T.W.7108=27 July 1821 & 304 A. by
T.W.10,481=29 Oct 1830 Joseph & James Williams 1094 A. in Hardy Co. on
Pattersons Cr. adj. heirs of George Gilpin, hiers of Peter Babb, said William's
Mill lot, Samuel Babb, Charles A. Turley, heirs of Abraham Baker, James Bosley?.
5 Mar 1833 [Dl'd Col. Mullen 6 Mar 1833]

D2-225: Surv. 12 Mar 1831, 300 A. by T.W.10,297=14 Sep 1829 & 80 A. by 10,505=6
Jan 1831 John Bayliss 380 A. in Culpeper Co. adj. Francis Tyler, Marshall
Johnson, Bakers Mt., Philip Irons now Peter Pierce, Wolf Mt., Jones, Henry
Tyler. 23 Mar 1833 [Dl'd Mr. Broaddus 25 Mar 1833]

D2-226:   Surv. 9 Apr 1832 200 A. by T.W.7309=15 Oct 1822 & 29 A. by
T.W.10,477=21 Dec 1831 George Lynn 229 A. in Hardy Co. on Trout Run, Trough Rg.
adj. Henry Wilson, Newman, Maker, Daniel Babb, Campbell. 6 July 1833 [Sent by
mail 6 July 1833]

D2-227:   Surv. 29 July 1831 by T.W.9131=20 Jan 1827 & by decree of Superior
Court of Morgan Co. Samuel Grove 39 A. in Morgan Co. on Middle fork of Sleepy
Cr. adj. William Smith, Hurbeit Humes, Grove. 27 Sep 1833 [By mail 1 Oct 1833]

D2-228:   Surv. 3 Nov 1832, 700 A. by T.W.10,313=6 Oct 1829 & 15 A. by
T.W.10,442=4 May 1830 Valentine Simmons 715 A. in Hardy Co. on N. Mt. adj.
William Maxwell formerly Robert Means of City of Richmond, Daniel Call,
Greenbrier Br., LampLick hollow, David Ogden, Dog Gap, Benjamin Williams heirs.
30 Oct 1833 [Dl'd to Rec't 5 Nov 1833]

D2-229: Surv. 20 June 1832 by T.W.10,362=13 Jan 1830 Travis D. Croston 21 A. in
Hampshire Co. on N. R. adj. Christopher Heiskill, said Croston, Alexander
Deavour/Deavor dec'd. 4 Nov 1833 [Vance 1834]

D2-230:   Surv. 7 Sep 1831, 100 A. by T.W.10,403=18 Feb 1830 & 58 A. by
T.W.10,602=6 July 1831 Joseph Shockey 158 A. in Hampshire Co. on Saw Mill Run of
S. Br. of Potomac adj. Jacob Shank, John Pancake, Little Mt., Isaac Pancake. 10
Nov 1833 [Mr. Vance 1835]

D2-231:   Surv. 12 June 1832 by T.W.10,752=21 Mar 1832 Nathan Kerns(of George)

175 A. in Hampshire & Frederick Cos. on Timber Rg. adj. William Parish's smith shop, Daniel Oats formerly Mason, Peter Mauzy, John Rosenberger heirs, McKee, Casper Alleman, Griffin. 4 Nov 1833 [Dl'd Col. J?.D.B. Smith 1834]

D2-232:   Surv. 8 June 1830 by T.W.10,422=23 Feb 1830 Jacob Cline 20 1/2 A. in Hardy Co. on Big Rg. near Capon waters adj. his own land, Benjamin Moore. 26 Jan 1833 [Mullen 1834]

D2-232:   Surv. 26 Jan 1832 by T.W.10,501=27 Dec 1830 Samuel McMechen 100 A. in Hardy Co. on Pattersons Cr. Mt. adj. his own land. 14 Nov 1833 [Mullen 1834]

D2-233: Surv. 26 Apr 1832 by T.W.10,422=23 Feb 1830 Benjamin Moore 60 A. in Hardy Co. on Big Rg. adj. said Moore, Littlejohn, Thomas Moore. 1 Nov 1833 [Mullen 1834]

D2-233:   Surv. 21 Jan 1833, 76 3/8 A. by T.W.9131=20 Jan 1827 & 20 5/8 A. by T.W.10,427=15 Aug 1832 Henry Bruner & George Ziler 97 A. in Morgan Co. on Sidling Hill adj. Aaron Harlan. 28 Nov 1833 [Dl'd Mr. Buck 1834]

D2-234:   Surv. 3 Sep 1832 by T.W.7044=28 Feb 1821 Jacob Smith 17 A. in Morgan Co. on Indian Run of Sleepy Cr. adj. Mathias Rezer, John Miller, Philip C. Pendleton, Daniel Fernoe. 15 Nov 1833 [Buck 1834]

D2-235: Surv. 26 Oct 1832 by T.W.10,507=10 Jan 1831 Isaiah Buck 50 A. in Morgan Co. on Sleepy Cr. adj. said Buck, Simeon Rankin, Robert Buck, Peter Youst, Andrew Michael. 15 Nov 1833 [Dl'd Mr. Buck 1834]

D2-236:   Surv. 21 May 1832 by T.W.10,710=2 Mar 1832 David Alderton 83 A. in Morgan Co. on Big Run of Potomac R. adj. John Ester, David Alderton. 28 Nov 1833 [Dl'd Mr. Buck 1834]

D2-236:   Surv. 22 May 1832 by T.W.10,710=2 Mar 1832 Jacob Alderton 117 A. in Morgan Co. on Powtomac R. adj. David Alderton/Alderson, his former surv., Mary Alderson, heirs of William Alderton. 28 Nov 1833 [Dl'd Mr. Buck 1834]

D2-237:   Surv. 17 Mar 1832 by T.W.10,677=21 Dec 1831 Jonathan Henline 70 A. in Hardy Co. on Alleghany Mt., Abrahams Cr., main Rd., adj. Solomen Michael. 14 Nov 1833 [Mullen 1834]

D2-238:   Surv. 8 June 1830 by T.W.10,422=23 Feb 1830 John Stewart 5 A. in Hardy Co. near Cacapeon adj. his own land, Jacob Cline. 1 Nov 1833 [Mullen 1834]

D2-239:   Surv. 22 June 1832 by T.W.10,677=21 Dec 1831 George Michael 350 A. in Hardy & Hampshire Cos. adj. Pick, Michael Switzer, Ohaver, Elk hill, Rollar, Jacob Saunnet. 14 Nov 1833 [Mullen 1834]

D2-240:   Surv. 24 Apr 1832 by T.W.10,043=25 Feb 1828 Jacob Keller 224 A. 3 Ro. 25 Per. in Shenandoah Co. in Powells Big Fork adj. John Clem, S. Fork Mt., Jacob Smith, Henry Hockman. 14 Nov 1833 [Dl'd Col. Bare]

D2-240:   Surv. 17 July 1833 by T.W.10,852=12 Dec 1832 John Sherrard 245 A. in Morgan Co. on Rock Gap run & Sleepy Cr. adj. Robert Gustin, Thomson Elzey, Warm spring Rg., Williams. 27 Feb 1834 [Dl'd Mr. Buck 1834]

D2-241:   Surv. 10 July 1832 by T.W.10,649=27 Jan 1832 Daniel Snyder 455 A. in Jefferson Co. on Shenandoah R. by Key's ferry landing, adj. John Vestal, Gersham Keys, Brown, James Lang, Carlyle now Lang. 14 Nov 1833 [Dl'd Mr. Gallaher 1834]

D2-242: Surv. 17 June 1830, 100 A. by T.W.7501=30 Sep 1825 & 75 A. by T.W.10,032 =23 Feb 1828 Samuel Vandiver 175 A. in Hampshire Co. on New Cr. adj. Vincent Vandiver bought of Samuel Vandiver, Vincent's Moreley tract. 3 Dec 1833 [Vance 1834]

D2-243:   Surv. 25 Nov 1831, 150 A. by T.W.10,585=2 June 1831 & 57 1/2 A. by T.W.10,640=21 Oct 1831 Samuel B. Davis Jr. 201 1/2 A. in Hampshire Co. on Mill Run & Pattersons Cr. adj. Mary Harrison. 1 Nov 1833 [Vance 1834]

154

D2-243: Surv. 23 Nov 1821, 50 A. by T.W.10,489=9 Dec 1830 & 11 A. by T.W.10,640=21 Oct 1831 Henry Harrison 61 A. in Hampshire Co. on New Cr. Mt. adj. William Duling Jr., Frank's Gap, said Henry Harrison. 1 Nov 1833 [Vance 1834]

D2-244: Surv. 11 Sep 1832 by T.W.10,752=21 Mar 1832 Branson Poston 93 A. 1 Ro. in Hampshire Co. on Craigs run of N. R. adj. N. R. Mt. adj. said Poston, Jacob Hammock. 15 Nov 1833 [Vance 1834]

D2-244: Surv. 29 Mar 1832 by T.W.10,640=21 Oct 1831 William Bailey 25 A. in Hampshire Co. on Cabbin Run adj. Said Bailey, Samuel Dobbins, Cabbin Run Hill. 14 Nov 1833 [Vance 1834]

D2-245: Surv. 22 May 1832 by T.W.10,640=21 Oct 1831 Samuel Vandiver 30 A. in Hampshire & Hardy Cos. on Alleghany Mt., Hogeland Glade Run of Abraham's Cr. adj. Emanuel Arnold, Parsons, Hugh Murphy. 14 Nov 1833 [Vance 1834]

D2-245: Surv. 11 Sep 1832 by T.W.10,752=21 Mar 1832 Branson Poston 4 3/4 A. in Hampshire Co. on N. R. adj. his land. 15 Nov 1833 [Vance 1834]

D2-246: Surv. 12 Sep 1832 by T.W.10,585=2 June 1831 Bronson Poston 40 A. in Hampshire Co. on N. R. Mt. adj. said Poston. 15 Nov 1833 [Vance 1834]

D2-246: Surv. 6 June 1832 by T.W.10,752=21 Mar 1832 Charles Carlyle 6 A. 3 Ro. in Hampshire Co. on Great Cacaphon. 15 Nov 1833 [Vance 1834]

D2-247: Surv. 20 July 1827 vy T.W.7419=19 Feb 1823 Wm. Ely Sr. & Betsy Ann Dew 154 1/4 A. in Hampshire Co. on Little Cacapehon adj. George Thompson, Stephen Ganoe heirs, said Ely, Parry Drew, Drew now Alexder Patterson. 15 Nov 1833 [Vance 1834]

D2-247: Surv. 21 June 1832 100 A. by T.W.10,640=21 Oct 1831 & 76 1/2 A. by T.W.12,772=30 Apr 1832 James B. Watkins 176 1/2 A. in Hampshire Co. on S. fork of Little Cacaphon adj. his own land, Fredinand Guelick/Gulick, Harrison Watkins, Creamer. 14 Nov 1833 [Vance 1834]

D2-248: Surv. 1 June 1832 by T.W.10,772=30 Apr 1832 Abraham Reed asne. of John C. Utt Jr. 76 A. in Hampshire Co. on Pattersons Cr. adj. John C. Utt Sr., Dry Run. 15 Nov 1833 [Vance 1834]

D2-248: Surv. 6 June 1832 by T.W.10,752=21 Mar 1832 Charles Carlyle 9 1/2 A. in Hampshire Co. on Great Cacaphon adj. Portin heirs, John Cheshire heirs, Bear Garden Mt., Evan Candy. 15 Nov 1833 [Vance 1834]

D2-249: Surv. 25 Nov 1828 by T.W.9988=11 Jan 1828 John Ruckman 11 A. 11 Po. in Hampshire Co. on Little Cacaphon adj. his own land, Bell?, William Loy. 15 Nov 1833 [Vance 1834]

D2-249: Surv. 20 June 1829 by T.W.9997=22 Jan 1828 John Beeler 50 A. in Shenandoah Co. on Little N. Mt. adj. his land, William Lyvert?, Martin Hupp asne. of heirs of Philip Brobrek? dec'd, John Himmen, Phinres Cradorff. 14 Nov 1833 [Col. Bare 1834]

D2-250: Surv. 18 June 1832 by T.W.6878=22 Mar 1832 Abraham Funkhouser 42 A. 1 Ro. in Shenandoah Co. on N. Mt. & Stony Cr. adj. Jacob Funkhouser, Peter Baker, Abraham Rosenbarger, heirs of Paul Harminson dec'd. 14 Nov 1833 [Col. Bare 1834

D2-250: Surv. 16 Mar 1832 by T.W.6387=26 Oct 1816 Adam Rudolph asne. of John Bealer 99 1/3 A. in Shenandoah Co. on Little N. Mt. adj. Isaac Hartmyrs, said Rudolph, Abraham Sevirt?. 14 Nov 1833 [Col. Bare 1834]

D2-251: Surv. 26 Apr 1832 by T.W.9159=21 Feb 1827 Richard Carrier 58 3/4 A. in Shenandoah Co. on Stony Cr. adj. John Struts dec'd heirs, John Basey. 14 Nov 1833 [Col. Bare 1834]

D2-251: Surv. 14 Jan 1832 by Surv. 9173=5 Mar 1827 John G. Teller? asne. of Thomas Windell 84 1/2 A. in Shenandoah Co. on Little N. Mt. adj. Lawrence

Keller, George Keller. 14 Nov 1833 [Col. Bare 1834]

D2-252: Surv. 1 Dec 1830 30 A. by T.W.4762=1 Aug 1811 & 44 A. =2 Nov 1830 Richard Short 74 A. in Hampshire Co. on Brakeneck Mt. adj. Isaac Short heirs, Taylor. 10 Nov 1833 [Sloan 1834]

D2-252: Surv. 22 May 1832 by T.W.10,640=21 Oct 1831 Samuel Vandiver 105 1/2 A. in Hampshire Co. on Abrahams Cr. & Alleghany Mt. adj. Buffington heirs, Higgins heirs, Hugh Murphy, Greenley. 10 Nov 1833 [Sloan 1834]

D2-253: Surv. 31 May 1833 T.W.7484=23 July 1823, T.W.7109=27 July 1820 & T.W.7373=26 Dec 1822 Vincent Vandiver 312 A. in Hampshire Co. on Dry Run of Pattersons Cr. adj. Joseph Vanmeter, Inias Moore, John C. Utt. Jr. bought of Robert Parker, John C. Utt Sr., Pusley's Run. Nov 1833 [Sloan 1834]

D2-253: Surv. 13 Apr 1832 by T.W.7373=26 Dec 1822 Vincent Vandiver 66 A. in Hampshire Co. on Pattersons Cr. adj. Jesse Bane devised to George Bane, Samuel Cockerill, Daniel Fink. 4 Nov 1833 [Sloan 1834]

D2-254: Surv. 31 Oct 1832 by T.W.10,489=9 Dec 1830 & 10,373=16 Jan 1830 Benjamin N. Roberts 185 A. in Hampshire Co. on Mikes Run adj. Gersham Roberts heirs, Abraham Doll, Vanmeter. 1 Nov 1833 [Sloan 1834]

D2-254: Surv. 20 Nov 1830 30 A. by T.W.10,585=2 June 1831 & 33 A. by T.W.10,640=21 Oct 1831 George Shoemaker 63 A. in Hampshire Co. on Mill Cr. adj. Frederick High, said George Shoemaker, Patrick's heirs, Frederick Purget. Nov 1833 [Sloan 1834]

D2-255: Surv. 13 Mar 1832 123 A. by T.W.7660=23 Feb 1824 & 122 A. by T.W.10,669 =13 Dec 1831 Lander Shores 245 A. in Hampshire Co. on S. Br. of Potomack adj. Lishes heirs, John Earson formerly Woodrow. 14 Nov 1833 [Mr. Vance 1835]

D2-256: Surv. 7 Aug 1832 by T.W.10,752=21 Mar 1832 John Brant 1 1/2 A. in Hampshire Co. on N. Br. of Potomack & Alleghany Mt. adj. George G. Tasker, said Brant. 1 Nov 1833 [Sloan 1834]

D2-256: Surv. 16 Nov 1832 by T.W.10,772=30 Apr 1832 Joseph Inskeep 180 A. in Hampshire Co. on Patterson's Cr. adj. his Bush land, McGrary heirs, Parker run, William Naylor, Inskeep's Carlyle land. 4 Nov 1833 [Sloan 1834]

D2-257: Surv. 22 Apr 1831 by T.W. 9089=2 Nov 1826 Josius Moore 37 A. in Hampshire Co. on Dry Run of Pattersons Cr. adj. Joseph Vanmeter. 10 Nov 1833 [1834]

D2-257: Surv. 28 Mar 1832 by T.W.6787=5 Feb 1820 Daniel Hollenback 29 1/2 A. in Hampshire Co. on Middle Rg. & Pattersons Cr., Thompsons Run, adj. Ashford Pierc? bought of John Singleton, said Riss bought of said Singleton, Andrew Lure now Jacob & Elizabeth Lure, Brinin. 14 Nov 1833 [Sloan 1834]

D2-258: Surv. 14 May 1831 by T.W.10,489=9 Dec 1830 Philip Umstot 40 A. in Hampshire Co. on Knobley Mt. adj. James Rundell, said Umstot, William Culp. Nov 1833 [Sloan 1834]

D2-259: Surv. 14 Apr 1829 by T.W.10,135=14 Oct 1828 Philip Umstot 12 3/4 A. in Hampshire Co. on Cabbin Run hill adj. his own land, Abraham Leatherman, Samuel Dobbins. 1 Nov 1833 [Sloan 1834]

D2-259: Surv. 14 May 1831 by T.W.=14 Oct 1828 Philip Umstot 15 1/2 A. in Hampshire Co. on Horseshoe Rg. adj. Peter Harrell Sr., William Armstrong. 1 Nov 1833 [Sloan 1834]

D2-260: Surv. 30 Oct 1832 by T.W.10,773=30 Apr 1832 Abraham Doll 105 A. in Hampshire Co. on Mikes Run adj. said Doll, Gersham Roberts heirs, Vanmeter, Josias Moore. 4 Nov 1833 [Sloan 1834]

D2-260: Surv. 28 Feb 1832 100 A. by T.W.10,640=21 Oct 1831 & 45 A. by T.W.10,669 =13 Dec 1831 John Smith 145 A. in Hampshire Co. on Little Cacaphon adj. said

Smith, James McBride bought of Christopher Heiskill, John McBride heirs, Jacob Stein, Barlow Suroot formerly John Williamson. 1 Nov 1833 [Sloan 1834]

D2-261: Surv. 14 Mar 1832 by T.W.10,602=6 July 1831 George Horn 83 A. in Hampshire Co. on Green Spring hollow of S. Br. of Potomack, Middle Rg., adj. Leslie's heirs, Fonis? heirs. 1 Nov 1833 [Sloan 1834]

D2-262: Surv. 19 Sep 1832 by T.W.10,773=30 Apr 1832 William Staggs 50 A. in Hampshire Co. on Cabin Run, Paddy town Run adj. Frederick Sheetz, Samuel Hammock heirs, said Staggs. 4 Nov 1833 [Mr. Vance Mar 1835]

D2-262: Surv. 7 Nov 1832 by T.W.10,773=30 Apr 1832 William Bennett 49 A. in Hampshire Co. on N. R. adj. William Torrence, Owen Deliplane, Offord, Conrod, Minser, Bilse?, Wharton, Armpieller. 4 Nov 1833 [Mr. Vance Mar 1835]

D2-263: Surv. 3 Nov 1832 by T.W.10,027=22 Feb 1828 William Vanbuskirk 74 1/2 A. in Hampshire Co. on Johnsons Run adj. his land. 1 Nov 1833 [Mr. Vance Mar 1835]

D2-263: Surv. 21 June 1832, 15 A. by T.W.6145=20 Jan 1818, 5 A. by T.W.10,032=23 Feb 1828, 50 A. by T.W.6661=7 June 1819 & 26 A. by T.W.10,773=30 Apr 1832 John Arnold 96 A. in Hampshire Co. on Chesnut Rg. & Little Cacaphon, adj. said Arnold bought of Knott heirs, Samuel Hott, Cornelius Williamson, Daniel Haines. 1 Nov 1833 [Mr. Vance Mar 1835]

D2-264: Surv. 30 Oct 1832, 40 3/4 A. by T.W.9997=22 Jan 1828 & 87 1/2 A. by 7851=29 Jan 1825 Jacob Strickler 128 1/4 A. in Shenandoah Co. on Massanotton Mt. adj. Benjamin Pennybacker heirs, John Keigy/Kugey, Reuben Walton. 14 Nov 1833 [Dl'd Col. Bare Mar 1836]

D2-265: Surv. 24 Apr 1832, 100 A. by 9087=31 Oct 1826 & 192 A. by T.W.6878=22 Mar 1820 Reuben Walton asne. of Solomon Biller 292 A. in Shenandoah & Rockingham Cos. on Supenlick Mt. & Bear Run Hollow, adj. said Biller, John Coffman, Michael Pheazlis, John Biller, Dellinger, Christian Overholser. 28 Nov 1833

D2-266: Surv. 23 Apr 1832 by T.W.6878=22 Mar 1820 Andrew Pitman & Lawrence Pitman Jr. 107 A. 1 Ro. 18 Po. in Shenandoah Co. on Messannotton Mt. adj. heirs of _?_ Allen dec'd, James Hawkins, Joseph H. Samuels, Joseph Pitman, John Pitman. 15 Nov 1833

D2-267: Surv. 15 June 1832 by T.W.6878=22 Mar 1832 John Walker 122 A. 1 Ro. in Shenandoah Co. on N. Mt. adj. Jacob Barb, George Lee, David Webb, Walker purchased of Abraham Sonnafrank, Peter Bakis. 15 Nov 1833

D2-267: Surv. 31 Oct 1832 by T.W.9198=8 Mar 1827 Michael Neff 116 1/2 A. in Shenandoah Co. on Massanotton Mt. & Short Arse Mt. adj. Elijah Evans, Benjamin Pennybarker heirs. 14 Nov 1833

D2-268: Surv. 25 Apr 1832, 50 A. by T.W.7572=21 Jan 1824, 50 A. by T.W.7573=21 Jan 1824 & 100 A. by T.W.6878=22 Mar 1820 John Basey 200 A. in Shenandoah Co. on Stoney Cr. adj. Orkney Spring tract, Walter Newman, Adam Barb, heirs of John Sheets dec'd. 14 Nov 1833 [Dl'd Mr. Rinkin 17 Dec 1835]

D2-269: Surv. 20 Sep 1932 30 A. by 10,373=16 Jan 1830 & 44 A. by T.W.10,773=30 Apr 1832 William VanBuskirk 74 A. in Hampshire Co. on Dry Run adj. his own land, Vincent Vandiver, John Kabrick. 1 Nov 1833 [Mr. Vance Mar 1835]

D2-270: Surv. 9 Nov 1830 by T.W.10,403=18 Feb 1830 John Ludwick 22 A. 3 Ro. in Hampshire Co. on Mill Cr. adj. Wharton, Nailor, James Reed heirs, Muddy Run, John Foley heirs. 4 Nov 1833 [Mr. Vance Mar 1835]

D2-270: Surv. 2 Sep 1831 by T.W.7382=6 Jan 1823 William N. Scott 72 A. in Hardy Co. on Looneys Cr. adj. his own land, Job Walton, the Manor line, land he bought of Anthony Read heirs, his Norman line. 1 Nov 1833 [Dl'd Mr. Gordon 1834]

D2-271: Surv. 9 Apr 1832 gy T.W.10,677=21 Dec 1831 William Stone 140 A. in Hardy Co. on Hanging Rock Rg. adj. Rd. from Wardersville to Moresfield, James

Stone 1796 grant. 14 Nov 1833

D2-271:   Surv. 2 Feb 1832 by T.W.10,500=27 Dec 1830 David Vanmeter 277 A. in Hardy Co. on Mud lick Run adj. Isaac Vanmeter formerly John Foley. 14 Nov 1833 [Dl'd Mr. Mullen 20 Jan 1835]

D2-272:   Surv. 29 Nov 1832 by T.W.6653=27 May 1819 Hannibal Pugh 70 A. in Hardy Co. adj. Moses Hutton, Seymour, George Harness, Abel Seymour, Michael Neff, Peter Hiebloed? 14 Nov 1833

D2-273:   Surv. 16 Apr 1832 by T.W.10,677=21 Dec 1831 Michael Switzer 50 A. in Hardy Co. on Big Rg. adj. Michael Switzer, Daniel or David Landaires. 1 Nov 1833

D2-273:   Surv. 2 Feb 1832 by T.W.10,500=27 Dec 1830 David Vanmeter 7 A. in Hardy Co. on Mud lick Run adj. said David Vanmeter formerly Joseph Vanmeter, David Vanmeter formerly Hite. 5 Nov 1833 [Dl'd Mr. Mullen 20 Jan 1835]

D2-274: Surv. 8 Feb 1832, 12 1/2 A. by T.W.6295=8 June 1818, 50 A. by T.W.10,267 =29 Apr 1829 & 6 1/2 A. by T.W.10,640=21 Oct 1831 John Parker 69 A. in Hampshire Co. on Mill Cr. adj. Jacob Parker, Edward Taylor bought of Mary Huffman, Jacob Parker bought of Jonathan Parker, John Parker's Titus place. 1 Nov 1833 [Mr. Vance 1835]

D2-275:   Surv. 7 Feb 1832, 50 A. by T.W.10,267=29 Apr 1829 & 19 A. by T.W.10,640=21 Oct 1827 John Parker 69 A. in Hampshire Co. on Middle Rg. adj. his own land, Abraham Parker, Edward Taylor, William Peepy 1794 grant, Thomas Beusny? now said John Parker. 1 Nov 1833 [Mr. Vance Mar 1835]

D2-275:   Surv. 23 May 18?2 by T.W.10,772=30 Apr 1832 James Murphy 111 1/2 A. in Hampshire Co. on Alleghany Mt. & Abraham's Cr. adj. Buffington heirs, Greenley, Samuel Vandiver, Higgins heirs, William Harvey, Bensna? Cassady. 3 Dec 1833 [Dl'd Mr. Vance Mar 1835]

D2-276:   Surv. 21 Sep 1832 by Surv. 10,373=16 Jan 1830 Henry Sulser 100 A. in Hampshire & Hardy Cos. on Mill Cr. & Mud Lick Run adj. Frederick High, David Gibson, Henry Purget, Isaac Vanmeter. 1 Nov 1833 [Mr. Vance Mar 1835]

D2-277:   Surv. 2 Mar 1832 by T.W.10,669=13 Dec 1831 Joseph Stump 65 A. in Hampshire Co. on Little Cacaphon adj. William M. Sterritt, William Pool. 4 Nov 1833 [Mr. Vance Mar 1835]

D2-277:   Surv. 31 Oct 1832, 100 A. by T.W.9965=17 Dec 1827 & 15 1/2 A. by T.W.7692=9 Mar 1824 Randal Largeant & George McDonald 115 1/2 A. in Morgan Co. on Potomack R. adj. Meeting house, Jacob Alderton, Col. Finney, John Portmess?, John Easter, David Alderton. 15 Nov 1833 [Dl'd Maj. Sherrard]

D2-278:   Surv. 1 May 1832 100 A. by 9965=17 Dec 1827 & 58 3/4 A. =10 Jan 1831 Aaron Faris & James Smith 158 3/4 A. in Morgan Co. on Potomack R. adj. Gassaoway Cross, Valentine Smith, John Young formerly James Shearer, line formerly Dimnutt. 28 Nov 1833 [Dl'd Maj. Sherrard]

D2-279:   Surv. 10 Oct 1832 by T.W.10,427=15 Aug 1832 Aaron Farris 64 A. in Morgan Co. adj. Gassaway Cross, Ferris & Smith. 15 Nov 1833 [Dl'd Maj. Sherrard]

D2-279:   Surv. 9 Jan 1833 by T.W.10,852=12 Dec 1832 Absalom Flora 88 1/2 A. in Morgan Co. on Potomack R. adj. heirs of Thomas Flora dec'd, S. Castler?, heirs of James Tidball dec'd, Abraham Gross. 15 Nov 1833 [Dl'd Maj. Sherrard]

D2-280:   Surv. 3 Oct 1832, 14 1/2 A. by T.W.7467=12 May 1823, 50 A. by T.W.10,176=6 Jan 1829 & 6 1/2 A. by T.W.10,427=15 Aug 1832 Samuel Rankin 71 A. in Morgan Co. adj. his land, William Rankin, Mathias Swin, John Sherrard. 15 Nov 1833 [Dl'd Maj. Sherrard]

D2-281:   Surv. 3 Oct 1932 by T.W.10,176=6 Jan 1829 Simeon Rankin 20 A. in Morgan Co. on Sleepy Cr. adj. Swim, Samuel Rankin, Conrad Sulman. 15 Nov 1833 [Dl'd Maj. Sherrard]

D2-281:   Surv. 18 Feb 1832 by T.W.10,508=10 Jan 1831 Isaac Dawson Jr. 14 1/4 A. in Morgan Co. on Cacapeon Mt. adj. Isaac Dawson Sr., said Dawson Jr., Henry Mires. 15 Nov 1833 [Dl'd Maj. Sherrard]

D2-282:   Surv. 3 Oct 1832 by T.W.10,427=15 Aug 1832 Samuel Rankin 21 A. in Morgan Co. on Sleepy Cr. adj. Christian Courtney, said Rankin.   15 Nov 1833 [Dl'd Maj. Sherrard]

D2-282:   Surv. 8 Jan 1833 by T.W.10,882=26 Dec 1832 George Euller 1 A. 2 Ro. 12 Per. in Jefferson Co. adj. said Euller, heirs of Benora? Swearingen, on the Potomack R., Blackford's Ferry landing, Hessey?. 14 Nov 1833

D2-283:   Surv. 29 Mar 1832 by T.W.10,693=2 Feb 1832 Jesse Howell 15 A. 3 Ro. 19 Po. in Loudoun Co. on Blue Rg. adj. McIlhaney's heirs, Howel's purchase of Jesse Janney, Howell's purchase of Fairfax, John Jugrain/Jorgrum. 14 Nov 1833

D2-284:   Surv. 4 Sep 1832 by T.W.7149=17 Nov 1821 Benjamin Shreve Jr. 5 A. 39 Po. in Loudoun Co. on Secolin Br. on Rd. from Leesburg? to Whiteley's ford, Elgan/Elgin, said Shreve purchase of William A. Binns, Greenup, Chs. Binns. 15 Nov 1833 [Dl'd Mr. Janey 11 Feb 1835]

D2-284:   Surv. 28 May 1830 by order of Monroe Co. Ct. Andrew Wylie 137 A. in Monroe Co. adj. Martin Shery, Henry Kelly Sr., Thomas Wylie, William Adare, James Wylie, William Lynch, 1787 grant to John King now said Wylie, George King now Wylie by deed of Robert King, grant of Samuel Black to Robert Wylie who deeded to Andrew Wylie who conveyed 44 A. to William Lynch. 20 Feb 1834 [Dl'd Mr. Alexander 18 Jan 1835]

D2-286:   Surv. 29 Aug 1832 by T.W.10,430=21 Aug 1832 Thomas G. Clarke 18 1/8 A. in Hanover Co. adj. land formerly Isaac Oliver now said Thomas G. Clarke, Bowling Starke, John Oliver. 10 Nov 1833

D2-287:   John Allen 246 A. Alleghany Co. "Wrong Book"

D2-288:   Surv. 7 Jan 1828 by T.W.8053=7 Feb 1826 John B. White & Samuel Cockrell Exrs. of Samuel Dew dec'd 150 A. in Hampshire Co. on Mill Cr. Knobs & Mill Cr. adj. Thomas Taylor, Father House Knob, Hugh Malone, George Haynes, George Liller, Grassy Knob. 12 Aug 1834 [Sent by mail Aug 1834]

D2-289:   Surv. 10 Pct 1833 by T.W.11,014=31 July 1833 William S. Calguhaun 20 A. 1 Ro. 3 Po. in Pr. William Co on Quantico Cr. adj. Bullett, Miller heirs.   16 Aug 1834

D2-289:   Surv. 10 July 1833 by T.W.10709=1 Mar 1832 Andrew Hoak 33 sq.Po.   in Page Co. adj. Crum, Peter Prince, John Verner, Andrew Hoak, Balser Sawer.   29 Sep 1834 [Sent by mail Sep 1834]

D2-290:   Surv. 1 Dec 1833 by T.W.10,709=1 Mar 1832 Andrew Hoak 17 A. 3 Ro. 37:28 Po. in Page Co. on big Hawksbill Cr. adj. Andrew Hoak, Peter Prince, Crum, Hoak's Balser Sower Piney Mt. tract, Adam Rodefer, Abram Prince, Samuel Short. 29 Sep 1834 [Sent by mail Sep 1834]

D2-291:   Surv. 1 June 1833 by T.W.10,985=24 Apr 1833 James R. Tinder & James Canady 30 A. in Culpeper Co. near Mt. Dumpling adj. Peter Hansborough, William Kemper, Andrew Glassell, Thomas Fitzhugh, Thornton's Rd. 19 Nov 1834

D2-292:   Surv. 12 Mar 1833 by T.W.7303=1 Oct 1822 Daniel Sibert 1 A. 53 Per. in Shenandoah Co. in Powel Big Ft. adj. said Sibert, John Clem.   22 Nov 1834 [Col.Bare Mar 1835]

D2-292:   Surv. 14 Nov 1832 by T.W.9997=22 Jan 1828 John Orndurff 100 A. in Shenandoah Co. on Tea Mt., Cedar Cr. adj. James Conner, Jacob Orndurff. 24 Nov 1834 [Dl'd Col. Bare Mar 1836]

D2-293:   Surv. 21 Mar 1832 by T.W.6747=6 Dec 1819 Jacob Clem (s. of David) 17 A. 1 Ro. 9 Per. in Shenandoah Co. in Powells Big Ft. adj. Philip Fogle, Elsy, David

& George McInturf, Michael Ligler?. 24 Nov 1834 [Dl'd to Rec't]

D2-293: Surv. 5 Jan 1833 by T.W.9087 George Grandstaff 200 A. in Shenandoah Co. on Tree Top Mt. adj. Horn's gully, Horn's run, George Rynard, Thomas Hampston, Peter Snyder, Benjamin Hawkins formerly Byrd, Lawrence Pitman Sr. 20 Nov 1834 [Mr. Pennybacker Mar 1835]

D2-294: Surv. 28 Oct 1833 by T.W.10,316 Shadrick Fleming 22 1/4 A. in Shenandoah Co. on Short Arse Mt. & Smiths Cr. adj. said Fleming, Solomon Kingree, Charles L. Morris dec'd heirs. 20 Nov 1834 [Mr. Pennybecker Mar 1835]

D2-295: Surv. 18 Dec 1832 by T.Ws.6878 & 5209 John Basey 234 3/4 A. in Shenandoah Co. on Stony Cr. Little N. Mt. adj. Jacob Barb, John Walker, Lee, Dry Run, Peter Williams. 20 Nov 1834 [Dl'd Mr. Rinkin 17 Oct? 1835]

D2-295: Surv. 27 Apr 1832 by T.Ws.6386 & 10,042 John Funkhouser 116 A. in Shenandoah Co. on Stony Cr. adj. said Jacob Funkhouser, John Basey, Powder Spring Knob, Walter Newman. 22 Nov 1834 [Col. Bare Mar 1835]

D2-296: Surv. 29 Aug 1832 by T.W.6878 Daniel Ridenour 122 1/2 A. in Shenandoah Co. in Powells Big Fork, on N. Mt. adj. Robert Scott, Dilbeck's run, Henry Hickman, Adam Ridenour. 22 Nov 1834 [Col. Bare Mar 1835]

D2-297: Surv. 17 May 1833 by T.W.6878 Lawrence Pitman Jr. & Andrew Pitman 135 A. in Shenandoah Co. on Three Top Mt. adj. George Grandstaff, Joseph Arthur & Co., George Rynard. 18 Nov 1834 [Mr. Pennybecker Mar 1835]

D2-297: Surv. 25 Feb 1833 by T.W.6113 George Stubblefield 40 A. in Jefferson Co. inc. a part of the R. of Shenandoah, some Islands above Hardings ferry landing, adj. United States lumber yard, Joseph L. Smith & Co., Mars Necessary, Capt. Hall's works. 22 Nov 1834

D2-298: Surv. 30 May 1833 by T.Ws.10,109, 10,972 & 10,754 George Hottel 780 A. in Hardy & Frederick Cos. adj. Ohaver, Thomas Woods, Paddys Mt., Paddy's Run, Martin. 22 Nov 1834 [Col. Bare Mar 1835]

D2-299: Surv. 15 June 1832 by T.W.10,669 Thomas Edwards 30 A. in Hampshire Co. on Slanes Knob adj. John Loy, Benjamin Slane, John Combs, McPherson. 20 Nov 1834 [Dl'd Mr. Nixon Mar 1836]

D2-300: Surv. 30 Sep 1833 by T.W.10,602 William Clark 50 A. in Hampshire Co. on Knobley Mt. adj. William Welsh, Henry Liller, John Welsh, John Head, N. Western Turnpike Rd. 20 Nov 1834 [Dl'd Mr. Sloan 16 Feb 1836]

D2-300: Surv. 2 Nov 1832 by T.Ws.10,640 & 10,373 Elias Jones 8 A. in Hampshire Co. on New Cr. adj. Abram's Rg., said Jones, Ball, Henry Harrison. 20 Nov 1834 [Dl'd Mr. Sloan 20 Jan 1836]

D2-301: Surv. 1 Nov 1832 by T.Ws.10,602 & 10,373 Elias Jones 174 A. in Hampshire Co. on New Cr. adj. John Kelly, John Ward. 20 Nov 1834 [Mr. Sloan 20 Jan 1836]

D2-301: Surv. 23 May 1832 by T.W.10,772 John Sheilds 18 A. in Hampshire Co. on Abrahams Cr. & Alleghany Mt. adj. James Murphy, Higgin's heirs, William Harvey, Clinton?. 20 Nov 1834 [Dl'd Mr. Sloan 16 Feb 1836]

D2-302: Surv. 28 Feb 1833 by T.W.10,032 Elisha Gulick 15 A. in Hampshire Co. on Little Cacaphon adj. Ferdinand Gulick, John Powelson heirs, said Elisha Gulick, Zorobable Galloway, Gassoway Cross. 18 Nov 1834 [Dl'd Mr. Sloan 20 Jan 1836]

D2-302: Surv. 18 June 1832 by T.W.10,489 & 10,773 William Johnson 81 A. in Hampshire Co. on Great Cacaphon adj. Robert Sherrard, Lewis Largent Sr. 20 Nov 1834 [Dl'd to Nixon 1836]

D2-303: Surv. 18 Nov 1833 by T.W.10,948 John Sheilds 40 A. in Hampshire Co. on Alleghany Mt. & Emmery's run adj. Sineon Simmmon's heirs, Robert Sherrard. 20 Nov 1834 [Dl'd Mr. Sloan 18 Dec 1836]

D2-303: Surv. 2 May 1833 by T.W.7104 William Welsh exr. of Samuel Hammock dec'd 50 A. in Hampshire Co. on Knobley Mt. adj. Peter Leatherman, John Rogers. 20 Nov 1834 [Dl'd Mr. Sloan 20 Jan 1836]

D2-304: Surv. 28 Feb 1833 by T.W.10,032 Elisha Gulick 50 A. in Hampshire Co. on Bald Hill & Little Cacaphen adj. Albert Carder, John Hansborough formerly Ruckman, William Naylor, William Vance formerly Burch. 18 Nov 1834 [Mr. Sloan 20 Jan 1836]

D2-305: Surv. 3 Apr 1833 by T.W.10,373 & 9091 Washington Cross 20 1/2 A. in Hampshire Co. on Little Cacapheon adj. Indian Camp, Susannah Ruckman, Watkins heirs, his own land bought of James Patterson, Harrison Watkins, John Creamer. 18 Nov 1834 [Dl'd Mr. Sloan 20 Jan 1836]

D2-305: Surv. 28 May 1831 by T.W.10,489 & 10,539 John W. Largent asne. of James Largent 120 A. in Hampshire Co. on Great Cacaphon & Little Mt. adj. Abraham Dawson heirs. 20 Nov 1834 [Dl'd Mr. Vance Mar 1835]

D2-306: Surv. 8 Apr 1833 by T.W.10,373 John Gritton 185 A. in Hampshire Co. on Sidling hill adj. Jacob Jenkins heirs, Silus Prathers, Pearse Noland. 20 Nov 1834 [Mr. Vance Mar 1835]

D2-306: Surv. 18 Mar 1833 by T.W.10,032 & 10,948 Elisha Gulick 64 A. in Hampshire Co. on Little Cacaphon adj. Town hill, John Doman?, Hannah, Gassoway Cross, Washington Cross. 18 Nov 1834 [Mr. Vance Mar 1835]

D2-307: Surv. 27 Feb 1833 by T.W.10,032 Elisha Gulick 174 A. in Hampshire Co. adj. N.fork of Little Cacaphon Robert McBride, Gassoway Cross, Joel Wolverton, William Naylor, Drew, Watkins, John Patterson heirs. 18 Nov 1834 [Mr. Vance Mar 1835]

D2-308: Surv. 19 June 1832 by T.W.10,773 William Johnson 122 A. in Hampshire Co. on Wolf Run of Great Cacaphon adj. Lewis Largent Sr., Jacob Probasco, Bruner. 20 Nov 1834 [Mr. Vance Mar 1835]

D2-308: Surv. 7 Feb 1833 by T.W.10,539 Samuel Ruckman(of John) & Branson Petters 104 A. in Hampshire Co. on Tear Coat adj. John Horn, Samuel Ruckman, Moses Hunter, Sutton. 18 Nov 1834 [Mr. Vance Mar 1835]

D2-309: Surv. 19 Mar 1833 by T.W.10,373 Stephen Hannah 66 A. in Hampshire Co. on S. Br. of Potomac adj. Bald hill, John McDowel, Thomas Muledy, John Jack, Heiskell heirs, Elisha Gulick, John Handsbrough formerly Ruckman. 18 Nov 1834 [Mr. Vance Mar 1835]

D2-310: Surv. 2 May 1833 by T.W.10,772 William Welsh Exr. of Samuel Hammock dec'd 100 A. in Hampshire Co. adj. Knobley Mt., John Rogers, Daniel Taylor, Vincent Vandiver. 18 Nov 1834 [Mr. Vance Mar 1835]

D2-310: Surv. 8 Nov 1833 by T.W.10,948 John Ludwick 47 A. in Hampshire Co. on Mill Cr. adj. John Henry, Millar's heirs, John Foley's heirs, John Leatherman, Henry Hartman heirs. 20 Nov 1834 [Mr. Vance Mar 1835]

D2-311: Surv. 4 Feb 1833 by T.W.6735 Gassoway Cross 100 A. in Hampshire Co. on Town hill adj. his surv. bought of John Pownall, John Powelson? heirs, William M. Powel heirs. 18 Nov 1834 [Mr. Vance Mar 1835]

D2-312: Surv. 6 Aug 1831 by T.W.10,289 & 10,773 Thomas Abernathy 41 A. in Hampshire Co. on Stony Run & Alleghany Mt. near the Meeting house, adj. Tasker, James McCormack, John Abernathy heirs. 18 Nov 1834 [Mr. Vance Mar 1835]

D2-312: Surv. 6 Mar 1832 by 10,539, 10,489 & 10,669 James Abernathy 122 A. in Hampshire Co. on Swishers Mt. adj. John Earsom, Chapman heirs, John Maxwell, Elizabeth Savage, John Long. 18 Nov 1834 [Mr. Vance Mar 1835]

D2-313: Surv. 5 Feb 1833 by T.W.10,373 Washington Cross 34 1/2 A. in Hampshire Co. on Town hill adj. John Doman, William Doman, John Arnold, Powell heirs,

Gassaway Cross. 18 Nov 1834 [Mr. Vance Mar 1835]

D2-313: Surv. 23 June 1832 by T.W.10,032 Elisha Gulick 15 1/2 A. in Hampshire Co. on Little Cacaphon adj. John Powelson heirs, Ferdinand Gulick, Cloe Ann Powelson. 18 Nov 1834 [Mr. Vance Mar 1835]

D2-314: Surv. 22 Aug 1832 by T.W.10,752 Nicholas Caylor 35 A. in Hampshire Co. on Little Cacaphon adj. Gordon Allison, George Sharp, Sarah Moon. 18 Nov 1834 [Mr. Vance Mar 1835]

D2-314: Surv. 5 Feb 1833 by T.W.10,773 John Doman 30 A. in Hampshire Co. on Town hill adj. William Doman, Urton?, Hannah. 18 Nov 1834 [Mr. Vance Mar 1835]

D2-315: Surv. 8 Feb 1833 by T.W.10,539 Samuel Ruckman(of John) & Branson Petters 146 A. in Hampshire Co. on Tear Coat & Short Arse Mt. adj. Moses Hunter, Sutton. 18 Nov 1834 [Mr. Vance Mar 1835]

D2-315: Surv. 22 May 1833 by T.W.10,752, 10,773 & 10,948 John Brant 39 A. in Hampshire Co. on N. Br. of Potomac, Alleghany Mt. adj. Alexaner Riley heirs, McChesney. 18 Nov 1834 [Mr. Vance Mar 1835]

D2-316: Surv. 23 May 1833 by T.W.10,948 John Brant 100 A. in Hampshire Co. on Alleghany Mt. adj. his land bought of Rees' Exr., Martin. 18 Nov 1834 [Mr. Vance Mar 1835]

D2-316: Surv. 6 Apr 1833 by T.W.10,586 John Critton 200 A. in Hampshire Co. bet. Spring Gap Mt. & Sideling hill adj. Silas Prather formerly Sutton. 20 Nov 1834 [Mr. Vance Mar 1835]

D2-317: Surv. 17 Mar 1832 by T.W.10,677=21 Dec 1831 Hendricks Clark 115 A. in Hardy Co. on Allegany Mt. & Abrams Cr. adj. his own land, Emanuel Arnold. 18 Nov 1834 [Dl'd Mr. Mullen Mar 1835]

D2-317: Surv. 25 June 1833 by T.W.10,972=9 Mar 1833 Abraham Inskeep 200 A. in Hardy Co. on Timber Rg. adj. Valentine Simmons, James Miles, William Heath. 19 Nov 1834 [Dl'd Mr. Mullen]

D2-318: Surv. 17 Mar 1832 by T.W.10,677=1 Dec 1831 Emanuel Arnold 22 A. in Hardy Co. on Allegany Mt. & Abram's Cr. adj. his own land. 19 Nov 1834 [Dl'd Mr. Mullen]

D2-318: Surv. 16 June 1832 195 A. by T.W.10,669=13 Dec 1831 & 31 A. by 10,773=30 Apr 1832 John Simpson 226 A. in Hampshire Co. on Great Cacaphon adj. James Largent, Thomas Allen. 22 Nov 1834 [Mr. Vance Mar 1835]

D2-319: Surv. 13 May 1830 by T.W.10,403=18 Feb 1830 William Largent 100 A. in Hampshire Co. on N. R. adj. Benjamin McDonald, Joseph & Jeremiah Huff/Hutt. 22 Nov 1834 [Mr. Vance Mar 1835]

D2-319: Surv. 2 Nov 1832 by T.W.10,640=21 Oct 1831 William Welch asne. of Thomas Jones 50 A. in Hampshire Co. on Knobley Mt. adj. Samuel Jones heirs. 19 Nov 1834 [Mr. Vance Mar 1835]

D2-320: Surv. 26 Sep 1833, 25 A. by T.W.10,373=16 Jan 1830 & 48 A. by T.W.10,752=21 Mar 1832 Philip Malick 73 A. in Hampshire Co. on Tear coat Cr. adj. Thompson's lick, his own land, Samuel Loy, George Carner heirs. 20 Nov 1834 [Mr. Vance Mar 1835]

D2-320: Surv. 25 Mar 1832 by T.W.=10 Feb 1829 Farmer Johnson 40 A. in Culpeper Co. adj. Jabez Jones, Francis Dies. 19 Nov 1834 [Dl'd Mr. Smith 9 Apr 39]

D2-321: Surv. 2 May 1826 by T.W.6602=11 Mar 1819 John L. Smith & John G. Brent 27 1/2 A. in Frederick & Shenandoah Cos. adj. John W. Bayliss, Lewis?, , Cedar Cr., Paul Frunan now Charles Brent. 24 Nov 1834 [Dl'd Col. Smith Mar 1836]

D2-321: Surv. 17 Apr 1829 by T.W.6943=2 Sep 1820 John Tharp & Alexander Evans

400 A. in Hardy Co. on Mt. run adj. said Tharp & Evans, David Vanmeter, Robert Davidson, Joseph Tucker, said Evans, said Tharp. 6 Nov 1834 [Dl'd Mr. Mullen]

D2-322: Surv. 23 Nov 1833 by T.W.9038 &10,354 Reuben Booton 156 A. in Madison Co. adj. William Pickett grant Feb 1737, Garth's spring Rg., Peter Jarrett?. 21 Nov 1834 [Mr. Banks Mar 1835]

D2-323: Surv. 28 Apr 1833 by T.W.10,591 James Lodman 1 A. 3 Ro. 8 sq.Po. in Berkeley Co. adj. Jonathan Wandling. 18 Nov 1834 [Dl'd Mr. Hunter Feb 1835]

D2-323: Surv. 28 Sep 1833 by T.W.10,591 Ehud Turner asne. of Washington Evans 1 A. 1 Ro. 22 Po. in Berkeley Co. on Swam Pond Run adj. John Butts heirs, E. Turner, Zane now Rawleigh Morgan heirs. 20 Nov 1834 [Mr. Hunter Feb 1835]

D2-324: Surv. 10 June 1833 by T.W.10,179=12 Jan 1829 Hueley Groves 12 A. in Pr. William Co. on Little Cr. adj. s'd Groves. 19 Nov 1834 [Mr. Williams Mar 1835]

D2-324: Surv. 5 Feb 1833, 300 A. by T.W.10853 & 31 1/2 A. by T.W.10,852 both=12 Dec 1832 William Neely & John Sherrard (asnes. of William Neely for 100 A.) 331 1/2 A. in Morgan Co. adj. Azeil Johnson, Gassoway Cross, James House, John Mitchell, John Eustis Jr. 21 Nov 1834 [Dl'd Maj. Sherrard]

D2-325: Surv. 7 Nov 1826 by T.W.4309=27 Jan 1806 George Knap asne. of James Rader asne. of William Parsons 100 A. in Mason Co. on Big Mill Run adj. Cluckburgh Rd., Qilliam L. Parsons. 25 Nov 1834 [Dl'd Col. Wagner 27 Jan 1836]

D2-326: Surv. 25 Nov 1833 by T.W.9038=15 June 1826 Henry F. Baker 10 A. in Madison Co. adj. William Kirby 1805 surv., Francis Collins, Francis Kirby 1749 grant. 19 Nov 1834 [Mr. Banks Mar 1835]

D2-326: Surv. 10 Feb 1834 by T.W.11,122=9 Jan 1834 Elijah Griffith 9 A. in Fauquier Co. adj. John Glascock, Thomas Baron, Enoch Ennis now Grayham, Mirier. 21 Nov 1834 [Dl'd Bearer of Rec't(Elias Edmonds) 7 Feb 1839]

D2-327: Surv. 2 Feb 1833 by T.W.10,709=1 Mar 1832 Philip Long & John Beaver 50 A. in Page Co. on Shenandoah R. & Massennetton Mt. adj. Reubin Long, John Beaver, Philip Long, Jones. 22 Nov 1834 [Dl'd Dr. Robertson]

D2-327: Surv. 5 Apr 1833 by T.W.10,709=1 Mar 1832 Daniel Miller 2 A. 2 Ro. 35 27/100 Po. in Page Co. on S. fork of Shenandoah R. adj. David Lauderback, Isaac Koontz. 22 Nov 1834 [Dl'd Dr. Robertson]

D2-328: Surv. 18 Juny 1831 by T.W.3944=24 May 1817 John Bromback 8 A. in Piney Mt. in Page Co. adj. heirs of John Kiblinger dec'd, Adam Rodeffer purchase of Henry Prince. 19 Nov 1834 [Dl'd Dr. Robertson]

D2-328: Surv. 31 Mar 1833 by T.W.10,971=9 Mar 1833 William Hershy 75 A. in Hardy Co. on Pattersons Cr. adj. Williams, Berry. 19 Nov 1834 [Mr. Mullen]

D2-329: Surv. 14 Sep 1833 by T.W.10,677=21 Dec 1831 Jacob Getts 133 A. in Hardy Co. Co. on Middle Mt. adj. his own land, Frederick Sites, George Harness. 21 Nov 1834 [Dl'd Mr. Mullen]

D2-329: Surv. 17 July 1832 by T.W.10,677=21 Dec 1831 John Sites asne. of Daniel Sites 50 A. in Hardy Co. on Salt peter Knob adj. his own land, heirs of Peter Briglr?, heirs of Jacob Landrs. 21 Nov 1834 [Mr. Mullen Mar 1835]

D2-330: Surv. 2 Feb 1832 by T.W.10,677=21 Feb 1831 Elijah Stonestreit 28 A. in Hardy Co. on S. Br. adj. his own land bought of William Hause, Welsh, Stroud. 21 Nov 1834 [Dl'd Mr. Mullen]

D2-331: Surv. 17 Mar 1832 by T.W.10,677=21 Dec 1831 Jacob Gills 234 A. in Hardy Co. on ? Mt. adj. his land, James & David Morrow, Spilman, Harness. 21 Nov 1834 [Dl'd Mr. Mullen]

D2-331: Surv. 16 May 1832 by T.W.10,677=21 Dec 1831 Nathan & Caleb Hinkel 155

A. in Hardy Co. bet. S. Forks & S. Br. on Middle Mt. adj. Cowger, their own land. 21 Nov 1834 [Dl'd Mr. Mullen]

D2-332: Surv. 6 Apr 1831 500 A. by T.W.7179=21 Jan 1822, 300 A. by 10,313=6 Oct 1829 & 82 A. by 10,463=7 Aug 1830 James Sterritt 882 A. in Hardy Co. on Big Capon adj. Wilson, heirs of Robert Mins dec'd, Waits Run, Wilson, N. Mt. 25 Nov 1834 [Dl'd Mr. Mullen]

D2-333: Surv. 16 Mar 1832 by T.W.10,677=21 Dec 1831 William Hershey 160 A. in Hardy Co. on Allegany Mt., Stoney R. below Lindseycombs cabin. 19 Nov 1834 [Dl'd Mr. Mullen]

D2-334: Surv. 4 Jan 1833 by T.W.10,463=7 Aug 1830 John Johnson 133 A. 15 Po. in Hardy Co. on Lost R. adj. the Big Rg., Jeremiah Inskeep, William Baker, Josiah Clagett. 21 Nov 1834 [Dl'd Mr. Mullen]

D2-335: Surv. 11 Nov 1833 by T.W.10,971=9 Mar 1833 Jacob Tetrick 100 A. in Hardy Co. adj. his land, Jacob Barkdall, Abraham Sites. 21 Nov 1834 [Mr. Mullen]

D2-335: Surv. 22 June 1832, 19 A. by T.W.6724=25 Oct 1819 & 16 A. by T.W.10,677=21 Dec 1831 William Stone 35 A. in Hardy Co. on Three Spring Run of Lost R. adj. James Stone's purchase of William Warden, said William Stone, Abraham Baker heirs. 21 Nov 1834 [Dl'd Mr. Mullen]

D2-336: Surv. 11 Apr 1832 by T.W.6349=18 Aug 1818 Martin Dellinger 60 A. in Hardy Co. on Breakneck Mt. adj. James Stone formerly William Warden, Abraham Dillinger, his own land, William Stone. 25 Nov 1834

D2-337: Surv. 4 Sep 1833 by T.W.10,677=21 Dec 1831 William Shillingbury Sr. 23 A. in Hardy Co. on Allegany Mt. adj. Abram's Cr. his own land, Emanuel Arnold, Hendricks Clark. 18 Nov 1834 [Dl'd Mr. Mullen]

D2-337: Surv. 14 Mar 1833 by T.W.10,971=9 Mar 1833 William Campbell 143 A. in Hardy Co. on Chesnut Rg. adj. heirs of Robert Pew dec'd, William Babb. 21 Jan 1835 [Dl'd Mr. Mullen]

D2-338: Surv. 5 Sep 1833 by T.W.7312=21 Oct 1822 Thomas J. Bullett 40 A. 1 Ro. in Pr. William Co. on Ward's Br. of Quantico Run adj. said Bullett. 21 Jan 1835 [Mr. Williams Mar 1835]

D2-338: Surv. 4 Aug 1831 by 10,463=7 Aug 1830 Elizabeth Vanmeter 791 A. in Hardy Co. on Patterson's Cr. Mt. adj. the Mill lot, her old tract, Vincent Williams heirs, Abram Roby. 4 Mar 1835 [Mr. Mullen Mar 1835]

D2-339: Surv. 24 Mar 1828 by T.W.9925=18 May 1827 Isaac C. Miller & Corbin W. Miller 186 A. in Hardy Co. on Lost R. adj. Levi Claypole, Catherine Paul, See, Stone Lick Run. 13 Mar 1835 [Dl'd Col. Mullen 19 Jan 1836]

D2-340: Surv. 4 May 1830 by T.W.10,013=7 Feb 1828 Daniel Hacker 200 A. in Hardy Co. on Frys Run of Great Cacapeon adj. Isaac Strosnider. 13 Mar 1835 [Dl'd Col. Mullen Jan 1836]

D2-340: Surv. 11 Apr 1834 by T.W.10,856 Isaac H. Huff 100 A. in Rappahannock Co. near the Blue Rg., on Peaked Mt. adj. Daniel Mason, Turkey Run, Johnston, said Huff, Dearing. 21 Apr 1835 [Dl'd to Rec't 22 May 1835]

D2-341: Surv. 19 Apr 1834 by T.W.9110? John McFarlin 150 A. in Rappahannock Co. adj. N. Br. of Little or Hasty's R., John Finnel, CrabApple Br. 21 Apr 1835 [Dl'd to Rec't 22 May 1835]

D2-341: Surv. 18 Sep 1829 by T.W.9089=2 Nov 1826 Philip Moore 25 A. in Hampshire Co. on Mill Cr. adj. said Philip Moore, Frederick High's Heath land, Magill heirs. 11 Oct 1834 [Mr. Vance Mar 1836]

D2-342: Surv. 2 Nov 1832 by T.W.10,692=13 Jan 1832 & Exg. T.W.2353=28 Sep 1820 Joel Pennybaker 505 1/4 A. in Shenandoah Co. on Massanotton Mt. adj. Evans, heirs of Benjamin Pennybacker dec'd, Davis Allen spring. 11 Oct 1835

D2-343: Surv. 2 Sep 1834 by T.W.10,677 & T.W.12,226 Francis Idleman 85 A. in Hardy Co. on Stony R. adj. his own land, Bruce, Davis path. 8 May 1835 [To rec't 30 Oct 1835]

D2-343: Surv. 4 Jan 1833 by T.W.5517 James Gray 190 A. in Hardy Co. on Charlie's Knob adj. Aaron Wetten, heirs of Abel Seymour, the manor line, Charles Johnson. 8 May 1835 [Dl'd to rec't 30 Oct 1835]

D2-344: Surv. 10 Jan 1833 by T.W.5518 James Gray 40 A. in Hardy Co. on N. fork & Frenchman's Run adj. his own land, lot formerly Val. Powers, N. N. Line, Hackey. 8 May 1835 [Dl'd to rec't 30 Oct 1835]

D2-344: Surv. 3 Oct 1834 by T.W.12,239 John Kismiller 36 A. in Hardy Co. on Alleghany Mt. adj. his own land, Stoney R. Makim/McKim, Joseph Nevel. 8 May 1835 [Dl'd to rec't 30 Oct 1835]

D2-345: Surv. 11 June 1834 by T.W.7484 Frederick Mauk 70 A. on M. R. adj. Samuel Good, Hezekiah Lintsecum, Isaac Willson, George Haws, his own land, William Housman, John F. Willson, Robert Means. 8 May 1835 [Dl'd to rec't 30 Oct 1835]

D2-345: Surv. 27 May 1834 by T.W.6723 Martain Mcnamara 62 A. in Hardy Co. on Patterson's Cr. adj. Daniel McNeill, McMacheon. 9 May 1835 [Rec't 30 Oct 1835]

D2-346: Surv. 6 Oct 1834 by T.W.12,239 Thomas Stingley & George Shell 250 A. in Hardy Co. on Patterson's Cr. adj. John Miles, Solomon Cunningham heirs, Peter Hutton. 8 May 1835 [Dl'd to rec't 30 Oct 1835]

D2-347: Surv. 9 June 1834 by T.W.10,752 Margaret Leigh 50 A. in Hampshire Co. on Grassy lick Run adj. Samuel Kercheval, Bush lick. 10 June 1835 [Dl'd Mr. Sloan 16 Feb 1836]

D2-347: Surv. 1 July 1834 by 10,948 John Simpson 53 A. in Hampshire Co. on N. R. adj. Joseph Spotts, Jonathan Hiet, Charles Blue formerly White, N.W. Turnpike, Alexander Poston. 10 June 1835 [Dl'd Col. Nixon Mar 1836]

D2-348: Surv. 26 Mar 1831 by T.W.10,217 & 10,489 William H. Moreland 118 A. in Hampshire Co. on Dellin's Run & Park's Rg. adj. George Deaver, Pugh, Moreland bought of William Carlyle, Marr, Foreman, Ingle. 10 June 1835 [Mr.Nixon Mar 1836

D2-349: Surv. 22 May 1833 by T.W.10,948 Layton S. Cundiff 192 A. in Hampshire Co. on N. Br. of Potomac & Alleghany Mt. adj. John Brant, Oliver bought of Jessee Sharpless, Montgomery's Run, Henry Barrick. 12 Sep 1835 [30 Sep 1835]

D2-350: Surv. 6 Sep 1833 by T.W.10,752 John Hawse 105 A. in Hampshire Co. on Tear Coat Cr. adj. William Loy, Aroon Rogers. 20 Aug 1835 [Mr.Sloan 17 Feb 1836]

D2-350: Surv. 19 Nov 1833 by T.W.11,061 Elijah Harvey 25 A. in Hampshire Co. on Alleghany Mt. & Abram's Cr. adj. land he bought of Clinton's heirs, McKim. 25 Aug 1835 [Dl'd Mr. Sloan 20 Jan 1836]

D2-351: Surv. 15 Apr 1834 by T.W.10,948 Benjamin McDonald 46 3/4 A. in Hampshire Co. on N. R. & Sidling Hill, adj. Robert Sherrard, his own land bought of Probasco, William Largent. 25 Aug 1835 [Dl'd Mr. Nixon Mar 1836]

D2-352: Surv. 7 May 1834 by T.W.10,051 Thomas Taylor 14 A. in Hampshire Co. in Hentman Pasture gap adj. Hugh Malone, said Taylor. 25 Aug 1835 [Dl'd Mr. Sloan 17 Feb 1836]

D2-352: Surv. 4 July 1834 by T.W.10,948 James Candy 75 A. in Hampshire Co. on Cacaphon Mt. adj. Robert Pugh, William H. Moreland. 25 Aug 1835

D2-353: Surv. 23 Apr 1834 by T.W.10,948 Catherine Ginnevan 120 A. in Hampshire Co. on Spring gap Mt. adj. Alla Calors, John Critton, Silas Prather, Samuel Largent. 25 Aug 1835 [Dl'd Nixon Mar 1836]

D2-354: Surv. 6 May 1834 by T.Ws.10,051 & 11,062 Ephraim Herroit 16 A. in Hampshire Co. on Mill Cr. adj. his own land, James Hamilton bought of Utt's heirs, Isaac Means heirs, Fox heirs. 25 Aug 1835 [Dl'd Mr. Sloan 20 Jan 1836]

D2-354: Surv. 8 Dec 1829 by T.W.10,321 David Pugh 22 A. in Hampshire Co. on Big Cacaphon Mt. adj. his own land bought of Levi Arnold heirs, Crisswell, Mishall Pugh. 25 Aug 1835 [Dl'd Mr. Nixon 27 Dec 1835]

D2-355: Surv. 18 Aug 1834 by T.W.10,948 John Loy 2 A. 2 Ro. 28 Po. in Hampshire Co. on Sandy Rg. adj. his land bought of Daniel Loy. 25 Aug 1835 [Dl'd Mr. Nixon Mar 1836]

D2-356: Surv. Surv. 18 Aug 1834 by T.W.10,948 & 11,199 John Loy 6 1/2 A. in Hampshire Co. on Great Cacaphon adj. Slanes Knob, said Loy, Thomas Edwards, Benjamin Slain, John Kidwell, Cold stream Run. 25 Aug 1835 [Mr. Nixon Mar 1836]

D2-356: Surv. 9 June 1834 by T.W.10,051 Solomon Tharp 40 A. in Hampshire Co. on Horn Camp Run adj. John Tharp heirs. 25 Aug 1835 [Dl'd Mr. Sloan 20 Jan 1836]

D2-357: Surv. 17 Sep 1834 by T.W.11,199 John Greenwalt 30 A. in Hampshire Co. on Staggs Run of Patterson's Cr. adj. his own land, Christopher Stagg. 25 Aug 1835 [Dl'd Mr. Sloan 20 Jan 1836]

D2-358: Surv. 21 May 1834 by T.W.11,062 William F. Taylor 35 A. in Hampshire Co. on S. Br. Mt. adj. his land bought of George W. Deveeman. 25 Aug 1835

D2-358: Surv. 24 Oct 1833 by T.W.10,773 Catherine Utt asne. of John Utt Sr. 50 A. in Hampshire Co. on Dry Run of Mikes Run adj. John C. Utt Sr., John C. Utt Jr. 25 Aug 1835 [Dl'd Mr. Sloan 20 Jan 1836]

D2-359: Surv. 7 Oct 1834 by T.W.7166, 11,0628 & 11,199 Isaac Woolverton 78 A. in Hampshire Co. on Tear Coat & Bear Waller adj. Samuel Stewart, Thomas Bloxham, John Hott, Grant or Whitsill, Jacob Baker bought of John Brown heirs. 25 Aug 1835 [Dl'd Mr. Sloan 17 Feb 1836]

D2-360: Surv. 2 Oct 1834 by T.W.11,199 Daniel McLaughlin 50 A.in Hampshire Co. on Dobson's Knob adj. The Pedlars path, Daniel Mclaughlin heirs. 25 Aug 1835 [Dl'd to Rec't 1835]

D2-360: Surv. 16 Nov 1833 by T.W.16,061 Elijah Harvey 145 A. in Hampshire Co. on Abram's Cr. adj. his land bought of William Harvey, McKim, Elijah Harvey bought of Clinton's heirs. 25 Aug 1835 [Dl'd Mr. Sloan 20 Jan 1836]

D2-361: Surv. 26 Apr 1834 by T.W.10,752 & 11,062 John Brady 15 A. in Hampshire Co. on S. Br. of Potomac inc. an Island. 25 Aug 1835 [Mr. Sloan 20 Jan 1836]

D2-362: Surv. 8 Aug 1834 by T.W.10,373, 10,948 & 11,199 Elijah Vanbuskirk 213 A. in Hampshire Co. on Deep Run of Pattersons Cr. 25 Aug 1835 [Dl'd Mr. Sloan 16 Feb 1836]

D2-362: Surv. 1 July 1834 by T.W.10,772 James Stewart Sr. 24 1/2 A. in Hampshire Co. on Burshy Rg. adj. Thomas Bloxham, John Carter. 25 Aug 1835 [Dl'd Mr. Nixon Mar 1836]

D2-363: Surv. 7 June 1834 by T.W.10,752 &11,062 Elisha Gulick in his own right & as asne. of Francis Piles 177 A. in Hampshire Co. on N. R. & Davis Rg. adj. John Parker. 25 Aug 1835 [Dl'd Mr. Sloan 20 Jan 1836]

D2-364: Surv. 19 Apr 1834 by T.W.11,061 & 11,062 John Critton asne. of Samuel Sutton 356 A. in Hampshire Co. bet. Sidling hill & Spring Gap Mt. adj. said John Critton. 25 Aug 1835 [Dl'd Mr. Nixon Mar 1836]

D2-364: Surv. 25 Sep 1833 by T.W.10,948 & 10,669 David Hott & George Hott 250 A. in Hampshire Co. on Hairy Mt. & Grassey Lick Run adj. Daniel Corbin heirs, French's heirs, Joseph Shockey. 25 Aug 1835 [Dl'd Mr. Sloan 17 Feb 1836]

D2-365:   Surv. 28 Mar 1833 by T.W.7903 & 10,852 Sarah Jacques 40 A. in Morgan Co. on Sleepy Cr. adj. said Sarah Jacques, Jacob Ash. 1 Sep 1835 [Dl'd to Rec't 19 Mar 1836]

D2-366:   Surv. 6 June 1834 by T.W.10,051 & 11,062 James Combs 67 A. in Hampshire Co. on Cove Mt. adj. Charles Doyles, said Combs. 25 Aug 1835 [Dl'd Mr. Sloan 17 Feb 1836]

D2-367:   Surv. 21 Apr 1834 by T.W.11,061 & 11,062 Cornelius Vannosdall in his own right & as asne. of Samuel Sutton 562 A. in Hampshire Co. on the Big Mt. inc. Tea Table Rg. adj. Little's heirs. 25 Aug 1835 [Mr. Sloan 20 Jan 1836]

D2-368:   Surv. 26 Sep 1833 by T.W.10,403, 10,752 & 7101 John Starkey & Gipson Ruckman 283 A. in Hampshire Co. on Tear Coat Cr. adj. Jacob Lewis heirs, Philip Malick, Thompson heirs, Clay lick Rg. 25 Aug 1835 [Mr. Sloan 17 Feb 1836]

D2-368:   Surv. 29 May 1834 by T.W.7326 William Duling Jr. 82 A. in Hampshire Co. on New Cr. adj. his own land, New Cr. Mt., George Banick, Duling's Matteny land. 25 Aug 1835 [Dl'd Mr. Sloan 20 Jan 1836]

D2-369:   Surv. 22 July 1834 by T.W.7106 John Mulin 22 A. in Hardy Co. on Paterson's Cr. Mt. adj. Elizabeth Vanmeter, James Williams, his own land. 12 Sep 1835 [Dl'd to Rec't Mar 1836]

D2-370:   Surv. 22 Sep 1834 by T.W.7382 John Rohraban 91 A. in Hardy Co. on Mill Cr. adj. William Weare, his own land, heirs of Jacob Landes. 25 Aug 1835 [Dl'd to Rec't Mar 1834?]

D2-370:   Surv. 13 June 1834 by T.W.12,226 George Miller 37 A. in Hardy Co. on Lost R. adj. Chilket, his own land, Kimsey's Run. 25 Sep 1835 [Dl'd Col. Mullen 19 Jan 1836]

D2-371:   Surv. 23 Aug 1834 by T.W.12,239 John Roberts & Abram Rotruck 270 A. in Hardy Co. on Patterson's Cr. on Dividing Rg., Johnson's Rg. 25 Aug 1835 [Dl'd to Rec't Mar 1836]

D2-372:   Surv. 29 Apr 1834 by T.W.11,006 Micheal Simons 80 A. in Hardy Co. on S. fork adj. Coffman, his own land, Leonard Desher. 25 Aug 1835 [To Rec't Mar 1836]

D2-372:   Surv. 8 July 1834 by T.W.7271 Joseph Arnold 108 A. in Hardy Co. on Patterson's Cr. Mt., Mill Cr. & Arnold's Run. 19 Sep 1835 [To Rec't Mar 1836]

D2-373:   Surv. 14 May 1834 by T.W.11,207 Jacob Nimrod & Clary Kitterman, heirs of John Kitterman, 52 A. in Hardy Co. on S. Mill Cr. adj. Jacob Barkdall, Harness. 12 Sep 1835 [Dl'd to Rec't Mar 1836]

D2-374:   Surv. 16 Nov 1833 by T.W.10,430 Henson Veatch Sr. 50 A. in Hardy Co. on Loonies Cr. adj. Elijah Veatch, heirs of Abel Seymour, heirs of Anthony Read. 12 Sep 1835 [Dl'd to Rec't Mar 1836]

D2-374:   Surv. 10 Nov 1834 by T.W.5516 & 11,111 Francis Idleman 17 A. in Hardy Co. on Alleghany Mt. & Stoney R. adj. Fisher Inskeep, his own land. 12 Sep 1835 [Dl'd Col. Mullen Jan 1836]

D2-375:   Surv. 12 Nov 1834 by T.W.11,111 Nimrod Judy 48 A. in Hardy Co. on S. Mill Cr. adj. his own land, Valentine Cooper, Judy's heirs. 10 Sep 1835 [Dl'd to Rec't Mar 1836]

D2-376:   Surv. 28 Apr 1834 by T.W.11,207 Jacob Tetrick 21 A. in Hardy Co. adj. his own land on S. Mill Cr., the Buzzard Nob. 12 Sep 1835 [To Rec't Mar 1836]

D2-376:   Surv. 16 Nov 1818 by T.W.212 Jacob Fisher 235 A. in Hardy Co. on Elk horn Br. of S. Mill Cr. adj. his land, heirs of Jacob Borer, Joseph Crites, Philip Crites, Elias Shewmaker. 12 Sep 1835 [Dl'd to Rec't Mar 1836]

D2-377:   Surv. 7 July 1834 by T.W.7271 Joseph Arnold 292 A. in Hardy Co. adj.

James Williams, Miss Vanmeter, heirs of Isaac Hite, Jacob Vanmeter, his own land on Patterson's Cr. Mt. 12 Sep 1835 [Dl'd to Rec't Mar 1836]

D2-378: Surv. 29 July 1834 by T.W.12,226 John Rotruck 67 A. in Hardy Co. adj. John Bacorn, his own land on Paterson's Cr., Abraham Rotruck, Snip's Rg. 10 Sep 1835 [Dl'd to Rec't Mar 1836]

D2-379: Surv. 5 Aug 1833 by T.W.10,971 Daniel Landacre 445 A. in Hardy Co. on Oldham's Run, Big Rg., adj. Michaeal Switzer, Nicholas Moore, Joseph Landacre, Jonny Cake Gap. 12 Sep 1835 [Dl'd to Rec't Mar 1836]

D2-380: Surv. 6 July 1834 by T.W.10,422 George Miller 175 A. in Hardy Co. adj. his land on Mud Lick Run of King's Run of Lost R. of Great Cacaphon.12 Sep 1835 [Dl'd Col. Mullen 17 Jan 1836]

D2-381: Surv. 14 May 1834 by T.W.11,006 Jacob Kitterman 85 A. in Hardy Co. adj. his own land, Harness, on S. Mill Cr., King. 25 Aug 1835 [To Rec't Mar 1836]

D2-382: Surv. 13 May 1834 by T.W.11,006 Jacob Kitterman 148 A. in Hardy Co. on S. Fork adj. Jones Green, his own land. 25 Aug 1835 [To Rec't Mar 1836]

D2-383: Surv. 5 Dec 1833 by T.W.10,709 William Maze 4 A. 1 Ro. 24 & 25/100 Po. in Page Co. near Mill Run adj. Charles Dovil, William Maze, Christian Aleshire. 1 Sep 1835 [Dl'd Mr. Almond Mar 1836]

D2-384: Surv. 22 Feb 1834 by T.W.10,709 Henry Micham 7 A. 2 Ro. 20 Po. in Page Co. on S. R. adj. Reuben Long dec'd, Barbour. 1 Sep 1835

D2-385: Surv. 27 Feb 1834 by T.W.10,709 Jacob Freeze 26 A. 3 Ro. 20 Po. in Page Co. bet. Dry Run & Pass Run on Piney Rg. adj. Benjamin Blackford, Adam Fox, John Freeze, John Hockman Sr. dec'd. 1 Sep 1835 [Dl'd Col. Almond 31 Mar 1837]

D2-385: Surv. 22 Nov 1834 by T.W.5650 John Griffy 26 A. 3 Ro. 37 3/100 Po. in Page Co. on Dry Run adj. Daniel Baker Sr., John Griffy, Smith, land formerly owned by David Griffy Sr. 1 Sep 1835 [Dl'd Col. Almond 31 Mar 1837]

D2-386: Surv. 10 Mar 1834 by T.W.11,126 Benjamin Blackford & Thomas T. Blackford 413 A. in Page Co. on S. R. Mt. & the second Mt. on Passage Cr. adj Benjamin Blackford formerly Shanks, Charles Dunkham. 1 Sep 1835 [Dl'd Col. Almond 31 Mar 1837]

D2-387: Surv. 12 Mar 1834 by T.W.10,043 Jacob Keller & Henry Hockman 267 A. in Shenandoah Co. in Powels Big Ft. adj. Daniel Ridenour, Merry Shearman, Henry Hockman. 25 Aug 1835 [Dl'd Col. Bare 10 Jan 1836]

D2-388: Surv. 8 Apr 1834 by T.W.6878 Jacob Peer 150 A. in Shenandoah Co. on Little N. Mt. adj. John Wilkin, land formerly George & John Cline. 25 Aug 1835 [Dl'd Col. Bare 9 Jan 1836]

D2-389: Surv. 14 Mar 1834 by T.W.6878 Henry McInturff 77 1/2 A. in Shenandoah Co. on Powel's Big Ft. adj. David McInturff, Jacob Golliday. 25 Aug 1835 [Dl'd Col. Bare 9 Jan 1836]

D2-390: Surv. 19 Sep 1834 by T.W.10,977 Adam Olinzer 21 1/2 A. in Shenandoah Co. on Massanatoen Mt. adj. said Olinzer purchase of Charles Pence, William Weeks. 25 Aug 1835 [Dl'd Col. Bare Mar 1836]

D2-391: Surv. 28 Nov 1833 by T.W.6878 George Hebron 69 1/4 A. in Shenandoah Co. in Powel's Big Ft. adj. George Sibert, William Moredock, William Elsy. 25 Aug 1835 [Dl'd Col. Bare Mar 1836]

D2-391: Surv. 1 Mar 1834 by T.W.9990 & 10,977 William Weeks 115 1/2 A. in Shenandoah Co. on Massanotten Mt. adj. Solomon Hinkle, Joseph Click, Charles Pence. Rockingham Co. line. 25 Aug 1835 [Dl'd Col. Bare Mar 1836]

D2-393: Surv. 21 Mar 1834 by T.W.9189 Isaac Walter asne. of George McInturff &

David McInturff 152 sq. Po. in Shenandoah Co. in Powel's Big Ft. adj. Daniel Sybert, Isaac Walter, Jacob Cline. 25 Aug 1835 [Dl'd Col. Bare 9 Jan 1836]

D2-393: Surv. 14 June 1834 by T.W.10,591 John S. Light 2 A. 2 Ro. 22 Po. in Berkeley Co. on Opeckon Cr. adj. Henry Myers formerly Thompson, Jacob Myers, John S. Light. 25 Aug 1835 [Dl'd Rec't 19 Mar 1836]

D2-394: Surv. 7 May 1834 by T.W.11,112 John & Jacob Sharff 202 A. 10 Po. in Berkeley Co. on Third Hill Mt. adj. their(Cormain's surv.), Dr. Henry Sneibly heirs (William Morgan surv.), Richard McSherry heirs, George Everheart now James Faulkner, Elisha Boyd, land formerly Vanmeter's. 12 Sep 1835 [18 Mar 1836]

D2-395: Surv. 2 June 1834 by T.W.11,151 John & Jacob Sharff 1405 A. in Berkeley Co. on third Hill Mt. adj. Richard McSherry heirs, Dr. Henry Sneibly heirs, John Myers, (Corman's surv.), Jonas Hedge, heirs of James S. Lane formerly Forman, William Morgan, David Hunter heirs, Joseph & John R. Hedges, Burns heirs, John McCleary now John Row, Ephraim Gather, Elon Miller now R. Snodgrass, Amos Tharp, James T. Polack now Koneky & Rateen. 12 Sep 1835 [Dl'd 18 Mar 1836]

D2-397: Surv. 20 Apr 1835 by T.Ws. 11,085,11,086, 11087, 11088, 11,089 & 11,090 each=5 Dec 1833 Edward Colston & Philip C. Pendleton 1891 A. in Berkeley Co. on Meadow Br., at Locks of Sleepy Cr. & Third Hill Mt. adj. Elisha Boyd, Richard Beason now heirs of Andrew Waggoner dec'd, John & Jacob Sharff formerly George Corman, Collins & Roberts, Anderson & Hunter, Sleepy Cr. Mt., line bet. Berkeley & Morgan Cos., Paul Taylor, Little Brush Cr., John Roberts, Henry Everheart. 6 Nov 1835 [Mailed to Mr. Pendleton 5 Nov 1835]

D2-400: Surv. 20, 22 & 23 Nov & 2 & 3 Dec 1834 by T.Ws.11,145, 11,146, 11,147 & 11,148 Edward Colston & Philip C. Pendleton asnes. of John R. Cooke & Thomas M. Colston 777 A. 1 Ro. 2 Po. in Morgan Co. on Meadow Br., Sleepy Cr. & Third Hill Mt. adj. John Smith formerly Thomas Payne, Morgan & Berkeley Cos. line, Edward Smoot, Pendleton h'rs, Rumsy, Gill, Thomas Swearingin, John McClary. 20 Nov 1835

D2-401: Surv. 28 Apr 1834 by T.W.11,207 Abram Henkel 40 A. in Hardy Co. adj. his own land, John Cooper, Solomon & William Wease, S. Mill Cr., his land originally Woods & Green, Valentine Cooper. 20 Mar 1836 [Dl'd Col. Mullen 19 Jan 1836]

D2-402: Surv. 1 May 1833 by T.W.10,018=8 Feb 1828 Jeremiah Stewart 96 A. in Hardy Co. on Baker's Mt. & Moors Run of Great Capecapeon R. adj. William Rodgers, near Furnace Dam, Francis Goodlove, Jacob Cline, Baker, Littler, Abraham Fry. 21 Jan 1836 [Dl'd Col. Mullen]

D2-403: Surv. 21 May 1835 by T.W.12,313 Nicholas Baker, William Baker, Anthony Baker & Elizabeth Baker 600 A. in Hardy Co. on S. Fork & Middle Mt. adj. their own land, Leonard Stump heirs. 20 Jan 1836 [Dl'd to Mullen Mar 1836]

D2-404: Surv. 20 July 1834 by T.W.12,226 Hanson Veach 92 A. in Hardy Co. adj. John Pool, Thomas Bryant, McKim on Counies Cr., Big spring Run. 19 Mar 1836 [Dl'd Col. Mulin Mar 1835]

D2-405: Surv. 17 Oct 1835 by T.W.10,678 John Rust 11 A. 3 Ro, 12 Po. in Warren Co. late part of Frederick Co. near Island ford Mill, adj. Jno. Rust, Col. James Bowen. 1 May 1836 [Dl'd Mr. Cost? May 1836]

D2-405: Surv. 8 Nov 1835 by Exg.T.W. 2657 Philip C. Pendleton 144 A. 2 Ro. 38 Po. in Berkeley Co. on third Hill Mt. & place called Locks adj. Paul Taylor, Abraham Shockey surv. granted Peter Harbour, Edward Colston & Philip C. Pendleton, Little Brush Cr. 1 July 1836 [Dl'd to Recp't July 1836]

D2-406: Surv. 31 July 1835 by T.W.11,056 William Wease 21 A. in Hardy Co. on S. Mill Cr. adj. his own land. 1 June 1836 [Dl'd Mr. McNamar 31 Oct 1836]

D2-407: Surv. 8 June 1835 by T.W.6349 William Reed 42 A. in Hardy Co. on Lost R. adj. his own land formerly Oldacres, Pound Mill Run, Jacob Baker. 1 June 1836 [Dl'd Mr. McNamar 31 Oct 1836]

D2-408:   Surv. 30 June 1828 T.W.4968 Elias Browning 60 A. in Hampshire Co. on Alleghany Mt. adj. his own, Blackburn formerly Elzey & Stewart. 1 June 1836 [Dl'd Col. Sloane 27 Mar 1837]

D2-409:   Surv. 26 July 1835 by Exg.T.W.2665 & T.W.10,971 Joseph Landacre 300 A. in Hardy Co. on Lost R. adj. Adam Howdyshell, his own land, Henry Baker, Daniel Landacre, Oldacre. 1 June 1836 [Dl'd Mr. McNamar 31 Oct 1836]

D2-410:   Surv. 8 Apr 1834 by T.W.10463 Joseph McNamara 57 A. in Hardy Co. adj. Joseph Arnold, his own land on Paterson's Cr., George Rankin heirs. 1 June 1836 [Dl'd Mr. McNamar 31 Oct 1836]

D2-411:   Surv. 30 June 1830 by T.Ws.6724 & 9925 James Gray 391 A. in Hardy Co. on S. Fork of Radcliffs Run adj. Micheal Break, Morrow, Kettarman, Borrer, N.N. Line. 1 June 1836 [Dl'd Mr. McNamar 31 Oct 1836]

D2-412:   Surv. 11 June 1835 by T.W.10,897 George Haws & George Wolf 100 A. in Hampshire Co. on Tear Coat Cr. & Short arse Mt. adj. Samuel Ruckman, Branson Peters, Stump formerly Sutton. 21 July 1836 [Dl'd Col. Sloane 27 Mar 1837]

D2-412:   Surv. 26 Mar 1835 by T.W.11,199 Marquis Monroe 450 A. in Hampshire Co. on Plum lick Run of N. R. adj. Benjamin Corbin, Peter Poland, Elisha Gulick. 21 July 1836 [Dl'd Col. Sloane 27 Mar 1837]

D2-413:   Surv. 16 Aug 1834 by T.W.10373 Adam Loy asne. of John W. Largent 40 A. in Hampshire Co. on Great Cacaphon Mt. adj. John Copsey, John Largent. 21 July 1836 [Dl'd Col. Sloane 28 Mar 1837]

D2-414:   Surv. 19 June 1832 by T.Ws.10,585 & 10,773 Lewis Largent Jr. 78 3/4 A. in Hampshire Co. on Great Cacaphon adj. his own land, Jacob Probasco, Largent's Boyd surv. 21 July 1836 [Dl'd Col. Sloane 27 Mar 1837]

D2-414:   Surv. 9 Mar 1835 by T.Ws.11,061 & 12,264 David Ellis 172 A. in Hampshire Co. on Sidling Hill adj. William Wilison, William Daugherty, Cox heirs, Robert Sherrard. 21 July 1836 [Dl'd Col. Sloane 27 Mar 1837]

D2-415:   Surv. 3 Aug 1835 by T.Ws.10,373 & 12,374 Adam Loy asne. of John W. Largent 110 A. in Hampshire Co. on Great Cacaphon Mt. adj. John Copsey, John W. Largent, John Largent(of Lewis), Caudy's Castle.   21 July 1836   [Dl'd Col. Sloane 28 Mar 1837]

D2-416:   Surv. 10 Oct 1833 by T.W.10,948 David Ellis 150 A. in Hampshire Co. on Sidling Hill Mt. adj. Robert Sherrard, Cox, Jacob Jenkins heirs, John Critton, Silas Prather.   21 July 1836 [Dl'd Col. Sloane 27 Mar 1837]

D2-416:   Surv. 5 Aug 1835 by T.Ws.12,265 & 11,063 David Ellis 6 1/2 A. in Hampshire Co. on N. R. adj. Berry heirs, Benjamin McDonald, Titus Probasco heirs. 21 July 1836 [Dl'd Col. Sloane 27 Mar 1837]

D2-417:   Surv. 13 Mar 1833 by T.W.10,773 William French Jr. 50 A. in Hampshire Co. on Potomac adj. James Taylor, his land. 21 July 1836 [Col. Sloane 27 Mar 1837]

D2-418:   Surv. 24 Apr 1830 by T.W.4863 John Largent(of Lewis) 73 A. in Hampshire Co. on N. R. Mt. adj. his own land, John Largent. 21 July 1836 [Dl'd Col. Sloane 27 Mar 1837]

D2-418:   Surv. 4 June 1835 by T.Ws.10,403 & 11,063 Thomas Walker 10 1/2 A. in Hampshire Co. on N. Br. of Potomac adj. James Taylor, John Mitchell. 21 July 1836 [Dl'd to Rec't 24 Jan 1837]

D2-419:   Surv. 28 Apr 1834 by T.W.10,054 John Finnell 70 A. in Rappahannock Co. adj. Finnell, Gordon, Bryant, John McFarlin. 21 July 1836 [Dl'd to me 26 Oct 1837 C?. H. Brown]

D2-419:   Surv. 9 Sep 1835 by T.W.6878 Daniel Sybert 21 1/2 A. in Shenandoah Co.

in Powels Big Ft. adj. Jacob Golladay, George Sybert, Bruner & Galladay bought of John Artz & others, Wm. Elsy, Jacob Clem, Isaac Waller. 21 July 1836 [Dl'd Col. Bare 14 Feb 1837]

D2-420: Surv. 20 Mar 1832 by T.W.6386 David Knisely 17 A. 17 Po. in Shenandoah Co. in Powel's Big Ft. adj. George Knisely heirs, Henry Vanmeter, Daniel Munch, Elsy. 21 July 1836 [Dl'd Col. Bare 14 Feb 1837]

D2-421: Surv. 13 Aug 1835 by T.W.12,384 Samuel Painter & Philip Smucker 42 1/4 A. in Shenandoah Co. on Little Ft. Mt., Rd. from Huddle's plantation on the Shenandoah R. to Powels Ft., Eliazer Downey purchase of William Ellzey, Frederick McInturff. 21 July 1836 [Dl'd Col. Bare 14 Feb 1837]

D2-422: Surv. 30 Apr 1834 by T.W.8072 Jonas Hedges 63 A. 7 Po. in Berkeley Co. adj. Robert Pinkerton, Ellen Miller now Robertson, Jacob Weddle. 21 July 1836 [To Rec't 20 Feb 1837]

D2-422: Surv. 29 Apr 1834 by T.W.8072 Jonas Hedges 86 A. 3 Ro. 33 Po. in Berkeley Co. adj. Pinkerton heirs now Palmer, Robertson. 21 July 1836 [To Rec't 20 Feb 1837]

D2-423: Surv. 1 Apr 1835 by T.W.12,264 Thomas Bloxham 19 A. in Hampshire Co. on Pine draught Run of N. R. adj. Dunmore's heirs, Joseph Shinholt bought of Hannah Thornton, John Carter. 30 July 1836 [Dl'd Col. Sloane 27 Mar 1837]

D2-423: Surv. 18 July 1835 by T.W.10,669 Thomas Shores 22 1/2 A. in Hampshire Co. on Alleghany Mt. adj. Stewart heirs, John Abernathy heirs, Riley, N. Br. of Potonac. 30 July 1836 [Dl'd Col. Sloane 28 Mar 1837]

D2-424: Surv. 15 Apr 1835 by T.W.11,063 John Vandiver 22 A. in Hampshire Co. on Docker's Glade Run & Alleghany Mt. adj. Nathaniel Kuykendall, said Vandiver. 30 July 1836 [Dl'd Col. Sloane 27 Mar 1837]

D2-425: Surv. 25 Mar 1831 by T.Ws.9117 & 10,489 William Largent 113 A. in Hampshire Co. on N. R. Mt. adj. John Largent, Joseph Largent, John Largent(of Lewis). 30 July 1836 [Dl'd Col. Sloane 27 Mar 1837]

D2-425: Surv. 28 Mar 1835 by T.Ws.11,199 & 10,602 Joel Ward 73 A. in Hampshire Co. on Park's holow adj. George Oats, said Ward, Samuel Guard, Jonathan Barret. 30 July 1836 [Dl'd Col. Sloane 27 Mar 1837]

D2-426: Surv. 28 Oct 1835 by T.W.10,362 Thomas Carscadon 150 A. in Hampshire Co. on Knobley Mt. adj. John's Gap, Vincent Vandiver, Michael Thrush, the Nutt Surv. 30 July 1836 [Dl'd Col. Sloane 28 Mar 1837]

D2-427: Surv. 4 June 1835 by T.W.11,063 William Abernathy(of Sam'l) 48 A. in Hampshire Co. on S. Br. adj. James Abernathy, John Peper, Craig heirs, Woodrow heirs. 30 July 1836 [Dl'd Col. Sloane 28 Mar 1837]

D2-427: Surv. 18 July 1835 by T.W.11,063 Joseph Dixon 44 A. in Hampshire Co. in Alleghany Mt. on Emory's run adj. Isaac Vanmeter, Elijah Harvey, Linton. 30 July 1836 [Dl'd Col. Sloane 28 Mar 1837]

D2-428: Surv. 11 Mar 1835 by T.W.7501 James Meckins 14 1/2 A. in Hampshire Co. on Town Hill adj. Cartmill, said Meckin. 30 July 1836 [Col. Sloane 27 Mar 1837]

D2-428: Surv. 16 Sep 1834 by T.W.10,373 John Hagarty asne. of Isaac Hull 50 A. in Hampshire Co. on Knobley Mt. adj. said Hull, Matheny Plaer?, Vincent Vandiver. 30 July 1836 [Dl'd Col. Sloane 27 Mar 1837]

D2-429: Surv. 17 Nov 1835 by T.W.12,374 Benj'n Junkins 20 3/4 A. in Hampshire Co. on N. Br. of Potomac in Alleghany Mt. adj. said Junkins. 30 July 1836 [Dl'd Col. Sloane 28 Mar 1837]

D2-429: Surv. 16 Dec 1834 by T.W.6295 Elijah High asne. of Frederick High 46 A. in Hampshire Co. on Mill Cr. adj. said High, Vincent Vandiver, George Liller.

30 July 1836 [Dl'd Col. Sloane 27 Mar 1837]

D2-430: Surv. 29 July 1835 by T.Ws.10,373 & 11,013? Thomas Welch 98 3/4 A. in Hampshire Co. on Cabin Run & Cabin Run Rg., adj. Nesbit, said Welsh, Taylor, Joseph Cropley. 30 July 1836 [Dl'd Col. Sloane 27 Mar 1837]

D2-431: Surv. 24 Sep 1835 by T.Ws.10,897 & 12,374 Solomon Elifrits 194 A. in Hampshire Co. on Cabin Run Rg. & Pattersons Cr. adj. Okey Johnson, Samuel Hammock heirs, said Elifrits, Samuel Dobbins. 30 July 1836 [Dl'd Col. Sloane 27 Mar 1837]

D2-432: Surv. 23 Sep 1835 by T.Ws.9215 & 12,374 Okey Johnson 316 A. in Hampshire Co. on Sheetz Run of Patterson's Cr. adj. Samuel Hammock heirs, said Johnson. 30 July 1836 [Dl'd Col. Sloane 27 Mar 1837]

D2-432: Surv. 14 Mar 1835 by T.Ws.10,373 ,10669 &12,264 James Abernathy 400 A. in Hampshire Co. on S. Br. adj. Philip Graer's? heirs, Woodrow heirs, Craig heirs. 30 July 1836 [Dl'd Col. Sloane 27 Mar 1837]

D2-433: Surv. 10 Mar 1835 by T.W.12,264 John Milison 74 A. in Hampshire Co. on Sideling Hill adj. William Milison, Adam's heirs, Thomas Slain, William Sherrard. 30 July 1836 [Dl'd Col. Sloane 27 Mar 1837]

D2-434: Surv. 29 Mar 1835 by T.W.12,264 William Milison 165 A. in Hampshire Co. on Sidling hill adj. his own land, David Ellis. 30 July 1836 [Dl'd Col. Sloane 27 Mar 1837]

D2-434: Surv. 29 Oct 1835 by T.W.11,104 John Thrush 147 A. in Hampshire Co. on Abram's Rg. adj. William Armstrong. 30 July 1836 [Col. Sloane 28 Mar 1837]

D2-435: Surv. 14 Nov 1835 by T.W.12,374 Thomas Abernathy 23 A. in Hampshire Co. on Stony Run of N. Br. of Potomac on Alleghany Mt. adj. John Abernathy heirs, Stewart heirs, James McCormick, said Thomas Abernathy. 30 July 1836 [Dl'd Col. Sloane 27 Mar 1837]

D2-436: Surv. 17 July 1835 by T.Ws.10,373 & 10948 John Brant 49 A. in Hampshire Co. on the Alleghany Mt. adj. Layton S. Cundiff, Oliver, Colston & Co. 30 July 1836 [Dl'd Col. Sloane 28 Mar 1837]

D2-436: Surv. 17 Mar 1835 by T.W.10,669 James Abernathy 86 A. in Hampshire Co. on Swishers run, Swisher's Mt. adj. Chapman heirs. 30 July 1836 [Dl'd Col. Sloane 27 Mar 1837]

D2-437: Surv. 3 June 1835 by T.W.11,063 James Abernathy 50 A. in Hampshire Co. on S. Br. Mt. adj. John Higgins & Michael Laubinger, Dobson's Knob. 30 July 1836 [Dl'd Col. Sloane 27 Mar 1837]

D2-438: Surv. 23 Jan 1835 by T.W.12,264 Joseph Arnold 84 A. in Hampshire Co. on Patterson Cr. Mt. adj. said Arnold, Lucy Colston, William Naylor, John Pearse, Job Wilton heirs. 30 July 1836 [Dl'd Col. Sloane 27 Mar 1837]

D2-438: Surv. 24 May 1833 by T.Ws.10,897 & 10,948 George G. & Benjamin Tasker asnes. of Benjamin Junkins 76 A. in Hampshire Co. on N. Br. of Potomac & Alleghany Mt., adj. Alexander Sinclair. 30 July 1836 [Col. Sloane 27 Mar 1837]

D2-439: Surv. 12 Nov 1833 by T.Ws.11,061 & 10,897 George G. Tasker in his own right & as asne. of Benjamin Junkins, & Benjamin Tasker 86 A. in Hampshire Co. on Allegany Mt., Deep Run, Howell's Run, Howell's Rg., adj. said Junkin, Thomas Davis, Stewart heirs, Alexander Sinc'air. 30 July 1836 [Col. Sloane 27 Mar 1837]

D2-440: Surv. 19 Nov 1835 by T.W.12,374 James Junkins, Benjamin Junkins, George G. Tasker & Benjamin Tasker 110 A. in Hampshire Co. on Howell's run, main house Run in Alleghany Mt. adj. James Junkins, Stewart heirs, Alexander King, W. Kine or McKine?. 30 July 1836 [Dl'd Col. Sloane 27 Mar 1837]

D2-441: Surv. 14 July 1835 by T.W.12,233 Nathaniel KuyKendall 260 A. in

Hampshire & Hardy Cos. on Alleghany Mt. adj. said KuyKendall, Robert Sherrard. 30 July 1836 [Dl'd Col. Sloane 27 Mar 1837]

D2-441: Surv. 26 Oct 1833 by T.W.10,373 Nathaniel KuyKindall asne of William Hull 100 A. in Hampshire Co. on Knobley Mt. adj. said Nathaniel KuyKindall, Peter Leatherman Jr. 30 July 1836 [Dl'd Col. Sloane 27 Mar 1837]

D2-442: Surv. 14 Nov 1935 by T.W.12,374 Thomas Shores Jr. 50 A. in Hampshire Co. on Alleghany Mt. adj. Stewart heirs, James McCormick, Benjamin Junkins, Thomas Shores. 30 July 1836 [Dl'd Col. Sloane 27 Mar 1837]

D2-443: Surv. 13 Nov 1833 by T.Ws. 10897 & 11,061 Benjamin Junkins 109 A. in Hampshire Co. on N. Br. of Potomac & Alleghany Mt. adj. his land, Rd. to Davis's Mill, Joseph Davis heirs, Thomas Davis heirs. 30 July 1836 [Dl'd Col. Sloane 27 Mar 1837]

D2-444: Surv. 20 July 1835 by T.W.11,111 Abram Kitteman 28 A. in Hardy Co. on N. Mill Cr. adj. his own land, Jacob Barkdall, Middle Mt., Monse's heirs. 30 July 1836 [Dl'd Col. Mullen 31 Mar 1837]

D2-444: Surv. 30 Apr 1835 by T.W.11,207 Hannah Rohraban & Elizabeth Rohraban 42 A. in Hardy Co. on Middle Mt., S. Mill Cr. adj. Jacob Barkdall, Jacob Zandes now Crites, John G. Robertson. 30 July 1836 [Dl'd Col. Mullen 31 Mar 1837]

D2-445: Surv. 30 Sep 1835 by Surv. 12,226 & 11,207 Aaron Barkdall 22 A. in Hardy Co. on Middle Mt. & S. Mill Cr. adj. Jacob Tetrick, Jacob Barkdall. 30 July 1836 [Dl'd Col. Mullen 31 Mar 1837]

D2-445: Surv. 8 July 1835 by T.W.11,200 John Barkdall 100 A. in Hardy Co. bet. N. & S. Mill Crs. adj. Jacob Barkdall, his own land, N.N. line. 30 July 1836 [Dl'd Col. Mullen 31 Mar 1837]

D2-446: Surv. 12 June 1835 by T.W.11,063 & 9089 Powel Powelson 200 A. in Hampshire Co. on Clay Lick fork of Little Cacaphon adj. Chloe Ann Powelson, Henry Watkins bought of William Cool?, John Nelson, Josiah Corbin, Harburt Park. 30 July 1836 [Dl'd Col. Sloane 27 Mar 1837]

D2-446: Surv. 26 Nov 1834 by T.Ws.7404 & 11,111 Henry Baker 175 A. in Hardy Co. on Lost R. adj. Daniel Landaire, Joseph Landaire, Nicholas Mor/Moor. 39 July 1836 [Dl'd Col. Mullen 31 Mar 1837]

D2-447: Surv. 4 May 1835 by T.Ws.10,480 & 10,927 Jones Green 1000 A. in Hardy Co. on Middle Mt. adj. Anthony Baker heirs, Jacob Kitteman. 30 July 1836 [Dl'd Col. Mullen 31 Mar 1837]

D2-448: Surv. 30 Apr 1835 by T.W.11,207 Christian Rohraban 90 A. in Hardy Co. on S. Mill Cr., Middle Mt. adj. his own land, Frederick Letise heirs, Martain Radabang. 30 July 1836 [Dl'd Col. Mullen 31 Mar 1837]

D2-449: Surv. 6 July 1835 by T.W.10,591 Thomas Lemen 26 A. 3 Ro 23 Po. in Berkeley Co. on Big Run adj. French heirs formerly Jacob Houkr, Robert Jack heirs, John White heirs, Michael Houkr heirs. 30 July 1836 [Rec't 20 Feb 1837]

D2-450: Surv. 12 May 1835 by T.W.11,207 John Sceres 5 A. in Hardy Co. adj. McKim, Joshua Orahood, Loonies Cr. 39 Sep 1836 [Dl'd Col. Mullen 31 Mar 1837]

D2-450: Surv. 4 June 1830 by T.W.10,422 Hezekiah Claget 27 A. in Hardy Co. on Bakers Run of Lost R. adj. his land. 30 Sep 1836 [Col. Mullen 31 Mar 1837]

D2-451: Surv. 29 Mar 1835 by T.W.10,501 Bennet Bean 3d 95 A. in Hardy Co. on N. R. adj. his own land, Davis heirs, Peter Poland. 30 Sep 1836 [Dl'd Col. Mullen 31 Mar 1837]

D2-451: Surv. 25 Nov 1835 by T.W.2350 Jacob Fisher 330 A. in Hardy Co. on Middle Mt. inc. Byrn's Knob & Byrn's Run adj. William Cunningham heirs, Anthony Baker heirs formerly See, Cassel. 30 Sep 1836 [Dl'd Col. Mullen 31 Mar 1837]

D2-452:   Surv. 20 Oct 1835 by T.Ws.12,313 & 12,361 Jacob Vanmeter 183 A. in Hardy Co. on High knob Mt. adj. Isaac Vanmeter formerly Hite, David Vanmeter, Higgins, Isaac Vanmeter now Garret, Joseph Vanmeter now David's, Abraham & Garret Vanmeter. 30 Sep 1836 [Dl'd Col. Mullen 31 Mar 1837]

D2-453:   Surv. 1 Mar 1835 by T.W.11,207 James Williams 158 A. in Hardy Co. on Patterson's Cr. Mt. adj. Miss Vanmeter, Abram Robey, Joseph Arnold, his own land, Vanmeter's Mill lot. 30 Sep 1836 [Dl'd Col. Mullen 31 Mar 1837]

D2-454:   Surv. 1 May 1835 by T.W.11,207 Van C. Dawson 140 A. in Hardy Co. adj. Martin Judy heirs, Mill Cr., Jacob Judy, Stone Lick Run.   30 Sep 1836 [Dl'd Col. Mullen 31 Mar 1837]

D2-454:   Surv. 10 Mar 1835 by T.W.11,200 Andrew Garret 140 A. in Hardy Co. on Lost R. & Flat Rg., Hanging Rock Rg., Stone. 30 Sep 1836 [Dl'd Col. Mullen 31 Mar 1837]

D2-455:   Surv. 23 July 1835 by T.W.7951 Henry Strawthurman 61 A. in Hardy Co. adj. Thomas Bassager, Adam See, Shireman, Lost R.   30 Sep 1836 [Dl'd Col. Mullen 31 Mar 1837]

D2-456:   Surv. 9 May 1834 by T.W.6724 Jacob Cornell 50 A. in Hardy Co. adj. Joseph McNamar, his own land on Patterson's Cr., George Rankin.   30 Sep 1836 [Col. Mullen 31 Mar 1837]

D2-456:   Surv. 5 July 1834 by T.W.9157 Thomas Campbell 6 1/2 A. in Frederick Co. on Opequon adj. George Payne, said Campbell, James Ridgway. 30 Sep 1836 [Dl'd Mr. J. Lovet 14 Feb 1845]

D2-457:   Surv. 8 May 1834 by T.W.8072 George Everhart 100 A. in Berkeley Co. on Mill Cr. adj. Konekey heirs, Tevener heirs, John Walput?. 30 Sep 1836 [Rec't 20 Feb 1837]

D2-457:   Surv. 15 Aug 1832 by T.W.10,758 Valentine Seachrist 83 A. in Hampshire Co. on Great Cacaphon, in Yellow Spring hollow, adj. said Seachrist, John Swisher. 30 Sep 1836 [Dl'd Col. Sloan 28 Mar 1837]

D2-458:   Surv. 13 Feb 1826 by T.W.2510 Thomas Hoomes 30 A. in Pr. William Co. adj. Margareth Hoomes, Carr. 30 Sep 1836 [Dl'd Mr. Williams 27 Mar 1837]

D2-459:   Surv. 5 Mar 1834 by T.Ws.10,709 & 11,143 Peter M. Gordon & Henry S. Rose 280 A. in Page Co. bet. N. & Middle Mts. on Passage Cr., on Spring Br. adj. Allin & Clemm, John Larey. 30 Sep 1836 [Dl'd Col. Almond 31 Mar 1837]

D2-460:   Surv. 1 Apr 1836 by T.W.2350 Elizabeth Vanmeter 20 A. in Hardy Co. on Paterson's Cr. adj. her own land, William Dorron/Doron, Abram Vanmeter. 28 Feb 1837 [Dl'd Col. Mullen 31 Mar 1837]

D2-460:   Surv. 26 Apr 1836 by T.W.12,384 Philip Stickley 4 A. 3 Ro. 23 Po. in Shenandoah Co. near town of Strasburg adj. Jacob Everly, Grabel, George Hupp. 28 Feb 1837 [Dl'd Mr. Rinker 14 Mar 1837]

D2-461:   Surv. 21 Nov 1835 by T.W.12,384 Zachariah Shirly 8 3/4 A. in Shenandoah Co. on Smith's Cr. adj. heirs of Christian Kaggy dec'd, John Hess, said Shirly. 28 Feb 1837 [Dl'd Mr. Rinker 14 Mar 1837]

D2-462:   Surv. 16 Mar 1836 by T.W.10,977 Henry Hockman 200 A. in Shenandoah Co. in Powel's Big Ft. adj. said Hockman & others, Jacob Smith. 28 Feb 1837 [Dl'd Mr. Rinker 14 Mar 1837]

D2-463:   7 July 1835 by T.W.10,501 Jacob Backdall 5 A. in Hardy Co. on S. Mill Cr. & Middle Mt. adj. his own land. 28 Feb 1837 [Dl'd Col. Mullen 31 Mar 1937]

D2-463:   Surv. 19 Aug 1834 by T.W.7375 George Sharf asne. of John Orr 27 A. in Hampshire Co. on Riggs hollow, N. R. Mt. adj. said George Sharff, Richard Moreland, George Little. 28 Feb 1837 [Dl'd Col. Sloane 27 Mar 1837]

D2-464:   Surv. 16 July 1835 by T.Ws.9089, 11,063 & 10602 Philip Urias asne. of Reuben Davis 274 A. in Hampshire Co. on Alleghany Mt. & Deep Run adj. William Bosley, Bosley's Coal mine, Elk Garden surv., Elias Browning, Stuart heirs, Cramberry Run, Joseph Dixon. 28 Feb 1837 [Dl'd Col. Sloane 27 Mar 1837]

D2-465: Surv. 10,11,& 12 Nov 1835 by T.Ws.10,801, 10,811, 10,800 & 10,798 George Huddle asne. of Wm. W. Payne 1197 1/4 A. in Shenandoah Co. on Little N. Mt. adj. John Kingan, John Swarr/Swar, John Withers, John G. Feller, Henry Keller, George Huddle, Jacob Huddle, Abraham Windel formerly Brobeck, William Sybert, John Bealer, Philip P. Baker. 28 Feb 1837 [Dl'd to Rec't 10 Mar 1837]

D2-467:   Surv. 26 Dec 1834 by T.W.12,271 William Watson 16 A. 2 Ro. 2 Po. in Berkeley & Jefferson Co. on Opequon Cr. adj. Priest's lot, William Cameron dec'd now John Whitehall, Mitchell, Anthony Rosenberger now said William Watson, Mill Cr., Sebastian Eatz? now Jacob Gilbert. 30 Jan 1837 [Mr. Gallaher 22 July 1837]

D2-468:   Surv. 10 Sep 1833 by T.W.9997 John Wilkin 76 1/4 A. in Shenandoah Co. on Little N. Mt. & Toms Cr. adj. Jacob Parrot, George Windel, George Keller, Coffman, Thomas Wendel. 28 Feb 1837 [Dl'd Mr. Rankin 14 Mar 1837]

D2-469:   Surv. 10 Sep 1833 by T.W.9997 John Wilkin 73 3/4 A. in Shenandoah Co. on Little N. Mt. adj. Joseph Layman Sr., Christian Gouchenour, George Fellow, Martin Funkhouser. 28 Feb 1837 [Dl'd Mr. Rankin 14 Mar 1837]

D2-470:   Surv. 1 Oct 1835 by T.Ws.10,442 & 12,361 Adam Howdyshell 390 A. in Hardy Co. on Lost R. and Flat Rg. adj. Joseph Landacre, Lucretia Oldacre, others, Pixler now Harris. 1 Apr 1837 [Dl'd Mr. Mullen 14 Apr 1838]

D2-471:   Surv. 13 Sep 1836 by T.W.10,927 John D. Miles 250 A. in Hardy Co. on Middle Fork of Patersons Cr. adj. George Strout, Thomas Stingley, Abert G. Watson. 1 Apr 1837 [Dl'd Mr. Mullen 4 Apr 1838]

D2-472:   Surv. 18 Apr 1834 by T.W.11,060 Thomas Johnson 85 A. in Hampshire Co. on Bloomery Run adj. Robert Sherrard, Leeth, Weaver, Poplar Hollow. 1 Apr 1837 [Dl'd Mr. ODell Apr 1839]

D2-473:   Surv. 26 Apr 1834 by T.Ws.11,061 & 11060 Thomas Johnson 212 A. in Hampshire Co. on Great Cacaphon adj. Dawson heirs, Lewis Largent Sr., Woodrow heirs, John W. Largent. 1 Apr 1837 [Dl'd Mr. ODell Apr 1839]

D2-474: Surv. 10 Nov 1836 by T.W.12,696 Elizabeth Vanmeter 4 A. in Hardy Co. on Patersons Cr. adj. Abram Vanmeter. 6 June 1837 [Dl'd to Rec't 18 June 1837]

D2-474:   Surv. 16 June 1836 by T.W.11,200 Henry Baughman 105 A. in Hardy Co. on Lost R. adj. George Claypool, his land formerly John Haman. 1 July 1837 [Dl'd Mr. Mullen 4 Apr 1838]

D2-475:   Surv. 23 Sep 1836 by T.W.12,591 Thomas Wilson 50 A. in Hardy Co. adj. George Hulver heirs, Abram Switzer, his own land, Lost R. 1 July 1837 [Dl'd Mr. Mullen 4 Apr 1838]

D2-475:   Surv. 26 Oct 1836 by T.W.12,655 William Hershy 180 A. in Hardy Co. on Patterson's Cr. Mt. adj. his own land, John Moore. 1 July 1837 [Dl'd Mr. Mullen 4 Apr 1838]

D2-476:   Surv. 3 Oct 1834 by T.W.12,229 Abram & Isaac Inskeep 14 A. in Hardy Co. on Stony R. adj. his own land, the Public Rd., Idleman. 16 Oct 1837 [Dl'd Mr. Mullen 4 Apr 1838]

D2-476:   Surv. 20 Sep 1836 by T.W.12,665 Conrod Shireman 67 A. in Hardy Co. in Upper Cove adj. John Chrisman, his own land, N. Mt., Conrod Segar formerly Roberts. 16 Oct 1837 [Dl'd Mr. Mullen 4 Apr 1838]

D2-477:   Surv. 13 Apr 1836 by T.W.11,202 John Birch 26 A. in Hardy Co. adj. his own land, 91 Spring Lick, Coburns Knob. 16 Oct 1837 [Mr. Mullen 4 Apr 1838]

D2-477:   Surv. 23 Sep 1835 by T.W.12,226 Archibald Cornell 150 A. in Hardy Co. adj. Davisson, Marcus, Balb, John Smith, on Pattersons Cr., Bishop, Cornell. 16 Oct 1837 [Dl'd Mr. Mullen 4 Apr 1838]

D2-478:   Surv. 25 May 1831 by T.W.10,539 William McDougin 52 1/2 A. in Hampshire Co. on N. R., on Sandy Rg. adj. Brown, Knob Rg., John Largent (of Lewis). 1 July 1937 [Dl'd Mr. ODell Apr 1839]

D2-478:   Surv. 14 May 1830 by T.W.10,247 James Richmond 97 A. in Hampshire Co. on Great Cacaphon, White Rock Mt. 1 July 1937 [Dl'd Mr. Odell Apr 1839]

D2-479:   Surv. 24 May 1831 by T.W.10,539 William McDougin 115 A. in Hampshire Co. on Sandy Rg., Great Cacaphon & N. R. adj. Candy's Castle, John Largent(of Lewis) Peter Shinholt bought of Richard Relfe, David Ellis. 1 July 1937 [Dl'd Mr. ODell Apr 1839]

D2-479:   Surv. 11 Apr 1836 by T.W.6878 John Koontz 3 A. 9 Po. in Shenandoah Co. on McNeeses Run adj. John Hossenfluck?, said Koontz. 6 July 1837 [Dl'd J. Koontz 28 Oct 1837]

D2-480:   Surv. 16 May 1832 by T.W.10,769 Zedekiah Kidwell 24 1/2 A. in Fairfax Co. near Falls Church adj. Pearsons now Cloud, Leesburg & Alexandria Rd., four mile run, John Wrenn heirs. 6 July 1837 [Dl'd to rec't 9 July 1838]

D2-481:   Surv. 10 Oct 1836 by T.W.10,861 George Aullabaugh & Archibald Waugh 334 1/2 A. in Morgan Co. on Sleepy Cr. adj. George Miller, William Bailey. 16 Oct 1837 [Col. Buck 4 Apr 1838]

D2-481:   Surv. 19 Nov 1835 by T.W.5650 Jacob Freeze 5 A. 1 Ro. 15 Po. in Page Co. on Dry Run adj. Jacob Smith, Philip Sowers, David Griffy dec'd. 16 Oct 1837 [Dr. Robertson 3 Apr 1839]

D2-482:   Surv. 8 Sep 1836 by T.W.11,143 Addison A. Jones 5 A. 10 Po. in Page Co. on S. fork of Shenandoah R. adj. heirs of Elisha Odell dec'd, Benjamin Blackford, old grant line. 6 July 1837 [Dl'd Jno. Koontz 28 Oct 1837]

D2-482:   Surv. 12 May 1835 by T.W.11,143 Addison A. Jones 86 A. 1 Ro. 16 Po. in Page Co. on S. fork of Shenandoah R. adj. George Keeser/Keyser, old Grant line now Reuben Bell, Benjamin Blackford, John Kidwell formerly Samuel Odell dec'd, Elsy. 6 July 1837 [Dl'd J. Koontz 28 Oct 1837]

D2-483:   Surv. 3 Sep 1836 by T.W.11,143 Addison A. Jones 9 A. in Page Co. on Dry Run & Hawksbill Cr. adj. William C. Lauck formerly Holdaman, Jacob Coffman. 6 July 1837 [Dl'd J. Koontz 28 Oct 1837]

D2-484:   Surv. 28 May 1834 by T.W.10,062 George Barrick 89 A. in Hampshire Co. on Abrams Rg. adj. his land, Hooker heirs. 12 Oct 1837 [Col. Park 30 Mar 1838]

D2-484:   Surv. 15 Nov 1836 by T.W.12,456 Richard Baker 57 A. 1 Ro. in Hampshire Co. on Knobby Mt. near Ash Cabin Run. 16 Oct 1837 [Dl'd Mr. Odell Apr 1839]

D2-485:   Surv. 12 Oct 1836 by T.W.10,640 Samuel Dobbins 40 1/2 A. in Hampshire Co. on Cabin Run hill adj. Joseph Palmer, Samuel Totten, said Dobbins Wharton land, Dobbins Hatten land. 16 Oct 1837 [Dl'd Col. Park 2 Feb 1839]

D2-485:   Surv. 27 Feb 1836 by T.W.12,374 William French 51 A. in Hampshire Co. on Little Cacapehon, Dog Run hollow, adj. his own land, William Cool, N.W. Turnpike Rd., John Powelson heirs. 16 Oct 1837 [Dl'd Mr. Odell Apr 1839]

D2-486:   Surv. 19 Nov 1835 by T.W.12,374 Samuel Harvey 50 A. in Hampshire Co. on N. Br. of Potomac, in Alleghany Mt. adj. Reyson Harvey. 16 Oct 1837 [Dl'd Mr. Odell Apr 1839]

D2-486:   Surv. 19 Apr 1836 by T.W.6295 Frederick High 32 A. in Hampshire Co. on Mill Cr. adj. said High, Lewis U.? Everitt. 16 Oct 1837 [Col. Park 30 Mar 1838]

D2-487: Surv. 14 May 1836 by T.Ws.10,373 & 12,590 James Haggerty 153 A. in Hampshire Co. on Spring Gap Mt. adj. Moses Cox, Silas Prather. 16 Oct 1837 [Dl'd Mr. Odell Apr 1839]

D2-487: Surv. 16 Nov 1825 by T.Ws.5441 & 6662 Samuel Loy asne. of John Loy Jr. 279 1/4 A. in Hampshire Co. on Stony lick Run of Tear Coat Cr. adj. Hood & Ray formerly Pigman, John Thompson heirs, John Loy. 16 Oct 1837 [Mr. Odell Apr 1839]

D2-488: Surv. 16 May 1836 by T.Ws.12,374 & 12,590 Adam Loy 28 A. in Hampshire Co. on N. R. adj. said Loy, N. R. Mt., John Largent of Lewis. 16 Oct 1837 [Dl'd Mr. Odell Apr 1839]

D2-489: Surv. 5 Aug 1836 by T.W.12,590 Richard Moreland 16 1/4 A. in Hampshire Co. on Taylors run of Little Cacapehon adj. his own land, Jacob Woolery, Thomas Slane. 16 Oct 1837 [Dl'd Mr. Odell Apr 1839]

D2-489: Surv. 5 Mar 1832 by T.Ws.10,585 & 10,669 Isaac Pownall 48 1/2 A. in Hampshire Co. on Town Hill adj. Thomas Burkett, William M. Sterritt. 16 Oct 1837 [Dl'd Mr. Odell Apr 1839]

D2-490: Surv. 10 June 1834 by T.Ws.10,403, 7485 & 11,062 Aaron Poland 219 A. in Hampshire & Hardy Cos. on Little Mt., Saw Mill Run, Bear Wallow, adj. Michael Miller formerly Sutton, said Poland. 16 Oct 1837 [Dl'd Mr. Odell Apr 1839]

D2-490: Surv. 3 Jan 1833 by T.Ws.10,640, 10,669 & 10,373 Isaac Pownall 74 A. in Hampshire Co. on S. Br. Mt. adj. Isaac Pownall heirs, James Higgins. 16 Oct 1837 [Dl'd Mr. Odell Apr 1839]

D2-491: Surv. 11 Oct 1836 by T.W.12,589 Joseph Palmer 58 1/2 A. in Hampshire Co. on Cabin Run Rg. adj. Samuel Tottin heirs, John Rankin heirs. 16 Oct 1837 [Dl'd Mr. Odell Apr 1839]

D2-491: Surv. 20 July 1836 by T.Ws.10,162, 10,362 & 12,590 Abraham Secrest 90 A. in Hampshire Co. on Yellow Spring Run of Great Cacapehon adj. Moorefield Rd., Valentine Secrest, Cacapehon Mt. 16 Oct 1837 [Dl'd Mr. Odell Apr 1839]

D2-492: Surv. 23 Sep 1836 by T.W.11,063 Asa Simons 25 A. in Hampshire Co. on Little Cacapehon adj. William Loy, Adam Rudolph, Horn?. 16 Oct 1837 [Dl'd Mr. Odell Apr 1839]

D2-492: Surv. 30 June 1836 by T.W.10,897 Tobias Stickley 28 A. in Hampshire Co. on Mikes Run, Knobby Mt. adj. Jacob Bacorn heirs, Solomon Leatherman formerly Terry. 16 Oct 1837 [Dl'd Mr. Odell Apr 1839]

D2-493: Surv. 13 Oct 1836 by T.W.12,590 John Spencer Jr. 34 A. in Hampshire Co. on Knobby Mt. adj. John Spencer Sr., Jacob Fleck, George Mice, Urice. 16 Oct 1837 [Dl'd Mr. Odell Apr 1839]

D2-493: Surv. 12 Nov 1835 by T.W.11,104 David Thrush asne. of John Thrush 68 1/2 A. in Hampshire Co. on Abrams Rg. adj. his land, Nathaniel KuyKendall. 16 Oct 1837 [Dl'd Mr. Odell Apr 1839]

D2-494: Surv. 22 June 1836 by T.W.10,655 Thomas Anderson & Bartholomew McKee 22 A. in Frederick Co. adj. said Anderson, Routs heirs, on Timber Rg. & Back Cr., the Moorfield Rd. 2 Aug 1837 [To Rec't 25 Oct 1837]

D2-494: Surv. 19 Oct 1808 by T.Ws.17,109 & 17,206 Joseph Longacre 5534 1/2 A. in Shenandoah, Hampshire & Hardy Cos. on Great N. Mt. & Cedar Cr. adj. John Rudolph, John Wilson, Jacob Rudolph, Michael Strosnider, George Wymer, Archibald Findley, John Wymer, David Miller, Col. Isaac Zane, Pear, Thomas Wood, Samuel Wicks, Henry Robinson. 20 Aug 1837 [By mail 30 Oct 1837]

D2-496: Surv. 11 June 1836 by T.W.10,655 Bartholomew McKee 5 A. 3 Ro. 12 Po. in Frederick Co. adj. his own land, George Kearns, others. 20 Aug 1837 [To Rec't 28 Oct 1837]

D2-496:   Surv. 30 Dec 1836 by T.W.10,969 Samuel Dailey 358 A. 2 Ro. 15 Po. in Frederick Co. adj. said Dailey, Joseph Baker heirs, Andrew Mason, Samuel Goodnight, Co. bet. Frederick & Morgan, Hail or Hoil, E. Boyd. 20 Oct 1837 [Dl'd Mr. OFarrel 15 July 1839]

D2-497:   Surv. 7 Sep 1836 by T.W.10,671 Mathias Rutter 167 3/4 A. in Frederick Co. on Hunting Rg., Hog Cr. adj. John Hart, William Clark, Enoch Fenton, Eli Smith. 20 Aug 1837 [Dl'd Mr. Wood 4 Jan 1838]

D2-497:   Surv. 30 Jan 1837 by T.W.12,734 Job Armantrout 27 A. in Hardy Co. on N. Mill Cr. adj. his own land, John Cunningham heirs, John Welton, The Manor line. 21 Oct 1837 [Dl'd Mr. Mullen 4 Apr 1838]

D2-498:   Surv. 26 Sep 1836 by T.W.12,361 George Bean 90 A. in Hardy Co. on N. R. adj. his own land, Rd. from Moorefield to Winchester, Thomas Birches, Ball. 21 Oct 1837 [Dl'd Mr. Mullen 4 Apr 1838]

D2-498:   Surv. 18 May 1836 by T.W.11,110 Bennet Bean 2nd 100 A. in Hardy Co. on N. R. adj. his own land, Elija Dyers, James Bean, Hoggins, William Clark, Hunting Rg., the Marshall line tract. 21 Oct 1837 [Dl'd Mr. Mullen 4 Apr 1838]

D2-499:   Surv. 20 Sep 1836 by T.W.12,591 Bennet Bean 1st 51 A. in Hardy Co. on N. R. & Spring Lick Rg., David Vanmeter, Buckley, Joseph Bean. 21 Oct 1837 [Dl'd Mr. Mullen 4 Apr 1838]

D2-499:   Surv. 18 Mar 1835 by T.W.4703 Daniel Minull 8 A. in Hardy Co. on Timber Rg. & Walnut Bottom Run of S. Br. of Potomac adj. Perry, Vanmeter. 21 Oct 1837 [Dl'd Mr. Mullen 4 Apr 1838]

D2-500:   Surv. 20 Sep 1836 by T.Ws.7106 & 12,665 John Mullin 90 A. in Hardy Co. on Hickory Run & Patersons Cr. Mt. adj. Joseph Vanmeter, John Smith, Isaac Hite, John Webb. 21 Oct 1837 [Dl'd Mr. Mullen 4 Apr 1838]

D2-500:   Surv. 5 Apr 1836 by T.W.11,202 Thomas S. Davisson 196 A. in Hardy Co. on N. R. adj. said Davisson, Spring Lick Rg., Vanmeter. 21 Oct 1837 [Dl'd Mr. Mullen 4 Apr 1838]

D2-501:   Surv. 26 Oct 1836 by T.W.12,696 Jonathan Seymore 200 A. in Hardy Co. on Lounies Cr., Creek Mt. adj. Felix Seymore, Thomas Seymore, Powell, Randal, Idleman. 21 Oct 1837 [Dl'd Mr. Mullen 4 Apr 1838]

D2-501:   Surv. 18 Mar 1837 by T.Ws.11,111 & 12,841 Isaac Snyder 355 A. in Hardy rCo. on N. fork, of Cove Run adj. his own land, Anthony Fout, Big Lick, John Fout, N. Mt. 21 Oct 1837 [Dl'd Mr. Mullen 4 Apr 1838]

D2-502:   10 Sep 1836 by T.Ws.12,242, 10,500 & 12,591 David Vanmeter 1000 A. in Hardy Co. adj. his own land inc. Upper Little Mt., Saw Mill Run, his Foley flat surv., Wharton, Widener. 21 Oct 1837 [Dl'd Mr. Mullen 4 Apr 1838]

D2-502:   Surv. 10 Sep 1836 by T.W.12,696 Joseph Williams 250 A. in Hardy Co. on Patersons Cr. adj. his own land formerly Ryan, James Ryan, James Williams. 21 Oct 1837 [Dl'd Mr. Mullen 4 Apr 1838]

D2-503:   Surv. 8 Feb 1837 by T.W.12,734 Archibald & Able Welton 400 A. in Hardy Co. on Creek Mt. inc. Weltons Knob, the Manor line, Job Welton, Able Seymore. 21 Oct 1837 [Dl'd Mr. Mullen 4 Apr 1838]

D2-503:   Surv. 27 Aug 1832 by T.W.6878 Isaac Skelton 39 A. in Shenandoah Co. in the Blue Rg., S. Br. of Happy Cr. adj. Lazarous Taylor, said Skelton, Mary H. Roes or Ross. 21 Oct 1837 [Dl'd to Rec't Jan '39]

D2-504:   Surv. 8 Mar 1836 by T.Ws.6878 & 9992 George & David McInturff 123 1/4 A. in Shenandoah Co. in Powells Big Ft. on N. Ft. Mt. adj. said George & David McInturff, Martin Kibler, Woodstock Rd., BenJamin Blackford & son. 21 Oct 1837 [Dl'd 3 Apr 1839]

D2-504:   Surv. 10 Nov 1829 by T.Ws.7390 & 5117 William Smith asne. of Jno. S. &
R.G. Smith 75 1/4 A. in Shenandoah Co. on Turkey Run adj. Daniel Funkhouser,
Thomas Frazer, John Russell formerly Zane, Joseph Longacre heirs.   1 Oct 1837
[Dl'd Jno Koontz 28 Oct 1837]

D2-505:   Surv. 9 June 1835 by T.Ws.11,199 & 11,063 William Cool & Harburt Park
97 A. in Hampshire Co. on Black Lick Run & Clay Lick fork of Little Cacapehon
adj. Cloe Ann Powelson, Harburt Cool heirs, Josias Corbin. 1 Oct 1837 [Dl'd
Mr. G. Park 23 Jan 1838]

D2-506:   Surv. 20 Nov 1836 by T.W.2350 James Bean 32 A. in Hardy Co. on N. R.
adj. his own land, Bennet Bean the 1st, Thos. S. Davisson formerly Benedict
Jarbo?. 1 Dec 1837 [Dl'd Mr. Mullen 4 Apr 1838]

D2-506:   Surv. 22 Nov 1836 by T.W.12,696 James Bean 300 A. in Hardy Co. adj John
Birch, George Bishop, said Bean. 1 Dec 1837 [Dl'd Mr. Mullen 4 Apr 1838]

D2-507:   Surv. 10 Apr 1835 by T.W.4703 Daniel McNeill 100 A. in Hardy Co. on S.
Br., the High Knob Mt. adj. his own land, Kuykindall. 1 Dec 1837 [Dl'd Mr.
Mullen 4 Apr 1838]

D2-507:   Surv. 20 Oct 1835 by T.Ws.10,971 & 12,361 John Scott 85 A. in Hardy Co.
on Patersons Cr. Mt. adj. James Williams, Joseph Arnold formerly Foley. 1 Dec
1837 [Dl'd Mr. Mullen 4 Apr 1838]

D2-508:   Surv. 5 Sep 1834 by T.W.12,226 Notly McDavid 17 A. in Hardy Co. on
Walkers Rg., adj. Sinking spring Surv., Hite, Leon. 1 Jan 1838 [Dl'd Mr.
Mullen 4 Apr 1838]

D2-508:   Surv. 1 June 1837 by T.W.6989 John Mullin 48 A. in Hardy Co. on
Patersons Cr. Mt. adj. his own land, Oglesby, his Foley surv. 1 Jan 1838 [Dl'd
Mr. Mullen 4 Apr 1838]

D2-509:   Surv. 23 Apr 1837 by T.W.11,110 William McDaniel 13 A. in Hardy Co. on
Loonies Cr. adj. Adam Harness, Aaron Wellton, Little Mt. 1 Jan 1838 [Dl'd Mr.
Mullen 4 Apr 1838]

D2-509:   Surv. 16 May 1837 by T.W.6989 Soloman Michael 64 A. in Hardy Co. on
Walkers Rg. adj. George Michael, See or Lee big surv. 1 Jan 1838 [Dl'd Mr.
Mullen 4 Apr 1838]

D2-510:   Surv. 3 May 1837 by T.W.12,384 Joseph P. Mahaney 85 A. in Shenandoah
Co. on Little N. Mt. adj. Adam & Tobias Eshleman. 1 Jan 1838 [Mr. Lones? 3 Oct
1839]

D2-510:   Surv. 7 Dec 1835 by T.W.12,361 William Cunningham 120 A. in Hardy Co.
on Middle Mt. adj. Thomas & Miles Parsons, Anthony Baker heirs formerly See, his
own land. 1 Jan 1838 [Dl'd Mr. Mullen 4 Apr 1838]

D2-511:   Surv. 12 Apr 1837 by T.W.12,239 John Kretsinger 75 A. in Hardy Co. on
Waits Run adj. Daniel Call formerly Robert Means, Benjamin Dean, Andersons Rg.
1 Jan 1838 [Dl'd Mr. Mullen 4 Apr 1838]

D2-511:   Surv. 4 Mau 1837 by T.Ws.10,602 & 12,899 William Loy 191 A. in
Hampshire Co. on Tear Coat Cr. adj. his own land, Aaron Rogers, Gravely Lick
Run, Samuel Loy. 1 Jan 1838 [Dl'd Mr. Odell Apr 1839]

D2-512:   Surv. 5 May 1837 by T.Ws.10,563 & 2261 George Shevirs 130 A. 1 Ro. 33
Po. in Frederick Co. on Hoge Cr. adj. Mathias Ritter, Enoch Fenton, John Hart,
Adam Hart, C. Loy. 1 Jan 1838 [Dl'd to Rec't 11 Jan 1838]

D2-512:   Surv. 27 Feb 1837 by T.W.10,563 George Sevires 33 A. 3 Ro. 19 Po. in
Frederick Co. adj. Paul Taylor, James Pine, Samuel Strobridge heirs, Rd. from
Winchester to Bath, Nicholas Purtle heirs, Bear Wallow. 1 Jan 1838 [Dl'd to
Rec't 11 Jan 1838]

D2-513: Surv. 26 May 1837 by T.W.11,201 William Snodgrass 258 A. in Hardy Co. on Loonies Cr. adj. George Shell, Reeve's land, his own land formerly Stephen Ratliff, Welton, Diamond Lick surv., the Forge Tract, Ashby, 1 Jan 1838 [Dl'd Mr. Mullen 12 Feb 1838]

D2-513: Surv. 10 May 1837 by T.W.12,939 Daniel Tucker & Christopher Martin 175 A. in Hardy Co. bet. Knobby & New Cr. Mts. adj. Henry Martin, Martin McNemar. 1 Jan 1838 [Dl'd Mr. Mullen 4 Apr 1838]

D2-514: Surv. 31 Mar 1837 by T.W.12,841 Elija Weese 96 A. in Hardy Co. on N. Mill Cr. adj. said Weese. 1 Jan 1838 [Dl'd Mr. Mullen 4 Apr 1838]

D2-514: Surv. 17 Feb 1837 by T.W.7134 George Sevire 70 A. 3 Ro. 10 Po. in Frederick Co. on E. Fork of Brush Cr. & Little Mt. adj. James Pine formerly A. S. Tidball Exr. of Martin Rilly, Ruller now Rezin Mason, Pack Horse Rd., Ruble, Stone, Paul Taylor. 1 Jan 1838 [Dl'd to Rec't 11 Jan 1838]

D2-515: Surv. 5 Oct 1836 by T.W.11,065 William Harvie 5 A. in Nelson Co. in the 2nd hundred bet. S. Brs. of Ruckers Run & N. Brs. of Black Cr. adj. his own land, James Martin, James D. Brent. 8 Jan 1837 [See Book 87 page 750]

End Book D2 1829 - 1837

E2-1:   Surv.24 Nov 1834 by T.W.11,207 Stephen Reynolds 275 A. in Hardy Co. adj. Daniel Harris, Lost R., Lucretia Oldacres, Harris formerly Pixler, Stone. 25 May 1838 [Mailed to Philip Williams 28 May 1838]

E2-2: Surv.23 July 1835 by T.W.10,800 Hancock Lee 33 1/4 A. in Fauquier Co. bet. Edmund Jennings & Murdock near Rappahannock R. 9 June 1838 [Mailed 9 June 1838]

E2-3:   Surv.11 Nov 1837 by T.W.12,952 John Sloan 1877 A. in Hampshire Co. on Pine Swamp Run & Alleghany Mt. adj. John Brant, Middle Rg., Alexander King, Dr. Stewart heirs, George G. & Benjamin Tasker, Hezekiah Nally, Solomon Smith of Benjamin, George R. Tasker, Benjamin Dawson heirs. Angus W. McDonald, Edward McCarty. 30 Oct 1838 [Mailed to Prop'r 1 Dec 1838]

E2-4: Surv.27 Jan 1838 by T.W.10,879 & 12,824 Eli Smith 284 A. in Frederick Co. on Hoge Cr. adj. John Hart, Andrew Robinson, on Hunting Rg., Samuel Jackson, John Fenton heirs, Mathias Ritter. 30 Nov 1838 [Dl'd Mr. Sherrard 5 Apr 1839]

E2-5:   Surv.10 Mar 1837 by T.W.12,734 Jacob Barkdall 39 A. in Hardy Co. on S. Mill Cr. adj. his own land. 30 Nov 1838 [Dl'd Mr. Seymoure 27 Mar 1839]

E2-6:   Surv.5 Sep 1837 by T.W.12,591 John Bosley 300 A. in Hardy Co. on Pattersons Cr. Mt. adj. William Dorson, James Williams Green Spring Surv. 30 Nov 1838 [Dl'd Mr. Seymoure 27 Mar 1839]

E2-7: Surv.20 Nov 1837 by T.W.7271 Joel Crites 76 A. in Hardy Co. on Spring Run Rg. 30 Nov 1838 [Dl'd Mr. Seymoure 27 Mar 1839]

E2-8: Surv.12 June 1837 by T.W.10,442 & 12,939 Henry W. Fry 350 A. in Hardy Co. adj. Baker on Bakers Mt., Capcapeon, Samuel Baker now his own, Thomas Littler now Baker, Jeremiah Stewart, Cline. 30 Nov 1838 [Dl'd Mr. Seymoure 28 Mar 1839]

E2-9:   Surv. 5 Dec 1837 by T.W.12,665 James Gray 32 A. in Hardy Co. on N. Mill Cr. adj. Frederick K. Ford, Philip Yoakum, Stomboug, Peter Lauderman, Boots. 30 Nov 1838 [Dl'd Mr. Seymoure 27 Mar 1839]

E2-10: Surv.5 Dec 1837 by T.W.5519 James Gray 10 A. in Hardy Co. on N. Mill Cr. adj. Frederick K. Ford & others, Christopher Harmon. 30 Nov 1838 [Dl'd Mr. Seymoure 27 Mar 1839]

E2-11: Surv.29 Nov 1837 by T.W.6989 Jeremiah Inskeep 21 A. in Hardy Co. on Lost R. & Cr. Hill adj. his own land, lands formerly Robinson/Robison & Ruddle. 30 Nov 1838 [Dl'd Mr. Seymoure 27 Mar 1839]

E2-12: Surv.23 Feb 1837 by T.W.5798 & 11,006 Charles Lobb 286 A. in Hardy Co. on Middle Mt. & S. fork of S. Br. adj. George Nave, William Cunningham, Charles Lobb, Cragen, Navis, George Harness 3rd, Fisher & Bozard. 4 May 1838 [Dl'd Mr. Seymoure 27 Mar 1839]

E2-13: Surv.11 Nov 1837 by T.W.6723 & 6989 Martin McNemar & William Idleman 73 A. in Hardy Co. on Pattersons Cr. Mt. adj. McMechen heirs, said McNemara. 30 Nov 1838 [Dl'd Mr. Seymoure 28 Mar 1839]

E2-14:   Surv.11 Nov 1835 bt T.W.10,018 & 12,361 Simon Switzer 160 A. in Hardy Co. on N. Mt. & Great Capcapeon adj. Valentine Simmons, Tevalt now Clark, Williams, Bridge Run. 30 Nov 1838 [Dl'd Mr. Seymoure 23 Mar 1839]

E2-15:   Surv.21 Nov 1836 by T.W.12,665 Daniel Sites Jr. 65 A. in Hardy Co. on Middle Mt. adj. Jacob Ketteman, James Morrow, N.N. line. 30 Nov 1838 [Dl'd Mr. Seymoure 27 Mar 1839]

E2-16:   Surv.25 June 1837 by T.W.12,841 & 6989 George Shell 92 A. in Hardy Co. on Patersons Cr. Mt. adj. John Moor, Hershy, Solomon Cunningham heirs, James Williams. 4 May 1838 [Dl'd Mr. Seymoure 27 Mar 1839]

E2-17:   Surv.20 Mar 1837 by T.W.10,852 & 7695 Mathias Swain 28 A. 2 Ro. in Morgan Co. on Sleepy Cr. adj. Sherard heirs, Swain, Rankin. 30 Nov 1838 [Mr. O'Farrell 4 Apr 1839]

E2-18:   Surv.10 Oct 1837 by T.W.7147 George Reynolds & Jacob Brosius 35 A. in Morgan Co. on Sideling Hill adj. Entlee?, Harlan. 30 Nov 1838 [Dl'd to rec't 18 Feb 1839]

E2-19:   Surv.18 Nov 1837 by T.W.12,331 George Reynolds 166 A. in Morgan Co. adj. Barnet/Barnett, Reynolds, Rd. Rg., Marmaduke. 30 Nov 1838 [To Mr. Reynolds 4 Apr 1839]

E2-20:   12 Sep 1837 by T.W.12,331 George Reynolds & Jacob Brosius 151 A. in Morgan Co. on Cacapeon Cr. & Canalaway Hill adj. Bilmire, Reynolds, Young, Harlan, Sherard or Crop. 30 Nov 1838 [Dl'd to Rec't 18 Feb 1839]

E2-21:   Surv.18 Nov 1837 by T.W.12,331 George Reynolds 18 A. in Morgan Co. at foot of Sideling Hill adj. Marmaduke. 30 Nov 1838 [Dl'd to Rec't 18 Feb 1839]

E2-22:   Surv.25 Apr 1837 by T.W.10,507 Andrew Michael 21 1/2 A. in Morgan Co. on Sleepy Cr. adj. Pendleton, Michael. 30 Nov 1838 [Dl'd Mr. OFarrall 4 Apr '39]

E2-23:   Surv.13 Nov 1837 by T.W.7695 John Huff 50 A. in Morgan Co. on Cacapeon Mt. 30 Nov 1838 [Dl'd Mr. OFarrall 4 Apr '39]

E2-24:   Surv.10 Dec 1837 by T.W.12,331 Lemuel Crop 12 A. in Morgan Co. bet. Potomac R. & Cacapeon Cr. adj. Allen, Cross heirs, Still House farm, Red horse Cr. 30 Nov 1838 [Dl'd Mr. OFarrall 4 Apr '39]

E2-25:   Surv.20 Nov 1837 by T.W.7695 Henry Bruner 32 A. 1 Ro. in Morgan Co. on Cacapeon Cr. adj. Harlan, Bruner. 30 Nov 1838 [Mr. OFarrall 4 Apr '39]

E2-26:   Surv.20 Mar 1837 by T.W.12,791 Daniel Williams 100 A. in Hampshire Co. on Little Cacaphon adj. George Sharp, Samuel J. Stump, James Meekin, Sterritt. 30 Nov 1838 [Dl'd Mr. Odell Apr 1839]

E2-27:   Surv.7 Dec 1836 by T.W.12,590 Conrad Umstot 1 A. 1 Ro. in Hampshire Co. on Beaver Run adj. John Miller heirs, said Umstot, Umstot's Smith Surv. 4 May 1838 [Dl'd Mr. Odell Apr 1839]

E2-28:   Surv.22 Nov 1837 by T.W.12,899 Isaac Lochmiller 3 A. 1 Ro. in Hampshire Co. on Dillons Run adj. Jesse Lupton, his own land, Adam Cooper, William Lupton. 30 Nov 1838 [Dl'd Mr. Odell Apr 1839]

E2-29:   Surv.15 Nov 1836 by T.W.12,374 David Long 28 A. in Hampshire Co. on Martin's Rg. & N. Br. of Potomac adj. John Martin, Richard Baker, said Long known as the Ohio Co. surv., Cresap heirs. 30 Nov 1838 [Dl'd Mr. Odell Apr 1839]

E2-30:   Surv.14 Apr 1837 byT.W.12,589 & 12,899 Solomon Leatherman 60 A. in Hampshire Co. on Mikes Run adj. Thomas Dye, said Leatherman formerly Josiah Morris, Bacorn, Roberts heirs. 30 Nov 1838 [Dl'd Mr. Odell Apr 1839]

E2-31:   Surv.13 Sep 1831 by T.W.10,585 & 4863 Aaron Largent 173 A. in Hampshire Co. on Great Cacaphon adj. Lewis Largent, land formerly Rinker & Largent, Joseph Baker, Hutchinson, Lewis Largent Sr. 4 May 1838 [Dl'd Mr. Odell Apr 1839]

E2-32:   Surv.26 Feb 1836 by T.W.12,374 Nathan Kerns 5 1/2 A. in Hampshire Co. on Timber Rg. adj. Kerns, George Mauzey. 30 Nov 1838 [Dl'd Mr. Odell Apr 1839]

E2-33:   Surv.28 Sep 1837 by T.W.12,899 & 12,936 George Haws 175 A. in Hampshire Co. on S fork of Little Cacaphon & Cove Mt. adj. his own land, Elisha Bell. 30 Nov 1838 [Dl'd Mr. Odell Apr 1839]

E2-34:   Surv.6 Sep 1837 by T.W.12,899 & 12,565 John Dye 107 A. in Hampshire Co. on Knobley Mt. adj. Thomas Dye, Tobias Stickley, Daniel & George W. Doll. 30 Nov 1838 [Dl'd Mr. Odell Apr 1839]

E2-35:   Surv.8 Nov 1837 by T.W.12,565 Thomas Davy 100 A. in Hampshire Co. on High Knob adj. Abraham Vanmeter, Garret Vanmeter, High Knob Gap, Rush Spring Gap. 30 Nov 1838 [Dl'd Mr. Odell Apr 1839]

E2-36:   Surv.21 Nov 1837 by T.W.12,590 Adam Cooper 14 A. in Hampshire Co. on Dillons Run adj. his land, Jesse Lupton, Isaac Lockmiller. 30 Nov 1838 [Dl'd Mr. Odell Apr 1839]

E2-37:   Surv.16 Apr 1835 by T.W.11,051 William Boseley 61 A. in Hampshire Co. on New Cr. Mt. adj. Elizabeth Boseley, his own land, John Ward. 30 Nov 1838 [Dl'd Mr. Odell Apr 1839]

E2-38:   Surv.14 Mar 1837 by T.W.12,791 Archibald Babb 110 Po. in Hampshire Co. on S. Br. of Potowmack adj. Garret J? Blue & Uriah Blue, Henry Powelson. 30 Nov 1838 [Dl'd Mr. Odell Apr 1839]

E2-39:   Surv.6 Jan 1837 by T.W.9106 & 10,267 John W. Blue 51 1/2 A. in Hampshire Co. on Stone or Rock Mt. adj. Henry Powellson, Garret J.? Blue, Michael Blue. 30 Nov 1838 [Dl'd to Rec't 18 Feb 1839]

E2-40: Surv.22 Mar 1837 by T.W.12,791 John Ambler 99 A. in Hampshire Co. on Pine Cabin Run adj. Trouton, Buzzard, Ambler, Ambrose. ___ 1838 [Mr. Odell Apr 1839]

E2-41:   Surv.14 Dec 1836 by T.W.12,382 Noah Sigler 14 A. 3 Ro. in Page Co. on Stoney Run adj. heirs of John Nauman dec'd, Hetick. 30 Nov 1838   [To Dr. Robertson 3 Apr 1839]

E2-42:   Surv.14 Dec 1836 by T.W.12,382 Jacob Sigler 14 A. 1 Ro. in Page Co. on Stoney Run adj. Abram Spitler, heirs of John Nauman dec'd, John Cave formerly Henry Aleshire?. 30 Nov 1838 [To Dr. Robertson 3 Apr 1839]

E2-43: Surv.19 Dec 1837 by T.W.14,461 Adam Sowers 82 A. 2 Ro. 9 Po. in Page Co. on Blue Rg., head of Dry Run adj. Charles Weaver, John Prince. 30 Nov 1838 [To Dr. Robertson 3 Apr 1839]

E2-44:   Surv.5 Apr 1836 by T.W.5650 Adam Rineheart 9 A. 3 Ro. 4 Po. in Page Co. on Shenandoah R. adj. Ambrose Huffman, Stephen Price formerly Thomas Goodwin. 30 Nov 1838 [To Dr. Robertson 3 Apr 1839]

E2-45:   Surv.22 Mar 1837 by T.W.12,382 William Breeding 11 A. 3 Ro. 20 Po. in Page Co. on Little Line Run adj. John Keyser, William Breeding, hiers of John Nauman dec'd, Leoy Lucus. 30 Nov 1838 [To Dr. Robertson 3 Apr 1839]

E2-46:   Surv.29 May 1836 by T.W.5650 Tobias Beem 20 A. 2 Ro. 9 Po. in Page Co. on Blue Rg. & Pass Run adj. Martin Clizer, James H. Lehew, Abram Beem, Geo. Briton heirs. 30 Nov 1838 [To Dr. Robertson 3 Apr 1839]

E2-47:   Surv.30 Feb 1837 by T.W.12,491 & 12,753 John Brown 13 1/2 A. in Rappahanock Co. adj. Robert Hudson, Robert Jones, said Brown, Alexander Hudson, Red Oak Mt. 30 Nov 1838 [Dl'd Maj. Broadus 1 Feb 1839]

E2-48:   Surv.18 Apr 1837 by T.W.11,127 Benjamin & Thomas S. Blackford 100 A. in Shenandoah Co. on Mt. bet. Powells Big & Little Forts, adj. Pennybacker. 30 Nov 1838 [To Mr Conn 3 Apr 1839]

E2-49:   Surv.23 Nov 1836 by T.W.9992 Thomas McCan 2 A. 1 Ro. 6 Po. in Shenandoah Co. on Smith's Cr. adj. Joseph Click, Hinkle. Jacob Summers. 30 Nov 1838 [To Mr Conn 3 Apr 1839]

E2-50:   Surv.14 Apr 1837 by T.W.6878 Henry Ridenour 46 1/2 A. in Shenandoah Co. on Three Topt Mt. adj. Jacob Coffman, Ridenour. 30 Nov 1838 [Mr Conn 3 Apr 1839]

E2-51:   Surv.20 Dec 1837 by T.W.12,717 George Washington Sibert as asne. one undivided half & Lorenzo D. Sibert remaining undivided half, 838 3/4 A. in Shenandoah Co. on Cedar Cr.& Paddy Mt., adj. s'd Siberts, John Hamilton, Samuel Boehm, John Swaney, John Koontz, Rocky Rg. 30 Nov 1838 [Col. Bare 15 Feb 1839]

E2-52:   Surv.29 Mar 1836 by T.W.10,978 Philip Funk asne of James Rowzee 170 A. in Shenandoah Co. in Creces Ft. adj. Daniel Munch, Solomon Veach. 30 Nov 1838 [To Mr Conn 3 Apr 1839]

E2-53:   Surv.23 Sep 1837 by T.W.3240 Henry Wisecarver 9 A. 12 sq. Po. in Frederick Co. on Cedar Cr. adj. his own land, Joseph Fawcet, Isaac Longacre, John G. Gaugh. 26 Nov 1838 [Dl'd Mr. Sherrard 27 Mar 1839]

E2-54:   Surv.8 July 1837 by T.W.12,899 Thomas Downey 82 A. in Hampshire Co. on N. Br. of Potomac opposite mouth of Georges Cr., adj. Philadelphia Burns, Clement Smith. 2 July 1839 [Mailed to Prop'r 7 Mar 1840]

E2-55:   Surv.14 May 1838 by T.W.2751 Adam Bolener 200 A. in Hardy Co. on Thorn Bottom on Back Mt. & Bean's Mt. adj. Jacob Pugh, Devils Hole Mt. 30 Nov 1839 [Dl'd Mr. McNamar 16 Dec 1839]

E2-56:   Surv.3 Aug 1838 by T.W.2751 William Branson 100 A. in Hardy Co. on Lost R. adj. his own land, his Smith Surv., his Fravel land. 30 Nov 1839 [Dl'd Mr. Seymour 9 Mar 1840]

E2-57:   Surv.13 June 1836 by T.W.12,591 John Beckhorn 3 1/2 A. in Hardy Co. on Pattersons Cr. adj. James Mile, James Williams, his own land, Doron. 30 Nov 1839 [Dl'd to Rec't 16 Dec 1839]

E2-58:   Surv.24 May 1838 by T.W.2751 John Bosley 32 A. in Hardy Co. on Patersons Cr. Mt. adj. Hershy, Williams, said Bosley, Sugar Camp hollow. 30 Nov 1839 [Dl'd to Rec't 16 Dec 1839]

E2-59:   Surv.18 May 1838 by T.W.2751 Ezra Clark 38 A. in Hardy Co. on Big Rg., near his own land. 30 Nov 1839 [Dl'd to Rec't 16 Dec 1839]

E2-60:   Surv.24 May 1838 by T.W.2751 Ananias Constable 76 A. in Hardy Co. on N. R. bet. N. Mt. & Brushy Rg. adj. Robert Means, Huffman formerly William G. Hagar, Abraham Constable. 30 Nov 1839 [Dl'd Mr. Seymore 9 Mar 1840]

E2-61:   Surv.18 May 1838 by T.W.2751 Adam & Henry Costner 48 A. in Hardy Co. on Loonies Cr. adj. his own land, John L. Miller, Elzey, Miller formerly Bishop. 30 Nov 1839 [Dl'd to Rec't 16 Dec 1839]

E2-62:   Surv.10 July 1837 by T.W.11,056 & 6989 Reubin Davis 95 A. in Hardy Co. on Walker's Rg. adj. James Bosly, Christain Hilky, Benjamin Chambers, James McDavid. 30 Nov 1839 [Dl'd Mr. McNamar 16 Dec 1839]

E2-63:   Surv.26 Aug 1838 by T.W.2751 Jacob H. Fisher asne. of George N. Fisher 85 A. in Hardy Co. on Lounies Cr. adj. Babb, Valentine Simmons, Daniel Shell, William McDaniel, John L. Miller formerly Bishop. 30 Nov 1839 [Dl'd Mr. Seymour 7 Mar 1840]

E2-64:   Surv.24 May 1838 by T.W.2751 Felix Henkle 67 A. in Hardy Co. on S. Mill Cr. adj. Caleb & Nathan Henkle, his own land, near Deep Spring, the Conrod Salt place. 30 Nov 1839 [Dl'd Mr. Seymour 7 Mar 1840]

E2-65:   Surv.21 Aug 1838 by T.W.12,632 Henry Hockman 41 A. in Shenandoah Co. in Powel's Big Ft. on S. Ft. Mt. adj. said Hockman, William Derflinger formerly A. Stickley. 30 Nov 1839 [Dl'd Col. Bare 20 Feb 1840]

E2-66:   Surv.20 Aug 1838 by T.W.12,632 Henry Hockman 159 A. in Shenandoah Co. in Powels Big Ft. on N. Ft. Mt. adj. his own land, William Derflinger formerly Abraham Stickley, Passage Cr. 30 Nov 1839 [Dl'd Col. Bare 20 Feb 1840]

E2-67:   Surv.14 May 1838 by T.W.2751 William McDaniel & Daniel Shell 60 A. in Hardy Co. on Lounies Cr. adj. Ashby, Gaven, Nimrod Ashby, Bishop now John L. Miller. 30 Nov 1839 [Dl'd to Recp't 16 Dec 1839]

E2-68:   Surv.3 July 1837 by T.W.12,361 Joseph Nevill 55 A. in Hardy Co. on Alleghany Mt. adj. Byrn's heirs formerly Lyas? Roby, McKim. 30 Nov 1839 [Dl'd

Mr. Seymore 9 Mar 1840]

E2-69:   Surv.24 May 1838 by T.W.2751 Joseph Nevill 300 A. in Hardy Co. on Alleghany Mt. & Stoney R. adj. Abram & Isaac Inskeep, McNiell & others, Inskeep formerly John Cogsten, surv. made by Fisher & Bogard, Meneell?, Andrew Bruice now George Cunningham, Henline. 30 Nov 1839 [Dl'd Mr. Seymore 9 Mar 1840]

E2-70:   Surv.24 May 1838 by T.W.2751 Joseph Nevill 400 A. in Hardy Co. on Alleghany Mt. & Stoney R. adj. Michael Hider, Strile? Cunningham formerly Nevill, Hoy, Francis Deakins, Joseph Nevill now Michael Hider, Bruice now McKim. 30 Nov 1839 (Deed marked out. See Book 90 p.757)

E2-71:   Surv.25 May 1838 by T.W.2751 Aaron Poland 92 A. in Hardy Co. on Water Lick Run of N. R., Fox lick Rg. 30 Nov 1839 [Dl'd Mr. McNamar 16 Dec 1839]

E2-72:   Surv.25 May 1838 by T.W.2751 Elizabeth Rohrabau 60 A. in Hardy Co. on Ash Run of S. Mill Cr. adj. George Sites, Jacob Ketteman, Guidean Sites, Flat Rg. 30 Nov 1839 [Dl'd Mr. Seymore 9 Mar 1840]

E2-73:   Surv.11 May 1838 by T.W.2751 Jacob Smith 65 A. in Hardy Co. on N. Fork adj. land he ght of Jacob Hans, Stroud. 30 Nov 1839 [Mr. Seymore 9 Mar 1840]

E2-74:   Surv.28 Nov 1838 by T.W.2751 Daniel, James, Philip, William, Rachael, & Jonathan Smith 365 A. in Hardy Co. on N. R. adj. John Dyer heirs, Baretown Spring, Warden's Rg. 30 Nov 1839 [Dl'd to Rec't 16 Dec 1839]

E2-75:   Surv.15 Dec 1835 by T.W.10,463 Valentine Simmons 120 A. in Hardy Co. inc. Halmark Gap head adj. John Snodgrass heirs, John Snodgrass, S. Br. Manner, Huckleberry Rg., David Welton heirs. 30 Nov 1839 [Dl'd Mr. Seymore 9 Mar 1840]

E2-76:   Surv.26 Aug 1838 by T.W.2751 & 11,201 Valentine Simmons 600 A. in Hardy Co. on Patersons & Lounies Crs. adj. Francis Idleman, Joseph McNamar, Babb & others, Miller, Tear Coat Run, McNamar formerly Thomas Wilson. 30 Nov 1839 [Dl'd Mr. Seymore 9 Mar 1840]

E2-77:   Surv.26 Aug 1838 by T.W.12,696 Daniel Vanmeter 40 A. in Hardy Co. on Walnut Bottom Run of S. Br. adj. his own land, James Miles, grant from Fairfax to Mercer now his own, Daniel Marviell, Meniel, Jacob Vanmeter 1789 grant. 30 Nov 1839 [Dl'd to Rec'pt 16 Dec 1839]

E2-78: Surv.24 May 1838 by T.W.2751 Charles A. Turley 42 A. in Hardy Co. on Saw Mill Run & lower Little Mt. adj. Straus? hunting camp, David Vanmeter's Foley flat surv. 30 Nov 1839 [Dl'd Mr. Seymore 9 Mar 1840]

E2-79:   Surv.31 Aug 1837 by T.W.10463 Valentine Simmons 525 A. in Hardy Co. on Patersons & Lounies Crs. adj. Joseph McNamar, Babb, McNamar's Thomas Wilson surv., Jacob Cornell, William Cornell, Bishop's Thorn Run surv., John Smith. 30 Nov 1839 [Dl'd Mr. Seymore 9 Mar 1840]

E2-80:   Surv.24 May 1838 by T.W.2751 John Shell 200 A. in Hardy Co. adj. his own land, Peter Babb on Little Mt., Tucker, Stingley, Francis I. Combs, Bishop, Middle fork Gap. 30 Nov 1839 [Dl'd Mr. McNamar 16 Dec 1839]

E2-81:   Surv.29 Aug 1838 by T.W.2751 Elizabeth Vanmeter 180 A. in Hardy Co. on Patterson's Cr. & Patterson's Cr. Mt. adj. John Smith, John Moore. 30 Nov 1839 [Dl'd Mr. McNamar 16 Dec 1839]

E2-82:   Surv.16 Jan 1839 by T.W.2751 William Wease 24 A. in Hardy Co. on Fork Mt. & S. Mill Cr. adj. Sites, Abram Hinkel formerly McCord. 30 Nov 1839 [Dl'd Mr. McNamar 16 Dec 1839]

E2-83:   Surv.25 Mar 1837 by T.W.12,791 John Rannell & John B. Miller 19 A. in Hampshire Co. on Little Cacaphon adj. their tract, Sam'l Vandiver, Stephen Geno? 1789 grant. 30 Nov 1839 [Dl'd Col. Gilson 10 Mar 1840]

E2-84:   Surv.5 June 1837 by T.W.12,589 Solomon Smith (of Benjamin) 50 A. in

Hampshire Co. on Alleghany Mt. adj. said Smith, George R. Tasker, Nally. 30 Nov 1839 [Dl'd Col. Gilson 10 Mar 1840]

E2-85:   Surv.22 Nov 1836 by T.W.12,589 George R. Tasker & Solomon Smith (of Benjamin) 300 A. in Hampshire Co. on Alleghany Mt. & Pine Swamp Run. 30 Nov 1839 [Dl'd Col. Gilson 10 Mar 1840]

E2-86:   Surv.13 June 1838 by T.W.11,062 & 13,050 William Welch 57 A. in Hampshire Co. on Knobley Mt. adj. John Harison originally Stradler, Samuel Jones now Harison, Wm. Hogan heirs. 30 Nov 1839 [Dl'd Col. Gilson 10 Mar 1840]

E2-87:   Surv.12 June 1838 by T.W.6558 Wyet Allen 10 A. in Loudoun Co. on Goose Cr. adj. Robert Carter now George Carter, Samuel Fillet, Jonathan Carter. 19 Nov 1839 [Dl'd to Rec't 19 Nov 1839]

E2-88:   Surv.20 Feb 1837 by T.W.6558 James Mount 1 1/4 A. in Loudoun Co. adj. Catesby Cocke, James Rust?, said James Mount, Thomas Rees, Thomas Owsley. 19 Nov 1839 [Dl'd to Rec't 19 Nov 1839]

E2-89:   Surv. 25 Sep 1838 by T.W.10,852 & 13,096 John Huff 80 A. in Morgan Co. on Cacapeon Cr. adj. said Huff, John Hardy, Dawson. 30 Nov 1839 [Dl'd Col. Orrick 23 Feb 1842]

E2-90:   Surv.31 Mar 1838 by T.W.13,025 Jacob Steegle asne. of Moses Walton 17 1/2 A. in Shenandoah Co. near Boiling Spring adj. Jacob Steegle, Wine, heirs of John Branner dec'd. 5 Nov 1839 [Dl'd Mr. James Hardin 5 Nov 1839]

E2-91:   Surv.7 May 1838 by T.W.13,089 Joseph Stickler 31 1/4 A. in Shenandoah Co. on Massanottan Mt. adj. Jacob Bushong, said Walton, Abraham Savage. 30 Nov 1839 [Dl'd Col. Bare 20 Feb 1840]

E2-92:   Surv.30 & 31 May 1838 by T.W.10,978 & 14,020 Samuel G. Henkle 461 3/4 A. in Shenandoah Co. on Massanotten Mt., on Shenandoah & Rockingham Cos. line, adj. Wm. Weeks Jr., Adam Olinger, Olinger's purchase of Charles Pence?, Moses Zirkle, James Barber. 30 Nov 1839 [Dl'd Col. Bare 20 Feb 1840]

E2-93:   Surv.24 Feb 1816 by T.W.5650 Ambrose Huffman 50 A. in Page Co. on S. Fork of Shenandoah R. adj. Colin Micham now Stephen Price, heirs of Reuben Long dec'd, said Ambrose Huffman. 30 Nov 1839 [Dl'd Col. McPherson 22 Dec 1841]

E2-94:   Surv.16 Jan 1839 by T.W.2350 John Shell, Philip Shell, Daniel Shell, George Shell, Elizabeth Shell now Elizabeth Bradford, Mary Shell now Mary McDaniel, & Catherine Shell now Catherine Tucker, heirs of George Shell dec'd, 130 A. in Hardy Co. on Alleghany Mt. & Stony R. above Welton, adj. Bruice. 20 Dec 1839 [Dl'd Col. Mullen 3 Feb 1841]

E2-95:   Surv.20 Feb 1839 by T.W.13,025 Joseph Schmucker 137 sq. Per., an Island in N. Br. of Shenandoah R. in Shenandoah Co. adj. Johathan Gochenour, Fredinand Schmucker, Levi Gochenour. 15 Jan 1840 [Dl'd Col. Bare 20 Feb 1840]

E2-96:   Surv.30 Nov 1838 by Exg.T.W.2300 Capt. George Wallis 85 A. in Culpeper Co. adj. John C. Gordon's Lovell & Gordon tract, said Wallis Foley Tract. 1 Feb 1840 [Dl'd Maj. Broadus 18 Feb 1840]

E2-97:   Surv.8 Feb 1838 by T.W.10773 James W. Alban asne. of Enoch Park 2 A. 3 Ro. 22 Po. in Hampshire Co. on Bushes Run of Tear Coat adj. George Park, Hunting Rg., John Petters. 30 June 1840 [Dl'd Col. Vance 16 Mar 1841]

E2-98:   Surv.22 Apr 1839 by T.W.13,049 & 10,948 Adam Cooper 132 A. in Hampshire Co. on Sandy Rg. near Bens Knob adj. said Cooper, Isaac Lupton, Jesse Lupton, Isaac Carlyle. 30 June 1840 [Dl'd Col. Vance 16 Mar 1841]

E2-99:   Surv.5 Sep 1837 by T.W.12,565 Daniel Doll & George W. Doll 56 1/2 A. in Hampshire Co. on Knobly Mt. adj. their own land, Hamrick. 30 June 1840 [Dl'd Col. Vance 16 Mar 1841]

E2-100: Surv.9 Aug 1839 by T.W.12,936 & 14,172 Reuben Davis 449 A. in Hampshire Co. on New Cr. Mt. alias Abrahams Rg. adj. said Davis, John Ward, Elias Jones, Josias Smoot, Henry Harrison formerly Adam Hider?, Samuel B. Davis, Thomazin Grayson, John Neff heirs, John Mitchel Jr., Hogan heirs. 30 June 1840 [Dl'd Col. Vance 16 Mar 1841]

E2-101: Surv.15 Mar 1838 by T.W.12,936 & 13,050 David Hott & George Hott 49 A. in Hampshire Co. on Stony Mt. & Grassy lick Rd., adj. their land bought of William Reed & Robert French heirs, Margaret Leigh. 30 June 1840 [Dl'd Col. Vance 16 Mar 1841]

E2-102: Surv.8 Mar 1839 by T.W.10,373 & 13,049 Stephen Hannah 67 A. in Hampshire Co. on S. Br. of Potomac, S.E. of Romney adj. Christopher Heiskill now s'd Hannah, Abbik Carder, Vance. 30 June 1840 [Dl'd Col. Vance 16 Mar 1841]

E2-103: Surv.10 Aug 1839 by T.W.11,199 Thomas Jones 50 A. in Hampshire Co. on Abram's Rg. adj. Elias Jones, Josias Smoot, Reuben Davis, 30 June 1840 [Dl'd Col. Vance 16 Mar 1841]

E2-104: Surv.5 Sep 1837 by T.W.12,399 Michael Lickens Jr. asne. of Robert Parker asne. of Eli Moore 75 A. in Hampshire & Hardy Cos. on Dry Cow Hollow of Mikes Run, adj. Solomon Leatherman. 30 June 1840 [Dl'd Col. Vance 16 Mar 1841]

E2-105: Surv.16 Mar 1838 by T.W.12,050 John Lochner 122 A. in Hampshire & Hardy Cos. on Big Mt. adj. his own land. 30 June 1840 [Dl'd Col. Vance 16 Mar 1841]

E2-106: Surv.15 Nov 1839 by T.Ws.12,590 & 14,172 Solomon Leatherman 421 A. in Hampshire Co. on Knobley Mt. adj. Thomas Camell, Doll heirs, John Bland, Hogan heirs, Thomazen Grayson, Hamricks Gap. 30 June 1840 [Col. Vance 16 Mar 1841]

E2-107: Surv.30 Mar 1839 by T.W.13,049 Nicholas Leatherman 5 3/4 A. in Hampshire Co. on Mill Cr. adj. Leonard Boncrotz, Adam Sulser, Philip Moore. 30 June 1840 [Dl'd Col. Vance 16 Mar 1841]

E2-108: Surv.25 Sep 1839 by T.W.10,373 James Moorhead 34 A. in Hampshire Co. on Little Cacaphon adj. John Pettitt, Norman Uston heirs, Enias Everett, Asa Everett, Richard Hall. 30 June 1840 [Dl'd Col. Vance 16 Mar 1841]

E2-109: Surv.1 May 1839 by T.W.10,373 James Moorhead 47 A. in Hampshire Co. on S. Br. Mt. adj. James Parsons, Jack Scoovey?, Gibson, Throckmorton heirs, William Inskeep. 30 June 1840 [Dl'd Col. Vance 16 Mar 1841]

E2-110: Surv.20 Nov 1839 by T.W.13,096 Adam Bohrer 9 1/2 A. in Morgan Co. on Sleepy Cr. adj. Dawson, Bohrer. 30 June 1840 [Dl'd Col. Orrick 23 Feb 1842]

E2-111: Surv.18 Sep 1839 by T.W.10,812 William Catlett 9 A. in Morgan Co. on Cacapeon Cr. adj. Cross heirs. 30 June 1840 [Dl'd Col. Orrick 23 Feb 1842]

E2-112: Surv.30 July 1839 by T.W.13,049 Elijah Rinehart 42 A. in Hampshire Co. on Pattersons Cr. adj. said Rinehart, Abraham Rinehart. 30 June 1840 [Dl'd Col. Vance 16 Mar 1841]

E2-113: Surv.8 Aug 1839 by T.W.12,565 John Ward 50 A. in Hampshire Co. on New Cr. Mt. adj. his own land, William Boseley, Elizabeth Boseley, Reubin Davis. 30 June 1840 [Dl'd Col. Vance 16 Mar 1841]

E2-114: Surv.29 May 1838 by T.W.2751 Philip Shell 160 A. in Hardy Co. adj. George Shell on Little Mt., Joseph Tucker, Shell Run, Stingley. 30 June 1840 [Dl'd Col. Mullen 3 Feb 1841]

E2-115: Surv.9 Nov 1839 by T.W.2751 John Smith 100 A. in Hardy Co. adj. Samuel Babb, heirs of John Bishop, on Pattersons Cr., Brushey Run, Marlaser?, Cornell, Bishop. 30 June 1840 [Dl'd Col. Mullen 3 Feb 1841]

E2-116: Surv.24 May 1838 by T.W.2751 John Sites Jr. 5 1/2 A. in Hardy Co. on S. Mill Cr. adj. Adam Sites, McMeekin heirs. 30 June 1840 [Col. Mullen 3 Feb 1841]

E2-117:   Surv.12 Oct 1838 by T.W.2751 John Kitsmiller 9 A. in Hardy Co. on Alleghany Mt. adj. Morgan Byrns heirs, Nevill, Bruice, Byrns' Roby Tract. 30 June 1840 [Dl'd Col. Mullen 3 Feb 1841]

E2-118:   Surv.10 May 1838 by T.W.12,591 William Horseman 18 A. in Hardy Co. on N. R. adj. his land, Frederick Mauck, his land formerly William Thompson. 30 June 1840 [Dl'd Col. Vance 16 Mar 1841]

E2-119:   Surv.25 Feb 1839 by T.W.2751 Johnson Cavanovan 122 A. in Hardy Co. on Alleghany Mt. adj. Kuykendall, Barnhouse, Co. line. 30 June 1840 [Dl'd Col. Mullen 3 Feb 1841]

E2-120:   Surv.24 Apr 1839 by T.W.12,841 Jacob Bosley 2 A. in Hardy Co. adj. Christopher Martin, his own land formerly James Ryan. 30 June 1840 [Dl'd Col. Mullen 3 Feb 1841]

E2-121:   Surv.28 Dec 1838 by T.W.12,664 James Stinson 7 A. 3 Ro. in Warren Co. an island in S. R. 30 June 1840 [Dl'd Col. Carson 30 Dec 1841]

E2-122: Surv.7 Oct 1839 by T.W.14,147 Charles Shackelford 210 A. in Rappahannock Co. on Bluff Mt. adj. Buck formerly Dade, Warner formerly Duke, Barber now Mason, Eastham R., s'd Shackelford now Clark. 30 June 1840 [Rec't 22 Dec 1840]

E2-123:   Surv.6 Apr 1834 by T.W.10754 John Cooper 67 A. in Hardy Co. adj. Abram Hinkle, his own land, on S. Mill Cr., McCord now Hinkle. 25 Apr 1840 [Dl'd Col. Mullen 3 Feb 1841]

E2-124:   Surv.5 June 1837 by T.W. 12,226, 6349 & 10,927 Jesse Hutton & James R. Heiskill & Co. 240 A. in Hardy Co. on N. Fork adj. Elisha Stonestreet inc. the Meba? House. Sheat. 25 Apr 1840 [Dl'd Col. Mullen 3 Feb 1841]

E2-125:   Surv.22 Oct 1839 by T.W.11,143 Addison A. Jones 23 A. in Page Co. adj. Benjamin Blackford, heirs of Wharton Jones dec'd, Jerrymys run. 30 July 1840 [Sent by mail 28 Oct 1840]

E2-126:   Surv.6 Oct 1835 by T.W.1764 Anthony Funkhouser asne. of Isaac W. Longacre 15 A. 2 Ro. 8 Po. in Frederick Co. adj. Anthony Funkhouser, Fawcett now Funkhouser, Lupton. 30 July 1840 [Dl'd Mr. Bird 3 Jan 1842]

E2-127:   Surv.16 Nov 1839 by T.W.12,824 George Kearns 10 A. 26 Po. in Frederick Co. on Tmber Rg. adj. his land, James Fletcher & others. 30 July 1840 [Dl'd Mr. Woods 5 Jan 1841]

E2-128:   Surv.16 Dec 1839 by T.W.10,671 Malon S. Lovett 4 A. in Frederick Co. on Timber Rg. adj. Mure, Millison, J.? Lovett. 30 July 1840 [Mr. Bird 3 Jan 1842]

E2-129:   Surv.25 July 1838 by T.W.2293 George Sevire Jr. & John Clarke 133 A. 3 Ro. 14 Po. in Frederick Co. on Brush Cr. adj. Elzra Grover, Jacob Null, David Null, Peter Ashton formerly Joseph Sexton, Lukes lick, Job Dehoven formerly Wharton. 30 July 1840 [Dl'd Bird 3 Jan 1842]

E2-130:   Surv.10 May 1838 by T.W.2751 George Bradford 86 A. in Hardy Co. on Pattersons Cr. & New Cr. Mt. adj. his own land, Abram Rotruck, Shell. 31 Aug 1840 [To Col. Mullen 3 Feb 1841]

E2-131:   Surv.2 Mar 1838 by T.W.10,927 Joseph H. Buckley 94 A. in Hardy Co. on N. R. adj. his own land, in Tommies lick hollow, Marshall. 31 Aug 1840 [To Col. Mullen 3 Feb 1841]

E2-132:   Surv.16 Feb 1837 by T.W.10,927 Godfrey & Adam See Jr. 65 A. in Hardy Co. on Middle Mt. adj. Jacob Fisher, Adam See Sr. 31 Aug 1840 [Col. Mullen 3 Feb 1841]

E2-133:   Surv.3 Sep 1839 by T.W.2751 Thomas George 20 A. in Hardy Co. on Patersons Cr. adj. his own land formerly Zachariah Lenton, Hall, Haggerty. 31 Aug 1840 [To Col. Mullen 3 Feb 1841]

E2-134: Surv.22 Oct 1835 by T.W.12,226 & 12,361 George Lynn 126 A. in Hardy Co. on Chesnut Rg. adj. Sterrett heirs, Pugh & others, Lee formerly Machir. 31 Aug 1840 [To Col. Mullen 3 Feb 1841]

E2-135: Surv.15 Feb 1837 by T.W.11,202 Adam See Sr. 21 A. in Hardy Co. on Middle Mt. adj. Stover, Sugar Camp hollow. 31 Aug 1840 [Col. Mullen 3 Feb 1841]

E2-136: Surv.7 Mar 1837 by T.W.12,841 Jacob Wire 71 A. in Hardy Co. on Branch Mt. 31 Aug 1840 [To Col. Mullen 3 Feb 1841]

E2-137: Surv.18 Feb 1840 by T.W.2751 John Welton & Alexander Scott 280 A. in Hardy Co. on Litttle Mt. adj. Scott, Benjamin Roby, Martain Lance, Sulphur Lick Run. 31 Aug 1840 [To Col. Mullen 3 Feb 1841]

E2-138: Surv.10 Oct 1839 by T.W.2751 Elijah Weare 197 A. in Hardy Co. adj. S. Mill Cr. Judy heirs formerly Luke Smith. 31 Aug 1840 [Col. Mullen 3 Feb 1841]

E2-139: Surv.14 Apr 1839 by T.W.5846 James Curtis 149 A. in Berkeley Co. on Tilehanseys Br. & Third Hill Mt. adj. John & Jacob Sharff, McClung, Robertson, Jonas Hedges, Jacob Widdle, Pinkerton heirs. 31 Aug 1840 [By mail 16 Oct 1840]

E2-140: Surv.15 Mar 1838 by T.W.10,753 Joshua Hooper 95 A. in Rappahannock Co. adj. Anna Cox, Joshua Hooper, Mrs. Dean, on Peaked Mt., John Miller, Daniel Jackson. 31 Aug 1840 [Dl'd Mr. Strother 23 Dec 1840]

E2-141: Surv.9 Apr 1838 by T.W.13,042 Farmer Johnson 3 A. 1 Ro. 30 Per. in Rappahannock Co. adj. Tyler now Hopper, Harris, Turkey Run, Samuel Miller now Harris, S.fork of Rush R. 31 Aug 1840 [Iss'd Jas. F. Strother Esq. 3 Dec 1940]

E2-142: Surv.24 Nov 1839 by T.W.5535 George Fitzer 5 1/4 A. in Shenandoah Co. near Toms Brook adj. Christopher Wendel's 1750 patent, John Swan formerly Ulrrick Stoner, John Black. 30 Sep 1840. [Dl'd Mr. Williams 12 Dec 1840]

E2-143: Surv.22 July 1839 by T.W.12,616 Levi Gochenour 1 A. 1 Ro. 30 Po. in Shenandoah Co., Is. in N. Shenandoah R. 30 Sep 1840. [Mr. Williams 12 Dec 1840]

E2-144: Surv.26 Apr 1838 by T.W.9992 David McInturff 19 A. in Shenandoah Co. in Powells Big Ft. near Passage Cr. adj. said McInturff, David Ross. 30 Sep 1840. [Dl'd Mr. Williams 12 Dec 1840]

E2-145: Surv.25 Apr 1838 by T.W.9992 Solomon Veach 49 A. in Shenandoah Co. in Creare Ft. adj. S. Ft. Mt., said Veach, James Rouzee now Philip Funk. 30 Sep 1840. [Dl'd Mr. Williams 12 Dec 1840]

E2-146: Surv.11 Apr 1838 by T.W.9189 Elijah Estep 50 A. in Shenandoah Co. on Sup and lick Mt. adj. said Estep, Adam Barb. 30 Sep 1840. [Dl'd Mr. Williams 12 Dec 1840] [Dl'd Col. Cann 23 Dec 1840]

E2-147: Surv.13 June 1834 by T.W.10,948 Christian Huffman 44 A. in Hampshire Co. on high knob adj. Leonard Bomerotz, Adam Sulser, William Bomeratz, said Christian Huffman & his sons bought of John Foley heirs, Jacob Hartman heirs. 30 Sep 1840 [Dl'd Col. Vance 16 Mar 1841]

E2-148: Surv.28 Nov 1839 by T.W.2751 William Baker 88 A. in Hardy Co. on N. R. adj. William Reed, Lost R. hill, Samuel Baker, William Reed formerly Warden, Willson. 30 Sep 1840. [To Col. Mullen 3 Feb 1841]

E2-149: Surv.12 June 1837 by T.W.12,239 Abraham Constable 98 A. in Hardy Co. on Water Lick Run & Brushy Run adj. Ananias Constable, Fox Lick Run. 30 Sep 1840 [To Col. Mullen 3 Feb 1841]

E2-150: Surv.20 Mar 1835 by T.W.12,313 John Dyer 240 A. in Hardy Co. adj. his own land, heirs of Alexander Smith dec'd on Wardens Rg. & Flat Rg. 30 Sep 1840. [To Col. Mullen 3 Feb 1841]

E2-151: Surv.12 June 1838 by T.W.2751 Herbert & Andrew Dyer 17 A. in Hardy Co.

on N. Mill Cr. adj. Van C. Dawson. 30 Sep 1840. [To Col. Mullen 3 Feb 1841]

E2-152: Surv.9 Oct 1839 by T.W.2751 Simeon Detrick 14 A. in Hardy Co. on Fork Mt. adj. s'd Detrick, Deep Spring Surv. 30 Sep 1840. [Col. Mullen 3 Feb 1841]

E2-153: Surv.24 May 1838 by T.W.2751 Jacob Dietrick 108 A. in Hardy Co. on S. Mill Cr. adj. his own land. 30 Sep 1840. [To Col. Mullen 3 Feb 1841]

E2-154: Surv.12 Nov 1838 by T.W.2751 Henry Feaster 100 A. in Hardy Co. on Little Mt. adj. his own land formerly Bishop. 30 Sep 1840. [Col. Mullen 3 Feb 1841]

E2-155: Surv.3 Sep 1839 by T.W.2751 Jacob Hull 115 A. in Hardy Co. on Patersons Cr. adj. his land, Henry Black formerly Stephen Ross, Thomas George formerly Paul Hagerty, Gilpin. 30 Sep 1840. [Dl'd Col. Mullen 3 Feb 1841]

E2-156: Surv.9 Oct 1839 by T.W.2751 Felix Henkel 350 A. in Hardy Co. on S. Mill Cr. adj. his land, his McCord corner, Deep Spring Run, Detrick, Jacob Detrick, Sites, Nimrod Judy, Valentine Cooper, Judy heirs. 30 Sep 1840. [Dl'd Col. Mullen 3 Feb 1841]

E2-157: Surv.29 Oct 1839 by T.W.2751 Adam Harness 140 A. in Hardy Co. on Lounies Cr. adj. his land formerly Badgaly. 30 Sep 1840. [Dl'd Col. Mullen 3 Feb 1841]

E2-158: Surv.5 Oct 1839 by T.W.2751 Elijah Judy 100 A. in Hardy Co. on Fork Mt. adj. his own land, Woods & Green, Booer, Nimrod Judy. 30 Sep 1840. [Dl'd Col. Mullen 3 Feb 1841]

E2-159: Surv.30 Apr 1839 by T.W.11,207 Jacob Judy 54 A. in Hardy Co. on N. Mill Cr. adj. his own land. 30 Sep 1840. [Dl'd Col. Mullen 3 Feb 1841]

E2-160: Surv.29 Oct 1839 by T.W.2751 Benjamin Roby 160 A. in Hardy Co. bet. New Cr. & Little Mt. adj. surv. by James Machir. 30 Sep 1840. [Col.Mullen 3 Feb 1841

E2-161: Surv.20 Nov 1839 by T.W.2751 Henry Swisher 180 A. in Hardy Co. on N. R. & Little Rg. adj. Michael now Swisher. 30 Sep 1840. [Col. Mullen 3 Feb 1841]

E2-162: Surv.31 Oct 1839 by T.W.2751 Daniel Shell 225 A. in Hardy Co. on Little Mt. adj. his land, Feaster formerly Stingley, George Stingley, John Mays. 30 Sep 1840. [Dl'd Col. Mullen 3 Feb 1841]

E2-163: Surv.20 June 1838 by T.W.2751 Conrod Sites 48 A. in Hardy Co. on Eymans Spring Run of S. Mill Cr. adj. Harness formerly Eyman, N.N. line, Jacob Barkdall Jr. 30 Sep 1840. [Dl'd Col. Mullen 3 Feb 1841]

E2-164: Surv.12 Nov 1839 by T.W.13,070 David Vanmeter 500 A. in Hardy Co. on High knob adj. his own land, his Joseph Vanmeter surv., Garret Vanmeter. 30 Sep 1840. [Dl'd Col. Mullen 3 Feb 1841]

E2-165: Surv.10 Oct 1839 by T.W.2751 William Weare 26 A. in Hardy Co. on S. Mill Cr. adj. Solomon Weare, Abram Hinkel, his own land, Swamp Run. 30 Sep 1840. [Dl'd Col. Mullen 3 Feb 1841]

E2-166: Surv.2 Sep 1839 by T.W.12,226 Solomon Weare & William Weare 252 A. in Hardy Co. adj. Valentine Cooper, their own land on S. Mill Cr., John Rohrabar. 30 Sep 1840. [Dl'd Col. Mullen 3 Feb 1841]

E2-167: Surv.3 Sep 1839 by T.W.2751 William Willson 347 A. in Hardy Co. adj. Daniel McNiel/McMeill, Peter Hatton, Bishop, Black Oak Rg., S. fork of Patersons Cr. 30 Sep 1840. [Dl'd Col. Mullen 3 Feb 1841]

E2-168: Surv.7 Dec 1839 by T.W.2751 John Welton 187 A. in Hardy Co. bet. N. Fork & S. Br. adj. his land, Morgan Byrns heirs, R. Mt., Lancerco, Been. 30 Sep 1840. [Dl'd Col. Mullen 3 Feb 1841]

E2-169: Surv.10 Feb 1840 by T.W.11,043 John Lock 4 1/2 A. 8 Po. in Frederick & Clarke Cos. adj. Opequon Cr. Isaac Pedger?. 30 Sep 1840 [Col.Burwell 24 Feb 1841

E2-170:   Surv.13 May 1840 by T.W.13,010 Richard Caton asne. of Wm. Carroll 185 A. in Morgan Co. on Sideling Hill adj. Potomac R., George Catlett. 30 Nov 1840 [Sent to Prop'r 23 Feb 1841]

E2-171:   Surv.18 Apr 1840 by T.W.12,616 Isaac Boehm & John Copenhaver 48 A. in Shenandoah Co. adj. Alexander B. Feely, Daniel Funkhouser on Little N. Mt. 30 Nov 1840 [Dl'd Mr. Williams 12 Dec 1840]

E2-172:   Surv.10 July 1840 by T.W.12,361 George Lynn 35 A. in Hardy Co. on Capecapeon adj. Yost & Long, David Ogden. 30 Apr 1841 [Mailed to Prop'r 4 Sep 1841]

E2-173:   Surv.10 July 1840 by T.W.2751 George Lynn 150 A. in Hardy Co. on Chesnut Rg. adj. Babb & others, Pugh. 30 Apr 1841 [Mailed to Prop'r 4 Sep 1841]

E2-174:   Surv.14 Aug 1839 by T.W.11,051, 12,590, 12,589 & 14,172 William Boseley 248 A. in Hampshire Co. on Alleghany Mt. & Deep Run adj. said Boseley, Reuben Davis, John Boseley, William Thomas, Joseph Dixon.   30 Apr 1841 [Dl'd Col. Vance 31 Jan 1846]

E2-175:   "Mistake. Copied on page 174."

E2-176:   Surv.28 Feb 1840 by T.W.12,616 & 13,044 Henry Coulers 756 A. in Shenandoah & Warren Cos. in Powels Big Ft. on S. Ft. Mt., adj. Solomon Veach, said Coulers, Daniel Munch, Wm. Ellzey, John Clem dec'd, Adam Shearman, Michael Kniesley, John Shipes. 30 Apr 1841 [Dl'd to Recp't 7 Dec 1841]

E2-177:   Surv.25 Feb 1840 by T.W.12,516 & 13,044 Isaac Coverstone 242 1/4 A. in Shenandoah Co. in Powels Big Ft. on N. Ft. Mt. adj. Philip Kibler, Philip Fogle, Wm. Ellzey, Faisins run, George McInturff. 30 Apr 1841 [Dl'd Col. Crawford 14 Feb 1844]

E2-178:   Surv.27 Feb 1840 by T.W.13,056 Daniel Munch 124 3/4 A. in Shenandoah Co. in Powells Big Ft. on S. Ft. Mt. adj. Wm. Ellzey, said Munch, Philip Funk. 30 Apr 1841 [Dl'd to Rec't 30 Jan 1843]

E2-179:   Surv.27 Feb 1840 by T.W.13,089 John Shipe 41 1/4 A. in Shenandoah Co. in Powells Big Ft. on S. Ft. Mt. adj. said Shipe, Solomon Veach, Philip Funk, Peter Courston, Mill Run. 30 Apr 1841 [Dl'd Col. Crawford 14 Feb 1844]

E2-180:   Surv.23 Nov 1839 by T.W.7951 & 2751 John Strawderman 89 A. in Hardy Co. on Lost R. adj. Eli Lehew, Jacob Chrisman. 30 June 1841 [To Rec't 31 Jan 1842]

E2-181:   Surv.26 Aug 1840 by T.W.13,044 Isaac Boehm & John Copenhaver 133 3/4 A. in Shenandoah Co. on Little N. Mt. adj. said Boehm & Copenhaver, Daniel Funkhouser. 30 June 1841 [Dl'd to rec't 30 Jan 1843]

E2-182:   Surv.17 Nov 1840 by T.W.6989 John Hopewell 166 A. in Hardy Co. on Alleghany Mt. adj. his own land, Laurel Run, Hendrix Clark. 30 June 1841 [Dl'd to Rec't 21 Dec 1841]

E2-183:   Surv.12 Nov 1839 by T.W.10754 David Vanmeter 49 A. in Hardy Co. on Still house Rg. adj. his own land, James Miles, his Mercer surv., his Foley surv. 30 June 1841 [Dl'd Col. Mullen 31 Jan 1842]

E2-184:   Surv.11 Mar 1840 by T.W.8072 William Hedges 41 A. in Berkeley Co. on Third Hill Mt. and Tilehanse's Br. adj. Daniel Lunuster? formerly Margaret Pinkerton, Jacob Weddle, Jonas Hedges, James Robinson, Chs. & Jacob Coffinbarger. 30 June 1841 [Dl'd to Rec't 8 Dec 1841]

E2-185:   Surv.28 Mar 1835 by T.W.11,061 & 12,264 Jonathan Barrett 65 1/2 A. in Hampshire Co. on Pack's hollow adj. George Oats, said Barrett, Joel Ward. 30 June 1841 [Dl'd Col. Vance 31 Jan 1842]

E2-186:   Surv.24 Mar 1831 by T.W.10,489 Joseph Largent 73 A. in Hampshire Co. on N. R. Mt. & Nulls R. Mt. adj. John Largent, John Largent(of Lewis). 30 June 1841 [Dl'd Col. Vance 31 Jan 1842]

E2-187: Surv.18 Nov 1837 by T.W.12,936 & 12,899 Joseph Largent 18 1/2 A. in Hampshire Co. on Jerrys run of N. R. adj. his own land, John Copsey, Hiett. 30 June 1841 [Dl'd Col. Vance 31 Jan 1842]

E2-188: Surv.3 Apr 1840 by T.W.13,049 Jared McDonald 8 A. in Hampshire Co. on Great Cacapeon near Beck's Gap on Little Mt. adj. Joseph Cackley, George Stonaker, Twiford, Branson Parill. 30 June 1841 [Dl'd Col. Vance 31 Jan 1842]

E2-189: Surv.22 Apr 1839 by T.W.13,049 Jared McDonald 8 A. in Hampshire Co. on Sandy Rg. adj. his own land, Isaac Lupton, Joseph Cackley. 30 June 1841 [Dl'd Col. Vance 31 Jan 1842]

E2-190: Surv.2 Apr 1840 by T.W.13,049 Enoch Pennington 12 3/4 A. in Hampshire Co. on Lonanis Br. of Big Cacapeon adj. Samuel Milslagel, Samuel Davis, John Seivert heirs, Samuel Beckwith heirs. 30 June 1841 [Col. Vance 31 Jan 1842]

E2-191: Surv.14 Oct 1840 by T.W.10,507, 10,812 & 14,354 Jacob Ash 92 A. in Morgan Co. on Sleepy Cr. adj. Hodge, Jacob Courtney, Loman, Pendleton. 30 June 1841 [Dl'd Col. Orrick 8 Dec 1841]

E2-192: Surv.14 Nov 1840 by T.W.14,354 Absalom Kisler 26 A. in Morgan Co. on Potomac R. adj. Thomas Flora heirs. 30 June 1841 [Dl'd Col. Orrick 23 Feb 1842]

E2-193: Surv.5 Oct 1840 by T.W.10,852 Charles Hunn? 27 A. in Morgan Co. on Sleepy Cr., Sleepy Cr. Mt. adj. William Rankin, Matthias Swaim. 30 June 1841 [Dl'd Col. Orrick 23 Feb 1842]

E2-194: Surv.18 Nov 1840 by T.W.14,269 Overton A. Hieronimus & George Crowl 346 A. in Morgan Co. on Sleepy Cr. Mt. adj. Spratman, Hunter & Anderson, Bohrer, Newberry. 30 June 1841 [Dl'd Col. Orrick 10 Dec 1842]

E2-195: Surv.10 Oct 1840 by T.W.13,098 Simeon Rankin 82 A. in Morgan Co. on Sleepy Cr. adj. Keysicker, McKowan, Johnson heirs. 30 June 1841 [Dl'd Col. Orrick 23 Feb 1842]

E2-196: Surv.16 Nov 1840 by T.W.14,161 Peter Spratman 350 A. in Morgan Co. on Sleepy Cr. adj. George Bohrer, Hunter & Anderson, Newberry. 30 June 1841 [Dl'd Col. Orrick 23 Feb 1842]

E2-197: Surv.2 June 1840 by T.W.6952 & 14,261 Jacob Whitsle 34 A. 24 Po. in Frederick Co. adj. said Whitsle, M. Bean & Joseph Longacre, James B. Ha_?, John Whitsle heirs, Henry Wisecarrer. 30 July 1841 [By mail to surveyor 2 Oct 1841]

E2-198: Surv.14 Nov 1840 by T.W.12,885 James Burner 4 A. 2 Ro. 27 Po. in Shenandoah Co. on N. Fork of Shenandoah R. 30 July 1841 [To Rec't 30 Jan 1843]

E2-199: Surv.15 Feb 1840 by T.W.10,007 Charles A. Arrundle 1 A. 2 Ro. 34 Po. in Fairfax Co. on The Ase Rd. S. of said Co. C.H. adj. James Tillett, Loughborough now estate of John Arrundale dec'd, William Offritt, C.A. Arrundle formerly John Coffer. 30 July 1841 [Mailed to Prop'r 8 Sep 1841]

E2-200: Surv.18 Dec 1837 by T.W.12,366 Joseph Williams 200 A. in Hardy Co. in hills W. of Patterson's Cr. adj. his own land, John Cross, his Ryan surv. 30 Aug 1841 [Dl'd Col. Mullen 31 Jan 1842]

E2-201: Surv.20 July 1932 by T.W.10,422 Daniel Sites 193 A. in Hardy Co. This is copied see page 253.

E2-202: Surv.24 Apr 1840 by T.W.2751 George Fisher 250 A. in Hardy Co. on Cattale Run adj. his own land, Dr. Jacob Fisher, the Manor line, Pringle, Crites heirs. 30 Aug 1841 [Dl'd Col. Mullen 31 Jan 1842]

E2-203: Surv.21 Dec 1840 by T.W.10,852 Walter McAtee 100 A. in Morgan Co. on Spring Gap, adj. William Alderton, McCrackin, Coulston, Grindstone Mt. 30 Aug 1841 [Dl'd Col. Orrick 23 Feb 1842]

E2-204: Surv.24 Dec 1840 by T.W.7903 & 13,096 John P. Gardner asne. of James C. Higgins 48 A. in Morgan Co. on Lick Run & Sleepy Cr. Mt. adj. Tritafro?, Philip C. Pendleton. 30 Aug 1841 [Dl'd Col. Orrick 23 Feb 1842]

E2-205: Surv.10 May 1837 by T.W.12,791 Benjamin Ely 91 A. in Hampshire Co. on Little Cacaphon adj. Peter McBride, William Dougherty, Thomas Burkett, Samuel Berry, said Ely. 30 Sep 1841 [Dl'd Col. Vance 31 Jan 1842]

E2-206: Surv.12 Mar 1840 by T.W.14,234 William Duling 21 A. in Hampshire Co. on Abrams Rg. adj. said Duling, John Kelly, Duling's Matheny place. 30 Sep 1841 [Dl'd Col. Vance 31 Jan 1842]

E2-207: Surv.14 Apr 1840 by T.W.13,049 & 14,234 Joseph Martin 32 1/2 A. in Hampshire Co. on N. R. adj. his own land, Lord Dunmore heirs. 30 Sep 1841 [Dl'd Col. Vance 31 Jan 1842]

E2-208: Surv.27 Feb 1840 by T.W.12,791 & 10,772 Henry H. Leigh 105 A. in Hampshire Co. on Stony Mt. adj. George & David Hott, Margaret Leigh. 30 Sep 1841 [Dl'd Col. Vance 31 Jan 1842]

E2-209: Surv.27 Feb 1840 by T.W.14,172 & 10,772 Benjamin Corbin 180 A. in Hampshire Co. on N. R. & Grassy Lick Mt. adj. Jacob Park, Marquis Monroe, said Corbin. 30 Sep 1841 [Dl'd Col. Vance 31 Jan 1842]

E2-210: Surv.10 Nov 1840 by T.W.14,234 Andrew Shannon 24 3/4 A. in Hampshire Co. on Rg. bet. John Long's Green Spring Valley & Narny Wall, Chadwick heirs, Long formerly Savage, Thomas Baker. 30 Sep 1841 [Dl'd Col. Vance 31 Jan 1842]

E2-211: Surv.7 May 1840 by T.W.13,049 & 14,234 Eli D. Chadwick 82 1/4 A. in Hampshire Co. on Little Cacaphon adj. Ransom Day, Thomas Patterson, Little Cacaphon Mt., David Hains, Chadwick's Heiskill land. 30 Sep 1841 [Dl'd Col. Vance 31 Jan 1842]

E2-212: Surv.4 Mar 1940 by T.W.12,456 George G. Tasker 33 1/4 A. in Hampshire Co. on Abram's Rg. adj. George Baruck, Hooker heirs, William Duling, John Kelly. 30 Sep 1841 [Dl'd Col. Vance 31 Jan 1842]

E2-213: Surv.16 Aug 1834 by T.W.10,051 David Ellis asne. of John W. Largent 10 A. in Hampshire Co. on Great Cacaphon adj. Samuel Largent. 30 Sep 1841 [Dl'd Col. Vance 31 Jan 1842]

E2-214: Surv.19 May 1831 by T.W.10,539 David Ellis 51 A. in Hampshire Co. in Spring Gap on Spring Gap Mt. adj. Frances Farmer land she bought of Robert Rogers, Samuel Largent, Sutton, Jacob Jenkins heirs. 30 Sep 1841 [Dl'd Col. Vance 31 Jan 1842]

E2-215: Surv.11 Nov 1840 by T.W.13,049 James Abernathy 15 A. in Hampshire Co. on Campell's Mt. adj. his own land, George Calmes?, Abernathy bought of Smith. 30 Sep 1841 [Dl'd Col. Vance 31 Jan 1842]

E2-216: Surv.12 May 1838 by T.W.10,772 & 13,050 James Stewart Jr. 32 A. in Hampshire Co. on Tear Coat Cr. adj. George Warfield, William Morrow, Isaac Wolverton, Jonathan Pugh Jr. 30 Sep 1841 [Dl'd Col. Vance 31 Jan 1842]

E2-217: Surv.27 Aug 1840 by T.W.14,202 James Stewart Jr. 50 A. on forked Knob & Bear Knob adj. Philip Moore, William Mills heirs. 30 Sep 1841 [Dl'd Col. Vance 31 Jan 1842]

E2-218: Surv.26 Feb 1840 by T.W.13,050 Adam Rudloph 2 A. in Hampshire Co. on Little Cacaphon adj. his own land, Thomas Ruckman. 30 Sep 1841 [Dl'd Col. Vance 31 Jan 1842]

E2-219: Surv.4 May 1840 by T.W. 7968, 7268 & 7419 Joseph Blackburn 300 A. in Hampshire Co. on Dry Run & Mike's Run of Patterson's Cr. adj. Joseph Arnold, Absalom Fox, John Vandiver, Christian Utt, Utt's heirs, McDonald. 30 Sep 1841 [Dl'd Col. Vance 31 Jan 1842]

E2-220:   Surv.7 May 1840 by T.W.13,049 Samuel Leatherman 40 A. in Hampshire Co. on Cabin Run adj. Elisha VanBuskirk formerly Stolabarger, Thomas Welch, Joseph Crosley, John Rogers, Peter Leatherman, Benjamin N. Roberts. 30 Sep 1841 [Dl'd Col. Vance 31 Jan 1842]

E2-221: Surv.12 Mar 1835 by T.W.10,640 & 12,264 Peter McBride 103 A. in Hampshire Co. on Little Cacaphon adj. Benjamin Ely. 30 Sep 1841 [Dl'd Col. Vance 31 Jan 1842]

E2-222: Surv.11 Nov 1840 by T.W.12,899 & 14,360 John Vandiver 93 A. in Hampshire Co. on Dry Run adj. the Manor line, James B. Pugh & Co., George Hill, John Kabrick, Peter Good, Stephen Pilcher. 30 Sep 1841 [Dl'd Col. Vance 31 Jan 1842]

E2-223: Surv.27 Aug 1840 by T.W.12,565 John Lear asne. of Abraham Lear 25 A. in Hampshire Co. on S. Br. of Potomac adj. Isaac Pancake, William Mills heirs, Thomas Taylor Jr. 30 Sep 1841 [Dl'd Col. Vance 31 Jan 1842]

E2-224:   Surv.10 Feb 1841 by T.W.14,172 & 14,234 Stephen Hannah 151 A. in Hampshire Co. on Little Cacapon adj. William Foreman, James Moerhead, Richard Hall, John J. Pownak. 30 Sep 1841 [Dl'd to Col. Vance per order 29 Oct 1841]

E2-225: Surv.13 Jan 1841 by T.W.13,049 Stephen Hannah 10 A. in Hampshire Co. on Little Cacaphon, on N.W. Turnpike Rd. S.E. of Romney adj. William Foreman, John Powelson. 30 Sep 1841 [Dl'd Col. Vance 31 Jan 1842]

E2-226:   Surv.23 Oct 1840 by T.W.14,172 Silas Rees & Reason Harvey 22 3/4 A. in Hampshire Co. on N. Br. of Potomac in Alleghany Mt. adj. Edward Smith, Samuel Harvey, ___ Roberts, Bell's bottom. 30 Sep 1841 [Dl'd Col. Vance 31 Jan 1842]

E2-227:   Surv.4 May 1837 by T.W.12,791 & 12,899 Branson Peters 113 A. in Hampshire Co. on Tear Coat Cr. adj. Aaron Rogers, William Loy, Gravelly lick run, George Haw. 30 Sep 1841 [Dl'd Col. Vance 31 Jan 1842]

E2-228:   Surv.6 Apr 1840 by T.W.12,952 Joseph Huffman 80 A. in Hampshire Co. on Marshall's Rg. adj. Peter Poland, John W. Simpson, Lock's heirs, said Huffman. 30 Sep 1841 [Dl'd Col. Vance 31 Jan 1842]

E2-229:   Surv.23 Oct 1840 by T.W.14,172 Siles Rees & Reason Harvey 44 1/4 A. in Hampshire Co. on Alleghany Mt. adj. Edward Smith & others, Cooper. 30 Sep 1841 [Dl'd Col. Vance 31 Jan 1842]

E2-230:   Surv.6 Apr 1840 by T.W.13,049 & 14,234 Peter Poland 131 A. in Hampshire Co. on Marshall's Rg. & Mud lick run, adj. his own land, John W. Simpson. 30 Sep 1841 [Dl'd Col. Vance 31 Jan 1842]

E2-231:   Surv.3 Aug 1835 by T.W.10,051 & 10,602 John W. Largent asne of James Largent 112 A. in Hampshire Co. on Great Cacaphon adj. Robert Sherrard, John W. Largent, John Simpson. 30 Sep 1841 [Dl'd Col. Vance 31 Jan 1842]

E2-232:   Surv.27 Apr 1840 by T.W.14,258 William Partlow 23 A. in Rappahannock Co. on Blue Rg. adj. Elisha Partlow. 30 Sep 1841 [Dl'd Mr. John Green 2 Mar 1843]

E2-233: Surv.28 Apr 1840 by T.W. 14,258 Elisha Partlow 93 A. in Rappahannock Co. on Gravelly Spring of Rush R. & Blue Rg. 30 Sep 1841 [John Green 2 Mar 1843]

E2-234: Surv.27 Apr 1840 by T.W.14,258 Elisha Partlow 58 A. in Rappahannock Co. adj. Polly Richardson, Isham Cornwell. 30 Sep 1841 [Dl'd Mr. John Green 2 Mar 1843] (Surveyor made a mistake. It should be 38 A. instead of 58)

E2-235:   Surv.23 Aug 1834 by T.W.12,239 Abram Roby 47 A. in Hardy Co. adj. Elizabeth Vanmeter, Abram Arnold on Paterson's Cr. Mt., Joseph Arnold. 30 Sep 1841 [Dl'd Col. Mullen 31 Jan 1842]

E2-236:   Surv.17 Dec 1837 by T.W.10,442 Jesse Landes 310 A. in Hardy Co. on N. Mill Cr. opposite Nicholas Judy. 30 Sep 1841 [Dl'd Col. Mullen 31 Jan 1842]

E2-237:   Surv.14 Apr 1840 by T.W.2751 Joseph McNamar 125 A. in Hardy Co. on New Cr. Mt. adj. his land, John Harris. 30 Sep 1841 [Dl'd Col. Mullen 31 Jan 1842]

E2-238:   Surv.18 Sep 1840 by T.W.2751 Joseph Arnold 220 A. in Hardy Co. on Patterson's Cr. Mt. adj. his own land, Fravel, his Foley surv., the Elk ponds. 30 Sep 1841 [Dl'd Col. Mullen 31 Jan 1842]

E2-239:   Surv.5 Oct 1840 by T.W.2751 Elijah Wease 74 A. in Hardy Co. on S. Mill Cr. adj. his own land, Hours, William & Solomon Wease. 30 Sep 1841 [Dl'd Col. Mullen 31 Jan 1842]

E2-240:   Surv.1 May 1840 by T.W.2751 Cephas Childs 17 A. in Hardy Co. on Lost R. adj. his own land, Baker's heirs, Inskeep, Johnson (now his own). 30 Sep 1841 [Dl'd to rec't 31 Jan 1842]

E2-241:   Surv.9 May 1837 by T.W.12,734 Samuel Bean 10 A. in Hardy Co. on Sagg's run adj. his land, John Birch, Thomas Birch. 30 Sep 1841 [To rec't 31 Jan 1842]

E2-242:   Surv.3 Mar 1840 by T.W.12,589 & 14,234 James Paris 114 A. in Hampshire Co. on Abrams Rg. adj. the Canby field, Angus W. McDonald, Brian Bruin, Duff Green, N. Kuykendall, William Duling heirs, said Paris. 30 Sep 1841 [Dl'd Col. Vance 31 Jan 1842]

E2-243:   Surv.3 Mar 1840 by T.W.13,049 & 14,234 James Paris 36 A. in Hampshire Co. on New Cr. Mt. & Mauk's run, adj. Jenny's heirs, said Paris, Angus W. McDonald, Brian Bruin. 30 Sep 1841 [Dl'd Col. Vance 31 Jan 1842]

E2-244:   Surv.9 Nov 1837 by T.W.12,899 Mitchell Mills asne. of Jacob Shockey 50 A. in Hampshire Co. on S. Br. of Potomac adj. Philip Moore bought of Abraham Vanmeter. 30 Sep 1841 [Dl'd Col. Vance 31 Jan 1842]

E2-245:   Surv.5 Oct 1837 by T.W.12,589 & 12,936 Thomas Blue & Stephen Bird 144 A. in Hampshire Co. on S. Br. of Potomac adj. said Blue, John Myers, S. Br. Mt., Simon Taylor. 30 June 1841 [Dl'd to me 7 Aug 1841 S. D. Brady]

E2-246:   Surv.14 Nov 1837 by T.W.10,373, 12,589 & 12,936 Stephen Bird 83 A. in Hampshire Co. on S. Br. of Potomac adj. Simon Taylor, William F. Taylor, James Watson. 30 June 1841 [Dl'd to me 7 Aug 1841 S. D. Brady]

E2-247:   Surv.23 July 1836 by T.W.10,422 John See 80 A. in Hardy Co. adj. George Edmund See, his own land on Lost R. opposite Rush lick run. 12 Jan 1842 [Dl'd Maj. Shook 15 Jan 1842]

E2-248:   Surv.1 Sep 1840 by T.W.14,240 William Miller 240 A. in Hardy Co. on Saw Mill Mt. & S. Br. adj. Kuykendall & others, Wharton now Miller. 31 Jan 1842 [Dl'd Col. Vance 19 Feb 1842]

E2-249:   Surv.2 Dec 1840 by T.W.14,240 David Vanmeter 295 A. in Hardy Co. on Saw Mill Mt. adj. his own land, Daniel McNiell, on S. Br., the Manner line, Tuckers run, the main Rd., his Folely tract, his Widner tract, his Gilchrist tract. 31 Jan 1842 [Dl'd Col. Vance 19 Feb 1842]

E2-250:   Surv.15 Dec 1838 by T.W.14,064 John Sherman 54 A. 2 Ro. 32 Po. in Frederick Co. on Crooked run adj. Stephen Grubbs, Colin Leach, David Devo, said Sherman formerly Dr. Dunbarr, Rd. from Newtown to Ninevah. 28 Feb 1842 [Dl'd Col. Byrd 22 Mar 1842]

E2-251:   Surv.21 Oct 1840 by T.W.14,234 Joseph Davis 62 A. 1 Ro. in Hampshire Co. on Alleghany Mt. adj. his own land, Robert Sherrard, John Vandiver, N. Kuykendall, Martin. 28 Feb 1942 [Dl'd Col. Vance 21 Mar 1842]

E2-252:   Surv.1 Apr 1840 by T.W.2751 & 1114 George Bean 50 A. in Hardy Co. on N. R. adj. Vanmeter, Thomas S. Davisson, David Vanmeter, Buckley, Tommy's hollow. 30 Apr 1842 [Dl'd Col. Miles 24 Mar 1843]

E2-253:   Surv.20 July 1832 by T.W.10,422 Daniel Sites 193 A. in Hardy Co. on

Middle Mt. & S. Mill Cr. adj. his own land, Cooper now Sites, Briggles. 11 Apr 1842 [Dl'd Jacob H. Fisher 15 Apr 1842]

E2-254: Surv.7 July 1834 by T.W.12,239 Joseph Arnold 110 A. in Hardy Co. on Patterson's Cr. adj. Miss Vanmeter, his own land, Pattersons Cr. Mt., Williams. 1 July 1842 [Dl'd to rec't 20 Dec 1842]

E2-255: Surv.12 Aug 1841 by T.W.2751 Jesse Davis 200 A. in Hardy Co. on New Cr. adj. his own land, Hilky, Kettle Lick Rg., Joseph Davis heirs, Hite, Ignatius Wheler. 1 July 1842 [Dl'd Col. Miles 8 Dec 1842]

E2-256: Surv.23 Nov 1839 by T.W.2751 William Danner 16 A. in Hardy Co. on N. R. on Bush's Rg. adj. his own land formerly Ohover, Gouchenhour. 20 July 1842 [Dl'd to rec't 10 Dec 1842]

E2-257: Surv.23 Nov 1839 by T.W.2751 William Danner 30 A. in Hardy Co. on Short House Mt. adj. his land, Samuel Gouchenhour. 1 July 1842 [To rec't 10 Dec 1842]

E2-258: Surv.13 Oct 1837 by T.W.12,841 Joseph Arnold 50 A. in Hardy Co. on Paterson's Cr. Mt. N. of the Elk Ponds. 1 July 1842 [To rec't 20 Dec 1842]

E2-259: Surv.13 Oct 1837 by T.W.12,841 Joseph Arnold 90 A. in Hardy Co. on Paterson's Cr. Mt. adj. his own land, blue John Roby. 1 July 1842 [Dl'd to rec't 20 Dec 1842]

E2-260: Surv.25 Nov 1841 by T.W.13,025 Jacob B. Keller 16 1/4 A. in Shenandoah Co. on Little N. Mt. adj. Good, the Co. line, Peter Wilts, Abraham Jones, John Hulva, Patrick OHenley. 1 July 1842 [Dl'd Col. Crawford 14 Feb 1844]

E2-261: Surv.15 June 1841 by T.W.12,968 Samuel Hopewell 65 1/4 A. in Shenandoah Co. in Powell's big Ft. on Stoney run adj. John Moore now Benjamin Blackford & son, Daniel McInturff. 1 July 1842 [Dl'd Col. Crawford 14 Feb 1844]

E2-262: Surv.16 May 1838 by T.W.12,934 & 13,050 Joseph Hannum 107 1/2 A. in Hampshire Co. on Lonam's Br. of Big Cacaphon adj. Jesse Anderson heirs, Thomas Racy heirs, John Sevier, John Reed, Amos Anderson, Amos Marker. 1 July 1842 [Dl'd Col. Blue 15 Feb 1843]

E2-263: Surv.17 Dec 1840 by T.W.14,355, 14,354 & 10,861 Christian Courtney 296 A. in Morgan Co. on Sleepy Cr. adj. Rankin, Keysicker, Sleepy Cr. Mt., near Pendleton, Sporr, said Courtney, Goodman. 1 July 1842 [To rec't 7 Dec 1842]

E2-264: Surv.15 Oct 1841 by T.W.14,508 Peter Yost 32 1/2 A. in Morgan Co. on Sleepy Cr. Mt. adj. Yost, Richard Wood. 1 July 1842 [Col. Yeache? 8 Dec 1842]

E2-265: 2 Dec 1841 by T.W.14,664 Algernon R. Wood 300 A. in Frederick & Hampshire Cos. adj. Wm. McIntire, Joshua Gore, St. John's Rd. from Sleepy Cr. to Col. Robert Sherrard's store, Thomas Nasmith, James Summerville. 1 July 1842 [Dl'd Col. Wood 9 Dec 1842]

E2-266: Surv.11 Sep 1841 by T.W.14,3267? Robert V. Lockhart 975 A. in Frederick Co. on N. Mt. adj. Mrs. Howard?, Frederick & Hampshire Cos. line, Joseph Hannum, Felix Good, Pinacle Mt., Gen. Josiah Lockhart, William Elliott, heirs of Thomas Brown, Jonathan Lovet. 1 July 1842 [Dl'd Mr. J. Lovet 14 Feb 1845]

E2-267: Surv.10 Mar 1841 by T.W.12,824 William Elliott 22 A. in Frederick Co. on Back Cr. adj. heirs of Thomas Brown, Gen. Josiah Lockhart, said Elliott. 1 July 1842 [Dl'd Mr. J. Lovet 14 Feb 1845]

E2-268: Surv.21 July 1838 by T.W.14,083 John Shierly 133 A. 3 Ro. in Frederick & Morgan Cos. on Brush Cr. adj. said Shierly, George Hail, Samuel Dailey & others, Winchester - Bath Rd. 1 July 1842 [Mailed Jos. Hackney Esq. 2 Sep 1842]

E2-269: Surv.22 Mar 1840 by T.W.2751 Gideon Morrow 95 A. in Hardy Co. on Middle Mt. adj. his own land. 1 Aug 1842 [Dl'd to rec't 18 Aug 1842]

E2-270:   Surv.17 Sep 1840 by T.W.2751 Pious Combs 315 A. in Hardy Co. on Big Rg. on Clalypole run of Lost R. adj. Link formerly Kons. no date! (This grant is defective the last course left out)

E2-271:   Surv.22 Dec 1841 by T.W.12,475 Isaiah Buck 187 A. in Morgan Co. adj. Boyd heirs, Brosires, Bechtol, Havermill. 1 Aug 1842 [Dl'd Prop'r 19 Oct 1842]

E2-272:   Surv.30 July 1841 by T.W.14,573 William Critton 279 A. in Hampshire Co. on Long Hill adj. Cornelius Vaunasdall, Silas Prather, said Critton, Keith's gap. 1 Aug 1842 [Dl'd Col. Blue 15 Feb 1843]

E2-273:   Surv.10 June 1840 by T.W.13,050 John Hall 26 1/2 A. in Hampshire Co. on S. Br. of Potomac adj. Christopher Heiskell, Stephen Calvin heirs, Radolph Hardy. 1 Aug 1842 [Dl'd Col. Blue 15 Feb 1843]

E2-274:   Surv.15 June 1841 by T.W.14,360 & 14,574 Walter McAtee 61 A. in Hampshire Co. on Spring Gap Mt. adj. his tract, Maccae line. 1 Aug 1842 [Dl'd Col. Blue 15 Feb 1843]

E2-275:   Surv.4 Aug 1841 by T.W.14,574 Bene S. Pigman 22 A. in Hampshire Co. on N. Br. of Potomac adj. said Pigman. 1 Aug 1842 [Dl'd Col. Blue 15 Feb 1843]

E2-276:   Surv.6 July 1841 by T.W.14,172 Reuben Davis 88 A. in Hampshire Co. on New Cr. & New Cr. Mt. adj. Silas Rees, William Duling, Josias Smoot, John's gap now Harrisson's Gap, Samuel B. Davis. 1 Aug 1842 [Dl'd Col. Blue 15 Feb 1843]

E2-277:   Surv.16 Aug 1841 by T.W.14,360 William P. Stump 28 1/2 A. in Hampshire Co. on S. Br. Mt. adj. Solomon D. Parker late Solomon Parker heirs, John Thompson, Benjamin E. Wills. 1 Aug 1842 [Dl'd Col. Sloan 23 Jan 1843]

E2-278:   Surv.16 Feb 1841 by T.W.10,373 & 14,234 Samuel C. Ruckman 75 A. in Hampshire Co. on S. fork of Little Cacapeon adj. Susan Cramer, said Ruckman, John Arnold, Corbin, John Nelson, James B. Watkins. 1 Aug 1842 [Dl'd Col. Blue 15 Feb 1843]

E2-279:   Surv.10 June 1840 by T.W.13,049 William McDonald 7 1/4 A. in Hampshire Co. on Little CapeCapon adj. Daniel Haynes, John Smoot, Joseph Snapp. 1 Aug 1842 [Dl'd Col. Blue 15 Feb 1843]

E2-280:   Surv.27 May 1841 by T.W.14,202 John Malick 16 1/2 A. in Hampshire Co. on Tear Coat Cr. adj. said Malick, Frederick Pepper, Henry Wolford. 1 Aug 1842 [Dl'd Col. Blue 15 Feb 1843]

E2-281:   Surv.5 Apr 1839 by T.W.13,050 Jacob Buzzard 10 1/2 A. in Hampshire Co. on Pine Cabbin run of Tear Coat adj. Henry Powell, Barney Kearn, Addison McCauley, Robinson heirs. 1 Aug 1842 [Dl'd Col. Blue 15 Feb 1843]

E2-282:   Surv.29 May 1841 by T.W.12,936 & 14,574 Edmund Buzzard 161 A. in Hampshire Co. on Little CapeCapon Mt. adj. George Thompson, Wm. Ely, Matthew Hare. 1 Aug 1842 [Dl'd Col. Blue 15 Feb 1843]

E2-283:   Surv.21 Oct 1840 byT.W.12,791 & 14,202 Andrew Bogle 67 A. in Hampshire Co. on Alleghany Mt. on N.W.Turnpike Rd. adj. Nathaniel Kuykendall. 1 Aug 1842 [Dl'd Col. Blue 15 Feb 1843]

E2-284:   Surv.12 May 1840 by T.W.10,373 Joseph Haynes 47 1/2 A. in Hampshire Co. on Little Cacapeon adj. Bald hill, William Vance, Abbet Carder, Thomas Malledy, Isaac Haynes formerly Drew, Heiskell heirs. 1 Aug 1842 [Col. Blue 15 Feb 1843]

E2-285:   Surv.8 Apr 1841 by T.W.14,202 & 14,360 Daniel Haines 351 A. in Hampshire Co. on Piny Mt. & N. R. on Grassy lick run adj. his own tract, Robert Davison, George Gilpin, Michael Millar, Horn Camp Run, Hott. 1 Aug 1842 [Dl'd Col. Blue 15 Feb 1843]

E2-286:   Surv.4 Aug 1841 by T.W.13,049 & 4,573 Bene S. Pigman 160 A. in Hampshire Co. adj. N. Br. of Potomac, his land. 1 Aug 1842 [Col. Blue 15 Feb 1843]

E2-287: Surv.11 Nov 1841 by T.W.14,623 Joseph Davis 85 A. in Hampshire Co. on Alleghany Mt. near Whitemans Lick Run adj. John Hoye, Edward Smith. 1 Aug 1842 [Dl'd Col. Blue 15 Feb 1843]

E2-288: Surv.26 Feb 1840 by T.W.10,772 Thomas Ruckman 75 A. in Hampshire Co. on Stoney Mt. adj. George Haws, Samuel Ruckman heirs. 1 Aug 1842 [rec't 7 Feb 1843]

E2-289: Surv.1 Apr 1841 by T.W.14,360 Daniel Taylor Jr. 43 1/2 A. in Hampshire Co. on Cabbin run of Patterson's Cr. adj. Samuel Hammack heirs, said Taylor. 1 Aug 1842 [Dl'd Col. Blue 15 Feb 1843]

E2-290: Surv.28 May 1841 by T.W.2751 Solomon Leatherman 190 A. in Hardy Co. on Mikes run of Patersons Cr. adj. Bacorn & others, Snips Rg., John Rotruck, Likins. 1 Aug 1842 [Dl'd Col. Blue 15 Feb 1843]

E2-291: Surv.10 Nov 1841 by T.W.14,234, 10,897 & 14,623 Joseph Davis & Francis Murphy 740 A. in Hampshire & Hardy Cos. on N. Br. of Potomac on Alleghany Mt., adj. John Hoye, Gibson & White, mouth of Stony R., Michel Hider heirs, George Cunningham. 1 Aug 1842 [Dl'd Col. Blue 15 Feb 1843]

E2-292: Surv.2 Apr 1841 by Surv.10,752 Jacob Miller Jr. 28 A. in Hampshire Co. on Knobley Mt. inc. head spring of Ash Cabbin run, adj. his own land. 1 Aug 1842 [Dl'd Col. Blue 15 Feb 1843]

E2-293: Surv.2 July 1841 by T.W.14,172 Reubin Davis 60 A. in Hampshire Co. on New Cr. Mt. adj. Josiah Smoot, N.W.Turnpike Rd., Henry Harrisson formerly Hider, Roe-lick run, Reubin Davis, Elias Jones. 1 Aug 1842 [Col. Blue 15 Feb 1843]

E2-294: Surv.21 June 1841 by T.W.13,049, 12,456 & 14,574 Benjamin Taylor 144 A. in Hampshire Co. on Potomac R. opposite mouth of Town Cr. adj. Isaac Taylor, the Baltimore & Ohio Railroad Co. bought of James Allonder, Malcom's heirs, William Malcom, Simon Taylor. 30 Sep 1842 [Dl'd Col. Blue 15 Feb 1843]

E2-295: Surv.19 May 1838 by T.W.12,791 & 13,050 Harbert Park 18 A. in Hampshire Co. on Tear Coat Cr. adj. his own land, John Peters, Dunmore heirs, Uriah Cheshire. 30 Sep 1842 [Dl'd Col. Blue 15 Feb 1843]

E2-296: Surv.20 Mar 1837 by T.W.12,791 Augustus J.? Stump 57 A. in Hampshire Co. on Little Cacaphon adj. George Sharfe, Daniel Williams, James Meekins. 30 Sep 1842 [Dl'd Col. Blue 15 Feb 1843]

E2-297: Surv.27 Feb 1840 by T.W.13,050 & 14,234 Joseph Haines Jr. 130 A. in Hampshire Co. on Stoney Mt. adj. Margaret Leigh, his own land, Henry H. Leigh. 30 Sep 1842 [Dl'd Col. Blue 15 Feb 1843]

E2-298: Surv.15 Mar 1838 by T.W.12,791 & 13,050 George & David Hott 418 A. in Hampshire Co. on Piney Mt. adj. their land bought of William Reed, Margaret Leigh, Daniel Hains. 30 Sep 1842 [Dl'd Col. Blue 15 Feb 1843]

E2-299: Surv.6 Apr 1841 by T.W.14,234 & 14,360 James Combs Jr. 100 A. in Hampshire Co. on Stoney Mt. adj. 175 A. surv. for George Haws 28 Sep 1837, French heirs, Levi Shaver. 30 Sep 1842 [Dl'd Col. Blue 15 Feb 1843]

E2-300: Surv.29 May 1841 by T.W.13,099 George Thompson 184 A. in Hampshire Co. on Chesnut Rg. adj. Robert Thompson, John Arnold, Thompson formerly Williamson, Edmund Buzzard, his Alexander tract. 30 Sep 1842 [Col. Blue 15 Feb 1843]

E2-301: Surv.7 Mar 1842 by T.W.14,742 Harrison Bowers 150 6/8 Sq. Po. in Frederick Co. adj. George Boston & others, said Bowers. 30 Sep 1842 [Dl'd Mr. John T. Wall 29 Nov 1845]

E2-302: Surv.7 Mar 1842 by T.W.14,670 Azariah Pugh 1/2 A. in Frederick Co. adj. William Elliott, Mrs. Stephens' heirs, Carter? & others, Daniel Carver. 30 Sep 1842 [Dl'd Mr. J. Lovet 14 Feb 1845]

E2-303: Surv.5 May 1837 by T.W.7134 & 2293 George Sevire 206 A. in Frederick

Co. on Brush Cr. adj. James Pine, Puffenburger, Job Dehaven. 30 Sep 1842 [Dl'd Col. Wood 9 Dec 1842]

E2-304: Surv.11 Sep 1841 by T.W.14,261 John Bowen 13 A. 27 Po. in Frederick Co. on Opeckon adj. John & Joseph Cayle, Benjamin Thomas. 30 Sep 1842 [To Col. Wood 7 Dec 1842]

E2-305: Surv.26 Mar 1841 by T.W.12,382 John Frestoe 5 A. in Page Co. bet. Jereymys run & Gap run near Benjamin Blackfords old ore bank, said John Fristoe, John & Martain Kibler, tract formerly Dolton's. 30 Sep 1842 [Dl'd Col. McPherson 17 Jan 1844]

E2-306: Surv.5 Mar 1841 by T.W.14,061 Peter Keyser 6 A. 3 Ro. in Page Co. on Shenandoah R. on the Mt. adj. Wesly Bell, Benjamin H. Wood, Peter Keyser. 30 Sep 1842 [Dl'd Col. McPherson 26 Feb 1844]

E2-307: Surv.6 Feb 1842 by T.W.12,382 Chirubim Hershman 2 A. 2 Ro. in Page Co. on Shenandoah R. adj. Cherubim Hershman purchase of Henry Fowler, George Dovell purchase of Christopher Keyser. 30 Sep 1842 [Dl'd Col. McPherson 26 Feb 1844]

E2-308: Surv.28 Feb 1839 by T.W.12,382 Isaac Koontz 9 A. in Page Co. on Shenandoah R. adj. Isaac Koontz, Ambrose Huffman, Daniel Koontz. 30 Sep 1842 [Dl'd Col. Strode Delegah. 6 Feb 1843]

E2-309: Surv.4 Mar 1841 by T.W.14,061 Peter Keyser 30 A. 1 Ro 35 Po. in Page Co. on Shenandoah R. and the Mt. adj. Peter Keyser formerly Odell. 30 Sep 1842 [Dl'd Col. McPherson 26 Feb 1844]

E2-310: Surv.20 Jan 1841 by T.W.19,121 Daniel Dovell 150 A. in Page Co. on Shenandoah R. adj. Henry Fowler, heirs of David Dovell dec'd, Joel Smith, big Foltzes run. 30 Sep 1842 [Dl'd Col. McPherson 26 Feb 1844]

E2-311: Surv.24 Feb 1841 by T.W.12,382 John Kite(s. of Henry Kite) 31 1/2 A. in Page Co. on Shenandoah R. adj. land Christian Kite dec'd bequeathed to his wife Agnes Kite, Cutlip Eariff. 30 Sep 1842 [Dl'd Mr.Strode 8 Dec 1842]

E2-312: Surv.22 Nov 1839 by T.W.2751 Samuel Gauchenhour 90 A. in Hardy Co. on N. R. adj. George P. Dawson, Danner, said Gauchenhour. 30 Sep 1842 [Dl'd Col. Miles 6 Jan 1844]

E2-313: Surv.6 Dec 1838 by T.W.12,382 Charles Weaver 125 A. in Page Co. adj. Charles Weaver, Philip Shaffer, path across the Blue Rg. at the Stoney man, Adam Sowers. 30 Sep 1842 [Dl'd Col. McPherson 26 Feb 1844]

E2-314: Surv.5 Sep 1839 by T.W.12,591 James Been 250 A. in Hardy Co. on Varvells Rg. adj. his own land, Thomas Marshal, Staggs run, David VanMeter. 30 Sep 1842 [Dl'd to rec't 20 Dec 1842]

E2-315: Surv.15 Apr 1837 by T.W.12,841 John Hawk 141 A. in Hardy Co. on Little Mt. called the Brown Place adj. his own land, his Bodkins surv. 30 Sep 1842 [Dl'd to rec't 20 Dec 1842]

E2-316: Surv.30 Mar 1837 by T.W.12,665 George Rorabau 79 A. in Hardy Co. on New Cr. Mt. adj. Brethed. 31 Oct 1842 [Dl'd to rec't 6 Jan 1844]

E2-317: Surv.22 Aug 1838 by T.W.2751 David Coler 50 A. in Hardy Co. on Lounies Cr. adj. his own land, Cyrus Welton, Jonathan Seymore, Thomas Seymore, Elzy. 31 Oct 1842 [Dl'd to rec't 6 Jan 1844]

E2-318: Surv.26 May 1838 by T.W.2751 Jonathan Keplinger 33 A. in Hardy Co. on Lounies Cr. adj. his own land, Feaster, Aaron Welton. 31 Oct 1842 [6 Jan 1844]

E2-319: Surv.15 Dec 1837 by T.W.6989 Michael Simons 16 A. in Hardy Co. on Middle Mt. adj. his own land, Hinkol, Michael Cofman. 31 Oct 1842 [Dl'd to rec't 9 Dec 1843]

E2-320:   Surv.23 May 1837 by T.W.12,734 Suffere Whitmer 55 A. in Hardy Co. on upper cove run & Cove Mt. adj. Adam Halterman, Machir. 31 Oct 1842 [Dl'd Col. Miles 6 Jan 1844]

E2-321:   Surv.5 Oct 1840 by T.W.2751 John Basley 32 A. in Hardy Co. on Patersons Cr. adj. his own land, Hershy, William Green Spring line. 30 Sep 1842 [Dl'd to rec't 20 Dec 1842]

E2-322:   Surv.22 Nov 1839 by T.W.2751 Samuel Gauchenhour 64 A. in Hardy Co. on N. R. adj. Henry Swishir, John Sperry, Ludwick formerly Gauchenhour. 30 Sep 1842 [Dl'd to rec't 6 Jan 1844]

E2-323:   Surv.27 July 1841 by T.W.2751 Benjamin Warden 40 A. in Hardy Co. on Lost R. adj. his own land. 30 Sep 1842 [Dl'd Col. Miles 6 Jan 1844]

E2-324:   Surv.22 June 1840 by T.W.2751 Abram Barb 120 A. in Hardy Co. on Buck Mt. adj. David Gouchenour, Mophasis. 30 Sep 1842 [Dl'd Col. Miles 6 Jan 1844]

E2-325:   Surv.22 June 1840 by T.W.2751 Abram Barb 47 A. in Hardy Co. on Cape-Capeon adj. Maphas, Earl &c, Gauchenhour. 30 Sep 1842 [Col. Barb 6 Jan 1844]

E2-326:   Surv.12 Nov 1840 by T.W.2751 Jonathan Keplinger 18 A. in Hardy Co. on S. fork of Lounies Cr. adj. his own land, Adam Harness, Aaron Welton. 30 Sep 1842 [Dl'd to rec't 20 Dec 1842]

E2-327:   Surv.12 Nov 1840 by T.W.2751 John Delawder 9 A. in Hardy Co. on Lost R. in the big cove adj. Fitzwater now his own, Basore, Jac. Halterman, Shireman, Sager. 30 Sep 1842 [Dl'd to rec't 20 Dec 1842]

E2-328:   Surv.24 Nov 1837 by T.W.12,841 Jacob Kitteman Jr. 140 A. in Hardy Co. on S. Mill Cr. adj. his land formerly Pettliyone, John Sites, Jacob Barkdall, Harness, Frederick Sites, Jacob Sites. 30 Sep 1842 [Dl'd to rec't 20 Dec 1842]

E2-329:   Surv.1 Mar 1841 by T.W.14,472 William Catlett, Absalom Barney & Isaac Finck 300 A. in Frederick & Morgan Cos. at the Capon Mt. adj. William McIntire, David New, George Sevire & P. Siler now William McIntire, Foxcraft & Thompson. 30 Sep 1842 [Dl'd Col. Wood 19 Dec 1842]

E2-330: Surv.9 June 1842 by T.W.2751 Abram Wimer 160 A. in Hardy Co. on Welton's Knob adj. Valentine Simmons, John Snodgrass, the Mannor, Adam Harness formerly George Harness, Able & Archibald Welton. 30 Dec 1842 [Col. Miles 6 Jan 1844]

E2-331:   Surv.18 Nov 1840 by T.W.2751 Joseph Tucker 50 A. in Hardy Co. on Pattersons Cr. & Little Mt. adj. Babb, Bishop, Middle Fork of Patterson's Cr. 30 Dec 1842 [Dl'd to rec't 6 Jan 1844]

E2-332:   Surv.18 Oct 1837 by T.W.12,939 Joseph Arnold 130 A. in Hardy Co. on Paterson's Cr. Mt. adj. his land, Vanmeter. 28 Feb 1843 [Col. Miles 6 Jan 1844]

E2-333:   Surv.22 Nov 1837 by T.W.12,591 Joseph Crites 245 A. in Hardy Co. on Elk horn run of S. Mill Cr. adj. Sites formerly Borer, Sites formerly Fisher, Crites, Parson heirs, Jacob Barkdall. 28 Feb 1843 [Dl'd to rec't 20 Mar 1843]

E2-334:   Surv.5 Aug 1842 by T.W.2751 Robert Gomes 68 A. in Hardy Co. on S. Br. and Powder Spring Rg. adj. Cunningham & Seymore formerly Eaton & Rinker, Hamilton. 28 Feb 1943 [Mailed to prop'r 3 Aug 1843]

E2-335:   Surv.21 Apr 1842 by T.W.14776 James Yowel 89 A. in Madison Co. on Quaker Run adj. said Yowel, Jones, German Mt., Gallihue, Christopher Yowel heirs. 28 Feb 1943 [Dl'd Col. Bank 13 Mar 1843]

E2-336:   Surv.25 May 1838 by T.W.2751 Joel Ketterman 12 A. in Hardy Co. on S. Mill Cr. adj. Frederick Sites heirs, Christian Rohrback, his own land. 30 Mar 1843 [Dl'd to rec't 6 Jan 1844]

E2-337:   Surv.2 Apr 1840 by Exg.T.W.2751 Sarah Wilkin 70 A. in Hardy Co. on Lost

R. and Kimsey's run adj. John Miller, Sarah Fout on Big Rg.   30   Mar   1843
[Mailed to A. Wilkins 26 May 1843]

E2-338:   Surv.19 Aug 1842 by T.W.2751 Moses Wilkins 159 A. in Hardy Co. on Lost
R. adj. Sarah Fout, Fravel, Chilcot, Coby.   30 Mar 1843 [Mailed to Aaron
Wilkins 26 May 1843]

E2-339:   Surv.28 June 1842 by T.W.14,343 Richard Caton 125 A. in Morgan Co. on
Sideling hill on Potmac adj. Pendleton, said Caton, Shepherd.   30 Mar 1843
[Mailed to prop'r 3 Apr 1843]

E2-340:   Surv.30 June 1842 by T.W.14,343 Richard Caton 38 A. 2 Ro. in Morgan Co.
on Sideling hill on Potomac R. adj. his land, Catlett.   30 Mar 1843 [Mailed to
prop'r 3 Apr 1843]

E2-341:   Surv.13 Apr 1840 by T.W.12,361 John Snodgrass 143 A. in Hardy Co. on
the knobs opposite Charles Knob Mt. adj. Welton formerly Miles, Adam Harness
formerly George Harness, Keller's Spring.   1 June 1843 [Col. Miles 6 Jan 1844]

E2-342:   Surv.12 Aug 1841 by T.W.2751 Sarah Fout 200 A. in Hardy Co. on Lost R.
adj. her own land.   30 June 1843 [Dl'd to Rec't 6 Jan 1844]

E2-343:   Surv.13 June 1842 by T.W.2751 George C. Harness & John G. Harness 204
A. in Hardy Co. on Right hand fork of Town Ft. run adj. their own land, Thomas
McCarty now Green Lee.   30 June 1843 [Dl'd to rec't 6 Jan 1844]

E2-344: Surv.13 June 1842 by T.W.2751 George C. Harness & John G. Harness 446 A.
in Hardy Co. on Dividing Rg. bet. Town Ft. run & Sulphur Spring, adj. John G.
Harness, Nevill, McCarty.   30 June 1843 [Dl'd to rec't 6 Jan 1844]

E2-345:   Surv.4 Sept 1842 by T.W.2751 John Huse 2 1/2 A. in Hardy Co. adj.
Alexander Scott, Benjamin Roby, Christain Keplinger, Kembles.   30 June 1843
[Dl'd to rec't 6 Jan 1844]

E2-346:   Surv.9 Sep 1842 by T.W.2751 Michael Leavy 200 A. in Hardy Co. on N. R.
adj. his own land & others, Bean, Pugh lick drain, Ananias Constable, Garrett
formerly Hefman.   30 June 1843 [Dl'd to rec't 6 Jan 1844]

E2-347:   Surv.18 Sep 1841 by T.W.2751 Martin Miller 57 A. in Hardy Co. on Lost
R. & Buck Rg. adj. Mathias Wilkins, George Miller, Big Rg.   30 June 1843 [Dl'd
to rec't 6 Jan 1844]

E2-348:   Surv.13 June 1842 by T.W.2751 George Miller 120 A. in Hardy Co. on
Kemseys Run of Lost R. adj. his own land, his Javel tract, Chambers, Mudlick
spur, his Blaze Robertson tract.   30 June 1843 [Dl'd to rec't 6 Jan 1844]

E2-349:   Surv.24 Aug 1841 by T.W.2751 Jacob McNamar 85 A. in Hardy Co. on Knobly
Mt. adj. Joseph McNamar, Harris.   30 June 1843 [Dl'd to rec't 6 Jan 1844]

E2-350:   Surv.28 Oct 1841 by T.W.2751 Solomon Michael 27 A. in Hardy Co. on
Pattersons Cr. Walkers Rg. adj. Nicholas Michael's heirs, his own formerly Lee.
30 June 1843 [Dl'd to rec't 6 Jan 1844]

E2-351:   Surv.4 Sep 1842 by T.W.2751 Solomon Michael 17 A. in Hardy Co. adj. his
own land, in N. fork Gap, Evans.   30 June 1843 [Dl'd to rec't 6 Jan 1844]

E2-352:   Surv.26 Aug 1842 by T.W.2751 William McDaniel 80 A. in Hardy Co. on
Lounies Cr. adj. William Snodgrass, the Ashly land, the Forge Tract, Mays.   30
June 1843 [Dl'd to rec't 6 Jan 1844]

E2-353:   Surv.23 Aug 1842 by T.W.2751 William McDaniel 30 A. in Hardy Co. on
Lounies Cr. adj. Adam Harness, Cyrus Welton, Costner, Elzy now Cyrus Welton,
Harness formerly Bidgaly, his own land formerly Geroge Shell.   30 June 1843
[Dl'd to rec't 6 Jan 1844]

E2-354:   Surv.19 Dec 1841 by T.W.2751 William McDonald 2 A. 3 Ro. 35 Po. in

Hardy Co. on Lounies Cr. adj. Snodgrass, Welton, Harness formerly Badglay, his own formerly Shell, Diamond lick run. 30 June 1843 [Dl'd to rec't 6 Jan 1844]

E2-355: Surv.17 June 1842 by T.W.2751 James Webb 366 A. in Hardy Co. on N. R. & Br. Mt. adj. John Evans, Thomas Burch, Covington Burch. 30 June 1843 [Dl'd to rec't 6 Jan 1844]

E2-356: Surv.22 Nov 1842 by T.W.14,623, 14,360 & 14,234 Joseph Arnold 221 A. in Hampshire Co. on Miles Run adj. John Vandiver, A. W. McDonald, Elijah Roberts. 30 June 1843 [Dl'd Col. Ward 9 Feb 1844]

E2-357: Surv.22 June 1842 by T.W.14,781 & 14,574 James Abernathy 197 A. in Hampshire Co. on N.W. run of S. Br. of Potomac adj. Grace heirs, Gurlett? heirs, John Earsom, William P. Stump. 30 June 1843 [Dl'd Col. Ward 9 Feb 1844]

E2-358: Surv.9 Aug 1842 by T.W.14,573 & 14,782 Isaac Baker & Randolph Largent 124 A. in Hampshire Co. on Devils Nose Mt. adj. the Potomac, James Taylor, Mary J. Taylor, Walter McAtee. 30 June 1843 [Dl'd Col. Ward 9 Feb 1844]

E2-359: Surv.29 July 1842 by T.W.14,782 Thomas Baker 198 A. in Hampshire Co. on Green spring Run of N. Br. of Potomac adj. John Donaldson, Nancy Wall, said Baker. 30 June 1843 [Dl'd Col. Ward 9 Feb 1844]

E2-360: Surv.10 Aug 1842 by T.W.11,105 & 14,781 Henry Cowgill 50 A. in Hampshire Co. on Town hill adj. George Moreland, John A. Cox. 30 June 1843 [Dl'd Col. Ward 9 Feb 1844]

E2-361: Surv.31 July 1842 by T.W.14,717 & 14,782 John Donaldson 222 A. in Hampshire Co. on Green Spring Run of N. Br. of Potomac adj. William Donaldson, Donaldson formerly Vance, Thomas Baker. 30 June 1843 [Col. Ward 9 Feb 1844]

E2-362: Surv.6 July 1841 by T.W.12,899 John Green asne. of Andrew Barnhouse 122 A. in Hampshire Co. on Alleghany Mt. adj. John Barnhouse. 30 June 1843 [Dl'd Col. Ward 9 Feb 1844]

E2-363: Surv.28 July 1842 by T.W.14,202 David Gibson 121 A. in Hampshire Co. on Patersons Cr. & The Mt. adj. Ward's heirs, Garrett Blue heirs, Keller heirs. 30 June 1843 [Dl'd Col. Ward 9 Feb 1844]

E2-364: Surv.18 Aug 1842 by T.W.10,362 & 14,782 Peter Jones 31 A. in Hampshire Co. on S. Br. Mt. adj. Thomas Taylor, Hoffman heirs, Kuykendall. 30 June 1843 [Dl'd Col. Ward 9 Feb 1844]

E2-365: Surv.6 Aug 1842 by T.W.14,781 & 14,782 Frederick Kerns 82 A. in Hampshire Co. on Spring Gap Mt. adj. George Stump, Ginnavan heirs, David Alderton, Neal's run. 30 June 1843 [Dl'd Col. Ward 9 Feb 1844]

E2-366: Surv.1 Apr 1842 by T.W.14,624 & 14,717 Nicholas Leatherman 129 A. in Hampshire Co. on Mile Cr. knobs & Piss ant Hill, adj. said Leathermsn's Sulser land, Philip Moor/Moore, John Rinker, Leonard Bumcrots. 30 June 1843 [Dl'd Col. Ward 9 Feb 1844]

E2-367: Surv.6 Apr 1842 by T.W.14,574 William Loy 30 A. in Hampshire Co. on Tear coat Cr. adj. Charles Doyle, John Horn, Shepherd, said Loy. 30 June 1843 [Dl'd Col. Ward 9 Feb 1844]

E2-368: Surv.10 Aug 1842 by T.W.14,624 George Moreland 200 A. in Hampshire Co. on Town Hill adj. his land, John Portmess. 30 June 1843 [Col. Ward 9 Feb 1844]

E2-369: Surv.13 Oct 1842 by T.W.13,049 Daniel McLaughlin 77 A. in Hampshire Co. on S. Br. of Potomac & Dobson's knob adj. Anna McLaughlin, William French. 30 June 1843 [Dl'd Col. Ward 9 Feb 1844]

E2-370: Surv.11 Aug 1842 by T.W.14,781 James McDonald 96 A. in Hampshire Co. on Town hill near Old Town Rd. adj. said McDonald, John Stump, Wm. Pool, John & Jeremiah Pool. 30 June 1843 [Dl'd Col. Ward 9 Feb 1844]

E2-371:   Surv.4 Aug 1842 by T.W.14,781 & 14,782 John Portmess 142 A. in Hampshire Co. on Town Hill adj. his own land, Shaw, James Allender, John Kepler, John Critton heirs. 30 June 1843 [Dl'd Col. Ward 9 Feb 1844]

E2-372:   Surv.4 Aug 1842 T.W.14,781 John Portmess 28 A. in Hampshire Co. on Little Cacapon adj. his own land, John Critton heirs, George Stump, John Moreland. 30 June 1843 [Dl'd Col. Ward 9 Feb 1844]

E2-373:   Surv.10 Oct 1842 by T.W.14,623 John Parker 29 A. in Hampshire Co. adj. Mill Cr., Edward Taylor heirs, Vause Fox. 30 June 1843 [Col. Ward 9 Feb 1844]

E2-374:   Surv.31 Mar 1842 by T.W.14,624 & 14,717 George Shoemaker & Isaac Foley 275 A. in Hampshire & Hardy Cos. on Long Lick Mt. adj. Shoemaker bought of Frederick Purgott, Hampshire furnace lands, Elisha Smith bought of David Gibson, Frederick High now Jacob Statton, High now Joseph Frazier. 30 June 1843 [Dl'd Col. Ward 9 Feb 1844]

E2-375:   Surv.16 Nov 1842 by T.W.14,720 Peter Dyche 35 A. in Morgan Co. on Warm Spring Rg. adj. Cromwell Orrick. 30 June 1843 [Dl'd Mr. OFerrall 9 Feb 1844]

E2-376:   Surv.27 Feb 1842 by T.W.14,159 Jacob Cann 100 A. in Morgan Co. on Sideling hill adj. Doyle, Caton. 30 June 1843 [Dl'd Mr. OFerrall 9 Feb 1844]

E2-377: Surv.27 Feb 1842 by T.W.14,159 Jacob Cann 100 A. in Morgan Co. on Great Cacapon Cr. adj. Bell, Dawson & others. 30 June 1843 [Mr. OFerrall 9 Feb 1844]

E2-378:   Surv.25 Nov 1840 by T.W.14,473 George Catlett 150 A. in Morgan Co. on Potomac R. adj. Tidball, Catlett. 30 June 1843 [Dl'd Mr. OFerrall 9 Feb 1844]

E2-379:   Surv.19 Nov 1842 T.W.14,653 Samuel Rankin Sr. 57 A. in Morgan Co. on Sleepy Cr. adj. Dawson heirs. 30 June 1843 [Dl'd Mr. OFerrall 9 Feb 1844]

E2-380:   Surv.23 Mar 1842 by T.W.12,844 Rezin O. Smith 9 A. 3 Ro 24 Per. in Fairfax Co. on Difficult run above the Little Falls adj. Thomas Lewis, heirs of Samuel Smith dec'd, Fairfax now Comodore Jones. 30 June 1843 [Dl'd Ira Williams Esq. 8 July 1851]

E2-381:   Surv.2 Mar 1842 by T.W.2751 Charles Snyder 132 A. in Hardy Co. on N. Mt. & Cove Run adj. Isaia Tusing, Cove Mt., Charles Snyder, Lee. 31 July 1843 [Dl'd to rec't 11 Dec 1843]

E2-382:   Surv.21 Mar 1842 by T.W.2751 Charles Snider 72 A. in Hardy Co. adj. his own land, Cove Mt. 31 July 1843 [Dl'd to rec't 11 Dec 1843]

E2-383:   Surv.2 Mar 1842 by T.W.2751 Isaac Tusing 145 A. in Hardy Co. on Lost R. & N. Mt. adj. Charles Snyder, Cove run. 31 July 1843 [Dl'd rec't 11 Dec 1843]

E2-384:   Surv.22 Apr 1842 by T.W.14,623 & 14,781 Abraham Doll 61 A. in Hampshire Co. on Mikes run Rg. adj. Thomas Dye, Thomas Ferebee, Dye's Fuller land, said Doll. 31 July 1843 [Dl'd Col. Ward 9 Feb 1844]

E2-385:   Surv.22 Apr 1842 T.W.14,781 Abraham Doll 19 A. in Hampshire Co. on Mikes run Rg. adj. said Doll, Thomas Dye's Fuller land, Dye's McDowells land. 31 July 1843 [Dl'd Col. Ward 9 Feb 1844]

E2-386: Surv.5 Sep 1842 by T.W.2751 Benjamin Cunningham 5 A. in Hardy Co. on S. fork adj. Felix Seymore, David & Garrett Vanmeter, the Manner line, Daniel McNiell. 30 Sep 1843 [Dl'd to rec't 6 Jan 1844]

E2-387:   Surv.11 Oct 1842 by T.W.2751 Henry W. Coler & George W. Coler 7 A. in Hardy Co. on Lounies Cr. bet. N. & S. fork of said Cr. adj. Cyrus Welton, Jonathan Seymour. 30 Sep 1843 [Dl'd Col. Miles 6 Jan 1844]

E2-388:   Surv.18 Mar 1842 by T.W.2751 Isaac H. May 90 A. in Hardy Co. in Upper Cove on Lost R. adj. Adam Halterman, Conrad Lager, Whitmer, Lindemood, Jenkins. 30 Sep 1843 [Dl'd Col. Miles 6 Jan 1844]

E2-389: Surv.25 Mar 1842 by T.W.2751 John Willson 40 A. in Hardy Co. on Lost R. adj. his own land, Mill Mt., Rounsville, Elswick. 30 Sep 1843 [Dl'd Col. Miles 6 Jan 1844]

E2-390: Surv.25 Jan 1841 by T.W.2751 Joseph Willson 70 S. in Hardy Co. on Mill Run of Lost R. adj. Mill Mt., his own corner, Michael Wise, his Elswick surv. 30 Sep 1843 [Dl'd Col. Miles 6 Jan 1844]

E2-391: Surv.4 June 1841 by T.W.2751 Aaron Seymour 65 A. in Hardy Co. on Lounies Cr. adj. Jonathan Seymour, Coler, Thomas Seymour, his own land. 30 Sep 1843 [Dl'd Col. Miles 6 Jan 1844]

E2-392: Surv.2 Mar 1842 by T.W.2751 Mary Snyder 33 A. in Hardy Co. in upper Cove on N. Mt. adj. Lee, the Sulpher Spring. 30 Sep 1843 [To rec't 11 Dec 1843]

E2-393: Surv.22 Feb 1842 by T.W.14,720 Jacob Ash 84 A. in Morgan Co. on Sleepy Cr. adj. Keysicker heirs, Shriver heirs, Clacomb heirs, Wolvington heirs. 30 Sep 1843 [Dl'd Mr. OFerrall 9 Feb 1844]

E2-394: Surv.6 June 1842 by T.W.14,739 Nancy Calvert 100 A. in Rappahannock Co. on Blue Rg. adj. Absolom Eastes, Nancy Calvert, William Jackson, Mrs. Francess Burgess, Marshall Johnson. 30 Sep 1843 [Dl'd Mr. Hedrick 11 Dec 1843]

E2-395: Surv.15 June 1842 by T.W.12,735 Solomon Henkle 3 3/4 A. in Shenandoah Co. on Massanotten Mt. adj. said Solomon Henkle, Adam Olinger, Wm. Week. 30 Sep 1843 [Dl'd Col. Crawford 14 Feb 1844]

E2-396: Surv.14 May 1836 by T.W.10,162 Silas Prather 25 A. in Hampshire Co. on Spring Gap Mt. adj. Cox, Sampson Henderson heirs. 30 Sep 1843 [Dl'd Col. Ward 9 Feb 1844]

E2-397: Surv.6 Apr 1842 by T.W.14,574 John Horn 5 1/2 A. in Hampshire Co. on Tare Coat Cr. adj. said Horn, Charles Doyle, William Loy. 30 Sep 1843 [Dl'd Col. Ward 9 Feb 1844]

E2-398: Surv.6 Apr 1842 by T.W.14,574 John Horn 5 1/2 A. in Hampshire Co. on Tare Coat Cr. adj. said Horn, William Loy. 30 Sep 1843 [Col. Ward 9 Feb 1844]

E2-399: Surv.1 Aug 1842 by T.W.14,782 John Myers 7 1/4 A. in Hampshire Co. on S. Br. of Potomac and S. Br. Mt. adj. his own land. 30 Sep 1843 [Dl'd Col. Ward 9 Feb 1844]

E2-400: Surv.13 Oct 1842 by T.W.14,782 John Myers 36 A. in Hampshire Co. on S. Br. Mt. adj. said Myers, Stephen Bird. 30 Sep 1843 [Dl'd Col. Ward 9 Feb 1844]

E2-401: Surv.14 Oct 1842 by T.W.12,936 Stephen Bird 46 A. in Hampshire Co. on S. Br. Mt. adj. Tully, Bird, John Myers. 30 Sep 1843 [Col. Ward 9 Feb 1844]

E2-402: Surv.30 Nov 1841 by T.W.2751 Philip Walker asne. of Lafinton Huffman 55 A. in Hardy Co. on N. R. adj. his own land. 30 Sep 1843 [Col. Miles 6 Jan 1844]

E2-403: Surv.18 Aug 1842 by T.W.2751 Solomon Leatherman 270 A. in Hardy Co. on Knobly Mt. adj. his own land, Stickley's Still house, Bacorn, Bly. 30 Sep 1843 [Dl'd Col. Miles 6 Jan 1844]

E2-404: Surv.2 Aug 1842 by T.W.12,936 Stephen Bird 17 A. in Hampshire Co. on S. Br. Mt. adj. Thomas Burkit, said Bird, Taylor, Haas & Baker. 30 Sep 1843 [Dl'd Col. Ward 9 Feb 1844]

E2-405: Surv.7 June 1842 by T.W.14,624 & 14,781 Richard Blue 147 A. in Hampshire Co. on S. Br. Mt. adj. said Blue, Samuel Larrimore, John Thompson, Newmantown Rd. 30 Dec 1843 [Dl'd Col. Ward 9 Feb 1844]

E2-406: Surv.19 July 1842 by T.W.2751 George Lynn 185 A. in Hardy Co. on Great Capecapeon adj. Isaac Strosnider, Williams, Clark, Jacob Kesner, Daniel Hacker. 30 Dec 1843 [Dl'd Col. Miles 6 Jan 1844]

E2-407: Surv.4 Aug 1843 by T.W.2751 Thomas Stingley 446 A. in Hardy Co. on Middle Fork of Patterson's Cr. adj. Cunningham, Peter Hutten, Hutton's Wilson land, Wilson, Cornwell, Lewis, Shrout, Jno. D. Miles & his own land. 29 Feb 1844 [Dl'd by mail to Prop'r 8 Mar 1844]

E2-408: Surv.18 July 1842 by Exg.T.W.2751 George Lynn & John Vance 155 A. in Hardy Co. on Slate rock Run of Great Capecapeon adj. Benjamin Williams, Clark, Rd. to Wardensville, James Ornduff, Funkhouser. 30 Apr 1844 [Rec't 10 Dec 1844]

E2-409: Surv.1 Sep 1842 by T.W.2751 Charles Linch 50 A. in Hardy Co. on Powder Spring Knob adj. Bullet & Higgins, Linch now George Harness, McCarty. 30 Apr 1844 [Dl'd Mr. Lee 10 Dec 1844]

E2-410: Surv.6 Apr 1843 by T.W.2751 Peter Babb 100 A. in Hardy Co. on N. Fork of Patterson's Cr. below Hazzard forge adj. Samuel Babb, James Miles, Harness & Turley Forge tract, Gilpin, Gilpin's George land, his own land. 30 Apr 1844 [Dl'd to order 10 Dec 1844]

E2-411: Surv.23 Nov 1840 by T.W.2751 Hugh Shillenburg & William Fout 600 A. in Hardy Co. on Allegany Mt. adj. Prier S. Roby, Burgess on Abrams Cr. 29 June 1844 [Dl'd Mr. Lee 10 Dec 1844]

E2-412: Surv.28 July 1843 by T.W.14,720 & 14,508 James King 128 A. in Morgan Co. on Grindstone Mt. adj. Alderton. 29 June 1844 [Col. OFerrall 10 Feb 1845]

E2-413: Surv.16 June 1843 by T.W.13,059 Wm. R. Ashby, Marcus C. Richardson, Thomas F. Buck & John Buck 123 1/4 A. in Shenandoah Co. in Powell's Big Ft. on Passage Cr. adj. Isaac Coverstone, the Ft. Rd., S. Ft. Mt. 29 June 1844 [Dl'd Mr. D. Stickley 2 Dec 1844]

E2-414: Surv.11 June 1842 by T.W.14,624 John & Jeremiah Pool 75 A. in Hampshire Co. on Town hill adj. William Pool, John A. Cox. 29 June 1844 [Dl'd Col. Sloan 2 Dec 1844]

E2-415: Surv.13 June 1842 by T.W.10,031 & 10,481 John Stump 80 A. in Hampshire Co. on Town hill adj. his own tract, John & Jeremiah Pool. 29 June 1844 [Dl'd Col. Blue 24 Feb 1845]

E2-416: Surv.12 Oct 1843 by T.W.14,712 Gen. John Mason of Clermont 230 1/2 A. in Fairfax Co. S.W. of Alexandria adj. Peter Fesler, Ezra Lunt dec'd now Samuel Lunt, Clermont now Mason, Josiah Watson now Rich. M. Scott, Benj. Dulany now Clermont tract, Scott & late Wm. Simms dec'd now Mrs. Reed one of heirs of Simms, Wm. Reed her son, Dennis Johnson, John T. Frible, Judge Cranch now Robert Jemison, Lunt. 15 July 1844 [By mail to Prop'r 16 July 1844]

E2-417: Surv.14 Nov 1843 by T.W.2751 William Branson 137 1/2 A. in Hardy Co. on Lost R., Fraivel's Run, Wilson's Run & the Big Rg., adj. Coby, Moses Wilken, his own land, his Baker surv. formerly Claypool. 10 Aug 1844 [To rec't 10 Dec 1844]

E2-418: Surv.13 Nov 1843 by T.W.2751 William Branson 278 1/4 A. in Hardy Co. on Lost R. & Little Rg. bet. Wilson's run & Fraivel's run adj. his land, his Fraivel land, his Baker land. 10 Aug 1844 [Dl'd to rec't 10 Dec 1844]

E2-419: Surv.14 June 1842 by T.W.2751 John Coby 65 A. in Hardy Co. on Fraivel's run of Lost R. & Big Rg. adj. his own land, Baker formerly Claypool, Miller's lick, Claypool's saw mill run. 10 Aug 1844 [Dl'd to rec't 10 Dec 1844]

E2-420: Surv.14 June 1842 by T.W.2751 John Coby 78 A. in Hardy Co. on Fraivel's Run of Lost R. & the Big Rg. adj. his own land. 10 Aug 1844

E2-421: Surv.17 Sep 1840 by T.W.2751 Pious Combs 315 A. in Hardy Co. on Big Rg. and Claypool's run of Lost R. adj. Link formerly Kens. 10 Aug 1844 [Dl'd Mr. Lee 10 Dec 1844]

E2-422: Surv.24 Nov 1843 by T.W.2751 Lewis Frederick 26 A. in Hardy Co. on Tearcoat run of Lounie's Cr. adj. Adam & Henry Cosner, Powell, his own formerly

Bishop, Eldsey. 10 Aug 1844 [Dl'd Mr. Lee 10 Dec 1844]

E2-423: Surv.24 Nov 1843 by T.W.6989 George M. Fisher 18 3/4 A. in Hardy Co. on Lounies Cr. adj. Samuel H. Alexander formerly Snodgrass and known as the Ratcliff land, Adan & Henry Cosner, Lewis Frederick formerly Bishop. 10 Aug 1844 [Dl'd Mr. Lee 10 Dec 1844]

E2-424: Surv.18 July 1842 by T.W.2751 George Fisher 100 A. in Hardy Co. on Walker's Rg. adj. his own land, Adam Harness formerly Valentine. 10 Aug 1844 [Dl'd Mr. Lee 10 Dec 1844]

E2-425: Surv.24 June 1843 by T.W.10,860 Peter Hutton 9 3/4 A. in Hardy Co. on Patterson's Cr. in Frasure Lick Hollow adj. his own land, McNeill, his Wilson land. 10 Aug 1844 [Dl'd to rec't 10 Dec 1844]

E2-426: Surv.16 Nov 1843 by T.W.2751 Abraham Link 154 1/2 A. in Hardy Co. on Lost R. adj. Wilson's run, Inskeep's run on Big Rg., Baker, Inskeep, Pios Cooms, Peter Cooms, Inskeep's Riddle surv. 10 Aug 1844 [Dl'd Mr. Lee 10 Dec 1844]

E2-427: Surv.1 Nov 1843 by T.W.11,006 Charles Lobb 20 3/4 A. in Hardy Co. on Dividing Rg. bet. Town Ft. run & Cornwall's run adj. John G. Harness's Nevill land, resurv. of Jno. G. & George C. Harness formerly McCarty, Jonathan Melton now Seymour, Lall. 10 Aug 1844 [Dl'd to Rec't 10 Dec 1844]

E2-428: Surv.27 Jan 1843 by T.W.2751 Solomon Michael asne. of Nicholas Michael 67 3/4 A. in Hardy Co. on Walker's Rg. & N. Fork of Patterson's Cr. adj. Henry Smith, heirs of Elisha Mooreland. 10 Aug 1844 [Dl'd to rec't 10 Dec 1844]

E2-429: Surv.3 Sep 1843 by T.W.2751 Nicholas Michael asne. of Solomon Michael 37 3/4 A. in Hardy Co. on Patterspn's Cr. & New Cr. Mt. adj. Henry Smith, Griffin. 10 Aug 1844 [Dl'd to rec't 10 Dec 1844]

E2-430: Surv.6 Jan 1843 by T.W.2751 Daniel Shell 140 1/2 A. in Hardy Co. on Lounies Cr., New Cr. Mt., Little Mt. adj. Philip Shell, Feaster, his own land, Feaster Herbough. 10 Aug 1844 [Dl'd Mr. Lee 10 Dec 1844]

E2-431: Surv.11 May 1843 by T.W.12,990 James Miles 9 3/4 A. in Hardy Co. on Hutton's run, Coal Mt. adj. Baker formerly Welton, heirs of William Heath dec'd, heirs of James Snodgrass dec'd known as Tibbs' land. 10 Aug 1844 [Dl'd to Rec't 10 Dec 1844]

E2-432: Surv.1 May 1836 by T.W.12,226 & 11,207 John G. Robertson 125 A. in Hardy Co. on Middle Mt. & S. Mill Cr. adj. John Mangold, Christain Roheabaw, his own land, Daniel Sites. 10 Aug 1844 [Dl'd Mr. Lee 10 Dec 1844]

E2-433: Surv.23 Oct 1843 by T.W.2751 Nancy Nipper 129 A. in Hardy Co. on Tearcoat Rg. bet. Tearcoat run & Brushy Run adj. Powell, Idleman, McNemar formerly Shepherd, Simmons, Frederick formerly Bishop. 10 Aug 1844 [Dl'd to rec't 10 Dec 1844]

E2-434: Surv.2 Aug 1842 by T.W.12,939 & 12,734 Joseph McNemar & George Fisher 250 A. in Hardy Co. on Alleghany Mt. & Abram's Cr. 10 Aug 1844 [Dl'd to rec't 10 Dec 1844]

E2-435: Surv.3 Nov 1843 by T.W.2751 Thomas Stingley 18 A. in Hardy Co. on Patterson's Cr., S. of Indian Grave hollow, adj. Hearshey, Jno. G. Harness, Peter Hutten, Hershey's Ross surv. 10 Aug 1844 [Dl'd to rec't 10 Dec 1844]

E2-436: Surv.12 Aug 1843 by T.W.2751 Thomas Stingley 38 1/4 A. in Hardy Co. on Main Rg. bet. S. & Middle forks of Patterson's Cr. adj. Henry Hearshey, John D. Miles, Miles' Smith land. 10 Aug 1844 [Dl'd to rec't 10 Dec 1844]

E2-437: Surv.16 Oct 1843 by T.W.2751 Thomas Stingley 267 1/4 A. in Hardy Co. on Patterspn's Cr. & Patterson's Cr. Mt. bet. Hearshey's gap & Phoebus' gap, adj. Hershey, Vanmeter, Samuel McMichen heirs, McNeill. 10 Aug 1844 [Dl'd to rec't 10 Dec 1844]

E2-438:   Surv.22 Oct 1838 by T.W.2751 Joseph Tucker 50 A. in Hardy Co. on Patterson's Cr. adj. his land, Cornel, Babb. 10 Aug 1844 [Dl'd 10 Dec 1844]

E2-439:   Surv.22 June 1842 by T.W.2751 David Tucker 72 A. in Hardy Co. on Mt. run of N. R. & Br. Mt. adj. Joseph Tucker, Alexander Evans formerly Obannon, Jonathan Burch's Rg. 10 Aug 1844 [Dl'd to rec't 10 Dec 1844]

E2-440:   Surv.12 Dec 1842 by T.W.12,734 Joseph Walker 101 A. in Hardy Co. on Little Mt. bet. N. fork & Middle Fork of Patterson's Cr. adj. heirs of Joseph Walker dec'd, Peter & Samuel Babb, Joseph Tucker, the Bishop land. 10 Aug 1844 [Dl'd Mr. Lee 10 Dec 1844]

E2-441:   Surv.15 June 1842 by T.W.2751 Mathias Wilkin 255 A. in Hardy Co. on Fraivels run formerly Scott's run of Lost R., Big Rg. adj. his own land. John Coby, Lee, George Miller, Martin Miller. 10 Aug 1844 [Dl'd rec't 10 Dec 1844]

E2-442: Surv.19 Aug 1842 by T.W.2751 Moses Wilkins 27 A. in Hardy Co. on Big Rg. adj. Chiliot, Mathias Wilkins. 10 Aug 1844 [Dl'd to rec't 10 Dec 1844]

E2-443:   Surv.14 June 1843 by T.W.6848 Henry Larrick 12 A. 3 Ro. 31 Per. in Frederick Co. on N. Mt. adj. Joseph B. Parker, William Rozenberger, Pealey Ramey, Hetrick. 10 Aug 1844 [Dl'd Mr. J. Lovet 14 Feb 1845]

E2-444:   Surv.26 July 1843 by T.W.14,449 & 6848 William Howard 60 1/4 A. in Frederick Co. on Hoge Cr. adj. James Cather, Gabriel Darlinton heirs & others, George Lukins, Pertlebaugh. 10 Aug 1844 [Dl'd Mr. J. Lovet 14 Feb 1845]

E2-445:   Surv.2 Oct 1843 by T.W.14,722 George D. Miller 3/4 A. in Berkeley Co. adj. heirs of Samuel Chenowith, West, his own land, William Kroesen, Henry Couchman. 10 Aug 1844 [Dl'd Encl'd to Jno. P. Kearfott 14 June 1849]

E2-446:   Surv.25 Nov 1843 by T.W.14,594 George Aullabough & Archibald Waugh 20 A. in Morgan Co. on Sleepy Cr. adj. Thornburg, Smith, Waugh. 10 Aug 1844 [Dl'd Col. OFerrall 10 Feb 1845]

E2-447: Surv.20 June 1843 by T.W.14,266 John Coverstone 10 1/2 A. in Shenandoah Co. on Passage Cr. in Powel's Big Ft. adj. said Coverstone, David McInturff, Gideon Clem, Joshua Clem. 10 Aug 1844 [Dl'd Mr. Crawford 24 Feb 1845]

E2-448:   Surv.21 June 1843 by T.W.12,968 Mary Conner 15 A. in Shenandoah Co. in Powel's Big Ft. on Passage Cr. adj. George & Daniel McInturff, land formerly Benjamin Blackford. 10 Aug 1844 [Dl'd Mr. Crawford 24 Feb 1845]

E2-449:   Surv.6 June 1843 by T.W.14,266 Abraham Funkhouser 5 A. in Shenandoah Co. on Stoney Cr. adj. John Basey, Jacob Funkhouser, Christian Funkhouser. 10 Aug 1844 [Dl'd Mr. Crawford 24 Feb 1845]

E2-450:   Surv.13 July 1843 by T.W.13,044 John Orndurff 14 1/4 A. in Shenandoah Co. on Cedar Cr. adj. Lorenzo & Washington Sibert formerly John Hamilton, Samuel Beam. 10 Aug 1844 [Dl'd Mr. Crawford 24 Feb 1845]

E2-451:   Surv.31 Aug 1842 by T.W.14,782 Robert Carmichael 7 1/4 A. in Hampshire Co. on N. R. adj. his tract, John Wolford, John Martin. 31 Aug 1844 [Dl'd Col. Blue 24 Feb 1845]

E2-452:   Surv.29 Feb 1840 by T.W.12,589 Charles Dial asne. of James Malick 24 1/2 A. in Hampshire Co. on Little Cacaphon adj. Charles Dial, Samuel Ruckman heirs. 31 Aug 1844 [Dl'd Col. Blue 24 Feb 1845]

E2-453:   Surv.12 June 1843 by T.W.14,897 John Delaplane 13 A. in Hampshire Co. on Little CapeCapen adj. Philip Swisher, Eli Delaplane, Sam'l C. Ruckman, Adam Rudolph, said Delaplane. 31 Aug 1844 [Dl'd Col. Blue 24 Feb 1845]

E2-454:   Surv.21 Feb 1843 by T.W.14,574 Isaac Lockwood & James G. Clark asnes. of Angus W. McDonald Exr. &c, 446 A. in Hampshire Co. on Patterson's Cr. & Mill Cr. adj. George Ludwick, Hampshire Furnace lands, Mud run, Colsten's Salt=peter

Cave tract, Bishop. 31 Aug 1844 [Dl'd Col. Blue 24 Feb 1845]

E2-455: Surv.16 June 1842 by T.W.14,234, 14,574, 14,623, 14,781 & 14,624 Samuel Larrimore 115 A. in Hampshire Co. on S. Br. Mt. adj. his own land, Richard Blue, John Thompson. 31 Aug 1844 [Dl'd Col. Blue 24 Feb 1845]

E2-456: Surv.18 Jan 1837 by T.W.12,264 John Mileson 10 1/4 A. in Hampshire Co. on Spring Gap Mt. adj. Richard Moreland, William Mileson. 31 Aug 1844 [Dl'd Col. Blue 24 Feb 1845]

E2-457: Surv.6 June 1843 by T.W.15,031 Philip Long 25 A. in Hampshire Co. on Plum Lick Run of Patterson's Cr. adj. George Lickliter, John Cranfice?, said Long. 31 Aug 1844 [Dl'd Col. Blue 24 Feb 1845]

E2-458: Surv.17 Jan 1843 by T.W.12,791 Alexander Poston 33 A. in Hampshire Co. on N. R. Mt. adj. Jacob Hammack, Hammack's Mill race. 31 Aug 1844 [Dl'd Col. Blue 24 Feb 1845]

E2-459: Surv.7 Dec 1841 by T.W.13,049 Robert M. Powell the Third 9 A. in Hampshire Co. on N. R. Mt. adj. Adam Loy, said Powell. 31 Aug 1844 [Dl'd Col. Blue 24 Feb 1845]

E2-460: Surv.13 June 1843 T.W.14,624, 11,105 & 15,031 Samuel C. Ruckman 239 A. in Hampshire Co. on Piny Mt. adj. Amos Poland heirs, Joseph Haines. 31 Aug 1844 [Dl'd Col. Blue 24 Feb 1845]

E2-461: Surv.7 Apr 1842 by T.W.14,623 & 14,781 David Hott 65 A. in Hampshire Co. on Hairy Mt. adj. said Hott, William French, Grassy Lick run. 30 Oct 1844 [Dl'd Col. Blue 24 Feb 1845]

E2-462: Surv.15 Aug 1843 by T.W.7151 Col. George Minor 28 A. 2 Ro. 15 Per. in Fairfax Co. on Potomac R. above Little Falls Bridge adj. Falls Bridge Turnpike Rd., Thomas Lee, Cloe Gordon's purchase of Turberville heirs, William Nelson Jr. showed corner of said Gordon's purchase, place shown by old Robert Reid as corner of Lee now Grants. 30 Oct 1844 [Dl'd to rec't 11 Dec 1844]

E2-463: Surv.24 Apr 1844 by T.W.10,523 Churchill Berry 2 3/4 A. in Rappahannock Co. on Bersy Bell Mt. adj. Robert Hisle, Rose & Lenith Dial, Hedgman Campbell, Mark Reid, Rose Deal. 30 Nov 1844 [Dl'd Col J. F. Strother 17 Jan 1849]

E2-464: Surv.16 Apr 1844 by T.W.12,664 William Carson 200 A. in Warren Co. adj. said Carson, John Carson asne. of Abraham Millar, heirs of John Catlett & Wm. R. Ashby dec'd agreeable to recent surv. by order of Warren Co., Alex. Machie & William Jennings, on Cabin run, the Rg. Rd., Charles Pierce, Raimy. 30 Nov 1844 [Dl'd Gen'l Carson 24 Dec 1844]

E2-465: Surv.20 June 1842 by T.W.2751 Jeremiah Veach 35 A. in Hardy Co. adj. Alexander Aurahood, Feaster, Jackson now Feaster. 31 Dec 1844 [Dl'd to rec't 12 Dec 1845]

E2-466: Surv.24 May 1842 by T.W.2751 Jacob Sites 4th, Jacob Gils & Abram Sites 43 A. in Hardy Co. adj. their own lands, Christian Rohrabau, Solomon Sites, Jacob Sites. 31 Dec 1844 [Dl'd to rec't 12 Dec 1845]

E2-467: Surv.8 June 1842 by T.W.2751 Adam Ketteman 138 A. in Hardy Co. on S. fork & Forked Mt. adj. James Gray, Sites, his own land, his Borer land, Daniel Sites. 31 Dec 1844 [Dl'd to rec't 12 Dec 1845]

E2-468: 30 June 1843 by T.W.2751 James Davidson 163 3/4 A. in Hardy Co. bet. Mud Lick Hollow & N. R. adj. Marshall, Wise formerly Davis, Arnold, Cunningham. 31 Dec 1844 [Dl'd Col. Charles Blue 24 Feb 1845]

E2-469: Surv.21 June 1844 by T.W.2869 Aaron Bechtol & John W. Breathed 920 A. in Morgan Co. on Dry Run adj. Gustin's heirs, Swaim, Shank, Ambrose, Smith. 30 Apr 1845 [Mailed to Mr. OFerrell 3 May 1845]

E2-470:   Surv.7 Feb 1837 by T.W.12,734 Conrad Sites 103 A. in Hardy Co. on S. Mill Cr. & Elk horn Mt. inc. the Cedar Knob adj. Sites land, Jacob Ketterman formerly Dehart, Eyman. 30 May 1845 [Dl'd to rec't 12 Dec 1845]

E2-471:   Surv.2 Oct 1844 by T.W.13,025 John Wine Sr. asne. of Henry Carrier 22 1/4 A. in Shenandoah Co. on Sup & Lick Mt. adj. Elijah Estep, said Carrier. 30 June 1845 [Dl'd Col. Crawford 13 Dec 1845]

E2-472:   Surv.30 May 1844 by T.W.14,266 Christian Comer 45 1/2 A. in Shenandoah Co. on Ft. Mt. adj. William C. Williams. 30 June 1845 [Mr. Denison 10 Dec 1845]

E2-473:   Surv.8 Oct 1844 by T.W.2751 Elijah Judy 111 A. in Hardy Co. on Middle Mt. bet. N. & S. Mill Crs. adj. Isaac Shobe formerly Strader, the manor. 30 June 1845 [Dl'd Mr. C.C. Lee 11 Feb 1846]

E2-474: Surv.24 May 1838 by T.W.2751 Solomon & Abraham Sites Jr. 55 A. in Hardy Co. on Water Ash Run of S. mill Cr. adj. their own lands inc. the Seder Knob, said Abram Sites. 30 June 1845 [Dl'd Mr. C.C. Lee 11 Feb 1846]

E2-475:   Surv.26 Mar 1844 by T.W.2751 Christopher Martin 82 1/4 A. in Hardy Co. on Salt spring Knob of Knobley Mt. bet. Thorn run & Salt Spring Run of Pattersons Cr. adj. heirs of Christopher Martin dec'd, heirs of Michael Liken dec'd, James Roberts, Sarah Reed, Robert Putnam, Liken formerly Noel & Reed. 30 June 1845 [Dl'd to rec't 12 Dec 1845]

E2-476:   Surv.14 Nov 1839 by T.W.2751 Elizabeth Sites 25 A. in Hardy Co. on S. Mill Cr. adj. said Sites, Christian Rohrback, Jacob Ketterman Jr., Harness formerly Elyman, Sites' Jordon surv., Richardson's run of S. Mill Cr. 30 June 1845 [Dl'd to rec't 12 Dec 1845]

E2-477:   Surv.27 Sep 1844 by T.W.2751 Henry Feaster 17 A. 112 Po. in Hardy Co. on Wolf Thicket bet. N. & S. prongs of Norman's run of Lounies Cr. adj. Veach, Orrowhood, Big surv. of Holmes, Gale & Harness, his own land. 30 June 1845 [Dl'd to rec't 12 Dec 1845]

E2-478:   Surv.9 May 1842 by T.W.2751 John Y., Elizabeth A., Rebecca M., Frances T., Jemima T., James A., Mary Matilda, & William M. S. Newhouse asnes. of James A. Newhouse 130 A. in Hardy Co. on Town Ft. run adj. Petty, his own, E. of the Waggon Rd., Cunningham, McCearty's run, Harness. 30 June 1845 [Dl'd Col. McNemar, Sheriff of Hardy Co., 12 Dec 1845]

E2-479:   Surv.16 Feb 1842 by T.W.2433 Isaac Dehaven 56 3/4 A. in Frederick Co. adj. George Swire, Strobridge heirs, Job Dehaven, Brush Cr. 30 June 1845 [Dl'd to rec't 5 Mar 1846]

E2-480:   Surv.9 June 1843 by T.W.2433 William & Josephus Mason 159 A. 1 Ro. 29 Per. in Frederick Co. on Brush Cr. adj. said Mason, McGowan heirs, Puffenbarger heirs, Burton, Old Warm Spring Rd., Jesse Colbert. 30 June 1845 [Dl'd Mr. Long 15 Dec 1845]

E2-481:   Surv.25 Jan 1844 by T.W.15,243 Jacob F. Seibert 16 A. in Frederick Co. on Back Cr. adj. said Seibert, George F. Dent. 30 June 1845 [Dl'd 2 Dec 1845]

E2-482:   Surv.10 Sep 1844 by T.W.15,243 & 6848 Jonathan Lovett 19 3/4 A. in Frederick Co. adj. his own land, William Millison, M.S. Lovett, Eli Hicks purchase of Lockhart, Millison's purchase of Giffin. 30 June 1845 [Dl'd A. R. Wood Esq. 31 May 1849]

E2-483:   Surv.13 Nov 1844 by T.W.15,273, 6848 & 15,425 James A. Russell 249 A. 1 Ro. 9 Po. in Frederick & Hampshire Cos. near top of N. Mt. adj. said Russell's Beaty surv. in the Little Cove, William Deakins, the Capon Spring Rd. 30 June 1845 [Dl'd Mr. Wall 2 Mar 1848]

E2-484:   Surv.7 Oct 1843 by T.W.15,031 John Ridgway 18 3/4 A. in Hampshire Co. on Big Cacapehon adj. Abram Brill bought of John Ridgway, McKeever heirs, Adam Kline. 30 June 1845 [Dl'd Mr. Asa Hiett 5 Feb 1846]

E2-485: Surv.30 Oct 1844 by 15,050 Samuel Arnold 19 A. in Hampshire Co. on New Cr. & New Cr. Mt.adj. Brian Bruen, James Inskeep, said Arnols. 31 July 1845 [Dl'd Mr. Asa Hiett 5 Feb 1846]

E2-486: Surv.7 May 1844 by T.W.15,031 & 15,270 John Brady 221 A. in Hampshire Co. on Middle Rg. adj. his own land, Carr, John Hoy. 31 July 1845 [Dl'd Mr. Asa Hiett 5 Feb 1846]

E2-487: Surv.10 May 1842 by T.W.14,360 James Carter 3 A. 20 Per. in Hampshire Co. on Pine Draft run of N. R. adj. John Carter, Andrew Emmit, George R. Dye. 31 July 1845 [Dl'd Mr. Asa Hiett 5 Feb 1846]

E2-488: Surv.20 Mar 1844 by T.W.15,031 Abraham Emmitt 4 1/2 A. in Hampshire Co. on N. R. adj. his own land, Joseph Smith, Jacob Hammock. 31 July 1845 [Dl'd Mr. Asa Hiett 5 Feb 1846]

E2-489: Surv.24 Sep 1844 by T.W.15,054 Philip Fahs 5 1/4 A. in Hampshire Co. on Two Lick run adj. his own land bought of Matthew Heare, Samuel Allen heirs, Wesley Iliff. 31 July 1845 [Dl'd Mr. Asa Hiett 5 Feb 1846]

E2-490: Surv.7 Apr 1842 by T.W.10,752, 14,623 & 14,781 William French asne. of John Hawse 34 A. in Hampshire Co. on Stony Mt. adj. William French, David Hott, Henry H. Leigh. 31 July 1845 [Dl'd Mr. Asa Hiett 5 Feb 1846]

E2-491: Surv.15 May 1844 by T.W.14,202 David Gibson 14 A. in Hampshire Co. on Mt. near mouth of Pattersons Cr. adj. his late surv., Henry Ward, Patterson Cr. Mt. 31 July 1845 [Dl'd Mr. Asa Hiett 5 Feb 1846]

E2-492: Surv.8 Apr 1841 by T.W.14,360 & 10752 John Hawse 41 A. in Hampshire Co. on Clay Lick run adj. his land formerly Nelson, John Lock heirs. 31 July 1845 [Dl'd Mr. Asa Hiett 5 Feb 1846]

E2-493: Surv.17 June 1843 by T.W.14,781 & 15,031 John Hannahs 58 A. in Hampshire Co. on Little Capecapon Mt. adj. Matthew Hare, James Patterson, Edmund Buzzard. 31 July 1845 [Dl'd Mr. Asa Hiett 5 Feb 1846]

E2-494: Surv.17 Sep 1844 by T.W.14,780 Elisha P. Heare 100 A. in Hampshire Co. on S. Br. of the Potomac adj. Saw Mill run, Elisha C. Dicks, Michael Miller. 31 July 1845 [Dl'd Mr. Asa Hiett 5 Feb 1846]

E2-495: Surv.3 May 1844 by T.W.14,897 Luke Kuykendall 13 A. in Hampshire Co. on Knob S. W. of Rd. from Kuykendall's Mill to Mill Cr. adj. Isaac Pancake, said Kuykendall. 31 July 1845 [Dl'd Mr. Asa Hiett 5 Feb 1846]

E2-496: Surv.13 July 1844 by T.W.15,031 & 15,270 Jacob Lear 109 A. in Hampshire Co. on Bear Knob adj. Nicholas Leatherman, James Stewart, said Lear. 31 July 1845 [Dl'd Mr. Asa Hiett 5 Feb 1846]

E2-497: Surv.6 Dec 1841 by T.W.14,202 & 14,624 William H. Moreland 32 A. in Hampshire Co. on Dillon's Run of Big Cacapehon adj. Jesse Pugh, said Moreland. 31 July 1845 [Dl'd Mr. Asa Hiett 5 Feb 1846]

E2-498: Surv.6 Oct 1843 by T.W.14,624 William Moreland 100 A. in Hampshire Co. on Park's Mt. adj. William H. Moreland, his tract of 126 A., George Oats, Jesse Pugh, Slonacre. 31 July 1845 [Dl'd Mr. Asa Hiett 5 Feb 1846]

E2-499: Surv.18 Apr 1844 by T.W.15,050 David Malick 47 1/2 A. in Hampshire Co. on N. R. adj. his own land. 31 July 1845 [Dl'd Mr. Asa Hiett 5 Feb 1846]

E2-500: Surv.18 Apr 1844 by T.W.15,050 Philip Malick 131 1/2 A. in Hampshire Co. on N. R. adj. Patterson, said Malick, David Malick. 31 July 1845 [Dl'd Mr. Asa Hiett 5 Feb 1846]

E2-501: Surv.1 May 1844 by T.W.14,239 & 15,270 Michael Miller 1322 A. in Hampshire & Hardy Cos. on Mt. S.E. of Trough, Little Mt. adj. Jno. Lockner, David Vanmeter, said Miller, Wm. Miller. 31 July 1845 [Mr. Asa Hiett 5 Feb 1846]

E2-502:   Surv.29 July 1844 by T.W.15,270 The Overseers of the Poor of Hampshire Co. 6 1/4 A. in Hampshire Co. on S. Br. Mt. adj. Wm. Mill's heirs, another tract of said Overseers. 31 July 1845 [Dl'd Mr. Asa Hiett 5 Feb 1846]

E2-503:   Surv.14 Jan 1845 by T.W.15,474 & 15,404 James Parris 85 A. in Hampshire Co. on New Cr. Mt. adj. James Inskeep, Brian Bruen now Parris, John Singleton heirs formerly Armstrong. 31 July 1845 [Dl'd Mr. Asa Hiett 5 Feb 1846]

E2-504:   Surv.13 May 1844 by T.W.14,717 & 14,360 John J. Pownall 257 A. in Hampshire Co. on S. Br. of Potomac adj. Isaac Pownall, Henry Cowgill, Edward Trickle, Bird heirs, Hass, Baker. 31 July 1845 [Dl'd Mr. Asa Hiett 5 Feb 1846]

E2-505:   Surv.14 Jan 1843 by T.W.14,782 & 14234 Peter Rawlings 162 A. in Hampshire Co. on Stovers Run of Patterson's Cr. adj. Peter Rotruck, Demcy Welch, Peter Thrush. 31 July 1845 [Dl'd Mr. Asa Hiett 5 Feb 1846]

E2-506:   Surv.6 Apr 1844 by T.W.14,781 & 15,050 Joseph Ruckman 46 A. in Hampshire Co. on Little Cacapeon adj. Susan Cramer, James B. Watkins, Harrison Watkins. 31 July 1845 [Dl'd Mr. Asa Hiett 5 Feb 1846]

E2-507:   Surv.14 June 1843 by T.W.15031 John Ruckman 305 A. in Hampshire Co. on Stony Mt. adj. Amos Poland heirs, Mauzey heirs, Philip B. Street. 31 July 1845 [Dl'd Mr. Asa Hiett 5 Feb 1846]

E2-508:   Surv.8 May 1844 by T.W.15,050 Wm. P. Stump & Wm. Walker 235 A. in Hampshire Co. bet. Green Spring Valley & N. Br. of Potomac on Round Bottom hollow adj. Holmes. 31 July 1845 [Dl'd Mr. Asa Hiett 5 Feb 1846]

E2-509:   Surv.7 May 1844 by T.W.15,050 & 15,270 William P. Stump 160 A. in Hampshire Co. on Middle Rg. adj. Holmes, Carr, Jno. Brady, John Hoy. 31 July 1845 [Dl'd Mr. Asa Hiett 5 Feb 1846]

E2-510:   Surv.2 June 1843 by T.W.14,623 William P. Stump 15 1/2 A. in Hampshire Co. on S. Br. Mt. adj. John Thompson, Solomon D. Parker, said Stump. 31 July 1845 [Dl'd Mr. Asa Hiett 5 Feb 1846]

E2-511:   Surv.2 June 1843 by T.W.14,360 & 14,623 William P. Stump 54 A. in Hampshire Co. on S. Br. Mt. adj. Robert Parker's heirs, an Island formerly Isaac Newman's corner, Uriah L. Blue. 31 July 1845 [Dl'd Mr. Asa Hiett 5 Feb 1846]

E2-512:   Surv.3 Mar 1843 by T.W.13,050 & 14,897 John Taylor asne. of Strother Gannon 214 A. in Hampshire Co. on Mill Cr. Knobs adj. FotherHouse Knob, Thomas Taylor, John Taylor, Catherine Gannon. 31 July 1845 [Mr. Asa Hiett 5 Feb 1846]

E2-513:   Surv.10 Dec 1844 by T.W.14,717 & 15,270 David Vanmeter 277 A. in Hampshire Co. on Abram's Cr. & Alleghany Mt. adj. said Vanmeter, McKim, Garrett & Jacob Vannmeter's Elk Garden tract, Emory's run. 31 July 1845 [Dl'd Mr. A. Hiett 5 Feb 1846]

E2-514:   Surv.14 Mar 1843 by T.W.2751 Joseph Arnold asne. of Robert D. Arnold 31 3/4 A. in Hardy Co. on Mud Lick & Elm Lick runs adj. Elisha Smith, Joseph Arnold, John Foley now Jacob Vanmeter, Henry Sulser, Huffman. 31 July 1845 [Dl'd Mr. C.C.Lee 11 Feb 1846]

E2-515:   Surv.12 Jan 1844 by T.W.2751 Covington Burch 90 5/8 A. in Hardy Co. on N. R. & Spring Lick Rg. adj. Webb, Buckley, his own land. 31 July 1845 [Dl'd Mr. C.C.Lee 11 Feb 1846]

E2-516:   Surv.11 Mar 1842 by T.W.2751 Benjamin F. Baker 160 A. in Hardy Co. on Lost R. adj. his own land, Wilson, his Davis Surv.31 July 1845 [Dl'd Mr. C.C.Lee 11 Feb 1846]

E2-517:   Surv.22 July 1844 by T.W.2751 Jacob A. Davidson 624 A. in Hardy Co. on Big Arn & S.E. side of Cobourn's Knob of Br. Mt., Mud lick run of Baker's Run adj. Burch, Davidson, heirs of Thomas Bobo dec'd, John Burch. 31 July 1845 [Dl'd Mr. C.C.Lee 11 Feb 1846]

E2-518:   Surv.15 Sep 1841 by T.W.2751 William Cobey 125 A. in Hardy Co. on Kemsey's Run of Lost R., on Laurel Lick Hill bet. Hunting Rg. & Buck Rg. adj. Miller, Lee. 31 July 1845 [Dl'd Mr. C.C.Lee 11 Feb 1846]

E2-519:   Surv.2 June 1842 by T.W.12,990 Cyrus Hutton 5 A. in Hardy Co. on S. fork adj. his own land. 31 July 1845 [Dl'd Mr. C.C.Lee 11 Feb 1846]

E2-520:   Surv.28 Mar 1844 by T.W.2751 John G. Harness 2 A. 1 Ro. 29 Po. in Hardy Co. on Pattersons Cr. adj. his own land, Peter Hutton. 31 July 1845 [Dl'd Mr. C.C.Lee 11 Feb 1846]

E2-521:   Surv.1 Aug 1844 by T.W.2751 Abraham Link 422 A. in Hardy Co. on Ruddle's run of Lost R. bet. Little & Big Ridges adj. Inskeep, Cooms formerly Bell, Clark, Childs. 31 July 1845 [Dl'd Mr. C.C.Lee 11 Feb 1846]

E2-522:   Surv.2 Aug 1844 by T.W.2751 Abraham Link 80 1/2 A. in Hardy Co. on Little Rg. & Ruddlel's run of Lost R. adj. Jeremiah Inskeep, the Ruddle tract, Kidner. 31 July 1845 [Dl'd Mr. C.C.Lee 11 Feb 1846]

E2-523:   Surv.26 July 1841 by T.W.2751 John Lockner 258 A. in Hardy Co. on Miller's Saw mill run of S. Br. bet. Br. Mt. & Little Mt. adj. his own land, his Poland land. 31 July 1845 [Dl'd Mr. C.C.Lee 11 Feb 1846]

E2-524:   Surv.26 Jan 1843 by T.W.2751 Solomon Michael asne. of Isaac Mooreland, Basil Mooreland, Elisha Mooreland & John Mooreland & in his own right 7 1/4 A. in Hardy Co. on N. fork of N. fork of Patterson's Cr. & Alleghany Mt. adj. Elisha Mooreland dec'd, Thomas Dent, Archibald Stewart, Chamber's 36,000 A. surv. 31 July 1845 [Dl'd Mr. C.C.Lee 11 Feb 1846]

E2-525:   Surv.3 May 1844 by T.W.2751 Sandford Y. Simmons asne. of Solomon Michael 715 1/2 A. in Hardy Co. on New Cr. Mt. bet. Hawk's gap & N. fork gap on Patterson's & Lounies Crs. adj. John Shell, Philip Shell, Daniel Shell, The Beverly Surv., the Lee Surv, the Bishop land, John Shell's Comb's land, Morgantown Rd., Ellzey. 31 July 1845 [Dl'd Mr. C.C.Lee 11 Feb 1846]

E2-526:   Surv.19 May 1838 by T.W. 2751 Daniel & Joseph Tucker 70 A. in Hardy Co. on Little Mt. & Lounies Cr. adj. Babb, Feaster, Morgantown Rd., Stingly, Philip Shell, John Shell. 31 July 1845 [Dl'd Mr. C.C.Lee 11 Feb 1846]

E2-527:   Surv.15 Oct 1844 by T.W.2751 Samuel Thomas 15 A. 136 Po. in Hardy Co. on Hutton's run formerly called Adar Swamp run bet. Coal Mt. & the Round Knob adj. Miles, heirs of Owen Thomas dec'd, heirs of Wm Heath dec'd, Simmons formerly Bishop, Snodgrass. 31 July 1845 [Dl'd Mr. C.C.Lee 11 Feb 1846]

E2-528:   Surv.31 Aug 1844 by T.W.11,201 Aaron Wilkin & Archibald Wilkin 6 5/8 A. in Hardy Co. on Kimsey's run & Lost R. inc. the Big hill adj. Fout, Lehugh, Wilson formerly heirs of Godfrey Wilkin dec'd, heirs of Joseph Wilkin dec'd. 31 July 1845 [Dl'd Mr. C.C.Lee 11 Feb 1846]

E2-529:   Surv.10 Sep 1844 by T.W.2751 & 7951 Henry Wise 60 A. 56 Per. in Hardy Co. on S. fork of N. R. & Warden's Rg. adj. his own land, heirs of Henry Gouchenour dec'd, his Simmon's tract, Smith's path. 31 July 1845 [Dl'd Mr. C.C.Lee 11 Feb 1846]

E2-530:   Surv.10 Apr 1844 by T.W.13,044 Tobias Eshelman 19 1/2 A. in Shenandoah Co. on Little N. Mt. adj. William Supinger & John Mowery, heirs of Wm. Allison dec'd, said Eshelman. 31 July 1845 [Dl'd Col. Crawford 13 Dec 1845]

E2-531:   Surv.11 Apr 1844 by T.W.12,968 John & Ephraim Mowery 62 1/2 A. in Shenandoah Co. on Little N. Mt. adj. Frederick R. Mowery, John Hockman, Isaac Beam, John Copenhaver, John Richards. 31 July 1845 [Col. Crawford 13 Dec 1845]

E2-532:   Surv.10 Apr 1844 by T.W.13,056 John S. Mowery & William Supinger 49 A. in Shenandoah Co. on Little N. Mt. adj. heirs of William Allison dec'd, Conrad Myley. 31 July 1845 [Dl'd Col. Crawford 13 Dec 1845]

E2-533:   Surv.28 May 1844 by T.W.12,937 Henry Ridenour 241 A. in Shenandoah Co. on Green Mt. in Powel's Big Ft., adj. David McInturff, Henry McInturff, Munch's Gap. 31 July 1845 [Dl'd Col. Crawford 13 Dec 1845]

E2-534:   Surv.16 Sep 1844 by T.W.14,720 Aaron Harlan 9 A. in Morgan Co. on Cacapeon Mt. adj. his own land, Richard Caton. 30 Aug 1845 [Rec't 2 Dec 1845]

E2-535:   Surv.16 Nov 1844 by T.W.13,057 John Young 13 A. in Morgan Co. adj. Sherar's heirs, Coulston. 30 Aug 1845 [Dl'd Col. Michael 16 Feb 1846]

E2-536:   Surv.5 July 1843 by T.W.14,720 Peter Spealman 23 A. in Morgan Co. on Little Mt. adj. Varnasdol, Hutchison. 30 Aug 1845 [Col. Michael 16 Feb 1846]

E2-537:   Surv.17 Sep 1844 by T.W.14,720 Adam Steinback asne. of Aaron Harlon 14 A. in Morgan Co. on Sideling hill adj. Richard Caton, Adam Steinback. 30 Aug 1845 [Dl'd to rec't 2 Dec 1845]

E2-538:   Surv.2 Mar 1842 by T.W.14,158 Charles K. Bruce & William Cross 400 A. in Morgan Co. on Canolaway hill & Rd. Rg. adj. Neely, Reynolds. 30 Aug 1845 [Mailed Jno. OFearral 12 Sep 1845]

E2-539:   Surv.5 Jan 1844 by T.W.14,720 Isaac Clark Jr. asne. of Joshua Clark 13 A. 3 Ro. in Morgan Co. on Sleepy Cr. adj. said Clark, McBee, Caw. 30 Aug 1845 [Mailed to J.D. OFerrall 29 Sep 1845]

E2-540:   Surv.30 Dec 1841 by T.W.14,354 Samuel Johnston 5 1/4 A. in Morgan Co. on Timber Rg. adj. Washington Unger, Henry Farber, John Bailie's heirs, William Cattlett heirs. 30 Aug 1845 [Dl'd Col. Michael 16 Feb 1846]

E2-541: Surv.30 Jan 1844 by T.W.12,929 Taliaferro Berryman 3 A. 1 Ro. 34 Po. in Fauquier Co. on Tinpot run adj. William Berryman purchase of William Bower, Cashenberry now William Franklin, Thornton now William A. Bowen. 30 Aug 1845

E2-542: Surv.23 Feb 1844 by T.W.2751 William Idleman 133 1/4 A. in Hardy Co. on Bald Rg. bet. Taylor's run or Long Hollow & Sugar Camp run of Vanmeter Mill run adj. Jacob Vanmeter, Cornwell, Taylor. 30 Aug 1845 [Mr. C.C.Lee 11 Feb 1846]

E2-543: Surv.20 Mar 1839 by T.W.12,264 Wilson McBride 40 A. in Hampshire Co. on Little Cacaponon Mt. adj. John Smith, Christopher Heiskill, Isaac Hains, Charles S. Taylor. 29 Nov 1845 [Dl'd Mr. A. Hiett 5 Feb 1846]

E2-544: Surv.2 May 1845 by T.W.15,579 Thomas W. Chapman 17 A. in Madison Co. on Quaker run adj. Bohannon, Yowell. 29 Nov 1845 [Mailed to Prop'r 16 Jan 1846]

E2-545:   Surv.17 Nov 1842 by T.W.14,720 Jesse Fryer 3 1/2 A. in Morgan Co. on Sideling Hill adj. D. Alderton, Richard Caton. 30 Jan 1846 [Dl'd Col. Michael 16 Feb 1846]

E2-546:   Surv.4 Sep 1842 by T.W.2751 Isaac W. Kuykendall 75 A. in Hardy Co. on Middle Mt. adj. Wease, the Mine surv. 30 Mar 1846 [Dl'd to rec't 20 Feb 1847]

E2-547:   Surv.22 Nov 1842 by T.W.14,698 Samuel L. Lewis 10 A. 3 Ro. 17 Po. in Fairfax Co. on Great Rocky Cedar Run called Talbott's old Mill Lot, adj. Capt. James L. Triplett. 30 Apr 1846 [Mailed to Alfred Moss 14 June 1850]

E2-548:   Surv.6 Aug 1844 by T.W.15,398 Nicholas Perkey 35 A. in Page Co. being an Island in S. R. 20 mi. S. of Luray. 30 May 1846 [Dl'd to rec't 6 Jan 1846]

E2-549:   Surv.20 July 1841 by T.W.2751 Isaac Groves 62 A. in Hardy Co. on Lounie's Cr. & Little Mt. adj. his own land formerly Bodkin & Brown. 30 June 1846 [Dl'd C.C. Lee 20 Feb 1847]

E2-550:   Surv.31 Mar 1845 by T.W.2751 Jacob Sites 66 7/8 A. in Hardy Co. on Mt. bet. S. fork & S. Mill Cr. called Buffetts or Richardson's Run adj. Getry, heirs of Frederick Sites dec'd, Rohrabaugh, his own & Co., Harness's Eyman land. 30 June 1846 [Dl'd to rec't 15 Dec 1846]

E2-551:   Surv.23 July 1844 by T.W.11,201 Valentine Simmons 418 3/4 A. in Hardy
Co. on Long Lick & Mud Lick of Baker's Run, on Hunting Rg. adj. Bobo's heirs,
John Burch, heirs of James Bean dec'd, Means, Burch's Bishop land, Hoggen. 30
June 1846 [Dl'd C.C. Lee 20 Feb 1847]

E2-552:   Surv.23 Feb 1844 by T.W.2751 John Cornwell 202 A. in Hardy Co. on
Patterson's Cr. Mt. adj. Taylor's run, Ashby's Spring run of Vanmeter Mill Run,
Jacob Vanmeter, his own land. 30 June 1846 [Dl'd to rec't 15 Dec 46]

E2-553:   Surv.18 Apr 1845 by T.W.4897 & 6184 John W. Murphy 195 A. in Berkeley
Co. on Telehances Br. adj. Joseph Harper, James Shields, John Siler, Davis,
Joseph Johnson. 30 June 1846 [Dl'd Mr. Boak? 8 Dec 1846]

E2-554: Surv.10 Mar 1842 by T.W.14,720 & 14,354 Samuel Johnston 47 A. in Morgan
Co. on Cacapeon Mt. 30 June 1846 [Dl'd Col. Michael 24 Mar 1848] Signature of
Governor affixed Sept. 20th, 1920. by Jno W. Richardson, Register of Land Office

E2-555: Surv.1 Feb 1845 by T.W.15,398 Gideon T. Jones 13 A. 1 Ro. 32 Po. in Page
Co. on main Rd. from Big Spring Meeting house to Milford adj. Benjamin H. Wood,
Joshua Wood, Bear & Jordan. 30 June 1846 [Sent to prop'r by mail 6 Feb 1847]

E2-556:   Surv.22 Mar 1845 by T.W.15,398 & 15,442 Samuel H. Shink 9 A. 2 Ro. 20
Po. in Page Co. adj. Shink's purchase of Benjamin Blackford & Sons Trustees,
wid. Ann Shink dower land. 30 June 1846 [Dl'd Mr. Tho's Bushnell 30 Apr 1848]

E2-557:   Surv.5 Sep 1845 by T.W.15,640 & 11,143 Cyrus W. Murray 14 A. in Page
Co. on S. R. near Luray adj. Lauderback, Reuben Fultz, Cyrus W. Murray, Bruin.
30 June 1846 [Mailed to prop'r 13 Aug 1846]

E2-558: Surv.19 July 1845 by T.W.15,243 Lewis P. Coontz 18 A. 2 Ro. 14 7/10 Po.
in Frederick Co. adj. Peter Bailey, James R. BrocKing, Henry Seever Jr., Mauk,
Sulphur Spring Rd. 30 June 1846 [Dl'd to Rec't 10 Dec 1846]

E2-559:   Surv.5 Oct 1841 by T.W.14,573 Jacob Jones 38 A. in Hampshire Co. on
Middle Rg. adj. Taylor's heirs, John Parker formerly Frederick Fink. 30 June
1846 [Dl'd Mr. A. Hiett 12 Mar 1847]

E2-560:   Surv.7 Apr 1842 by T.W.14,781 & 12,936 John Herbaugh asne. of Andrew
J.? Leigh 50 A. in Hampshire Co. on Stony Lick Rg. adj. Joseph Hains, Margaret
Leigh, David Hott. 30 June 1846 [Dl'd Mr. A. Hiett 12 Mar 1847]

E2-561:   Surv.11 Aug 1842 by T.W.14,781 Isaac Pownall 50 A. in Hampshire Co. on
Town hill adj. Henry Cowgill, John A. Cox, Geo. Moreland, John Stump, John &
Jeremiah Pool. 30 June 1846 [Dl'd Mr. Sloan 7 Dec 1846]

E2-562:   Surv.3 Jan 1845 by T.W.15,404 Joseph Martin 9 A. in Hampshire Co. on N.
R. adj. George Carter of Oatlands, said Martin, Joseph Huffman. 30 June 1846
[Dl'd Mr. A. Hiett 12 Mar 1847]

E2-563:   Surv.2 May 1845 by T.W.15,404 George Gilbert 52 A. in Hampshire Co. on
Middle Rg. adj. Gilbert, George Banes. 30 June 1846 [Mr. A. Hiett 12 Mar 1847]

E2-564:   Surv.13 May 1844 by 15,270 Henry Cowgill 3 3/4 A. in Hampshire Co. on
Town hill adj. said Cowgill, George Moreland, John A. Cox, Edward Trickle. 30
June 1846 [Dl'd Mr. A. Hiett 12 Mar 1847]

E2-565:   Surv.4 Jan 1845 by T.W.15,404 Joseph Huffman 8 1/2 A. in Hampshire Co.
on N. R. in Stack's Gap adj. said Huffman, Cutliffe heirs. 30 June 1846 [Dl'd
Mr. A. Hiett 12 Mar 1847]

E2-566:   Surv.20 June 1845 by T.W.12,936 & 15,554 Cornelius Vanosdal & Jeremiah
Vanosdal 136 A. in Hampshire Co. on Great Cacaphon adj. Doyle, Joseph F. Baker
h's, Daniel Kains, Daniel Royce 1796 grant. 30 June 1846 [Mr. Hiett 12 Mar 1847]

E2-567:   Surv.5 Sep 1844 by T.W.14,623, 14,781, 14,234 & 15,270 James Liller 145
A. in Hampshire Co. on Mill Run adj. Henry Liller, their Putman land, John T.

Hickman, Nathaniel Kuykendall, Edward Culp, Benjamin Rawlings, Liller's Elzey land. 30 June 1846 [Dl'd Mr. A. Hiett 12 Mar 1847]

E2-568: Surv.25 Aug 1845 by T.W.15,554 Levis Passmore 325 A, in Hampshire Co. on Bloomery Run of Great Cacaphon R. & Mt. S.E. of said R. adj. John Copsey, Robert Sherrard heirs, John W. Largent, Thomas Johnson, said Passmore. 30 June 1846 [Dl'd Col. Tho's Sloan 22 Feb 1847]

E2-569: Surv.14 Apr 1845 by T.W.15,436 Isaac Brill 23 A. 3 Ro. 23 Po. in Frederick Co. adj. his other land, Henry Richard's Gravel spring tract, Bull's purchase of Russell. 31 July 1846 [Dl'd James R. M. Sydnor? 19 Dec 1848]

E2-570: Surv.31 Jan 1846 by T.W.15,480 James G. Ficklin 6 A. 3 Ro 14 Po. in Frederick Co. adj. said Ficklin, Carter heirs, Jesse Wood. 31 July 1846 [Mailed to Jno. F. Ficklin 17 Aug 1846]

E2-571: Surv.11 Nov 1844 by T.W.15,050 Wm. D. Rees asne. of Nimrod Pugh one moiety & William Leese one moiety in his own right 200 A. in Hampshire Co. on Middle Rg. adj. Abram Rinehart, George W. Washington. 31 July 1846 [Dl'd Mr. A. Hiett 12 Mar 1847]

E2-572: Surv.17 June 1845 by T.W.14,360 Levis Passmore asne. of John W. Largent 20 1/2 A. in Hampshire Co. on Great Cacaphon adj. David Ellis, Samuel Largent, Absolam Kessler. 31 July 1846 [Dl'd Col. Tho's Sloan 22 Feb 1847]

E2-573: Surv.18 Oct 1845 by T.W.14,594 & 13,057 William Harmison asne. of William Young 165 A. in Morgan Co. on Great Cacapeon Cr. adj. Caton, Harlan, Sherard, Canoloway hill. 31 July 1846

E2-574: Surv.26 Jan 1846 by T.W.15,876 Archibald Sherwood 3 A. 16 Po. in Fairfax Co. adj. John Trammell, Pearson now Harsey, Thompson, Fish's heirs, Gunnell now Fish, Pearson now Fish's heirs. 31 July 1846 [Mr. Love 19 Dec 1846]

E2-575: Surv.21 Sep 1844 by T.W.14,701 Richard B. Horner 16 A. 1 Ro. 8 Po. in Fauquier Co. near head of E. Br. of Carter's run adj. John Earley, George Chapman heirs, Patton & Swann now William Fletcher, Scott, Chapman, Thomas L. Moore now Earley, Fairfax. 31 July 1846 [Dl'd Gen. Wallace 26 Jan 1847]

E2-576: Surv.7 Aug 1841 by T.W.14,574 Samuel Bonham 17 A. in Hampshire Co. on Baker's Run of Potomac R. adj. William Malcum, his own land. 31 Aug 1846 [Dl'd Mr. A. Hiett 12 Mar 1847]

E2-577: Surv.26 Apr 1845 by T.W.15,554 John Rannells 1 7/8 A. in Hampshire Co. on Town hill adj. his Berry Land, land he bought of Musetter?, William Carder. 31 Aug 1846 [Dl'd Mr. A. Hiett 12 Mar 1847]

E2-578: Surv.1 Apr 1845 by T.W.15,404 Wm. Thomas 142 A. in Hampshire Co. bet. Spring gap Mt. & Sideling hill adj. David Ellis, Swisher, Hagerty heirs, McDonald. 31 Aug 1846 [Dl'd Mr. A. Hiett 12 Mar 1847]

E2-579: Surv.20 Apr 1844 by T.W.14,781 Daniel Williams 39 A. in Hampshire Co. on Little Cacapon & Town hill adj. his own land, John Swisher, James Meckin, George Sharfe. 31 Aug 1846 [Dl'd Mr. A. Hiett 12 Mar 1847]

E2-580: Surv.26 Oct 1842 by T.W.12,899 Daniel Shawen 30 A. in Hampshire Co. on Little Cacapehon adj. John J.? Pownall, said Shawen, Richard Hall. 31 Aug 1846 [Dl'd Mr. A. Hiett 12 Mar 1847]

E2-581: Surv.1 Apr 1845 by T.W.15,404 Silas Milleson 50 A. in Hampshire Co. bet. Spring Gap Mt. & Sideling hill adj. Williams Thomas, David Ellis, Robert Sherrard heirs, McDonald. 31 Aug 1846 [Dl'd Mr. A. Hiett 12 Mar 1847]

E2-582: Surv.17 Jan 1843 by T.W.14,782 & 12,456 William Poston 92 A. in Hampshire Co. on N. R. Mt. adj. surv. originally Branson Poston. 31 Aug 1846 [Dl'd Mr. Hiett 12 Mar 1847]

E2-583: Surv.6 Apr 1844 by T.W.15,031 Henry Watkins 44 A. in Hampshire Co. on Little Cacapeon adj. James B. Watkins, Wm. French. 31 Aug 1846 [Dl'd Mr. A. Hiett 12 Mar 1847]

E2-584: Surv.1 Apr 1845 by T.W.15,404 Silas Milleson 102 A. in Hampshire Co. bet. Spring Gap Mt. & Sideling hill adj. McDonald, Jenkins heirs, Wm. Thomas. 31 Aug 1846 [Dl'd Mr. A. Hiett 12 Mar 1847]

E2-585: Surv.2 Apr 1845 by T.W.15,404 Silas Milleson 5 1/2 A. in Hampshire Co. on Little Cacaphon adj. his tract, Peter McBride. 31 Aug 1846 [Dl'd Mr. Hiett 12 Mar 1847]

E2-586: Surv.14 Dec 1843 by T.W.2751 George Strawtherman 58 5/8 A. in Hardy Co. on Lost run adj. John Wilson Jr. formerly Wilkins, on Little Rg. 31 Aug 1846 [Dl'd C.C.Lee Esq. 20 Feb 1847]

E2-587: 18 May 1842 by T.W.2751 George P. Daudson 350 A. in Hardy Co. on N. R. adj. Michael Swisher, Benjamin Warden, Little Rg. 31 Aug 1846 [Dl'd C.C.Lee Esq. 20 Feb 1847]

E2-588: Surv.21 Aug 1844 by T.W.11,201 David Ornduff & James Ornduff 9 A. 3 Ro 33 Po. in Hardy Co. on Zane's Rg. bet. Slate Rock & Pine Lick Runs of Cacapeon, adj. their own land, Funkhouser. 31 Aug 1846 [Dl'd C.C.Lee Esq. 20 Feb 1847]

E2-589: Surv.20 Nov 1840 by T.W.2751 George P. Dadson & Philip Ludwick 300 A. in Hardy Co. on N. R. adj. his own land formerly Gouchenhour, Samuel Gouchenhour, Henry Swisher. 31 Aug 1846 [Dl'd C.C.Lee Esq. 20 Feb 1847]

E2-590: Surv.7 Apr 1845 by T.W.2751 John N. Baughman 39 1/4 A. in Hardy Co. on Lost R. & run through Kidner's Gap, Limestone Rg. adj. Inskeep, Link, Inskeep's Robinson tract, Henry Baughman, Jacob Baughman, Robison, Kidner, Baker's Wise land now Baughman. 31 Aug 1846 [Dl'd C.C.Lee Esq. 20 Feb 1847]

E2-591: Surv.8 Apr 1845 by T.W.2751 William Slater & Henry Baughman 52 A. 71 Po. in Hardy Co. on Lost R. & R. hill adj. Tho's Wilson, Hulver, Inskeep, Clark's & Wilson's Runs, surv. formerly Baker. 31 Aug 1846 [C.C.Lee Esq. 20 Feb 1847]

E2-592: Surv.29 Oct 1844 by T.W.2751 William Baker 42 1/2 A. in Hardy Co. on Flat & Rocky Ridges on Lost R. at place known as the Racoon Ponds, adj. Dellinger, Lee, Reed. 31 Aug 1846 [Dl'd C.C.Lee Esq. 20 Feb 1847]

E2-593: Surv.29 Apr 1845 by T.W.2751 Nicholas Baker asne. of Moses Jones 28 A. 103 Po. in Hardy Co. on Marsh's Run of Hutton's run of S. Br. of Patterson's Cr. Mt. Coal Mt., Keller's Spring adj. Harness, Baker, Snodgrass, heirs of Wm Heath dec'd. 31 Aug 1846 [Dl'd C.C.Lee Esq. 20 Feb 1847]

E2-594: Surv.20 Aug 1844 by 2751 Hezekiah Clagett 233 7/8 A. in Hardy Co. on Waits run & Cacapeon, on N. Mt. adj. Valentine Simmons, Yoast & Long, Ornduff, heirs of Benjamin Williams, Robert Means, Zane now Ornduff. 31 Aug 1846 [Dl'd C.C.Lee Esq. 20 Feb 1847]

E2-595: Surv.5 Aug 1836 by T.W.12,591 William Hose 18 A. in Hardy Co. on Lost R. adj. Wilson/Willson, Switzer, Wm. Reed. 31 Aug 1846 [C.C.Lee Esq. 20 Feb 1847]

E2-596: Surv.28 Dec 1842 by T.W.10,709, 14,461, 5650 & 11,100 John Griffith & Adam Griffith 21 A. 2 Ro. 16 Po. in Page Co. on Piney Mt. & Dry Run adj. John Smith, Abraham & Henry Heastin, Martain Stumbock. 30 Sep 1846 [Dl'd Col. McPherson 31 May 1847]

E2-597: Surv.5 Sep 1837 by T.W.12,626 Robert Ratcliffe 35 A. 69 Po. in Fairfax Co. adj. Edward Embs now John Gunnell, Reed now John Jackson heirs, Jenkins now heirs of Spencer Jackson dec'd, Embs & Harles now James Roberts. 30 Sep 1846 [Dl'd Gen. Rogers 10 Feb 1847]

E2-598: Surv.30 Dec 1845 by T.W.15,836 John Vaughan 7 A. in Culpeper Co. adj. John Vaughan formerly Russell Vaughan, Joseph B. Redd, heirs of Edward Brown dec'd, William H. Ward formerly Presley White, Mt. Poney. 30 Sep 1846 [Dl'd Mr. Mauzy 8 Feb '57]

E2-599: Surv.31 May 1845 by T.W.11,143 & 15,640 Samuel Judd 20 1/4 A in Page Co. on Piney Mt. near Pass run about 5 mi. E. of Luray adj. Alexander Rider, Samuel Judd, Martin Stemback, John Hockman, John Fraze. 30 Sep 1846 [Dl'd Mr. Thomas 3 Apr 1848]

E2-600: Surv.9 Apr 1845 by T.W.2751 William Baker 37 A. in Hardy Co. on Lost R. at Baker's run, Creek Hill adj. Wilson, James Baker, his own surv. 31 Oct 1846 [Dl'd C.C.Lee Esq. 20 Feb 1847]

E2-601: Surv.15 Nov 1843 by T.W.2751 John Coby asne. of Peter Cooms 257 1/4 A. in Hardy Co. on Wilson's run of Lost R. adj. Baker, Branson formerly Baker, Coby, Pios Cooms, the Big Rg. 31 Oct 1846 [Dl'd C.C.Lee Esq. 20 Feb 1847]

E2-602: Surv.1 Nov 1844 by T.W.2751 John Hulver 4 A. 142 Po. in Hardy Co. on Lost R. & Clark's Run adj. Creek hill, Indian hill, heirs of George Hulver dec'd, Switzer, Inskeep. 31 Oct 1846 [Dl'd C.C.Lee Esq. 20 Feb 1847]

E2-603: Surv.18 Nov 1843 by T.W.2751 John Wilson Jr. asne. of George Harper 1 A. 22 Po. in Hardy Co. on Lost R. & Kimsey's run adj. Heirs of Joseph Wilkin dec'd, John Wilson Jr. formerly Godfrey Wilkin heirs. 31 Oct 1846 [Dl'd C.C.Lee Esq. 20 Feb 1847]

E2-604: Surv.17 Nov 1845 by T.W.2751 John Wilson Jr. 77 A. in Hardy Co. on Kimsey's run of Lost R. & Kimsey's knob adj. Fout, Branson, his own, heirs of Joseph Wilkins dec'd. 31 Oct 1846 [Dl'd C.C.Lee Esq. 20 Feb 1847]

E2-605: Surv.22 June 1840 by T.W.2751 John Willson & David Willson 238 A. in Hardy Co. on Mill Mt. adj. their own lands, Wise, Isaac Wilson, John Wilson, Joseph Willson. 31 Oct 1846 [Dl'd C.C.Lee Esq. 20 Feb 1847]

E2-606: Surv.29 June 1829 by T.W.9925 Charles Wese/Weese 107 A. in Hardy Co. on N. Mill Cr. adj. Philip Yokum, Stump, Boot. 31 Oct 1846 [C.C.Lee 20 Feb 1847]

E2-607: Surv.4 June 1841 by T.W.2751 Abram Rotruck 50 A. in Hardy Co. on Knobly Mt. adj. his own land, his Martain surv., Martain McNamar, Herris, Christopher Martain Heirs. 31 Dec 1846 [Dl'd C.C.Lee Esq. 20 Feb 1847]

E2-608: Surv.8 Dec 1838 by T.W.12,382 John Tuckwiller & Henry Miller 92 A. 2 Ro in Page Co. on Blue Rg. & Dry run adj. Philip Shaffer. 11 Mar 1847 [Dl'd Col. McPherson 12 Mar 1847]

E2-609: Surv.14 Apr 1846 by T.W.14,755 Richard Harris 75 A. 39 Po. in Rappahannock Co. on Peaked Mt. adj. Joshua Hopper, Daniel Jackson, Warner Miller, Franklin Miller, said Harris, Isaac H. Hough. 13 Mar 1847

E2-610: Surv.25 June 1846 by T.W.12,664 & 16,083 Samuel Rogers Jr. & John Rogers 356 A. in Warren Co. adj. John S. Davidson, heirs of Jonathan Lukins, heirs of Elisha Catlett, John Carson, William Little, Samuel R. Rogers. 30 Mar 1847 [Dl'd Mr. Wall of Fred'k 15 Jan 1848]

E2-611: Surv.6 May 1846 by T.W.15,843 & 2751 Jesse Stump 254 A. in Hardy Co. on Middle Mt. & N. Mill Cr. of Long run adj. Yoakum, Tho. McMechen, Stump & Boots, Elijah Wan. 30 Mar 1847 [Mailed to Tho's Martin 27 May 1847]

E2-612: Surv.29 Jan 1844 by T.W.11,100 David C. Prince 1 A. 1 Ro. 33 Po. in Page Co. on Hawksbill Cr. adj. the Lutheran & Calvinist Church M.H., John Prince, John & Joseph Verner, Boracker. 22 Mar 1847 [Dl'd Col. McPherson 22 Mar 1847]

E2-613: Surv.22 Apr 1846 by T.W.15,611 & 12,855 William Thomas 700 A. in Pr. William Co. on Powells run adj. Bland, Cannon, Weaver, Taylor, Evans, Groves & Stonnel, John Thomas, Dumfries & Brentsville Rd., Bacon Race Rd., Grandison Cannon. 10 May 1847 [Mailed to Prop'r 10 May 1847]

E2-614:   Surv.6 Feb 1846 by T.W.14,897 Samuel Leatherman 42 A. in Hampshire Co. on Cabbin Run Rg. adj. James Welch, Abraham Good heirs, said Leatherman. 30 June 1847 [Dl'd Col. Hiett 17 Mar 1848]

E2-615:   Surv.9 Nov 1846 by T.W.15,875 Jesse Spurling 53 A. in Hampshire Co. on Mill Cr. on Brier Run Rg. adj. Elijah High, High's Magill land, Wm. S. Foley heirs, George Hartman. 30 June 1847 [Dl'd Col. Hiett 17 Mar 1848]

E2-616:   Surv.29 May 1846 by 15,875 Thomas Dobbins 5 A. 3 Ro. in Hampshire Co. on Cabbin Run hill adj. the Wharton Tract, his own land, the Hatten tract, Samuel Dobbins legatees. 30 June 1847 [Dl'd Col. Hiett 17 Mar 1848]

E2-617:   Surv.2 May 1846 by T.W.15,554 William Loy Jr. 35 A. 3 Ro. in Hampshire Co. on Tear Coat Cr. adj. Branson Petters, Samuel Loy, George Haws. 30 June 1847 [Dl'd Col. Hiett 17 Mar 1848]

E2-618:   Surv.5 Nov 1842 by T.W.11,199 Henry Harrison asne. of Tho's Jones 50 A. in Hampshire Co. on New Cr. adj. Elias Jones, said Harrison. 30 June 1847 [Dl'd Col. Hiett 17 Mar 1848]

E2-619:   Surv.8 Oct 1846 by T.W.15,966 James Shutz 11 A. in Hampshire Co. on Parker's Run adj. Carshaden, Parker, said Shutz, Frederick Shutz, Samuel Cockerel, Parker's heirs. 30 June 1847 [Dl'd Col. Hiett 17 Mar 1848]

E2-620:   Surv.4 May 1846 by T.W.13,050 & 15,875 Adam Rudloph 14 A. in Hampshire Co. on Little Cacaphon adj. his own land, Jacob Ruckman. 30 June 1847 [Dl'd Col. Hiett 17 Mar 1848]

E2-621:   Surv.21 Nov 1845 by T.W.15,270 & 14,782 James Sloan 67 A. in Hampshire Co. on Mill Cr. adj. Andrew Ludwick, Richard Sloan heirs, Jacob Biser, Abraham Mosley 1789 grant. 30 June 1847 [Dl'd Col. Hiett 17 Mar 1848]

E2-622:   Surv.29 Oct 1844 by T.W.14,716 Jacob Knabenshoe 122 A. in Hampshire Co. on New Cr. adj. Block house run adj. Barrick heirs, said Knabenshoe, Wm. Duling's Baker land, Thomas Seagull, Joseph Frazier. 30 June 1847 [Dl'd Col. Hiett 17 Mar 1848]

E2-623:   Surv.18 Apr 1846 by T.W.15,713 & 15,875 Vanse Dobbins 22 A. 3 Ro. in Hampshire Co. on Cabin Run Rg. adj. Solomon Elifrits, Samuel Dobbins legatees, said Vanse Dobbins, Thomas Allen. 30 June 1847 [Dl'd Col. Hiett 17 Mar 1848]

E2-624: Surv.14 Apr 1846 by T.W.2472 & 14,722 John M. Small & John Kilmer 50 A. in Berkeley Co. on N. Mt. adj. John Gross, Wm. Lamar, Gen. Boyd heirs, John Tabb, John Walters. 30 June 1847 [Dl'd to Rec't 14 Dec 1847]

E2-625:(1) Surv.8 Apr 1837 by T.W.10,801, 10,799, 6784, 10,042 & 9173 George Hottel & Henry S. Wunder 852 3/4 A. in Shenandoah Co. on Little N. Mt. adj. Wm. W. Payne, Kingan, Philip C. Jones, James Copelan, John Rudolph, Adam Rudolph, Abraham Secrist?, Joseph P. Mahany, William & John L. Smith, Scott. 30 Nov 1838 [Dl'd to Mr. Conn 3 Apr 1839]

E2-626:(2) Surv.bet. 13 & 20 Dec 1837 by T.W.12,659 & 12,717 Lorenzo D. Sybert 3050 A. in Shenandoah Co. on Cedar Cr. & Little N. Mt. adj. said Sybert, Holmes, Isaac Zane, John Kingan, Rd. from Cr. to Woodstock, Jacob Ott, Joseph Fawver, Joseph Parker, John Wilkin, Jacob Peer, Jacob Hoover, Wendel, John Sra__?, George Hottel, Philip C. Jones, James Cannire?, John Ornduff, Couler Run, Lewis Ornduff, foot of Cupola. 30 Nov 1838 [Dl'd Col. Bare 11 Apr 1839]

E2-628:(4) By judgment of Co. Ct. of Clark Co. 26 Jan 1846 in case of Thomas Whiting's Creditors; Mann R. Page Escheator, was directed to pay Creditors by sale of Escheated estate.   Grant to Elizabeth Cary Hay 1/4 A. in town of Berryville in Clark Co. Land conveyed to Thomas Whiting by deed from Treadwell Smith & Ann C., his w., 3 Feb 1829, recorded in Frederick Co. Inquisition of escheat held 29 May 1841. 31 July 1846. [Mailed to Mrs. Hay 3 Aug 1846]

End Grants E No. 2 1838 '46

F2-1: Surv.30 May 1846 by T.W.13044 John & William Evans 14 A. in Shenandoah Co. on Three-toped Mt. adj. Philip Stover, John Artz. 30 June 1847 [5 Feb 1848]

F2-2:   Surv.10 Apr 1846 by T.W.13,025 George Shaver 1 A. in Shenandoah Co. on Tom's Brook adj. Daniel Jacobs, said Shaver, Beckford Parish.   30 June 1847 [Dl'd Mr. Hill 7 Feb 1848]

F2-3:   Surv.27 May 1846 by T.W.15,713, 15,875 & 15,894 Michael Millar 605 A. in Hampshire Co. on S. Fork of Potomac adj. said Millar, Wm. Millar, Little Mt., John M. Pancake, Wm. Taylor, Buffaloe Run S. fork below Narrows, Isaac Pancake, Friend Gray, Luke Kuykendall. 30 June 1847 [Dl'd Col. Hiett 17 Mar 1848]

F2-4:   Surv.20 Apr 1846 by T.W.15,173 John Judd 15 A. 2 Ro. 7 Po. in Rappa-hannock Co. on Naked Mt., adj. Behem's Gap Rd., said Judd, William Bowen. 30 June 1847 [Dl'd Mr. J. F.Strother 11 Dec 1847]

F2-5:   Surv.21 Nov 1846 by T.W.10,812 William G. Catlett 1 A. 22 Po. in Morgan Co. on Cacapeon Cr. adj. Henry Myers, Dawson heirs. 30 June 1847 [Dl'd Col. Michael 24 Mar 1848]

F2-6: Surv.21 Oct 1845 by T.W.13,057 Benjamin Largent 14 3/4 A. in Morgan Co. on Potomac R. adj. his land, Alderton, Easter. 30 June 1847 [Col.Michael 24 Mar'48]

F2-7:   Surv.3 Nov 1846 by T.W.14,729 Wesley J. Easter 40 A. in Morgan Co. on Grindstone Mt. adj. King. 30 June 1847 [Dl'd Col. Michael 24 Mar 1848]

F2-8:   Surv.21 Nov 1846 by T.W.14,004 & 14,531 Jacob Cann 140 A. in Morgan Co. on Cacapeon Cr. 30 June 1847 [Dl'd Col. Michael 24 Mar 1848]

F2-9:   Surv.4 Nov 1846 by T.W.13,057 William G. Catlett 140 A. in Morgan Co. on Cacapeon Cr. & Cacapeon Mt. adj. heirs of Isaac Dawson, said Catlett, Sherard's heirs, Harmison, Harlan. 30 June 1847 [Dl'd Col. Michael 24 Mar 1848]

F2-10: Surv.20 Dec 1843 by T.W.2751 Benjamen Roby 27 3/4 A. in Hardy Co. on Big Spring Run of Lounie's Cr. foot of Little Mt. adj. Polly Scott, McKem, McCave, his land formerly Pool. 30 June 1847 [Dl'd Mr. G.T. Barbee 25 Feb 1848]

F2-11:   Surv.9 Mar 1846 by T.W.2751 John Stingley 127 A. in Hardy Co. on Little Mt., S. fork of Lounie's Cr. adj. Welton, his own formerly Badgley, Graves, McDonald, Cosner, Groves called the Brown tract.   30 June 1847 [Dl'd Mr. Seymour 25 Feb 1848]

F2-12:   Surv.20 Dec 1845 by T.W.2751 Abraham A. Inskeep 29 5/8 A. in Hardy Co. on Cr. Hill & Lost R., in Ruddles' Gap adj. his own land, Hulver, his Ruddle tract. 30 June 1847 [Dl'd Mr. Wm. Seymour 11 Mar 1848]

F2-13:   Surv.12 Mar 1846 by T.W.2751 Benjamen Roby 27 3/4 A. in Hardy Co. on Little Mt. & Meadow Run adj. Holmes, Gale & Harness Big Surv., Clark, Lentz, Welton. 30 June 1847 [Dl'd Mr. G.T. Barbee 25 Feb 1848]

F2-14:   Surv.13 Aug 1844 by T.W.2751 Aaron Baker asne. of Jacob Thrasher 3 1/4 A. in Hardy Co. on Thorn run & Knobby Rd. adj. Gilpin, heirs of Abraham Baker dec'd(old Stone lick surv.), old Ross Surv. 30 June 1847 [Dl'd Mr. Wm. Seymour 11 Mar 1848]

F2-15:   Surv.1 Aug 1845 by T.W.2751 Josiah Bland 43 A. in Hardy Co. bet. Lounie's Cr. & Tearcoat adj. Jesse Welton, Tho's Ellzey, Coler & Powell, Seymour.   30 June 1847 [Dl'd Mr. G.T. Barbee 25 Feb 1848]

F2-16: Surv.9 Jan 1846 by T.W.2751 David Vanmeter 30 A. 150 Po. in Hardy Co. on Vanmeter's Mill Run adj. Jacob Vanmeter's Hite Tract, the Foley tract, his Berry or Humphrey tract, Joseph Vanmeter, Watson, Claylick run, Neal. 30 June 1847 [Dl'd Mr. Wm. Seymour 11 Mar 1848]

F2-17: Surv.11 Nov 1845 by T.W.2751 Elijah Judy 93 3/4 A. in Hardy Co. on Middle Mt. bet. N. & S. Mill Crs. adj. his land, N.N. line, Strader Hollow, Powder lick. 30 June 1847 [Dl'd Mr. G.T. Barbee 25 Feb 1848]

F2-18: Surv.15 Dec 1837 by T.W.2751 Valentine Simmons asne. of John Summers 295 A. in Hardy Co. on Lost R. adj. Jacob Snider/Snyder, Reuben Fravel, Lee formerly Machir, Jacob Chrisman, Jonathan Bransen, Lionel Bransen. 31 July 1847 [Dl'd Mr. G.T. Barbee 25 Feb 1848]

F2-19: Surv.10 Jan 1846 by T.W.12,990 Daniel Smith asne. of Van Jacobs 19 1/2 A. in Hardy Co. near Patterson's Cr. Mt. on Vanmeter's Mill Run, adj. the Foley Tract now Vanmeter, Cade or Higgin's tract now Jacob Vanmeter. 31 July 1847 [Dl'd Mr. Wm. Seymour 11 Mar 1848]

F2-20: Surv.27 Oct 1845 by T.W.15,744 Lewis Western asne. of Robert Ratcliff asne. of Charles W. Lindsay 15 A. 109 Po. in Fairfax Co. adj. Bourn, Giles Tillett, Harris & Baxter, the Ox Rd., heirs of Peter Watener dec'd, Lindsay heirs. 31 July 1847 [Dl'd Mr. Moss 6 Dec 1847]

F2-21: Surv.11 Jan 1847 by T.W.15,875 & 15,966 Elijah Lyon 90 A. in Hampshire Co. on Knobby Mt. adj. Michael Baker, said Lyon's Hoddy tract, George Baker. 31 July 1847 [Dl'd Col. Hiett 17 Mar 1848]

F2-22: Surv.5 Jan 1847 by T.W.2995 John Hoye 118 A. in Hampshire Co. on Myers Run of Patterson's Cr. adj. Jacob Wagoner, John M. Wagoner's Legatees, Jesse Rice, George Smith. 31 July 1847 [Mailed to Prop'r 13 Aug 1847]

F2-23: Surv.9 Apr 1846 by T.W.15,299 Jacob Cook 135 A. in Shenandoah Co. in Powell's Little Ft. adj. Jacob Beydler, Three Toped Mt. 31 Aug 1847 [Dl'd Mr. Hill 7 Feb 1848]

F2-24: Surv.21 Nov 1845 by T.W.15,600 & 2751 William Kile 208 1/2 A. in Hardy Co. in Big Cove adj. Snyder, Harper, Chrisman, Davis, Pepper, Cove Mt. 30 Aug 1847 [Dl'd Mr. Wm. Seymour 11 Mar 1848]

F2-25: Surv.14 Oct 1845 by T.W.2751 John G. Harness 247 A. in Hardy Co. on Sugar Loaf Mt. bet. Mannon's & Town Ft. Runs of S. Br. adj. Carson, Lobb, Cain, his own land. his Nevill land, Balthas, McNeill. 30 Aug 1847 [Dl'd Mr. G.T. Baarbee 25 Feb 1848]

F2-26: Surv.20 Nov 1845 by T.W.15,600 Isaac Snyder 75 A. in Hardy Co. in Big Cove on N. Mt. adj. his own land, Harper, John Snyder, James Laughlin, Davis, Claypool. 31 Aug 1847 [Mr. Wm Seymour 11 Mar 1848]

F2-27: Surv.26 Apr 1845 by T.W.15,404 William Carder 14 1/4 A. in Hampshire Co. on Little Cacapeon adj. Philip Fahs, John Burkett, Benjamin Ely, John Rannell. 31 Aug 1847 [Dl'd Col. Hiett 17 Mar 1848]

F2-28: Surv.19 Sep 1846 by T.W.5527 Sperry Catlett 35 A. in Warren Co. on Cabin Run adj. Wm. Bennet, Richard Ridgeway, Tho's Leach, Catlett heirs. 31 Aug 1847 [Mailed to Prop'r 11 Nov 1847]

F2-29: Surv.23 Sug 1843 by T.W.14,573 Bazel Sybole asne. of Jacob Sybole 61 A. in Hampshire Co. on Little Mt. on Falling Spring Run adj. James Sybole formerly Boyd, David & Thomas Alderton. 30 Sep 1847 [Dl'd Col. Hiett 17 Mar 1848]

F2-30: Surv.13 Mar 1844 by T.W.15,031 Samuel Bumgarner 47 1/2 A. in Hampshire Co. S.W. of Great Cacapeon adj. said Bumgarner's Cacapeon tract, Wm. Taylor, Throckmorton, Winterton, Enoch Pennington. 30 Sep 1847 [Col. Hiett 17 Mar 1848]

F2-31: Surv.1 July 1842 by T.W.14,781 George Wolf 6 1/2 A. in Hampshire Co. on Tear Coat Cr. adj. John Peters, William Doran, said Wolf. 30 Sep 1847 [Dl'd Col. Hiett 17 Mar 1848]

F2-32: Surv.17 May 1846 by T.W.15,875 John Cheshir of Obadiah 22 A. 3 Ro. in Hampshire Co. on N. R. Mt. adj. Obadiah Cheshir, John Swisher, Samuel J.? Stump.

30 Sep 1847 [Dl'd Col. Hiett 17 Mar 1848]

F2-33: Surv.27 Feb 1847 by T.W.14,172, 15,966 & 16,350 Emmer Stalcup Jr. 246 A. in Hampshire Co. on N. Br. of Potomac & Knobley Mt. adj. Emmer Stalcup, George House, top of Morentz's Rocks, Falling Spring Run. 30 Sep 1847 [Dl'd Col. Hiett 17 Mar 1848]

F2-34: Surv.20 Oct 1845 by T.W.10,427 John Dawson 148 A. in Morgan Co. on Great Cacapeon Cr., Canolaway Hill adj. Reynolds. 30 Sep 1847 [Col.Michael 24 Mar 1848

F2-35: Surv.2 Jan 1847 by T.W.15,480 Washington Cather 5 A. in Frederick Co. bet. his own land & John Cather, adj. McNeill & Mitchell now John Cather, Joseph Fisher. 30 Sep 1847 [Dl'd Mr. Baker 2 June 1852]

F2-36: Surv.5 Aug 1846 by T.W.12,990 George A. Lynch 2 A. in Hardy Co. on S. Fork & Stoker Lick of Town Ft. Run near Morefield, adj. Hamilton, Moore now Seymour, Harness's Reed Tract. 30 Sep 1847 [Dl'd Mr. Wm. Seymour 11 Mar 1848]

F2-37: Surv.29 Oct 1846 by T.W.2751 Francis Godlove 77 Po. in Hardy Co. on Cacapehon R. at Anderson's Rg. adj. Rd. bet. Wardensville & Fry's tan yard, Switzer, his land formerly Pugh. 30 Sep 1847 [Dl'd Mr. Wm. Seymour 11 Mar 1848]

F2-38: Surv.22 Mar 1845 by T.W.2751 Christopher Martin 3 A. 142 Po. in Hardy Co. on Stone Lick or Thorn Run adj. Boseley, Roberts, his own land formerly Reed & Cantor. 30 Sep 1847 [Dl'd Mr. Wm. Seymour 11 Mar 1848]

F2-39: Surv.16 Mar 1846 by T.W.2751 Christopher Martin 95 A. in Hardy Co. on Pine Rg. bet. Stone Lick & Salt Spring Runs of Patterson's Cr. adj. Boseley, Harris, the Big Surv., George Rotruck, Jas. Roberts, his own land, Reed & Cantor now George's, John Rotruck. 30 Sep 1847 [Dl'd Mr. W. Seymour 11 Mar 1848]

F2-40: Surv.24 Jan 1846 by T.W.2751 Anthony Hunous 22 3/8 A. in Hardy Co. on Fox Lick & Water Lick runs, Fox Lick Rg., Short Arse Mt. adj. Tusing, the Big Surv., Poland, his own land formerly Constable. 30 Sep 1847 [Dl'd F.B.Welton 16 Mar 1849]

F2-41: Surv.9 Apr 1846 by T.W.2751 Sanford Y. Simons asne. of John Stingley 365 A. in Hardy Co. on Little Mt. & Reels Gap, S. Fork of Lounies Cr. adj. Zahn, Badgley, Holmes, Gale, Harness, Benj'n Roby, Groves, s'd Simons, Cosner, New Cr. Mt., Reel, Beverly, Stingley. 30 Sep 1847 [Dl'd Mr. G.T. Barbee 25 Feb 1848]

F2-42: Surv.29 May 1845 by T.W.11,143 George Printz 37 A. 2 Ro. 18 Po. in Page Co. on Blue Rg. in Kettle Hollow adj. Isaac Printz Sr., Spunk Run. 30 Nov 1847 [Dl'd Mr. Tho's Buswell 3 Apr 1848]

F2-43: Surv.3 Apr 1847 by T.W.15,442 Peter Printz 251 A. in Page Co. on Big Hawk-Bill Cr. at Blue Rg. near Luray adj. Peter Printz, wid. Shaffer, Abram Printz, Jacob Smith, Jno. Verner. 30 Nov 1847 [Dl'd Tho's Buswell 3 Apr 1848]

F2-44: Surv.8 Apr 1847 by T.W.15,640 Valentine Deats 14 1/2 A. in Page Co. on Big Naked Cr. near Blue Rg. S. of Loray adj. Valentine Deats, Daneil Monica. 30 Nov 1847 [Dl'd Mr. Tho's Buswell 3 Apr 1848]

F2-45: Surv.3 June 1846 by Surv.15,640 John Prince Jr. 7 3/4 A. in Page Co. on Big Hawksbill Cr. at foot of Blue Rg. S. of Luray adj. John Varner, John Miller heirs, John Prince Sr. 30 Nov 1847 [Dl'd Mr. Tho's Buswell 3 Apr 1848]

F2-46: Surv.23 Apr 1847 by T.W.15,640 & 16,531 Henry Sours 51 A. in Page Co. on Kettle Rg. E. of Luray adj. Nicholas Houser, John Verner, John Printz. 30 Nov 1847 [Dl'd Mr. Tho's Buswell 3 Apr 1848]

F2-47: Surv.12 Oct 1846 by T.W.15,667 & 2751 Abraham Ketterman 301 1/2 A. in Hardy Co. on Middle Mt. bet. N. & S. Mill Crs. on Three Mile Lick run of N. Mill Cr. adj. Ayres, Mouze, Iman. 30 Nov 1848 [Dl'd Mr. G.T.Barbee 25 Feb 1848]

F2-48: Surv.28 Oct 1846 by T.W.2751 Samuel Harper 79 3/4 A. in Hardy Co. on

Still run of Lost R. bet. Big & Little Cove Mts. adj. A.M. Woods, Dunbar. 30
Nov 1847 [Dl'd Mr. W. Seymour 11 Mar 1848]

F2-49: Surv.28 Oct 1846 by T.W.2751 Angus M. Wood 41 3/4 A. in Hardy Co. on
Lost R. adj. his own land formerly Branson, Little Cove Mt., Dunbar. 30 Nov
1847 [Dl'd Mr. W. Seymour 11 Mar 1848]

F2-50: Surv.27 Mar 1846 by T.W.2751 Samuel Harper 162 A. in Hardy Co. on Lost
R. bet. Mill Run & Still Run on Grindstone Mt. adj. Claypool, Wood formerly
Branson, his own land, Wilken now Harper & Claypool, Rd. to Woodstock, Wood's
Swingling Mill tract. 30 Nov 1847 [Dl'd Mr. W. Seymour 11 Mar 1848]

F2-51: Surv.8 Oct 1846 by T.W.16,185 & 2751 Joshua Mouse 157 1/4 A. in Hardy
Co. on Middle Mt. bet. N. & S. Mill Crs., Mile Lick run of N. Mill Cr. adj.
Ayres, Landers, Slate lick Hollow, Iman's path. 30 Nov 1847 [Dl'd Mr. G.T.
Barbee 25 Feb 1848]

F2-52: Surv.7 Oct 1846 by T.W.15,670 & 10,860 John Ayres 120 A. in Hardy Co. in
Middle Mt. bet. N. & S. Mill Crs., Spruce Lick & Three Mile Lick Runs of N. Mill
Cr. adj. Bergdall, Ketterman, Landers, Iman's Path. 31 Dec 1847 [Dl'd Mr. G.T.
Barbee 25 Feb 1848]

F2-53: Surv.9 Oct 1846 by T.W.15,786 John Ayres 189 1/2 A. in Hardy Co. on
Island Rg. & Joe Lick Rg. of Middle Mt. bet. N. & S. Mill Crs., Joe Lick Run of
N. Mill Cr. adj. Bergdall, Yoakum's Weese surv., Weese. 31 Dec 1847 [Dl'd Mr.
G.T. Barbee 25 Feb 1848]

F2-54: Surv.5 May 1847 by T.W.16,500 Teter Everhart asne. of Nathan Everheart
105 A. in Berkeley Co. on third hill Mt. adj. Ganoe, Butler land, Campbell
heirs, Leading Rg., John Roberts, Good, Everhart, Henry Everhart. 31 Jan 1848
[Dl'd Col. Brown 4 Apr 1848]

F2-55: Surv.30 July 1847 by T.W.14,461 & 16,531 Edward A. William & Joseph M.
Roads 150 A. in Page Co. on Middle Mt. in Powel's Ft. on Passage Cr. W. of Luray
adj. Frederick A. Marye. 29 Feb 1848 [Dl'd Tho's Buswell Esq. 3 Apr 1848]

F2-56: Surv.8 Apr 1847 by T.W.15,640 & 16,531 William Merica & Daniel Merica 6
1/4 A. in Page Co. on Big Naked Cr. near the Blue Rg. S. of Luray adj. Valentine
Deats, William Merica. 29 Feb 1848 [Dl'd Tho's Buswell Esq. 3 Apr 1848]

F2-57: Surv.20 Mar 1846 by T.W.2751 Daniel S. Tucker 6 3/4 A. in Hardy Co. on
Thorn Run of Patterson's Cr. adj. his own land, George formerly Gilpin, Harris
heirs, his Haggarty tract, Reed & Canter now George and Harriss heirs. 29 Feb
1848 [Dl'd G.T. Barbee 9 Mar 1849]

F2-58: Surv.20 Mar 1846 by T.W.2751 Daniel S. Tucker 62 3/4 A. in Hardy Co. on
Ross Run of Patterson's Cr. adj. George, his own land formerly Haggarty, his
Ross land, his Hurskey land. 29 Feb 1848 [Dl'd G.T. Barbee 9 Mar 1849]

F2-59: Surv.1 Oct 1847 by T.W.10,591 Jacob Schoppert 1 A. 1 Ro. 22 Per. in
Berkeley Co. on Opequon Cr. adj. Abraham & Asahel Vanmeter, Colbert Anderson
formerly Hunter heirs, said Schoppert. 30 June 1848

F2-60: Surv.16 Mar 1847 by T.W.15,875 John Arnold 4 A. in Hampshire Co. on Bear
Wallow run adj. Robert McBride, Wm. Grant, said Arnold's Mason tract. 30 June
1848 [Dl'd Jas. Allen Esq. 15 Mar 1849]

F2-61: Surv.4 Aug 1847 by T.W.16,493 David Arnold 45 A. in Hampshire Co. on S.
Br. Mt. or Dobson's Knob adj. Robert Martin, Daniel McLaughlin. 30 June 1848
[Dl'd Jas. Allen 15 Mar 1849]

F2-62: Surv.17 Nov 1847 by T.W.16,350 Samuel Arnold 19 1/2 A. in Hampshire Co.
on New Cr. adj. William Janney, John Winow, John Barnhouse, the Crevey Surv.30
June 1848 [Dl'd Col. J. Allen 15 Mar 1849]

F2-63: Surv.31 Oct 1844 by T.W.15031 William Grayson 15 A. in Hampshire Co. on

New Cr. adj. Sarah Grayson, Chamber's Big Surv., William Fout. 30 June 1848 [Dl'd Col. J. Allen 15 Mar 1849]

F2-64:   Surv.14 June 1847 by T.W.16,493 John Hiett & Evan Hiett 35 A. in Hampshire Co. on N. R. Mt. adj. their tract. 30 June 1848 [Col. A.Hiett 13 Mar 1849]

F2-65:   Surv.18 Mar 1847 by T.W.16,350 & 15,966 Thomas F. Henderson 607 A. in Hampshire Co. on N. R. & Timber Mt. in Rigg's hollow adj. George Little heirs, George Sharf, Wood, George McCauley, Milslagle, Cooper, John Ingle. 30 June 1848 [Mailed Prop'r 13 July 1848]

F2-66:   Surv.30 Nov 1847 by T.W.2995 John Hoye 326 1/2 A. in Hampshire Co. on Knobley Mt. adj. George Calmes legatees, said Hoye, Honess Gap. 30 June 1848 [Mailed to Prop'r 14 Mar 1849]

F2-67:   Surv.3 June 1847 by T.W.15,966 Silas Milleson 16 1/2 A. in Hampshire Co. on Little Cacaphon adj. his tracts, John Smith. 30 June 1848 [Dl'd Col. A. Hiett 13 Mar 1849]

F2-68:   Surv.3 June 1847 by T.W.15,404 & 15,966 Silas Milleson 11 A. in Hampshire Co. on Little Cacaphon Mt. adj. said Milleson, Wilson McBride, John Smoot. 30 June 1848 [Dl'd Col. A. Hiett 13 Mar 1849]

F2-69:   Surv.31 Aug 1842 by T.W.14,624 Samuel J. Stump 36 1/2 A. in Hampshire Co. on N. R. Mt. adj. Richard Wood, George Little. 30 June 1848 [Dl'd Col. A. Hiett 13 Mar 1849]

F2-70:   Surv.10 June 1847 by T.W.16,493 James Starns 6 A. in Hampshire Co. on Spring Gap Mt. adj. John Critton heirs, Catherine Ginevan, his own land. 30 June 1848 [Dl'd Col. A. Hiett 13 Mar 1849]

F2-71:   Surv.9 Apr 1844 by T.W.14,360 John Starkey 65 A. in Hampshire Co. on Tear Coat Cr., Middle fork Clay Lick Run adj. John Lock heirs, John Hawse, said Starkey. 30 June 1848 [Dl'd Jas. Allen Esq. 15 Mar 1849]

F2-72:   Surv.11 Mar 1847 by T.W.14,234 Henry Trout 43 A. in Hampshire Co. on Knobley Mt. adj. Alexander Riley, said Trout, Wm. Hull Jr., Jonas Chamberlain. 30 June 1848 [Dl'd Col. Jas. Allen 15 Mar 1849]

F2-73:   Surv.12 Mar 1847 by T.W.14,234 & (erased) Henry Trout 41 A. in Hampshire Co. on Knobly Mt. adj. Jonas Chamberlain, Wm. Hagan heirs, Thomazin Grayson heirs, said Trout. 30 June 1848 [Dl'd Col. Jas. Allen 15 Mar 1849]

F2-74:   Surv.2 Apr 1845 by T.W.15,404 William Troutin 12 A. in Hampshire Co. on Crooked run adj. Joseph Snapp, William McDonald, John Moreland. 30 June 1848 [Dl'd Col. A. Hiett 13 Mar 1849]

F2-75:   Surv.29 July 1847 by T.W.15,966 & 16,493 James Twigg 245 A. in Hampshire Co. on N. Br. of Potomac adj. Bene S. Pigman, Wm. P. Stump, Round bottom hollow, the Big Surv., said Twigg bought of Patterson. 30 June 1848 [Dl'd Col. Jas. Allen 15 Mar 1849]

F2-76:   Surv.27 Nov 1847 by T.W.14,266 Thomas J. Miller 16 3/4 A. in Shenandoah Co. on N. fork of Shenandoah R. above Cedar Cr. adj. said Thomas J. Miller, Bowman. 30 June 1848 [Dl'd Mr. Philip Pitman 10 July 1849]

F2-77:   Surv.3 Apr 1847 by T.W.14,522 Jonathan Hiett asne. of Job Pugh 15 A. 2 Ro. 22 Po. in Frederick Co. on Brush Cr. adj. George P. Chrisman, said Pugh, Shade. 30 June 1848 [Dl'd Col. A. Hiett 3 Dec 1848]

F2-78:   Surv.11 Mar 1847 by T.W.2751 Henry Feaster 85 A. in Hardy Co. on Little Mt. bet. N. & S. forks of Lounies Cr. adj. McDonald, his own land, Groves' Brown tract, Groves' Bodkin tract. 30 June 1848 [Dl'd Mr. McNamar 12 Dec 1848]

F2-79:   Surv.13 June 1846 by T.W.2751 Henry Feaster Jr. 123 1/4 A. in Hardy Co. on New Cr. Mt., N. fork of Lounies Cr. bet. Morgantown Rd. & Hawk's Gap, adj.

Shell, Simmons, the Beverly surv., his own land. 30 June 1848 [Dl'd Jos. McNamar 12 Dec 1848]

F2-80: Surv.28 Dec 1846 by T.W.2751 Abraham A. Inskeep 95 A. in Hardy Co. on Lost R., Creek hill, Ruddles Gap adj. Inskeep, Slater, Baughman, Hulver, Kinder, Robinson, Collins, McHendry. 30 June 1848 [Dl'd G.T. Barbee Esq. 9 Mar 1849]

F2-81: Surv.27 Nov 1846 by T.W.2751 Adam Nave 190 A. in Hardy Co. on Lost R. on Little Cove Mt. adj. Wood, Harper, Chrisman, Miller. the Cove tract, Big Cove Mt., Dunbar. 30 June 1848 [Dl'd F.B. Welton 16 Mar 1849]

F2-82: Surv.28 Nov 1846 by T.W.15,728 & 2751 Jacob R. Pope 263 A. in Hardy Co. on Buck & Brush Lick Runs of Lost R., Rd. to Brock's Gap adj. Henry Halterman, Christian Halterman, heirs of Caldwell, drain of Shenandoah R. 30 June 1848 [Dl'd F.B. Welton 16 Mar 1849]

F2-83: Surv.21 Nov 1840 by T.W.2751 Joseph Nevill 237 S. in Hardy Co. on Alleghany Mt. & Stony R. adj. George Cunningham formerly McKim. 30 June 1848 [Mailed to Prop'r 8 Aug 1848]

F2-84: Surv.8 June 1846 by T.W.2751 Henry Smith 57 A. in Hardy Co. on N. fork of S. Br. of Potomac at the Narrows adj. his own land bought of Cunningham, the Big Island tract. 30 June 1848 [Dl'd Mr. McNamar 12 Dec 1848]

F2-85: Surv.27 July 1841 by T.W.2751 Henry Smith 257 A. in Hardy Co. on Crow run of N. Fork, on Alleghany Mt. and known by The Richwoods. 30 June 1848 [Dl'd Mr. McNamar 12 Dec 1848]

F2-86: Surv.9 Sep 1846 by T.W.10,860 & 15,805 John Snyder 59 A. in Hardy Co. on Middle Mt. bet. S. fork & S. Mill Cr. adj. his land formerly Siver, Bergdall, Rorabaugh, his Robertson tract. 30 June 1848 [Dl'd G.T. Barbee 7 Nov 1848]

F2-87: Surv.9 Jan 1846 by T.W.15,640 Mason Jobe 1 3/4 A. in Page Co. on S. Shenandoah R. near Luray, adj. John Ruffner, David Strickler Sr. 30 June 1848 [Dl'd Mr. Buswell 22 Dec 1848]

F2-88: Surv.8 July 1845 by T.W.15,640 Reuben Summers 92 A. in Page Co. on Blue Rg., on Hawkbill SE of Luray adj. John Prince's "Kettle tract", George Printz, Isaac Printz. 30 June 1848 [Dl'd Mr. Buswell 22 Dec 1848]

F2-89: Surv.26 Apr 1847 by T.W.14,461, 15,640, 15,442 & 16531 Reuben Somers & Isaac Somers 225 1/2 A. in Page Co. on Big Hawksbill Cr. on Blue Rg. near Luray adj. Jacob Smith. 30 June 1848 [Dl'd Thos. Buswell 22 Dec 1848]

F2-90: Surv.15 Apr 1847 by T.W.16,500 Henry Barns 12 A. 2 Ro.16 Po. in Berkeley Co. adj. said Barns, Walter Jones, Colston heirs, Foose, Bowers. 31 July 1848

F2-91: Surv.9 Feb 1847 by T.W.15,513 Mahala J.? Shimp 73 A. in Berkeley Co. on Tilehanzes Br. near third hill Mt. adj. George Coffenberger, Jacob Coffenberger, Jonas Hedges, John & Jacob Sharff. Koneky h's. 31 July 1848 [Dl'd Lewis Grantham 4 Dec 1849]

F2-92: Surv.3 Nov 1847 by T.W.16,500 William Butt 25 A. in Berkeley Co. on N. Mt. adj. James Wilson, Joseph Minginni heirs. 31 July 1848 [Prop'r 6 June 1849]

F2-93: Surv.30 July 1847 by T.W.16,493 William P. Stump 488 A. in Hampshire Co. on N. Br. of Potomac adj. Jones heirs, James Twigg, Joseph Waggoner, Buck Island run, George Smith, Donaldson, said Stump. 31 July 1848 [James Allen 15 Mar'49]

F2-94: Surv.27 May 1847 by T.W.15,713 William P. Stump 148 A. in Hampshire Co. on N. Br. of Potomac, Middle Rg., Round Bottom hollow, adj. James Twigg formerly Holmes, Holmes heirs Big surv. 31 July 1848 [Dl'd James Allen Esq. 15 Mar 1849]

F2-95: Surv.20 Jan 1848 by T.W.16,800 & 12,616 Alexander Anderson 448 1/4 A. in Shenandoah Co. on Stony Cr. called Zion's Church land, adj. John Tisinger, Israel Rinker, Stephen Showman, Cashes. 31 Aug 1848 [Mailed Prop't 30 Sep 1848]

F2-96: Surv.13 Jan 1847 by T.W.15,966 James Allen 54 A. in Hampshire Co. on Patterson's Cr. adj. Thomas Hollenback, said Allen. 31 Aug 1848 [Dl'd to Prop'r 12 Mar 1849]

F2-97: Surv.10 June 1847 by T.W.16,170 Washington McCulty 25 A. in Hardy Co. on Rabbit Lick Run of N. Mill Cr. and Middle Mt., to Haggler Knob adj. Landers. 31 Aug 1848 [Dl'd G.T. Barbee 9 Mar 1849]

F2-98: Surv.19 Apr 1847 by T.W.2751 Christopher Martin 3 7/8 A. in Hardy Co. on Limestone Run of Thorn Run of Patterson's Cr. at Little Mt. near Rotruck's Gap adj. Baker & Gilpin (formerly). 31 Aug 1848 [Dl'd F.B. Walton 16 Mar 1849]

F2-99: Surv.10 Mar 1846 by T.W.2751 John Hughes 15 A. 127 sq. Per. in Hardy Co. bet. Diamond Lick Run & S. fork of Lounie's Cr. adj. Stingley formerly Badgely, Welton's Brewin land, Wiley. 31 Aug 1848 [Dl'd G.T. Barbee 9 Mar 1849]

F2-100: Surv.31 Aug 1838 by T.W.13,049 Nacy Waters 7 A. in Hampshire Co. on Little Cacaphon adj. said Waters, Peter Stump, Philip Shinholt, William Milison, Alex. Monroe. 31 Aug 1848 [Dl'd James Allen Esq. 15 Mar 1849]

F2-101: Surv.15 Jan 1846 by T.W.2751 Bennet Bean(Secundus) 116 A. in Hardy Co. on Bolens run of Scagg's run & on Hunting Rg. adj. heirs of James Bean dec'd called Hoggen tract, Simmons, Burch's Bishop land, Robt. Bean, his own land. 30 Sep 1848 [Dl'd F.B. Welton Esq. 16 Mar 1849]

F2-102: Surv.26 Jan 1847 by T.W.2751 & 14,240 David Vanmeter 498 A. in Hardy Co. on Mud Lick run of S. Br. & High Knob Mt. adj. James Vanmeter, Leatherman, his own land, Combs now Foss, John Godfrey. 30 Sep 1848 [G.T.Barbee 9 Mar 1849]

F2-103: Surv.28 May 1844 by T.W.2751 Christopher C. Yoakum asne. of Michael Yoakum 57 A. in Hardy Co. on Jordan's & Broad Runs of N. fork bet. Walker's Rg. & the Alleghany Mt. adj. the Chamber surv., his own land formerly White's, Holmes, Gale & Harness, Rohrabaugh. 30 Sep 1848 [Dl'd Mr. Welton 14 Dec 1848]

F2-104: Surv.7 Jan 1847 by T.W.2751 Moses Arnold 102 1/2 A. in Hardy Co. on Patterson's Cr. Mt., Elk Ponds adj. Joseph Arnold, Foley. 30 Sep 1848 [Dl'd F.B. Welton 16 Mar 1849]

F2-105: Surv.30 July 1847 by T.W.16,459 William Baker 56 3/4 A. in Hardy Co. on Baker's run of Lost R. & Brushy Spur of Short Arse Mt. adj. his own land, James Baker. 30 Sep 1848 [Dl'd F.B. Welton 16 Mar 1849]

F2-106: Surv.2 Aug 1847 by T.W.16,456 & 16,459 William Baker 165 3/4 A. in Hardy Co. on Lost R. & Little Rg. adj. Warden, his own land, Means. 30 Sep 1848 [Dl'd F.B. Welton 16 Mar 1849]

F2-107: Surv.29 May 1845 by T.W.11,100 & 15,640 Jacob Freeze 5 A. 1 Ro. 10 Per. in Page Co. on Dry Run adj. Adam Griffith, Heaston, John Smith, Joseph Griffith. 30 Sep 1848 [Dl'd Mr. Buswell 22 Dec 1848]

F2-108: Surv.12 Feb 1848 by T.W.16,531 George B. Chadduck 3 A. 12 1/2 Po. in Page Co. on the Big Hill S.E. of Luray adj. Abraham Shenk, Chaney Brook. 30 Sep 1848 [Dl'd Mailed to Eli Chadduck 28 Oct 1848]

F2-109: Surv.28 Jan 1848 by T.W.16,531 Paschal Graves 2 A. 3 Ro. 8 Po. in Page Co. on Little Hawkbill Cr. S.E. of Luray adj. Paschal Graves, Isaac Overall heirs. 30 Sep 1848 [Dl'd to rec't 8 Jan 1849]

F2-110: Surv.20 Nov 1847 by T.W.12,664 James Stinson 21 A. in Warren Co. adj. said Stinson, Forrie, Silas Fristoe, the Grant line. 30 Sep 1848 [Dl'd Mr. Giles Cook 5 May 1851]

F2-111: Surv.22 Mar 1848 by T.W.17,003 Lewis Grantham 42 A. 1 Ro. in Berkeley Co. adj. Nathan Everhart, Peter Jones h's. 31 Oct 1848 [Dl'd Prop'r 4 Dec 1849]

F2-112: Surv.29 May 1835 by T.W.11,063 Peter Harsel Jr. 17 1/2 A. in Hampshire

Co. on Johnson's Run of Patterson's Cr. adj. Okey Johnson, John Lambert, said Harsel. 30 Nov 1848 [Dl'd Mr. Allen 9 Dec 1848]

F2-113: Surv.29 May 1846 by T.W.15,713 John Dobbins 3 1/2 A. in Hampshire Co. on Patterson's Cr. adj. Kesiah Lambert, Dobbins. 30 Nov 1848 [Mr. Allen 9 Dec 1848]

F2-114: Surv.28 July 1847 by T.W.15,729 Hezekaiah Clagett 175 A. in Hardy Co. on Sandy Rg. at place called the Coaling, on Moore's Run adj. Godlove, Stewart, his own land. formerly Rogers, Pearson now Godlove. 30 Nov 1848 [Dl'd F.B. Welton 16 Mar 1849]

F2-115: Surv.18 May 1848 by T.W.12,382 & 16,531 Henry Miller 37 A. 30 sq. Po. in Page Co. on Blue Rg. & Dry Run S.E. of Luray adj. Philip Shaffer. 22 Dec 1848 [Dl'd Mr. Buswell 23 Dec 1848]

F2-116: Surv.12 Mar 1840 by T.W.14,172 & 14,234 Elias Jones 34 A. in Hampshire Co. on New Cr. Mt. adj. said Jones, Josias Smoot. 10 Jan 1849 [Dl'd James Allen Esq. 15 Mar 1849]

F2-117: Surv.5 Nov 1842 by T.W.14,234 Elias Jones 74 A. in Hampshire Co. on New Cr. adj. his land, Thomas Jones, Henry Harrison, Reuben Davis, Thomazin Grayson. 10 Jan 1849 [Dl'd James Allen Esq. 15 Mar 1849]

F2-118: Surv.23 May 1848 by T.W.16,531 Joseph Snell 44 1/4 A. in Page Co. in Piney woods S. of Luray adj. John Pendegrast, Henry Snell heirs, M. Piedlas, Dan'l Flinn, Marshall Yowal, Rodham Mazes. 10 Jan 1849 [John Kenny 17 Jan 1851]

F2-119: Surv.22 Aug 1842 by T.W.2751 Abraham Delauder 30 A. in Hardy Co. in upper Cove on N. Mt. adj. Machir, Abraham Delauder Sr., Adam Halterman, Campbell. 30 Apr 1849 [Dl'd Wm. Seymour 2 Nov 1850]

F2-120: Surv.2 Dec 1846 by T.W.2751 Jesse Whetzel 33 5/8 A. in Hardy Co. on Lost R. adj. Caldwell heirs, Cleaver, Lee, See. 13 Apr 1849 [Dl'd C.C. Lee Esq. 1 July 1850]

F2-121: Surv.16 May 1842 by T.W.2751 Benjamin Roby 45 A. in Hardy Co. in Fleming's Gap adj. Bell & Harness, Reel. 30 May 1849 G.T.Barbee 13 Dec 1849]

F2-122: Surv.8 Mar 1848 by T.W.10,451 Jacob Loy asne. of Conrod Loy 36 A. 1 Ro. 30 Per. in Frederick Co. on Hunting Rg. adj. said Loy, Matthew Ritter, David Davis, David Fries, John Hart. 30 May 1849 [Dl'd Rich. E. Burd Esq. 25 Apr 1851]

F2-123: Surv.7 Aug 1848 by T.W.16,854 Henry Brill 15 A. in Hampshire Co. on Timber Rg. & Dry Run adj. said Brill, Joseph Hannum, Samuel Brill, Isaac Brill. 30 June 1849 [Dl'd Wm. P. Stump 7 Mar 1850]

F2-124: Surv.5 Aug 1848 by T.W.16,854 Henry Brill 57 A. in Hampshire Co. on Timber Rg. & Lonam's Br. adj. his land, Jesse Anderson heirs, Thomas Racy heirs, John Laffollette, James Kelsoe. 30 June 1849 [Dl'd Wm. P. Stump 7 Mar 1850]

F2-125: Surv.2 Aug 1848 by T.W.15,966 & 16,854 Jacob Cump 75 A. in Hampshire Co. on Great Cacaphon adj. his land, John Siver heirs, Isaac Brill formerly Rudolph Bumgarner, Abraham Secrist's Taylor tract. 30 June 1849 [Dl'd Rob. M. Powell 17 Dec 1849]

F2-126: Surv.20 Aug 1839 by T.W.13,089 Joel Pennybaker asne. of Mounce Byrd & Edward Walton 50 A. in Shenandoah Co. on Smith's Cr. adj. John Kingree, George & Joel Pennybacker, Byrd now Joel Pennybaker. 31 May 1849 [Dl'd Prop'r 8 Dec 1849]

F2-127: Surv.18 Nov 1847 by T.W.16,630 William Duling 192 A. in Hampshire Co. on New Cr. & Knobley Mt. adj. his land, his Turner land, his Baker tract. 30 June 1849 [Dl'd Wm. P. Stump 7 Mar 1850]

F2-128: Surv.12 Oct 1848 by T.W.17,107 David Hott 124 A. in Hampshire Co. on Piney Mt. adj. David & George Hott 1842 patent. 30 June 1849 [Dl'd Wm. P. Stump 7 Mar 1850]

F2-129:   Surv.3 Aug 1848 by T.W.16,493 Andrew Kump 35 A. in Hampshire   Co.   on
Great Cacaphon adj. Valentine Secrest, Abraham Secrest, Jacob Cump.   30 June
1849 [Dl'd R.M. Powell 17 Dec 1849]

F2-130:   Surv.2 Aug 1848 by T.W.16,493 Andrew Kump 8 1/2 A. in Hampshire Co. on
Great Cacaphon adj. Jacob Kump, Joel Ellis heirs.   30 June 1849 [Dl'd R.M.
Powell 17 Dec 1849]

F2-131: Surv.14 Aug 1848 by T.W.16,854 Jacob Kline 3 1/4 A. in Hampshire Co. on
S.E. foot of Cacaphon Mt. adj. Kizner/Kisner, John Kline heirs.   Frederick
Conrod's grant 1 Dec 1770.   30 June 1849 [Dl'd W.P.Stump 7 Mar 1850]

F2-132:   Surv.18 July 1848 by T.W.11,105 Nicholas Leatherman 15 A. in Hampshire
Co. on High knob adj. land he bought of Vanmeter, Thomas Davy, Page. 30 June
1849 [Dl'd W.P.Stump 7 Mar 1850]

F2-133:   Surv.13 Oct 1848 by T.W.17,107 James Malick 128 A. in Hampshire Co. on
Short Ass Mt. adj. Samuel J. Stump, Philip Malick, Philip Swisher, William Loy,
George Hawse.   30 June 1849 [Dl'd W.P.Stump 7 Mar 1850]

F2-134:   Surv.29 Sep 1837 by T.W.12,899 & 12,589 James Malick & Gibson Ruckman
108 A. in Hampshire Co. on Tear Coat Cr. adj. George Haws, said Ruckman, John
Starkey, Philip Malick, Samuel Loy. 30 June 1849 [Dl'd W.P.Stump 7 Mar 1850]

F2-135: Surv.3 June 1847 by T.W.14,782 Daniel Williams 6 1/2 A. in Hampshire Co.
on Little Cacaphon adj. Silas Milleson, said Williams, Abraham Detrick. 30 June
1849 [Dl'd W.P.Stump 7 Mar 1850]

F2-136: Surv.10 Oct 1848 by T.W.16,493 & 17,107 Peter Poland 16 A. in Hampshire
Co. on Plum Lick Rg. adj. Henry Timbook/Timbrook, his own land, Joseph Chitter.
30 June 1849 [Dl'd W.P.Stump 7 Mar 1850]

F2-137:   Surv.11 Oct 1848 by T.W.17,107 Peter Poland 89 A. in Hampshire Co. on
N. R. adj. his own land, Thomas M. Marshall, Bennit Bean the third. 30 June
1849 [Dl'd W.P.Stump 7 Mar 1850]

F2-138:   Surv.6 Mar 1845 by T.W.14,897 Frederick Sheetz asne. of Michael Paugh
42 1/2 A. in Hampshire Co. on Leaffy Rg. & Patterson's Cr. adj. Dobbins,
Johnson, William Ree's heirs, Elijah Greenwell's legatees, Solomon Elifrits.   30
June 1849 [Dl'd W.P.Stump 7 Mar 1850]

F2-139:   Surv.10 Oct 1848 by T.W.16,854 & 17,107 Joseph S. Simpson asne. of
Peter Poland 122 A. in Hampshire Co. on Marshall's Rg. & N. R. by Mud lick run
adj. said Polland, Thomas M. Marshall, Samuel Marshall, William Sherrard heirs,
Parker. 30 June 1849 [Dl'd W.P.Stump 7 Mar 1850]

F2-140:   Surv.27 Sep 1845 by T.W.2751 Samuel Bromback 172 A. in Hardy Co. on
Stony R. adj. Baker, Bonness, Shell heirs, Spruce Rg., William Bonness. 30 June
1849 [Dl'd G.T.Barbee 13 Dec 1849]

F2-141:   Surv.30 May 1848 by T.W.2751 Henry W. Fry 99 1/2 A. in Hardy Co. on
Moore's Run of Cacapeon R. & the Big Rg. adj. his own land, Murray, his Moore
tract. 30 June 1849 [Dl'd Wm. Seymour 2 Nov 1850]

F2-142:   Surv.16 Jan 1847 by T.W.15,804 Amos Huffman 16 A. in Hardy Co. on S.
fork of N. R. adj. Sperry, Ludwick. 30 June 1849   [Dl'd Wm. Seymour 2 Nov 1850]

F2-143:   Surv.26 Apr 1848 by T.W.12,734 George Strawderman 39 5/8 A. in Hardy
Co. on Big Rg. & Kimsey's Run adj. Moses Wilkin, Mathias Wilkin, Fout, Chilcott.
30 June 1849   [Dl'd Wm. Seymour 2 Nov 1850]

F2-144:   Surv.1 Apr 1845 by T.W.2751 Henry Shepler 75 1/4 A. in Hardy Co. on
Brake's Mill Run of S. Fork & Forked Mt., White oak flats, Fearn Spring adj.
Simons, Deep Spring or Mine Surv.30 June 1849 [Mr. G.T. Barbee 13 Dec 1849]

F2-145:   Surv.20 Apr 1848 by T.W.14,722 Robert V. Snodgrass 2 A. 3 Ro. 16 sq.

227

Po. in Berkeley Co. adj. Henry G. Kitchen, Col. Snodgrass other land, Robert Murphy. 30 June 1849 [Dl'd C.J. Faulkner Esq. 22 Apr 1851]

F2-146: Surv.20 Apr 1848 by T.W.16,500 Robert V. Snodgrass 10 A. in Berkeley Co. on Back Cr., adj. Lowry, John Myers, Col. Snodgrass other land. 30 June 1849 [Dl'd C.J. Faulkner Esq. 22 Apr 1851]

F2-147: Surv.8 Apr 1848 by T.W.16,500 William S. Miller 4 A. 12 sq. Po. in Berkeley Co. adj. said Miller, James L. Campbell, George M. Bowers formerly Lemon, Lemon's reps. 30 June 1849 [Dl'd Jno. P. Kearfott Esq. 21 July 1849]

F2-148: Surv.28 Aug 1848 by T.W.13,025 Jonathan Crabill 1 A. 2 eRo. 21 Po. in Shenandoah Co. adj. Jacob Haun, Socksman, Andrew Bushong. 30 June 1849 [Dl'd Mr. Pitman 16 Mar 1850]

F2-149: Surv.21 Apr 1848 by T.W.16,215 George Miller 190 A. in Shenandoah Co. on Little Stony Cr. & Mill Cr. Mt. adj. Joseph Miller. 30 June 1849 [Dl'd Mr. Pitman 16 Mar 1850]

F2-150: Surv.15 June 1848 by T.W.14,775 Martin F. Miley 2 1/4 A. in Shenandoah Co. adj. Jacob Layman, said Miley's purchase of Abraham Whisson formerly Cline, Eli Saum formerly Wolf. 30 June 1849 [Dl'd Mr. Pitman 16 Mar 1850]

F2-151: Surv.8 Nov 1848 by T.W.14,926 John Story 27 A. in Madison Co. on Long Mt. adj. Elijah Yowell, Allen Yowell, John Story formerly Leonard Barnes, John L. Rider formerly William Early. 30 June 1849 [Dl'd Gen'l Banks 12 Mar 1850]

F2-152: Surv.20 May 1841 by T.W.12,361 Andrew Skidmore asne. of Elisha Stonestreet 50 A. in Hardy Co. on N. Fork adj. his own land, Andrew Skidmore, Elisha Stonestreet, Broad Run. 30 July 1849 [Dl'd Mr. G.T. Barbee 13 Dec 1849]

F2-153: Surv.15 Nov 1848 by T.W.14,594 William Neely 23 A. 2 Ro. in Morgan Co. on Warm Spring Rg. adj. Wm. Thompson, Miller, Gray, McKewan. 31 Aug 1849 [Dl'd Mr. Duckwall 14 Mar 1850]

F2-154: Surv.6 Sep 1848 by T.W.14,004 Henry Davis 14 A. 3 Ro. in Morgan Co. on Sideling Hill in Hardey's line, adj. said Davis, Richard Vannorsall. 31 Aug 1849 [Dl'd Mr. Duckwalt 14 Mar 1850]

F2-155: Surv.28 July 1848 by T.W.14,720 & 14,729 David Alderton 20 A. in Morgan Co. on Potomac R. adj. his own land, James King, Largent, William Alderton, W. Easter. 31 Aug 1849 [Dl'd Mr. Duckwalt 14 Mar 1850]

F2-156: Surv.21 Feb 1848 by T.W.14,720 Michael Rooney 4 A. 16 per. in Morgan Co. on Potomac R. below Sleepy Cr. 31 Aug 1849 [Dl'd Mr. Duckwalt 14 Mar 1850]

F2-157: Surv.29 July 1848 by T.W.13,057 & 10,852 Peter Gross 31 A. in Morgan Co. on Sideling Hill adj. Rodgers Heirs, side of Owl hollow, McDonald. 31 Aug 1849 [Dl'd Mr. Duckwalt 14 Mar 1850]

F2-158: Surv.5 Oct 1848 by T.W.12,791 Jacob Cann 510 A. in Morgan Co. on Cacapeon Mt. adj. Sherard heirs, path across the Mt. 31 Aug 1849 [Dl'd Mr. Duckwalt 14 Mar 1850]

F2-159: Surv.21 Apr 1848 by T.W.12,616 & 15,665 George F. Hupp asne. of Joseph Miller 92 A. in Shenandoah Co. on Little Stony Cr., Little Sluss Mt., adj. Walter Newman, Mill Cr. Mt. 31 Aug 1849 [Dl'd Mr. Pitman 16 Mar 1850]

F2-160: Surv.19 Feb 1844 by T.W.11,143 & 11,100 Gideon C. Brubaker 7 A. 2 Ro. 34 Po. in Page Co. on Shenandoah R. at foot of Massanotten Mt. adj. John Beever, Philip Long, s'd Gideon C. Brubaker, Barbour. 31 Aug 1849 [Dl'd Mr. Tho's Buswell 19 Mar 1850]

F2-161: Surv.13 Nov 1847 by T.W.14,729 John T. Dawson & Horatio R. Dawson asnes. of W.G. Catlett & John H. Kindle 178 A. in Morgan Co. on Sideling Hill adj. Pendleton, Reynolds, Harmison. 31 Jan 1850 [Dl'd Mr. Duckwall 14 Mar 1850]

F2-162: Surv.25 Nov 1848 by T.W.17,201 John H. Gaskins 2 Ro. 22 Po. in Fauquier Co. adj. Isham Keith formerly Pickett, John F. Chinn formerly Samuel Torbert, said John H. Gaskins, on Carter's Run. 29 Sep 1849

F2-163: Surv.15 Nov 1847 by T.W.14,729 & 14,720 William G. Catlett & John H. Kindle 222 A. in Morgan Co. on Rd. Rg. adj. Pendleton, Bennett's Run, Harmison. 1 Oct 1849 [Dl'd Mr. Duckwall 14 Mar 1850]

F2-164: Surv.21 Nov 1837 by T.W.12,665 Philip Crites & Jonathan Crites in their own right & as asnes. of Mary Crites & Barbry Crites 352 A. in Hardy Co. on Little Knob adj. Thomas Parson heirs, Wm. Taylor formerly Hincles, Bald Rg.. 1 Oct 1849 [Dl'd G.T. Barbee 13 Dec 1849]

F2-165: Surv.3 Sep 1842 by T.W.2751 Mordecai Strosnider in his own right & Henry W. Fry asne. of said Mordecai Strosnider 350 A. in Hardy Co. on N. Mt. adj. his father, Simon Surtzer, Henry Fry, Daniel Hacker, Isaac Strosnider. 31 Oct 1849 [Dl'd Wm. Seymour 2 Nov 1850]

F2-166: Surv.19 Mar 1849 by T.W.6184, 5832 & 16,356 Moses S. Grantham 291 A. in Berkeley Co. on N. Mt. adj. Capt. John Lyle, said Grantham, James Parke, Tate, Rob't Daniels, Dr. Coe, Round Top Mt. 30 Nov 1849 [M.S. Grantham 12 Jan 1850]

F2-167: Surv.18 Sep 1848 by T.W.16,456 William Baker 53 1/2 A. in Hardy Co. on Lost R. & Brown Loaf Mt. adj. his own land, Reed, Warden heirs, Moore. 30 Nov 1849 [Dl'd Wm. Seymour 2 Nov 1850]

F2-168: Surv.18 Sep 1848 by T.W.16,456 William Baker 24 5/8 A. in Hardy Co. on Lost R. & Brownioaf Mt., Rocky Rg. adj. his own land, heirs of Wm Reed dec'd, Lacell's hollow. 30 Nov 1849 [Dl'd Wm. Seymour 2 Nov 1850]

F2-169: Surv.7 Aug 1841 by T.W.14,573 David Ellis 151 A. in Hampshire Co. on Bakers Run of Potomac R. adj. Benjamin Taylor, Valentine King(28 Dec 1791 grant), Sam'l Bonham, Daniel McDonald(5 Apr 1790 grant). 30 Nov 1849 [Dl'd Mr. Powell 13 Mar 1850]

F2-170: Surv.21 Mar 1846 by T.W.2751 Joseph Williams asne. of John Crose 65 1/4 A. in Hardy Co. on Patterson's Cr. and Swimm's hollow adj. George formerly Y. Linton, his own, Williams. 30 Nov 1849 [Dl'd Wm. Seymour 2 Nov 1850]

F2-171: Surv.27 May 1848 by T.W.17,196 Ephraim Link 70 3/4 A. in Hardy Co. on Lost R. & Little Rg. adj. Baker, Inskeep, Link, Slater, Kidner. 30 Nov 1849 [Dl'd Wm. Seymour 2 Nov 1850]

F2-172: Surv.20 Jan 1848 by T.W.2751 Daniel S. Tucker 14 A. in Hardy Co. on Ross Run of Patterson's Cr. adj. his own land, Welch, Geo. Gilpin now Welsh, his Ross land. 30 Nov 1849 [Dl'd Wm. Seymour 2 Nov 1850]

F2-173: Surv.10 Apr 1849 by T.W.16,531 Martin Alther 5 1/4 A. in Page Co. on the Blue Rg. E. of Luray adj. James Kibler, Martin Alther, George Shenk, John Fox, Johathan Grandstaff. 30 Nov 1849 [Dl'd Mr. Tho's Buswell 19 Mar 1850]

F2-174: Surv.11 Nov 1847 by T.W.10,852 Peter Dyche & John Young asnes. of William Harmison 26 A. in Morgan Co. on Conolaway hill adj. Cross heirs, John Sherard heirs. 15 Dec 1849 [Dl'd Mr. Duckwall 16 Jan 1850]

F2-175: Surv.4 May 1849 by T.W.14,926 J.B. Gray, A.G. Grinnan & David S. Jones 63 A. in Madison Co. on Stony Man Mt. & the Blue Rg. near Page & Madison Cos. line, adj. Philip Slaughter. 31 Dec 1849 [Dl'd Mr. Newman 23 Jan 1850]

F2-176: Surv.24 May 1849 by T.W.17,628 Jefferson Hart 76 A. in Madison Co. adj. Great Ragged Mt., Mark Fink, Joel Hart?, Richard Burdine 1767 grant. 31 Dec 1849

F2-177: Surv.28 Nov 1848 by T.W.15,458 & 2945 Jesse J. Pugh 249 1/2 A. in Hardy Co. on Lost R., Flat Rg., Hanging Rock Rg. & Wardin's Rg. adj. Reed, Dyer, Hawdershell, Landacre, Bixler, Garrett, Poundmill Run, Smith. 31 Dec 1849 [Dl'd Mr. A.R. Wood 19 Mar 1850]

F2-178: Surv.14 June 1847 by T.W.15,875 & 16,493 James Croston & William Croston asnes. of Christopher Heiskill 14 A. in Hampshire Co. on N. R. & Cacaphon, N. Br. Turnpike Rd., adj. said Heiskill, Croston's Compton tract, Croston's Deaver land. 31 Dec 1849 [Dl'd Mr. Powell 13 Mar 1850]

F2-179: Surv.17 Jan 1849 by T.W.15,875 Elijah High asne. of Strother Gannon 42 1/2 A. in Hampshire Co. on Mill Cr. adj. Elijah High, Henry M. High, Stephen Fuller, Lewis W. Everitt. 31 Dec 1849 [Dl'd Mr. Powell 13 Mar 1850]

F2-180: Surv.31 May 1849 by T.W.16,469, 17,294 & 17,003 Archibald Myers 102 A. in Berkeley Co. near Third Hill Mt. adj. Campbell's Little Yates tract, Arick, Ganoe's heirs, Teter Everhart. 31 Dec 1849 [Dl'd M.S. Grantham 12 Jan 1850]

F2-181: Surv.15 June 1849 by T.W.17,521 Henry Quaintance 108 3/4 A. in Madison Co. adj. Nimrod Jenkins, land formerly Peter Fox, Gt. Ragged Mt., Rocky Run. 31 Jan 1850 [Dl'd M.D. Newman 4 Mar 1850]

F2-182: Surv.12 June 1849 by T.W.17,294 Henry Miller 21 A. in Berkeley Co. adj. Jones, Gantt formerly Burcham, said Miller. 31 Jan 1850 [Dl'd Mr A.G. Hammond 13 Mar 1850]

F2-183: Surv.15 June 1847 by T.W.14,004 Jacob Cann 76 A. in Morgan Co. on Cacapeon Mt. adj. Edland, Vannorsdall, Harlan, Ziler. 31 Jan 1850 [Dl'd Mr. Duckwall 14 Mar 1850]

F2-184: Surv.15 June 1847 by T.W.14,004 Jacob Cann 56 A. in Morgan Co. on Cacapeon Cr. & Little Mt. adj. land formerly Jonathan Morgan. 31 Jan 1850 [Dl'd Mr. Duckwall 14 Mar 1850]

F2-185: Surv.9 Nov 1847 by T.W.14,004 Jacob Cann 22 1/4 A. in Morgan Co. on Cacapeon Cr. bet. Little Mt. & Cacapeon Mt. adj. Edland, Vannorsdall. 31 Jan 1850 [Dl'd Mr. Duckwall 14 Mar 1850]

F2-186: Surv.14 June 1849 by T.W.17,770 George Keesacker 7 A. in Berkeley Co. adj. said Keesacker, Jonas Hedge, John Zorn, Keesacker's Robinson land. 1 Mar 1850 [Dl'd Mr. Lewis Grantham 13 Mar 1850]

F2-187: Surv.19 Apr 1849 by T.W.17,414 Isaiah Corbin asne. of Henry Corbin 186 A. in Hampshire Co. on Buck Mt. adj. Isaiah Corbin, Abraham J. Alger, Elizabeth Powell, William French (of Rob't). 1 Mar 1850 [Dl'd Mr. Powell 13 Mar 1850]

F2-188: Surv.8 June 1849 by T.W.17,236 Benjamin P. Newman 857 A. in Hardy & Shenandoah Cos. on N. Mt. & Devil's hole Valley, Moorefield to Woodstock Rd. adj. Moyers, Tibbit, Newman, Timber Hill. 1 May 1850 [Wm. Seymour 2 Nov 1850]

F2-189: Surv.20 June 1849 by T.W.17,514 Rowland Yowell 124 A. in Madison Co. on Rocky Run & Fork Mt. adj. Peter Fox, Jenkins, Story's Spring Br., Henry Quaintnce. 1 May 1850 [Dl'd Gen. Banks 14 Apr 1853]

F2-190: Surv.22 June 1849 by T.W.17,514 Roland Yowell 122 A. in Madison Co. on Story's Spring Br. & Rocky Run adj. said Yowell, Henry Quaintance. 1 May 1850 [Dl'd Gen. Banks 14 Apr 1853]

F2-191: Surv.22 Nov 1849 by T.W.15,665 John Coffman 7 A. in Shenandoah Co. on N. Fork of Shenandoah R. adj. Philip Zirkle & Henry Kips purchase of Lilbert, being an island in s'd R. 1 July 1850 [Dl'd Sam'l C. Williams Esq. 31 Oct 1850]

F2-192: Surv.10 May 1849 by T.W.9053 Philip Dellinger 143 A. in Shenandoah Co. on Stoney Cr. & N. Mt. adj. land formerly Isaac Funkhouser, Christian Dellinger formerly Lindemood, Walter Newman, Conrad Sayger. 1 July 1850 [Dl'd Sam'l C. Williams Esq. 31 Oct 1850]

F2-193: Surv.15 Nov 1849 by T.W.12,968 Jonathan Hollar 1 1/2 A. in Shenandoah Co. in Pine Woods N. of Stoney Cr. adj. John Burk, said Hollar's purchase of Dennison, James Dicuts, Hollar's purchase of John Koonty. 1 July 1850 [Dl'd Sam'l C. Williams Esq. 31 Oct 1850]

F2-194:   Surv.23 May 1849 by T.W.12,937 Adam Tusing 42 A. in Shenandoah Co. adj. the Co. line bet. Rockingham & Shenandoah Cos., said Adam Tusing, Machir now Lee, Adam Barb. 1 July 1850 [Dl'd Sam'l C. Williams Esq. 31 Oct 1850]

F2-195:   Surv.18 Nov 1849 by T.W.12,937 Henry Ridenour 65 A. in Shenandoah Co. on Treetopped Mt. adj. said Ridenour, heirs of Michael Spiegle dec'd. 1 July 1850 [Dl'd Sam'l C. Williams Esq. 31 Oct 1850]

F2-196:   Surv.21 Nov 1849 by T.W.17,290 Jacob Stirewalt 11 A. in Shenandoah Co. on Turnpile Rd. from New Market to Luray on Massanotten Mt. adj. James Barbour, Peter Fogle, Moses Zirkle. 1 July 1850 [Sam'l C. Williams Esq. 31 Oct 1850]

F2-197:   Surv.17 May 1849 by T.W.12,616 Joshua Sine 34 3/4 A. in Shenandoah Co. on Stoney Cr. adj. Walter Newman, Lee, Jacob Barb, Lewis Naselrod. 1 July 1850 [Dl'd Sam'l C. Williams Esq. 31 Oct 1850]

F2-198:   Surv.22 May 1849 by T.W.13,025 & 14,266 Edward Walton 151 A. in Shenandoah Co. on Short Hills & Sup and lick Mt. adj. Jacob Wine, Estep. 1 July 1850 [Dl'd Sam'l C. Williams Esq. 31 Oct 1850]

F2-199: Surv.11 June 1849 by T.W.17,173 John M. Barb 51 A. in Hardy Co. on Trout run valley, N. Mt. adj. Moyers, Smith, Lee. 1 July 1850 [Wm. Seymour 2 Nov'50]

F2-200: Surv.16 Sep 1848 by T.W.15,804 Henry Baughman asne. of David Reed 22 A. in Hardy Co. on Flat Rg. & Lost R. near Hanging Rock, adj. heirs of Wm. Reed dec'd, Lee. 1 July 1850 [Dl'd Wm. Seymour 2 Nov 1850]

F2-201:   Surv.23 Apr 1849 by T.W.11,056 & 11,201 Archibald Cornwell 348 A. in Hardy Co. on Patterson's Cr. Mt. bet. Thomas & Randall's Gaps adj. Bergdall, Seymour, land he purchased of Heath, Martin's Gap, the Frenchman's Hollow. 1 July 1850 [Dl'd Wm. Seymour 2 Nov 1850]

F2-202:   Surv.21 June 1849 by T.W.17,196 Jacob A. Chrisman 34 1/4 A. in Hardy Co. on Lost R. & Little Rg. adj. Lee, Wood, his own land, Dunbar. 1 July 1850 [Dl'd Wm. Seymour 2 Nov 1850]

F2-203:   Surv.5 Nov 1849 by T.W.15,771 George Fisher 161 A. in Hardy Co. on New Cr. Mt. S. of Hawks Gap adj. Cosner, Idleman, his own land, Lounies Cr., the Beverly land, Mill Tract. 1 July 1850 [Dl'd Wm. Seymour 2 Nov 1850]

F2-204:   Surv.26 Sep 1849 by T.W.15,804 William Idleman 4 1/2 A. in Hardy Co. on Patterson's Cr. Mt. & Bald Rg. adj. McMechen heirs, McNemar Vanmeter, his own land, McNemar, Renick. 1 July 1850 [Dl'd Wm. Seymour 2 Nov 1850]

F2-205:   31 Oct 1849 by T.W.17,343 Michail Simons 40 A. in Hardy Co. on S. Fork adj. Radabough, Christian Simon, the Big Surv., Dasher's Simon's place. 1 July 1850 [Dl'd Wm. Seymour 2 Nov 1850]

F2-206:   Surv.12 July 1849 by T.W.15,729 Isaac V. Seymour 2 7/8 A. in Hardy Co. on S. Fork adj. his own land, Felix Seymour, the Thicket, F. Seymour's Race field. 1 July 1850 [Dl'd Wm. Seymour 2 Nov 1850]

F2-207:   Surv.31 Oct 1848 by T.W.15,804 Aaron & Archibald Wilkin 9 1/2 A. in Hardy Co. on Little Rg. & Kimsey's Run of Lost R. adj. Harper, Wilson, Lee, Lehugh heirs, Little Back Run. 1 July 1850 [Dl'd Wm. Seymour 2 Nov 1850]

F2-208:   Surv.3 July 1848 by T.W.12,734 Mathias Wilkin 9 A. in Hardy Co. on Big Rg. adj. his own land, Miller, Moses Wilkin, Strawderman. 1 July 1850 [Dl'd Wm. Seymour 2 Nov 1850]

F2-209:   Surv.2 Feb 1849 by T.W.16,531 Henry Clizer 4 A. 20 Per. in Page Co. on Jeremies Run at foot of Blue Rg. N.E. of Luray adj. George Jones, Isaac Overall heirs. 1 July 1850 [Dl'd Mr. Buswell 3 Apr 1851]

F2-210:   Surv.10 Oct 1848 by T.W.14,004 & 12,791 Jacob Cann 134 A. in Morgan Co. on Sideling hill. 1 July 1850 [Dl'd L. Vanarsdale Esq. 31 Mar 1851]

F2-211:   Surv.10 Nov 1847 by T.W.14,004 Jeremiah Harlan & Aaron Harlan Jr. 108
A. in Morgan Co. on Capapeon Mt. adj. Aaron Harland/Harlan Sr., Geo. Ziler. 1
July 1850 [Dl'd L. Vanarsdale Esq. 31 Mar 1851]

F2-212: Surv.5 Apr 1842 by T.W.14,360 Wm. Hammach asne. of George Haws 86 A. in
Hampshire Co. on S. Fork of Little Cacapon adj. James Coombs, Coombs tract
bought of Smoot, Charles Doyle. 1 July 1850 [Dl'd Col. C. Blue 4 Mar 1851]

F2-213: Surv.3 Feb 1849 by T.W.16,350 William Jenney 6 A. in Hampshire Co. on
New Cr. adj. said Jenney, Samuel Arnold. 1 July 1850 [Wm.P. Stump 24 Mar 1851]

F2-214: Surv.4 May 1849 by T.W.14,202, 17,545 & 10,772 Benjamin Junkins 216 A.
in Hampshire Co. on Alleghany Mt. adj. Vanse, Abram's Cr., Elijah Harvey heirs,
Clinton, Inskeep. 1 July 1850 [Dl'd Wm.P. Stump Esq. 24 Mar 1851]

F2-215: Surv.5 May 1849 by T.W.17,545 William Junkins 136 A. in Hampshire Co.
on Alleghany Mt. adj. Martin, Elijah Harvey heirs "Linton" tract, Abram's Cr.,
Clinton. 1 July 1850

F2-216: Surv.14 Dec 1846 by T.W.15,404 George Thompson 17 A. 3 Ro. in Hampshire
Co. on Little Cacapeon Mt. adj. his land, John Arnold, Sam'l Hott heirs, Edmond
Buzzard heirs. 1 July 1850 [Dl'd Wm.P. Stump Esq. 24 Mar 1851]

F2-217: Surv.4 May 1849 by T.W.17,545 George G. Tasker & William Junkins 173 A.
in Hampshire Co. on Alleghany Mt. bet. Abram's Cr. & the N. Br. adj. Benjamin
Junkins, Inskeep, Vause. 1 July 1850 [Dl'd Wm.P. Stump Esq. 24 Mar 1851]

F2-218:   Surv.30 Oct 1849 by T.W.15,966 George G. Tasker & Benjamin Junkins 100
A. in Hampshire Co. on Alleghany Mt. bet. N. Br. of Potomac & Abram's Cr. adj.
Vause, George G. Tasker & William Junkins, Inskeep, tract formerly Clinton's,
William & Francis Deakins. 1 July 1850 [Dl'd Wm.P. Stump Esq. 24 Mar 1851]

F2-219:   Surv.27 Oct 1849 by T.W.17,279 James W. F. Allen & Mortimer D. Nevill
119 1/2 A. in Hardy Co. on Hay's Rg. of Alleghany Mt. bet. Difficult & N. Br. &
Buffaloe. adj. Kidd Hays. 9 Aug 1850 [Mailed to Prop'r 13 Aug 1850]

F2-220: Surv.3 Apr 1846 by T.W.10,860 Henry Funkhouser asne. of William Slater
17 1/4 A. in Hardy Co. on Little Rg. S. of Ruddles Run of Lost R. adj. Inskeep's
Robinson or Collins tract, Inskeep's McHendry tract. 1 Aug 1850 [Dl'd Mr.
Welton 28 Mar 1851]

F2-221:   Surv.24 May 1838 by T.W.2751 Isaac W. Kuykendall asne. of Solomon
Crites 93 A. in Hardy Co. on Water Ash Run adj. Landes heirs, Jacob Barkdall. 1
Aug 1850 [Dl'd Mr. Welton 28 Mar 1851]

F2-222:   Surv.3 Apr 1846 by T.W.15,616 & 10,860 Henry Funkhouser asne. of
William Slater 67 A. in Hardy Co. on Lower Little Rg. & Ruddles Run of Lost R.
adj. Link, Inskeep, grant to William Baker by Fairfax now Inskeep & Wardens,
Inskeep's Home or McHendry tract. 1 Aug 1850 [Dl'd Mr. Welton 28 Mar 1851]

F2-223: Surv.21 Sep 1849 by T.W.17,917 Mordicai B. Sinclair & James M. Sinclair
8 A. 3 Ro. 33 1/2 Po. in Pr. William Co. adj. their own land, William W. Davis,
John H. Austin & wife, Occoquon R., Long Br. 1 Aug 1850

F2-224: Surv.10 Apr 1848 by T.W.10,451 Peter Ashton 111 1/2 A. in Frederick Co.
on Brush Cr. adj. Lamp, Bailey, Null &c., said Ashton, Green spring Rd., Null
now Barak Dehaven, Job Dehaven, William Dehaven. 1 Aug 1850 [Dl'd J. F. Wall
Esq. 18 Mar 1851]

F2-225:   Surv.23 May 1849 by T.W.13,025, 14,266, 17,290, 12,937 & 15,665 Israel
Tusing 404 1/2 A. in Shenandoah Co. on Sup and Lick Mt., adj. Shenandoah &
Rockingham Cos. line, Tunis Cr., adj. Nicholas Dusing, Adam Barb Jr., Christian
Biller. 1 Aug 1850 [Dl'd Mason Base Esq. 24 Dec 1852]

F2-226: Surv.5 June 1849 by T.W.16,602 & 16,301 Thomas Berryman Looker 205 A.
in Rockingham Co. on Peaked Mt. adj. Mauzy, Ammons, John Comrad/Conrad, Kirtley,

232

Rinehart, Great Mt. Surv.1 Aug 1850 [Dl'd to br. of rec't 22 Oct 1851]

F2-227:   Surv.26 Jan 1849 by T.W.17220 William F. Pifer 155 A. in Hardy Co. on
Fork Mt. & Brakes Mill Run adj. Morrow, heirs of James Gray dec'd. 31 Aug 1850
[Dl'd G.T.Barbee Esq. 31 Oct 1850]

F2-228:   Surv.23 May 1840 by T.W.2751 George Simons 175 A. in Hardy Co. adj. his
land on Middle Mt., Leonard Dasher, Randell. 31 Aug 1850 [Mr. Welton 28 Mar 1851

F2-229:   Surv.1 Sep 1841 by T.W.2751 Isaac Dasher 127 A. in Hardy Co. on Middle
Mt. adj. his own land, Peter Simons, his John Brake tract, N.N. line. 31 Aug
1850 [Dl'd Mr. Welton 28 Mar 1851]

F2-230:   Surv.31 Oct 1848 by T.W.17,083 & 17,196 William Smith 107 1/2 A. in
Hardy Co. on Flat Rg. & Lost R. adj. Warden's heirs, Reed's heirs, Whitzel. 31
Aug 1850 [Dl'd Mr. Welton 28 Mar 1851]

F2-231:   Surv.12 June 1846 T.W.2751 William McDonald 115 A. in Hardy Co. on
Little Mt. bet. N.& S. forks of Lounies Cr. adj. Feaster, Groves, Stingley,
Welton, his own land, his Forge tract, Feaster's Bishop land, Grove's Brown
tract. 31 Aug 1850 [Dl'd Mr. Welton 28 Mar 1851]

F2-232:   Surv.9 Nov 1847 by T.W.14,232 John Dawson 21 A. 3 Ro. in Morgan Co. on
Warm Spring Rg. adj. Neely, Hamlin. 1 Oct 1850 [Dl'd L. Vanorsdale 31 Mar 1851]

F2-233:   Surv.6 Oct 1849 by T.W.11,099 Rezin Reynolds 77 A. in Morgan Co. on
Sideling Hill, adj. Hite, Beatty. 1 Oct 1850 [Dl'd L. Vanorsdale 31 Mar 1851]

F2-234:   Surv.24 Nov 1848 by T.W.17,302 Henry Swisher 166 1/2 A. in Hardy Co. on
S. fork of N. R. adj. Warden, Bradfield, Stover, his own land, Wardens Rg. 1
Oct 1850 [Dl'd Mr. Welton 28 Mar 1851]

F2-235:   Surv.9 Aug 1848 by T.W.16,854 Joseph Hannum 57 A. in Hampshire Co. on
Timber Rg. & Lonams Br. adj. John Perril, James Kelsoe, Johathan Lukin's heirs.
1 Oct 1850   [Dl'd Alex. Monroe Esq. 24 Mar 1851]

F2-236: Surv.10 Aug 1848 by T.W.16,854 Joseph Hannum 25 1/2 A. in Hampshire Co.
on Timber Rg. & N. Mt. adj. Johathan Lukin's hiers, said Hannum, James Kelsoe,
John Farmer. 1 Oct 1850 [Dl'd Alex. Monroe Esq. 24 Mar 1851]

F2-237: Surv.7 Aug 1848 by T.W.16,854 Joseph Hannum 48 1/2 A. in Hampshire Co.
on Timber Rg. & Dry Run adj. his land, Henry Brill, Isaac Brill. 1 Oct 1850
[Dl'd Alex. Monroe Esq. 24 Mar 1851]

F2-238:   Surv.18 May 1849 by T.W.17,414, 17,545 & 17,107 Frederick W. Brill 395
A. in Hampshire Co. on Spring Run near Farrington's Br. of Great Cacaphon adj.
John Rosebrough, Addison Cooper, Roger's heirs, Joseph Watson, the Spring Rg. 1
Oct 1850 [Dl'd Alex. Monroe Esq. 24 Mar 1851]

F2-239:   Surv.10 Aug 1848 by T.W.16,854 John Brill 10 A. in Hampshire Co. on
Great Cacaphon adj. his own line, Jacob Crump?, Joel Ellis heirs. 1 Oct 1850
[Dl'd Alex. Monroe Esq. 24 Mar 1851]

F2-240:   Surv.18 May 1849 by T.W.17,414 Henry Brill 50 A. in Hampshire Co. on
Great Cacaphon near Farringtons Br. & Spring Rg. adj. Frederick W. Brill, said
Henry Brill, John L. Smith, John Rosbrough. 1 Oct 1850 [Dl'd Alex. Monroe Esq.
24 Mar 1851]

F2-241:   Surv.18 May 1849 by T.W.16,335 Henry Brill & John L. Smith 200 A. in
Hampshire & Hardy Cos. on Farringtons Br. of Great Cacaphon, foot of Spring Rg.
adj. John Inskeep, John Rosbrough. 1 Oct 1850 [Dl'd Alex. Monroe 24 Mar 1851]

F2-242:   Surv.30 Mar 1850 by T.W.18,347 William C. Worthington Trustee for
Robert Worthington 8 A. 1 Ro. 25 Per. in Jefferson Co. adj. Mrs. L. Washington's
dower, Bryant O'Bannon, Geo. B. Beall, Alldridge, Smithfield, Charlestown &
Harpers Ferry Turnpike, Rt. Worthington. 1 Nov 1850 [Mailed to Wm. C.

Worthington Esq. 6 Nov 1850]

F2-243: Surv.2 Apr 1850 by T.W.13,122 Perry I.? Eggborn 49 1/2 A. in Culpeper Co. on Muddy Run Mt. adj. John Scott formerly Fairfax, Dulaney, Combs now Connors, Savage now Stewart, Fauc. 1 Nov 1850 [Mailed to Prop'r 19 Dec 1850]

F2-244: Surv.27 Jan 1849 by T.W.16,646 Adam Wolfe Jr. 43 1/2 A. in Hardy Co. on S. Fork & Shooks Run, it being land surveyed for Hite, Branch Mt. 1 Nov 1850

F2-245: Surv.19 Aug 1835 by T.W.12,361 Christipher Armantrout 25 A. in Hardy Co. on N. Mill Cr. adj. John & Henry Armantrout, Christopher Armantrout now Job Armantrout, Stombaw now Henry Armantrout heirs (Harmantrout). 1 Nov 1850 [Dl'd Mr. Welton 28 Mar 1851]

F2-246: Surv.18 Apr 1849 by T.W.16,493 & 17,545 William French of Robert 13 A. in Hampshire Co. on Little Cacaphon near his saw mill, adj. said French, Robert McBride heirs, French formerly Elisha Gulick. 1 Nov 1850 [Dl'd W.P. Stump Esq. 24 Mar 1851]

F2-247: Surv.6 Apr 1850 by T.W.17,956 John, David & George Sours 35 A. in Page Co. on Hawk's bill & Blue Rg. S.W. of Luray adj. Reuben Somers, David S. Jones, David Sours, Isaac Printz. 30 Nov 1850 [Dl'd Mr. Buswell 3 Apr 1851]

F2-248: Surv.27 Apr 1850 by T.W.17,956 & 18,442 John Sours, David Sours & George Sours 101 1/2 A. in Page Co. on Blue Rg. on Miller's head S.W. of Luray adj. David C. Printz, D.S. Jones, Peter Printz, Abraham Printz. 30 Nov 1850 [Dl'd Mr. Buswell 3 Apr 1851]

F2-249: Surv.22 Feb 1850 by T.W.18,205 Alpheus Gaunt 27 1/2 A. in Rappahannock Co. on Pignut Mt. adj. Andrew Gaunt, Alpheus Gaunt. 1 Jan 1851 [Dl'd James H. Morrison 22 Apr 1852]

F2-250: Surv.6 Apr 1850 by T.W.17,956 John, David & George Sours 79 1/2 A. in Page Co. on Dry Run & Blue Rg. S.E. of Luray adj. John Griffith, head of the Falls, John Sours, Frederick Sours, John Printz. 1 Jan 1851

F2-251: Surv.23 Mar 1842 by T.W.2751 Abram Steelee 45 A. in Hardy Co. on Cove Mt. adj. Branson's heirs, James Machir 1795 grant. 1 Feb 1851 [Dl'd Wm. Seymour 22 Jan 1851]

F2-252: Surv.17 Sep 1849 by T.W. 14,004 William Dawson 34 A. in Morgan Co. on Sideling Hill & Mill Rd. adj. Cann. 1 Jan 1851 [L. Vanorsdale Esq. 31 Mar 1851]

F2-253: Surv.28 May 1850 by T.W.17,132 Adam B. Doval 1 A. 3 Ro. 31 Po. in Page Co. on Shenandoah R. S.W. of Luray adj. Adam B. Doval, John Kite. 1 Jan 1851 [Dl'd Mr. Buswell 4 Apr 1851]

F2-254: Surv.25 June 1850 by T.W.18,442 Charles Duncan 131 A. 3 Ro. in Page Co. on Middle Mt. in Powels Ft. N.W. of Luray adj. Charles Duncan, Marstons Lantz. 1 Feb 1851

F2-255: Surv.12 Dec 1843 by T.W.2751 John Delawder 27 1/2 A. in Hardy Co. in Upper Cove on Cove Mt. adj. Benjamin Basore, Jacob Halterman. 1 Feb 1851 [Dl'd Wm. Seymour 22 July 1851]

F2-256: Surv.3 May 1850 by T.W.18,082 & 17,770 Moses S. Grantham 91 A. in Berkeley Co. adj. Butler, Campbell, Adam Fry, said Grantham. 1 Feb 1851 [Dl'd to Prop'r 13 Jan 1852]

F2-257: Surv.27 Aug 1849 by T.W.15,804 Samuel & Zachariah Arnold 9 5/8 A. in Hardy Co. on Alleghany Mt. adj. My Lords Meadows, their own land, Shillingsberg, the Germans formerly Chambers. 1 Apr 1851 [Dl'd Wm. Seymour 22 July 1851]

F2-258: Surv.27 June 1849 by T.W.17,125 Jonas Brock 103 A. in Hardy Co. on Hunting Rg. bet. Pain's run & Camp Br. adj. his own land formerly Cook, Whetzel, the Big Surv., Coon Lee. 1 May 1851 [Dl'd Wm. Seymour 22 July 1851]

F2-259:   Surv.11 Oct 1849 by T.W.16,458 & 17,173 Cephas Childs 112 A. in Hardy Co. on Lost R., Little Rg. adj. Inskeep, Link, Funkhouser, Warden, his own land, Charlotte's hollow, his Johnson tract. 1 May 1851 [Wm. Seymour 22 July 1851]

F2-260:   Surv.15 Dec 1846 by T.W.2751 Michael Tusing 145 A. in Hardy Co. on Brushy Rg. bet. Buck lick & Water Lick runs of N. R. adj. Hammick, Walker, Hunous, his own land formerly Mawk. 1 May 1851 [Dl'd Wm. Seymour 22 July 1851]

F2-261:   Surv.3 Nov 1849 by T.W.10,885 Corneluis Shuler 6 A. 13 1/2 sq. Po. in Frederick Co. on Timber Rg. adj. George Whitacre, John Rinehart, Jackson, land formerly Adam's. 1 May 1851 [Dl'd Rich'd E. Byrd Esq. 14 July 1851]

F2-262:   Surv.18 Apr 1849 by T.W.15,031 Ann Elizabeth Watkins wid., James Thomas, Francis Marion, Elizabeth Harriet, Henry Madison, Benjamin Franklin & John Williams Watkins, ch. & heirs of Henry Watkins dec'd, 12 A. in Hampshire Co. on Little Cacaphon adj. 108 A. he bought of William French, John Powelson heirs. 1 May 1851 [Dl'd Mr. T.B.White 15 Apr 1853]

F2-263:   Surv.18 Apr 1849 by T.W.16,854 Ann Elizabeth Watkins wid., James Thomas, Francis Marion, Elizabeth Harriet, Henry Madison, Benjamin Franklin & John Williams Watkins, ch. & heirs of Henry Watkins dec'd, 22 A. in Hampshire Co. on Little Cacaphon adj. Robert McBride heirs, William French of Rob't, said Watkins bought of French, Simon Baker. 1 May 1851 [Mr. T.B. White 15 Apr 1853]

F2-264:   Surv.28 Oct 1850 by T.W.15,928 Joseph W. Hollis 16 1/2 A. in Berkeley & Frederick Cos. on N. Mt. adj. Joseph W. Hollis, Suver heirs, P. H. Rouse. 1 June 1851 [Dl'd Mr. Gray 13 Jan 13/52]

F2-265:   Surv.2 May 1846 by T.W.14,202 & 15,875 George Haws 25 A. 2 Ro. in Hampshire Co. on Tear Coat Cr. adj. William Loy. 1 Aug 1851 [Dl'd Thomas White Esq. 14 Feb 1852]

F2-266:   Surv.19 June 1850 by T.W.17,770 John French 5 A. in Berkeley Co. adj. Strous, Henry French heirs. 1 Aug 1851 [Dl'd Mr. Newkirk 13 Jan '52]

F2-267:   Surv.14 Oct 1850 by T.W.15,480 Joseph Sidebottom 32 1/4 A. in Frederick Co. on Gap Run & N.W. Turnpike adj. Zane now Sidebottoms heirs, J. H. Campbell, Bruce, William Rinker. 1 Aug 1851 [Dl'd Jos. Barrett Esq. 2 Mar '54]

F2-268:   Surv.23 Mar 1850 by T.W.12,791 & 14,004 Isaac Fawver & John H. Kindle 118 A. in Morgan Co. on Willotts Run, Rd. Rg. adj. Sampson Sagle, Dermoody, Pendleton, Catlett, Kindle. 28 July 1851 [Dl'd A. Michael Jr. 2 June '52]

F2-269:   Surv.1 Feb 1849 by T.W.16,976 William Schitzer 48 3/8 A. in Hardy Co. on Rg. bet. N. & Middle forks of Patterson's Cr. adj. Babb, Shrout, James Miles. 1 Aug 1851 [Dl'd Mr. Price 24 Mar '52]

F2-270:   Surv.23 Dec 1850 by T.W.18,702 Jacob B. Brown & Jacob Nisswaner 39 A. 2 Ro. in Jefferson Co. at confluence of Potomac & Shenandoah Rs. adj. Jacob B. Brown, Robert Harper, Shenandoah Street near office formerly occupied by U.S. super't, U. S. Canal. 29 July 1851 [Mailed to Andrew Hunter Esq. 1 Aug 1851]

F2-271:   Surv.24 Jan 1850 by T.W.15,824 William Welch 55 1/2 A. in Hardy Co. on Ridges Bet. Thorn & Ross Runs of Patterson's Cr. adj. George's Heirs, Harriss, Tucker. 1 Aug 1851 [Dl'd Jno. H. Cassin Esq. 1 Mar 1854]

F2-272:   Surv.23 Jan 1850 by T.W.17,345 James Roberts 10 A. in Hardy Co. on Salt Spring Run of Thorn Run, on Knobly Rd. adj. his own land, Reed & Canter, Noel, his tract, Doll. 1 Aug 1851 [Dl'd John C. Mulloy Esq. 3 Mar '54]

F2-273:   Surv.2 June 1850 by T.W.14,775 George Keller asne. of John Keller 8 3/4 A. in Shenandoah Co. in Powell's Big Ft. adj. Jacob Burner, George Keller. 1 Sep 1851 [Dl'd Mr. Gatewood 7 Feb '54]

F2-274:   Surv.20 June 1850 by T.W.17,248 Jackson Smith 250 A. in Shenandoah Co. on Head Springs of Jumping Run adj. Frederick Hoffman, John J. Allen, Isaac

Painter, Abraham Painter. 1 Sep 1851 [Dl'd Mr. Pitman 6 Mar '52]

F2-275: Surv.5 Feb 1851 by T.W.11,112, 6184 & 18,963 Nathan Everhart 464 A. in Berkeley Co. on Third Hill Mt. adj. Faulkner, Sharff, Boyd. 1 Sep 1851 [Dl'd M.S. Grantham 13 Jan '52]

F2-276: Surv.3 Feb 1851 by T.W.14,654 John Burk 124 A. in Morgan Co. on Warm Spring Rg. & Sir John's Run adj. Marcus, Offerall, Barrett, Vanorsdall, Dyche. 1 Sep 1851 [Mailed to Prop'r c/o J. S. Duckwall 15 Nov 1851]

F2-277: Surv.23 May 1850 by T.W.17,290 Joshua Sine 38 1/4 A. in Shenandoah Co. on Gossip's Run of Stoney Cr. adj. Lewis Nesselrod, Barb, Abraham Sayger, Philip Lindamood, said Barb formerly Christie, Jacob Barb Sr. 1 Sep 1851 [Dl'd Mr. Pitman 21 Dec '55]

F2-278: Surv.31 Oct 1850 by T.W.16,854 & 18,352 Jacob McIlwee 303 A. in Hampshire Co. on Great Cacapon & Horseshoe Hill adj. John Inskeep, Henry Brill, Rudolph, John Rosebrough, Frye. 1 Sep 1851 [Dl'd Mr. T.B. White 15 Apr 1853]

F2-279: Surv.6 Feb 1851 by T.W.14,004 Jacob Cann 94 A. in Morgan Co. on Little Mt. & Cacapon Cr. adj. Pasmore, Effland, his own line. 1 Sep 1851 [Dl'd Mr. Michael 20 Feb '52]

F2-280: Surv.31 Oct 1850 by T.W.17,414 Henry Brill 225 A. in Hampshire Co. on Faninds Br. of Great Cacapon, near Fryes Run adj. Rudolph, John Rosebrough 1800 grant, Hawks Run. 1 Sep 1851 [Dl'd Mr. T.B. White 15 Apr '53]

F2-281: Surv.12 Mar 1850 by T.W.17,126 Jesse Landers 19 A. in Hardy Co. adj. S. Mill Cr., S. Br. Manor, Stump, Bergdall. 1 Oct 1851 [J.B. Kee Esq. 16 Feb 1853]

F2-282: Surv.4 Mar 1850 by T.W.17,956 Daniel Weaver 114 A. in Page Co. on Blue Rg.S.E.of Luray adj. Sheltons path, Charles Weaver, Adam Sours heirs. 1 Oct 1851

F2-283: Surv.23 Dec 1850 by T.W.4994 Andrew Riner 35 A. in Berkeley Co. on Elk Lick Run near Third Hill adj. Cherry formerly David Hunter, Walpertz formerly Gasper Snider, Henry Everhart, Baker, Stookey formerly Scott. 1 Oct 1851 [Dl'd M.S. Grantham 13 Jan 1852]

F2-284: Surv.23 Dec 1850 by T.W.4994 Henry Everhart 23 A. in Berkeley Co. on Elk Lick Run & Third Hill adj. Stookey formerly Scott, Jinkins now John Keys, Cherry formerly David Hunter. 1 Oct 1851 [Dl'd M.S. Grantham 13 Jan 1852]

F2-285: Surv.11 Nov 1850 by T.W.18,748 Philip Lindamood 9 1/2 A. in Shenandoah Co. on Stony Cr. adj. said Lindamood, Godfrey Miller, Lewis Naselrod. 1 Nov 1851 [Dl'd Mr. Pitman 21 Dec '55]

F2-286: Surv.10 Nov 1850 by T.W.18,748 Lewis Naselrod 76 1/2 A. in Shenandoah Co. on Stony Cr. adj. formerly Peter Drums, said Naselrod, Adam Sayger, Abraham Sonnafrank formerly Peter Williams. 1 Nov 1851 [Dl'd Mr. Pitman 21 Dec '55]

F2-287: Surv.20 Mar 1851 by T.W.14,710 Henry H. Halley 6 A. 2 Ro. 37 1/2 Po. in Fairfax Co. adj. Wm. Fairfax now heirs of Mor. Miller, said Holley formerly Wm. Stabler, Wm. Swam, Halley's purchase of Gunnell. 1 Nov 1851

F2-288: Surv.8 Apr 1850 by T.W.16,218 Sandford Y. Simmons asne. of William Slaten 267 A. in Hardy Co. bet. Paines & Mud Lick Runs of Bakers Run adj. Davis, McCarty, Simmons' Wharton tract. 1 Jan 1852 [Dl'd John Cassin Esq. 28 Feb '54]

F2-289: Surv.11 June 1850 by T.W.17,206 George F. Hupp 150 A. in Hardy Co. on Waites Run adj. said Hupp, Means heirs, the 44,300 A. surv., N. Mt., Martin now Wilson, s'd Hupp formerly Orndoff. 1 Jan 1852

F2-290: Surv.10 June 1850 by T.W.17,206 George F. Hupp 267 A. in Hardy Co. on Trout Run & Waites Run adj. Wilson, Means heirs, the 44,300 A. surv, Gochenour, Tasco. 1 Jan 1852

F2-291: Surv.12 Apr 1850 by T.W.17,343 David Tucker & William Timbrook 5 1/4 A. in Hardy Co. on Stone Lick Run of N. R. adj. Bean heirs, Evans, Tucker, Obannon. 1 Jan 1852 .[Dl'd Mr. Thos.B. White 15 Apr 1853]

F2-292: Surv.12 Apr 1850 by T.W.17,343 David Tucker & William Timbrook 79 1/2 A. in Hardy Co. on Br. Mt. & N. R. adj. Tharp heirs, Joseph Tucker, James Tucker. 1 Jan 1852 [Dl'd Mr. T.B. White 15 Apr 1853]

F2-293: Surv.1 May 1832 by T.W.7434 Frederick Mauk 131 A. in Hardy Co. on Short house Mt. & Waites Run of N. R. of Cacapeon adj. Jonathan Tailor, Williams heirs, Robert Means, said Mauk, Good. 1 Jan 1852 [Dl'd Thos. White 26 Apr '52]

F2-294: Surv.8 Aug 1850 by T.W.16,959 & 17,004 James Foster 305 A. 39 Po. in Pr. William Co. on Crooked Br. of Hovis Cr. on Occoquon Rd. adj. Reed, Selecman, Jos. Savage, Daniel Witbeck, Albert Arrington, Wm. Reed. 1 Jan 1852 [Dl'd N.H. Saunders Esq. 1 May 1852]

F2-295: Surv.1 Nov 1850 by T.W.17,545 Peter Urice 100 A. in Hampshire Co. on Knobly Mt. adj. said Urice, John Spencer. 1 Jan 1852 [Mr. T.B. White 15 Apr '53]

F2-296: Surv.5 Dec 1850 by T.W.15,966 James Twigg 150 A. in Hampshire Co. on N. Br. of Potomac opposite Prathers island, adj. Homes heirs, John J. Jacobs, said Twigg. 1 Jan 1852 [Dl'd Mr. T.B. White 15 Apr '53]

F2-297: Surv.13 Jan 1851 by T.W.17,705 & 14,665 James Twigg 200 A. in Hampshire Co. on N. Br. of Potomac adj. his land. 1 Jan 1852 [Mr. T.B. White 15 Apr '53]

F2-298: Surv.16 Apr 1850 by T.W.14,537 John Shac. Green 42 1/2 A. in Rappa-hannock Co. on N. fork of Thornton's R. adj. Wm. Bowen, Stanfield Waters, T.B. Dwyre, J.Y. Menefee. 1 Jan 1852

F2-299: Surv.5 Apr 1850 by T.W.17,180 & 16,976 Cyrus W. Vannort 262 1/2 A. in Hardy Co. on Lost R., Pound Mill Run, Wardens Rg. & Hanging Rock Rg. adj. Pugh, Wardens heirs, Reed, his own land. 1 Jan 1852 [Dl'd Mr. Price 12 Feb '52]

F2-300: Surv.24 Nov 1848 by T.W.17,302 Abraham Stover 223 1/2 A. in Hardy Co. on S. fork of N. R., Wardens Rg. adj. his land, Wise, Swisher, Ludwick. 1 Jan 1852

F2-301: Surv.29 Apr 1850 by T.W.17,500 Simion Detrick & A.B. Risk 200 A. in Hardy Co. on Fork Mt. & Deep Spring adj. Detrick, Henkle. 1 Jan 1852 [Dl'd Geo: R.C. Price Esq. 17 Feb 1852]

F2-302: Surv.30 Dec 1849 by T.W.12,990 Ferdinand Lewis 2 A. 1 Ro. 32 Po. in Hardy Co. on Middle fork of Pattersons Cr. adj. his own land, Babb, Shrout. 1 Jan 1852 [Dl'd John H. Cassin Esq. 28 Feb '54]

F2-303: Surv.22 June 1842 by T.W.2751 George Cline 8 A. in Hardy Co. on Great Capecapeon adj. Funkhouser, Fry, John Devalt, Funkhouser's Switzer tract. 2 Feb 1852 [Dl'd Mr. George R.C. Price 3 Mar 1852]

F2-304: Surv.17 May 1850 by T.W.17,235 Francis Idleman 129 1/2 A. in Hardy Co. in the Alleghany Mt. on Oil Run & Abram's Cr. adj. his own land, Gibson, Smith, Davis path, Bogart & Fisher, the Pike. 2 Feb 1852 [Dl'd Mr. Price 3 Mar 1852]

F2-305: Surv.17 Feb 1851 by T.W.18,748 Abraham Strickler 11 A. in Shenandoah Co. on N. Shenandoah R. adj. Denton, Baudennan now Strickler. 2 Feb 1852 [Dl'd Mr. Gatewood 29 Mar '52]

F2-306: Surv.17 Feb 1851 by T.W.12968 Abraham Beydler 4 A. 1 Ro. 30 Po. in Shenandoah Co. on N. Shenandoah R. adj. Denton, Isaac Beydler. 2 Feb 1852 [Dl'd Mr. Gatewood 29 Mar '52]

F2-307: Surv.17 Feb 1851 by T.W.12968 Abraham Beydler 1 A. 2 Ro. 27 Po. in Shenandoah Co. on N. Shenandoah R. adj. the old Patent line. 2 Feb 1852 [Dl'd Mr. Gatewood 29 Mar '52]

F2-308: Surv.17 Feb 1851 by T.W.12,968 Isaac Beydler 25 A. in Shenandoah Co. on N. Shenandoah R. adj. Jacob Beydler, Denton. 2 Feb 1852 [Mr. Gatewood 29 Mar'52]

F2-309: Surv.17 Feb 1851 by T.W.18,748 Henry Ridenour 3 A. 10 Sq. Po. in Shenandoah Co. on N. Shenandoah R. adj. Denton, Amos Crabill. 2 Feb 1852 [Dl'd Mr. Gatewood 29 Mar '52]

F2-310: Surv.4 Feb 1850 by T.W.17,196 Angus M. Wood 95 A. in Hardy Co. on Lost R. & Little Rg. adj. his own land, Chrisman, Strawderman, Wilson. 2 Feb 1852 [Dl'd Jno. C. Mullen Esq. 3 Mar '54]

F2-311: Surv.12 Apr 1850 by T.W.18,124 Alexander Evans 33 1/4 A. in Hardy Co. on Stone Lick Run of N. R. adj. his Wise land, Bean's heirs, Tucker & Timbrook, Arnold, Davidson. 2 Feb 1852 [Dl'd John H. Cassin Esq. 28 Feb '54]

F2-312: Surv.13 Apr 1850 by T.W.18,124 Alexander Evans 7 5/8 A. in Hardy Co. on N. R. adj. his Wise land, Cunningham, Davidson, Davis path. 2 Feb 1852 [Dl'd John H. Cassin Esq. 28 Feb '54]

F2-313: Surv.27 Jan 1850 by T.W.16,952 Adam Strawderman 41 3/4 A. in Hardy Co. on the Wagon Rd. Br. of Lost R. adj. Lee, Himes, Lowry, Little Rg.. 2 Feb 1852 [Dl'd Jno. C. Mullen Esq. 3 Mar '54]

F2-314: Surv.12 Dec 1850 by T.W.17,705 & 14,665 Reuben Davis 251 A. in Hampshire Co. on Abrams Cr. & Alleghany Mt. adj. Ellzey, Vincent Vandiver, Joseph & Reuben Davis, Deacon, Tasker & Junkins, Vause, Fox. 2 Feb 1852 [Mr. J. Allen 11 May'52]

F2-315: Surv.29 Nov 1850 by T.W.10,948, 16,240 & 17,705 Joseph Davis & Reuben Davis 150 A. in Hampshire Co. on Abrams Cr. & Alleghany Mt. adj. Vincent Vandiver, F. & Wm. Deacon, Charles Clinton, N. Br. of Potomac, Macher. 2 Feb 1852 [Dl'd Mr. J. Allen 11 May '52]

F2-316: Surv.23 Mar 1850 by T.W.16,976 Samuel Harper 28 A. in Hardy Co. on Lost R., Still Run & Big Spring adj. Branson, Beverly, his own land. 2 Feb 1852 [Dl'd Jno. C. Miller Esq. 3 Mar '54]

F2-317: Surv.6 Apr 1850 by T.W.17,174, 16,680 & 17,175 Samuel Baker & William Slater 608 A. in Hardy Co. on Lost R. & N. R. & Little Rg., Wardens Rg. adj. Dotson, Warden heirs, the Big Surv., Baker, Big Lick Run, Wm. Baker, Reeds path, Swisher. 2 Feb 1852 [Dl'd Jno. C. Miller Esq. 3 Mar '54]

F2-318: Surv.15 Mar 1850 by T.W.17,923 Gideon Bergdall 36 A. in Hardy Co. on Waterfall Knob bet. the falls & White Walnut Bottom Run of S. Mill Cr. adj. his land, Sites, Deep Spring Rd. 2 Feb 1852 [Dl'd John C.B. Mullin Esq. 9 Dec 1853]

F2-319: Surv.14 June 1850 by T.W.17,173 Isaac L. Fry 75 A. in Hardy Co. near Hampshire Co. line on Frys & Littlers Runs of Cacapeon R. adj. Fry heirs, Warden Heirs. 2 Feb 1852 [Dl'd Jno. C. Mullen 3 Mar '54]

F2-320: Surv.19 Apr 1850 by T.W.17,516 George Fisher 101 3/4 A. in Hardy Co. on Bodkins Run of S. Fork of Luneys Cr., New Cr. Mt. adj. his own land, Roby, Groves. 2 Feb 1852 [Dl'd John H. Cassin Esq. 28 Feb '54]

F2-321: Surv.25 Mar 1850 by T.W.17,303 John Heingardner 182 A. in Hardy Co. on Lost R. above Little Cove Mt. adj. his own land, See, Miller, Rocky Run, Bottom. 1 Mar 1852 [Dl'd Mr. Bull br. of rct' 6 June 1853]

F2-322: "ERROR: Vide folio ante (321)"

F2-323: Surv.13 Nov 1850 by T.W.13,050 Richard Baker 139 A. in Hampshire Co. on Knobly Mt. & N. Br. of Potomac adj. his land, Hooper, Deacon. 1 Apr 1852 [Dl'd Mr. T. B. White 15 Apr '53]

F2-324: Surv.19 Oct 1850 by T.W.16,854 & 17,107 John Culp 179 1/2 A. in Hampshire Co. on Knobly Mt. adj. McDonald, Ann Culp, James Culp. 1 Apr 1852 [Dl'd Mr. T. B. White 15 Apr '53]

F2-325:   Surv.9 Sep 1851 by T.W.14,722 James S. Pitzer 5 A. 34 Po. in Berkeley
Co. at N. Mt. adj. Henry Bowers h'rs, Nicholas Hess Hs., John Lyle, Robert Lyle,
James Fisher formerly Taylor. 1 Apr 1852 [Dl'd J.P. Kearfott Esq. 30 Sep '54]

F2-326:   Surv.21 Feb 1850 by T.W.18,205 Alpheus Gaunt, Daniel Gaunt, William
Gaunt, Isaiah Gaunt, Elizabeth Groves, Ellen Swindler, Sarah Corbin w. of James
N. Corbin, Nancy Turley w. of Charles Turley, & Rebecca Corbin w. of Wm. Corbin
heirs of Andrew Gaunt dec'd 60 A. in Rappahannock Co. on Pignut Mt. adj. William
Gray, Andrew Gaunt. 10 May 1852 [Dl'd John H. Morrison Esq. 12 May '52]

F2-327:   Surv.15 Nov 1850 by T.W.18,352 John W. Taylor 34 A. in Hampshire Co. on
Cabin Run adj. Daniel Taylor, Solomon Elifritz, Rd. from Sheetz's Mills to Paddy
Town. 1 May 1852 [Dl'd T.B. White 15 Apr '53]

F2-328:   Surv.26 Aug 1851 by T.W.12,994 David Scothran 199 A. 1 Ro. 27 Po. in
Page Co. on Passage Cr. on Powels Ft. N.W. of Luray adj. heirs of Joseph
Scothran dec'd, Middle Mt., Page & Shenandoah Co. line. 1 June 1852

F2-329:   Surv.25 Aug 1851 by T.W.17,132 & 18,583 Samuel Neff 193 A. 3 Ro. 25 Po.
in Page Co. in Powel's Ft. on Passage Cr. bet. West & Middle Ft. Mts. N.W. of
Luray adj. John Leary heirs, s'd Scothran. 1 June 1852

F2-330:   Surv.15 Nov 1850 by T.W.16,854 Solomon Elifrits 50 A. in Hampshire Co.
on Cabin Run adj. Hammack's heirs, Rd. from Sheetz Mills to Paddy Town, adj.
Hammock, Wealch formerly Crossley. 1 June 1852 [Dl'd Mr. T.B. White 15 Apr 1853]

F2-331:   Surv.23 Jan 1851 by T.W.16,493 Daniel Michael asne. of Uriah Ohesher 40
A. in Hampshire Co. on Elk Rg. & Flat Rg. adj. lands formerly Ohaver, Michael's
Somet tract. 2 Aug 1852   [Dl'd Mr. T.B. White 15 Apr 1853]

F2-332:   Surv.28 Feb 1851 by T.W.18,932 William Loy Sr. 27 A. in Hampshire Co.
on Big Run of Little Cacaphon & Hunting Rg. adj. Samuel Ruckman, Adam
Howdyshell. 2 Aug 1852   [Dl'd Mr. T.B. White 15 Apr 1853]

F2-333:   Surv.13 Nov 1851 by T.W.19,254 David Moreland asne. of Wm. H. Moreland
200 A. in Hampshire Co. on Spring Gap Mt. adj. Francis Farmer, his 1830 surv.,
Richard Moreland, William Henderson, Silas Prather, Jacob Jinkins heirs, David
Ellis. 2 Aug 1852   [Dl'd Mr. T.B. White 15 Apr 1853]

F2-334:   Surv.7 Mar 1851 by T.W.18,352 Wm. Combs asne. of Sam'l Ruckman(of John)
20 A. in Hampshire Co. on Cove Mt. & Little Cacaphon adj. Mathew Combs, heirs of
James Combs, Wm. Combs, Rodgers heirs. 2 Aug 1852 [Mr. T.B. White 15 Apr 1853]

F2-335:   Surv.6 Mar 1851 by T.W.18,352 William Combs 31 A. in Hampshire Co. on
Cove Mt. adj. Aaron Rodgers' heirs, Samuel Ruckman of John, James Combs heirs,
Doile. 2 Aug 1852   [Dl'd Mr. T.B. White 15 Apr 1853]

F2-336:   Surv.25 June 1851 by T.W.19,254 Johnson Dobbins 200 A. in Hampshire Co.
on Knobly Mt. adj. Jacob Fleck, John Fridley, Samuel Biser, John & Wm. Urice,
John Spencer Jr., John M. Spencer. 2 Aug 1852 [Dl'd Mr. T.B. White 15 Apr 1853]

F2-337:   Surv.29 Jan 1851 by T.W.18,352 Samuel Ruckman of John 12 A. in
Hampshire Co. on Cove Mt. adj. William Loy Sr., his own land, Aaron Rodgers, Wm.
Loy Jr. 2 Aug 1852   [Dl'd Mr. T.B. White 15 Apr 1853]

F2-338:   Surv.3 Apr 1844 by T.W.14,360 & 15,050 George Hartman 20 A. in
Hampshire Co. on Tear Coat Cr. adj. Moses Hunter, Branson Peters, George Hawes,
Charles Deal heirs. 2 Aug 1852   [Dl'd Mr. T.B. White 15 Apr 1853]

F2-339:   Surv.29 May 1851 by T.W.12,899 Israil Hardy 10 3/4 A. in Hampshire Co.
on Great Cacaphon adj. Thomas Largent, Samuel A. Pancost. 2 Aug 1852 [Dl'd Mr.
Sherrard Dec 1853]

F2-340:   Surv.10 Nov 1851 by T.W.14,897 John W. Johnson one moiety & Frederick
Royce asne. of said John W. Johnson the other moiety of 14 5/8 A. in Hampshire
Co. on Great Cacaphon adj. Israel Hardy, John Royce 1773 grant. 2 Aug 1852

F2-341:   Surv.12 Oct 1848 by T.W.16,350 George Loy 15 A. in Hampshire Co. on Tare Coat Cr. adj. John Horn, William Loy, Benjamin Pugh. 2 Aug 1852 [Dl'd Thos. B. White 6 Oct 1853]

F2-342:   Surv.19 Feb 1841 by T.W.12,589 Samuel Ruckman of John 10 A. 3 Ro. 30 Po. in Hampshire Co. on Little Cacapeon adj. his own land, land he bought of Thomas Ruckman. 2 Aug 1852   [Dl'd Mr. T.B. White 15 Apr 1853]

F2-343:   Surv.28 Jan 1851 by T.W.14,665 Richard M. Slonaker? asne. of Susan Dew 116 A. in Hampshire Co. on Dillon's Mt. & Big Cacapon adj. Richard M. Sloanacre, Monroe, Wm. Morelan. 2 Aug 1852   [Dl'd Mr. T.B. White 15 Apr 1853]

F2-344:   Surv.25 June 1851 by T.W.18,352 John N. Spencer 150 A. in Hampshire Co. on Knobly Mt. adj. John Spencer Jr., Isaac Adams, Peter Urice. 2 Aug 1852 [Dl'd Thos.B. White 15 Apr 1853]

F2-345:   Surv.22 Apr 1851 by T.W.15,031 & 2995 John Umpstot 96 1/2 A. in Hampshire Co. on Knobly Mt. adj. his own land, Henry Fleck, John Urice, Peter Urice. 2 Aug 1852 [Dl'd James Allen ESq. 22 Mar 1853]

F2-346:   Surv.9 Aug 1851 by T.W.17,956 David C. Printz 1 A. 1 Ro. 12 93/100 Po. in Page Co. on Baker's Run adj. John Printz Sr., George Printz & David C. Printz, Mt. Calvary Church. 2 Aug 1852 [Mailed Thos. Buswell Esq. 16 Oct 1854]

F2-347:   Surv.9 Aug 1851 by T.W.18,442 Aaron Printz 1 A. 1 Ro 31 46/100 Po. in Page Co. on Big Hawksbill Cr. S.E. of Luray adj. David Printz Sr., Daniel Blasser, John & Joseph Verner, Elias Houser. 2 Aug 1852 [Mailed E. Chadduck 29 Nov '54]

F2-348:   Surv.13 Oct 1851 by T.W.19,696 S. Howell Brown 5 1/2 A. in Jefferson Co. near town of Bolivar adj. Robert Harper now United States, Susan Downey, John Lambough, William Smallwood. 2 Aug 1852 [Mailed the Prop'r 2 Sep 1852]

F2-349:   Surv.23 May 1851 by T.W.19,148 Jacob Bushong 48 1/2 A. in Shenandoah Co. on Smiths Cr. & Massanotten Mt. adj. Daniel Bannamen now heirs of Abraham Gouchenour dec'd, Ephraim Wood, Pennybaker sold to Daniel Branaman, David Neff, Jacob Kagey, John Kagey. 2 Aug 1852 [Dl'd Mr. Pitman 24 Dec 1852]

F2-350:   Surv.11 Nov 1851 by T.W.18,830 Francis Johnston 26 A. 1 Ro. 20 Po. in Fairfax Co. adj. Mathews now C. B. Mason & Magnadier? Mason, Dogue Run, Reid. 2 Aug 1852 [Mailed H.W. Thomas 15 Oct 1852]

F2-351: Surv.10 Oct 1851 by T.W.19,103 Howard Lillard & Benjamin F. Smith 19 A. in Madison Co. adj. Wm. C. Nicholson, said Smith, Ragged Mt. 2 Aug 1852

F2-352:   Surv.13 May 1850 by T.W.16,961 & 15,771 David Vanmeter 386 A. in Hardy Co. on Tucker's & Mannon's Runs, Harriss Rg., Potatoe row Mt. adj. his Harriss land, Phils Knob, Cooms Knob. 2 Aug 1852 [Dl'd Robt. J. Tilden Esq. 27 Feb 1854]

F2-353:   Surv.15 Mar 1851 by T.W.16,854 Matthew Combs 45 A. in Hampshire Co. on Hase Rg. adj. Abraham Combs, Levi Shaffer, Lock, Isaiah Heares. 1 Sep 1852 [Dl'd Mr. T.B. White 11 Apr 1853]

F2-354:   Surv.1 Mar 1851 by T.W.14,665 David Doran asne. of James J. Starkey 14 A. in Hampshire Co. on Clay Lick Run adj. his land, Gibson Rudkman, James Malick. 1 Sep 1852   [Dl'd Mr. T.B. White 15 Apr 1853]

F2-355:   Surv.5 Mar 1851 by T.W.18,932 George Haws 20 A. in Hampshire Co. on Little Cacaphon adj. Samuel Ruckman, Adam Howdyshell, William Hammock. 1 Sep 1852   [Dl'd Mr. T.B. White 15 Apr 1853]

F2-356:   Surv.24 Oct 1850 by T.W.16,854 Samuel House Jr. 32 1/2 A. in Hampshire Co. on N. Br. of Potomac adj. his land, his Monroe tract, Monroe, John Gamber. 1 Sep 1852   [Dl'd Mr. T.B. White 15 Apr 1853]

F2-357: Surv.26 Mar 1851 by T.W.15,875 Isaac Haines asne. of John Shingleton 22 1/2 A. in Hampshire Co. on Little Stoney Mt., N. fork of Little Cacaphon adj. Isaac Haines, Jesse Pownell, Shaffer, Powelson, George W. Cooper, William French heirs. 1 Sep 1852 [Dl'd Mr. T.B. White 15 Apr 1853]

F2-358: Surv.25 Mar 1851 by T.W.10,948 John Hansbrough asne. of W. B. McNemar 2 3/4 A. in Hampshire Co. on Rush Run adj. his land, John Hansbrough, Anthony Hammock. 1 Sep 1852 [Dl'd Mr. T.B. White 15 Apr 1853]

F2-359: Surv.10 Feb 1851 by T.W.15,031 Abraham Johnson 36 1/2 A. in Hampshire Co. on Patterson's Cr. adj. his land, Abraham Leatherman, Johnson's Hopkin Surv. 1 Sep 1852 [Dl'd Mr. T.B. White 15 Apr 1853]

F2-360: Surv.3 Mar 1851 by 17,705 John Park 38 A. in Hampshire Co. on Brier Lick Run & Grassy Lick Mt. adj. his land, James Pepper, Solomon Tharp, Plum Lick Mt. 1 Sep 1852 [Dl'd Mr. T.B. White 15 Apr 1853]

F2-361: Surv.16 Aug 1851 by T.W.17,545 & 18,932 Isaac Pear 123 1/4 A. in Hampshire Co. adj. Sutton, tract vested in trustees of Watson Town, John R. Rickard, Joseph Johnson. 1 Sep 1852 [Dl'd Mr. T.B. White 15 Apr 1853]

F2-362: Surv.26 Mar 1851 by T.W.17,545 John Shingleton asne. of Isaac Haines 52 3/4 A. in Hampshire Co. on S. Br. of Potomac adj. Amos Poling heirs, William Shingleton, Lewis Run, Carlton F. Jack. 1 Sep 1852 [Mr. T.B. White 15 Apr 1853]

F2-363: Surv.18 Mar 1851 by T.W.17,705, 18,932 & 14,781 Solomon Tharp 200 A. in Hampshire & Hardy Cos. on N. R. adj. his own land, James Davison, Arnold, Street. 1 Sep 1852 [Dl'd Mr. T.B. White 15 Apr 1853]

F2-364: Surv.19 Mar 1851 by T.W.18,352 & 18,932 Solomon Tharp 69 1/4 A. in Hampshire Co. on Hairy Mt. adj. his own land, Pepper, Elisha P. Heare, George Hott, Daniel Haines. 1 Sep 1852 [Dl'd Mr. T.B. White 15 Apr 1853]

F2-365: Surv.15 Dec 1851 by T.W.19,028 Middleton Duckwall 21 A. 3 Ro. in Morgan Co. on Sleepy Cr. adj. Duckwall, Mendenhall, Lutman, P. C. Pendleton, Abernathy. 1 Sep 1852 [Dl'd Mr. Michael 18 Dec 1852]

F2-366: Surv.29 Nov 1851 by T.W.14,232 Wm. Hobday Jr. 208 A. in Morgan Co. on Cacapeon Mt. adj. Henry Dawson, on Indian Run. 1 Sep 1852 [Dl'd Mr. Michael 18 Dec 1852]

F2-367: Surv.1 Jan 1852 by T.W.19,715 Lewis Merchant 100 A. in Morgan Co. on Sleepy Cr. Mt. adj. Samuel Merchant, Aullabough, Buck, Hunter, Anderson. 1 Sep 1852 [Mailed to A. Michael Jr. 4 Nov 1852]

F2-368: Surv.22 Nov 1851 by T.W.12,791 & 19,028 Adam Shade 420 A. in Morgan Co. on Sleepy Cr. Mt. adj. Talbot, Col. Hill, Lutrell, Baker heirs. 1 Sep 1852 [Mr. Michael 18 Dec 1852]

F2-369: Surv.29 May 1851 by T.W.18,748 Andrew Funkhouser 90 sq. Po. in Shenandoah Co. on Mill Cr. adj. Rosena Pennywitt, said Funkhouser, Levi Rinker, Wm. Lutz. 1 Sep 1852 [Dl'd G.S. Meem Esq. 25 Nov 1852]

F2-370: Surv.16 Jan 1851 by T.W.15,480 George Wright 1/4 A. in Frederick Co. in Middletown (Lot # 57) on Jefferson St., Slate Alley. 1 Oct 1852 [Dl'd Mr. John S. Davison 8 Dec '52]

F2-371: Surv.16 Feb 1852 by T.W.19,458 George G. Tasker 56 7/8 A. in Hampshire Co. on Alleghany Mt. on Montgummary's run adj. Duff Green, Miller & Cooper formerly Barrack heirs, Oliver ODonald. 1 Oct 1852 [Dl'd T.B. White 15 Apr '53]

F2-372: Surv.3 Aug 1835 by T.W.12,374 John W. Largent 17 1/2 A. in Hampshire Co. on N. R. adj. John Largent heirs, Peter Millar, Red Stone Rd., Berry heirs. 1 Oct 1852 [Dl'd Mr. Sherrard Dec 1852]

F2-373: Surv.4 Mar 1852 by T.W.19,904 William W. Triplett 21 A. 3 Po. in

Fairfax Co. on Dogue Run adj. Col. Mason, Michael Ashford now Triplett, Thompson Lavin, Monroe. 1 Oct 1852

F2-374:   Surv.2 Apr 1850 by T.W.17,235 Isaac W. Link 31 3/4 A. in Hardy Co. on Lost R., Ruddles Run adj. his own land, Inskeep, Abm. Link, E. Link, the Bottom Tract, Slater, Funkhouser. 1 Oct 1852 [Mailed to Prop'r 23 Mar '53]

F2-375:   Surv.30 July 1850 by T.W.16,344 Sandford Y. Simmons 221 A. in Hardy Co. on Alleghany Mt: bet. Abrans Cr. & Stony R. adj. Deakins, Neville, Prior S. Roby, Branson, Robinett, Fox. 1 Oct 1852 [Dl'd John H. Cassin Esq. 28 Feb '54]

F2-376:   Surv.9 Apr 1851 by T.W.18,748 John Carrier 34 A. in Shenandoah Co. in the Short Hills on Stoney Cr. adj. John Fout dec'd, Elizabeth Fry, Abraham Good, John Ryman, Ryal's run. 1 Nov 1852 [Dl'd G.S. Meem Esq. 24 Nov 1852]

F2-377:   Surv.5 Mar 1851 by T.W.18,748 John Haymon 120 1/2 A. in Shenandoah Co. on Timber Rg. adj. Christian Rupert, Jacob Profate, Samuel Tusing, Henry Hess. 1 Nov 1852 [Dl'd G.S. Meem Esq. 24 Nov 1852]

F2-378:   Surv.7 May 1851 by T.W.18,748 Thomas Lloyd 1 A. 3 Ro. 28 Po. in Shenandoah Co. on Rd. from Forrestville to Solomon's Church in the Forrest, adj. Sarah Pence, John Peters, Jacob Bowers. 1 Nov 1852 [Dl'd G.S. Meem Esq. 24 Nov 1852]

F2-379:   Surv.10 Nov 1850 by T.W.18,748 Christian Biller 81 1/2 A. in Shenandoah Co. in the Short Hills adj. said Biller, Gideon Estep. 1 Nov 1852 [Dl'd G.S. Meem Esq. 24 Nov 1852]

F2-380:   Surv.6 Mar 1851 by T.W.18,748 Henry Hepner asne. of John Haymons 101 1/2 A. in Shenandoah Co. on Sup & Lick Rg. adj. Elijah Estep, Edward Walton dec'd, Abraham Funkhouser. 1 Nov 1852 [Dl'd G.S. Meem Esq. 24 Nov 1852]

F2-381:   Surv.22 Jan 1851 by T.W.18,352 Stephen Smith 55 3/4 A. in Hampshire Co. on Tare Coat Cr. adj. Benjamin F. Pepper, said Stephen Smith, Chesshire. 1 Nov 1852 [Dl'd T.B.White 15 Apr '53]

F2-382:   Surv.24 Jan 1851 by T.W.17,414 Obadiah Cheshir 100 A. in Hampshire Co. on Hammock's Mt. adj. his land, Huff. 1 Nov 1852 [Dl'd Thos.B.White 15 Apr '53]

F2-383:   Surv.22 Mar 1851 by T.W.14,360 Samuel Haines 35 A. in Hampshire Co. on Little Mt. adj. Jonah Lupton, Adam Cooper, Heatherol. 1 Nov 1852 [Dl'd T.B. White 15 Apr '53]

F2-384:   Surv.19 Feb 1852 by T.W.17,770 Henry Keesacker 8 3/4 A. in Berkeley Co. adj. said Keesacker, Robert Johnson, Bennet Sylor, Jacob Barnes. 1 Nov 1852 [Dl'd G.H. McClure Esq. 2 Mar 1853]

F2-385:   Surv.14 Jan 1852 by T.W.15,480 John Rhodes 1 A. in Frederick Co. in Middletown(Lot #35) on Main St, adj. Dr. Ahlenfeldt, Cross St.   1 Nov 1852 [Dl'd Mr. Jno. S. Davison 8 Dec 1852]

F2-386:   Surv.13 Sep 1850 by T.W.18,620 James M. Nicholson 23 A. in Madison Co. on Bear Church Mt. adj. Gen. Robert A. Banks & others, David Nicholson. 2 Dec 1852 [Dl'd Mr. Newman 8 Dec '52]

F2-387:   Surv.27 Apr 1852 by T.W.20,123 J. L. Kinzer 1 3/4 A.in Fairfax Co. on Great Hunting Cr. adj. John Churchman, J. H. McVeigh. 1 Dec 1852 [Dl'd Wm. D. Massey Esq. 22 Dec 1852]

F2-388:   Surv.25 Nov 1839 by T.W.2750 William O. Bond asne. of James Smith 500 A. in Hardy Co. on N. R. adj. Smith's heirs, Henry Baker, on Wardens Rg., Alexander Smith heirs, near Bear town Spring, Flat Rg., Ohover, Cutloaf, Wise, Rd. from N. R. to Wardens Ville. 1 Dec 1852 [Dl'd Thos. White Esq. 16 Mar '53]

F2-389:   Surv.10 May 1850 by T.W.16,976 Valentine Powers 38 1/2 A. in Hardy Co. on N. Fork & Linestone Rg. bet. Lavelle's hollow & the Manor Line adj. James Gray dec'd, Gray's heirs. 1 Dec 1852 [Dl'd Jno. C. Mullen Esq. 3 Mar '54]

242

F2-390: Surv.31 July 1850 by T.W.2751 Lewis Frederick 44 1/2 A. in Hardy Co. on N. drain of N. fork of Lunys Cr. adj. his own land, Stickley, Jas. B. Frederick, Yaman, Shell. 1 Dec 1852 [Dl'd Robert J. Tilden Esq. 27 Feb '54]

F2-391: Surv.30 Mar 1847 by T.W.15,824 John Mullin 232 3/4 A. in Hardy Co. on Patterson Cr. Mt. & Main Rd. adj. Arnold, Williams, his own land, Smith or Arnold. 1 Dec 1852 [Mailed to Prop'r 29 Jan 1853]

F2-392: Surv.31 Mar 1847 by T.W.2751 John Mullin 55 A. in Hardy Co. on Patterson's Cr. Mt. adj. his own land, on Devils Peak, Oglivie, John Webb. 1 Dec 1852 [Mailed to Prop'r 29 Jan 1853]

F2-393: Surv.28 Jan 1851 by T.W.14,665 Samuel Haines 100 A. in Hampshire Co. on Dillons Mt. adj. Richard M. Slonacre, his own land, Philip Cline, Susan Due. 1 Dec 1852 [Dl'd T.B. White Esq. 15 Apr '53]

F2-394: Surv.2 Dec 1850 by T.W.16,854 William Wagoner 26 A. in Hampshire Co. on Middle Rg., Wards Run adj. Joseph Wagoner, Wm. P. Stump. 1 Dec 1852 [Dl'd T.B. White Esq. 15 Apr '53]

F2-395: Surv.17 Apr 1852 by T.W.18,063 Samuel G. Henkel & Jacob Stirwalt 409 3/4 A. in Page & Shenandoah Cos. on Middle Ft. Mt., W. of Luray, on Turnpike Rd. below toll gate on Massanotton Mt., adj. Peter Fogle, Jacob Stinwalt, Jacob Bushong, David Scothran, Barbour. 1 Dec 1852 [Dl'd Mr. Miller of Frederick Co. 18 Feb 1853]

F2-397: Surv.31 Oct 1851 by T.W.19,729 Uriel Carpenter 2 3/8 A. in Madison Co. adj. heirs of B. Crisler & heirs of Jonas Wayman both dec'd, Elias Blankebeker, said Uriel Carpenter. 1 Jan 1853

F2-398: Surv.13 Feb 1851 by T.W.14,004 Jacob Cann 12 1/4 A. in Morgan Co. on Sideling Hill adj. Ziler, Craigan. 1 Jan 1853 [Mailed to Prop'r 3 June '59]

F2-399: Surv.18 Nov 1851 by T.W.14,720 & 14,594 Michael Rooney 142 A. 3 Ro. 24 Po. in Morgan Co. on Third Hill Mt. adj. Barrett, Ensminger, Anderson. 1 Jan 1853 [Dl'd Henry I. Sirbert Esq. 5 Jan 1854]

F2-400: Surv.15 Feb 1851 by T.W.14,004 Thomas Gale 21 A. in Morgan Co. on Potomac R. adj. Walter McAtee, his own land, McDonald, near Western Mouth of the Tunnel. 1 Jan 1853

F2-401: Surv.3 Apr 1852 by T.W.18,593 Richard Pickering 1 A. 38 Po. in Page Co. on Big Naked Cr. S. of Luray adj. Wm. Merica, Henry Deetz. 1 Jan 1853 [Dl'd Jno. H. Shock Esq. 11 Aug 1853]

F2-402: Surv.3 Apr 1850 by T.W.17,196 Sandford Y. Simmons asne. of William Smith 56 A. in Hardy Co. on Bakers Run & Big Rg. adj. Inskeep, Childs, Johnson, Clagett, the Big Surv., his own land bought of Link, Ketner. 1 Jan 1853 [Dl'd John H. Cassin Esq. 28 Feb '54]

F2-403: Surv.22 Mar 1851 by T.W.18,932 Isaac Lochmiller 12 1/2 A. in Hampshire Co. on Ben's Knob adj. Jesse Lupton's heirs, his own land. 1 Feb 1853 [Dl'd Jesse Lupton Esq. 15 Dec 1853]

F2-404: Surv.27 Jan 1851 by T.W.17,414 Spencer R. Gray 191 1/2 A. in Hampshire Co. on Dillons Run & Hammocks Mt. adj. his tract, Huff, Obediah Cheshire, Wardensville to Dillons Run Rd. 1 Feb 1853 [Dl'd Jesse Lupton Esq. 15 Dec 1853]

F2-405: Surv.6 Feb 1852 by T.W.10,451 Robert A. Colston 10 A. 2 Ro. 13 Po. in Frederick & Clark Cos. adj. Johnson Furr, George F. Calmes, s'd Colston purchase of Carter heirs, Knight, Gibbons. 1 Mar 1853 [Dl'd Mr. Morgan 16 Jan 1854]

F2-406: Surv.5 May 1852 by T.W.18,693 William Shane 82 7/10 sq. Po. in Frederick Co. in Gainesborough adj. Doct. Brown. 1 Apr 1853 [Prop'r 14 July'53]

F2-407: Surv.5 May 1852 by T.W.18,693 William Shane 31 A. 2 Ro. 15 Po. in

Frederick Co. adj. Thomas Adams heirs, Henry Fout, Shutt, David Adams. 1 Apr 1853 [Mailed to Prop'r 14 July '53]

F2-408: Surv.9 Sep 1851 by T.W.18,352 John W. Taylor 23 1/4 A. in Hampshire Co. on Cabin Run & State Rd. adj. Solomon Elifrets, Daniel Taylor, William Wealch. 1 Apr 1853 [Dl'd Isaac Parsons 17 Mar '56]

F2-409: Surv.15 Jan 1851 by T.W.11,056 Sandford Y. Simmons asne. of William P. Heath 186 1/4 A. in Hardy Co. on Patterson's Cr. Mt. & Cove Hollow adj. Vanmeter, Miles, Heath, his new Surv., Coler. 1 Apr 1853 [Dl'd John H. Cassin Esq. 28 Feb '54]

F2-410: Surv.15 Jan 1851 by T.W.11,056 William C. McNiell, Daniel R. McNiell & Benjamin S. McNiell asnes. of William P. Heath 195 3/4 A. in Hardy Co. on Patterson's Cr. Mt. at Colars Knob on Cove hollow adj. Coler, Vanmeter formerly Heath, his new Surv., McMechin formerly Vanmeter. 1 Apr 1852 [Dl'd Jno. C. Mullen Esq. 3 Mar '54]

F2-411: Surv.23 July 1852 by T.W.4109 & 20,054 John H. Crawford 200 A. in Pr. William Co. on N. run of Neabsco adj. Mrs. Williams, heirs of Philip Hedges, Francis Arington. 2 May 1853 [Mailed to G. S.? Minn Esq. 18 Sep 1854]

F2-412: Surv.8 Oct 1852 by T.W.17,004 Joseph M. Savage 13 A. 3 Ro. 18 Po. in Pr. William Co. adj. Jas' Foster, Collins, Selectman now Pambroke Reed. 1 June 1853 [Dl'd Isaiah Fisher Esq. 13 July '54]

F2-413: Surv.14 Jan 1851 by T.W.16,962 Sandford Y. Simmons asne. of Wm. P. Heath 113 A. in Hardy Co. on Pattersons Cr. Mt. adj. his Wolf land, McMechen, Wilson, McNeill, Cunningham, Willis, Sugar Camp Run, Wolfs Gap. 1 June 1853 [Dl'd John H. Cassin Esq. 28 Feb '54]

F2-414: Surv.19 Oct 1852 by T.W.14,146 Otho W. Ridgway 2 1/2 A. in Warren Co. on Shenandoah R. & Cabin Run adj. William Ridgway formerly Horn, Richard Ridgway dec'd (patented to Jno. Poker & Thos. Buck Sr.), Jno. Horn now Philip E. Frederick in part. 1 June 1853 [Dl'd Jno. A. Thornhill 24 Mar '54]

F2-415: Surv.13 June 1852 by T.W.16,854 James Haines 5 1/2 A. in Hampshire Co. on Tare Coat Cr. adj. Bryan Kern, Peter Shickle, Daniel Shelly formerly Buzzard. 1 July 1853 [Mailed to Prop'r 28 July 1853]

F2-416: Surv.17 Sep 1851 by T.W.17,545 Abraham J. Alger 21 3/4 A. in Hampshire Co. on Little Cacaphon adj. Robert Thompson, his own land, Isaiah Corbin, Elizabeth Powell. 1 July 1853 [Dl'd Isaac Parsons 17 Mar '56]

F2-417: Surv.9 1852 by T.W.18,694 Adam Peters 15 1/4 A. in Shenandoah Co. in Powell's Big Ft. on Peters Mill Run, adj. Luke Thomas, Peter Peters, said Adam Peters. 1 July 1853 [Dl'd Mr. Pitman 19 Mar '56]

F2-418: Surv.7 June 1852 by T.W.19,254 John H. Largent 11 1/2 A. in Hampshire Co. on Cedar Hill & Big Cacaphon adj. Caspar Rinker & John Largent patent of 26 June 1789, Samuel Largent formerly Copsy, Thomas Allen. 1 July 1853 [Dl'd Isaac Parsons 17 Mar '56]

F2-419: Surv.16 Apr 1852 by T.W.18,748 John Basey 60 A. in Shenandoah Co. in Hills near Orkney Springs adj. John Sheetz. 1 July 1853 [Prop'r 4 Oct 1854]

F2-420: Surv.16 Jan 1852 by T.W.18,694 Adam Peters 7 1/4 A. in Shenandoah Co. on Hornsberry Run in Powell's Big Ft. adj. John Keller, said Adam Peters, John McInturff, Luke Thomas now John Keller. 1 July 1853 [Dl'd Mr. Pitman 19 Mar '56]

F2-421: Surv.7 Apr 1852 by T.W.19,148 Philip Lindamood 23 1/4 A. in Shenandoah Co. on Stony Cr. adj. Joshua Sine, Jacob Barb, said Philip Lindamood. 1 July 1853 [Dl'd Mr. Pitman 21 Dec '55]

F2-422: Surv.2 Jan 2852 by T.W.19,148 Elias Ridenour 3 1/4 A. in Shenandoah Co. an island in N. Shenandoah R. 1 July 1853 [Dl'd Mr. Pitman 21 Dec '55]

F2-423: Surv.27 Nov 1851 by T.W.18,694 & 19,148 Peter Gilham 108 1/4 A. in Shenandoah Co. on Cedar Cr. called Presbyterian Church land, adj. Absalom Funkhouser, Valentine Rhodes, Copp. 1 July 1853 [Dl'd to Rec't 6 Feb 1854]

F2-424: Surv.12 Feb 1852 by T.W.18,932 James Dixon 38 3/16 A. in Hampshire Co. on Alleghany Mt. adj. Reason Harvey now his own land, Vincent Vandiver, Frederick Nethkin. 1 July 1853 [Dl'd Isaac Parsons 17 Mar '56]

F2-425: Surv.19 Aug 1851 by T.W.17,705 James Powelson 8 5/8 A. in Hampshire Co. on Little Cacaphon adj. John Powelson heirs, William French heirs. 1 July 1853 [Dl'd Jesse Lupton Esq. 31 Jan 1854]

F2-426: Surv.6 May 1852 by T.W.18,694 John W. Bochm & Isaac Watson 50 A. in Shenandoah Co. on Little N. Mt. adj. John S. Mowery, Wm. Supinger, Tobias Eshelman. 1 July 1853 [Dl'd Mr. Gatewood 14 Jan '54]

F2-427: Surv.1 June 1852 by T.W.12,968 John McInturff 7 A. in Shenandoah Co. in Powell's Big Ft. adj. Adam Peters, said McInturff. 1 July 1853 [Dl'd Mr. Buswell 18 Jan '54]

F2-428: Surv.19 Jan 1852 by T.W.19,148 Simon Barb 6 1/2 A. in Shenandoah Co. on Stony Cr. adj. David Barb, Henry Tusing, Lee. 1 July 1853 [Prop'r 5 June'54]

F2-429: Surv.1 June 1852 by T.W.19,254 David Arnold 4 3/8 A. in Hampshire Co. on Potomac R. & Little Cacaphon adj. his tract. 1 Aug 1853 [Dl'd Isaac Parsons Esq. 27 Feb '54]

F2-430: Surv.22 Dec 1852 by T.W.17,356 Jonathan Rinker 23 A. in Warren Co. adj. John Cooley formerly Nicholas Sperry, Jacob Rinker, Reuben & George Rinker, Miers. 1 Aug 1853 [Dl'd Jno. A. Thornhill Esq. 24 Mar '54]

F2-431: Surv.15 Sep 1852 by T.W.19,729 Joseph Story 22 A. in Madison Co. adj. John Harlow, Morgan Jenkins, said Joseph Story, on Long Mt., John Story heirs, Lutheran Congregation. 1 Aug 1853

F2-432: Surv.16 Jan 1851 by T.W.18,694 John Biller (son of George) 75 A. in Shenandoah Co. on Mill Cr. adj. Daniel Rupert, Shenandoah & Rockingham Cos. line, said Biller. 1 Aug 1853 [Dl'd Mr. Pitman 19 Mar '56]

F2-433: Surv.19 June 1852 by T.W.18,932 & 19,458 David Arnold 49 A. in Hampshire Co. on Break Neck Mt. adj. Walter Davis 1812 surv., Daniel Suder, Isaac Taylor heirs, S. Br. of Potomac. 1 Aug 1853 [Dl'd Isaac Parsons Esq. 27 Feb '54]

F2-434: Surv.21 Mar 1850 by T.W.18,059 Conrad Basore 6 7/8 A. in Hardy Co. on N. Mt. adj. his own land, Benjamin Basore, Leeor See now Basore. 1 Sep 1853 [Dl'd Jno. C. Mullen Esq. 3 Mar '54]

F2-435: Surv.1 Apr 1851 by T.W.18,059 Conrad Basore 1 7/8 A. in Hardy Co. on Lost R. in lower Cove Gap adj. Cove & Chrisman Run, adj. Chrisman, Harper, Pepper, Dunbar, Mill lot. 1 Sep 1853 [Dl'd Jno. C. Mullen Esq. 3 Mar '54]

F2-436: Surv.28 Mar 1850 by T.W.18,059 Benjamin Basore 136 3/4 A. in Hardy Co. on Cove Run bet. Little & Big Cove Mts. adj. his own land, See or Lee. 1 Sep 1853 [Dl'd Jno. C. Mullen Esq. 3 Mar '54]

F2-437: Surv.18 June 1851 by T.W.17,705 Levi Snyder asne. of Lemuel Nixon 30 A. in Hampshire Co. on Town hill adj. land Nixon sold Levi Snyder, Jacob Swisher, William Malcom. 1 Sep 1853 [Dl'd Jesse Lupton Esq. 1 Mar '54]

F2-438: Surv.2 June 1852 by T.W.19,254 Thomas Allender 6 A. 3 Ro. 11 Per. in Hampshire Co. on S. Br. Mt. adj. Rudolph Hardy heirs, William Allender. 1 Sep 1853 [Dl'd Jesse Lupton Esq. 16 Jan 1854]

F2-439: Surv.9 Oct 1852 by T.W.20,510 Lucien Peyton, Mammia Craven & John F. Peyton heirs of John S. Peyton dec'd 75 A. in Fairfax Co. adj. James Green, Watkins, William Cleaveland, the Theological Seminary, old Leesburg Rd., Edgar

Snowden, Wm. D. Nutt, Middle Turnpike Rd., Masters, Adkinsons. 1 Sep 1853 [Mailed to J. Louis Kenzie, Alexandria 5 Jan 1854]

F2-440:   Surv.8 Mar 1852 by T.W.19,997 John L. Lohman 22 A. in Fairfax Co. adj. Bailey, Benson purchase of Whiting near a school house, Fairfax & Alexandria Cos. dividing line, Bladen. 1 Sep 1853 [Mailled to Jas. Thrift 17 Jan '57]

F2-441:   Surv.7 Dec 1852 by T.W.15,538 Lorenzo Oats 84 sq. Po. in Frederick Co. on Timber Rg. adj. Samuel Griffin heirs, L. Oats other land, Bartholomas H. McKee. 1 Sep 1853

F2-442:   Surv.14 Dec 1853 by T.W.20,274 Alfred Orndorff 14 A. in Frederick Co. adj. Manganese Tract, Elenor Orndorff, Jacob Rudolph, A. Nicholas. 1 Sep 1853

F2-443:   Surv.15 Nov 1852 by T.W.17,356 John A. Thornhill asne. of Thomas F. Buck 30 A. in Warren Co. near Ft. Mt. adj. Charles Sexton/Saxton, Wm. Elzea's Mt. surv., John Shawl, land formerly Martin Doctor, Henry Davis. 1 Oct 1853 [Mailed to Jno. A. Thornhill Esq. 24 Mar '54]

F2-444:   Surv.8 Jan 1850 by T.W.14,004 Basil E. Shockey 8 A. in Morgan Co. on Sleepy Cr. adj. Widnyer, Hobday. 1 Nov 1853 [Dl'd Mr. Dyche 24 Feb '54]

F2-445:   Surv.15 Feb 1853 by T.W.20,653 Benjamin Grubb 3 Ro. 1 Per. in Loudoun Co. adj. said Benjamin Grubb, Rd. to Stone Church, Virt. 30 Nov 1853

F2-446:   Surv.16 June 1852 by T.W.14,234 Alexander Saunders 46 A. in Hampshire Co. on S. Br. of Potomac on Rd. from Romney to Winchester, Town run, land lately Naylor's heirs, William H. Foote, John M. Snyder. 1 Nov 1853 [Mailed J. B. White 5 Mar 1855]

F2-447: Surv.18 Aug 1851 by T.W.16,854 Benjamin F. Darby 78 3/4 A. in Hampshire Co. on Sandy Rg. adj. his own land, George Park's heirs, heirs of Jacob Milslagle, Charles Blue. 1 Nov 1853 [Dl'd Jesse Lupton Esq. 31 Jan 1854]

F2-448: Surv.29 Oct 1851 by T.W.18,352 Edward Armstrong, admr. of Strawther Gannon dec'd asne. of William B. Polling 40 1/2 A. in Hampshire Co. on Island Hill adj. Isaac Pancake, Sarah Mills, Michael Miller. 1 Nov 1853 [Dl'd Isaac Parsons 17 Mar '56]

F2-449: Surv.8 Dec 1852 by T.W.19,458 John Loy 20 A. 20 Po. in Hampshire Co. on the Knob Rg. adj. Joel Ward, said Loy, Knob Mt. 1 Nov 1853 [Dl'd Jesse Lupton Esq. 31 Jan 1854]

F2-450:   Surv.13 Mar 1851 by T.W.17,107 Samuel C. Ruckman 100 A. in Hampshire Co. on Piny Mt. adj. William Poling bought of John B. White. 1 Nov 1853 [Dl'd Jesse Lupton Esq. 31 Jan 1854]

F2-451:   Surv.14 Mar 1844 by T.W.7136 Peter Evans 50 A. in Hampshire Co. on Dillons Run adj. Rachel Parrill, Joseph P. Clutter, said Evans, Rudolph. 1 Nov 1853 [Dl'd Jesse Lupton Esq. 31 Jan 1854]

F2-452:   Surv.19 Feb 1841 by T.W.12,899 Samuel Ruckman of John 28 1/2 A. in Hampshire Co. on Little Cacapehon adj. James Combs, Cove Mt., his own land, land he bought of Thomas Ruckman. 1 Nov 1853 [Dl'd Jesse Lupton Esq. 31 Jan 1854]

F2-453: Surv.8 Apr 1853 by T.W.17,956 Benjamin H. Wood 1 A. 35 9/10 Po. in Page Co. on Jeremies run N. of Luray adj. Nelsons Br., heirs of Harrison Wood, Edward W. Wood, Turnpike Rd. 1 Dec 1853 [Mailed to E. Chadduck Esq. 27 May 1854]

F2-454: Surv.8 Mar 1853 by T.W.18,593 Emanuel Grove & David H. Brumback 11 A. 3 Ro. 3 Po. in Page Co. on Punk Run S.E. of Luray adj. John Verner, Samuel Lowe, Isaac Printz, said Grove & Brumback, Frederick Sours. 1 Dec 1853 [Mailed to E. Chadduck Esq. 27 May 1854]

F2-455: Surv.1 Aug 1852 by T.W.20,018 John Pearson asne. of Thomas M. Ewing 28 A. 1 Ro. 19 Po. in Pr. William Co. adj. James Arnold, Fitzhugh, Fraser, Jno. R.

Arington, Matthew Priest. 1 Feb 1854 [Mailed Tho's N. Carter Esq. 20 Apr 1854]

F2-456: Surv.1 Aug 1852 by T.W.20,018 Thomas N. Carter asne. of Thomas M. Ewing 7 A. 3 Ro. 20 Po. in Pr. William Co. adj. William Fraser, Dane, Caleb Simpson, Maddox, John Clarke. 1 Feb 1854 [Mailed to Prop'r 20 Apr 20 1854]

F2-457: Surv.8 Mar 1851 by T.W.18,113 Daniel R. McNeill, Benjamin S. McNeill & William C. McNeill 90 3.4 A. in Hardy Co. on Pattersons Cr. Mt. & S. Fork of Patterson's Cr. adj. McMechin, Stingley, their own land, on Little Knob, Wilson, McNemar & Idleman, Pond Knob. 1 Feb 1854 [Dl'd P. T. Welton Esq. 12 Dec '55]

F2-458: Surv.18 June 1853 by T.W.21,362 Thomas Smith trustee of Sarah G. Smith & her ch. 15 A. 2 Ro 25 Per. in Stafford Co. known as John Smith's Big Island in Rappahannock R. 1 Mar 1854 [Mailed to E. Conway Esq. 15 May '54]

F2-459: Surv.18 June 1853 by T.W.21,362 Thomas Smith Trustee of Sarah G. Smith & her Ch. 4 A. 3 Ro. in Stafford Co. in Rappahannock R. known as Point of Fork island N.W. of Big Island. 1 Mar 1854 [Mailed to E. Conway Esq. 15 May '54]

F2-460: Surv.23 July 1853 by T.W.21,422 John Hutchison 113 3/4 A. in Pr. William Co. adj. Johnsburg/Johnsburgh tract belonging to heirs of Alexander C. Bullett, said Hutchison, Tebbs Dale, Quantico Cr. 1 Mar 1854

F2-461: Surv.12 Sep 1853 by T.W.21,615 John Monroe Jr. 4 A. 3 Ro. 12 Per. in Stafford Co. adj. said Monroe, Whitfield Monroe, Daniel Monroe. 1 Apr 1854 [Mailed to E. Conway Esq. 15 May '54]

F2-462: Surv.31 May 1853 by T.W.17,356 Robert McFarland 12 1/2 A. in Warren Co. adj. Silas Fristoe's McKoy grant, James Stinson, Hawkins tract, Rd. fron Ft. Royal to Luray, James Stinson's Alexander Mathews grant. 1 Apr 1854 [Dl'd M.D. Newman pardner of F.C. Hill 12 Nov 1855]

F2-463: Surv.23 July 1853 by T.W.21,441 Charles Roby 3 A. 2 Ro. 24 Per. in Fairfax Co. adj. Samuel Wilson, Stephen Lewis, Wolf Trap run, George Town Rd., Broadwater. 1 Apr 1854 [Mailed to Prop'r c/o Spencer Junkins? 2 June 1854]

F2-464: Surv.8 Mar 1852 by T.W.11,112 William Snyder 22 A. in Berkeley Co. on N. Mt. adj. William Snyder, Boyd, James Myers, Back Cr., Stookey, Snyder's heirs. 1 May 1854 [Mailed to J. P. Kearfott 21 June 1871?]

F2-465: Surv.24 Sep 1853 by T.W.14,147 John W. Lockhart 76 A. in Rappahannock Co. on Oven top Mt. adj. William McLearan, John W. Lockhart, William Pullin. 1 May 1854 [Mailed to Prop'r 23 Aug '54]

F2-466: Surv.18 Dec 1852 by T.W.20,388 Samuel C. Collins 16 A. 3 Ro. 38 Po. in Pr. William Co. on Brentsville & Occoquan Rd. adj. land formerly J.? M. Savage, James Bradley. 1 May 1854 [Mailed to Prop'r 28 Oct '54]

F2-467: Surv.3 Nov 1853 by T.W.20,374 Jacob B. Brown 21 A. 2 Ro. 30 Po. in Jefferson Co. adj. Potomac R. & Government Canal, Samuel Strider, Robert Harper, Wm. Smallwood, Government line. 1 June 1854 [Mailed to Prop'r 10 June 1854]

F2-468: Surv.7 Aug 1852 by T.W.18,684 Chapman Renoe 55 A. 2 Ro. 15 Po. in Pr. William Co. adj. Brentville & Dunfries Rd. & Long Br. of Occoquan, Lewis Cole, Washington, Forbes, Henry A. Barron. 1 June 1854 [Mailed to Chas. E. St.Clair Esq. 16 June '54]

F2-469: Surv.12 Aug 1852 by T.W.18,407 Samuel Bromback 84 A. in Hardy Co. on Alleghany Mt. & Stony R. at mouth of Four Mile Run adj. Deakins, Washington, Boness. 1 June 1854 [Mailed the Prop'r 25 Sep '54]

F2-470: Surv.12 Aug 1852 by T.W.18,407 Samuel Bromback 120 A. in Hardy Co. on Stony R. in the Alleghany Mt. adj. his own land, Bonness, Washington, Deakins, Shell heirs. 1 June 1854 [Mailed the Prop'r 25 Sep '54]

F2-471: Surv.8 Apr 1853 by T.W.18,620 Henry Batten 3 7/8 A. in Madison Co. adj.

James Taylor, A.H. Carpenter, heirs of Lewis Aylor dec'd, Gen. R. A. Banks, John Batten heirs. 1 June 1854

F2-472: Surv.18 Dec 1840 by T.W.14,232 Elijah Hovermill 252 A. in Morgan Co. on Indian Run on Cacapeon Mt. 1 July 1854

F2-473: Surv.3 Oct 1853 by T.W.15,538 Henry W. Richards 32 A. in Frederick Co. on Paddy's Run in Little Cove adj. Richards formerly Lewis T. Moore. 1 July 1854

F2-474: Surv.8 Mar 1853 by T.W.17,421 & 15,538 John A. Hart 90 A. in Frederick Co. adj. Adam Hart's purchase of Trisham Ewin, Conrad Loy formerly John Holliday, said John Hart. 1 July 1854 [Mailed L. S. Miller Esq. 16 Dec '54]

F2-475: Surv.3 Sep 1851 by T.W.18,583 Benjamin F. Thomas & Joseph Offenbacker 46 A. 3 Ro. 37 Po. in Page Co. on Naked Cr. S. of Luray. 1 July 1854 [Mailed cto Eli Chadduck 29 Nov '54]

F2-476: Surv.15 June 1853 by T.W.20,170 Thomas Holmes 28 A. 3 Ro. 1 Po. in Pr. William Co. near Lucky Run adj. Holmes, Bridewell, Elizabeth Holmes. 1 July 1854 [Dl'd to rec't 28 Feb '56]

F2-477: Surv.12 Feb 1850 by T.W.18,076 Isaiah Fisher 7 A. 21 Po. in Pr. William Co. on Rd. from Brentsville to Occoquon Mills adj. Francis Hanna, William Selecman, Joseph Janney. 1 July 1854 [Dl'd Mr. John H. Fisher Jan 23/55]

F2-478: Surv.13 Mar 1853 by T.W.18,352 Garrett J. Blue asne. of Richard W. Varden 37 Per. in Hampshire Co. on S. Br. of Potomac R. adj. Garrett J. Blue, John Hardy. 1 July 1854 [Dl'd I. Parsons 17 Mar T.W.56]

F2-479: Surv.25 Jan 1851 by T.W.14,665 Abel Evans 50 A. in Hampshire Co. on N. R. Mt. adj. Henry Wise, Benjamin Fry, said Evans. 1 July 1854 [Dl'd Isaac Parsons 17 Mar'56]

F2-480: Surv.11 Apr 1853 by T.W.18,932 & 21,111 Jacob Hynes asne. of George Loy 110 1/2 A. in Hampshire Co. on Stony Mt., adj. John Ruckman, James Combs heirs, Christopher Deliplain, Samuel McDonald, Thomas Piles, William Cool, Henderson. 1 July 1854 [Dl'd Isaac Parsons 1 Dec 1856]

F2-481: Surv.23 Sep 1851 by T.W.17,545 & 19,254 John S. Kidwell 71 1/4 A. in Hampshire Co. on N. R. & N. R. Mt. adj. James Hawking, Ralph now his & said Hawking's land, Foreman formerly Slain's heirs, Samuel A.Kidwell, Benjamin McDonald. 1 July 1854 [Dl'd Isaac Parsons 17 Mar 56]

F2-482: Surv.14 Mar 1851 by T.W.16,493 George Loy asne. of William Cod 75 A. in Hampshire Co. on Stony Mt. adj. Philip B. Streit, Samuel J.? Ruckman, Thomas Ruckman, Samuel C. Ruckman, Thomas Piles. 1 July 1854 [Isaac Parsons 17 Mar 56]

F2-483: Surv.10 May 1853 by T.W.17,545 Abraham Milslagle & Jonathan W. Albright 1 1/2 A. in Hampshire Co. on Sandy Rg. adj. said Milslagle & Albright, Park. 1 July 1854 [Dl'd Isaac Parsons 17 Mar'56]

F2-484: Surv.24 Mar 1851 by Surv.14,624 & 18,932 William Moreland 315 A. in Hampshire Co. on Dillon's Mt. adj. Swan Due, Abraham Creswell, his Cale surv., William Nixon, Robert Pugh heirs, George Chamberlain, William H. Moreland. 1 July 1854 [Dl'd Isaac Parsons 17 Mar 56]

F2-485: Surv.19 June 1851 by T.W.4982, 5775, 10,027 & 7985 Margery Moreland wid. of Basil Moreland dec'd, George W. Moreland, Benjamin W. Moreland, Sarah C. Moreland, Mary E. Moreland, & Basil N. Moreland ch. & infant heirs of said Basil Moreland dec'd, 73 A. in Hampshire Co. on Little Cacaphon adj. George Moreland heirs, John Caylor, John Jenkins heirs, John Largent, John Critton heirs, James Sterns. 1 July 1854 [Dl'd Isaac Parsons 17 Mar 56]

F2-486: Surv.17 Feb 1863 by T.W.19,458 Joseph F. Parrill 37 A. in Hampshire Co. on Dillon's Run on Little Mt. adj. Peter Evans, Linthicum heirs, Rice Hawkins bought of Hezekiah Clegett. 1 July 1854 [Dl'd Isaac Parsons 17 Mar 56]

F2-487: Surv.29 June 1853 by T.W.10,640 George Riley 37 1/4 A. in Hampshire Co. on Alleghany Mt. & Little N. Br. of Potomac R. adj. Neal's Sugar Camp Run adj. said Riley, Alexander Riley, John Abernathy heirs, Thomas Shore. 1 July 1854 [Mailed Prop'r 9 Oct 1854]

F2-488: Surv.16 Mar 1853 by T.W.20,864 & 19,438 Emmer Stalcup 112 A. in Hampshire Co. on Nobley Mt. adj. George House, Samuel House, Hanes. 1 July 1854 [Dl'd Isaac Parsons 25 Jan 1856]

F2-489: Surv.23 Feb 1853 by T.W.19,458 Emmor Stallcup Jr. 23 A. in Hampshire Co. on N. Br. of Potomac R.adj. Samuel House, said Stallcup. 1 July 1854 [Dl'd Isaac Parsons 25 Jan 1856]

F2-490: Surv.5 Apr 1853 by T.W.17,545 Jacob Short 15 1/2 A. in Hampshire Co. on Grape Vine Rg. adj. John Engle, George Sharff, Robert Carmichael. 1 July 1854 [Dl'd Isaac Parsons 17 Mar '56]

F2-491: Surv.29 Nov 1853 by T.W.16,531 Joseph Baker 1 A. 20 8/10 Po. in Page Co. N. of Luray adj. Pass Run, William Kibler, Springfield-Thornton's Gap Rd., Joseph Baker, Martin Kibler heirs. 1 Aug 1854 [Dl'd Eli Chadduck 29 Nov '54]

F2-492: Surv.29 Oct 1853 by T.W.18,593 James W. Chadduck 3 Ro. 35 Po. in Page Co. N. of Luray adj. John Lionberger, Thompson Vaughn, Eli Chadduck. 1 Aug 1854 [Dl'd Eli Chadduck 29 Nov '54]

F2-493: Surv.3 Dec 1852 by T.W.19,458 Thomas Connor 3 A. in Hampshire Co. on Little Cacapon adj. said Connor, Samuel Ruckman, Washington Alben. 1 Aug 1854 [Mailed to Prop'r 25 July '55]

F2-494: Surv.4 Mar 1853 by T.W.19,458 & 20,864 William Hanes & John Starnes 634 A. in Hampshire Co. on Lewis run of S. Br. of Potomac adj. Amos Poland heirs, John McDowel, David Gibson, Carpenter's Lick Rg., Parsons, Kuykendall. 1 Aug 1854 [Dl'd to Isaac Parsons 17 Mar 56]

F2-495: Surv.13 Feb 1852 by T.W.18,593 Joel Fultz 7 A. 1 Ro. 38 Po. in Page Co. on Shenandoah R. S.W. of Luray adj. John Strole. 1 Aug 1854 [Chadduck 29 Nov'54]

F2-496: Surv.7 Apr 1853 by T.W.12,791 Joseph McBride asne. of Peter McBride 15 1/2 A. in Hampshire Co. on Little Capon adj. Silas Mileson, John Smith. 1 Sep 1854 [Dl'd Isaac Parsons 17 Mar 56]

F2-497: Surv.6 Apr 1853 by T.W.17,545 & 20,864 John McBride of Peter 27 1/2 A. in Hampshire Co. on Little Capon adj. Silas Mileson, John Pence, Isaac Miller. 1 Sep 1854 [Dl'd Isaac Parsons 17 Mar 56]

F2-498: Surv.17 June 1851 by T.W.16,350 Samuel Bonham 24 3/4 A. in Hampshire Co. on Potomac R. hill & Town hill adj. his land bought of Daniel McDonald heirs, Snider bought of Nixon, Jacob Swisher. 1 Sep 1854 [Dl'd Isaac Parsons 17 Mar'56]

F2-499: Surv.8 Dec 1853 by T.W.18,290 James Williams 58 A. in Hampshire Co. on Patterson's Cr. & Patterson's Cr. Mt. adj. said Williams, Isaac Johnson heirs, Jacob Johnson, Vandiver. 1 Sep 1854 [Dl'd Isaac Parsons 17 Mar'56]

F2-500: Surv.30 Sep 1851 by T.W.19,254 Samuel Bonham 10 1/4 A. in Hampshire Co. on Potomac R. & R. hill adj. Jacob Swisher, his own land bought of McDonald heirs. 1 Sep 1854 [Dl'd Isaac Parsons 17 Mar '56]

F2-501: Surv.22 Jan 1850 by T.W.16,948 John Tucker Jr. & John Smith of Sarah 450 A. in Hardy Co. on Little Mt. & Salt Spring Run adj. Roberts, Rotruck, Tucker & Martin, Gilpin, Harriss, David Roberts, Knobley Mt., Jas. Roberts's Putnam tract, Martin's Taylor tract. 1 Sep 1854 [Jno. Tucker Jr. 2 Aug '55]

F2-502: Surv.21 Mar 1854 by T.W.22,051 John M. Kight 6 1/2 A. in Hampshire Co. on N. Br. of Potomac R. below Baltimore & Ohio RR. Bridge, adj. said Kite, mouth of Savage. 30 Oct 1854 [Dl'd to Prop'r 1 Nov 1854]

F2-503: Surv.23 Mar 1854 by T.W.22,051 John M. Kight 355 1/4 A. in Hampshire Co. on N. Br. of Potomac R. adj. said Kight, Hampshire Coal & Iron Co., George G. Tasker, Montgomery run, Baltimore & Ohio RR. 30 Oct 1854 [Prop'r 1 Nov 1854]

F2-504: Surv.20 Mar 1854 by T.W.22,051 John M. Kight 265 1/4 A. in Hampshire Co. on N. Br. of Potomac R. adj. Oliver, Baltimore & Ohio RR. Bridge, Macker, Montgomery's Run. 30 Oct 1854 [Dl'd to Prop'r 1 Nov 1854]

F2-505: Surv.3 June 1853 by T.W.17,205 Christopher Armantrout 6 A. in Hardy Co. on S. Br. & Mill Cr. adj. his own & Hires lands, Stombough, Gray's heirs. 2 Oct 1854 [Dl'd G.T.Barbee Esq. 13 Nov 1854]

F2-506: Surv.24 Mar 1853 by T.W.17,414 Jacob Swisher 7 1/2 A. in Hampshire Co. on Little Capon adj. Christy, Watson heirs. 2 Oct 1854 [Isaac Parsons 17 Mar'56]

F2-507: Surv.24 Mar 1853 by T.W.17,414 Jacob Swisher 6 A. in Hampshire Co. on Little Capon adj. said Swisher, John Detrick, Christy. 2 Oct 1854 [Dl'd Isaac Parsons 17 Mar '56]

F2-508: Surv.19 Oct 1853 by T.W.19,254 Isaac Brill 7 3/4 A. in Hampshire Co. on Lonan's Br. adj. said Brill, Joseph Hannum, Daniel & William Anderson. 2 Oct 1854 [Dl'd Isaac Parsons 17 Mar '56]

F2-509: Surv.19 Nov 1852 by T.W.19458 Josiah Caylor 6 3/4 A. in Hampshire Co. on Spring Gap Mt. & Neals Run of Little Cacapon adj. Boman, Caylor, John Ginevan. 2 Oct 1854 [Dl'd Isaac Parsons 17 Mar '56]

F2-510: Surv.28 Feb 1853 by T.W.19,458 Richard M. Slonaker 3 A. 2 Ro. 13 Po. in Hampshire Co. on Mt. bet. Parkes Valley & Dillons Run adj. said Slonaker, Jesse Lupton, Geo. Corly, Pendleton Murphey, Christopher Oats, George Slonaker, Richard M. Slonaker. 2 Oct 1854 [Dl'd Isaac Parsons 17 Mar '56]

F2-511: Surv.14 Feb 1854 by T.W. 18,352 Jacob Ullery 16 1/4 A. in Hampshire Co. on Little Capon, & Br. Mt. adj. said Ullery, Watson heirs. 2 Oct 1854 [Dl'd Isaac Parsons 17 Mar '56]

F2-512: Surv.9 Dec 1853 by T.W.21,111 & 21,653 Joseph Arnold 127 3/4 A. in Hampshire Co. on Pattersons Cr. Mt. by Salt Petre Gap Run, adj. said Arnold, Job Welton heirs, Richard Holiday heirs, Colston mannor. 2 Oct 1854 [Mailed Prop'r 15 Dec 1854]

F2-513: Surv.22 Oct 1853 by T.W.15,875 John Spade 2 A. in Hampshire Co. on Rg. E. of Great Cacapon R. adj. said Spade, Philip Kline, George Spade. 2 Oct 1854 [Dl'd Isaac Parsons 17 Mar '56]

F2-514: Surv.18 May 1853 by T.W.15,875 George Spade 3 1/2 A. in Hampshire Co. on Great Cacapon adj. said Spade, Thos. McGraw heirs. 2 Oct 1854 [Dl'd Isaac Parsons 17 Mar '56]

F2-515: Surv.18 Nov 1852 by T.W.14,574 & 19,458 Thomas Henderson & John Ginevan 46 3/4 A. in Hampshire Co. on Spring Gap Mt. adj. Henderson, George Stump, George Boman. 2 Oct 1854 [Dl'd Isaac Parsons 17 Mar '56]

F2-516: Surv.25 Mar 1853 by T.W.19,254 John Deiterick 4 A. 2 Ro. 13 Po. in Hampshire Co. on Little Capon adj. Nicholas Caylor, said Deiterick, Jacob Swisher. 2 Oct 1854 [Dl'd Isaac Parsons 17 Mar '56]

F2-517: Surv.20 Oct 1853 by T.W.19,458 Jacob McKiver 26 1/4 A. in Hampshire Co. near Capon Springs adj. Julious C. Waddle, Trustees of Watson Town, Bear Rg., John Racey, Daniel & William Anderson. 2 Oct 1854 [Isaac Parsons 17 Mar '56]

F2-518: Surv.17 May 1852 by T.W.18,189 Charles Brown 39 1/2 A. in Hardy Co. on Tucker's Run, on the divides of N.R. drains adj. his own land, Masham Bean. 2 Oct 1854 [Dl'd Geo. Shultz 7 May '55]

F2-519: Surv.17 Nov 1853 by T.W.18,189 Horatio Bean & Richard Bean 100 A. in

Hardy Co. on Philo Lick Run & Br. Mt. adj. their own land, Burch. 2 Oct 1854 [Dl'd Geo. Shultz 7 May '55]

F2-520: Surv.23 Mar 1853 by T.W.17,517 Jacob Cornell 5 A. in Hardy Co. on Powder Lick Drain of Patterson's Cr. adj. his own land, Rankin. 2 Oct. 1954 [Dl'd J.H. Cassin 6 Mar'58]

F2-521: Surv.13 May 1852 by T.W.18,188 Masham Bean 19 5/8 A. in Hardy Co. on Tuckers Run on W. side of the Bean Settlement adj. Brown, Burch. 2 Oct 1854 [Dl'd Geo. Shultz 7 May '55]

F2-522: Surv.15 Nov 1853 by T.W.2751 Ezekial Bean 224 A. in Hardy Co. on Tucker's Run & Branch Mt. adj. Jno. Evans, Brown, Burch. 2 Oct 1854 [Dl'd Geo. Shultz 7 May '55]

F2-523: Surv.7 Dec 1853 by T.W.18,290 Jacob Johnson 154 A. in Hampshire Co. on Patterson's Cr. & Patterson's Cr. Mt. adj. James Williams, Vandiver, Isaac Johnson heirs, Hardy Co. line. 1 Dec 1854 [Mailed Prop'r 16 Jan '55]

F2-524: Surv.3 June 1854 by T.W.22,215 James W. Green 9549 A. in Hardy Co. on Stony R., Alleghany Mt. adj. Grassy Rg. George Seymour, Chambers, David Badgley, Ramp patch, Baker, Stingleys run, Deakins. Beaver fork of Blackwater, Holmes, Gale & Harness surv., George Seymour. 12 Dec 1854 [Mailed Prop'r 13 Dec 1854]

F2-525: Surv.8 Oct 1852 by T.W.15,902 Jesse Davis 12 A. in Hardy Co. on New Cr. bet. Walkers Rg. & New Cr. Mt. adj. his own land, Griffin. 2 Oct 1854 [Dl'd Hugh Perrell 3 Mar '58]

F2-526: Surv.28 Feb 1853 by T.W.18,188 & 17,236 Erasmus Bean 276 A. in Hardy Co. on Philo Lick & Tucker's Runs adj. Harness & Seymore. 2 Oct 1854 [Dl'd Geo. Shultz 7 May '55]

F2-527: Surv.16 Nov 1853 by T.W.18,189 Samuel Bean 50 A. in Hardy Co. on Cobourns Knob & Scagg's Run adj. his land. 2 Oct 1854 [Geo. Shultz 7 May '55]

F2-528: Surv.22 Mar 1853 by T.W.17,517 Jacob Cornell 15 A. in Hardy Co. on Patterson's Cr. Mt. near the Turnpike Rd., adj. his McMechen land, McNemar, Coler. 2 Oct 1854 [Dl'd J.H. Cassin 6 Mar '58]

F2-529: Surv.14 Nov 1853 by T.W.2751 John Evans 227 A. in Hardy Co. on Br. Mt. & head drains of N. R. & Tucker's Run adj. his own land, Webb, Bean, Ships, Brown. 2 Oct 1854 [Dl'd Geo. Shultz 7 May '55]

F2-530: Surv.18 Jan 1851 by T.W.17,158 Jacob Cornwell 27 1/2 A. in Hardy Co. on S. Fork of Patterson's Cr. adj. his own land, Rankin. 2 Oct 1854 [Dl'd J.H. Cassin 6 Mar '58]

F2-531: Surv.7 May 1852 by T.W.18,113 Peter Bean 13 1/4 A. in Hardy Co. on N. R. & Varvels Rg. adj. his own land, Davidson, Cunningham, Thompson, Jarbo. 2 Oct 1854 [Dl'd Geo. Shultz 7 May '55]

F2-532: Surv.8 Mar 1853 by T.W.14,232 & 13,096 William Hobday 74 3/4 A. in Morgan Co. on Cacapon Mt. along Indian Run, adj. his late surv. 2 Oct 1854

F2-533: Surv.2 June 1845 by T.W.15,640 Paschal W. Cave 11 A. in Page Co. on Little Hawksbill adj. Roberts heirs, Andrew F. Grayson. 2 Oct 1854 [Mailed Prop'r 21 May'58]

F2-534: Surv.20 May 1852 by T.W.18,113 George Heishman 40 1/2 A. in Hardy Co. on Cacapeon R. adj. his own land. 1 Nov 1854 [Mailed Prop'r 16 May '55]

F2-535: Surv.18 Feb 1853 by T.W.17,236 George Hishman 6 3/4 A. in Hardy Co. on Lost R. adj. his own land, James Alban, Gillett & Russell. 1 Nov 1854 [Mailed Prop'r 16 May '55]

F2-536: Surv.1 Apr 1853 by T.W.16,962 David Whitzel 65 1/2 A. in Hardy Co. on

Pine Rg. & Rocky Br. of Lost R. adj. Kemble Bradfield, Reed heirs, his land,
Hardy Co. & Winchester pike. 1 Nov 1854 [Mailed Prop'r 20 Aug 1855]

F2-537:   Surv.11 Nov 1853 by T.W.21,658 Isabella Bennett 21 A. in Hampshire Co.
near N. R. adj. Sions Church, Cornelious A. Baker, Jacob Wolford, said Bennett,
Adam Wolford, Bruin, Robert Carmichael. 1 Nov 1854 [Isaac Parsons 17 Mar '56]

F2-538:   Surv.30 Nov 1853 by T.W.20,354 Jonathan Miller 14 A. in Shenandoah Co.
on Stony Cr. & Stony Cr. Rg. adj. said Miller, Christian Muoman. 1 Nov 1854
[Dl'd Mr. Pitman 21 Dec 1855]

F2-539:   Surv.1 Dec 1853 by T.W.18,694 Andrew Funkhouser 1 A. 1 Ro. 31 Po. in
Shenandoah Co. on Mill Cr. adj. Erasmus Rinker, said Funkhouser formerly John
Zehring. 1 Nov 1854 [Dl'd Mr. Pitman 21 Dec '55]

F2-540:   Surv.2 Feb 1854 by T.W.17,076 Isaac Sour of Philip 3 A. 2 Ro. 36 Po. in
Page Co. on Blue Rg. S.E. of Luray adj. Adam Smelser, Peter Judd, Isaac Sour. 1
Dec 1854 [Mailed E. Chadduck 28 Feb '55]

F2-541:   Surv.5 Apr 1850 by T.W.19,028 William Neely 11 1/2 A. in Morgan Co. E.
of Cacapeon Mt. adj. his land, Rhinehart. 1 Dec 1854 [Mailed Prop'r 7 June'58]

F2-542:   Surv.25 Apr 1854 by T.W.17,076 Isaac Somers & Reuben Somers 23 A. 3 Ro.
32 Po. in Page Co. on Big Hawksbill S.E. of Luray adj. Peter Printz, Isaac
Somers, Jones & Co. 1 Dec 1854 [Mailed E. Chadduck 28 Feb '55]

F2-543:   Surv.12 Feb 1852 by T.W.18,593 Simeon L. Huffman asne. of James M.
Andrews 3 A. 2 Ro. 26 Po. in Page Co. on Shenandoah R. adj. Joel Fultz, Geo.
Kite. 1 Jan 1855 [Mailed E. Chadduck 28 Feb '55]

F2-544:   Surv.29 May 1854 by T.W.17,956 John Smith 20 A. 2 Ro. 9 Po. in Page Co.
on Dry run S.E. of Luray adj. John Smith, Henry Shaffer, Daniel Sour. 1 Jan
1855 [Mailed E. Chadduck 28 Feb '55]

F2-545:   Surv.4 Apr 1854 by T.W.18,593 John Dofflemyer 2 A. 2 Ro. 35 1/2 Po. in
Page Co. on Shenandoah R. S. of Luray adj. land Christopher Comer sold John
Strole. 1 Jan 1855 [Mailed E. Chadduck 28 Feb '55]

F2-546:   Surv.1 May 1854 by T.W.10,709 James Kibler 7 A. 39 Po. in Page Co. on
Piny Mt. N.E. of Luray adj. John A. Ponn, Jas. Kibler purchase of Williams,
Kibler purchased of Jno. Clizer. 1 Jan 1855 [Mailed E. Chadduck 28 Feb '55]

F2-547:   Surv.6 June 1854 by T.W.10,852 John Dawson 14 1/4 A. in Morgan Co. on
Rock Gap Run adj. John Fearnow, said Dawson, Warm Spring Rg. 1 Feb 1855 [Dl'd
P.T. Zeilor 15 May 1858]

F2-548:   Surv.18 Mar 1854 by T.W.17,076 Richard T. Brumback 10 A. in Page Co. on
Piny Mt. & Jeremies Run N. of Luray adj. Richard T. Blumback, said Brumback. 1
Feb 1855 [Dl'd M. Spitler Esq. 23 Feb 1856]

F2-549:   Surv.18 Mar 1854 by T.W.18,583 Henry A. Keyser & William H. Bheam 34 A.
2 Ro. 9 Po. in Page Co. on Piny Mt. & Jeremies Run N. of Luray adj. Moses Wood,
Rich. T. Brumback. 1 Feb 1855 [Mailed E. Chadduck 26 Feb 1857]

F2-550:   Surv.9 Feb 1854 by T.W.18,593 Daniel F. Brown 3 A. 3 Ro. 33 Po. in Page
Co. on Shenandoah R. near Grove Hill S. of Luray adj. Wm. C. Kite, Jacob Couger.
1 Mar 1855 [Dl'd Mr. M. Spitler 28 Jan 1858]

F2-551:   Surv.12 May 1854 by T.W.15,538 James R. Coburn 9 A. 2 Ro. 37 Po. in
Frederick Co. adj. Joseph P. Hollingworth, Anthony Funkhouser, James Afflick. 1
Mar 1855 [Mailed Prop'r 1 Aug 1855]

F2-552:   Surv.24 Dec 1852 by T.W.10,773 & 10,752 Michael Thrush 57 1/2 A. in
Hampshire Co. on Knobley Mt. & Rd. from Paddy Town to Romney, adj. said Thrush,
James Cascaddon, John Hoy heirs, Edward Ravenscraft. 1 Mar 1855

F2-553:   Surv.31 Aug 1854 by T.W.22,118 Henry Comer 50 A.   3 Ro. 25 Po. in Page
Co. in the Piny Woods S. of Luray adj. Henry Forrer.   2 Apr 1855

F2-554:   Surv.1 Sep 1854 by T.W.18,593 William M. Darrough 20 3/4 A. in Page Co.
in Piny Woods S. of Luray adj. John Comer, Henry Comer.   2 Apr 1855 [Mailed Eli
Chadduck 28 Feb '55]

F2-555:   Surv.9 Aug 1854 by T.W.22,215 & 22,245 James W.   Green 763 A. in Hardy
Co. on Alleghany Mt. & Stony R. adj. Fisher, Bruce, Hearshey, Badgley now
Welton, Chambers now the Germans, Abrahams Cr., Roby now Bruce heirs, Baker. 1
May 1855 [Mailed Prop'r 3 May 1855]

F2-556:   Surv.4 Feb 1854 by T.W.21,961 Christopher Metcalfe 4 1/4 A. in Fauquier
Co. on Piny Br. adj. George W. F. Smith, William Lawler, James Scott, Gabriel
Jordon, heirs of Edward Carter dec'd, Lawler formerly Scott. 1 May 1855 [Dl'd
Rich'd H. Carter Esq. 7 May 55]

F2-557:   Surv.7 Feb 1854 by T.W.18,593 John Short 13 A. 3 Ro. 18 Po. in Page Co.
adj. Paul Long, Enoch Eppard heirs, Shenandoah R. S. of Luray.   1 May 1855
[Mailed Eli Chadduck 16 Oct '55]

F2-558:   Surv.1 Mar 1838 by T.W.12,362; John H. Wallace by deed 20 May 1850 was
asne. as Trustee of Samuel Lants, Isaac P. Rinker & Joseph Marston who by deed 8
June 1842 were asnes. of Pres., Dirs. & Co. of Bank of Virginia & Pres., Dirs. &
Co. of the Farmer' Bank of Virginia who by deed 8 June 1842 were asnes. of Wm.
J. Roberts & Hugh M. Patton Trustees, who were by deed 7 Sep 1839 asnes of
Benjamin Blackford & Thomas T. Blackford; 37 1/2 A. in Shenandoah Co. on S. R.
Mt. & Passage Cr. in Powel's Big Ft. adj. David Ross. 1 June 1855 [Dl'd P.V.
Daniel Jr. Esq. 5 July '55]

F2-559:   Surv.14 June 1854 by T.W.12,272 John Gunnell 2 A. 1 Ro. 6 Per. in
Fairfax Co. adj. Parker. point shown by W. Ballenger as Carter's patent, Emmbs &
Harle, Fairfax. 1 June 1855 [Dl'd Prop'r 1 Nov '55]

F2-560:   Surv.25 Jan 1854 by T.W.21,853 Isaac Baker & Absalom Keslor 74 A. in
Morgan Co. on Sideling Hill adj. Robert Rogers heirs, the Big Surv., Floras
heirs. 1 June 1855

F2-561:   Surv.17 Nov 1851 by T.W.17,760 Samuel H. Alexander 34 A. in Hardy Co.
on Townfort Run & Mannon's Run, Potatoe Run & Sugar loaf Knob, adj. Carson,
Harness, the Big Surv., Lobb. 1 Aug 1855 [Dl'd Jno. H. Cassin 6 Mar '58]

F2-562:   Surv.17 Jan 1851 by T.W.17158 Joseph McNemar 2 1/2 A. in Hardy Co. on
Paterson's Cr. Mt. in head of Wagon Rd. Gap adj. McMechen, Idleman, McNemar,
Vanmeter. 1 June 1855 [Dl'd J. H. Cassin 6 Mar '58]

F2-563:   Surv.4 Apr 1854 by T.W.20,374 Jacob B. Brown 10 A. 2 Ro. in Jefferson
Co. on Shenandoah R. adj. Robert Harper 1751 grant, foot Bridge at the Guard
Gates of the Canal, RR Bridge, near Rifle Factory, Hugh Gilleece, the Govt.
line. 1 June 1855

F2-564:   Surv.27 July 1854 by T.W.22,245 James W. Green 71 A. in Hardy Co. on
Alleghany Mt. in Stoney R. adj. his own land, Baker, Bromback. 12 July 1855
[Mailed Prop'r 19 July '55]

F2-565:   Surv.6 Nov 1854 by T.W.21,096 William Hunter 150 A. in Morgan Co. on
Warm spring Run below town of Bath adj. P. Dyche, Crone, Jno. Sherard heirs. 1
Aug 1855 [Mailed Prop'r 16 Oct '55]

F2-566:   Surv.25 Oct 1854 by T.W.18,635 James W. Chadduck & Charles T. Chadduck
274 A. 1 Ro. 37 Po. in Page Co. in Powell's Ft. on Middle Mt. W. of Luray adj.
John Leary. 1 June 1855 [Dl'd Mr. Spitler 10 Dec 1855]

F2-567:   Surv.29 Nov 1854 by T.W.16,531 Martin Beidler 17 A. 2 Ro. 15 Po. in
Page Co. in Piney Woods S. of Luray adj. John Reedy, John Pendegast, Noah
Painter, Martin Beidler. 2 July 1855 [Dl'd Mr. Spitler Esq. 3 Jan 1856]

F2-568: Surv.27 July 1853 by T.W.17,956 Elizabeth P. Wood 4 A. 1 Ro. 10 Po. in Page Co. N. of Luray adj. Joseph Robinson, Elizabeth P. Wood, David Bumgarner. 1 Aug 1855

F2-569: Surv.17 Mar 1854 by T.W.17,076 Peter Keyser 1 Ro. 26 Po. in Page Co. on Luray & Front Royal Turnpike Rd. N. of Luray, adj. Mary Fleming, Harrison Wood, Peter Keyser. 1 Sep 1855 [Mailed Eli Chadduck 17 Feb '57]

F2-570: Surv.3 Aug 1851 by T.W.17,158 Abraham Willis 25 A. in Hardy Co. on Pattersons Cr. Mt., Patterson's Cr. adj. his own land, the Wolf tract, Heath, his land formerly Shepherd. 1 June 1855 [Mailed S. Y. Simmons surv'r of Hardy Co. W. Va. 11 July 1879]

F2-571: Surv.28 Apr 1854 by T.W.15,640 Adam Smelser 16 A. 29 Po. in Page Co. on Blue Rg. E. of Luray adj. Sylvanus Strickler, Shirley, Leading Rg., Adam Smelser. 2 July 1855 [Dl'd M. Spitler Esq. 3 Jan 1856]

F2-572: Surv.22 Nov 1854 by T.W.22,118 & 18,635 Joshua Clemm 299 A. in Page Co. in Powels Ft. W. of Luray, on Middle Mt. adj. Marston, Lantz & Co. 2 July 1855 [Mailed Eli Chadduck 17 Feb '57]

F2-573: Surv.12 Feb 1850 by T.W.18,076 Hugh Hammill asne. of Isaiah Fisher 87 A. in Pr. William Co. on Occoquon Run adj. Francis Hanna, Joseph Janney. 1 Aug 1855 [Mailed Prop'r 1 Oct '55]

F2-574: Surv.24 Jan 1855 by T.W.22,118 Charles M. Keyser 2 A. 18 Po. in Page Co. on Shenandoah R. below the Golden Rock N. of Luray adj. Peter Keyser, Mary Fleming. 1 Sep 1855

F2-575: Surv.20 Dec 1854 by T.W.22,118, 22,731, 18,442 & 18,593 Joshua Clemm 433 3/4 A. in Page Co. on Middle fork Mt. W. of Luray adj. Sam'l Neff, Meadow Br., John Leary heirs. 1 Sep 1855 [Mailed Eli Chadduck 17 Feb '57]

F2-576: Surv.8 May 1854 by T.W.19,102, 21,700 & 22,236 Jesse Nicholson 190 A. in Madison Co. on Raggged Mt. adj. said Nicholson, Thomas Cubbage, Benjamin F. Smith, heirs of Howard Lillard dec'd, Bridge hollow drain, William R. Robson. 1 Oct 1855 [Dl'd A. Newman Esq. 1 Oct 1855]

F2-577: Surv.12 Jan 1855 by T.W.21,822 George Sperow 4 A. 2 Ro. in Berkeley Co. on Potomac R. adj. Leamaster, George Sperow's other land. 1 Oct 1855 [Mailed Jno. P. Kearfott 6 Oct '55]

F2-578: Surv.24 Jan 1854 by T.W.16,493 & 21,658 William B. Poling 183 1/2 A. in Hampshire Co. on Haunted Lick Run of S. Br. of Potomac R., on Little Mt. adj. Isaac Pancake, David C. Parsons, Susanna Dew, John M. Pancake, Strather Gannon heirs. 1 Oct 1855 [Dl'd Isaac Parsons 17 Nov '56]

F2-579: Surv.15 Nov 1854 by T.W.19,729 Jeremiah Jarrell 25 5/8 A. in Madison Co. adj. Robert Taylor, James May, Elijah Eddins, Noel May. 1 Oct 1855 [Dl'd Jno. Z. Wharton 21 Aug 1856]

F2-580: Surv.11 Apr 1854 by T.W.20,721 William Berry 30 A. in Madison Co. adj. Benjamin F. Thomas, Ragged Mt., Roberson R. 1 Dec 1855 [J.L. Kemper 22 Dec'55]

F2-581: Surv.2 Sep 1851 by T.W.17,132 & 18,583 Joseph Hoffman & Samuel Verner 150 A. in Page Co. on Blue Rg. at Milan's Gap S. of Luray adj. Joseph Huffman purchase of Reuben Thomas, Coffman, Wallace, said Huffman & Verner. 1 Dec 1855 [Dl'd Mr. M. Spitler 28 Feb '56]

F2-582: Surv.21 Mar 1854 by T.W.16.344 Sandford Y. Simmons 155 1/2 A. in Hardy Co. on Mud Lick & Baker's Run of Lost R. adj. Simmons, Koon, Bobo, J. Davison, Means, Pain, V. Simmons' Wharton Tract. 1 Nov 1855 [Mailed Prop'r 5 Apr'56]

F2-583: Surv.28 July 1854 by T.W.20,920 John W. Bowen 23 A. 1 Ro. 21 Po. in Alexandria & Fairfax Cos. near Four Mile Run adj. Mrs. Ruth Scott, Shrewood, Holmes's Run, Steele. 1 Nov 1855 [Mailed the Prop'r 21 July '57]

F2-584:   Surv.3 Aug 1844 by T.W.12,990 Weston Miles 12 5/8 A. in Hardy Co. on Timber Rg. & Walnut Bottom Run adj. James Miles, Simmons, Inskeep, the old Fidler path. 10 Jan 1856 [Dl'd J.H. Cassin 6 Mar '58]

F2-585:   Surv.14 Oct 1854 by T.W.18,290 S. Y. Simmons 24 1/2 A. in Hardy Co. on Scott's Rg. at head of Helmick's Gap, Helmick's spring Run adj. V. Simmons, A.A. Inskeep's Wimer land, the Manor line. 10 Jan 1856 [Mailed prop'r 5 Apr '56]

F2-586:   Surv.25 Oct 1852 by T.W.18,931 Henry Roadcap & Martin Roadcap 470 A. in Hardy Co. on Basore's Mill Run & Lost R. adj. See, Whitmore, Mathias, Basore, Barnett, Cline. 10 Jan 1856

F2-587:   Surv.11 Oct 1852 by T.W.17,760 Solomon Keplinger asne. of Jonathan Keplinger 20 1/8 A. in Hardy Co. on Luney's Cr. adj. Hire, Welton, his own land, heirs of Wm. Welton dec'd, Hires formerly D. Badgley.   10 Jan 1856 [Mailed Prop'r 15 Feb '56]

F2-588:   Surv.6 Jan 1854 by T.W.19,458 & 14,803 Lewis T. Dunn 674 A. in Hampshire Co. on Patterson's Cr. & Middle Rg. adj. Inskeep, Michael Baker, Jonathan Baker, Robert Dennison, John Hoy, Dr. Thomas Dunn. 10 Jan 1856 [Dl'd Mr. Parsons 14 Feb 1856]

F2-589:   Surv.27 Apr 1854 by T.W.19,775, 21,792 & 21,815 William Stillwell 680 A. in Berkeley Co. on Back Cr. adj. Noland heirs, Fletcher heirs, Cunningham, Dehaven, Greer, Col. Davenport, Third Hill Mt., Paul Taylor, Daniel Gano heirs. 1 Feb 1856 [Mailed prop'r 23 Feb '56]

F2-590:   Surv.11 July 1854 by T.W.21,658 & 22,358 William Abernathy 23 1/2 A. in Hampshire Co. on Alleghany Mt. & N. Br. of Potomac R. adj. George Riley now New Cr. Co., Isaac Kalbaugh, Thomas Shore. 1 Feb 1856 [Dl'd R.M. Powell 4 Mar'58]

F2-591:   Surv.12 May 1854 by T.W.2751 Adam Sions 600 A. in Hardy Co. on High Knob adj. Co. line, Jac. Vanmeter, McNeill, Kuykindall, Joseph Vanmeter, his own land formerly Vanmeter & Higgins. 1 Feb 1856 [Jno. P. Gardner 19 Sep 1857]

F2-592:   Surv.12 May 1854 by T.W.2751 John P. Gardner & M. P. Gardner asnes. of Adam Sions 100 A. in Hardy Co. in Trough on Saw Mill Mt. adj. Vanmeter, McNeill, Kuykendall, Miller, Trough Mt. 1 Feb 1856 [Mailed Jno. P. Gardner 19 Sep 1857]

F2-593:   Surv.8 Sep 1855 by T.W.22,236 William T. Simpson 79 A. in Madison Co. adj. Col. George H. Albers, Col. Edmund H. Lewis heirs, Battle F.T. Conway, Benjamin Simpson, Wm. T. Simpson, William J. Simpson, Noah Anderson. 1 May 1856

F2-594:   Surv.17 Dec 1853 by T.W.17,705 & 18,352 Isaac Slocum asne. of Perry Pepper 30 A. in Hampshire Co. on Crooked Run of Tear Coat Cr. adj. Henry Wolford's Flemming surv., Jonathan Pugh heirs. 1 May 1856 [R.M. Powell 4 Mar'58]

F2-595:   Surv.16 Aug 1855 by T.W.22,870 & 23,039 Thomas C. Williams 113 A. in Hampshire Co. on Alleghany Mt. & Montgomery Run of N. Br. of Potomac R. adj. James Machir, Bear Camp surv., Barrick. 2 June 1856 [Mailed prop'r 10 Oct 1856]

F2-596:   Surv.13 July 1855 by T.W.22,616 The New Creek Co. 8 A. 2 Ro. 30 Po. in Hampshire Co. on Alleghany Mt. near N. Br. of Potomac R. adj. Montgomery's Run, Richard Acton, the Oliver Surv. now Hampshire Coal & Iron Co., the Pea Vine Surv.2 June 1856 [Mailed Tho's C. Williams 10 Oct 1856]

F2-597:   Surv.18 Dec 1845 by T.W.2751 George High (of John) 26 A. 147 Po. in Hardy Co. on Mud Lick Run & Patterson's Cr. Mt. adj. Robey, Jno. Smith, land formerly Foley's, Slaty Rg., Dan'l J. Arnold, Jos. Arnold, Elisha Smith, Widow's dower. 1 July 1856 [Mailed Prop'r c/o Tho's Maslin 17 July '56]

F2-598:   Surv.19 Dec 1845 by T.W.2751 George High (of John) 37 A. 51 Po. in Hardy Co. on Mill Cr., Long Lick Mt. & Mud Run Mt. adj. Foley, Shoemaker, Smith, Arnold, Elisha Smith formerly David Gibson.   1 July 1856 [Mailed Prop'r c/o Tho's Maslin 17 July '56]

F2-599:   Surv.23 Nov 1855 by T.W.20,609 Michael Kerns 3 A. in Berkeley Co. on Mill Cr. of Back Cr. adj. Philip Everhart, Ruth Rawlings, Forbes, Riner's heirs, Shimp's heirs, Jacob Riner Jr., Michael Kerns, John Everhart. 1 July 1856 [Dl'd Jno P. Kearfoot 17 July '56]

F2-600:   Surv.1 Apr 1854 by T.W.17076 & 17,956 William Smith 63 A. 1 Ro. 28 Po. in Page Co. on Big Naked Cr. S. of Luray adj. Wesly Eppard, Wm. Smith, Fountain Utz/Ultz. 1 July 1856 [Mailed J.C. Walker 31 Oct 1856]

F2-601: Surv.28 Nov 1855 by T.W.22,154 Henry Hockman 1 3/4 A. in Warren Co. adj. Grant line, Obed Hockman, James Stinson. 1 July 1856 [Mailed Prop'r 29 Sep'56]

F2-602:   Surv.15 Aug 1855 by T.W.22,771 & 23,110 Gibson N. Roy 133 1/4 A. in Warren Co. adj. Norman, Cunningham, Calffee, G.N. Roy, J. S. Spingler, Lockhart heirs. 1 July 1856 [Mailed Prop'r 29 Sep'56]

F2-603:   Surv.16 Nov 1853 by T.W.21,658 & 19,254 Henry M. High 43 A. in Hampshire Co. on Fodderhouse Knob adj. Strather Gannon heirs, Andrew Ludwick. 1 July 1856 [Dl'd H. Perrell 3 Mar '58]

F2-604:   Surv.26 Jan 1854 by T.W.17,414 Elijah Wolford asne. of Jefferson Smith 10 1/4 A. in Hampshire Co. on N. R. adj. John Wolford heirs, Isabella Bennett, Bryan Bruin, Josiah Wolford. 1 July 1856 [Dl'd R.M.Powell 4 Mar '58]

F2-605:   Surv.17 Nov 1853 by T.W.19,458 & 21,658 Henry M. High 13 1/4 A. in Hampshire Co. on Mill Cr. adj. said High, Zacariah Arnold, John Flemming, High's McDonald land. 1 July 1856 [Dl'd Hugh Perrell 3 Mar '58]

F2-606:   Surv.17 May 1855 by T.W.22,876 James Carskadon 102 A. in Hampshire Co. on Middle Rg. adj. said Carskadon, Sheetz, Cockerel, Banes. 1 July 1856 [Dl'd Jas. D. Armstrong 10 Dec 1857]

F2-607:   Surv.19 Nov 1853 by T.W.17,705 James Powelson 18 A. 30 Po. in Hampshire Co. on Little Capon S. fork adj. William Vance, Samuel C. Ruckman, Martin Tutwiler, Powel Powelson, Henry Watkins. 1 July 1856 [R.M. Powell 4 Mar'58]

F2-608:   Surv.27 Jan 1854 by T.W.21,853 & 9131 John A. Hamilton 50 A. in Morgan Co. on Pursley Mt. & Potomac R. adj. Philip C. Pendleton, Catlett. 1 July 1856

F2-609: Surv.30 Jan 1854 by T.W.20,903 Jacob Cann 9 A. in Morgan Co. on Little Mt. & Cacapeon Mt. adj. said Cann, Dawson. 1 July 1856 [Mailed Prop'r 3 June'59]

F2-610:   Surv.30 Jan 1854 by T.W.20,276 Jacob Cann 317 A. in Morgan Co. on Sideling Hill adj. Benjamin Largent, Alderton, Cann, the Mill Path. 1 July 1856 [Mailed Prop'r 3 June 1859]

F2-611:   Surv.4 Feb 1854 by T.W.20,276 & 20,903 Jacob Cann 275 A. in Morgan Co. on Cacapeon Mt. on Chenowith's path, adj. said Cann, Dawson, Sink hole Run. 1 July 1856 [Mailed Prop'r 3 June 1859]

F2-612:   Surv.15 Dec 1854 by T.W.17,469, 17,514 & 22,236 Rowland Yowell 400 A. in Madison Co. on Great Ragged Mt. adj. Rowland Yowell, Rocky Run, Henry Quanintance, heirs of Nimrod Jenkins dec'd, Landrum run. 1 Aug 1856 [Mailed Jas. L. Kemper 4 Aug '56]

F2-613:   Surv.9 May 1854 by T.W.15,902 William F. Pifer 74 A. in Hardy Co. on New Cr. Mt. & Little Mt. on N. Fork adj. Gray heirs, Breathed, Hackney, N.N. line. 1 Aug 1856 [Mailed Prop'r 5 Feb '57]

F2-614:   Surv.2 Nov 1855 by T.W.22,616 John W. Athey 22 3/8 A. in Hampshire Co. on Mill Cr. adj. Job Parker now Parker's heirs, Rd. from Mehanicksburg to Sheet's Mills, said Athey, Jacob Parker heirs, Maj. James Parker. 1 Aug 1856 [Dl'd Jas. D. Armstrong 28 Dec '57]

F2-615:   Surv.22 June 1855 by T.W.20,864 Isaac Hanes 1 1/2 A. in Hampshire Co. near Barton's Meadow Run of W. fork of Little Cacapon adj. said Hanes, Joseph

Hanes heirs, Amos Poland heirs, Nancy Poland. 1 Aug 1856 [R.M.Powell 4 Mar'58]

F2-616: Surv.26 Apr 1853 by T.W.18,568 George W. Cooper asne. of Thomas French 5 3/4 A. in Hampshire Co. on N. Fork of Little Capon adj. said French, George W. Cooper. 1 Aug 1856 [Dl'd R.M.Powell 4 Mar '58]

F2-617: Surv.3 Oct 1855 by T.W.23,039 John W. Lawton 13 1/4 A. in Hampshire Co. on N. Br. of Potomac R. below Piedmont adj. Thomas C. Green's Gilpin surv., Pheonix Coal Co. Bridge, Baltimore & Ohio RR. 1 Aug 1856 [To Prop'r 9 Oct 1856]

F2-618: Surv.10 Apr 1855 by T.W.22,128 Joshua Dill 8 A. in Morgan Co. on Sleepy Cr. adj. Swain heirs, Walling, Dill. 1 Sep 1856 [Mailed Prop'r 27 Nov'56]

F2-619: Surv.22 Dec 1855 by T.W.22,154 Israel Lang 17 1/2 A. in Warren Co. on Punch Run adj. heirs of Christopher Kendrick/Hendrick, J.B. Cloud, Israel Lang, Bennett. 1 Sep 1856 [Mailed Jno. A. Thornhill 5 Nov '56]

F2-620: Surv.29 Jan 1855 by T.W.20354 Philip Lindamood 11 1/4 A. in Shenandoah Co. on Elk Run of Stony Cr. adj. Adam Weaver now Lewis Naselrodt, Abraham Sager, said Weaver & Gabriel Sager now Naselrodt. 1 Sep 1856 [Mailed Wm. Sisinger? 1 Feb 1859]

F2-621: Surv.25 Sep 1855 by T.W.23,039 Robert B. Sherrard 9 3/8 A. in Hampshire Co. on Bear Garden Rg. adj. Rogers heirs, William E. Hammack, John Keiter, Owen Rogers, William Unger formerly Peter Ougan. 1 Sep 1856 [Geo. Millison 28 May'57]

F2-622: Surv.25 Sep 1855 by T.W.23,039 Robert B. Sherrard 21 A. 60 Per. in Hampshire Co. on Bear Garden Rg. adj. said Sherrard, William Ungar, William E. Hammack, Rd. to Winchester, William Gaddis. 1 Sep 1856 [Dl'd Geo. Millison 28 May '57]

F2-623: Surv.23 Jan 1856 by T.W.23,039 Robert B. Sherrard 69 1/4 A. in Hampshire Co. on Bear Garden Rg. adj. William E. Hammack's Gaddis surv., said Sherrard, old Lemon line, Buzzard heirs. 1 Sep 1856 [Geo. Millison 28 May '57]

F2-624: Surv.26 Sep 1855 by T.W.23,039 Robert B. Sherrard 51 A. in Hampshire Co. on Owens Rg. adj. Charles Gill, said Sherrard bought of Christopher Slonaker, Jenkins heirs, the Meeting House lot, David Ellis, Isaac Kerns. 1 Sep 1856 [Dl'd Geo. Millison 28 May '57]

F2-625: Surv.1 Dec 1854 by T.W.21,936 John Wolf 58 A. in Frederick Co. on Babb's Run adj. Richard Barrett, William Bailey, John Sheerly/Shierly & others, Dangerfield, Chase. 12 Sep 1856 [Mailed Prop'r 16 Sep '56]

F2-626: Surv.23 Nov 1855 by T.W.22,876 James & John J. Morrison 13 1/2 A. in Hampshire Co. on N. Br. of Potomac R. adj. Benjamin Ashby Sr., Baltimore & Ohio RR. 15 Sep 1856 [Mailed John J. Morrison 20 Sep '56]

F2-627: Surv.16 July 1855 by T.W.22,957 Jacob Lantz & John J. Stoneburner 768 1/2 A. in Shenandoah Co. on Paddy Mt., Little Stony Cr. & Narrow Passage Cr. adj. Jacob Stultz, John Hepner, James S. Arthur. 20 Sep 1856 [Mailed Jno. Stoneburner Esq. 23 Sep 1856]

F2-628: Surv.29 June 1854 by T.W.19,458 & 22,358 Willim Cool 16 3/4 A. in Hampshire Co. on Dog Run of Little Capon adj. Hugh Murphy, John Arnold heirs, Adam Stump, N.W.Turnpike Rd., John Powelson heirs. 25 Sep 1856 [Dl'd Mr. Millison, Shff. 26 Sep 1856]

F2-629: Surv.11 Nov 1852 by T.W.19,458 Joel Cooper 8 1/2 A. in Hampshire Co. on N. R. adj. Timber Mt., s'd Cooper, John Engle. 1 Oct 1856 [R.M. Powell 4 Mar'58]

F2-630: Surv.13 Dec 1853 by T.W.17,346 Christipher Utta 27 1/4 A. in Hampshire Co. on Mikes Run of Patterson's Cr. adj. John C. Harrison, Aaron May, James Watson now David Dye. 1 Oct 1856 [Dl'd Hugh Perrill 3 Mar '58]

F2-631: Surv.8 May 1851 by T.W.15,554 Christopher Utta 50 A. in Hampshire Co.

on Mikes Run, Mikes Run Rg., adj. William Lessnby, John Vandiver, John Dye. 1 Oct 1856 [Dl'd Hugh Perrill 3 Mar '58]

F2-632: Surv.10 Dec 1853 by T.W.17,346 Christopher Utta 65 A. in Hampshire Co. on Mikes Run & Rg. adj. said Utta, John C. Harrison, Abner Banes, Josias More, George Gilpin, Utta's Parker surv. 1 Oct 1856 [Dl'd Hugh Perrill 3 Mar '58]

F2-633: Surv.15 June 1854 by T.W.14,624 Samuel J. Stump 12 1/2 A. in Hampshire Co. on N. R. Mt. adj. said Stump, James Shanholtzer, Wesley Smith. 1 Oct 1856 [Dl'd Geo. Millison 28 Nov '57]

F2-634: Surv.3 Jan 1855 by T.W.21,862 & 22,358 Isaac V. Inskeep 492 A. in Hampshire Co. on Middle Rg. & Patterson's Cr. adj. Robert Denneson, Lewis T. Dunn, John Hoy, Dr. Thomas Dunn, Thomas Cheney's Woodrow tract, Robert Cheney, Sliding Lick, William P. Stump, McAnaly, Jonathan Baker. 1 Oct 1856 [Mailed Prop'r 24 Feb 1857]

F2-635: Surv.20 Nov 1854 by T.W.14,623 Isaac V. Inskeep 1 1/2 A. 12 Per. in Hampshire Co. on Knobley Mt. adj. his own land, Angus W. McDonald, Dr. Perry. 1 Oct 1856 [Mailed Prop'r 24 Feb 1857]

F2-636: Surv.15 Dec 1853 by T.W.19,458 David Wolford 9 A. in Hampshire Co. on Tear Coat Cr. adj. Angus W. McDonald's Gilpin land, said Wolford, Samuel Ruckman, Branson Peters. 1 Oct 1856 [Dl'd Hugh Perrill 3 Mar '58]

F2-637: Surv.6 Jan 1855 by T.W.22,616 Clawsin Long 409 A. in Hampshire Co. on Keller's Run of Patterson's Cr. adj. Nimrod Furr, said Long, Joseph Inskeep heirs, Lewis T. Dunn, John Hoy now Dr. Thomas Dunn. 1 Oct 1856 [Mailed Prop'r 13 Mar '57]

F2-638: Surv.5 July 1854 by T.W.21,658 & 22,358 Stephen C. Rinehart 150 A. in Hampshire Co. on Middle Rg., Patterson's Cr. adj. Abraham Rinehart, James Allen, William Rees, William Leas, McNarey. 1 Oct 1856 [Dl'd R.M. Powell 4 Mar'58]

F2-639: Surv.11 Jan 1855 by T.W.20,198 & 22,216 Benjamin Williamson 158 A. in Hampshire Co. on Sidling Hill adj. said Williamson, Robert B. Fletcher, Hutt, Benjamin McDonald. 1 Oct 1856 [Dl'd Geo. Millisont 1 Dec 1854]

F2-640: Surv.5 Sep 1855 by T.W.22,616 John Deiterick 13 1/4 A. in Hampshire Co. on Little Cacapon adj. said Deiterick, Samuel J.? Stump, Jacob Swisher. 1 Oct 1856 [Dl'd R.M. Powell 3 Mar '58]

F2-641: Surv.12 Sep 1855 by T.W.22,876 Thomas S. Rigway, John McVey & Jacob Loose 4 7/8 A. in Hampshire Co. near N. Br. of Potomac R. adj. Robert K. Sheetz, their own land bought of Long, Ashby, Baziel Beall. 1 Oct 1856 [Dl'd R.M. Powell 3 Mar '58]

F2-642: Surv.18 Nov 1854 by T.W.20,864 & 15,875 Isaac Hollenback 54 A. in Hampshire Co. on Johnson's Run of Patterson's Cr. adj. said Hollenback, William D. Rees, Abraham Johnson, Solomon Ellifrits' Rankin surv., Grassy Lick, said Hollenback's Harsel surv. 1 Oct 1856 [Dl'd R.M. Powell 3 Mar '58]

F2-643: Surv.23 Jan 1855 by T.W.22,616 Evan McDonald 5 A. in Hampshire Co. on N. R. adj. Benjamin McDonald Sr., John S. Kidwell. 1 Oct 1856 [Dl'd R.M. Powell 4 Mar '58]

F2-644: Surv.8 Dec 1855 by T.W.23,039 Uriah Fletcher 8 1/4 A. in Hampshire Co. near Mills Br. on Bear Garden Rg. adj. Elijah Fletcher, Frederick Buzzard, Robert B. Sherrard's Kenney tract, the old Lemon line. 1 Oct 1856 [Dl'd R.M. Powell 4 Mar '58]

F2-645: Surv.10 Jan 1854 by T.W.21,658 Spencer R. Gray 176 A. in Hampshire Co. on Dillons Run adj. said Gray, Angust W. McDonald, Hammack, Zonley. 1 Oct 1856 [Dl'd R.M. Powell 4 Mar '58]

F2-646: Surv.28 May 1855 by T.W.22,616 & 22,876 William Moreland 72 A. in

Hampshire Co. on Cacapon Mt. adj. Robert Pugh heirs, John C. McDonald, said Moreland, Jesse Pugh, Eli Beall. 1 Oct 1856 [Dl'd R.M. Powell 4 Mar '58]

F2-647:   Surv.26 Sep 1855 by T.W.23,040 Christopher Neale asne. of Charles C. Smoot 4530 sq. ft. in Town of Alexandria adj. Conway, Pendleton St. 4 Nov 1856 [Mailed Prop'r 6 Oct 1856]

F2-648:   Surv.18 Sep 1854 by T.W.2751 Christian Cosner 103 A. in Hardy Co. on Abrams Cr. on the Alleghany Mt. adj. the German's, Cosner, Seymour, Bruce heirs, Sam'l H. Cosner, G. Cunningham. 1 Nov 1856 [Mailed Prop'r 15 Dec 1856]

F2-649:   Surv.22 May 1855 by T.W.18,290 Parson M. Taylor & Adam F. Miles 323 A. in Hardy Co. on Pattersons Cr. Mt. bet. Hershys Gap & Dapple hollow adj. Vanmeter, said Taylor bought of Boseley, Bruce, Taylor's Hershey tract, Vanmeter, Mullin's Foley tract, Jas. Bruce. 1 Nov 1856 [Mailed S.Y. Simmons 8 Aug '57]

F2-650:   Surv.21 May 1855 by T.W.18,290 Parson M. Taylor 32 A. in Hardy Co. on Patterson's Cr. & Patterson's Cr. Mt. adj. Bruce, Hershey, Williams, his own land, Littlefield hollow, Taylor formerly Boseley, William Boseley. 1 Nov 1856 [Mailed S.Y. Simmons 8 Aug '57]

F2-651:   Surv.22 Mar 1856 by T.W.17,132 Philip Long 8 A. in Page Co. on Massanuttin Mt. W. of Luray adj. said Long, the Big Surv., old Rd. formerly leading from Luray to New Market. 1 Nov 1856 [Dl'd R.P. Bell 25 Feb 1860]

F2-652:   Surv.14 Mar 1856 by T.W.14,643 Joseph Bumgarner 10 A. 2 Ro. 3 Per. in Page Co. on Massanuttin Mt. N. of Luray adj. Strickler, Andrew McKay, Christiah Bumgarner, the Deep Hollow. 1 Nov 1856 [Dl'd Mr. M. Spitler 28 Jan '58]

F2-653: Surv.25 Jan 1855 by T.W.22,616 Reasin King 4 3/4 A. in Hampshire Co. on N. R. adj. said King, Benjamin McDonald, McDonald's Sutton tract. 1 Nov 1856 [Dl'd R.M.Powell 4 Mar '58]

F2-654:   Surv.21 Nov 1854 by T.W.18,113 Henry W. Frye 100 A. in Hardy Co. on N. Mt. & Slate rock Run adj. his own land, Valentine Simmons, Simon Swisher, Dog Gap Run. 1 Dec 1856 [Mailed J. Didawick 2 Nov '57]

F2-655:   Surv.19 Nov 1853 by T.W.17,247 John Inskeep & J. L. Frye 46 1/2 A. in Hardy Co. on Fryes Run of Great Capon adj. their own land & others, Hecker. 1 Dec 1856 [Mailed J. Didawick 2 Nov '57]

F2-656:   Surv.25 Sep 1855 by T.W.22,777 Felix Richards 1 A. 1 Ro. 38 Per. in Fairfax Co. adj said Richards, heirs of Jane Monroe, line of Fairfax, Auld. 1 Dec 1856 [Dl'd to prop'r 29 May '57]

F2-657: Surv.21 Nov 1854 by T.W.14,782, 16,966, 21,111 & 22,616 James Berry 425 A. in Hampshire Co. on Georges Run of Pattersons Cr. adj. George Baker, Joseph Inskeep heirs, Jacob Adams, Samuel D. Brady, Anna Berry, James Berry. 1 Jan 1857 [Mailed J.B. Young 28 Mar 1857]

F2-658:   Surv.11 Jan 1847 by T.W.15,875 Anna Berry 30 A. in Hampshire Co. on Patterson's Cr. adj. her own land, James Berry. 1 Jan 1857 [Mailed J.B. Young 28 Mar 1857]

F2-659:   Surv.26 June 1855 by T.W.21,658 George Shoemaker 4 7/8 A. in Hampshire Co. on Mud Run of Mill Cr. adj. Larkin C. Kelley, said Shoemaker, Shoemaker's purchase of Ludwick heirs. 1 Jan 1857 [Dl'd R.M. Powell 6 Mar '58]

F2-660:   Surv.8 June 1855 by T.W.18,290 Daniel Arnold 560 A. in Hardy Co. on Patterson's Cr. Mt. near the Elk Ponds adj. heirs of Jos. Arnold dec'd, James Arnold, High, Slaty point, Smith, Dan'l J. Arnold, Vanmeter's Heath tract, Foley, Frazure's path. 1 Jan 1857 [Mailed Dennis Davis 16 Mqy '57]

F2-661:   Surv.19 Mar 1855 by T.W.18,290 Alfred Yoakum 205 A. in Hardy Co. on S. fork or Laurel run of Luney's Cr., bet. Alleghany Mt. & New Cr. Mt. on Flag

Meadow swamp adj. Walker's Rg. 2 Mar 1857 [Mailed S.Y. Simmons 8 Aug '57]

F2-662: Surv.8 Oct 1855 by T.W.21,869 Enos Cooper 50 A. in Hardy Co. on Alleghany Mt. & Johny Cake Run near Abrm's Cr. adj. N.W. turnpike, the Poenix Co., Clark originally Deakins, Fox, Wicough's Run, Gist. 2 Mar 1857 [Mailed to Jas. Cooper 23 Feb '59]

F2-663: Surv.6 June 1855 by T.W.12,264, 21,862 & 10,897 William Vance 100 A. in Hampshire Co. on Forked Knob near the Trough on S. Br. adj. Mitchell Mills, Jediah Carl, James Stuart, Lear. 1 Apr 1857 [Dl'd Geo. Millison 28 May '57]

F2-664: Surv.14 Sep 1855 by T.W.22,117 George W. Reedy, Andrew J. Grinnan & Rufus K. Fitzhugh 92 A. 3 Ro. in Page Co. on Blue Rg. S.E. of Luray adj. heirs of Asa Graves, Shenandoah & Rockingham Cos. line, Madison & Page Cos. line, Clore. 1 Apr 1857

F2-665: Surv.20 May 1856 by T.W.22,117 & 23,786 Andrew G. Grinnan & Rufus K. Fitzhugh 1717 A. in Page & Madison Cos. on Blue Rg. SE of Luray adj. Shelton's Gap, Shirley, Jones & Co., Daniel Weaver, John Saur, Charles Weaver, Hetick, Leading Rg. 1 Apr 1857 [Dl'd R.K. Fitzhugh 5 Aug 1857]

F2-666: Surv.17 Oct 1854 by T.W.15,875, 14,623 & 16,854 Reuben Davis asne. of Frances Murphy & Joseph Davis 49 A. in Hampshire Co. on Alleghany Mt., Abraham's Cr. adj. the Phenix Coal Co., Jones' heirs Martain's surv., John Shields, Jacob Kitsmiller, Buffington. 1 May 1857 [Dl'd Hny. R. Powell 3 Mar '58]

F2-667: Surv.1 Mar 1853 by T.W.18,932 & 20,864 Alexander Sanders 94 A. in Hampshire Co. on S. Br. of Potomac R. adj. Forman Inskeep, Buffalo hollow, Macher Inskeep, Isaac Parsons, said Sanders. 1 June 1857 [Dl'd R.M. Powell 4 Mar '58]

F2-668: Surv.2 Mar 1820 by T.W.6512 John Thompson 100 A. in Hampshire Co. on Sugar Run of S. Br. of Potomac R. adj. John Thompson Sr. dec'd bought of heirs of George & Isaaac Newman dec'd, John Newman patent of 5 Mar 1789, Richard Blue. 1 June 1857 [Mailed John B. White Esq. 16 Jan 1858]

F2-669: Surv.17 Sep 1851 by T.W.17,158 Samuel Rorobaugh asne. of Samuel H. Cosner 50 A. 3 Ro. in Hardy Co. on Alleghany Mt. & Abrahams Cr. adj. John Cosner, Cunningham now his own, Fern Spring, Roby, Bonness, McNeill. 1 June 1857 [Dl'd Jno. H. Cassin 6 Mar '58]

F2-670: Surv.14 May 1854 by T.W.15,824 Nancy Marshall & Mary Marshall 37 A. in Hardy Co. on N. R. adj. Thomas Marshall, Tucker's Run. 1 June 1857

F2-671: Surv.22 May 1855 by T.W.22876 David Cupp 10 A. 3 Ro. in Hampshire Co. on Dividing Rg. bet. Little Cacapon & Tear Coat Cr. adj. Locks heirs, Levi Shafer, his Beall land. 1 July 1857 [Mailed Prop'r 5 Sep '57]

F2-672: Surv.22 May 1855 by T.W.22,876 David Cupp 11 1/2 A. in Hampshire Co. on Dividing Rg. bet. Little Cacapon & Tear Coat Cr. adj. Mathew Combs, Levi Shafer's Beall tract. 1 July 1857 [Mailed Prop'r 5 Sep '57]

F2-673: Surv.19 June 1856 by T.W.23,386 Col. Isaac Parsons 67 A. 3 Ro. in Hampshire Co. in Green Spring Valley adj. John Donaldson, Bryan Bruin. 1 Aug 1857 [Mailed Prop'r 5 Oct '57]

F2-674: Surv.11 June 1856 by T.W.21,862 Amos Poland 49 1/2 A. in Hampshire Co. on S. Br. of Potomac R. adj. William H. McDowel, William Hanes, John Starnes. 1 Aug 1857 [Mailed Col. Isaac Parsons 5 Oct 1857]

F2-675: Surv.1 Dec 1856 by T.W.23,386 Theodore A. Krysher asne. of Abraham Smith 100 A. in Hampshire Co. on Great Cacapon adj. Samuel Sutton, Cornelius Vanosdall. 1 Aug 1857 [Mailed A. Smith Esq. 8 Oct '57]

F2-676: Surv.1 Feb 1856 by T.W.20,354 John Garber 60 sq. Po. in Shenandoah Co. on Mill Cr. adj. Joseph Osburn, William Wills heirs, Jacob Painter, Samuel

Wills. 1 Aug 1857 [Mailed Wm. Tisinger 1 May '58]

F2-677:   Surv.6 Feb 1856 by T.W.20,354 Abram Sager 1 A. 3 Ro. in Shenandoah Co. adj. Jacob Barb Sr., said Sager, Jacob Barb Jr.   1 Aug 1857   [Mailed Wm. Sainger? 1 Feb 1859]

F2-678:   Surv.1 Dec 1856 by T.W.21,294 Theodore A. Krysher asne. of Abraham Smith 100 A. in Hampshire Co. on High Top Mt. adj. John Heitty, Simeon Vanortwick. 1 Sep 1857 [Mailed A. Smith Esq. 8 Oct '57]

F2-679:   Surv.4 Nov 1856 by T.W.23,575 & 23,868 John J. Stoneburner 591 A. 2 Ro. 23 sq.Po. in Shenandoah Co. on Mt. bet. Powell's Big & Little Forts adj. John Shenk now Maston, Bush & Co., Samuel Hopewell, John Clem now Marston,Bush & Co. George & David McInturff, William C. Williams, Jacob Bowman.   1 Oct 1857 [Mailed Prop'r 16 Oct 1857]

F2-680:   Surv.20 June 1856 by T.W.23,700 David Neff 510 A. in Shenandoah & Page Cos. on Massanotten Mt. adj. Pennybacker, Elijah Evans, Jawbone Gap, Benjamin Blackford & son, Michael Neff.   1 Oct 1857   [Mailed Wm. Tisinger 7 May '58]

F2-681:   Surv.1 Apr 1856 by T.W.20,354 Levi Roads 11 1/8 A. in Shenandoah Co. on N. Fork of Shenandoah R. adj. Thomas Palmer now Levi Roads.   1 Oct 1857   [Mailed Wm. Tisinger 7 May '58]

F2-682:   Surv.17 Dec 1853 by T.W.19,458 & 20,864 Henry Wolford 25 1/2 A. in Hampshire Co. on Tear Coat Cr. adj. Jacob Wolford, said Henry Wolford, Crooked Run, Perry Pepper, Jonathan Pugh heirs, John Pugh.   2 Nov 1857 [Dl'd Hugh Perrill 3 Mar '58]

F2-683:   Surv.11 Nov 1853 by T.W.19,458 Henry Wolford 9 3/8 A. in Hampshire Co. on Tear Coat Cr. adj. said Wolford, John Malick heirs, William R. Kendall, James Stuart, Jacob Wolford.   2 Nov 1857   [Dl'd Hugh Perrill 3 Mar '58]

F2-684:   Surv.22 Aug 1856 by T.W.22,271 John McLanahan 9 A. 3 Ro. in Morgan Co. (Grant Marked out.) See Page 788.

F2-685:   Surv.18 Apr 1857 by T.W.23,979 Josiah H. Alexander 3 A. 3 Ro. 20 Po. in Berkeley Co. on N. Mt. adj. "Westenhaver" land, Daniel Leferre, E.G. Hedges.   16 Nov 1857   [Mailed Prop'r 21 Nov '57]

F2-686:   "[Mistake See page ante. 684] John McLanahan"

F2-687:   Surv.31 Aug 1855 by T.W.22,358 Joel Linthicum 87 A. in Hampshire Co. on N. R. adj. said Linthicum, Branson Poston, James Baker, N. R. Mt., Hammack. 1 Dec 1857 [Dl'd Geo. Millison 14 Dec '58]

F2-688:   Surv.22 May 1857 by T.W.23,039 Robert B. Sherrard 9 A. 20 Po. in Hampshire Co. on Bloomery Run adj. O.F. Heironimus, said Sherrard, Owen Rogers, John Keiter. 1 Dec 1857 [Dl'd Jas. D. Armstrong 29 Mar '58]

F2-689:   Surv.25 Jan 1855 by T.W.14,623 Reasin King 5 A. 3 Ro. 20 Per. in Hampshire Co. on N. R. adj. Benjamin McDonald, his Sutton Tract, said King. 1 Dec 1857 [Dl'd Chs. Blue 19 Mar '60]

F2-690:   Surv.13 Dec 1856 by T.W.23,983 Alexander E. Garrison 15 A. 2 Ro. 29 Po. in Stafford Co. adj. Mahorney, Callahan, Mountjoy, Rilley. 1 Feb 1858

F2-691:   Surv.2 June 1856 by T.W.17,406 John J. Shull 18 1/4 A. in Hardy Co. on Lost R. bet. Hanging Rock Rg. & Hardy & Winchester Pike adj. his own Mill lot, Benjamin Warden heirs, David Whetzel. 1 Jan 1858 [Dl'd Jno. Cassin 14 Mar '60]

F2-692:   Surv.3 June 1856 by T.W.17,406 John J. Shull 5 1/16 A. in Hardy Co. on Lost R. adj. his own land, David Whetzel, Benjamin Warden heirs, Hanging Rock Rg. 1 Jan 1858 [Dl'd J.H. Cassin 14 Mar '60]

F2-693:   Surv.27 Aug 1856 by T.W.18,121 Jacob R. Idleman & Lewis S. Idleman 13

1/2 A. in Hardy Co. on Alleghany Mt. bet. Mill Run & Abraham's Cr. adj. their own land, Cunningham, their Smith land, their Bogart & Fisher tract. 1 Jan 1858 [Mailed Prop'r 22 Sep '58]

F2-694: Surv.30 May 1857 by T.W.21,822 James Penteny 7 A. in Berkeley Co. on N. Mt. adj. Robert Penery, Elisha Butt. 1 Jan 1858 [Mailed Jno. P. Kearfott 23 Aug '58]

F2-695: Surv.15 July 1856 by T.W.16,854 Philip B. Streit 19 1/2 A. in Hampshire Co. on Alleghany Mt. & Abrams Cr. adj. Preston Coal & Iron Co., William Inskeep, Elijah Harvey, Bruice. 1 Feb 1858 [Dl'd J.D. Armstrong 26 Jan '60]

F2-696: Surv.16 July 1856 by T.W.22,616 Philip B. Streit 10 1/8 A. in Hampshire Co. on Alleghany Mt. & Deep Run adj. Thomazin Elzey, William Bosley now Preston Coal & Iron Co., Philip Urice. 1 Feb 1858 [Dl'd J.D. Armstrong 26 Jan '60]

F2-697: Surv.11 July 1856 by T.W.18,121 William Hall 28 1/4 A. in Hardy Co. on Alleghany Mt., Stoney R. & Coal Bank Run adj. Wm. S. Cunningham, Pheonix Co. formerly Nevill. 1 Feb 1858 [Dl'd J.H. Cassin 14 Mar '60]

F2-698: Surv.27 June 1855 by T.W.17,343 Charles Williams 26 A. in Hardy Co. on Patterson's Cr. & Croces Run adj. his own land, the Big Surv.known as Gilpin's, Linton, Joseph Williams dec'd. 1 Mar 1858 [Dl'd J.H. Cassin 14 Mar '60]

F2-699: Surv.1 Sep 1857 by T.W.17,331 Isaac Snyder 11 3/4 A. in Hardy Co. in lower Cove on N. Mt. adj. his own land, Erasmus Snyder, the Big Lick. 1 May 1858 [Mailed J. Didawick 9 Oct '58]

F2-700: Surv.29 Sep 1847 by T.W.16,300 Isaac Snyder 190 A. in Hardy Co. in Lower Cove on Cove Knob adj. his own land, Kele, Miller, Bear Wallow Rg., Davis, Laughlen, Atno. Miller. 1 May 1858 [Dl'd J. Didawick 8 Oct 1858]

F2-701: Surv.22 Apr 1857 by T.W.21,111 Col. Isaac Parsons 42 1/4 A. in Hampshire Co. on Valley Mt. adj. said Parsons, Bryan Bruin. 1 May 1858 [Dl'd to Prop'r 1 Dec 1858]

F2-702: Surv.30 May 1855 by T.W.17,760 Jacob Ketterman Jr. 16 1/4 A. in Hardy Co. on S. Mill Cr. & Long Run adj. his own land, Berkdall, his Brink tract, Jno. Sites. 1 June 1858 [Dl'd J.H. Cassin 14 Mar '60]

F2-703: Surv.28 May 1855 by T.W.17,760 Jacob Ketterman Jr. 29 1/4 A. in Hardy Co. on Long run of S. Mill Cr. adj. Berkdall heirs, heirs of George Harness dec'd, his own land, Nimrod Ketterman & Co., Harness Iman, Ketterman heirs. 1 June 1858 [Dl'd J.H. Cassin 14 Mar '60]

F2-704: Surv.29 May 1855 by T.W.2751 Hanah Bergdall asne. of Ashur Weese 137 A. in Hardy Co. on S. Mill Cr. & Eastern spurs of Middle Mt. adj. Rohrabough heirs, Cunningham, Welton, his own land, Weese. 1 June 1858 [Mailed Prop'r]

F2-705: Surv.1 Oct 1856 by T.W.16,214 Green B. Reed 8 3/4 A. in Hardy Co. on McDavits Mill Run on Alleghany Mt. adj. Chambers, Martin Leonard. 1 July 1858 [Dl'd J.H. Cassin 14 Mar '60]

F2-706: Surv.4 Oct 1856 by T.W.15,771 David Vanmeter 65 A. in Hardy Co. on Trough Mt. adj. his Carroll tract, his Gilchrist tract, Main Rd. to Romney, Wharton. 1 July 1858 [Dl'd J.H. Cassin 14 Mar '60]

F2-707: Surv.28 June 1856 by T.W.18,121 William C. Vanmeter 29 7/8 A. in Hardy Co. on Timber Rg. & Walnut Bottom Run adj. his own land, Whiting, Heath, his Mercer tract, Whiting's Miles land, Heath's Cranberry Pond tract. 1 July 1858 [Dl'd J.H. Cassin 14 Mar '60]

F2-708: Surv.28 June 1856 by T.W.18,212 James S. Whiting 66 1/4 A. in Hardy Co. on Timber Rg. adj. his Miles land, Inskeep, Vanmeter, Heath. 1 July 1858 [Dl'd J.H. Cassin 14 Mar '60]

F2-709: Surv.26 Oct 1849 by T.W.15,729 Lewis S. Idleman asne. of Upton Kitsmiller 1 A. 3 Ro. 18 Po. in Hardy Co. on Alleghany Mt. & Oil Run adj. Idleman, Gibson, Idleman's Hutton tract. 1 July 1858 [Mailed Prop'r 22 Sep'58]

F2-710: Surv.19 June 1856 by T.W.23,386 & 17,107 James Abernathy 133 A. in Hampshire Co. on Mt. W. of S. Br. called R. Mt. adj. his own land. 1 July 1858 [Dl'd J.D. Armstrong 28 Mar '60]

F2-711: Surv.10 May 1856 by T.W.13,050 Anthony Hammack asne. of John Simpson 23 1/4 A. in Hampshire Co. on S. fork of Hanging Rock Run & Sandy Rg. adj. Adam Cooper, Isaac Lupon now Anthony Hammack, Isaac Carlyle, Abraham Hammack, Jacob Baker, Charles Cooper. 1 July 1858 [Dl'd Ch's Blue 19 Mar '60]

F2-712: Surv.3 July 1857 by T.W.16,854 James Carskadon 31 A. in Hampshire Co. on New Cr. & New Cr. Mt. adj. Charles Creesap, Silas Rees, James Parris, Achiles Duling, Peter Smith. 1 July 1858 [Dl'd J.D. Armstrong 26 Jan '60]

F2-713: Surv.20 June 1854 by T.W.19,028 & 19,715 Samuel Johnston asne. of William Neely 22 A. in Morgan Co. on Cacapeon Mt. adj. Dawson, said Johnson. 1 July 1858

F2-714: Surv.9 June 1857 by T.W.15,538 Charles H. Barnes 80 sq. Po. in Frederick Co. in town of Stephensburg on Mulberry St. (2 Aug 1858 marked out) [The Governor refuses to sign this patent 18 Sep 1858]

F2-715: Surv.18 June 1855 by T.W.23,039 & 17,705 Solomon Tharp & A. Monroe 300 A. in Hampshire Co. on Pot Lick Run of N. R. adj. said Tharp's Martain surv., Benjamin Cubbage, Michael Milllar. 2 Aug 1858 [Dl'd Ch's Blue 19 Mar '60]

F2-716: Surv.12 June 1857 by T.W.22,385, 23,868 & 23,411 Joseph Maston, Isaac P. Rinker, Samuel M. Lantz, Charles Bush & George C. Lobdell 646 A. in Page Co. in Powell's Ft. on Passage Cr. adj. Marye, Carson, Charles Dunckham, John Leary, Carn Mt., line of Maston, Bush & Co., Ross, Messer alias Carson surv., Charles Dunckham, Middle Mt., Rhodes. 2 Aug 1858

F2-717: Surv.25 Apr 1856 by T.W.23,411 Benjamin F. Price 2 Ro. 9 Per. in Page Co. on Rd. from Shenandoah R. to head of Mill Cr. adj. Daniel Koontz, Thomas Higgs, S.W. of Luray. 1 Sep 1858 [Dl'd Dr. Kissr 7 July 1870]

F2-718: Surv.26 Jan 1858 by T.W.15,538 John Finch 68 A. 2 Ro. in Frederick Co. on Berkeley Co. line & Brush Cr. adj. Hyatt, Tilden Cogle, James White, Little Mt., William Dehaven, Pine. 1 Sep 1858 [To T.T. Fauntleroy Esq. 25 Feb 1859]

F2-719: Surv.3 June 1857 by T.W.17,688, 15,480, 15,936 & 15,538 Philip D.C. Jones 373 A. 2 Ro. 26 Po. in Frederick Co. adj. Harrison Cooper, Clark, N. Mt., Cooper's purchase of Rusell, Cove Mt., Hetrick, Paddy's Run, Turner, Henry Keller heirs, Winchester & Moorefield Grade. 1 Sep 1858 [Mailed R.H. Cockrell 11 Apr '58]

F2-720: Surv.26 Jan 1858 by T.W.11,112, 18,963 & 21,864 Nathan Everhart 213 A. 3 Ro. 30 Po. in Berkeley Co. adj. his other land, "Walper" land, Third Hill Mt., Boyd. 1 Sep 1858 [Mailed E.G. Albustir 29 May '69]

F2-721: Surv.16 Jan 1857 by T.W.22,705 John Wilkins 340 A. in Shenandoah Co. on Little N. Mt. adj. John Arthur, George Shrum, Paddy Mt. 1 Sep 1858

F2-722: Surv.3 July 1857 by T.W.12,456 Edward Bailey 21 1/2 A. in Hampshire Co. bet. Pattersons Cr. & Beaver Run, adj. the Manor line, said Bailey. 1 Sep 1858 [Dl'd J.D. Armstrong 26 Jan '60]

F2-723: Surv.19 June 1857 by T.W.24,353 James R. Smith & Benjamin F. Smith 176 A. in Hampshire & Hardy Cos. on Patterson's Cr. adj. said Smiths, George Williams heirs, Harness run, Elijah Vanbuskirk, James Williams. 1 Oct 1858 [Mailed Prop'r 19 Oct '58]

F2-724: Surv.1 June 1855 by T.W.22,616 John Cornell asne. of Philip Hartman 14

1/2 A. in Hampshire Co. on Mill Cr. adj. John Fleming, John Carnell, his own land, said Hartman bought of Henry M. High, John Carnell's old Hague surv. 1 Oct 1858 [Dl'd Cha's Blue 19 Mar'60]

F2-725: Surv.24 Feb 1857 by T.W.22,358 Elisha Powell 62 1/2 A. in Hampshire Co. on Diamond Rg. & Enoch's Br. of Great Cacapon adj. Robert M. Powell Jr., Robert M. Powell Sr., John Templer, Robert B. Sherrard. 1 Oct 1858 [Mailed Prop'r 17 June '59]

F2-726: Surv.22 Feb 1853 by T.W.18,932 Jacob Adams Sr. 10 3/4 A. in Hampshire Co. on Patterson's Cr. adj. Nimrod Furr, William Adams, said Jacob Adams, Denis Daniel. 1 Oct 1858 [Dl'd Geo. Millison 14 Dec '58]

F2-727: Surv.11 July 1856 by T.W.22,358 & 23,386 Hanibal P. Murphey & Davis N. Murphey 16 1/4 A. in Hampshire Co. on Alleghany Mt. & Whiteman's Lick Run of N. Br. of Potomac R. adj. Dunlap heirs, Abraham Inskeep's Randall surv., his Copper Spring tract, Jacob Vanmeter, Ravenscraft surv. part now James Murphy, part Nimrod Alkire. 1 Oct 1858 [Dl'd J.D. Armstrong 28 Mar '60]

F2-728: Surv.9 May 1855 by T.W.22,876 Samuel Hook 90 A. in Hampshire Co. on Bear Garden Rg. adj. said Hook, Eli Beall, David Heflebower, E. of Cacapon, Thomas Edwards. 1 Oct 1858 [Dl'd Geo. Millison 14 Dec '58]

F2-729: Surv.21 May 1856 by T.W.23,386 Robert M. Powell 3rd 5 A. in Hampshire Co. on Jerry's Run of Great Cacapon adj. John H. Largent, Samuel Largent, George Keiter, Jacob Alderton, said Powell. 1 Oct 1858 [Dl'd Cha's Blue 19 Mar '60]

F2-730: Surv.16 July 1856 by T.W.23,386 James Dixon 8 1/4 A. in Hampshire Co. on Alleghany Mt. near N. Br. of Potomac R. adj. Vandiver now Preston Coal & Iron Co., Reasin Harvey, Vanmetter's Elk Garden surv., Dixon's Harvey tract. 1 Oct 1858 [Dl'd D. Gibson 2 Apr '61]

F2-731: Surv.2 Dec 1853 by T.W.21,658 Richard Thrush 49 1/4 A. in Hampshire Co. on Rawlings Run of Patterson's Cr. adj. Michael Thrush, old Putnam surv., John Stagg, Sandy Lick. 1 Oct 1858 [Dl'd D. Gibson 2 Apr '61]

F2-732: Surv.27 June 1857 by T.W.23,386 & 24,353 Samuel Ruckman 50 A. in Hampshire Co. on Cove Mt. adj. Aaron Rogers heirs, Mathew Combs. 1 Oct 1858 [Dl'd D. Gibson 24 Jan '60]

F2-733: Surv.2 Apr 1853 by T.W.19,254 Samuel Hook 69 A. in Hampshire Co. on Stony Mt. adj. said Hook, John Ruckman, Joseph Hanes, Combs heirs. 1 Oct 1858 [Dl'd Geo. Millison 14 Dec '58]

F2-734: Surv.3 June 1857 by T.W.16,854 John Y. Baker 26 3/8 A. in Hampshire Co. near Green Spring Valley on Vances Run adj. John Donaldson now William Donaldson, Great Holmes surv., said Baker, Alen McGlathery. 1 Oct 1858 [Dl'd D. Gibson 30 Jan 1860]

F2-735: Surv.11 June 1856 by T.W.22,616 & 23,386 Amos Roberson 71 1/4 A. in Hampshire Co. on Piney Mt. & Little Cacapon adj. Sam'l C. Ruckman, said Roberson. 1 Oct 1858 [Dl'd Ch's Blue 19 Mar '60]

F2-736: Surv.4 Nov 1851 by T.W.18,932 Peter M. Thrush 17 A. 3 Ro. in Hampshire Co. on Patterson's Cr. in Burnt house hollow by Patterson's Cr. adj. his surv., John Vandiver, Dry run Hollow, John Hill Price 1805 grant. 1 Oct 1858 [Dl'd D. Gibson 2 Apr '61]

F2-738: Surv.3 Aug 1854 by T.W.21,658 Benjamin F. Pepper 100 A. in Hampshire Co. on Short Arse Mt. 1 Oct 1858 [Dl'd Cha's Blue 19 Mar '60]

F2-739: Surv.20 Nov 1856 by T.W.22,358 Catharine Ginevan 41 1/2 A. in Hampshire Co. on Little Capon adj. said Ginevan, Jacob Critton, Ginevan's old Stoker surv. 1 Oct 1858 [Dl'd Cha's Blue 19 Mar '60]

F2-740: Surv.19 Mar 1857 by T.W.2751 George Berkdall 39 A. in Hardy Co. on

Middle Mt. bet. N. & S. Mill Crs. adj. E. Judy, N.N. line, Manor line, Powder Lick. 1 Oct 1858 [Dl'd J.H.Cassin 14 Mar '60]

F2-741: Surv.13 Oct 1855 by T.W.18,121 Mortimore D. Neville 28 1/4 A. in Hardy Co. on Alleghany Mt. & Stony R., Coal Bank Run adj. William S. Cunningham, Phoenix Co., Neville now said Co. 11 Oct 1858 [Mailed Prop'r 21 Jan '59]

F2-742: Surv.10 June 1856 by T.W.18290 George W. Stump & Thomas French 2528 A. in Hardy Co. & probably Hampshire Co. on Br. Mt. bet. N. R. & Saw Mill Run adj. Means, Miller's Dick surv, Lochner, Tucker, Timbrook, Jos. Tucker, Birch now Cubbage, Sol'm Tharp, Pot Lick Run, Little & Big Mts., Lochner's Poland tract, Means heirs. 1 Oct 1858 [Dl'd J.H. Cassin 14 Mar '60]

F2-743: Surv.30 Jan 1846 by T.W.2751 Conrad Garrett 17 1/8 A. in Hardy Co. on Spring Lick Run of N. R., W. of Carwell's Rg. adj. Aaron & Peter Bean, T.S. Davidson, George Bean formerly Vanmeter, High Knob tract. 1 Oct 1858 [Dl'd J.H. Cassin 14 Mar '60]

F2-744: Surv.12 Nov 1856 by T.W.16,344 Felix Welton & John W. Welton 8 1/2 A. in Hardy Co. on Alleghany Mt. & Stony R. adj. their old Bruce tract, Deakins. 1 Nov 1858 [Dl'd J.H. Cassin 14 Mar '60]

F2-745: Surv.17 Feb 1857 by T.W.16,218 Simon Welton 65 A. in Hardy Co. on S. fork of Luneys Cr. & Flat Bush adj. his own land, Hughes, Stinley, Hire, Feaster, Collins, Bruin, Taylor, Elsey, Feaster's Brown tract formerly Seymour, Feaster's Jackson tract, Welton heirs, Heir's Badgley land. 1 Nov 1858 [Dl'd J.H. Cassin 14 Mar '60]

F2-746: Surv.26 Nov 1856 by T.W.11,143 Joshua Burucker 11 1/8 A. in Page Co. on Blue Rg. adj. Mann & William Snyder, Monroe Burucker, Jacob Aleshire. 1 Nov 1858 [Dl'd Th's B. Modesitt 4 Jan '60]

F2-747: Surv.31 May 1856 by T.W.17,076 Michael Scothorn, David Scothorn & Joseph Scothorn (said Michael Scothorn one half & David & Joseph Scothorn the other half) 45 A. 1 Ro. 10 Po. in Page Co. on Second Ft. Mt. adj. Joseph Scothorn. 1 Nov 1858

F2-748: Surv.13 Mar 1858 by T.W.23,411 Martin Ellis 5 A. 19 Per. in Page Co. on Pass Run at foot of Blue Rg. on New Market & Sperryville Turnpike adj. Michael Stomback, said Martin Ellis. 1 Nov 1858 [Dl'd R.P.Bell 6 Dec '59]

F2-749: Surv.13 May 1853 by T.W.19,144 Fredirick W. Miner asne. of Wileman Thomas 67 A. in Pr. William Co. bet. N. & S. forks of Quantico run or Cr. adj. said Thomas, Luke Cannon heirs. 1 Dec 1858 [Mailed Prop'r 10 Jan '59]

F2-750: Surv.21 Dec 1854 by T.W.22,698 R.P. Davis 5 A. in Fairfax Co. on Popes Head Run adj. Daniel B. Kincheloe, heirs of Cornelius Kincheloe. Date marked out. [The Governor will not sign this patent]

F2-751: Surv.9 July 1857 by T.W.20,573 John G. Biller 4 A. 33 sq. Po. in Shenandoah Co. on Mill Cr. adj. George Biller, John Holver now Peter Sprinkle, Martin Rupp. 1 Dec 1858 [Mailed Wm. Tisinger 17 Nov '59]

F2-752: Surv.9 July 1857 by T.W.20,354 John G. Biller 145 1/8 A. in Shenandoah Co. on Timber Rg. adj. John Hayman, Moses Ryman, John Cline, Six's heirs, Daniel Dellinger, PeeVee Run, George Biller, Holva, Martin Rupp. 1 Dec 1858 [Mailed Wm. Tisinger 17 Nov '59]

F2-753: Surv.10 July 1857 by T.W.20,573 John G. Biller 114 A. in Shenandoah Co. on Short hills & Elk Lick Hollow adj. Peter Sprinkle, John G. Biller, Daniel Rupert. 1 Dec 1858 [Mailed Wm. Tisinger 17 Nov '59]

F2-754: Surv.8 July 1857 by T.W.20,573 Solomon Biller 34 A. 3 Ro. 35 Po. in Shenandoah Co. on Supenlick Mt. adj. Israel Tusing, Christian Biller, Adam Barb, Elijah Esteep, Polly Esteep, John Wine Sr. 1 Dec 1858 [Mailed Wm. Tisinger 17 Nov '59]

F2-755: Surv.14 July 1857 by T.W.12,968 Levi Rinker 20 A. 110 Po. in Shenandoah Co. on Mill Cr. adj. Henry Baughman more recently Benjamin Hudson now John Beedle, Abraham Good, Lewis Fadley, Ulerick Nease. 1 Dec 1858 [Mailed Wm. Tisinger 17 Nov '59]

F2-756: Surv.13 Aug 1856 by T.W.22,616 Angus W. McDonald 26 A. 3 Ro. in Hampshire Co. on N. Br. of Potomac R. adj. the old Ashby surv. lately sold by Cornelius R. Long to Thomas S. Rigeway, Baltimore & Ohio RR, Hans Crevy, Robert K. Sheets. 1 Dec 1858 [Mailed Pro'r 29 July 1859]

F2-757: Surv.14 June 1854 by T.W.15,824 James Webb 1 1/2 A. in Hardy Co. on N. R. in the Tanyard hollow adj. Thomas Marshall, Jos. Hill, Nancy & Mary Marshall. 1 Jan 1859 [Dl'd J.H.Cassin 14 Mar '60]

F2-758: Surv.6 Nov 1856 by T.W.2751 George Webb 20 3/8 A. in Hardy Co. on N. R. & Spring Lick Rg. adj. Burch, Webb, Buckley. 1 Jan 1859 [J.H.Cassin 14 Mar '60]

F2-759: Surv.15 July 1856 by T.W.14,897 Marshall McDonald asne. of Angus W. McDonald 43 3/4 A. in Hampshire Co. on Abram's Cr. adj. Charles Clinton now Inskeep, Preston Coal & Iron Co. 1 Mar 1859 [Mailed Prop'r 29 July '59]

F2-760: Surv.22 Apr 1858 by T.W.24,742 John T. Peerce 3 A. 2 Ro. 30 Po. in Hampshire Co. on Alleghany Mt. adj. David Vanmeter bought of Davis, David Vanmeter's Simmons tract. 1 Apr 1859 [Dl'd D.Gibson 2 Apr '61]

F2-761: Surv.21 Apr 1858 by T.W.24,742 John T. Peerce 1 A. 2 Ro. 8 Po. in Hampshire Co. on Alleghany Mt. adj. Jacob & Garrett Vanmeter Elk Garden tract, their Elzy tract, David Vanmeter's Edwards tract, David Vanmeter's Parker surv. 1 Apr 1859 [Dl'd D.Gibson 2 Apr '61]

F2-762: Surv.24 Apr 1858 by T.W.23,411 George Printz 86 1/2 A. in Page Co. on Piny Mt. adj. Reuben Printz, John Griffith Sr., said George Printz, Isaac Printz. 1 Apr 1859 [Dl'd R.P.Bell 16 Mar '60]

F2-763: Surv.15 Sep 1858 by T.W.24,742 & 25,116 William Donaldson & Henry K. Hoffman 62 1/2 A. in Hampshire Co. on Green Spring Valley adj. Bruin, Holms, said Donaldson. 1 June 1859 [Dl'd J.D. Armstrong 28 Mar '60]

F2-764: Surv.8 Dec 1857 by T.W.20,573 James H. Orndorff 3 7/10 A. in Shenandoah Co. on Cedar Cr. adj. said Orndorff purchase of Watkins James, John Orndorff, Lewis Orndorff heirs. 1 June 1859 [Mailed Wm. Tisinger 17 Nov 1859]

F2-765: Surv.10 Nov 1858 by T.W.23,590 Jonas Hockman 39 1/2 A. in Warren Co. adj. Ephraim Leith's 1791 grant, Overall, Leith now Overall, Andrew McKoy now Silas Firstoe, James Stinson. 1 June 1859 [Mailed Prop'r 24 Jan 1860]

F2-766: Surv.10 Dec 1856 by T.W.23,039 & 23,386 William Donaldson 320 A. in Hampshire Co. near Green Spring Valley on Valley Mt. adj. Andrew Walker now Wm. W. Walker, James Abernathy, Bryan Bruin, James Donadlson, John Donaldson, Col. Isaac Parsons. 1 June 1859 [Dl'd J.D. Armstrong 28 Mar '60]

F2-767: Surv.9 June 1855 by T.W.17,760 Charles Miller 25 A. in Hardy Co. on Mud Run Mt. & Mill Cr. adj. High, his own land & others, Shoemaker. 1 July 1859 [Dl'd J.H.Cassin 14 Mar '60]

F2-768: Surv.27 June 1857 by T.W.24,353 Samuel Albright 1 A. 1 Ro. 32 Po. in Hampshire Co. on Little Cacapon adj. said Albright bought of Isaac Wolf, John Arnold heirs. 1 July 1859 [Dl'd Cha's Blue 19 Mar '60]

F2-769: Surv.4 May 1855 by T.W.16,418 John Hiett(of Joseph) 100 A. in Hampshire Co. on Ivy Run adj. said Hiett, Samuel A. Pancoast, Robert B. Sherrard, High Top Mt., Cornelius Vanasdall. 1 July 1859 [Dl'd Cha's Blue 19 Mar '60]

F2-770: Surv.10 June 1858 by T.W.23,386 Isaac Hite 7 A. 3 Ro. in Frederick & Hampshire Cos. on Bear Garden Rg. adj. his own land, Wm. S. Groves, Hite's Rogers tract, Packhorse Rd. 1 July 1859 [Dl'd Cha's Blue 19 Mar '60]

F2-771:   Surv.11 Feb 1858 by T.W.24,742 & 17,705 Samuel C. Ruckman 112 A. in Hampshire Co. on S. or Stone Lick Fork of Little Cacapon adj. Thomas Ruckman 1798 surv., John Arnold heirs, Beall now Ruckman, Stray Lick, Jacob Ruckman 1798 surv., Jacob & Peter Ruckman 1812 surv. 1 July 1859 [Cha's Blue 19 Mar '60]

F2-772:   Surv.30 June 1858 by T.W.24,742 Elizabeth Shank & Ann Shank 21 A. 3 Ro. in Hampshire Co. on Brushy Rg. adj. Elias Chesshir, James Orndorff, Stephen Shanholtzer, Wm. G. Shank. 1 July 1859 [Dl'd Cha's Blue 19 Mar '60]

F2-773:   Surv.7 Dec 1854 by T.W.21,658 John J. Salyards 100 A. in Hampshire Co. on Feritans Br., N. Mt. adj. Julius C. Waddle, Trustees of Watson Town, Isaac Pear, Sutton, Blakemore & Co. 1 July 1859 [Mailed Prop'r 8 Aug '59]

F2-774:   Surv.28 Nov 1857 by T.W.24,742 David Beery 39 A. 3 Ro. in Hampshire Co. on Little Capon on Town hill, adj. said Beery bought of Uriah Bowers, Abraham Miller, Thomas S. Cox. 1 Aug 1859 [Dl'd Cha's Blue 19 Mar '60]

F2-775:   Surv.30 Sep 1858 by T.W.25,116 & 24,959 A.M. Alverson 110 A. in Hampshire Co. on Knobly Mt. & N. Br. of Potomac adj. Peter Urice, Edward Gilpin, Angus W. McDonald, Cresap heirs, Urice's Bruen tract. 1 Sep 1859 [Dl'd D. Gibson 2 Apr '60]

F2-776:   Surv.12 Feb 1859 by T.W.23,110 G.W. Grayson 6 A. 3 Ro. 34 Po. in Warren Co. on Dry Run adj. said Grayson, Samuel Baker, M. Cleaver's Mill Tract. 1 Oct 1859 [Dl'd S.W. Thomas 10 Dec '59]

F2-777:   Surv.8 Dec 1857 by T.W.24,742 Simon Taylor 133 1/2 A. in Hampshire Co. on Valley Mt. adj. said Taylor, Isaac Johnson, John Long heirs, Walker & Raymond. 1 Oct 1859 [Mailed Prop'r 20 Dec '59]

F2-778:   Surv.18 Mar 1857 by T.W.23,039 Simon D. Taylor 27 A. in Hampshire Co. on S. Br. of Potomac R. adj. James Martin now Jeremiah Bonham, David Arnold heirs, Randolph Hardey heirs, Henry Cowgill, Joseph Hall. 1 Nov 1859 [Dl'd D. Gibson 2 Apr '60]

F2-779:   Surv.29 Jan 1858 by T.W.24,353 Samuel H. Yonley 100 A. in Hampshire Co. on White Rock Mt. adj. Samuel A. Pancoast, Pancoast's Relf surv., David Ellis, James Richmond. 1 Nov 1859 [Dl'd Col. D. Gibson 18 Feb '60]

F2-780:   Surv.22 Dec 1858 by T.W.25,176 Angus W. McDonald Jr. 40 1/2 A. in Hampshire Co. on Martin's Rg. & N. Br. of Potomac adj. Richard Baker, Cresap heirs, A. M. Alverson, F. & William Deakins. 1 Nov 1859 [D. Gibson 2 Apr '61]

F2-781:   Surv.7 June 1855 by T.W.22,876 George W. Stump & Thomas French 96 A. in Hampshire Co. on Stony Run of S. Br. adj. said Stump & French, the Glebe land, Michael Miller. 1 Nov 1859 [Dl'd D. Gibson 2 Apr '61]

F2-782:   Surv.29 Jan 1858 by T.W.24,353 Samuel H. Yonley 38 1/4 A. in Hampshire Co. on Great Cacapokn adj. old Enoch surv., Adam Loy, Castle Rock Mt., old Relf surv., Samuel A. Pancoast, near the Ice Spring. 1 Nov 1859 [Dl'd Col. D. Gibson 18 Feb '60]

F2-783:   Surv.29 Jan 1858 by T.W.24,353 Samuel H. Yonley 10 A. in Hampshire Co. on Great Cacapon R. inc. Candy's Castle Mt. adj. Adam Loy, Samuel A. Pancoast, McDugan heirs, George Hott, Pancoast's Relf surv., James Richmond. 1 Nov 1859 [Dl'd Col. D. Gibson 18 Feb '60]

F2-784:   Surv.9 Feb 1858 by T.W.24,742 Adam Stump 24 A. in Hampshire Co. on Mill Cr. Mt. adj. the Exchange lot for a mill seat from William Buffington to Lord Fairfax. 1 Nov 1859 [Mailed A.Smith 28 Feb '61]

F2-785:   Surv.9 Feb 1858 by T.W.24,742 Adam Stump 70 1/4 A. in Hampshire Co. on S. Br. of Potomac R. adj. Amos Poland, William Hanes, John Starnes, Thomas Mulady, James Brown, William Buffington. 1 Nov 1859 [Mailed A.Smith 28 Feb'61]

F2-786:   Surv.15 Jan 1848 by T.W.16,214 Angus M. Wood 75 A. in Hardy Co. on Cove

Run of Lost R. in Cove Gap adj. his Miller land, Chrisman, Nave, Harper. 1 Nov 1859 [Dl'd Jno.H. Cassin 7 Mar '60]

F2-787: Surv.7 May 1859 by T.W.25,066 & 18,290 Robert N. Harper, John H. Cassin & Aaron A. Welton 18,557 A. in Hardy Co. (part supposed in Tucker Co.), on Stony R., Red Cr., Blackwater Cr. adj. James W. Green's surveys of Holmes, Gale & Harness's heirs, the Breathed surv., & the Chamber's surv. on Canaan Rd., Holmes & Co., Canaan Mt., Fisher's Spring, Yoakum, N.N. line. 3 Jan 1860 [Dl'd J.H.Cassin Esq. 5 Jan 1860]

F2-788: [See 684] Surv.22 Aug 1856 by T.W.22,271 John McLanahan 9 A. 3 Ro. in Morgan Co. on Potomac adj. Jones h'rs, Minghinne, Steward, McLanahan. 2 Nov 1857

F2-789: Surv.4 Apr 1859 by T.W.25,343 Robert Calvin Garnett 2 A. in Madison Co. adj. said Garnett, Broadus Aylor, James Lillard. 3 Jan 1860

F2-790: Surv.26 Oct 1858 by T.W.20,927 Lucien Peyton 10 16/100 A. in Alexandria Co. on Leesburg & Alexandria Turnpike, adj. Mrs. Powell, Philip Huff. 1 Feb 1860 [Mailed Prop'r 22 Sep 1860]

F2-791: Surv.14 Apr 1859 by T.W.21,526 George M. Bohannon 5 3/4 A. in Madison Co. on Blue Rg. turnpike, adj. Miss Elizabeth C. Stover, Roberson R., said Bohannon. 1 Feb 1860

F2-792: Surv.14 Apr 1859 by T.W.21,526 George M. Bohannon 1 1/2 A. in Madison Co. on S. prong of Roberson R. adj. Miss Elizabeth C. Stover, said Bohannon. 1 Feb 1860

F2-793: Surv.15 Apr 1859 by T.W.24,904 Zachariah S. Smith 1 A. 1 Ro. 14 Po. in Madison Co. adj. Robert C. Garnett, heirs of Simeon Bates dec'd, N. prong of Roberson R. 1 Mar 1860

F2-794: Surv.13 May 1859 by T.W.25,100 George H. Baker 16 1/4 A. in Hampshire Co. on N. Br. of Potomac adj. John W. Shouse, John & Henry Smith, Abraham Inskeep heirs. 1 Mar 1860 [Mailed prop'r 10 Sep 1860]

F2-795: Surv.14 May 1859 by T.W.23,386 George H. Baker 90 A. in Hampshire Co. on Fairleys Run of Patterson's Cr. adj. Levi Baker, John W. Shouse, Baker formerly John Denham, Joseph Wagoner bought of King, Jacob I. Wagoner, Jackson Wagoner, Levi Baker formerly Gen. Shepherd. 1 Mar 1860 [To prop'r 10 Sep 1860]

F2-796: Surv.22 Dec 1858 by T.W.23,386 Nimrod Alkire 10 A. in Hampshire Co. on N. Br. of Potomac adj. Edward Gilpin, Peter Urice, John Ravenscraft, his own land. 1 Mar 1860 [Dl'd D.Gibson 2 Apr '61]

F2-797: Surv.19 Aug 1858 by T.W.21,924 & 18,290 Henry Bobo 353 A. in Hardy Co. on Br. Mt. at mouth of Bearhill on Pane's Run & Camp Br. adj. Coon, Renick, Coon's Pane land. 2 Apr 1860 [Mailed John J. Chipley(atty.) 11 June 1870]

F2-798: Surv.23 June 1857 by T.W.23,386 William Loy St. 2 1/4 A. in Hampshire Co. on Hunting Rg. adj. Asa Simons now Adam Rudolph, said Loy bought of John Horn. 3 July 1860 [Dl'd D. Gibson 2 Apr '61]

F2-799: Surv.13 May 1858 by T.W.24,353 William Hanes 10 A. 28 Po. in Hampshire Co. on Lewis Run of S. Br. of Potomac R. adj. said Hanes, John Starns, Charles Vowell heirs. 3 July 1860 [Dl'd D. Gibson 2 Apr '61]

F2-800: Surv.28 Dec 1854 by T.W.22,643 Samuel L. Lewis 9 A. 3 Ro. 12 Po. in Fairfax Co. on Great Rocky Cedar run near Edward Capal's Mill lot, Lewis Machen, Carter, Benjamin Cross. 21 July 1860 [Dl'd Mr. A. Moss 5 Apr '61]

F2-801: Surv.26 June 1857 by T.W.23,386 Oliver S. Dayton 5 1/4 A. in Hampshire Co. on Beaver Run of Patterson's Cr. adj. James Watz 1794 grant now said Dayton, old Parker line. 3 July 1860 [Dl'd D. Gibson 2 Apr '61]

F2-802: Surv.26 Sep 1859 by T.W.25,100 Henry Smith & John Smith 17 A. 3 Ro. 30

Po. in Hampshire Co. adj. said Henry & John Smith, John W. Shouse, Joseph Wagoner, James Martin, Little Cattail run. Wagoner's Bryan Bruin tract. 3 July 1860 [Mailed Prop'r 10 Sep '60]

F2-803: Surv.30 May 1859 by T.W.25,176 Santford Rawlings 196 A. in Hampshire Co. on Patterson's Cr. adj. Peter Rawlings, Peter Rotruck, Derney Welch, Johnson's Run of Patterson's Cr., Richard Thrush, Archibald Vandiver, Jacob M. Rutruck. 3 July 1860 [Dl'd D. Gibson 2 Apr '61]

F2-804: Surv.19 June 1858 by T.W.23,386 & 24,742 James & Isaac H. Carskadon asnes. of Reuben Davis 27 A. in Hampshire Co. on Mill run & New Cr. Mt. adj. Cardkaddon heirs, Davis, Wm. Hogan heirs, Benj'n Grayson. 1 Aug 1860 [Dl'd D. Gibson 2 Apr '61]

F2-805: Surv.12 Nov 1859 by T.W.25,471 Felix R. Seymour 43 1/2 A. in Hampshire Co. on N. Br. of Potomac R. adj. his own land, Spring Run drain, Stafford Tract. 1 Aug 1860 [Dl'd D. Gibson 2 Apr '61]

F2-806: Surv.14 Feb 1859 by T.W.24,742 & 25,261 A. Gerstell asne of Wm. Hall & G.M. Woodward 122 A. in Hampshire Co. on Knobby Mt. adj. Richard Baker, Angus W. McDonald formerly Deakins, Solomon Elifritz, Mason heirs, John Culp. 1 Aug 1860 [D. Gibson 2 Apr '61]

F2-807: Surv.19 Aug 1859 by T.W.22,876 J. H. Spencer asne. of John Spencer 13 A. 3 Ro. in Hampshire Co. on Cabin Run adj. Peter Urice, John Spencer heirs, Isaac Adams. 1 Aug 1860 [D. Gibson 2 Apr '61]

F2-808: Surv.1 Sep 1859 by T.W.25,427 Israel Updike 86 A. in Warren Co. adj. Leeds manor, 1778 Russell patent, Barbour. 1 Aug 1860 [S.W. Thomas 17 Jan '61]

F2-809:(1) Surv.7 Sep 1848 by T.W.17,275 & 16,218 Charles L. Cunningham & Job Welton Jr. 7470 A. in Hardy & Pendleton Cos. on Middle Mt. bet. N. & S. Mill Crs. adj. Stump, Ayres, Ketterman, Judy, Sites, Iman, Curtis McMechin, Island Rg., Boots, Bergdall, Mauze, Landers, McCulty, Woods Green, Dyer, Stone Lick Run, Borer, Weese, John Rohrabough, Wm. Weese. 30 May 1849 [Dl'd Mr. G.T. Barbee 13 Dec 1849]

F2-811:(3) Surv.21 Feb 1850 by T.W.17,426 Andrew J. Grinnam, J. B. Gray & David S. Jones 2308 A. in Page & Madison Cos. S.E. of Luray on Blue Rg. adj. Adam Sours heirs, Dry Run, Frederick Sours heirs, Reuben Somers, Punk Run, George Printz, Henry Sours, David C. Printz, Peter Printz, Hawksbill Cr., Jacob Smith, Madison Co. line, Stony Man Mt., David S. Jones, Sheltons path, Daniel Weaver. 31 Nov 1850 [Dl'd to Rec't 4 Dec 1850]

F2-812:(4) Surv.1 May 1849 by T.W.16,452, 16,638, 16,646, 16,739 & 16,805 Adam Wolfe Jr. 1205 A. in Hardy Co. on Middle Mt. bet. S. Fork & S. Br. adj. See, Baker, Fisher, Vanmeter, Cunningham, Baker's Spring Gap hollow, Bogart & Fisher, Parron, Neff, Shook, Green, Bryans Rg., Cassell, Stover, Greenwood, Rich Sugar Camp hollow, A. See, Godfrey, Adam See Jr., Salt petre Gap hollow. 1 Nov 1850

F2-814:(6) Surv.29 Apr 1805 by T.W.18,379 Abraham Printz, Reuben Somers & Isaac Somers 635 A. in Page Co. on Naked & Bird top Mt., on Blue Rg. S.E. of Luray adj. Edward Almond, John Vernin, Jacob Smith heirs, Reuben & Isaac Somers, George Jones, John Brumback. 30 Nov 1850 [Dl'd Mr. Buswell 13 Apr 1851]

F2-815:(7) By acts of Assembly in such case & by certificate of Auditor of Public Accounts, Purchase money paid by Philip Long. 33 A. in Page Co. adj. Gideon C. Brubaker, Philip Long & others. Robert Strickler died seized of said lot. Inquisition 29 Dec 1851 lot was found to escheat to Commonwealth. 22 Jan 1855 [Dl'd B.F. Grayson 22 Jan '55]

F2-815:(7) Surv.5 Jan 1838 by T.W.11,127 & 12,735 John H. Wallace by deed 20 May 1850 was asne. as Trustee of Samuel Lants, Isaac P. Rinker & Joseph Marston? who were by other deed (same date) asnes. of Pres., Dirs. & Co. of Bank of Virginia & Pres., Dirs. & Co. of the Farmer's Bank of Virginia, who 8 June 1842 were asnes. of Wm. J. Roberts & Hugh M. Patton trustees who 7 Sep 1839 were asnes. of

Benjamin Blackford & Thomas T. Blackford; 738 3/4 A. in Shenandoah & Page Cos. bet. Big & Little Forts, adj. Adam Ross, Passage Cr., Jacob Burner, John Teter Clem, said Blackford, William Steenin?, Pennybacker. 1 June 1855 [Dl'd P.N. Daniel Jr. 5 July '55]

F2-816:(8) Surv.23 Dec 1853 by T.W.19,458 & 21,658 William Alderton 73 1/2 A. in Hampshire Co. on Spring Gap Mt. adj. Thomas Gale, said Alderton, Walter McTee, Angus W. McDonald's Sutton land. 1 Jan 1855 [Isaac Parsons 17 Mar '56]

F2-817:(9) Surv.14 Nov 1855 by T.W.22117, 18635 & 17132 George W. Reedy, Andrew G. Grennan & Rufus K. Fitzhugh 8960 A. in Page Co. on Blue Rg. adj. Rockingham & Shenandoah Co. line, Big Hawksbill Cr. James Cubbage, Shirley, Overall, Little & Big line RunS, William Cubbage, Grindstone Mt., Outz Run, Sango Rg., Green Head Mt., Milam's Gap Rd., Little Hawksbill Run, Marsh Head Mt., New Market & Gordonsville Turnpike, Hetick, Joseph Varner, Smith, Weekly's quarter, Rowe's R., Franklin's Cliff, David's Spring, G.W. Reedy, Lewis Spring Br., Huffman, Reuben Thomas heirs, Frank's hollow, P. Graves, Milton Biedler, Paschal Breedon, Wallace's Quarter, Clore, Asa Graves. 1 May 1857 [R.K. Fitzhugh 5 Aug '57]

F2-820:(12) Surv.23 June 1855 by T.W.18,178 & 17,650 John G. Harness Jr. & Samuel A. McMechen asnes. of Adam Wolf Jr. one moiety & Lionel F. Branson the other moiety of 1700 A. in Hardy Co. on Fork Mt. adj. Simon, Deep Spring tract, Coffman now M. Simon, Dasher, Spohr, Peter Harness now Davis, Geo. Simon, Big Salt petre Cave, J. Dasher, N.N. line, Gray, W.F. Pifer, Seymour, Shepler. 1 Sep 1859 [Dl'd J.H. Cassin 14 Mar 1860]

End Book F2 1847-1859

NORTHERN NECK GRANTS Book G2 1860-1862

G2-1: Surv.1 Sep 1859 by T.W.25,427 Israel Updike 60 1/2 A. in Warren Co. adj. Russell, Barbour, Blue Rg., Cooksey, Marlow. 1 Aug 1860 [S.W. Thomas 17 Jan '61]

G2-2: Surv.4 Dec 1857 by T.W.24,742 William Junkins 17 3/4 A. in Hampshire Co. on Alleghany Mt. & Emory's Run adj. Vanmeter, said Junkins' Harvey tract, said Harvey. 1 Sep 1860 [Dl'd D.Gibson 2 Apr '61]

G2-3: Surv.16 Jan 1860 by T.W.25,556 George W. Leatherman 71 3/4 A. in Hampshire Co. on Stagg's & Middle Runs adj. Elijah, Benjamin & Santford Rawlings, Benjamin Leatherman, Santford Thrush, Richard Thrush. 1 Sep 1860 [Dl'd D. Gibson 2 Apr '61]

G2-4: Surv.27 Nov 1858 by T.W.24,959 The New Creek Co. asne. of Joseph B. Pugh 15 3/4 A. in Hampshire Co. on Alleghany Mt. adj. the New Cr. Co. 1 Sep 1860 [Dl'd D.Gibson 2 Apr '61]

G2-5: Surv.22 Nov 1859 by T.W.25,471 & 25,261 Isaac V. Inskeep 317 A. in Hampshire Co. on Patterson's Cr. & Middle Rg. adj. Joseph Inskeep heirs, Joshua Johnson, Rodgers run, Philip Rizer, Inskeep heirs Emmerson tract, Inskeep heirs Clark tract, Beall now Inskeep heirs & Nimrod Furr, Francis & William Deakins, Vause McNary. 1 Sep 1860 [Mailed J.B. Young 17 Oct '60]

G2-6: Surv.23 Dec 1858 by T.W.24,959 New Creek Co. asne. of Joseph B. Pugh 2 A. 1 Ro. 20 Po. in Hampshire Co. on N. Br. of Potomac adj. New Creek Co., Co.s Acton tract, Co.s Beckwith tract. 1 Sep 1860 [Dl'd D.Gibson 2 Apr '61]

G2-7: Surv.4 Mar 1859 by T.W.25,176 Simon D. Taylor 49 1/4 A. in Hampshire Co. on Potomac R. adj. Isaac Taylor heirs, his own land, Henry Swisher, Solomon Biser. 1 Oct 1860 [Dl'd D.Gibson 2 Apr '61]

G2-8: Surv.2 Nov 1857 by T.W.18,290 Charles Brown 88 A. in Hardy Co. on Branch Mt. & Tucker's Run, by Old Main Rd. from the Trough to head of N. R. adj. his own land, E. Bean, Burch, M. Bean. 1 Oct 1860

G2-9: Surv.9 July 1859 by T.W.18,290 Joseph Tucker 895 A. in Hardy Co. on New Cr. Mt. inc. N. Fork Gap of Patterson's Cr. adj. Simmons, Groves, Michael, Griffin, Old Main Rd., the Carter Beverly surv., Grove's Clark land, Michael's Hoy land, Stingley. 1 Oct 1860 [Dl'd Jos. McNemar 14 Dec '60]

G2-10: Surv.19 May 1859 by T.W.18,290 Archibald Wilkin 179 A. in Hardy Co. on Big Rg. & Kimsey's Run adj. Chilcott, Miller, Lee, heirs of Lehugh, his own land, his Fout land. 1 Oct 1860

G2-11: Surv.21 May 1859 by T.W.17,345 George Webb 14 A. in Hardy Co. on Br. Mt. & N. R. adj. James Webb, Martin Brill, Feller. 1 Oct 1860

G2-12: Surv.24 Feb 1859 by T.W.18,290 Samuel Bean 104 A. in Hardy Co. on Phils Lick Run & Combs Knob, Moorefield & Wardensville pike adj. E. Burche heirs, House Log Rg. 1 Oct 1860

G2-13: Surv.1 Aug 1859 by T.W.18,290 Isaac W. Brill 416 A. in Hardy Co. on Tucker's Run adj. E. Burch heirs, H. Ornduff, House Log Rg., Brill. 1 Oct 1860

G2-14: Surv.29 Sep 1852 by T.W.19,602 Nicholas Baker 1 A. 1 Ro. 14 Po. in Hardy Co. on Fork Mt. where Baker's path crosses the S. Fork adj. Cassell/Kessell, Fisher. 1 Oct 1860 [Dl'd prop'r 31 Mar 1864]

G2-15: Surv.29 Sep 1852 by T.W.19,602 Nicholas Baker 297 A. in Hardy Co. on Big Run & Byrn's Run of S. Br. on Byrn's Knob, Fork Mt. adj. his own land & others, Powder Spring Tract, Dr. Fisher, Scion's Rg. 1 Oct 1860 [To prop'r 31 Mar 1864]

G2-16: Surv.21 Nov 1854 by T.W.14,623 Jacob P. Daniels 9 1/4 A. in Hampshire Co. N.E. of Short Gap adj. his land, Philip Long. 1 Nov 1860 [D. Gibson 2 Apr '61]

G2-17: Surv.22 May 1957 by T.W.11,059 Susannah Powell wid. of Robert Powell Jr. dec'd, Josephus L. Powell, James F. Powell & Edmond L. Powell, an infant, heirs & legal reps. of Robert M. Powell dec'd 114 A. in Hampshire Co. on Big Cacapon & Big or Diamond Rg. adj. line formerly Robert M. Powell, Mary Leith, Joseph Leith, said heirs, William Mauzy now Robert Sims. 1 Nov 1860 [Mailed Mrs. S. Powell 13 Feb '61]

G2-18: Surv.27 Oct 1853 by T.W.21,658, 14,360 & 19,458 Samuel Hanes 54 A. in Hampshire Co. near Brushy Run adj. said Hanes, John Fulkimore, George Gilpin. 1 Nov 1860 [Dl'd D. Gibson 2 Apr '61]

G2-19: Surv.6 July 1859 by T.W.17,818 Larkin C. Kelly 184 A. in Hardy Co. on Patterson Cr. Mt. & Patterson Cr. adj. Jos Arnold dec'd, his & Moses Arnold, F. High, Elkpond Mt., Foley, Hite, Scott. 1 Nov 1860 [Cha's Williams 8 Feb 1862]

G2-20: Surv.1 Feb 1860 by T.W.25,553 Moses Albright 161 A. in Berkeley Co. on Tilehance's Br. adj. Coffingerger, Shemp's heirs, Rider, Zorn formerly Jonas Hedges, Richards, Leamaster. 1 Nov 1860 [Dl'd Mr. Mony 15 Jan '61]

G2-21: Surv.13 Mar 1858 by T.W.20,903 & 14,654 Jacob Cann 139 A. in Morgan Co. on Cacapon Mt. adj. A. Harlan dec'd, Jeremiah Harlan, A Harlan Sr., A. Harlan Jr., Ziler. 1 Nov 1860

G2-22: Surv.27 Apr 1856 by T.W.14,757, 22,271 & 22,036 Austin Newbrough 318 A. in Morgan Co. on Sleepy Cr. Mt. adj. Hunter, Anderson, Ruble, Berkeley & Morgan Co. line, Coulston, Pendleton, Paul Taylor, Overton. 1 Dec 1860 [Dl'd J.S. Duckwall 27 Mar '61]

G2-23: Surv.2 June 1859 by T.W.25,261 William H. High & John F. High asnes. of Philip Hartman 70 A. in Hampshire Co. on Mill Cr. adj. Thomas Taylor, John Rinker, Frederick S. High, said Hartman, said High's Moore tract. 1 Dec 1860 [Dl'd D. Gibson 2 Apr '61]

G2-24: Surv.13 Jan 1859 by T.W.24,742 James H.F. Patterson 8 1/4 A. in Hampshire Co. on Little Capon adj. his own land, Peter Alkire. 1 Dec 1860 [Dl'd D. Gibson 2 Apr '61]

G2-25: Surv.2 Dec 1857 by T.W.22,876 George G. Tasher 23 A. in Hampshire Co. on N. Br. of Potomac R. above Roberts bottom adj. Preston Coal & Iron Co., their Vandiver tract. 1 Dec 1860 [Dl'd D. Gibson 2 Apr '61]

G2-26: Surv.5 Apr 1860 by T.W.25,556 David Biser 132 A. in Hampshire Co. on Middle Rg. adj. James Parker & Brothers, James Carskaddon, George Gilbert, Abner Banes, Parker's Fink tract, Parker's Lazenby tract, Parker's Passgat? tract. 1 Jan 1861 [Mailed A. Smith Esq. 13 Feb 1861]

G2-27: Surv.15 Mar 1860 by T.W.25,471 & 25,556 Davis N. Murphy 45 1/2 A. in Hampshire Co. on Alleghany Mt. & N. Br. of Potomac R. adj. James Murphy, Nimrod Alkire, Dunlap, Whitman's Lick run, Preston Coal & Iron Co., Col. Dunlap formerly F. & W. Deakins. 1 Jan 1861 [Dl'd E.M. Armstrong 16 Feb '61]

G2-28: Surv.2 Dec 1857 by T.W.22,876 George G. Tasker 14 A. in Hampshire Co. on Alleghany Mt. bet. Deed Run & Cranberry Run adj. Joseph Dixon's Janey Spring tract, Preston Coal & Iron Co., Thomas, Elisha C. Dick. 1 Jan 1861 [Mailed Prop'r 21 Dec 1869]

G2-29: Surv.11 Dec 1856 by T.W.23,039 William W. Walker & Moses Raymond 170 A. in Hampshire Co. on Valley Mt. adj. James Abernathy, William Donaldson, Andrew Walker now William W. Walker. 1 Jan 1861

G2-30: Surv.14 Mar 1860 by T.W.25,471 Jacob Kitsmiller & Isaac Kitsmiller 348 A. in Hampshire Co. on N. Br. of Potomac adj. the Preston Coal & Iron Co., Richard Dixon, Garret Vanmeter heirs, Jacob Vanmeter, Reuben Davis & others, Slab Camp run, Silas Rees. 1 Jan 1861

G2-31: Surv.5 Jan 1858 by T.W.24,742 Abraham Smith 45 1/4 A. in Hampshire Co.

on Bloomary Run adj. Robert B. Sherrard, Ferin, Furnace tract patented to William Naylor 1820, Sherrard's Rogers' tract. 1 Jan 1861

G2-32: Surv.30 Aug 1859 by T.W.25,261 Randolph H. Kidwell 226 A. in Hampshire Co. on Sideling hill adj. Nathan Belsford, Johnston Mileson, Benjamin Williamson, Conrad Long & his own land, Long's Ellis tract. 1 Feb 1861 [Mailed R.H. Kidwell 11 Jan 1875]

G2-33: Surv.4 Apr 1860 by T.W.25,261 Frederick Biser one moiety in his own right & as asne. of David Biser the other moiety of 2 1/2 A. in Hampshire Co. on Mill Cr. adj. John Arnold heirs, James Whetman/Whiteman, John Carnell. 1 Feb 1861

G2-34: Surv.1 June 1860 by T.W.25.427 Israel Updike 48 A. in Warren Co. on Blue Rg. adj. the Manor lands & Barbour, Birkhead, Rose. 21 Feb 1861 [Dl'd S.W. Thomas 5 Mar '61]

G2-35: Surv.2 June 1860 by T.W.25,427 Israel Updike 59 A. in Warren Co. on Blue Rg. adj. heirs of Woodard, the Barbour surv., Birkhead, Cooksey, Santmyer. 21 Feb 1861 [Dl'd S.W. Thomas 5 Mar '61]

G2-36: Surv.29 May 1860 by T.W.25,427 Israel Updike 13 1/2 A. in Warren Co. on Gimlet Mt. adj. said Updike, G. N. Roy, Boston Gore patented to Nathan Job. 21 Feb 1861 [Dl'd S.W. Thomas 5 Mar '61]

G2-37: Surv.10 June 1858 by T.W.24,742 William McDonald 11 A. 2 Ro. 33 Po. in Hampshire Co. on S. Br. Mt. adj. Ewer, Cornwell, the big surv. 1 Mar 1861 [Ford. 20 June 1872]

G2-38: Surv.18 June 1858 by T.W.19,254 Samuel Doran asne. of Philip Malick Jr. 8 A. 1 Ro. 28 Po. in Hampshire Co. on Clay Lick Run of Tearcoat adj. James Malick, Andrew J. Martin, Samuel Park. 1 Mar 1861

G2-39: Surv.20 Apr 1860 by T.W.7044 Lewis W. Goodman 41 1/2 A. in Morgan Co. on Sleepy Cr. Mt. & Sleepy Cr. adj. Rumsey & Gill, Courtney, Pendleton. 1 Mar 1861

G2-40: Surv.27 Nov 1858 by T.W.16,214 Benjamin Cosner 37 3/4 A. in Hardy Co. on Alleghany Mt. & Mill Run adj. McNeill, Samuel Babb, The Phoenix Co. formerly Nevill. 1 Apr 1861

G2-41: Surv.26 May 1860 by T.W.25,628 Pascal Graves 7 1/2 A. in Page Co. on Tanner's Rg. near Little Hawksbill Cr. S. of Luray adj. Emanuel's Gray's heirs, said P. Graves. 1 Apr 1861 [Mailed 26 July 1872]

G2-42: Surv.27 Oct 1860 by T.W.15,538 John W. Smith 8 A. 3 Ro. 10 Per. in Frederick Co. in Gap run adj. William Rinker, Nathan Roberts, N.W. Turnpike. 1 June 1861 [Dl'd Mr. J. Vance Bell 30 Dec 1872]

G2-43: Surv.25 Nov 1856 by T.W.21,862 Charles Everrett 17 1/4 A. in Hampshire Co. on Jersey Mt. adj. Bathsheba Morehead, in Sugar Hollow, William Hall. 1 Aug 1861 [Mailed Party 26 Apr 1869]

G2-44: Surv.10 Mar 1860 by T.W.25,261, 24,742 & 25,556 Solomon Elifritz 80 A. in Hampshire Co. on Horse Shoe Rg. adj. his own land, Elifritz's Combs tract, Beall, William Armstrong Jr. now Peter Urice & others. 2 Sep 1861 [Mailed John Johnson 2 Apr 1867]

G2-45: Surv.13 Apr 1860 by T.W.21,822 John C. Blake 6 43/100 sq. Po. in Berkeley Co. on S. side of Berkeley & Hampshire grade, adj. Everhart Ryneal, Martinsburg & Winchester Turnpike Rd. 2 Sep 1861

G2-46: Surv.1 Oct 1858 by T.W.23,039 & 24,742 Solomon Elifritz 96 A.in Hampshire Co. on Knobly Mt. & Purgater run adj. his own land bought of Culp & Others, John Culp, Deakins. 2 Sep 1861 [Mailed John Johnson 2 Apr 1867]

G2-47: Surv.6 Feb 1856 by T.W.21,853 & 22,271 Dennis Grose 67 A. in Morgan Co. on Potomac R. adj. Long bottom tract of James House, land formerly Langham's or

McDonald's. 2 Sep 1861

G2-48: Surv.22 Apr 1856 by T.W.20198 Frederick Mauck 13 1/4 A. in Hampshire Co. on N. R. adj. his own land, John T. Wilson, George Haws, John D. Sutton now said Mauck. 1 Oct 1861

G2-49: Surv.23 Apr 1856 by T.W.23,386 Benjamin P. Fry 22 1/2 A. in Hampshire Co. on N. R. Mt. adj. said Fry, Fry's old Dunmore surv., Huffman now Haymaker. 1 Oct 1861

G2-50: Surv.20 Jan 1859 by T.W.18,620 Allen Yowell 14 1/2 A. in Madison Co. adj. heirs of William Henshaw dec'd, George A. Dulany, Miss Nancy Crow, said Yowell. 1 Oct 1861

G2-51: Surv.30 Sep 1860 by T.W.17,818 Thomas Maslin 3 A. 3 Ro. in Hardy Co. on Alleghany Mt. adj. his own land, Norman Bruce's 1791 surv. now E. K. Scott, his Martin tract, his McNiell tract. 1 Feb 1862 [Dl'd Ch's Williams 18 Mar '62]

G2-52: Surv.22 Feb 1861 by T.W.25,176 & 25,701 Silas Rees 50 A. in Hampshire Co. adj. his own land, Elisha C. Dick, Rees' Janney 1791 tract, Rees' Ramzey & Samuel Ravenscraft tracts, Alleghany Mt. 1 Feb 1862

G2-53: Surv.5 Feb 1861 by T.W.25,701 & 25,471 Andrew Horn 31 A. in Hampshire Co. on Middle Rg. & S. Br. of Potomac adj. George W. Washington, Michael & Lawson Blue formerly D.H. Kennedy, Fox's heirs, land Washington bought of George Horn. 1 May 1862

G2-54: Surv.28 June 1860 by T.W.21,094 William Clark 3 A. 3 Ro. 20 Per. in Frederick Co. on Parr's run adj. Street's heirs, Ruble, George S. Frieze, said William Clark. 2 June 1862 [Dl'd J.V. Bell 30 Dec '72]

G2-55: Surv.14 Aug 1840 by T.W.2751 Leonard Dasher 130 A. in Hardy Co. on Middle Mt. adj. his own land, Michael Simons, John W. Spohre. 1 Jan 1864 [Dl'd G.F. Page 29 Jan 1864]

G2-56: Surv.23 July 1867 by T.W.30,157, 30,159 & 30,161 Alfred Belt 8 A. 27 Per. in Loudoun Co. on Carortin Mt., S. of Valley Meeting house adj. James Fulton, John Umbaugh, Joshua Stock, Alfred Belt, Ebenezer Grubb, Joshua Pusey & Noble S. Brandon (Tennents in common), George Smith, Wilson Sanders. 1 Feb 1868 [Mailed Prop'r 15 Mar 1868]

G2-57: Surv.16 Apr 1867 by T.W.29,990 & 15,299 Samuel Tisinger 695 A. in Shenandoah Co. on Mill Run, Mill Run & Big N. Mts. adj. Walter Newman, Joseph Miller now John Wissler, Geo. Miller. 1 July 1868 [Dl'd Mr. S. McCanly 19 Mar 1870]

G2-58: Surv.21 Jan 1868 by T.W.23,590 John L. Murphy 6 A. 2 Ro. 20 Po. in Warren Co. on Round Mt. adj. said Murphy formerly Darby McCarty, Jennings heirs, James South formerly James Stimson, Philip Crunce?. 2 Nov 1868 [Mailed Prop'r 1 Jan 1869]

G2-59: Surv.23 Feb 1869 by T.W.30,114 Josiah C. Anderson & Wm. S. Johnson 100 A. in Frederick Co. on N. Mt. adj. Thomas Marpole, Lockheart heirs. 1 Nov 1869

G2-60: Surv.30 Oct 1868 by T.W.30,107 John Zimmerman 1 A. 3 Ro. 24 Po. in Rockingham Co. bet. lands formerly Abram Smith & Hugh Devies now Zimmerman & Senger on N. R. W. of Harrisonburg, Senger formerly Smith. 1 Jan 1870

G2-61: Surv.27 Oct 1868 by T.W.30,118 Michael Halterman 96 A. in Rockingham Co. on Pendleton Mt. N. of Harrisonburg, Michael's Spring Br., adj. Halterman. 1 Jan 1870

G2-62: Surv.4 Aug 1868 by T.W.30,164 Margaret A. Jackson 41 A. 20 Per. in London[sic] Co. on Potomac R. adj. Abner C. Tundle, heirs of Jacob Stonebruner dec'd, George W. Ball. 6 Mar 1870 [Mailed Prop'r 16 May 1870]

G2-63: Surv.17 Sep 1866 by T.W.24,914 & 10,451 John Ashton 106 A. in Frederick

Co. on Sleepy Cr. Mt. adj. John Shockey, George Mason, William Dehaven, Morgan
Co. line, Frederick & Berkeley Co. line. 1 Oct 1871 [Gen. Rogers 16 Dec 1871]

G2-64: Surv.1 May 1871 by T.W.22,966(iss'd 18 Apr 1844) H. C. Waldron 154 1/2
A. in London Co. on Blue Rg. adj. Jefferson Co. line, Mrs. Lydia Jones, Robert
Jones Jr., William Gore?, William Clendenning, Samuel Zimmerman's heirs. 18 Dec
1872 [Dl'd Wm. Matthew 21 Dec '72]

G2-65: Surv.1 May 1871 by T.W.22,966, 22,968(iss'd 18 Apr 1855) H. C. Waldron
184 A. in London Co. on Blue Rg. adj. Jefferson Co., W.Va. line, John Thompson,
William Clendenning, heirs of Nathan Neer, Hugh Thompson, Laurel Br., Herbert,
Shannendale Furnace Co. 18 Dec 1872 [Dl'd Wm. Matthews 21 Dec 1872]

G2-66: Surv.8 Feb 1869 by T.W.25,776 & 23,411 Joseph T. Strickler 80 A. in Page
Co. on Ft. Mt. adj. said Strickler, Joel Mauck, Miller Blunham, B. F. Coffman.
1 May 1873 [Mailed to Surveyor 11 May 1873]

G2-67: Surv.11 Mar 1869 by T.W.20,728 William J. Shenk 20 A. in Page Co. bet.
Shenandoah R. & Ft. Mt. adj. his father(Jacob Shenk), Benjamin T. Coffman,
Gatewood line. 1 May 1873 [Mailed Surv'r 3 May 1873]

G2-68: Surv.10 Jan 1871 by T.W.20,728 Abraham J. & John W. Rothgeb 2 A. 2 Ro.
15 Po. in Page Co. near Mud pike W. of Luray adj. said Rothgeb, Joshua Ruffner,
William C. Luck/Louck, Abraham Kendrick heirs, Reuben Dadiman?. 1 May 1873
[Mailed Surv'r 3 May 1873]

G2-69: Surv.12 Jan 1869 by T.W.25,776 Benjamin F. Coffman 135 A. in Page Co. on
Ft. Mt. adj. Joel Mauck, on Lick spring, Jacob Shenk, Isaac Miller, Miller
Blanham. 1 May 1873 [Mailed Surv'r 3 May 1873]

G2-70: Surv.1 June 1871 by T.W.25,776 Samuel Neff 30 A. in Page Co. on Middle
Mt. in Powells Ft. on Passage Cr. adj. Philip Christman, Joseph Marston, said
Neff. 1 May 1873 [Mailed Surv'r 3 May 1873]

G2-71: Surv.12 Sep 1878 by T.W.25,587 James R. Morrison 17 1/2 A. in Warren Co.
on Mathews Arm of Blue Rg. adj. Barbour, Walters, Lawrence, Wm. B. Overall, Roy
now Brown. 30 May 1879 [Mailed Prop'r, Front Royal 31 May '79]

G2-72: Surv.22 Apr 1878 by T.W.25,587 E. D. Thompson 5 1/2 A. in Warren Co. on
Flint Run bet. G. N. Roy now Rudolph W. Brown formerly Overall, heirs of James
Lawrence dec'd. 2 June 1879 [Mailed Prop'r 7 June 1879 Front Royal]

End Grants G2 1860-1862

276

Backer, Philip Peter 123
Bacorn, 182,198,204; Jacob
  177; John 168
Badgaly, 190
Badgely, 225
Badglay, 202
Badgley, 219,221,253,265; D.
  255; David 251
Bagart, 25
Bailey, 114,232,246; Benjamin
  100,141,145,151; Edward 263;
  George 61; John 12,24,104;
  Peter 214; William 6,155,
  176,257
Bailie, John 213
Bails, Henry 54
Baily, George 93
Bain, Abner 79
Baine, Jesse 85
Baisey, John 123
Bakehom, 67
Baker, 33,40,52,59,92,99,119,
  144,145,169,195,204,205,206,
  211,216,217,218,225,226,227,
  229,236,238,241,251,253,269;
  Aaron 219; Abraham 142,143,
  153,164,219; Adam 69,120,129
  Anthony 5,169,173,179;
  Benjamin F. 211; Cornelious
  A. 252; Daniel 39; Daniel
  Sr. 168; David 39; Elizabeth
  169; George 30,32,220,259;
  George H. 268; H. W. 42,44;
  Henry 13,14,22,41,49,53,137,
  170,173,242; Henry F. 163;
  Hieronymas 20; Isaac 144,
  202,253; Jacob 10,42,67,69,
  72,111,166,169,263; James
  217,225,261; John 12,30,47,
  66,69,86,92,110; John Y.264;
  Jonathan 255,258; Joseph 4,
  21,38,44,45,46,68,80,106,
  122,134,138,178,182,249;
  Joseph F. 214; Levi 268;
  Michael 96,220,255; Michel
  89; Mr. 221; Nicholas 37,
  169,216,271; Peter 51,129,
  130,155; Philip P. 175;
  Philip Peter 142,143; Richard
  96,176,182,238,267,269;
  Robert 40; Samuel 82,181,189,
  238,267; Simon 235; Thomas
  3,193,202; William 47,164,
  169,189,216,217,225,229,232;
  Wm. 238
Bakis, Peter 157
Balantine, Hugh 12
Balb, 176
Baldwin, 112; Cornelious 49;
  William 61
Baley, Benjamin 103
Ball, 160,178; Eli 130;
  Farling 1; Fayette 94;
  George W. 274; John 12,31;
  Spencer 56
Ballenger, W. 253
Balthas, 220
Bane, Abner Jr. 127; George
  127,156; Jesse 156
Banes, 256; Abner 258,272;
  George 214
Banett, 71
Banick, George 167
Banks, 86,147; Adam 33; Col.
  125; Gen'l 228; Gen. 230; L.
  62; Linn 61,73,85,86,88,106,
  109,122; Mr. 163; R. A. 248;
  Robert A. 242; Wm. T. 38

Bannamen, Daniel 240
Baracker, Michael 150
Barb, 236; Abraham 23,30,118,
  123,128; Abram 200; Adam 8,
  107,118,120,123,128,138,146,
  157,189,231,265; Adam Jr.
  39,74,123,232; Col. 200;
  David 39,74,146,245; Jacob
  8,107,128,157,160,231,244;
  Jacob Jr. 261; Jacob Sr. 36,
  236,261; John M. 231; Joshua
  118,138; Simon 245
Barbee, Andrew R. 142; G.T.
  219,220,221,222,224,225,226,
  227,228,229,233,250,269
Barber, 120,188; James 28,81,
  87,186; William 42
Barbour, 72,82,109,111,142,
  168,228,243,269,271,273,275;
  James 3,5,54,75,78,99,231
Barclay, Thomas 55
Bare, Col. 124,134,138,139,
  142,144,146,148,150,151,154,
  155,156,157,159,160,168,169,
  171,183,184,186,218; Mr.
  142,143,146,147; Sam'l 84,
  117; Samuel 103
Barett, Thomas 82
Bark, John 118
Barkdall, Aaron 173; Jacob
  164,167,173,181,200,232;
  Jacob Jr. 190; John 173
Barkdoll, 117; Jacob 114,129
Barker, Jacob 91; Jane 39;
  Leonard 87; William 11
Barkley, Micajah 9,10
Barnes, 69; Alexander Beale
  113,114; Catherine Ann 113,
  114; Charles 61; Charles H.
  263; Helen Mary 113,114;
  Jacob 242; Jos: 4; Leonard
  228; Richard H. 113,114;
  Teter 10; Thomas Beale 113,
  114; William 113,114
Barnet/Barnett, 182
Barnett, 255; Ambrose 50,69;
  George 69
Barney, Absalom 200; William
  129
Barnhouse, 188; Andrew 202;
  John 32,202,222
Barns, Henry 224; Teter 6
Baron, Thomas 163
Barr, James 112; William 28
Barrack, 241
Barret, 83; John 32; Jonathan
  171
Barrett, 2,236,243; Jonathan
  191,141; Jos. 235; Mary 64;
  Rachel 57; Richard 257;
  Thomas 82
Barrick, 218,255; George 176;
  Henry 147,165;
Barricks, Henry 127,140
Barron, Henry A. 247
Barry, 72
Barton, 38,59; James 93,113;
  Mary 56; Mr. 82,83; Roger
  56; Undrell 14
Baruck, George 193
Base, Mason 232
Basey, John 88,91,123,155,
  157,160,207,244
Basley, John 200
Basore, 52,200,255; Benjamin
  234,245; Conrad 245
Bassager, Thomas 174
Basy, John 123

Bates, Simeon 268
Batten, Henry 91,247;John 248
Battern, John 31
Baudennan, 237
Baugh, Henry 23
Baughman, 224; Henry 28,145,
  175,216,231,266; Jacob 216;
  John N. 216
Bauhman, Andrew 18,25
Baumcrotz, Leonard 147
Baumgardner, Christian 67
Bauncrotz, Leonard 150
Baxter, 37,220
Bayles, James 150
Baylis, 1
Bayliss, Henry 106; John 153;
  John W. 162
Baytes, James 45; Reuben 61
Beach, Alexander 42; Z'h 65
Beache, Alexander 42
Beadon, Robert 58
Beahm, Abraham Jr. 149;
  Jacob 149
Beakman, William 2
Beal, Bazel 35; Baziel 14;
  Elisha 21,36
Beale, Col. 62
Bealer, John 123,146,155,175
Beall, 260,267,271,273;
  Baziel 258; Eli 30,104,259,
  264; Geo. B. 233
Beals, 5
Beam, Daniel 20; Isaac 212;
  Jacob 27,81,86; Samuel 207;
  Tobias 27,65,74,81,86,183
Bean, 68,201,237,238,251;
  Aaron 265; Bennet (Secundus)
  225; Bennet 1st 178,179;
  Bennet 2nd 178; Bennet 3rd
  173; Bennit the third 227;
  Cloe 98; E. 271; Eli 136;
  Elizabeth 98; Erasmus 251;
  Ezekial 251; George 178,195,
  265; Horatio 250; James 88,
  98,109,178,179,214,225;
  Joseph 178; M. 192,271;
  Masham 250,251; Mordecai 7,
  45,108; Peter 251,265;
  Richard 250; Robt. 225;
  Samuel 195,251,271; William
  136,148; Wm. 137
Bear, 214; M. 114; Mr. 114;
  Peter 38
Beard, George 32,96; George
  Jr. 40; George Sr. 40
Beard, William 148
Bearly, Nicholas 53,97
Beason, Richard 22,169
Beats, Edward 34
Beatty, 233; George 15,89,111
Beaty, 53,209
Beaver, 72; John 110,163;
  Peter 32,105
Beavers, Robert 131,141
Bechtol, 197; Aaron 208
Beck, John 1
Beckett, John 69
Beckhorn, John 184
Beckwick, Samuel 152
Beckwith, 271; Newman 90,
  116,117; Samuel 192
Bedinger, Henry 66; Jacob 42;
  Joseph 128,135
Bedingers, H. 24
Beechm, 147
Beedle, John 266
Beeler, Benjamin 53; John
  117,155

277

Beelor, Christopher 21
Beem, Abram 183
Been, 190; Bennet 31; James 19,199
Beer, wid. 19
Beers, Amos 127; wid. 7,30
Beery, David 267
Beeson, 11; Edward 39,105
Beever, John 228
Beidler, Jacob 103; Martin 253
Beire, Samuel 107,108
Belford, Barney 95; Marjoram 136
Bell, 12,25,28,57,63,155,194, 203,212,226; Elisha 72,119, 182; George 6,33,47; Henry 33,47,48; J. Vance 273; J.V. 274; John 116; Joseph Sr. 8; R.P. 259,265,266; Reuben 176; Wesly 199; William D.14
Belsford, Nathan 273
Belt, Alfred 274
Benbridge, 76
Bennet, John 34; Sylvanus 92; Van 125; William 34; Wm. 220
Bennett, 34,37,39,136,257; Isabella 252,256; John 35; Thomas 39; William 13,157
Bennitt, 149
Benson, 246
Bergdall, 222,224,231,236, 262,269; George 264; Gideon 238; Hanah 262; Jacob 119
Berry, 58,163,170,215,219,241; Anna 259; C. 149; Churchill 149,208; James 259; Joseph 50; Lawson 110; Samuel 26, 193; Ths. 33; William 254
Berryman, 26,118; Taliaferro 213; William 213
Besher, Benjamin 83
Beshor, Benjamin 80
Bethel, 63; Joshua 116
Bethell, 141; George 52
Betz, Martin 4,18,28
Beur, 74
Beusny, Thomas 158
Beverley, Robert 36
Beverly, 22,212,221,224,231, 238,271; Robert 37
Beydler, Abraham 237; Isaac 237,238; Jacob 220,238
Bheam, William H. 252
Bickers, Andrew 84; James 84
Bidgaly, 201
Biedler, Milton 270
Biedner, Ulrick 149
Bigby, Ralls 37
Biggerstaff, Isaac 109; Samuel 109
Bill, William 125
Biller, Christian 232,242, 265; George 100,123,127,130, 245,265; John 157,245; John G. 265; Solomon 157,265
Billers, George 113
Bills, 79; William 55
Bilmire, 182; Martin 149
Bilse, 157
Bingham, 70
Binks, 85
Binner, Jacob 20
Binnes?, Jacob 20
Binns, Charles 13,14,15,49, 61,77,81,85; Charles Jr. 14; Chs. 159; Thomas 13; William A. 159

Birch, 136,265; John 175,179, 195; Thomas 90,195
Birches, Thomas 178
Bird, 211; Abraham 4,5,18,28; Jacob 70; Mr. 188; Stephen 148,195,204,
Birkhead, 273
Biser, 151; David 272,273; Frederick 273; Jacob 106,135, 141,147,218; Nicholas 147; Samuel 239; Solomon 271
Bishop, 56,89,99,176,184,185, 190,200,206,207,208,212,214, 225,233; George 31,135,179; Henry 2,88; Jacob 97; John 17,26,32,56,99,137,187;
Bitzer, Matthias 39; Michael 20
Biven, Stacy 95
Bixler, 229
Black, Daniel 51; Henry 190; John 189; Peter 14,18; Samuel 159
Blackborn, Thomas 37
Blackburn, 38,73,136,147,170; Edward L. 145; Joseph 193; Samuel 20
Blackford, 91,159; Arthur 78, 81; BenJamin 176,178; Ben-jamin & Sons 214; Benjamin 122,132,168,183,188,196,199, 207,253,261,270; Thomas S. 183; Thomas T. 168,253,270
Blackwell, 42,123,128; Armistead 71; George 15; Heritage 151; John 149; Joseph 71; Jos. 32; William 67
Blackwood, James 99; John 68, 110
Bladen, 246
Blair, Mr. 125; Thomas 109
Blake, John C. 273
Blakemore & Co.267; George 71
Blakey, Churchill 22,23,28; John 23,28; John Sr. 28; William 90
Blalkey, John 22
Blancumbaker, Michael 5,6
Bland, 217; Asbury 14; John 187; Josiah 219
Blanham, Miller 275
Blankebeker, Elias 243
Blankenbeker, 41; John 33,35; Samuel 36
Blankenber, John 36
Blasser, Daniel 240
Blauser, Peter 67,132; Peter Jr. 67
Blausser, Peter 75,87
Blew, 63
Blincoe, Joseph 20
Blizard, 56
Blohrer, Daniel 6
Blosser, Peter 75
Blotner, Daniel 26
Bloxham, Thomas 166,171
Blue, C. 232; Ch's 263,264; Cha's 264,266,267; Charles 165,208,246; Chs. 261; Col. 196,197,198,205,207; Garret J? 183; Garret W. Jr. 84; Garrett 202; Garrett J. 248; Isaac 132,152; John 2,80,84; John W. 183; Lawson 274; Michael 183,274; Nathaniel 66; Richard 51,57,62,116,152, 204,208,260; Thomas 195;

Uriah 80,85,183; Uriah L. 211; William K. 45
Blumback, Richard T. 252
Blunham, Miller 275
Bly, 204; John 123
Boak, Mr. 214; Wm. L. 139
Boardman, 92
Boarer, Adam 21,7175,88
Bobo, 214,254; Henry 268; Thomas 211
Bochm, John W. 245
Bodkin, 213,223
Bodkins, 199
Boehm, Isaac 191; Samuel 183
Bogan, 41
Bogard, 185
Bogart, 237,262,269
Boggess, 148
Bogle, Andrew 101,197; And'w 144
Bohannon, 213; George M. 268; Thomas 23,42,61,62,65
Bohrer, 192; Adam 75,187; George 192
Boiles 57
Bolener, Adam 184
Bolon, Mary 20
Bolsor, 84
Boman, 250; George 250
Bomcruts, Leonard 31
Bomeratz, William 189
Bomerotz, Leonard 189
Bomgarner, Rudolph 23,25
Boncrot, Leornard Jr. 113; Leornard Sr. 113
Boncrotz, Leonard 89,187
Bond, Isaac 4,6; Joseph 125; John 95; Thomas 30; William O. 242
Boness, 247
Bongamon, George 6,131
Bonham, Jeremiah 267; Samuel 215,249; Sam'l 229
Bonmoratz, William 152
Bonness, 227,247,260; William 227
Booer, 190
Boogher, Philip P. 10
Booker, George 8,43; John Philip 38; Philip P. 9
Booklass, 112; David 35
Booksright?, James 52
Boot, 217; John 75
Booten, William 22
Booth, William A.? 30
Booton, John 61; Reuben 163
Boots, 181,217,269; Adam 114
Boracker, 217
Borders, 57
Borem, 15
Borer, 200,208,269; Jacob 167
Borrer, 1701 Henry 69
Boseley, 221,259; Elizabeth 183,187; John 191; William 145,183,187,191,259
Bosley, Jacob 188; James 131, 153; James Sr.132; John 181, 184; William 175,262
Bosly, James 184
Boston, George 198
Botruck, Daniel 51
Bottom, 238
Botts, Alex'r 102; Benjamin 37; Bernard 29; James 149; Mr. 46; Thomas 52
Bough, Henry 65
Bouhman, Andrew 19
Bourn, 112,220

278

Bourne, Morton 112
Boush, Phillip 26; Henry 33
Bowcock, Henry 121
Bowell, William 61
Bowen, 58; James 52,169; John 37,62,199; John W. 254; William 14,19,111,120,219; William A. 213; Wm. 237
Bower, Henry 30,75,105; Henry Jr. 30,39; Henry Sr. 39; Jacob 127; John 30,118; William 32,213
Bowers, 116,224; George 42; George M. 228; Harrison 198; Henry 9,105,239; Jacob 242; John 113,123,124,138; Uriah 267
Bowman, 76,223; Alfred 143; Andrew 2; Daniel 107; George 115; Jacob 261; John 74; Bowness, William 5
Bowyers, Peter 139
Boyce, Nicholas 123,137
Boyd, 23,57,114,141,170,197, 220,236,247,263; E. 29,178; Elisha 4,8,11,24,27,28,29, 32,33,47,72,88,93,99,117, 169; Gen. 218; John 88; Sam'l 28; Samuel 3
Boyer, Peter 26,32,54,139; Philip 17
Boyle, And'w 144; Henry 118; James 52; William 118
Boyles, Stephen 52
Bozard, 181
Bozelley, Elizabeth 67
Bozzerman, Frederick Jr. 30; William 31
Bradfield, 233; George 31; Kemble 252; Leonard 137
Bradford, Daniel 61; Elizabeth 186; George 188; John 62; Simon 61
Bradigum, Benjamin 122,125; Gabriel 68
Bradley, James 247; William 153
Brady, John 103,143,166,210; Jno. 211; Samuel D. 259; S. D. 195
Bragg, Thomas 45
Brahan/Braham, Thom 3
Brake, Isaac 50; John 233; Michael 114
Branaman, Daniel 240
Brandom, Ezekiel 42; Francis 16,43; John 16
Brandon, Noble S. 274
Brandum, Ezekiel 120; Francis 111
Branfield, 139
Branner, John 186; Michael 69 William 121
Brannon, John 112; John Sr. 112
Bransen, Lionel 220; Jonathan 220
Branson, 217,222,234,238,242; Abraham 94; Jonathan 59,74, 119,120; Lionel 53,54,56,59; Lionel F. 270; William 184, 205
Brant, John 116,117,127,133, 156,162,165,172,181
Brawn, John 51
Breading, 86; Job 40
Break, Micheal 170
Breathard, 107

Breathed, 256,268; Edward 25; John W. 208
Breeding, 149; Spencer 4; William 183
Breedon, Paschal 270
Breetherd, R. 88
Breim, 80
Brekdoll, Jacob 139
Brelsford, Daniel 132;Majoram 143; Marjoram 143; Nathan B. 143
Brennaman, Daniel 100
Brenner, John 69
Brennon, John 34
Brent, 71; Charles 36,43,162; Chas. 42; George 24,26; James D. 180; John G. 162; Mr. 42,50
Brenton, 131
Brethed, 199
Brewbaker, John 110
Brewin, 225
Brian, John 103
Bridewell, 52,248
Briel, Henry 78; Henry Jr. 71; Henry Sr. 71; Michael 71,78
Briggles, 196
Briggs, D. 43,99; David 131
Briglr, Peter 163
Brill, 271; Abram 209; Frederick W. 233; Henry 116, 226,233,236; Isaac 215,226, 233,250; Isaac W. 271; John 233; Martin 271; Samuel 226
Bringman, Henry 68,70,75
Brinin, 156
Brink, 262
Briton, Geo. 183
Brittan, George 132
Britton, George 81,148; George Sr. 86
Brnes, Upton 71
Broaddus, Mr. 148,153; Will'm 36
Broadus, Maj. 183,186
Broadwater, 247; Guy 64
Brobeck, 175; Philip 117,155
BrocKing, James R. 214
Brock, John 1,12; Jonas 234; Rudolph 42
Bromback, 253; John 153,163; Samuel 227,247
Brook, Chaney 225; W. 6
Brooke, William 91
Brooks, 43
Broombock, 123; John 37
Broombrock, 128
Brosires, 197
Brosius, Jacob 182
Brouse, Andrew 2,34
Brown, 79,95,104,109,126,136, 154,213,219,223,251,265,275; C?. H. 170; Charles 250,271; Col. 222; Coleman 11; Daniel 17,87,109; Daniel F. 252; David 33; Doct. 243; Howell 240; Jacob B. 235,247,253; James 109,267; John 33,46, 49,57,68,83,91,111,117,166, 183; Jonathan 82; Matthew 89; Mr. 137; Richard 22; Rudolph W. 275; Thomas 196; Thos. 83; William 19
Browning, 36; Elias 144,170, 175; Joseph 17,94,108
Brownt, 233
Bruan, B. 12

Brubaker, Gideon C. 228,269
Bruce, 21,74,106,165,235,253, 259,265; Andrew 5; Charles 81,92,121; Charles K. 213; Jas. 259; Norman 22,274; Upton 101
Brucee, 259
Brue, 48
Bruen, 267; Brian 210,211
Bruice, 185,186,188,262; Andrew 185
Bruin, 32,34,95,214,252,265, 266; Brian 10,21,35,110,195; Bryan 10,11,16,19,23,41,104, 127,147,153,256,260,262,266, 269
Brumback, David H. 246; John 81,122,269; Richard T. 252; Rich. T. 252
Bruner, 91,161,171; Daniel 95, 119; George 141; Henry 48,91, 96,154,182; Jno. 133; Peter 24,29,31,57,95,101,141; Peter Jr. 101; Peter Sr. 79; Brunner, Henry 141
Bryan, Edward 61; James 44; Morgan 29; William 2,10,14, 16,18,19,23,36,37,42,43,65
Bryant, 170; James 81; Thomas 169
Bryants Meeting House, 111
Bryerley, Richard 70'
Bryerly, Thomas 70
Bryley, Richard 3
Bschm?, Samuel 125
Buck, 188,241; Anthoney 1; Charles 38; Col. 176; Isaiah 154,197; John 205; Mr. 154; Robert 1,154; Thomas 84,138; Thomas F. 205,246; Thos. Sr. 244
Bucker, Philip P. 47,48
Buckles, Robert 109
Buckley, 178,195,211,266; Joseph 97; Joseph H. 188
Buckner, 66,72; Col. 71,78; Mr. 58,61; Thornton 64,72
Buffenberger, Peter 97
Buffington, 156,158,260; Richard 133; Thomas 40; William 3,16,52,58,62,267
Bulkley, Joseph 101
Bull, 215; Dr. 82; Mr. 238; Nathan 35,38; Robert 35
Bullet, 73,205
Bullett, 159; Alexander C. 247; Thomas J. 114,164
Bumcrots, Leonard 202
Bumer, 91
BumGarner, 135
Bumgarner, 49; Christian 75, 87,94,259; David 254; Joseph 259; Rudolph 226; Samuel 220
Bumtgarner, Christian 146
Bunn, Peter 6
Burch, 135,136,138,161,211, 225,251,266,271 Covington 202,211; John 25,211,214; Jonathan 68,91,92,109,112, 207; Thomas 202
Burcham, 230
Burche, E. 271
Burchum, 6
Burd, Rich. E. 226
Burdine, Richard 229
Burdiue, Richard 44
Burges, William 103
Burgess, 205; Frances 204

Colson, 149
Colsten, 207
Colston, 145,172,224,250;
Edward 169; Lucy 172; Raw.
52; Rawleigh 8,22,34,80;
Robert A. 243; Thomas M. 169
Colvan, Joshua 7; Luther 7;
Samuel 7
Colvans, 3
Colven, 62
Colvill, 81; John 77
Colvin, Robert 49; Richard
131
Colvlle, Jno 94
Comb, 212
Combes, 31; John 19
Combs, 63,68,225,234,264,273;
Abraham 240; Aquilla 65;
Daniel 63,89; Francis 7,19;
Francis I. 185; Francis J.
135; Gilbert 16,36,37,42;
James 167,239,246,248; James
Jr. 198; John 92,109,118,160
Mahlon 38; Malon 34; Mary 92
Mathew 239,260,264; Matthew
240; Pious 197,205; Robert
D. 16; William 239; Wm. 239
Comer, Christian 209;
Christopher 105,252;
Elizabeth 11; Henry 253;
John 39,98,253; Samuel 11
Compston, Jacob 59
Compstone, 62
Compton, 29,83,230; Daniel
37,98,138; George 82,97;
Henry 109; Howard 110;
Isaac 39,90; Stephen 138;
Zebedee 148
Comrad, John 232
Conn, John 8; Mr. 183,184,218
Conner, 11,99; Edward 6,24;
Isaiah 120; James 128,159;
John 121; Lewis 4; Mary 207;
William 24,118
Connor, Thomas 249
Connors, 234
Conrad, 57; Frederick 32;
Henry 42,54; John 232
Conrod, 157; Frederick 227
Constable, 221; Abraham 184,
189; Ananias 184,189,201
Constant, John 55
Conway, 259; E. 247; Battle
F.T. 255; John 150; Peter
Sr. 61
Conwell, John 20
Cook, 65,84,234; Daniel 36;
Gen. 121; George 7; Giles
225; Hannah 80; Jacob 220;
John 4,48; Peter 42; Stephen
64
Cooksey, 271,273
Cool, Conrod 69; Harbert 21;
Harburt 145,179; Herbert 53,
63,101,104; John 69; Philip
107; William 173,176,179,
248; Willim 257
Cooley, John 245
Coombs, James 232
Coomes, 107
Cooms, 212; Peter 206,217;
Pios 206,217
Coon, 268
Coontz, Lewis P. 214
Cooper, 15,60,92,106,114,115,
136,194,196,223,241,263;
Adam 109,110,148,182,183,
186,242,263; Addison 233;

Alexander 65; Charles 263;
Enos 260; Frederick 25,46;
George 14; George W. 241,
257; Harrison 263; Jacob
148; James 16,31; Jas. 260;
Job 148; Joel 257; John 14,
48,69,112,148,169,188; Major
100; Stephen 144; Thomas 12;
Valentine 35,100,167,169,190
Cop, George 1
Copass, 93
Copejoy, 101
Copelan, James 128,218
Copeland, James 138
Copenhaver, 32; John 191,212
Copey, 66
Copp, 245; John 19; Joseph 19
Coppedge, William 53
Copper, John 30
Coppersone, Jacob 20
Copperstone, Jacob 20,69
Copsey, 60,96; John 53,125,
170,192,215
Copsy, 244
Corben, 63
Corban, David 7
Corbin, 197; Benjamin 170,
193; Daniel 5,21,31,36,44,
48,52,166; David 1,2,3,9,27,
37,41,92,117,137; Henry 230;
Humphrey 117; Isaiah 230,
244; Isaiah Sen.86; James N.
239; Josiah 173; Josias 179;
Rebecca 239; Sarah 239; Wm.
239; William 148
Corder, 25
Corlisl, 62
Corly, Geo. 250; John 30
Cormain, 169
Corman, 169; George 22,169
Cornal, John 137
Cornel, 207; Jacob 125;
William 56
Cornell, 176,187; Archibald
176; Jacob 135,174,185,251;
John 135,263; William 185
Cornwall, Wm. 99
Cornwell, 205,213,273; Archi-
bald 231; Charles 88; Isham
194; Jacob 251; John 214
Corrick, George 21
Corville, 11
Cosner, 219,221,231; Adam
205,206; Benjamin 273;
Christian 70,259; Henry 205,
206; John 260; Sam'l H. 259;
Samuel H. 260
Cost, Mr. 169
Costner, 201; Adam 184; Henry
184
Cotrill, 73
Cotter, John 11
Cotton, 6; William 14
Couchman, Henry 207
Couger, Jacob 252
Coulers, Henry 191
Coulson, 85,103
Coulston, 192,213,272; Mr.
112; Rawleigh 84; Peter 191
Courtney, 273; Jacob 88,146,
192; Christian 159,196
Coverstone, Isaac 191,205;
John 207; Peter 142,143
Coward, Jonathan 22,23,42,143
Cowden, James 12,61
Cowen, William 51
Cowger, 164
Cowgill, Henry 28,202,211,

214,267
Cowles, James 33
Cox, 78,81,136,170,204; Anna
189; Henry 35; Isaac 97;
James 78; John 35,92,107;
John A. 202,205,214; Moses
177; Thomas S. 267
Coyl, James 73
Crabb, Edward 2,22
Crabill, Amos 238; Jonas 79;
Jonathan 228
Crable, Jacob 26
Cradorff, Phinres 155
Crafford, Reuben 38
Crage, Dr. 22
Cragen, 181
Craick, Dr. 22
Craig, 171,172; Frederick
129; John 129; Peter 115,
128; William 129
Craigan, 243
Craigen, George 137; John
139,145
Craighill, William P. 62
Craigwell, Nathaniel 53
Craike, William 44
Cramer, 104; Susan 197,211
Crampton, Josiah 77
Cranch, Judge 205
Crane, 8,61; James 13
Cranfice?, John 208
Crapp, 138
Craven, Mammia 245
Crawfice, Margaret 47
Crawford, Col. 191,196,204,
209,212; David 134; John H.
244; Mr. 207
Craybill, 15
Creamer, 73,155; George 32;
Henry 65; John 140,161
Crebill, Christian 24; David
24
Creek, Stephen 9
Creeke, Jacob 76
Creel, John 17
Creesap, Charles 263
Cresap, 182,267; Michael 14
Creswell, Abraham 248
Crevey, 222
Crevy, Hans 266
Crews, Micajah 28
Crider, John 57
Crigler, Lewis 7
Criser, Christopher 4
Crisler, B. 243
Crisman, Isaac 42; Jacob 63;
Philip 63
Crissler, Deobald 6
Crissup, Robert 16
Crisswell, 166
Cristler, Adam 73,143; David
40; Henry 73
Criswell, Abraham 89,103,107,
131
Crites, 173,192,200; Barbry
229; Joel 181; Jonathan 229;
Joseph 167,200; Mary 229;
Philip 167,229; Solomon 232
Critten, Jacob 49; John Sr.49
Critton, Isaac 150; Jacob 264
John 97,103,150,162,165,166,
170,203,223,248; John Sr.49;
William 77,90,150,197
Crockwell, John 106
Cron, Fergus 115
Crone, 253; Henry 51; H. 8
Crooston, 62
Crop, 182; Lemuel 182

Cropley, Joseph 172
Crose, John 229
Crosley, Joseph 101,194
Cross, 182,187,229; Benjamin
268; G. 82,87,89; Gassaoway
158; Gassaway 123,139,162;
Gassoway 160,161,163; John
192; Mr. 125,133,134;
Washington 161; William 213
Crosser, Gassaway 133
Crossley, 239
Crosston, Travis D. 118
Croston, 138; Jacob 55; James
230; Travis D. 55,59,109,153
William 230
Croudson, John 32
Crouse, Michael 74
Crow, Dennis 7,33,45; Nancy
274; William 7,33
Crowger, Henry 148
Crowl, George 136,192
Crum, 106,159
Crump, 61; Jacob 233
Crumpton, 59
Crunce, Philip 274
Crupper, 12
Cubbage, 265; Benjamin 263;
James 270; Thomas 254;
William 270
Cullers, Daniel 130; Henry
130; Jacob 80
Culp, Ann 238; Edward 215;
George 60,63; James 238;
John 60,63,77,89,238,269,
273; William 156
Cummins, Willis 78
Cump, Jacob 152,226,227
Cumphers, John 108
Cumpton, John 53; Zebede 11
Cundiff, John 87,90,96; John
Jr. 98; Layton S. 165,172
Cunnard, James 91
Cunningham, 56,68,73,92,200,
205,208,209,238,244,251,255,
256,260,262,269; Benjamin
203; Charles L. 269; G. 259;
George 145,185,198,224;
James 17,41,44,51,69,83,97;
Jesse 82,90,97; Jessee 79;
John 16,33,178; Solomon 165,
181; William 90,145,173,179,
181; William Jr. 102; Wm.
145; William S.265; Wm.S.262
Cupp, David 260
Cure, Mrs. 71
Curl, James 57
Curtis, 121; James 189;
Thomas 52; Tobe 58
Custard, Conrad 127
Cutliffe, 214
Cutloaf, 242
Cuttin, John 153

Dabson, William 12
Dade, 82,134,188; Langhorn
43; Townsend 46
Dadiman, Reuben 275
Dadson, George P. 216
Dagg, John 64
Daggs, Hezekiah 4
Daicie, Michael 99
Dailey, James 44,68,80,83,84;
Samuel 178,196
Daily, 62; James 73,76,77;
Jas. 72,76
Dainty, Jonathan 11
Dalby, 139
Dale, Tebbs 247

Dance, Harrison 49
Dandridge, William 52
Dane, 247
Dangerfield, 257; Leroy 57
Daniel, 62; Denis 264; Peter
71,34; P.N. 62; P.N. Jr.
270; P.V. Jr. 253; Robert 66
Daniels, Jacob P. 271; Joshua
14; Robert 112; Rob't 229
Danner, 199; Jacob 129,130;
William 196
Darby, Benjamin F. 246; John
95,115
Daringer, Philip 28
Darke, William 24
Darlington, Meridith 38
Darlinton, Gabriel 207
Darnel, 58
Darr, Conrad 91
Darrough, William M. 253
Darrow, John 49
Dasher, 231,270; Isaac 233;
J. 270; Leonard 139,233,274
Daudson, George P. 216
Daugherty, John 24; Robert 51
William 126,143,170
Davenport, Braseton 109;
Braxton 72,73; Col. 255;
Samuel 73
David, Henry M. 124
Davidson, 211,238,251; Jacob
A. 211; James 208; John S.
217; Robert 163; T.S. 265
Davis, 12,26,59,71,110,124,
144,148,165,173,208,211,214,
220,236,237,238,262,266,269,
270; Absalon 100; B. R. 77;
Daniel 125; David 226;
Dennis 259; Ebenezar 44;
Hannah 125; Harmon 125;
Henry 228,246; Henry M. 145;
Jacob 34; James 34,55; Jesse
58,60,113,196,251; John 34,
43,52,65,70,75,89,120,125,
143; Joseph 7,15,58,60,113,
150,173,195,196,198,238,260;
Michael 2; R.P. 265; Reuben
101,175,187,191,197,226,238,
260,269,272; Reubin 131,132,
136,184,198; Richard 76;
Samuel 9,15,54,192; Samuel
B. 124,187,197; Samuel B.Jr.
154; Thomas 70,98,101,125,
131,132,136,147,172,173;
Thomas Sr. 125; Walter 60,
65,245; William 4,8,105;
William W. 232
Davison, J. 254; James 8,42,
241; Jno. S. 241,242; Robert
106,197
Davisson, 5,176; Thomas S.
178,195; Thos. S. 179
Davy, Thomas 183,227
Daw, 17; Mr. 50; Philip 29
Dawe, 105; James 10; Nancy
66; Ph: 33; Philip 66;
Philip Deverex 66; Phillip
6; William 66
Daws, Phillip 3
Dawson, 21,95,146,175,186,
187,203,219,256,263; Abraham
96,107,119,121,161; Abraham
Jr. 41; Abraham Sr. 41;
Abram 55; Benjamin 181;
George P. 199; Henry 125,
241; Horatio R. 228; Isaac
13,219; Isaac Jr. 159; Isaac
Sr. 159; Israel 119; John

18,221,233,252; John T. 228;
Van C. 174,190; William 234
Day, 68,146; Amary 72; Ransom
59,193; William 111
Dayton, 100,268; Oliver S.268
Deacon, 238; F. 238; Wm. 238
Deakins, 21,90,242,247,251,
260,265,269,273; F. 267,272;
Francis 5,21,185,232,271; W.
272; William 5,9,21,48,209,
232,267,271
Deal, Charles 239; Peter 16;
Rose 208
Dealey, Henry 81
Dean, BenJamin 179; Mrs. 189
Deane, Mr. 22; Thomas 101
Deanes, wid. 115
Deans, 132
Deant, 46
Dearing, 164
Deatheridge, William 36
Deats, Valentine 221,222
Deaver, 230; Alexander 138,
149; George 149,165; Richard
107; William 62,118
Deavers, 131; Gilbert 148;
William 109
Deavor, Alexander 153
Deavour, Alexander 153
Deavr, Alexander 149; George
149
Debut, 131
Debuts, 45
Decier, Frederick 87,99
Decious, Frederick 81
Decius, Frederick 26
Deck, John 88
Decke, 144
Decker, Ivea 111; Luke 111
Deeley, Henry 1
Deen, 76
Deetz, Henry 243
Dehart, 209; Abraham 40
Dehaven, 255; Barak 232;
Isaac 209; Job 199,209,232;
William 232,263,275
Dehoven, Job 188
Deiterick, John 250,258
Delany, Benjamin 47
Delaplain, Owen 149
Delaplane, Eli 207; John 207
Delauder, Abraham 226;Abraham
Sr. 226
Delawder, 53; Abraham 53;John
200,234
Delawter, Abraham 83
Delegah, Strode 199
Delenger, Martin 129
Deliplain, Christopher 248
Deliplane, Owen 157
Dellinger, 157,216; Benjamin
120; Christain 135,129,230;
Daniel 130,146,265; George
129; Martin 164; Philip 230
Deloder, Lawrence 139
Demmitt, John 46
Demoss, William 91
Denham, John 268
Denison, Mr. 209
Denneson, Robert 258
Dennis, Samuel 149; Thomas
C. 128
Dennison, 230; Robert 255
Denny, Wm. 134
Densil, 50
Dent, 10,65; George F. 209;
Thomas 15,69,75,212
Denton, 26,32,115,237,238;

284

Greenwell, 80; Elijah 11,107, 108,227
Greenwood, 269; William 139
Greer, 255
Greeves, Nath'l 3
Grennan, Andrew G. 270
Griffeth, John 11
Griffie, 120
Griffin, 154,206,251,271; Samuel 246
Griffith, Adam 216,225; Elijah 59,163; John 26,39,216,234; John Sr. 266; Joseph 225
Griffy, David 176; David Sr. 168; John 81,87,168
Grigby, John 105
Grigg, 12
Grigsby, Benjamin 68; Jesse 132; John 55
Grim, Peter 118
Grimsley, 11
Grinnam, Andrew J. 269
Grinnan, Andrew J. 260; A.G. 229
Grinstead, 27; James 39
Grist, 94
Gritton, John 161
Grose, Dennis 273
Gross, Abraham 124,158; John 218; Peter 228
Grove, 106,153,233; Christian 11; Emanuel 246; John 32; Samuel 153
Grover, Elzra 188
Groves, 6,99,121,217,219,221, 223,233,238,271; Elizabeth 239; Hueley 163; Isaac 213; Jacob 72; Joseph 47; Philip 30; Phillip 4; Solomon 74; Wm. S. 266
Grovier, 106
Grubb, 72; Benjamin 246; Daniel 120; Ebenezer 274; Stephen 195
Grymes, Philip 20
Guard, Samuel 171; Sam'l 130
Guelick, Ferdinand 155
Gulick, Elisha 95,160,161,162, 166,170,234; Ferdinand 35, 135,140,155,160,162
Gulley, Richard 55
Gunnel, 62; James 73
Gunnell, 15,215,236; Henry 64; John 216,253
Gurlett, 202
Gustim, 48
Gustin, 149,208; Alburdi 118; Doctor 75; John 2; R. 88; Robert 8,22,34,50,51,102,109, 118,154
Guston, John 15

Ha__?, James B. 192
Haas, 204; Michael 3,54
Hacker, Daniel 164,204,229
Hackey, 165,256
Hackney, Arron 57; Joseph 33, 57; Jos. 196; William 36
Haden, 117; Adam 141
Hagan, Wm. 223
Hagar, William G. 184
Hagarty, John 171
Hager, 104; William J. 7,19; William Jeinkins 107; William Jenkins 53
Hagerty, 43,215; John 99; Paul 6,190
Haggarty, 188,222

Haggerty, James 177
Hagler, Leonard 97
Hague, 61,264
Hahn, Jacob 139
Hail, 178; George 196
Hainer, Daniel 8
Haines, Daniel 157,197,241; George 89; Henry 57; Isaac 241; James 244; Joseph 139, 208; Joseph Jr. 198; Samuel 242,243
Hains, Daniel 198; David 193; George 31,40,89; Henry 28; Isaac 137,148,213;Joseph 214
Hainy, 61
Hair, Adam 1,57,63
Haiskell, Christopher 54
Hall, 78,80,87,95,128,146, 188; Adam 16,18,52,66,96; Bennett 15; Bennit 8; Capt. 160; Elijah 132; Jeremiah 78; John 197; Joseph 47,267; Richard 89,132,187,194,215; Samuel 57,123; Thomas 78,82, 85,99,124; William 262,273; Wm. 269
Halley, 78; Henry H. 78,236; Henry S. 77
Halliday, 112
Halterman, Adam 200,203,226; Christian 47,224; Christopher 53; Henry 224; Jac. 200; Jacob 53,234; Michael 274
Ham, Peter 70
Haman, John 175
Hamilton, 200,221; James 166; John 61,183,207; John A. 256; William 48,115
Hamlin, 233; Thomas 2
Hammack, 239,258,261; Abraham 263; Anthony 263; Jacob 208; John 69; Samuel 198; William E. 257
Hammach, Wm. 232
Hamman, George 74; Jacob 31, 74; Michael 1; Paul 51
Hammat, George 13,14,44
Hammick, 235
Hammill, Hugh 254
Hammis, 139
Hammitt, John 89
Hammock, 239; Anthony 241; Jacob 155,210; John 107,115, 127; Samuel 127,133,134,157, 161,172; William 240
Hammon, Powel 128; Thomas 130
Hammond, A.G. 230; James 16,53
Hampston, Thomas 160
Hampton, 72; John 65,139; Samuel 6
Hamrick, 186
Hand, William 88
Handsbrough, John 161
Handsecker, 71
Haner, Frederick 38; John 82
Hanes, 249; George 90; Isaac 256; Joseph 257,264; Samuel 272; William 249,260,267,268
Haney, George 82
Hanks, Thomas 25
Hanna, Francis 248,254
Hannah, 161,162,187; Stephen 161,187,194
Hannahs, John 210
Hannigan, Michael 17,44
Hannum, Joseph 196,226,233,250
Hans, Jacob 185

Hansbarger, John 127
Hansborough, Elijah 78; John 161; Peter 159; James 92; John 241
Hansford, Theodosius 55
Hanshaw, Levi 66
Harbaugh, Leonard 45
Harbough, Peter 112
Harbour, Peter 169
Hardey, Randolph 267
Hardin, James 186
Harding, 76,160; Henry 34
Hardy, Israil 239; John 96, 186,248; Radolph 197; Rudolph 245
Hare, Matthew 197,210
Hargis, William 12
Harison, 186; John 186
Harlan, 82,95,182,215,219, 230; A. 272; A. Jr. 272; A Sr. 272; Aaron 80,133,154, 213; Aaron Jr. 232; Aaron Sr. 232; Jeremiah 232,272; Jesse 67; Moses 24
Harland, Aaron Sr. 232; Jesse 31,57
Harle, 253
Harles, 216
Harlin, Aaron 98; Jesse 57; Moses 2
Harlon, Aaron 141,213
Harlow, John 245
Harman, Nicholas 52
Harmanson, William 94
Harmantrout, Henry 234
Harminson, Paul 155
Harmison, 219,228,229; James 71; William 215,229
Harmon, Christopher 181
Harnes, John 95
Harness, 163,167,168,190,200, 201,202,205,209,213,216,219, 221,225,226,251,253,268; Adam 99,136,179,190,200,201, 206; George 69,71,73,145, 158,163,200,201,205,262; George 3rd 181; George C. 201,206; George Sr. 71; John G. 90,201,206,212,220; John G. Jr. 270; Peter 270
Harper, 10,220,224,231,245, 268; Alexander 90; George 217; James 24; Joseph 214; Robert 235; Robert 97,240, 247,253; Robert N.268;Samuel 221,222,238; William 24
Harpine, Jonathan 127
Harrass, James 99
Harrell, Peter Sr. 156
Harriott, Ephraim 35,40; William 112
Harris, 175,189,201,220,221, 222; Cuthbert 99; Daniel 31, 181; James 99; John 195; Richard 217; William A. 121, 120; wid. 103
Harrision, 106
Harrison, 26,38,71,76,95,122, 127; Ann 115; George 36,40, 42,73,143; Henry 141,150,155, 160,187,218,226;James 96,115; Jesse 119; John 55; John C. 257,258;Joseph 105,115; Mary 105,154; Matthew 106; Mr.114; Robert 95; Samuel 75; Sarah Ann 115; Thomas 65; William B. 46; Wm.B. 19
Harriss, 222,235,240,249;

James 60; Mr. 139,142;
William 64
Harrisson, Henry 198
Harsel, 258; Peter Jr. 225
Harsell, Peter Sr. 141
Harsey, 215
Harshberger, Jacob 123
Hart, Adam 118,179,248;
Jefferson 229; Joel 229;
John 118,178,179,181,226;
John A. 248; Leonard 142
Hartley, John Sr. 109
Hartman, George 145,147,218,
239; Henry 30,31,60,126,140,
145,147,148,161; Jacob 40,
140,189; Peter 145,147;
Philip 263,272
Hartmyrs, Isaac 155
Hartstock, 113
Harvey, 271; Andrew 51;
Elijah 165,166,171,232,262;
Reasin 264; Reason 136,144,
145,147,194,245; Reazin 102;
Reyson 176; Samuel 176,194;
William 86,132,158,160,166
Harvie, 105; William 180
Haskiel, 99
Haskins, Christopher 44,47
Hass, 211; John 127
Hassel, 92
Hastings,John 5,9; William 25
Hasty, Clem 98
Hatick, George 1
Hatten, 176,218
Hatterman, Christopher 83
Hatton, David 60; Peter 190
Haufman, Jacob 148; Sam'l 148
Haun, George 150; Henry 134;
Jacob 228
Hause, William 163
Havermill, 197
Haw, Christian 152;George 194
Hawdershell, 229
Hawes, Aylett 4,12,13; George
239
Hawk, 80; Henry 40,58,137,147,
152; Jacob 71; John 61,124,
199; Martin 61,71,74
Hawke, Henry 140
Hawkin, Rice 248
Hawking, James 248;John Sr.54
Hawkins, 31,120,247; Benjamin
142,160; David 130; James
157; John 54,110,130; Joseph
4,5; William 130
Hawks, Henry 151; McNeal 151
Hawn, George 20
Haws, George 165,170,182,198,
218,227,232,235,240,274
Hawse, George 227; John 165,
210,223
Hawsthe, Dr. 19
Hay, Adam 2; Elizabeth Cary
218; John 21; Mrs. 218;
Peter 93
Hayden, Wm. 30
Hayes, James 94
Hayger, William J. 18
Haymaker, 274
Hayman, John 265
Haymon, John 242
Haymons, John 242
Haynes, Daniel 197; George
159; Isaac 197; Joseph 197
Haynie, George 91
Hays, 150; Alexis 64; Alexus
25; Gabriel 20; Kidd 232;
Peter 81

Haystings, John 9
Haywood, George Jr. 85
Hazel, Henry 117
Hazlerig, 37
Hazlett, 66
Hazzard, 205
Head, John 150,160; Nathan
Sr. 133
Heale, 50
Heare, Elisha P. 210,241;
Matthew 210
Heares, Isaiah 240
Hearshey, 206,253
Heasland, Abraham 147
Heastand, Abraham 4,110,147;
Peter 110,148; Peter Jr. 77
Heastant, John 17
Heastin, Abraham 216; Henry
216
Heaston, 225
Heath, 20,93,164,231,244,254,
259,262; James E. 77,113;
Jas. E. 76,94; Mr. 76;
William 73,75,93,99,103,162,
206; William P. 244; Wm 212,
216; Wm. P. 244
Heathe, James C. 46
Heatherol, 242
Heback, wid. 6
Hebner, George 100,104,127
Hebron, George 168
Hecker, 259
Heckson, John 99
Hedge, Jonas 169,230
Hedges, 71; E.G. 261; John 1,
39; John R. 1,10,11,13,18,
20,24,29,169; Jonas 104,171,
189,191,224,272; Joseph 1,
13,169; Philip 244; Samuel
the 3rd 105; Samuel the 4th
105; Siles 16; William 191
Heep, John 43
Heflebower, David 264
Hefman, 201
Heingardner, John 238
Heinzman, Henry 52,79,127
Heir, 265
Heironimus, O.F. 261
Heishman, George 251
Heiskel, C. 107; Christopher
118; Mr. 110
Heiskell, 33,161,197; Adam
52; Chris: 67,70; Christoper
33,68,93,197
Heiskill, 193; Christopher
153,157,187,213,230; James
R. 188; Mr. 38,86
Heitty, John 261
Heizkell, Isaac 92
Hellier, Robert 102
Helm, William Sr. 33
Helsley, Christipher 129
Hencock, Ann 76; Catherine S.
76; Margaret 76
Henderson, 7,50,71,72,73,77,
84,85,104,126,135,142,248;
Alex'r 29; Alexander 13,24,
35,44,77,129; David 1; John
2; Joseph 21; Moses 1;
Richard H. 38,56; Richard
Henry 77; Sampson 204;
Thomas 77,250; Thomas F.
223; Westley 56; William 239
Hendren, Samuel O. 88
Hendrick, Christopher 257;
Mr. 204
Hendrickson, Spencer 70
Hening, Robert 49; Wm. W.61,62

Henkel, Abram 169; Felix 190;
Samuel G. 243
Henkle, 237; Caleb 184; Felix
184; Nathan 184; Solomon
204; Samuel G. 186
Henline, 185; Jonathan 154
Henning, John 4; Mr. 79
Henry, Alexander 2; Bryan H.
110; Daniel 26,70; John 161;
John B. 42; Moses 99
Henshaw, Levi 99,103; William
274
Hentman, 165
Hepner, Henry 242; John 42,257
Herbaugh, John 214
Herberger, Frederick 3
Herbert, 275
Herbough, Feaster 206
Herriott, 148; Ephraim 112,140
Herris, 217
Herrod, 67
Herroit, Ephraim 166
Hersberger, Samuel 75
Hersha, William 25,99
Hershbarger, Henry 3
Hershberger, Jacob 28; Samuel
94
Hershey, 259; William 164
Hershman, 79; Chirubim 199
Hershy, 181,184,200; William
163,175
Hess, Caspard 108; Henry 242;
Jacob 39; John 174; Nicholas
105,239
Hessey, 159
Hetick, 152,183,260,270;
George 4,17,87,94,105,108,
122,148
Hetner, George 23
Hetrick, 207,263; George 75
Hewitt, 43,71
Heywood, Ichabod 45; Jebod 9
Hibs, 67
Hickel, 48; Christopher 125;
Henry 48; Samuel 25; Stephen
135
Hickman, 116; Henry 160; John
T. 215; Thomas 37
Hicks, Eli 209
Hickson, 34; John 88
Hicson, 129
Hider, 198; Adam 59,63,187;
Michel 198; Michael 185
Hidge, Jonas 49
Hidleback, Jacob 37
Hiebloed, Peter 158
Hientzman, 47
Hieronymus, Conrad 38
Hierronimus, Conrod 112;
Jacob 112
Hieronimus, Overton A. 192
Hieskell, Christopher 34
Hieshell, E? 58
Hiet, Jonathan 165
Hiett, 8,131,192; A. 213,214,
215,223; Asa 209,210,211;
Col.218,219,220,221; Even 85,
223; James 91; Jeremiah 143,
150; John 22,76,77,149,223,
266; John Sr. 126; Jonathan
85,146,149,223; Joseph 119,
143,266; Timothy 119
Higgens, John 135
Higgin, 160,220
Higgins, 73,84,138,139,156,
158,174,205,255; James 1,34,
55,177; James C. 193; James
Jr. 133; John 1,51,57,79,89,

58; Moses 216; Peter 99,132, 202,225; Philip C. 218; Philip D.C. 128,263; Robert 6,24,42,87,183; Robert Jr. 275; Samuel 10,87,90,162, 186; Stepthat? 145; Strother 34; Swan 24,35,46; Tho's 218; Thomas 3,5,10,18,19,23,84,98, 162,187,226; W. S. 134; Walter 224; Wharton 149,188; wid. 47; William 9
Jones & Co., 252,260
Jordan, 94,209,214; Gabriel 142,253; John 30
Jorgrum, John 159
Judd, John 219; Peirceson 39; Peter 252; Piercen 75,86,99, 110,132; Piersin 148; Samuel 217
Judy, 167,189,190,269; E.265; Elijah 190,209,220; George 74; Jacob 174,190; John 74; Martin 174; Nicholas 194; Nimrod 167,190
Jugrain, John 159
Julian, 58
Junckeson, 76
Junkin, James 153
Junkins, 238; Benjamin 102, 118,172,173,232; Benj'n 171; James 172; John 102,144; Spencer 247; William 232,271

Kabler, Frederick 35; William 9,35
Kabrick, John 157,194; Lickfrit 145; Peter 113,145; Peter Sr. 113
Kackley, Elias 9,10; Jacob 82,112
Kagays, 152
Kagey, Christian 123; Jacob 240; John 240
Kaggy, Christian 174
Kagy, Henry 115; Jacob 100; John 100; Rudolph 100,115
Kain, John 24
Kains, Daniel 214
Kalbaugh, Isaac 255
Kaler, Alla 151; John 151
Kalor, Alla 150; John 150
Karns, George 112
Karskaddon, Mr. 128
Kascadon, Mr. 133
Kauffman, Hawksbill Martin 86
Kaufman, Daniel 86; Jacob 110 Martin 77,78,91; Samuel 110; Kearan, 92; Barney 95; John 102
Kearfoot, Jno. P. 256
Kearfott, Jno. P. 207,228, 254,262; J.P. 239,247
Kearn, Barney 197; Thomas 59
Kearne, Henry 123
Kearnes, Frederick 140; George 112;
Kearns, Frederick 140; George 177,188; Henry 130
Keckley, Abraham 50; Joseph 123
Keder, John 8
Kee, J. B. 236
Keen, John 20; Richard 20
Keerean, Thos. 69
Kees, 12,59,69; Francis 22
Keesacker, George 230; Henry 242
Keeser, George 176

Keigy, John 157
Keiter, George 264; John 257,261
Keith, 57; Isham 229
Keizner, Jacob 95
Kelby, James 17
Kele, 262
Kellar, Joseph C. 77
Keller, 201,202; George 156, 175,235; Henry 175,263; Jacob 115,117,131,135,154, 168; Jacob B. 196; John 235, 244; Lawrence 147,156
Kellerman, Jacob 114
Kelley, 57; Cornelius 11,29; Larkin C. 259; James W. 66; John P. 67; Nancy 55; William 55
Kelly, Alex'd D.64; Cornelius 10; Edward 135,140; Henry Sr. 159; John 15,83,160,193; Larkin C. 272; Michael 87; Patrick 144; Thomas 150
Kelso, 55
Kelsoe, James 100,102,116, 226,233
Kembles, 201
Kemp, John 28
Kemper, 72; Charles Jr. 72; J.L. 254; Jas. L. 256; John 72; Peter 66; William 159
Kendal, James 78,124
KendallWilliam R. 261
Kendel, 36
Kendrick, Abraham 275; Christopher 257
Kenedy, David 32; Samuel 119
Kennaday, Daniel 29
Kennady, 9; Meridy 4; Kenneday, Daniel 113; Samuel 29
Kennedy, David 9; Daniel 9; D.H. 274; Meriday 1; Nancey C. 22; Robert Jr. 28; Robert Sr.28; Samuel 73; Thomas 119
Kenney, 258; Joseph 110,143
Kenniday, Daniel 29
Kenny, John 226
Kens, 205
Kenzie, J. Louis 246
Kepler, John 203
Keplinger, Christain 201; Jonathan 199,200,255; Solomon 255
Kerchaval, Mr. 109,136,137
Kercheval, Samuel 165
Kerchival, Mr. 135; Samuel 131; Samuel Jr. 132
Kerchivall, Mr. 126
Kerlin, David 127
Kern, 72; Bryan 244; Henry 26; Samuel 55
Kerney, 125; Anthony 108,125
Kerns, Frederick 202; George 153; Isaac 257; Jacob 95; Michael 256; Nathan 153,182; Samuel 70
Kerr, 42
Kerscadden, 67; Arthur 67,73; Thomas 67,73
Kesler, 97; John 58; John S. 63,86,109,153
Keslor, Absalom 253
Kesner, Jacob 204
Kessell, 271
Kessler, Absolam 215
Kessner, Solomon 54
Kessney, Solomon 75

Kester, John S. 138
Ketick, George 81
Ketner, 243
Kettarman, 170
Ketteman, Adam 208; Jacob 181,185
Ketterman, 222,269; Abraham 221; Jacob 40,209; Jacob Jr. 209,262; Joel 200; Nimrod 262
Kettick, George 81
Kettle, 224
Key, 92; James 131
Keyes, 11
Keys, Gersham 154; Isaac 93; John 236
Keyseeker, John 88
Keyser, 146; Andrew 122,146; Charles M. 254; Christopher 199; George 176; Henry A. 252; John 131,183; Peter 199,254
Keysicker, 192,196,204
Keysucker, John 105
Keyth, 59
Kibbiner, John 153
Kibler, James 229,252; Jas. 252; John 87,108,199; John Jr. 93,108; Martain 199; Martin 146,178,249; Peter 27; Philip 81,85,191; William 249
Kiblinger, John 86,94,108, 122,146,163
Kidner, 212,216,229
Kidwell, 120; John 119,166, 176; John S. 248,258; R.H. 273; Randolph H. 273; Samuel A. 248; Zedekiah 176
Kiger, Adam 6; George 35
Kight, John M. 249,250
Kile, 96; James 45; William 220
Kilgore, 125
Killgore, 125
Kilmer, John 218
Kilpatrick, 15
Kimble, Lambert 31
Kimbler, John 19
Kincheloe, Cornelius 265; Daniel 89; Daniel B. 265
Kindell, 36
Kinder, 224
Kindle, 235; John H. 228,229, 235
Kindrick, William 129
Kine 172
King, 117,168,219,268; A. 30, 51,55; Alex'r 33; Alexander 51,132,172,181; Alexandria 59; Charles 138; Col. 98, 104; George 159; James 42, 205,228; John 159; M.A. 51; Mr. 120; Reasin 259,261; Robert 159; Valentine 229; Wm B. 93
Kingan, 117,218; John 3,8,54, 123,175,218
Kingree, John 226; Solomon 113,146,160
Kinsey, Richard P. 98
Kinzer, J. L. 242
Kips, Henry 230
Kirby, Francis 163; William 163
Kirchavel, Samuel 132
Kirk, Patrick 89
Kirkendall, Nathaniel 3
Kirkley, William 40

293

294

Lucus, Elizabeth 125; Leoy 183
Ludwell, Phillip 83
Ludwick, 200,227,237,259; Andrew 218,256; George 207; Jacob 106; John 140,144,157, 161; Joseph 152; Leonard 133; Philip 151,216; wid. 47,51
Lukin, Johathan 233
Lukins, George 207; Jonathan 217
Lunt, 205; Ezra 205; Samuel 205
Lunuster, Daniel 191
Lupon, Isaac 263
Lupton, 50,188; David 39,72, 110; Isaac 40,116,186,192; Jesse 116,182,183,186,243, 245,246,250; John 15,44; Jonah 242; Jonathan 43; Mr. 123; William 39,182
Lure, Andrew 156; Elizabeth 156; Jacob 156
Lurtey, 50
Lutheran Congregation, 245
Lutheran M.H., 217
Lutman, 241; Conrod 103,109; George 103
Lutrell, 241; Robert 38
Lutsman, Conrod 20
Lutteral, 71
Luttrel, James 153
Luttrell, Edward 3; Robert 46
Luttz, Henry 128
Lutz, Wm. 241
Lyle, 114; John 56,105,114, 229,239; Robert 2,105,239
Lyler, George 120; John 90
Lyles, John 105; William 12
Lynch, George A. 221; William 159
Lyndsey, James 60
Lynn, Daniel 66,71; George 13, 153,191,204,205; John 50,77; Joseph R. 118; Moses 50; William 37,117
Lyon, Daniel 103; Elijah 220; Elisha 127; James 64; John 30,51; Richard 104; Thomas 151
Lyons, Daniel 65,90; Elijah 96; Elisha 65,77,89,96
Lyvert, William 155

M'Donal, 59
M'Donnal, 60
Mac-inturf, Frederick 27
Maccae, 197
Machen, Lewis 268
Macher, 238
Machi, Mr. 97,98
Machie, Alex. 208;James 142
Machin, James 39
Machir, 189,200,220,226,231; James 8,17,25,51,54,56,69, 76,102,107,137,190,234,255; Mr. 83,97
Macingturff, Daniel 122
Macinturf, Frederick 11,62,69
Macinturff, Frederick 21,67
Macker, 128,136,144,250
Mackey, Robert 3
Mackingturff, George 122
Mackinturff, Daniel 121
Macky, Robert 66
Macmillian, 27
Macrae, 93,121; John 10,86

Madden, 69
Maddox, 247
Maderea, Danl. 3
Madison, Gen.40; Mr.42; Wm.33
Mafees, Catharine 128
Magill, 144,147,164,218; A. 2,71; Archibald 8; Arch'd 14,57; Col. 7; Mr. 72,82,84; Thomas 7
Magills, 152
Magloclin, 80
Magowan, 55
Magruder, Dr. 130
Mahaney, Joseph P. 179
Mahany, Joseph P. 218
Mahony, Joseph P. 142
Mahorney, 261
Maize, William 108
Major, William 86
Maker, 153
Makim, 165
Malcom, 198; William 198,245
Malcum, William 215
Malic, John 83
Malick, David 210; James 207, 227,240,273; John 59,126, 197,261; Philip 162,167,210, 227; Philip Jr. 273
Malledy, Thomas 197
Mallory, John 60
Maloan, William 68
Malone, Hugh 32,159,165; John 27
Manefee, 65
Manganese, 246
Mangold, John 206
Manifee, Henry 14,18,19,27,37
Maphas, 200
March, 28
Marcus, 176,236
Margan, Richard 50
Mark, Daniel 4; John 13
Marker, Amos 196
Markes, John 86
Markham, 76
Marks, James 47; wid. 68
Marl, Jacob 70
Marlaser?, 187
Marll, Jacob 46
Marlow, 271
Marmaduke, 182
Marple, Northrop 45
Marples, Enoch 44; Ezekiel 44
Marpole, Joseph 148; Thomas 274
Marquess, James 63
Marquis, James 75; Richard 2, 13
Marr, 165; Daniel 67
Mars, 160
Marshal, Thomas 199
Marshall, 31,145,178,188,208; Benjamin 7,31,107; Jno. 35; John 41,125,131; Mary 260, 266; Nancy 260,266; Samuel 227; Thomas 25,97,98,101, 260,266; Thomas M. 106,227
Marston, 254,261; Joseph 253, 269,275
Martain, 217,260,263; Christopher 217
Martin, 44,54,98,121,153,160, 195,232,236,249,274; Andrew J. 273; Christopher 25,64, 180,188,209,221,225; Col. 105; Denny 52; Elias 54,64; Francis 49,67; George 39,48; George Jr. 1; George Sr. 39;

Henry 180; James 8,18,180, 267,269; Jephtha 94; Joel 43; John 85,98,111,135,140, 182,207; John Jr. 111; Joseph 76,111,144,193,214; Levi 94; Luther 80; Luther C. 133; Luther Jr. 79; Nehemiah 111; Philip 35; Rebecca 43; Robert 222; Tho's 217; Thomas Bryan 52;
Marviell, Daniel 185
Marye, 99,263; Frederick A. 222; William S. 78,122
Maslin, Thomas 274; Tho's 255
Mason, 38,68,85,138,150,154, 188,205,222,269; Andrew 178; C. B. 240; Col. 242; Daniel 164; Elenor 2; Enoch 34,121; George 98,275; George Jr. 79 John 4,102,205; Joseph 117; Josephus 209; Magnadier 240; Mr. 118; Rezin 180; Thomas 16,101,104; William 209
Massey, Wm. D. 242
Masters, 246;
Masters, Cassa 98; Diana 98; Ezekiel 98; Mary 98; Robert 98; Trefeny 98; William 98
Maston, 261; Joseph 263
Matheny, 193
Mathes, Benjamin 18; James 18; James Sr. 18
Mathew, Benjamin 26; Levi 26, 41
Mathews, 56,127,240; Alexander 67,247
Mathews, James 26,143
Mathias, 255; Jacob 143; John 56,84,143
Matteny, 167
Matthew, John 48,55; Wm. 275
Matthews, 38,77; John 50,91, 98; Levi 41
Matthias, John 84
Mattox, 61,134
Mauck, Frederick 188,274; John 108,117,124; Joel 275
Mauk, 54,134,214; Daniel 36; Frederick 165,237; Jonathan 17,23
Maulden, Richard 62
Mauze, 269
Mauzey, 211; George 182; Peter 62; Peter Jr. 95; Peter Sr. 95
Mauzy, 232; Henry 12,72; Henry Jr. 12; John 12; John Jr. 12; Mr. 217; Peter 154; Peter Sr. 150; William 272
Mavis, Adam 36; George 26; John 36
Mawk, 235
Maxwell, 44,145; John 161; William 43,153
May, Aaron 257; Isaac H. 203; James 254; Noel 254
Mayhall, 123,124
Mays, 201; John 190
Mayson, Reason 50
Maze, William 168
Mazes, Rodham 226
McAlister, Fentry 125; Jeremiah 125; James 51; Fenly 45
McAnaly, 258
McAtee, Walter 192,197,202,243
McBee, 61,213
McBride, 1,20,63,119; James

McCormack, Charles 46; Ch's 32; James 161
McCormick, 139; Charles 50, 57,139; Dawson 69; James 172,173
McCorneack, James 153
McCoy, 33; Daniel 80; Enos 15; Isaac 31; Jeremiah 30,31
McCrackin, 192
McCray, 135; Allen 132; John 50
McCrea, 6
McCulty, 269; Washington 225
McDaniel, 98; Mary 186; William 17,179,184,201; Will'm 54
McDavid, James 73,184; Notly 179
McDavit, James 25,64
McDonail, James 65
McDonal, Benjamin 73,75; Elinor 59
McDonald, 48,50,95,193,215, 216,219,223,228,238,243,256, 274; A.W. 202; Angus 14; Angus W. 152,181,195,207,258, 266,267,269,270; Angus W. Jr. 267; Angust W. 258; Ann 14; Benjamin 57,131,151,162,165, 170,248,258,259,261; Benjamin Sr. 258; Col. 124; Daniel 229,249; Evan 258; George 158; James 54,202; Jared 192; John C. 259; Marshall 266; Samuel 248; William 197,201,223,233,273
McDonnald, 60
McDonold, 133
McDougin, William 176
McDowel, John 161,249; William H. 260
McDowell, John 72,80,84,109; William 43
McDowells, 203
McDugan, 267
McElhaney, James 14
McEntyre, Charles 134; Wm.134
McFarlan, Elizabeth 32
McFarland, Robert 247
McFarlin, James 92; John 164, 170
McFee, John 108
McFeely, Joseph 105
McGath, 44
McGeath, 15
McGill, 144
McGinnis, James 13
McGlathery, Alen 264
McGowan, 209; James 24,28,94, 100; Phebe 68
McGrary, 156
McGraw, Morris 4; Thomas 4; Thos. 250
McGuire, 60,63; Edward 21,66; James 105
McHendry, 224,232
McIlhaney, 125,159; Mrs. 125
McIlwee, Jacob 236
McIntierf, David 146; George 146
McIntire, 43; Charles 105; Thomas 43; William 200; Wm. 196
McInturaf, David 159
McInturf, George 160
McInturff, Daniel 196,207; David 168,169,178,189,207, 213,261; Frederick 171;

George 168,178,191,207,261; Henry 168,213; John 244,245
McKay, 30; Andrew 67,94,259; David 151; Enos 58,149,151
McKeainin, 88
McKearnan, Laurence Jr. 2; Michael 19
McKee, 50,112,139,154; Bartholomas H. 246; Bartholomew 177; Robert 38; William 48,69
McKeever, 209; Paul 1
McKem, 219
McKenna, James L. 108
McKenney, 108
McKenny, John 12; Tully 73
McKerney, 54
McKever, Paul 25
McKewan, 114,118,228; Charles 50; Michael 8,11,12,19,24, 112,114,117,136; William 34
McKim, 165,166,169,173,184, 185,211,224
McKine, W. 172
McKiver, Jacob 250
McKnight, 146
McKowan, 192; Gilbert 61
McKown, John 83
McKoy, 247; Andrew 266
McLanahan, 268; John 261,268
McLaughlin, Anna 202; Daniel 166,202,222
McLearan, William 247
McMacheon, 165
McMaken, Alexander 61
McManing, George 51
McManus, Luke 69
McMasters, Thomas 37
McMechen, 181,231,244,251, 253; Samuel 154; Samuel A. 270; Tho. 217
McMeekin, 187,244,247
McMechin, Curtis 269
McMeckin, John 2,8,9,109
McMeil, John 32
McMeill, Daniel 190
McMichen, Samuel 206
McMillian, 3; John 35,36,46
McMurrin, Joseph 109
McNamar, 185; Jacob 201; Jos. 224; Joseph 174,185,195,201; Martain 217; Mr. 169,184, 185,223,224
McNamara, Joseph 170
Mcnamara, Martain 165
McNarey, 258
McNary, 119,131,132; Ebenezer 119,121,131,132; Vause 271
Mcnary, Eleenezer 117
McNeal, Strother 112
McNeale, 124
McNeill, 206,220,221,244,255, 260,273; Benjamin S. 247; Daniel 165,179; Daniel R. 247; William C. 247
McNemar, 206,231,247,251; Col. 209; Joseph 125,206, 253; Jos. 271; Martin 180, 181; W. B. 241
McNiel, Daniel 137,190
McNiell, 185,274; Benjamin S. 244; Daniel 195,203; Daniel R. 244; William C. 244
McNight, Emanuel 78
McPherson, 80,160; Col. 186, 199,216,217; Daniel 21; John 21; William 92
McPowell, William 77

McQuin, Samuel 43,58
McRae, Duncan 18; Mr. 125
McRay, Andrew 94; Enos 81,87
McSherry, Richard 27,169
McTee, Walter 270
McUan, Michael 95
McVay, Townsend 85
McVeigh, J. H. 242
McVey, John 258
McVicar, Duncan 32; William 11
McVicker, Duncan 23; John 116
Mead, 13,61; John 15
Means, 70,72,81,214,225,236, 254,265; Isaac 3,12,43,112, 130,140,147,166; Robert 1,7, 18,25,153,165,179,184,216, 237; Robt. 5; William 14,15
Meba?, 188
Meckin, James 215
Meckins, James 171
Medannil, 18
Medley, Ambrose 44
Meek, 14
Meekin, James 96,182
Meekins, James 97,143,147,198
James Sr. 143; Joseph 96
Meem, G.S. 241,242
Melcher, Wendel 39,85
Melick, 79; John 39
Melicks, John 57
Melton, 11; Jonathan 206
Mendenhall, 241
Meneell, 185
Menefee, Henry 111; Henry Sr. 120,123; John 111; Jonas 120
J.Y. 237
Mengham, 114
Meniel, 185
Menifee, 134; Henry Jr. 84; Henry Sr. 84
Menser, Cunrad 92
Mercer, 14,56,185,191,262; Edward 72; John 3; Richard 65,101; Tho. 90
Merchant, Lewis 241; Samuel 241
Merica, Daniel 222; William 222; Wm. 243
Meshe, John 3
Messer, 263; John 27
Metcalfe, Christopher 253
Metz, Peter Sr. 87
Mice, George 177
Michael, 137,190,239,271; A. Jr. 235,241; Andrew 2,154, 182; Col. 213,214,219,221; Daniel 239; Frederick 13,72; George 154,179; Henry 107; Mr. 236,241; Nicholas 201, 206; Peter 12; Solomon 71, 154,179,201,206,212
Micham, Colin 186; Henry 168
Michel, 80; John 62
Mickie, David 33
Mickmahon, 57
Micle, 149
Middlecalf, Jacob 39
Middleton, Thomas 24
Miers, 136,245
Milan, 42
Mildrum, Michael 66
Mile, James 184
Miles, 201,212,244,262; Adam F. 259; Col. 195,196,199, 200,201,203,204; David 7; George 6; James 99,107,150, 162,185,191,205,206,235,255;

John 165; Jno. D. 205; John
D. 175,206; Margaret 6;
Weston 255
Mileson, John 208; Johnston
273; Silas 249; William 208
Miley, Martin F. 228
Milhorn, Peter 70
Milison, John 172; William
172,225
Mill, Wm. 211
Millan, Geo. 78
Millar, 161; Abraham 208;
Absolam 151; Elon 6,21;
George 6,145,151; Henry 15;
Isaac 111; Michael 111,126,
127,197,219; Michel 147;
Peter 241; Reubin 15; Wm.
219; wid. 67
Millburn, William 39
Miller, 16,60,68,79,94,131,
159,185,195,212,224,228,230,
231,238,241,255,262,265,268,
271; Abraham 112,143,267;
Miller, Alexander 57; Anthony
56; Atno. 262; Casper 5,74;
Charles 266; Christian 19;
Corbin W. 164; Daniel 163;
David 177; Ellen 171; Elon
2,8,21,169; Ephraim 95;
Franklin 217; Geo. 41,274;
George 10,30,35,36,39,40,
114,116,123,124,127,138,142,
145,146,148,152,167,168,176,
201,207,228; George D. 207;
Godfrey 120,120,128,139,142;
Henry 9,10,30,36,37,142,217,
226,230; Isaac 249,275;
Isaac C. 164; Jacob 54,70,
73,74,80,90,100,102,118,120,
129,152; Jacob Jr. 150,198;
Jacob W. 130,135; James 85;
Jno. C. 238; John 2,11,20,
22,34,38,39,54,67,71,75,82,
87,88,137,146,148,154,182,
189,201,221; John B. 185;
John L. 184; Jonathan 142,
252; Joseph 4,61,134,228,
274; L. S. 248; Martin 151,
152,201,207; Mathias 129;
Michael 104,119,177,210,246,
267; Mor. 236; Mr. 119,120,
243; Philip 44; Phillip 2,
15,142; Robert 122; Samuel
110,189; Stephen 2; Thomas
J. 223; Warner 217; wid. 69;
William 27,195; William S.
228; Wm. 210; Zachariah 67;
Zachary 39;
Milleson, Silas 215,216,223,
227
Millhorm, Henry 38
Millison, 209; Geo. 257,258,
260,261,264; John 116,135;
Mr. 257; William 209
Millisont, Geo. 258
Milllar, Michael 263
Millor, John 24
Mills, 91; George 6; Henry
55; John 54,120; Mitchell
195,260; Sarah 246; William
6,13,36,80,80,111,193,194;
Williams 144; Wm. 147
Millshlagle, Jacob 119
Millslagel, Andrew 13,14,33;
George 1,16; Jacob 13,14,69
Milslagel, Samuel 192
Milslagle, 223; Abraham 248;
Jacob 246

Milton, Ebin 122
Miner, Fredirick W. 265
Ming, Charles 62
Minghinne, 268
Minginni, Joseph 224
Minifee, 128
Minn, G. S. 244
Minor, George 208; John 6
Mins, 153; Robert 149,164
Minser, 157
Minter, Joseph 61
Minull, Daniel 178
Mires, George 113; Henry 159;
John 124; William 59
Mirier, 163
Mishe, Benjamin 7
Mitcham, Collam 54,68; Collan
4,94
Mitchel, 85; John Jr. 26,187
Mitchell, 98,175,221; James
51; John 163,170; John Jr.
13,20,33,35,40; William 144
Mitchum, Collen 88
Moats?, Henry 100
Mock, Daniel 22,37
Modesitt, James 81; Th's B.
265
Moerhead, James 194
Mofett, Robert 85
Moffett, Rob't 77,81
Moler, Adam 103; David 103;
Frederick 101; Henry 103;
Mary 103
Molers, Frederic 65
Momrow, Robert 64
Moncure, 121; Wm. 17
Mongold, George 114
Monica, Daneil 221
Monroe, 64,72,84,240,242; A.
263; Alex'r 36; Alex. 225,
233; Alexander 21,22,31,135,
136,149; Daniel 247; James
58; Jane 259; Jeremiah 68;
John 82; John Jr. 247;
Marquis 170,193; Whitfield
247
Monrow, Andrew 63; Jeremiah 68
Monse, 173
Montgomery, Robert 106
Mony, Mr. 272
Moody, 48; Ann 19; Moses 23
Moon, Aaron 142; Sarah 162
Moor, John 181
Moor/Moore, 37; Philip 202
Moordock, William 115
Moore, 57,221,227,229,272;
Aaron 4,6,78; Benjamin 97,
98,154; Charles 78; Charles
L. 113,146; Eli 115,187;
George 58; Inias 156; Jacob
113; John 6,67,79,127,175,
185,196; John Jr. 4,5;
Joseph 17; Josias 156;
Josius 156; Lewis 4; Lewis
T. 248; Milly 140; Nicholas
94,124,168; Philip 164,187,
193,195; Reuben 8; Solomon
140; Thomas 97,98,154;
Thomas L. 115,215; W. H. 79;
William 6
Mooreland, Basil 212; Elisha
206,212; Isaac 212; John
212;
Moorhead, James 187
Moorland, Elisha 63;
William 49
Mophasis, 200
Mor/Moor, Nicholas 173

Mordock, William 20,55
More, Elizabeth 150; Josias
67,258; Nicholas R. 79;
Philip 126,140; Phillip 147
Moredock, William 168; Wm. 87
Morehead, Bathsheba 273; John
78; Samuel 58
Morelan, 63; Wm. 240
Moreland, 15; Basil 248;
Basil N. 248; Benjamin W.
248; David 239; Geo. 214;
George 150,151,202,214,248;
George W. 248; John 203,223;
Margery 248; Mary E. 248;
Richard 89,116,135,138,174,
177,208,239; Sarah C. 248;
William 104,210,248,258;
William H. 138,139,150,165,
210,248; Wm. H. 138,239
Moreley, 154
Mores, Philip 145
Morgan, 83; Abraham 42; Abram
58; Dan'l 73; Daniel 94,103,
125; Jacob 18,22,32; James
65; John 65; Jonathan 230;
Joseph 49; Mr. 243; Rawleigh
163; Richard 43,50,58; Thomas
12; wid. 32; William 169
Morison, John 134
Morlan, Richard 79
Morris, 56,69; Charles L.
160; Joshua 17; Josiah 182;
Philip 140; Richard 82;
Thomas 2,10,16
Morrison, James 257; James H.
234; James M. 138; James R.
275; John 82,134; John H.
239; John J. 257; John W.
138; William 69,137,138;
Wm. 70
Morrisson, Nathaniel 6
Morrow, 100,170,233; David
50,100,163; Gideon 196;
James 50,100,163,181;
William 193
Morse, Thomas 103
Morson, 43
Morton, 75; Mr. 117
Mosee, John 106
Moseley, 110; James 109,124
Mosley, Abraham 218
Moss, 62; A. 268; Alfred 213;
Mr.220; Robert 38; Thomas 14
Mott, George 51; John 51;
Sylvester 127
Mount, James 186
Mountjoy, 261
Mourer, John 113
Mouse, Joshua 222
Mouze, 221
Mowery, Ephraim 212; Frederick
R. 212; John 212; John S.
212,245
Mowrer, Loenard 36
Mowus, Frederick 146
Moyer, George 8; John Daniel
36,52
Moyers, 230,231; John D. 23
Muger, John 151
Mulady, Thomas 267
Muledy, Thomas 133,161
Mulin, John 167
Mulledy, Thomas 51,52,105,113,
127,131,133
Mullen, 154; Col. 61,75,153,
164,167,168,169,173,174,186,
187,188,189,190,191,192,194,
195; John 103; Jno. C. 238,

297

242,244,245; Mr. 114,125,129,
135,136,137,139,142,145,146,
151,152,158,162,163,164,175,
176,178,179,180
Mullidy, Thomas 51,132
Mullin, 259; Col. 152; John
178,179,243; J. 139; John
C.B. 238
Mulloy, John C. 235
Mumau, David 75
Mumaw, 128; Christian 142;
George 128,134
Mumew, David 146
Mumford, G.W. 138
Mummau, David 78
Munch, 213; Daniel 83,117,
129,130,171,184,191; wid. 20
Mundell, John 87
Mundle, John 81
Munford, Capt. 143,144
Muoman, Christian 252
Murdock, 181
Mure, 188
Murmaw, Christian 128
Murphey, 18,31; Davis N. 264;
Hanibal P. 264; Hugh 111;
James 2; Pendleton 250
Murphy, 67,80,95; Davis N.
272; Frances 260; Francis
144,148,198; Hugh 35,74,89,
155,156,257; James 6,21,41,
158,160,264,272; John 98;
John L. 274; John W. 214;
Robert 103,228
Murray, 227; Cyrus W. 214
Murury, James 117
Muse, Battaill 21; Robert 85,
143
Musetter, 215
Musselman, Christian 96
Muzey, John 33
Myars, George 52
Myer, John Daniel 48
Myer/Myers, John 75
Myers, 32; Archibald 230;
George 32,40,52,63,92; Henry
151,169,219; Isaac 127;
Jacob 86,92,151,169; James
247; John 66,105,195,204,
228; Joseph 106; Lewis 74;
Moses 28; Samuel 127;
Stephen 112
Myley, Conrad 212
Myre, George 63; Jacob 63
Myrtle, Benjamin 31

Naesselradt, Lewis 129
Naesselrodt, Lewis 130
Nail, William 3
Nailor, 157
Nalley, 153
Nally, 137,186; Hezekiah 181
Naselrod, Lewis 231,236
Naselrodt, Lewis 257
Nash, Thomas C. 55
Nasmith, Thomas 196
Nauman, John 183
Nave, 268; Adam 224; George
84,181; John 76
Navis, 181
Naylor, 246; William 18,51,66,
70,72,73,75,76,77,80,84,89,
91,93,80,102,107,111,113,143,
144,147,156,161,172,273; Wm.
121,147,148
Neal, 219; William 6
Neale, Christipher 259;
William 12

Neas, John 128; Michael 127
Nease, John 75; Ulrick 1;
Ulerick 266
Neasmith, Thomas 129
Neavill, 69
Neelson, Richard 9
Neely, 118,213,233; William
95,117,139,163,228,252,263
Neer, Nathan 275
Neff, 269; David 240,261;
John 37,122,151,187; Leonard
84,103,134,139; Michael 76,
157,158,261; Mr. 114,117;
Sam'l 254; Samuel 239,275
Neill, Abraham 32; Ann 32;
John 32
Neily, Wm. 136
Neiswander, Jacob 142
Nelson, 41,210; James 41,107;
John 78,173,197; John G. 21;
John Griffin 17; Rich'd 18;
Richard 2,17,21,107; T. Jr.
131; William Jr. 208
Neptune, John 101; wid. 101
Nesbet, 104; John 96
Nesbit, 172
Nesselrod, Lewis 236
Nethkin, Frederick 245
Nevel, 71; Joseph 165
Nevil, 50
Nevill, 71,188,201,206,220,
262,273; Jethro 61,90,91;
Joseph 1,7,48,184,185,224;
Mortimer D. 232; Mr. 97
Neville, 106,107,242; Joseph
71; Mortimore D. 265
New, David 200
Newberry, 192
Newbrough, Austin 272
Newell, Thomas 3,20,30,54,
142,143
Newhouse, Elizabeth A. 209;
Frances T. 209; James A.
209; Jemima T. 209; John Y.
209; Mary Matilda 209;
Rebecca M. 209; William M.
S. 209;
Newkirk, George 6; Isaac 6;
James 6; John 6; Joseph 6;
Margaret 6; Mr. 235; Reubin
6; Tunis 2,6
Newland, Daniel 18; William 5
Newman, 3,51,153; A. 254;
Benjamin P. 230; George 260;
Isaac 211,260; John 123,128,
260; M.D. 230,247; Mr. 229,
242; Muscoe 106; Solomon 7;
Walten 148; Walter 28,120,
123,135,138,139,142,157,160,
228,230,231,274
Newton, 52,81; William 22;
Willougby 38
Nicholas, 34; A. 246; Henry
59,69,73; Jacob 59; Tevault
47
Nichols, 53; Amos 29; Edwin
40; Eli 34; Isaac 15,131
Nicholson, David 242; Jesse
254; James M. 242; Thomas
95; Wm. C. 240
Nickols, 43
Niff, Adam 152
Nimrod, Jacob 167
Nipper, Nancy 206
Nisbet, Andrew 113
Nisbit, 113
Nisley, Henry 105
Nisswaner, Jacob 235

Niswander, 61
Niswanger, Christian 3
Niville, J. 99; S. 71
Nixon, 249; Col. 165; George
131; John 15; Lemuel 245;
Mr. 160,165,166; William
131,248
Nizely, Samuel 151
Noble, 139
Noel, 209,235
Noell, John 135
Noff, Abraham 40
Noland, 255; Obed 93; Pearce
150; Pearse 161; Thomas 24
Nooney, 20
Norden, Jacob 39
Norman, 34,68,85,157,256;
James 134; John 17,51;
Thomas 68; William 43
Normin, Benjamin 5; John 5
Norris, George H. 50,69;
Thaddeus 28
Norvell, Peyton 66
Nourse, Grabriel 14
Nowland, William 8
Nowman, John 86,87,108
Null, 232; David 105,106,129,
188; Jacob 80,188
Nutt, 91; Wm. D. 246
Nutts, 171

O'Bannon, Bryant 233
O'Farrell, Mr. 182; John 146
O'Ferrall, John 40
O'Ferrel, Ignatius 95
OBrian, Dennis 117
ODaniel, Stephen 79; William
79
ODell, Mr. 175,176
ODonald, Oliver 241
OFarrall, Mr. 182
OFarrel, Mr. 136,178
OFarrell, Mr. 139
OFearral, Jno. 213
OFerrall, Col. 205,207; J.D.
213
OFerrell, Mr. 141,142,203,204,
208
OHenley, Patrick 146,196
ONeal, 59
Oakley, George 78
Oar, Thomas 109
Oats, Christopher 250; Daniel
154; George 130,141,171,191,
210; Jacob 50; Lorenzo 246
Oayter, 85
Obannon, 207,237; Bryan 37;
Isham 72; Joseph 19,68,91
Odell, 5,199; Elisha 176;
Jeremiah 124; Mr. 102,116,
176,177,179,182,183; Samuel
94,176
Oden, 19; Elias 70
Oder, 58
Odles, 111
Oferbocher, John Jr. 81,108
Oferrall, John 20
Offenbacker, Joseph 248
Offerall, 236
Offerrall, Ignathius 124
Offerrell, Ignatius 141
Offiett, Eli 137
Offord, 157
Offritt, William 192
Ogan, 51; Peter 95,102
Ogden, David 68,153,191;
Thomas 137
Oglesby, 179

Oglivie, 243
Oglevie, Thomas 25,103,112
Ohaver, 154,160,239; George
14; Mary 48
Ohesher, Uriah 239
Ohio Co. Surv., 182
Ohover, 196,242
Okenlan, Patrick 100
Oldacre, 170; Lucretia 175
Oldacres, 169; Lucretia 181
Oldfield, Tullys 121
Olinger, Adam 186,204; David
114
Olinzer, Adam 168
Oliver, 165,172,250,255;
Isaac 159; John 159; wid. 1
Oneal, 47
Opie, Maj. 148
Orahood, Joshua 173
Oram, Henry 125
Orendorf, 108
Orm, James 101
Orme, James 68,91
Orndoff, 236; John 47,48,71;
Polly 147,149
Orndorf, John 42
Orndorff, 125; Alfred 246;
Elenor 246; Henry 94; Israel
118; James 267; James H.266;
John 8,266; Lewis 266;
Samuel 120,147
Ornduff, 216; David 216; H.
271; Lewis 218; James 205,
216; John 218; Samuel 134
Orndurff, 78; Jacob 159; John
207,159; Samuel 112
Oroark, David 69
Orr, 99; Anthony 118,131;
James 40; John 174; William
75
Orrich, George 117
Orrick, Benj. 123,124,125;
Benjamin 118; Col. 186,187,
192,193; Cromwell 149,203;
Mr. 120,124; Nicholas 53,75;
William 29
Orrowhood, 209; Joshua 135
Osborne, Joshua 125
Osburn, Joseph 260; William
24
Ott, Jacob 54,130,218; Jacob
Sr. 130
Ougan, Peter 20,257
Outz, Adam 16
Overall, 266,270,275; Isaac
30,49,58,78,83,104,108,225,
231; John 49,65,71,78;
William B. 99; Wm. B. 275
Overfelt, Martin 58
Overfield, 46
Overholser, Christian 128,130,
157; John 128; Samuel 63
Overton, 272; John 29,49;
Thomas B. 97
Owen, 257; Joshua 71
Owens, Reuben 50
Owsley, Thomas 186

Paddy, 112
Page, 95,105,119,227;
Alexander 152; G.F. 274;
Mann 12; Mann R. 218; Robert
12; William B. 53; Wm. 85
Pain, 254
Painter, Abraham 236; Isaac
34,236; Jacob 260; John 34;
John Jr. 28; Noah 253;
Samuel 171

Palmer, 2,24,171; John 47,48;
Joseph 176,177; Thomas 261
Panabaker, Adam 111
Pancake, 79; Isaac 107,112,
126,131,137,147,153,194,210,
219,246,254; John 2,37,153;
John M. 219,254
Pancoast, Samuel A. 266,267
Pancost, Samuel A. 239
Pane, 268
Parill, Branson 192
Paris, James 195
Parish, Beckford 219; William
154
Park, 121,248; Amos 118; Col.
176; Enoch 186; G. 179;
George 118,119,186,246;
Harbert 198; Harburt 173,
179; Jacob 193; John 33,52,
118,241; Samuel 53,273;
Solomn 33
Parke, James 229
Parker, 33,63,91,112,133,144,
218,227,258,266,268; Abraham
144,158; Absalom 40; Benjamin
35; Brothers 272; Jacob 53,
130,133,140,141,144,158,256;
James 118,256,272; Job 3,12,
13,36,43,133,256; John 105,
131,133,135,141,144,147,158,
166,203,214; Jonathan 36,
133,158; Joseph 130,142,218;
Joseph B. 207; Joseph M.119;
Nathaniel 119; Rich'd E. 56;
Robert 3,140,156,187,211;
Robert Jr. 43; Robert Sr.43;
Solomon D. 197,211; Thomas
33,48; William H. 56
Parkins, Jonathan 49,106;
Isaac 49
Parks, 63,68,72; Andrew 32;
George 140; John 22; Samuel
41,53,68,142
Parmer, John 33
Parnals, 52
Parrel, 69
Parril, 116
Parrill, Joseph 69; Joseph F.
248; Rachel 246
Parris, 211; James 211,263
Parrish, William 62
Parron, 269
Parrot, 110; Jacob 175
Parrott, Christopher 133
Parson, 62,200; James 16;
Mr. 110; Thomas 229
Parsons, 155,249; David 43,52,
66,83,101,111,127; David C.
254; David Jr. 131; George
17; Harriot 102; Harriot E.
102; I. 248; Isaac 244,245,
246,248,249,250,252,254,260,
262,266,270; James 47,83,
111,187; James Sr. 131,137;
Miles 179; Mr. 101,108,109,
110,111,114,115,116,117,255;
Qilliam L. 163; Solomon 102;
Thomas 139,179; William 163
Partlow, Benjamin 5,18,23,65;
Elisha 194; William 194
Pasmore, 236
Passgat?, 272
Passmore, Levis 215
Paterson, 59
Patick, 128
Patrick, 156
Patterson, 37,126,210,223;
Alexder 155; James 25,161,

210; James H.F. 272; John
126,140,161; Thomas 193
Patton, 215; Hugh M. 253,269;
Richard 5,8; Robert 78,85
Paugh, Michael 227; Nicholas
96
Paul, Andrew 81; Catherine
164
Pauner, John 6
Paw, 80
Payne, 121,124; Daniel 66;
George 174; John 121; Mr.29;
Thomas 10,24,169; Tully R.
62; William 6,12,62; Wm. 37;
Wm. W. 134,175,218
Peak, 120
Peake, 105; Craven 129; James
17,37; John 129; William 129
Peal, Bernard 28,43
Pear, 177; Isaac 241,267
Pears, 54
Pearsall, 121,132; John 2,117
Pearsaul, John 119
Pearse, John 172
Pearson, 38,55,215,226; Alex-
ander 30; John 246; Simon 62
Pearsons, 176
Peck, James 56
Pedger, Isaac 190
Pedrick, 61
Peepy, William 158
Peer, David 147; Jacob 168,
218; Philip 118
Peerce, John T. 266
Pell, William 37
Pemberton, George 73
Penabaker, Wm. 82
Pence, Charles 168,186;
Conrad 36,127; George Philip
75; Henry 1; Jacob 1,127;
John 127,249; Lewis 81;
Philip 127; Sarah 242
Pendegast, John 253
Pendegrast, John 226
Pendleton, 3,12,50,53,95,106,
182,192,196,201,228,229,235,
272,273; Edmund 22; Henry 6;
James 22; Jno: S. 134; Marie
22; Mr.169; P.C. 24,125,241;
Philip 16,18,20,22,49,57,95,
105; Philip C. 22,52,146,149,
154,169,193,256; Phillip 2,3,
5,20; Sarah 22; Wm. 72; Wm.
G. 74; Wm. Henry 22
Pendolton, 79
Penery, Robert 262
Pennebacker, Mr. 142
Penneybaker, William 38
Pennington, Abraham 41,85,104,
133; Elijah 102,116; Enoch
192,220; Jacob 41,104; James
116
Pennybacker, 183,261,270;
Benjamin 78,100,113,152,157,
165; George M. 113; Joel 113,
226; Mr. 160
Pennybaker, 93,152,240;
Benjamin 110; Derick 5;
Derrick 36; Joel 164,226;
William 10,29
Pennybarker, Benjamin 157
Pennybecker, Mr. 160
Pennywitt, Rosena 241
Penteny, James 262
Pentony, Luke 88,99; Michael
88,99
Peper, John 171
Pepper, 59,220,241,245;

299

Benjamin F. 242,264; Frederick 197; Henry 92; Jacob 92,142; James 241; John 69; John Jr. 92; John Sr. 92; Perry 255,261
Perkey, Nicholas 213
Perkins, 57
Perkipile, Christian 20; Michael 45
Perrel, Edward 69,112; John 9, 26,41; John Jr. 9; John Sr.9
Perrell, Edward 47; H. 256; Hugh 251,256; Joseph 47
Perril, John 102,233; William 102
Perrill, Hugh 257,258,261
Perry, 146,178; Dr. 258; Ignatious 33
Person, Isaac 3
Pertlebaugh, 207
Peters, Adam 244,245; Branson 170,194,239,258; Isaac 38; James 101,104; John 31,52, 68,198,220,242; Peter 26, 244; Tunie 101
Peterson, Martin 73,74,114
Petters, Branson 161,162,218; John 48,186
Pettit, Elijah 148; Elizabeth 148; John 81; Johnthan 148; Moses 92,107; Rachel 148
Pettitt, John 187; Thomas 143
Pettleyon, Peter 97
Pettliyone, 200
Petty,124,209; Marshall 78,85
Pew, Robert 164
Peyton, 139,148; Henry 22; Howe 46,50; John 42,44; John F. 245; John S. 245; Lucien 245,268; Valentine 17,52
Pheazlis, Michael 157
Philips, 7,33
Phillips, Plunket 2; William 91,92,151
Phogle, Philip 110
Pick, 154
Pickering, John 15; Richard 243
Picket, 10
Pickett, 61,229; George B.72; Martin 6,72; William 163
Pictall, 88
Pideler, Jacob 8
Piedlas, M. 226
Pierc?, Ashford 156
Pierce, Charles 208; Clement 58; Peter 153; Reubin 85
Pierpoint, Obed 61
Pierson, 145
Pifer, William F. 233,256; W.F. 270
Pigman, 5,104,177; Bene S. 197,223; Matthew 10,21,52
Pike, 22
Pilche, Stephen 36
Pilcher,John 106,109; Stephen 9,10,35,194; William 26
Piles, 46; Francis 166; Thomas 248
Pine, James 179,180,199
Pink, Perry 60
Pinkerton, 189; Margaret 191; Robert 10,11,13,171
Pinkins, Jacob 117
Pinkstone, 65
Piper, 107,108; Augustine 1, 105; Henry 41; John 139
Piser, Jacob 22,47,51

Pitman, 134; Andrew 157,160; David 123; John 131,157; Joseph 131,157; Lawrence 18, 131; Lawrence Jr. 157,160; Lawrence Sr.160; Mr.228,236, 240,244,245,252; Philip 223
Pittenger, 82
Pittman, Abraham 142,143
Pitzer, 2,75; James S. 239; Michael 81
Pixler, 175,181
Plaer, Matheny 171
Pleaudn, 147
Plodt, John 122,144
Plotner, Daniel 83
Plum, Abraham 152; John 26; John Sr. 40;
Plumb, 68; Abraham 100; John 8,26,35; John Sr. 80
Plume, Jacob 86
Poinder, Henry 18
Pointer, Eve 152; Joseph S.91
Poke, Adam 8,129; John 128; Jno. 244; Philip 78
Polack, James T. 169
Poland, 212,221,265; Aaron 177,185; Amos 19,33,64,73, 126,127,208,211,249,257,260, 267; John 19,30,64,73,126, 127; Nancy 257; Peter 170, 173,194,227; Richard 127; William 127
Poling, Amos 241; William 246; William B. 254
Pollard, Ro. 9; Thomas 51; Thos. 12; Thomas Jr. 28; Thos. Jr. 29
Polling, William B. 246
Pollock, Isaac 27
Ponn, John A. 252
Pool, 43,85,219; Henry 98, 127; Jeremiah 202,205,214; John 48,169,202,205,214; William 41,44,84,104,133, 158,205; Wm. 202
Poor, Overseers of 211
Pope, Jacob R. 224
Porter, John 76; William 58
Porterfield, 88; George 39, 40,65; James 122; Jas. 94; Jno. 88,92; John 88; Mr. 75, 82,83
Portin, 155
Portmess, John 158,202,203
Posten, Mr. 146
Poston, 89,139; Alexander 84, 112,165,208; Branson 118,155, 215,261; Bronson 155; Elias 34,138; Richard 111; Samuel 51; William 111,215
Potts, 125; John 52
Pough, 58
Poulison, John 33
Poulter, 58
Poutter, William 17
Powel, Joseph 132; William 22 William M. 161
Powell, 27,112,137,148,161, 178,205,206,219; Alfred H. 72; Ambrose 70; Burr 59; Dade 94,95,115; Edmond L. 272; Elias 98; Elisha 264; Elizabeth 230,244; Henry 197; Hny. R. 260; James 57, 104; James F. 272; John 93, 100; Joseph 79; Josephus L. 272; Leven 109; Mr. 229,230; Mrs. 268; R.M. 227,255,256,

257,258,259,260; Rob. M. 226; Robert 8,82,112; Robert Jr. 272; Robert M. 95,109, 272; Robert M. Jr. 264; Robert M. Sr. 264; Robert M. 3rd 208,264; Susannah 272; William M. 132
Powellson, 84; Henry 116,183
Powelson, 63,79,241; Charles 84; Chloe Ann 173; Cloe Ann 126,162,179; Henry 183;James 245,256; John 41,72,119,126, 137,160,161,162,176,194,235, 245,257; Powel 173,256
Power, Valentine 107
Powers, Stephen 59; Valentine 97,242; Val. 165
Powles, wid. 7
Pownak, John J. 194
Pownal, 62
Pownall, Isaac 177,211,214; John 63,152,161; John J. 211,215
Pownell, Isaac 41; James 57; Jesse 241; Jonathan 41
Powner, John 77; Joshua 80
Powson, 122
Prather, James 143; Silas 135, 150,162,165,170,177,197,204, 239
Prathers, Silus 161
Pratt, Jonathan 84
Praytor, James 25
Preston, 262; John 34
Price, Argalon 35; Arganal 115; Arjalon 86,90; Arjilon 117; Benjamin 53; Benjamin F. 263; Geo: R.C. 237; George R. C. 237; George W. 53; Henry 146; Jacob 8; John F. 23; John H. 92; John Hill 35,86, 90,264; Mr. 235,237; Philip 95; Stephen 183,186
Prichard, 59; Lewis 3; Rece 1; Stephen 46
Pridman, Benjamin 151
Priest, 175; Matthew 247
Prill, John 34,54
Prim, William 42
Primm, 115
Prince, Abraham 75,87,146; Abram 159; David C. 217; George 75,86,87,93,152,153; George Sr. 86; Goodlove 105; Henry 86,87,108,146,153,163; John 183,217,224; John Jr. 221; John Sr. 221; Peter 75, 87,146,159
Pringle, 192
Printz, Aaron 240; Abraham 234,269; Abram 221; David C. 234,240,269; David Sr. 240; George 221,224,240,266,269; Isaac 224,234,246,266; Isaac Sr. 221; John 221,234; John Sr. 240; Peter 221,234,252, 269; Reuben 266
Pritchard, Rees 92
Pritchett, William H. 37
Probasco, 165; Jacob 161,170; Samuel 75,120; Titus 170
Probst, Michael 122
Profate, Jacob 127,242
Prophet, Jacob 123
Prunty, John 83
Prutzman, Henry 40
Puffenbarger, 209
Puffengerger, John 106

Puffenburger, 199
Pugh, 114,136,143,165,189,191, 221,237; Abraham 53; Abram 39; Azariah 110,198; Benjamin 240; David 28,166; Hannah 28; Hannibal 158; Jacob 9,32,73,77,116,184; James B. 194; Jesse 28,30,48, 110,210,259; Jesse J. 229; Job 223; Johathan Sr. 128; John 146,261; Johnathan Jr. 146; Johnathan Sr. 146; Jonathan 85,92,255,261; Jonathan Jr. 128,193; Joseph 17; Joseph B.271; Mahlen 69; Melon 4,48; Michael 117; Mishall 166; Mr. 110,111; Nimrod 215; Rob't 131; Robert 165,248,259
Pullin, William 247
Pulse, 114;Jacob 6; Michael 8
Pumcrots, 89
Purcall, Jonathan 51,68,83
Purger, William 140
Purget, 60,63,80; Frederick 76,79,144,156; Henry 22,31, 89,140,158; Henry Jr. 144; Henry Sr. 140; Jacob 5,40; Sidney 140;
Purgett, Henry 140; Jacob 40
Purgott, Frederick 203
Purkepile, 124
Purkeypile, John 106
Purtle, Nicholas 179
Purtlebaugh, 44
Pusey, Joshua 274
Putman, 132,214; Jacob 86,90; Peter 10,16,30,104; Philip 16; 249,264; Robert 209
Putonun, Peter 64

Quaintance, Henry 230,
Quaintnce, Henry 230
Quanintance, Henry 256
Quarrier, Alexander 18
Queen, 138,139; John 57,79, 146; Jonas 57
Quick, James 24

Races, Thomas 143
Racey, John 250; Thomas 102;
Racy, Elizabeth 116; John 116; Lewis 116; Madison 116; Mana 116; Margaret 116; Nacy 116; Sarah 116; Thomas 116, 196,226
Radabang, Martain 173
Radabough, 231
Radcliff, William 50
Rader, James 163
Raimy, 208
Raish, Jacob 34
Ralls, George N.98; Hebron 46
Ralph, 91,110,248
Ralston, Robert 55
Ramey, Pealey 207
Ramzey, 274
Randal, 178
Randall, 264; Chilton 49; Jacob 7; James 87,126;
Randel, 56
Randell, 233; James 141
Randolph, George 142
Rankin, 182,196,251,258; George 56,170,174; John 85, 90,96,100,114,141,177; Mr. 175; Samuel 93,109,141,158, 159; Samuel Sr. 203; Simeon

154,158,192; William 22,50, 93,105,158,192
Rankins, George 70; William 12,19
Rannell, John 185,220
Rannells, 75; John 215
Ransbottom, Richard 81
Ratcalife, Richard 73
Ratcliff, 206; John 56; Richard 40; Robert 220
Ratcliffe, Richard 37,79; Robert 77,216
Rateen, 169
Ratliff, Stephen 180
Rattan, 55
Ravencroft, 5
Ravenscraft, 115,264; Charles 98; Edward 252; James 147; John 133,268; John D.133,147; Samuel 274; Samuel Jr. 30
Ravenscroft, John 48; James 47,48; William 65
Ravensworth, 11,148
Rawlings, Benjamin 35,96,117, 122,215,271; Elijah 117,122, 271; Peter 122,211,269; Ruth 256; Santford 269,271; Teter 117
Rawlins, 90
Rawlngs, Peter 96
Ray, 104,177
Raymond, 267; Moses 272
Razor, 70
Read, Anthony 157,167; Jacob 16,36;
Reader, Jacob 32; Nicholas 30
Reading, William 5
Reagan, John 44
Reager, 3; John 79
Reasoner, Jacob 11,100
Reaves, Peter 99
Rector, Conway 16,43; Wharton 10
Rector, W. 6
Redd, Joseph B. 216
Redeinck, Andrew 123
Reder, Catharine 100
Ree, William 227
Reece, Robert 37; William 5, 16
Reed, 103,126,209,216,221, 222,229,233,235,237,238,252; Abraham 112,116,145,155; David 231; George 102; Green B. 262; Jacob 145; James 11, 60,157; James H. 122; Jeremiah 51,102; John 196; Mrs.205; Pambroke 244; Sarah 64,209; William 145,169,187, 189,198; Wm. 205,216,229,231, 237
Reeder, Joseph 30
Reedy, George W. 260,270; John 253
Reel, 221,226
Rees, 59,162; Ashford 151,152 David 83; Jacob 83; Morris 46,54,55; Morris Sr. 55; Silas 194,197,263,272,274; Thomas 55,114,115,133,186; William 98,258; William D. 258; Wm. D. 215
Reese, 129; David 106; Esther 70; Morris 44;
Reeve, 180
Reeves, 31,56; Peter 7
Reichard, Jacob 117
Reid, 240; George 41,100;

Mark 208; Robert 208; Walker 70; Wallace 28
Reley, 134
Relf, 2,267
Relfe, 57; Richard 176
Relph, 17
Relphs, 15
Ren, 147
Rench, 2
Renchart, Michael 52
Renerfelt, John 27
Renick, 231,268; George 27
Renner, George 42
Rennick, George 47; William 1
Renno, Enoch 33; Enock 91
Rennoe, Enoch 71; Enock 109; George 71
Rennols, William 39
Reno, Enoch 3; John 55
Renoe, 43; Bayles 46; Chapman 247; Enoch 35,46
Renolds, George 141,149
Renow, Enoch 27
Renuer, Paul M. 32
Rester, John S. 138
Reyley, Alexander 66
Reynolds, 103,213,221,228; George 182; Patrick 80; Rezin 233; Stephen 181
Rezer, Mathias 154
Rhinehart, 252; Adam 128
Rhinetreat, Michael 146
Rhodes, 263; Abraham 134; John 242; Valentine 245
Riand, Rev's 34
Rice, 86; Benajah 40; Francis 94; Jesse 220
Richard, Henry 10,125,215
Richards, 26,272; Elijah 138; Felix 259; George 17; Henry 9,138; Henry W. 248; John 9, 112,212; wid. 5
Richardson, 153; John 38; Jno W. 214; Marcus C. 205; Polly 194; William 77
Richert/Richards, Henry 10
Richmond, James 143,176,267; William 143
Rickard, John R. 241
Rickets, Elisha 134
Rickey, 151
Riddle, 206
Ridenhour, John 71
Ridenour, Adam 69,160; Daniel 160,168; Elias 244; Henry 69,130,183,213,231,238; Jacob 130,135; John 71
Rider, 272; Alexander 3,217; Catharine 8,16,44,104; Christina 118; Jacob 8,16, 44; John L. 228; Mary 118; Peter 8,16,118
Ridgeway, Joseph 119; Richard 220
Ridgly, 133
Ridgway, James 174; John 209; Otho W. 244; Richard 244; William 244
Ridnour, Jacob 142
Ridwell, 126
Riffey, George 123,142
Rigeway, Thomas S. 266
Rigg, Richard 81
Riggs, 6
Right, Joseph 95
Rightenour, Henry 82
Rigway, Thomas S. 258
Riley, 94,100,105,171; Alex-

ander 117,223,249; Alexaner 162; George 249,255; Martin 83; wid. 89
Rilley, 261
Rilly, Martin 180
Rinckart, Abraham 33
Rinehart, 233; Abraham 110, 118,187,258; Abram 215; Elijah 187; Francis 11; George 28; John 235; Lewis 26; Michael 23,36; Stephen C. 258
Rineheart, Adam 87,132,183; George 87; Lewis 36
Riner, 256; Andrew 236; Christian 70; Ebehart 70; Henry 99; Jacob Jr. 256; John 70
Rinerfelt, 99
Riners, Henry 113
Rinker, 34,57,72,79,182,200; Absalom 83,106; Absolam 151; Barbara 106; Caspar 244; Casper 118,120; Ephraim 114, 120,127,135; Erasmus 252; Gaspar 89; George 28,245; Henry 1,120; Isaac P. 253, 263,269; Israel 224; Jac.74, 77; Jac. Jr. 74,77,78; Jacob 3,28,37,42,49,50,55,73,75, 89,129,130,135,137,142,245; Jacob Jr. 78,107; John 202, 272; Jonathan 245; Levi 241, 266; Mr. 174; Reuben 245; William 151,235,273
Rinkin, Mr. 157,160
Risk, A.B. 237
Riss, 156
Ritenour, Joseph 91
Ritter, Mathias 179,181; Matthew 226
Rizer, Philip 271
Roach, Robert 80
Road, Jacob 34; John 78; Joseph 146
Roadcap, 26; Henry 255; Martin 255
Roads, John 48; Joseph 110; Joseph M. 222; Joseph Sr. 94,108; Levi 261
Roberson, 79; Amos 264
Robert Sherrard 94
Roberts, 14,56,108,169,175, 182,194,221,249,251,272; Benjamin N. 156,194; David 249; Elijah 30,202; Gersham 40,156; James 209,216,235; Jas. 221,249; Jno. 37,43; John 24,45,49,167,169,222; Maj. 2,10,42,43,58,82; Mr. 36; Nathan 273; William 17, 30,70; Wm. J. 253,269
Robertson, 4,21,33,91,102,171, 189,224; Blaze 201; D. 149, 150; David 18; Dr. 148,149, 151,152,163,176,183; George 28,38; Israel 27,75,81; James 10,26,27,29,33,40; James R. 124,128,130; John G. 173,206; Mr. 105,129,134, 135,153
Robey, 255; Abram 174; Prior 5; Pryor S. 3
Robinett, 242
Robinson/Robison, 181
Robinson, 106,197,216,224,230, 232; Abraham 103; Andrew 181 Henry 177; Israel 67,82,83;

James 24,29,99,191; John 50; Joseph 254; Mitchell 78; Mr. 34; Thomas 99; William 19
Robison, 49,216; Charles 41; Robson, William R. 254
Roby, 188,238,253,260; Abram 164,194; Benj'n 221; Benjamen 219; Benjamin 189, 190,201,226; Charles 247; Elias 7; Lyas? 184; Prier S. 205; Prior 7; Prior S. 242; Samuel 64,74; blue John 196
Rodefer, Adam 159
Rodeffer, Adam 163
Rodeheffer, Samuel 77
Rodenheffer, David 26
Rodgers, 228,239; Aaron 239; John 50,76,101,122; Owen 50; Owing 95; Rhodham 101; Robert 95,102,124,138; William 74,169
Rodtruck, 22; Andrew 23,25
Roebuck, William 40
Roes, Mary H. 178
Roger, 233
Rogers, 111,226,257,266,273; Aaron 179,194,264; Achilles 90; Aroon 165; Daniel 26; Gen. 216,275; George 1; John 78,161,194,217; Joseph 44, 105; Owen 261; Robert 1,25, 30,61,70,138,193,253; Samuel Jr. 217; Samuel R. 217
Roheabaw, Christain 206
Rohraban, Christian 173; Elizabeth 173; Hannah 173; John 167
Rohrabar, John 190
Rohrabau, Christian 208; Elizabeth 185
Rohrabaugh, 213,225,262; John 269
Rohrback, Christian 200,209
Roice, 95
Roler, George 129; John 69
Rollar, 154
Rolls, 109
Romich, Michael 12,74
Romine, Peter 58
Romines, Thomas 8
Roney, Michael 83
Ront, John 139
Rooney, Michael 228,243
Rorabau, George 199
Rorabaugh, 224
Roraboh, Henry 119; John 97, 119
Rorer, Henry 123
Rorobaugh, Samuel 260
Rosbough, John 2,102
Rosbrough, John 23,25,233
Rose, 273; Col. 124; Henry S. 174; John 27
Rosebrough, John 26,33,86,135, 233,236
Rosenbarger, Abraham 155
Rosenberger, Anthony 175; Henry 117,123; John 154; Joseph 108; Rudolph 117,123
Rosey, Conrod 29
Ross, 52,54,102,206,219,222, 229,263; A. 57; Adam 27,121, 270; Alexander 33; David 67, 121,189,253; Gabriel 21; Mary H. 178; Nathan 82,93, 112; Reubin 121; Stephen 6, 25,190
Roszell, Stephen C. 22

Rothgeb, Abraham 94; Abraham J.275; George 85; John W.275
Rotruck, 249; Abraham 168; Abram 167,188,217; George 221; Jacob M. 269; John 168, 198,221; Peter 211,269
Rounsville, 204
Rouse, 65; George 7; P.H. 235
Roushe, Philip 74
Rout, 38,112
Routs, 177
Routsul, Henry 48
Routt, John 69,97
Rouzee, James 189; John 55
Row, George 45; John 169
Rowe, 270
Rowley, John 50; William 55
Rowzee, James 184
Roy, 275; Elijah 99,110; Gibson N. 256; G.N. 273,275
Royce, 102; Daniel 143,214; Frederick 239; John 239; Patrick 44
Roye, 59
Royer, Daneil 19,62
Rozell, Mr. 46
Rozenberger, William 207
Ruble, 49,56,180,272,274; Samuel 24,38
Ruckman, 72,81,161; Gibson 227; Gipson 167; Jacob 63,81, 144,218,267; John 119,155, 161,162,211,239,240,246,248, 264; Joseph 211; Peter 63,81, 267; Sam'l 239; Sam'l C. 207, 264; Samuel 29,104,107,109, 113,144,161,162,170,198,207, 239,240,246,249,258,264; Samuel C. 197,208,246,248, 256,267; Samuel J.? 248; Susanna 104; Susannah 161; Thomas 1,5,29,31,36,48,193, 198,240,246,248,267; Wilson 113
Ruddle, 181,212
Rudkman, Gibson 240
Rudolph, 86,112,236,246; Adam 155,177,193,207,218,268; Elizabeth 149; George 127, 135; Jacob 112,118,120,147, 177,246; John 48,112,134, 177,218; John Jr. 138
Rudy, John 129
Ruffner, Benjamin 85,91,101; David 105; John 224; Jonas 78,91; Joseph 150; Joshua 87,88,275; Peter 5
Rufner, Benjamin 11
Ruller, 180
Rumner, 48
Rumsey, 22,34,88,273; Edward 21
Rumsy, 169
Rundell, James 156
Runion, Jacob 100
Runner, William 94
Rup, Martin 17
Rupert, Christian 242; Daniel 245,265
Rupp, 101; Martin 265
Rusell, 263; James 39
Ruses, 114
Rush, John 31; William 92
Russaw, John 3
Russell, 4,37,46,113,215,251, 269,271; Andrew 97; Christopher 94; Elisha E. 77; James 53,62,71,76,83,137,

302

303

Shell, 188,202,224,227,243, 247; Catherine 186; Daniel 184,184,186,190,206,212; Elizabeth 186; George 74, 165,180,181,186,187; Geroge 201; John 185,186,212; Mary 186; Philip 186,187,206,212; Samuel 112,147,149
Shelley, Christian 54,75
Shells, George 60
Shelly, Daniel 244
Shemp, 272
Shenk, Abraham 225; George 229; Jacob 275; John 81, 101,148,261; Martin 74; William J. 275
Shenks, John 87; Martin 87
Shepard, Job 5,9,20,21
Shepherd, 53,201,202,206,254; Abraham 42; Gen. 268; Job 13,53; Thomas 100; Wm. 11
Shepler, 270; Henry 227
Sherar, 213
Sherard, 182,215,219,228; John 229; Jno. 253; Robert 110
Sherewood, 95
Sherffig, Abraham 12
Sherfig, Abraham 1
Sherman, John 195
Sherrard, Jno. 2,54,95,98; John 65,83,88,90,95,99,101, 103,105,105,154,158,163; Maj. 149,158,159,163; Mjr. 149, 150; Mr. 117,181,184,239, 240,241; Ro. 93; Robert 2,91, 93,96,102,138,143,160,165, 170,173,175,194,195,196,215; Robert B. 257,258,261,264, 266,273; William 93,102,117, 172,227
Sherreds, 61
Sherrerd, William 61
Sherwood, Archibald 215; John 19
Shery, Martin 159
Shevirs, George 179
Shewmaker, Elias 60,167; George 77; John 16
Shickle, Peter 244
Shield, James 90; John 67
Shields, 10; James 90,214; John 27,32,260; William 9, 67,131
Shierly, John 196,257
Shillenburg, Hugh 205
Shillingbury, William Sr. 164
Shillingsberg, 234
Shimp, 256; Mahala J.? 224
Shin, David 41,51,63
Shingleton, Absalom 80; John 241; William 241
Shinholt, Jacob 126; Joseph 171; Peter 93,126,144,149, 176; Philip 225; Smauel 126, 144
Shink, Ann 214; Samuel H. 214
Shinn, David 79; Samuel 79
Ship, Godfrey 60
Shipe, Christian 117;John 191
Shipes, John 191
Shipp, Capt. 112
Ships, 251; Asa 90
Shireman, 174,200; Conrod 175; George 106,119,135; Jacob 106,122,125,135
Shiriff, 153
Shirley, 254,260,270; Jervis

50; Thomas 9; Zacheus 9
Shirly, Zachariah 174
Shiveley, Michael 52
Shivers, John 141
Shobe, Isaac 209
Shock, Jno. H. 243
Shockey, Abraham 169; Basil E. 246; Jacob 43,195; John 275; Joseph 147,148,153,166; Lewis 71;
Shocky, Abraham 24,28
Shoe, Benjamin 1
Shoemaker, 255,266; Elias 117; George 1,8,17,23,44,144, 156,203,259; Michael 153
Shofe, John 76,80
Shook, 269; Jacob 134; Maj. 195
Shooke, Mr. 122
Shore, Thomas 12,249,255
Shores, Lander 156; Thomas 153,171,173; Thomas Jr. 173
Shorf, George 22
Short, 103; Isaac 156; Jacob 249; John 253; Michael 92; Richard 60,156; Samuel 159; Wm. 125
Shoter, Solomon 127
Shotwell, James 7,61,62; William 7
Shouse, John W. 268,269
Showalter, Jacob 119,129,130
Showler, 10
Showman, Stephen 224
Shreve, Benjamin Jr. 159
Shrewood, 254
Shriver, 204
Shrout, 205,235
Shrum, George 123,130,263
Shue, Abraham 146
Shular, 25
Shuler, Corneluis 235
Shull, Henry 48,112; John J. 261
Shultz, Geo. 250,251
Shumate, Talliafero 71
Shumucker, Nicholas 69
Shup, John 12
Shurley, Thomas 40; Zachary 40
Shutt, 244
Shutz, Frederick 218; James 218
Shwier, Jacob 104
Shwiers, Jacob 101
Sibert, Daniel 159; George 87, 124,168; George Washington 183; Jacob 90; Lorenzo 207; Lorenzo D. 183; Washington 207
Sidebottom, Joseph 235
Sidwell, Samuel 14
Siever, Moses 20,21,45
Sigler, Jacob 183; Noah 183
Silar, 29; Jacob 32
Siler, 57; John 214; P. 200
Silkmare, 17
Simmmon, Sineon 160
Simmon, 212
Simmons, 206,212,224,225,236, 255,266,271; Charles 117; Sandford Y. 212,236,242,243, 244,254; S.Y. 254,255,259, 260; V. 254,255; Valentine 149,153,162,181,184,185,200, 214,216,220,259; Van 17
Simms, Thomas 48; Wm. 205
Simon, 231,270; Christian 97,

231; Christian Sr. 136; George 129,135; Geo. 270; M. 270;
Simons, 71,227; Asa 177,268; Christ: 35; Christian 37,38, 135; George 139,233; Michael 199,274; Michail 231; Micheal 167; Mr. 68,71; Peter 233; Sanford Y. 221
Simpson, 28,55,76; Benjamin 255; Caleb 247; David 13; George 91,98,102; James 101; John 56,162,165,194,263; John W. 194; Jos. 102; Joseph 91; Joseph S. 227; Moses 91,98; Richard 91; Thomas 87; William 78; William J. 255; William T. 255
Sims, James 22; Reubin 85; Robert 272; Thomas 37
Sinclair, 53; Alexander 172; James M. 232; Mordicai B. 232; Mr. 118,120; Robert 90
Sinckler, William 58
Sine, Adam 115; John 23,115; Joshua 231,236,244; Peter 151
Singleton, 12; James 14,46, 70,137; John 87,96,156,211; Robert 6
Sions, Adam 255
Sirbert, Henry I. 243
Siron, Nathaniel 23
Sisinger?, Wm. 257
Sites, 185,190,208,238,269; Abraham 47,139,164; Abraham Jr. 209; Abram 120,208,209; Adam 187; Conrad 209; Conrod 190; Daniel 152,163,192,195, 206,208; Daniel Jr. 181; Elizabeth 209; Frederick 97, 163,200,213; George 47,74, 117,185; Guidean 185; Jacob 97,200,208,213; Jacob 4th 208; Jno. 262; John 163,200; John Jr.187; Solomon 208,209
Sittle, William 130
Sivel, Joseph 1
Siver, 224; John 124,226; Mosses 83
Sivy, Mathias 11
Six, 265; George 150; Isaac 129,130
Skelton, Isaac 178
Skidmore, Andrew 228
Skinker, 52
Skinner, Elijah 106; John 16, 42
Slack, 63
Slade, 153
Slagil?, wid. 53
Slain, 248; Benjamin 166; Daniel 95; James 23; Thomas 172
Slane, 59; Benjamin 91,92,118, 132,160; James 57,58,136,143 John 21,22,109; Thomas 65,92, 135,137,150,177
Slater, 224,229,242; Samuel 18; William 216,232,236,238
Slaughter, John 4,13; Mr. 43; Philip 78,98,229; Samuel 82; Smith 43; William 12,105
Sloan, 106,119,156,157; Col. 107,109,112,113,118,174,197, 205; George 131; James 218; John 72,181; Mr. 109,121,149,

150,151,152,160,161,165,166, 167,214; Richard 51,72,123, 126,132,133,140,151,152,218; Tho's 215
Sloanacre, Richard M. 240
Sloane, Col. 170,171,172,173, 175; John 106
Slocum, 126; Isaac 255; Robert 57,79
Slonacre, 210; Richard M. 243; Christopher 257; George 250; Richard M. 240,250
Slone, 17; Col. 113; John 54; M. 119; Richard 47
Small, John 291 John M. 218
Smallwood, William 240; Wm. 247
Smally, Joshua 111
Smawley, 72
Smelser, Adam 252,254
Smith, 2,6,26,53,58,64,65,71, 73,82,84,87,94,168,182,184, 193,206,207,208,212,229,231, 237,243,259,262,270; A. 260, 261,267,272; Abraham 260, 261,272; Abram 274; Adam 23, 39,123; Alexander 3,5,10,21, 22,74,83,189,242; Ann C.218; Augustine 71; Benjamin 181, 185,186; Benjamin F. 240, 254,263; Christian 54,128; Clement 146,184; Col. 48, 149,162; Conrod 27; D. 130; Daniel 185,220; David 19, 128; Downin 26; Edward 66, 194,198; Eli 178,181; Elisha 203,211,255; Francis 94; Gabriel 122; George 6,50,85, 86,91,129,220,224,274; George W. F. 253; Henry 74, 206,206,224,268; Isaac 40, 98; J.D.B. 154; Jackson 235; Jacob 120,154,174,176,185, 221,224,269; James 49,88, 158,185,242; James R. 263; Jefferson 256; Jno. 255; Jno. S. 179; Joel 199; John 15,20,32,52,73,75,90,98,103, 125,128,146,156,169,176,178, 185,187,213,216,223,225,247, 249,252,268; John L. 127, 139,142,162,218,233; John W. 273; Jonathan 137,185; Joseph 210; Joseph D. 58; Joseph L. 160; Levi 33,57; Luke 189; Michael 7,30; Mr. 162; Mrs. 73; Owen 14; Peter 6,56,263; Philip 185; R. G. 179; Rachael 185; Rezin O. 203; Rob. C. 76; Samuel 203; Sarah 79,249; Sarah G. 247; Solomon 181,185,186; Stephen 242; Thomas 53,107,247; Timothy 7,68,142; Treadwell 218; Valentine 139,158; Wesley 258; Will'm 54; William 3,7,10,18,29,32,34, 50,51,88,99,101,127,142,146, 147,153,179,185,218,233,243, 256; Willm. 47; Wm. 12,125; Zachariah S. 268
Smithfield, 233
Smoat, Josiah 40
Smoot, 53,58,59,232; Charles C. 259; Edward 169; John 197,223; Josiah 198; Josias 135,187,197,226
Smoots, Josias 132

Smootz, Matthias 77
Smucker, Philip 171
Smutz, Abraham 103
Smyth, Alexander 6,26,29; Isaac 29; John 29; Wm. 102
Snap, Jacob 8; Joseph 8; Mr. 18; P. 31; Philip 4,6,18,19, 22,26,30,31,48; Phillip 4,5
Snapp, 106; Adam 38; Geo: 82; Joseph 43,137,143,148,197, 223; P. 26; Philip 3,14,20, 21,24,25,26,27,33,36,38; Phillip 4
Sneibly, Henry 169
Snell, Henry 226; Joseph 226
Snicker, Edward 89
Snickers, 50
Snider, 249; Elizabeth 11; Gasper 236; Jacob 94,220; John 71,81,87,93; Peter 18
Sniveley, 18,24; Dr. 22; Henry 27,49
Snively, Henry 49
Snodgrass, 202,206,212,216; Col. 228; James 79,206; John 185,200,201; R. 169; Robert 9,16,29; Robert Jr. 16,94; Robert V.88,227,228; Stephen 26,81,82; William 20,180,201
Snowden, Edgar 246
Snyder, 220; Abraham 139; Adam 35; Charles 203; Daniel 154; David 26,122; Dr. 30; Erasmus 262; Gasper 2,11; Isaac 178,220,262; Jacob 83, 119,220; John 77,83,100,103, 126,220,224; John M. 246; Levi 245; Mann 265; Mary 204 Peter 160; William 247,265
Soan, Mr. 152
Socksman, 228; Adam 150
Sollars, Thomas 115
Somers, Isaac 224,252,269; Reuben 224,234,252,269
Somet, 239
Sommers, 11
Songster, James 28
Sonnafrank, Abraham 88,107, 157,236
Sour, Balsor 87; Daniel 252; Henry 152; Isaac 252
Sours, Adam 236,269; David 234; Frederick 234,246,269; George 234; Henry 221,269; John 234
South, James 274
Southard, John 148
Souther, Jacob 22,28
Southood, Edward 13
Southwood, 50; Edward 50,66
Sower, Balser 159; Frederick 98
Sowers, Adam 183,199; Frederick 62; Philip 176
Spade, George 250; John 250
Spangler, Joseph 65; Jos. S. 83,84; John 115; Philip 26
Spark, Samuel 53
Sparling, James 144
Speake, 59
Spealman, Peter 213
Speatman, 192
Specht, Charles 55
Speelman, Peter 129
Spence, 124; Dr. 118; Mary F. 86
Spencer, 63,105,114; J. H. 269; James 89; John 20,21,40,

59,141,152,237,269; John Jr. 177,239,240; John M. 239; John N. 240; John Sr. 177; Jr. 105;
Spengler, Anthony 124
Spero, George 67
Sperow, George 254
Sperry, 227; John 56,151,200; Nicholas 245; Peter 56
Sphor, David 103
Spicer, Randolph 36,44
Spidler, Abraham Jr. 86,87, 94,108; Abraham Sr. 94,99; Daniel 99
Spiecer, Randolph 12
Spiegle, Michael 20,231
Spilman, 163; Jacob 39
Spingler, J.S. 256; Philip 70
Spinner, John 5
Spitlar, John 115,128
Spitler, Abram 183; M. 252, 254,259; Mr. 253
Spohr, 270
Spohre, John W. 274
Spoore, Henry 1
Spore, John 57,104
Sporr, 196
Spotts, Joseph 146,165
Spratman, Peter 192
Sprigg, Osburn 2
Sprinkle, Peter 146,265
Spup, John 12
Spurling, Jesse 218
Squiles, 112
Sra_?, John 218
Srout, Peter 49
St.Clair, Chas. E. 247
StGeorge, Henry 105
Stabler, Wm. 236
Stafford, 269
Staffords, 145
Stagg, Christopher 133,166; George 67,73,96,133,134; John 264; William 133
Staggs, Christoper 127; George 90,127; William 157
Stalcup, Emmer 221,249; Emmer Jr. 221
Stallcup, Emmor Jr. 249; Israel 60,63
Stamback, Jacob 54
Stamp, Benjamin 150
Stananrd, Robt 99
Stanley, 22; Stephen 42
Stark, James 53; John 10
Starke, Bowling 159
Starkey, 116; Frederick 18, 104; James J. 240; John 167, 223,227
Starky, Frederick 107
Starn, John 58,59,65,70,75, 120; Joseph 269
Starns, 131; James 223
Starnes, John 249,260,267,268
Statton, Jacob 203
Staunton, Thomas 28
Steed, 97; Aaron 3; Aron 3
Steegle, Jacob 186
Steel, 5,21,33,36,63,72,81, 140; John 35; Thomas 15,42, 112
Steele, 254
Steelee, Abram 234
Steenbergen, Mr. 88; William 78
Steenin, William 270
Steer, Joseph 37
Steers, Joseph 39

305

Steffe, George 82
Steffle, Adam 82
Steglar, James 79
Stein, Jacob 157
Steinback, Adam 213
Steinbarger, Mr. 83
Stemback, Martin 217
Stepehs, David 114
Stephen, 60; Robert 6,52
Stephenfought, John 19
Stephens, 102; Henry 100;
Lewis 4,20,21,33,48,151;
Mrs. 198; Peter 112
Stephenson, 10,53,82,94;
James 1,2,13; William 21
Steritt, M. 147
Stern, Joseph 37
Sterns, James 248
Sterret, James 153; William
M. 9
Sterrett, 143,189; A.M. 149;
James 122,148; William 59;
William M. 26
Sterrit, 97
Sterritt, 133,182; James 164;
William M. 158,177
Steuart, Robert 70
Stevens, Henry 116
Stevenson, James 66; William
106
Steward, 268; John 27
Stewart, 170,171,172,173,226,
234; Archibald 64,212; Dr.
181; James 49,74,210; James
Jr. 193; James Sr. 77,166;
Jeremiah 153,169,181; John
154; Joseph 22; Samuel 166
Stickler, Joseph 186
Stickley, 204,243; A. 184;
Abraham 184; D. 205; Philip
174; Tobias 177,182
Stiegel, Jacob 26
Stillwell, William 255
Stimbel, Jost 22
Stimson, James 56,274
Stingley, 185,187,190,221,
225,233,247,271; George 190;
Jacob 5; John 137,219,221;
Thomas 165,175,205,206;
William 74,137
Stingly, 212,265; George 60,
73; William 64
Stinson, James 18,67,70,78,
110,188,225,247,256,266;
James Jr. 110; James Sr. 110
Stinwalt, Jacob 243
Stipe, John 91
Stirewalt, Jacob 231
Stirwalt, Jacob 243
Stock, Joshua 274
Stocks, Elizabeth 85; William
85
Stockslager, Alexander 70
Stoker, 264; John 84,97
Stolabarger, 194
Stollaberger, Mathias 141
Stomback, Michael 265
Stombaw, 234
Stomboug, 181
Stombough, 114,250; John 129
Stonaker, George 192
Stondemoyer, Barnett 153
Stone, 62,66,77,174,180,181;
Benjamin 2; Elijah 57; Isaac
36; Jacob 44; James 158,164;
Joseph 76,95,129; Josias 35;
Thomas 64,72; William 157,164
Stonebarger, Lewis 124

Stonebeger, Lewis 117
Stoneberger, Frederick 17,
105,108
Stonebridge, 122
Stonebruner, Jacob 274; John
J. 257,261
Stoneman, 125; Joshua 125
Stoner, Frederick Sr. 124;
Ulrrick 189
Stonestreet, Elisha 188,228
Stonestreit, Elijah 163
Stonnel, 217
Stookey, 236,247; Jacob 70
Stoolsman, John 1
Stophle, 2
Storey, John 137
Storm, Peter 12,49
Story, 230; John 245,228;
Joseph 245
Stoudemoier, Burnet 108
Stout, Daniel 115; Philip 65,
88
Stover, 70,120,189,233,269;
Abraham 237; Christian 27;
Daniel 86; David 31;
Elizabeth C. 268; Jacob 76,
79,139; John 4; Joseph 34,
61,67; Michael 8,20; Philip
219; Ulrich 20
Stovers, Joseph 72
Stowers, Mark 98
Strader, 209
Stradford, Thomas 60
Stradler, 186
Strasnider, Michael 147
Straus, 185
Strawderman, 231,238; Adam
238; George 227; John 191
Strawther, Mr. 35
Strawtherman, George 216;
Henry 174
Street, 241,274; Chas. 82;
Philip B. 211
Streit, Philip B. 248,262
Stribling, Francis 33
Strickler, 4,74,108,152,259;
Abraham 93,237; Benjamin 17;
David Sr. 224; Isaac 17,42,
74,75,86,87,88,93; Jacob 94,
157; John 5,86; Joseph 42,93,
100,105,110; Joseph T. 275;
Mr. 39; Robert 269; Samuel
115; Sylvanus 254
Strider, Henry 97; Samuel 247
Striekler, Joseph 108
Strile?, 185
Stringfellow, Thornton 78
Strobridge, 209; Samuel 83,
179
Strode,28,52,53,60,86; Edward
65; James 8,32,65; Jeremiah
29; Jno. 58; John 49,65; Mr.
199; Thomas 49,52
Strole, John 249,252
Strosnider, 118; Isaac 164,
204,229; Michael 149,177;
Mordecai 229
Strother, 111; Jas. F. 189;
J. F. 208,219; John 5,19,45;
Mr. 189
Stroud, 79,85,163,185
Strous, 235
Strout, George 64,175
Strownyder, Frederick 47
Strowsnyder, Frederick 42,47;
John F. 48
Struts, John 155
Stryder, 73

Stuart, 175; David 61; James
260,261
Stubblefield, George 160
Studdarth, 38
Stults, Jacob 39,257
Stumback, Martin 87,99,87,120
Stumbock, Martain 216
Stump, 170,217,217,236,269;
Adam 257,267; Augustus J.?
198; Benj. 150; Benjamin 90,
95,151; George 202,203,250;
George W. 265,267; Jesse 82,
114,151,217; John 59,84,137,
138,139,143,149,150,202,205,
214; Joseph 150,158; Leonard
169; Leonard Jr. 37,38,84;
Michael 37; Peter 95,150,225
Samuel J. 143,182,220,223,
227,258; William P. 197,202,
211,224,258; W.P. 227,234;
Wm. P. 211,223,226,232,243
Stuttz, Jacob 123
Sudden, 24
Suddeth, William 43
Suddoth, 52
Suden, 15
Suder, Daniel 245
Sugden, Samuel 17,74,75
Sugedut, John 153
Sulivant, Giles 83
Sullivant, Jeremiah 1
Sulman, Conrad 158
Sulser, 202; Adam 187,189;
Henry 158,211
Sultzer, Adam 150
Summer, Andrew 23
Summers, Jacob 183; John 220;
John T. 76,77,111; Joshua
152; Philip 11,39; Reuben
224; William 71
Summervill, James 95
Summerville, James 129,196
Supinger, William 212
Supinger, Wm. 245
Suroot, Barlow 157
Surtzer, Simon 229
Sutton, 75,126,127,131,135,
147,161,162,170,177,193,241,
259,261,267,270; Ebenezer 28
John D. 274; Samuel 166,167,
260; Zachariah 15
Suver, 235
Swaim, 208; Matthias 192;
Mathias 12
Swain, 257; Mathias 182
Swam, Wm. 236
Swan, John 189
Swaney, John 183
Swann, 215; Edward 61
Swany, Thomas 147
Swarr/Swar, John 175
Swartze, Joseph 150
Swayne, 125
Swearengen, 21
Swearingen, Andrew 24; Benora
159; Thomas 24; Van 24
Swearingin, Thomas 169
Swhier, George 134
Swift, Jonathan 147
Swim, 19,21,158; (third) 20;
John 34; Jr. 88; Mathias 22,
158; Mathias 3rd 105; Mathias
Jr. 34; Matth. 6; Matthias
(third) 19; Matthias 20,34,
50; Matthias Jr. 12,19,48;
Matthias Sr. 12,48;
Swindal, 109
Swindler, Ellen 239; Henry 18

307

Wait, 18
Walden, John 149
Waldon, Thomas 49
Waldron, H. C. 275
Walker, 34,53,70,235,267;
  Andrew 3,33,266,272; J.C.
  256; John 157,160; Joseph
  97,207; Robert 3,16; Thomas
  170; William W. 272; Wm. 211
Wm. W. 266
Wall, 38; John T. 198; J. F.
  232; Mr. 209,217; Nancy 202;
  Narny 193
Wallace, 35,40,60,61,254; Gen.
  215; Gustavus B. 50; John H.
  253,269; Michael 50,55;
  Thomas 42
Waller, Isaac 171
Walling, 257
Wallis, 35,120; George 186;
  John 16,23,29; William 92
Walper, 263
Walpertz, 236
Walput, John 174
Walter, Daniel 1; Henry 26,54,
  115; Isaac 168,169; Martin
  8,20,67,83; Nicholas 4,38;
  Richard C. 56
Walters, 275; Daneil 100,108,
  113,123,127; John 218;
  Nicholas 20,21,48; William
  S. 56
Walton, 186; Edward 127,226,
  231,242; F.B. 225; Job 157;
  Moses 30,94,98,99,100,101,
  104,115,152,186; Mr. 123,
  125,127,128,129,130; Reuben
  152,157; Samuel 104,123
Wan, Elijah 217
Wandling, Jonathan 163
Ward, 151,202; Col. 105,202,
  203,204; Henry 210; Joel 62,
  92,94,104,130,171,191,246;
  Joell 140; John 11,87,90,148,
  160,183,187; Richard 5;
  Robert G. 82; William H.
  217; Wm. 32
Warden, 189,225,229,233,233,
  235,238; Benjamin 200,216,
  261; William 64,164
Wardens, 232,237
Warder, Walter 54
Ware, James 134; William 121
Warfield, George 193
Warner, 12,15,49,65,134,188;
  John 82
Wartman, Jacob 80,81
Warton, 60,77; Moses 6
Warwick, John 117
Washington, 42,46,76,78,139,
  247; Augustine 83; Charles
  50; Edward 11; George 11,73;
  George W. 215,274; Henry 46,
  54; John 27; Laurence 83;
  Mrs. L. 233;
Washton, John 85
Watener, Peter 220
Waters, Nacy 225; Stanfield
  237; Richard 78
Watford, John 39
Watkins, 52,161,245; Ann 104;
  Ann Elizabeth 235; Benjamin
  Franklin 235; Elizabeth
  Harriet 235; Francis Marion
  235; Harrison 140,155,161,
  211; Henry 173,216,235,256;
  Henry Madison 235; James B.
  155,197,211,216; James

Thomas 235; John Williams
  235; Thomas 64
Watsdon, Henry 29
Watson, 7,23,30,147,219,250;
  Abert G. 175; Isaac 245;
  James 86,95,109,195,257;
  John 20; Jonathan 54,74,75;
  Joseph 10,25,33,46,47,233;
  Josiah 205; William 175
Watson Town, Trustees 250,267
Watt, Samuel 100
Watts, 35,92; Archibald 25;
  Frederick 35; James 17,103;
  James Sr. 79; Jonathan 25;
  Richard 27; Samuel 125
Watz, James 268
Waugh, 207; Archibald 176,
  207; David 73; James 37;
  Maj. 70
Wayland, Adam 33; Cornelius
  42; Joel 45
Waylands, Henry 40
Wayman, Henry 36,41; Jonas
  243
Weakley, 87
Wealch, 239; Thomas 127;
  William 244
Wealton, Job 107
Wear, Joseph 50
Weare, Elijah 189; Solomon
  190; William 167,190
Wease, 213; Elijah 195;
  Solomon 169; William 169,
  185,195
Weatherall, 7; Mrs 45
Weatherholt, Henry 8,11,44
Weaver, 131,175,217; Abraham
  95,129; Adam 257; Alfred
  143; Charles 183,199,236,260;
  Daniel 236,260,269; Elijah
  142; Elizabeth 143; Francis
  142; George 74; Jacob 15,34,
  38,46,66,67,131; Jacob Jr.
  71; James 142; Joell 142;
  John 60,95; Juliann 143;
  Larkin 142; Mathias 143;
  Peter 18; Sarah 142; Simeon
  143; Theodosha 142
Weavers, 48
Webb, 211,251; Daniel 1,8,11,
  17,118,128,134,139; David
  157; George 266,271; Herman
  118; James 202,266,271; John
  25,112,178,243
Webster, Andrew 10
Webyel, John 139
Weddle, Jacob 171,191
Week, Wm. 204
Weekly, 270
Weekley, Joseph 109
Weeks, John 4,5; Samuel 4,21;
  William 168; Wm. Jr. 186
Weese, 74,222,262,269; Ashur
  262; Elija 180; George 25;
  Wm. 269
Welch, 65,70,229; Benj. 134;
  Demcy 211; Derney 269; Isaac
  77,134,145; James 16,218;
  Sylvester 134; Thomas 96,
  172,194; William 162,186,
  235; Wm. 134
Welchance, Henry 32
Welche, Isaac 26
Wells, 27; Joseph 152;
  Richard 52
Wellton, Aaron 179
Welsh, 163; Demcy Sr. 133;
  James 132; John 160;

Sylvester 113,151; Thomas
  133; William 151,160,161
Welton, 180,186,201,202,206,
  219,225,233,253,255,262;
  Aaron 136,199,200; Aaron A.
  268; Able 178,200; Archibald
  178,200; Cyrus 199,201,203;
  David 4,25,79,185; F.B. 221,
  224,225,226; Felix 70,79,98,
  99,265; Jesse 219; Job 17,
  178,250; Job Jr. 269; John
  27,97,178,189,190; John W.
  265; Mr. 225,232,233,234;
  P.T. 247; Simon 265; Wm. 255
Welty, John 44
Wendel, 218; Christopher 189;
  Thomas 175
Were, William 121
Wese/Weese, Charles 217
West, 31,38,58,88,207;
  Benjamin 78; Hugh 69; John
  17,34; Stephen 44; Thomas 55
Western, Lewis 220
Wetherholt, Henry 129
Wetsail, 79
Wetsel, John 46,122
Wetten, Aaron 165
Wetzel, John 42,113
Wharton, 2,40,45,63,64,69,80,
  89,92,106,126,140,148,157,
  176,178,188,195,218,236,254,
  262; Jno. Z. 254; John 92;
  Joseph 44,46,68,74; Thomas
  74
Wheat, James W. 75
Wheatley, 58,61; George 52
Wheeler, George 59; Hezekiah
  Jr. 59; Ignatius 59;
  Richard 28
Wheler, Ignatius 196
Whetman, James 273
Whetzel, 234; David 261;
  Jesse 234
Whidmier, Michael 23
Whisner, Peter 38
Whisson, Abraham 228
Whitacre, George 235
White, 19,59,63,73,76,85,91,
  165,198,225; Armistead 37;
  Col. 84,89,90,91,92,102,104,
  105; F. 92,95,97,103;
  Frances? 59; Francis 9,11,
  21,49,91,93,94,95,115,126,
  132; George Jr. 121; Henry
  102; Isaac 147; J. B. 246;
  Jacob 7; James 263; James
  Taylor 45; Jodge Robert 42;
  John 44,173; John B. 146,
  159,246,260; Mordecai 8;
  Mr. 68,75,76,78,83,85,107,
  121; Nathaniel 35; Presley
  217; Robert 15,44; T. B.
  235,236,237,238,239,240,241,
  242,243; Thomas 235; Thos.
  242; Thos. B. 237,240,242
Whitecar, Thomas 47
Whitehall, John 175
Whitehead, 30,40
Whiteley, 159
Whitely, Francis 98
Whiteman, Jacob R. 8; James
  273; John 131,133; Rudolph
  42
Whitestone, Mordecai 82
Whiting, 246,262; James S.
  262; Thomas 218
Whitinger, Michael 29
Whitmer, 203; Suffere 200

309

Whitmire, Michael 43,65,119
Whitmore, 255
Whitsel, Christopher 101,107
Whitsill, 166
Whitsle, Jacob 192; John 192
Whitson, 106
Whitzel, 233; David 251; John 39,45
Whitzle, John 138
Wicks, Samuel 177
Wicough, 260
Widdle, Jacob 189
Widener, 178
Widmeyer, Michael 11
Widmire, 12
Widmyer, Michael 98,101
Widner, 195
Widnyer, 246
Wiggins, Archibald 36,95; Philip 109
Wildemy, 109
Wiley, 225; Abel 131; Benjamin 28,125,131,141; Gabriel 82; William M. 82; Wm. M. 82
Wilhoit, Michael 35
Wilhoite, Elizbeth 61
Wilison, William 170
Wilken, 222; Moses 205
Wilkin, Aaron 212,231; Archibald 212,231,271; George Sr. 64; Godfrey 113, 212,217; John 130,168,175, 218; Joseph 113,212,217; Mathias 207,227,231; Moses 227,231; Sarah 200
Wilkins, 64,216; A. 201; Aaron 201; George 64,74,90; Godfrey 151,152; John 263; Joseph 217; Mathias 53,201, 207; Matthias 74; Moses 201, 207
Will, John 8,37,50,127; George 127
Willey, Edward 17
William, Edward A. 222; P.151
Williams, 18,22,53,107,110, 154,163,184,196,204,229,237, 243,252,259; Abraham 65,71; Benjamin 46,112,118,153,205, 216; Ch's 274; Cha's 272; Charles 262; Daniel 143,149, 182,198,215,227; Edward G. 101; Edward O. 50,53,58,65, 88,139; Eliza 111; Geo. 28; George 29,50,263; Ira 203; James 26,92,153,167,168,174, 178,179,181,184,249,251,263; Jane 136; Jared 72; Jared Jr. 87; Jerome 21,50,105; Joel 118,147,149; John 13, 44; John W. 121,138; Jonas 58; Joseph 111,153,178,192, 229,262; Mr. 137,139,142, 163,164,174,189,191; Mrs. 244 Otho S. 87; Owen 7,104; Peter 18,35,40,99,107,112, 128,129,160,236; Philip 113, 181; Province 14; Rob't 14; Robert 5,130; Sam'l C. 230, 231; Thomas 11,13,39,54,57, 63,65,95,123; Thomas C. 255; Vincent 107,164; W.G. 124; William 21; William C. 2,3, 4,103,209,261; Wm. C. 81; Zedekiah 95
Williamson, 36,59,118,151, 198; Andrew 29; Benjamin

143,258,273; Cornelious 117; Cornelius 116,157; Elizabeth 29; Jacob 13; James 29; Jeremiah 29; John 37,50,120, 157 Margaret 29; Mary 29; Samuel 3,29,75,89,115,118; Sarah 29; Stone 75; Susanna 29; Thomas 9,16,25,29; Timothy 29; William 1,5,9, 23; William Jr. 5; wid. 16
Willis, 37,66,72,244; Abraham 254; Jacob 99
Wills, Benjamin E.197; George 63; Samuel 260; William 260
Willson, 189; David 4,217; Isaac 165; James 12,55; John 13,204,217; John F. 165; Joseph 204,217; Thomas 2; William 190
Wilson/Willson, 216
Wilson, 55,61,95,141,149,150, 153,164,205,206,211,212,217, 231,236,238,244,247; Armistead 148; Armstead 136; Charles 8; David 4,34; Fanny B. 102; Henry 18,153; Isaac 64,217; Isaac N. 147; James 8,11,61,73,224; Jeremiah 125 John 64,90,177,217; John Jr. 216,217; John T. 274; Jonathan 72; Richard 9,90, 102; Samuel 247; Tho's 216; Thomas 43,97,98,175,185; Walter 62,95; William 73,91, 92; wid. 87
Wilton, Job 70,172; John 107
Wilts, Peter 196
Wimer, 255; Abram 200; Andrew 35
Windel, Abraham 175; George 175
Windell, Thomas 155
Windsor, 87; Richard S. 78; Thomas 78
Wine, 186; Jacob 231; John Sr. 209,265
Winegardner, Adam 30; Herbert 30
Winn, 72; Minor Sr. 59
Winning, James 28; Samuel 16
Winow, John 222
Winston, 76
Winterton, 23,220; John 25 William 25
Wip, Daniel 67
Wire, Jacob 189
Wise, 151,208,216,217,237, 238,242; Frederick 152; Henry 152,212,248; Michael 204
Wisecarrer, Henry 184,192
Wisegarber, John 39
Wiseham, Wm. 18
Wisenberg, George 19,20
Wisenburgh, George 103
Wishart, Sydney 55
Wisman, George 69; Philip 149
Wisser, Peter 32
Wissler, John 274
Wiston, 36
Witbeck, Daniel 237
Withers, George 62; John 175; Spencer 98; William 26
Witson, 150
Wocker, Henry 74
Wodrow, Andrew 7,18,52; Col. 31
Wohlgemuth, Christian 30

Wolf, 228,244,254; Adam Jr. 270; George 23,170,220; Isaac 266; Jacob 39; John 15,257; Lewis 21,49
Wolfe, 50; Adam Jr. 234,269; George 46 Jacob 46,48,58,82, 112; Jacob the Elder 108; Lewis 35,50
Wolford, 63,77,99; Adam 252; David 258; Elijah 256; Henry 197,255,261; Jacob 71, 252,261; John 39,41,48,76, 207,256; Josiah 256
Wolvington, 204
Wolverton, Isaac 41,193; Joel 161
Wood, 53,79,86,222,223,224, 231; A. R. 209,230; Algernon R. 196; Angus M.222,238,267; Benjamin 48,71,78,83,86,149; Benjamin H. 199,214,246; Col. 196,199,200; Edward W. 246; Elizabeth P. 254; Ephraim 240; Harrison 246,254; James 37; Jesse 83,215; John 78,86; Joseph 7,14,47; Joshua 214; Moses 252; Mr. 178; Richard 60,81,85,109,196,223; Sarah 43; Thomas 48,54,177
Woodard, 273; James 45
Woodfin, 86
Woodrow, 156,171,172,175,258; Andrew 18,26,58,59
Woods, 65,114,131,169,190; A. M. 222; Benjamin 24; Joshua 124; Woods, Mr.188; Nehemiah 23; Richard 6; Thomas 160
Woodside, John 67
Woodson, 30
Woodward, G.M. 269; James 43
Woody, Wm. 14
Woolard, 125
Woolery, Jacob 177
Woolfe, Jacob 112
Woolford, John 111
Woolverton, Isaac 166; Isaac Sr. 109
Worden, Mr. 16
Wormley, Ralph 35
Worthington, Robert 233; William C. 233; Wm. C. 234
Woster, 11
Wrenn, John 176
Wright, 12,49; George 241; Isaac 94; Jno. 82; John 42, 56,82,104,107,145,148; Rebecca Margery 98; Reuben 52; Robert Lockhart 98; Sarah Ann 90,98
Wryht, 71
Wunder, Henry S. 218
Wydmire, Michael 11
Wylie, Andrew 159; James 159; Robert 159; Thomas 159
Wymar, John 147,177
Wymer, George 177
Wynekoop, Adrian 94; Garrett 94
Wyrmeer, George 147

Yager, 40,125; Benjamin 106, 109; Elizabeth 23; Joel 106; John 36; John A. 62; Michael 22
Yaman, 243
Yarnell, James 125
Yates, 148,230; Andrew 28; Charles 10,16,18; John 14,